MW01119458

Innovations in SMEs and Conducting E-Business:

Technologies, Trends and Solutions

Maria Manuela Cruz-Cunha
Polytechnic Insitute of Cavado and Ave, Portugal

João Varajão
University of Trás-os-Montes e Alto Douro, Portugal

Senior Editorial Director:	Kristin Klinger
Director of Book Publications:	Julia Mosemann
Editorial Director:	Lindsay Johnston
Acquisitions Editor:	Erika Carter
Development Editor:	Myla Harty
Production Editor:	Sean Woznicki
Typesetters:	Jennifer Romanchak, Milan Vracarich Jr., Deanna Zombro
Print Coordinator:	Jamie Snavely
Cover Design:	Nick Newcomer

Published in the United States of America by
Business Science Reference (an imprint of IGI Global)
701 E. Chocolate Avenue
Hershey PA 17033
Tel: 717-533-8845
Fax: 717-533-8661
E-mail: cust@igi-global.com
Web site: http://www.igi-global.com/reference

Library of Congress Cataloging-in-Publication Data

Innovations in SMEs and conducting e-business: technologies, trends and solutions / Maria Manuela Cruz-Cunha and Joao Varajao, editors.
       p. cm.
  Includes bibliographical references and index.
  Summary: "This book discusses the main issues, challenges, opportunities and solutions related to electronic business adoption with a special focus on SMEs, providing researchers, scholars, and professionals with some of the most advanced research developments, solutions and discussions of E-Business challenges, impacts and opportunities"--Provided by publisher.
  ISBN 978-1-60960-765-4 (hbk.) -- ISBN 978-1-60960-766-1 (ebook) -- ISBN 978-1-60960-767-8 (print & perpetual access) 1. Small business--Technological innovations. 2. Electronic commerce. I. Cruz-Cunha, Maria Manuela, 1964- II. Varajao, Joao, 1972- III. Title.
  HD2341.I554 2011
  658.8'72--dc22
                          2011011455

British Cataloguing in Publication Data
A Cataloguing in Publication record for this book is available from the British Library.

All work contributed to this book is new, previously-unpublished material. The views expressed in this book are those of the authors, but not necessarily of the publisher.

Editorial Advisory Board

List of Reviewers

Table of Contents

Section 1
Technological and Organizational Solutions

Section 3
Semantic Technologies

Section 4
Legal and Security Aspects

Detailed Table of Contents

Section 1
Technological and Organizational Solutions

    Alexis Barlow, Glasgow Caledonian University, UK
    Margaret McCann, Glasgow Caledonian University, UK
    Anne Smith, Glasgow Caledonian University, UK

This chapter critically analyses and assesses the concept and development of Web 2.0 within SMEs. Web 2.0 is changing the way that business can be conducted, offering SMEs opportunities for developing strategies, business models, and supply chains whilst adding value and gaining competitive advantage. There are many advantages for SMEs using Web 2.0, including them being easy to use, limited skills required, and relative low-cost, and there are a range of emerging applications in fields such as marketing, collaboration, knowledge transfer, enhancing products and services, and research. Equally, there is an array of operational and managerial challenges that need to be overcome. This chapter suggests a set of questions that SMEs may consider using as a guide if they are considering Web 2.0 as a competitive weapon for the future.

    Serdal Bayram, Siemens, Turkey
    Özalp Vayvay, Marmara University, Turkey

E-procurement accelerates SMEs at a reduced cost. The purpose of this chapter is to show that the adoption of an e-procurement system is essential in the supply chain for SMEs and to find solutions in order to make the use of this system as easy as possible. The adoption should be considered as a re-engineering process from an innovative perspective. An adoption plan is proposed within the study, consisting of three phases: 1) identification of the e-procurement process, 2) seeking integration points with other elements of the system, and 3) IT implementation of the integration areas. The study also proposes to use business process management tools that have workflow engines and Web service implementations for integration points. Although BPM tools are seen as quite expensive to SMEs, there are also dependable free licensed ones. The chapter is concluded with a case-study that is implemented with a free-licensed BPM tool for proof-of-concepts.

Chapter 3

Marlene Pinto, University of Trás-os-Montes e Alto Douro, Portugal
Ana Rodrigues, University of Trás-os-Montes e Alto Douro, Portugal
João Varajão, University of Trás-os-Montes e Alto Douro, Portugal
Ramiro Gonçalves, University of Trás-os-Montes e Alto Douro, Portugal

Today, e-commerce assumes particular importance due to the benefits that it may imply for companies. In this chapter the authors focus on business to business (B2B) e-commerce. B2B describes electronic commerce associated to operations of buying and selling products and services through the Internet or through the use of private networks shared between business partners, thus replacing the physical process around commercial transactions. There are several B2B solutions that enable companies to make transactions from buying and selling goods and services, to participating in auctions. The analysis of such solutions enabled the verification that there are major differences in the amount of the supported functionalities, and significant opportunities for development, with the aim of helping companies to evaluate their electronic commerce solutions and to conceive new and more complete systems. This chapter presents a new model of functionalities for the development of B2B solutions.

Chapter 4

Almudena Alcaide Raya, University Carlos III of Madrid, Spain
Jorge Blasco Alis, University Carlos III of Madrid, Spain
Eduardo Galán Herrero, University Carlos III of Madrid, Spain
Agustín Orfila Diaz-Pabón, University Carlos III of Madrid, Spain

This chapter is a comprehensive survey on a currently relevant security threat to Web applications: cross-site scripting (XSS). The rise of reported XSS vulnerabilities has made this family of attacks an interesting area for computer security researchers. XSS consists of the injection of code in Web pages. As injected code is client side scripts, it is executed at the user's Web browser. The main reason for the existence of this kind of vulnerabilities is the incorrect or insufficient handling of the input performed by Web applications. In this chapter, guidelines on proper input treatment for Web developers are offered. Additionally, existing proposals for XSS mitigations are exposed, and future lines of research are indicated to interested researchers and developers. Web applications are susceptible to vulnerabilities that may not only disrupt the provided service, but also facilitate private and personal information to an attacker. As these applications are usually public or even publicized, attacks are expected to be more and more frequent, making it necessary to supply the means to provide an adequate level of security in the utilization of Web applications.

Georgousopoulos Christos, INTRASOFT International S.A., Greece
Xenia Ziouvelou, Athens Information Technology, Greece
Gregory S. Yovanof, Athens Information Technology, Greece
Antonis Ramfos, INTRASOFT International S.A., Greece

Open Source Software (OSS) has gained a strong interest and an increased acceptance in the software industry, introducing wholly new means of software development and distribution, creating a significant impact on the evolution of numerous business processes. The chapter examines the impact of the open source paradigm in the e-Procurement evolution and identifies a trend towards Open Source e-Procurement Application Frameworks (AFs) which enable the development of tailored e-Procurement Solutions. Anchored in this notion, the authors present an Open-Source e-Procurement AF with a two-phase generation procedure, combining the Model Driven Engineering (MDE) approach with the Service-Oriented Architecture (SOA) paradigm for enabling the cost-effective production of e-Procurement Solutions by facilitating integration, interoperability, easy maintenance and management of possible changes in the European e-Procurement environment. The assessment process of the proposed AF and its resulting e-Procurement Solutions occurs in the context of G2B in the Western-Balkan European region. The evaluation yields positive results and further enhancing opportunities.

Rui Rijo, Institute for Systems and Computers Engineering at Coimbra & Research Center for Informatics and Communications- Polytechnic Institute of Leiria, Portugal

Often, small and medium enterprises consider the possibility of creating their own contact centre as a tool to improve the customer service. They pose some important questions about business and technical aspects: Why should we use a contact center solution? Which technologies, architectures, and solutions are available? Which key issues should be analyzed? The chapter provides specific information and practical guidelines about Contact Centers based on a literature review and interviews made to contact center business consultants specialized in the small and medium enterprises sector. The goal of the chapter is to help top management and Information Technology responsible in making the best technological choices and methodological approaches.

Gongjun Yan, Indiana University, USA
Stephan Olariu, Old Dominion University, USA
Weiming Yang, Old Dominion University, USA
Danda B. Rawat, Old Dominion University, USA

Parking is costly and limited in almost every major city in the world, and misparking aggravates the competition of parking slots. Innovative parking systems for meeting near-term parking demand are needed. The chapter proposes a novel parking system which adopts the wireless network and sensor technologies to provide an intelligent and automatic parking service, and presents the implementation and a probabilistic analysis of the new parking service. The drivers will be informed the detailed information, i.e. the vacant parking slots and the route to the slot. From the investor's view, the electronic parking system proposed in the chapter is an efficient and profitable system in utilization of slots and the maintenance cost.

Section 2
Marketing Strategies

Chapter 8

This chapter aims to add to the accumulative knowledge in the field of E-Marketing through conceptualising E-Marketing as a new marketing philosophy. The review of the literature has revealed that one of the main obstacles to developing E-Marketing potential is the absence of a clear conceptualisation of E-Marketing purpose and definition. The majority of researchers within the field misuse the term E-Marketing and are using the terms E-business, E-Marketing, E-Commerce and Internet-marketing interchangeably as if they are similar or have the same meaning, which is incorrect. The differences between these terms as well as the main components of E-Marketing are illustrated and discussed in detail within the chapter towards achieving a conceptualisation of E-Marketing as a new marketing philosophy and to build a ground base of understanding for these different concepts. The chapter will help researchers and scholars to have a clearer view towards this concept that in turn will contribute to the related accumulated knowledge in the field.

Chapter 9

This chapter demonstrates how adequate planning is fundamental in a SME to increase sales. The objective is to analyze the aspects that must be taken into consideration when developing a good e-marketing strategy and to study some of the different alternatives that the Internet and e-marketing make available to us: e-mail marketing, viral e-marketing, geomarketing, and positioning within search engines. Also the concept of Customer Relationship Management (CRM) will be analyzed. The leap into the global market is not easy and the reduction in budgets has inspired marketing professionals to adopt strategies which can be measured and the results controlled, pointing out that the online tactics and tools used by the vast majority of marketing professionals in their strategic plan are banners, search engines, and e-mail.

Chapter 10

Lisa M. Given, Charles Sturt University, Australia
Dinesh Rathi, University of Alberta, Canada

This chapter examines the possibilities of conducting market research in Web 2.0 environments, with a focus on implications for small to medium-sized companies. The chapter discusses how companies can undertake market research using Web 2.0 platforms, explores how these tools can facilitate successful and appropriate market research design, and examines the characteristics of qualitative and quantitative "Research 2.0" techniques appropriate to a Web 2.0 environment. The chapter also presents examples of companies that are using these tools successfully for market research and discusses advantages and barriers in adopting these tools, including privacy, ethics, and legal implications of this type of research.

Chapter 11

Nuno Manarte, University of Trás-os-Montes e Alto Douro, Portugal
Mário Sérgio Teixeira, University of Trás-os-Montes e Alto Douro, Portugal

In this chapter, the authors present e-marketing and the channels, tools, and techniques that can be used by SMEs, so that they can optimize the benefits of an online presence. Knowing its customers is the starting point for any firm's marketing activity, so the chapter introduces concepts related to the process of gathering information about e-customers. The company website is the gateway to Internet marketing, so it is important to promote it in a variety of ways that are also explained in the chapter. Selling online can be an interesting option, but this decision should only be taken after considering the pros and cons that it involves. To conclude, the authors discuss the e-marketing plan, which should guarantee that the objectives, strategies, and actions of online marketing are coherently integrated with the offline marketing plan.

Section 3
Semantic Technologies

Chapter 12

Ronald C Beckett, University of Western Sydney, Australia
Anni Rowland-Campbell, Semantic Transformations Pty Ltd, Australia
Paul Strahl, Semantic Transformations Pty Ltd, Australia

The purpose of this chapter is to explore opportunities offered by and issues associated with the use of emergent semantic technologies in enhancing an enterprise's business position. These technologies include a foundation level set of standards and descriptive languages supporting interpretive connections to applications. The chapter is more oriented towards applications and the human side of the human/machine interface. The authors draw on both the literature and case material available to them as active practitioners to illustrate benefits realized and potential barriers to the uptake of semantic technologies. Critical success factors are related to user learning capabilities, the establishment of trust in the technology and its providers, and factors influencing the nature of potential engagement with users and markets.

Chapter 13

Antonio Paredes-Moreno, University of Seville, Spain
Francisco J. Martínez-López, University of Granada, Spain
David G. Schwartz, Bar-Ilan University, Israel

Nowadays, firms need to refocus the way they manage the knowledge generated from business processes in order to optimize their information systems' performance. Business ontologies are an excellent tool for this. In this chapter, authors briefly treat and highlight how important it is for companies to invest efforts in a closer integration of their systems, with the aim of improving their performance and cooperation. This implies moving towards more efficient systems in their knowledge management. The big challenge for firms now is the semantic integration of information. Essential questions related to this question are synthetically introduced. Then, some of the most significant initiatives and projects on semantic integration of information are presented and compared with a business ontology that authors have developed for commercial use.

Chapter 14

Yi Zhao, Lehrgebiet Informationstechnik, Germany
Wolfgang A. Halang, Lehrgebiet Informationstechnik, Germany

With the increasing development of the Semantic Web technologies, the Semantic Web has been introduced to apply in the Web Services to integrate data across different applications. For the Semantic Web Services to succeed, it is essential to maintain the security of the organizations involved. To guarantee the security of the Web Services, security measures must be considered to protect against unauthorized disclosure, transfer, modification, or destruction, whether accidental or intentional. Access control is a kind of security measurements to guarantee the service processes, which is defined to allow resource owners to define, manage, and enforce the access conditions for each resource. In this chapter it is proposed an attribute based access control model with semantic mapping (SABAC) to specify access control over attributes defined in domain ontologies. The model is built on the basis of XACML policy language. Semantic mapping process is proved to be syntactical, semantic, and structural.

Business knowledge embodied in texts such as business news and companies profiles has become widely accessible to the business community, as well as to the general public, mostly due to the growing popularity of the Internet. The field of efficient information retrieval and knowledge discovery from textual data is an increasingly important research topic driven by the Internet growth and easy access to very large business directories on the Internet. To become acquainted with a particular domain and to better understand the underlying concepts, domain knowledge can be represented by ontologies. In addition, ontologies can be used for identification of potential links in virtual business communities and for decision support when searching for right business partners, which is very relevant to small to medium-sized enterprises. Potential applications range from dynamic supply chain configuration to building consortia as quick responses to business opportunities.

Section 4
Legal and Security Aspects

In order for a small to medium enterprise (SME) to conduct business electronically, that SME requires the establishment of a website. This requires agreements relating to (1) website development, (2) website hosting (3), Internet access, and (4) online content and advertising. The chapter will provide a practical guide from a UK law perspective for a SME in relation to the issues which should be considered when contracts for the above mentioned services are negotiated. The chapter does not cover the issues relating to how the SME should set up its arrangements with its own customers (for example, through website terms and conditions), nor does it consider e-commerce legislation required when conducting business on the Internet.

In cyberworld, intellectual property rights and the right to informational self determination have become two realities in tension. Nevertheless, they are two main concerns of the e-commerce stakeholders. From the industry point of view, new digital technologies, left unregulated, may allow a free flow of information and unauthorized access to contents both from consumers or competitors; from the consumers' perspective, security and privacy concerns are the major barriers to contracting online. The goal of the present chapter is to understand the relationship between anti-piracy oriented private electronic surveillance and consumers' privacy. If, on the one hand, the enforcement of intellectual property is a laudable activity – since the recognition of economic exclusive rights is an incentive to artistic or scientific creation and the protection of the investments is an ICT industry's legitimate interest –, on the other hand, the individual's privacy sphere is one of the most important values and personal freedoms that law, including intellectual property law, must preserve.

Chapter 18
José Gaivéo, Polytechnic Institute of Setubal, Portugal

Nowadays, when organizations, no matter what dimension they possess, are confronted with more exigent market challenges, they must change strategies and behaviors as needed to respond according to their new business positioning. If all organizations are affected by markets instability, SMEs suffer a greater impact due to a lack of suitable resources for the appropriate change of business strategy or even develop a new one, what reveals information and information security significance, and so the relevance of securing Information Systems that supports their flows through organizations. This chapter points information security issues that are important to SMEs' e-Business strategies, issues which could simultaneously guarantee organizational information privacy, and the chapter establishes guidelines which could also be applied to SMEs, allowing information security policies definitions.

Preface

ABOUT THE SUBJECT

Electronic business (e-business) plays a central goal in the economy, facilitating the exchange of information, goods, services, and payments. E-business is not exclusive for large enterprises. It propels productivity and competitiveness, and is accessible to all enterprises. Sophisticated systems like e-Marketplaces act as business integrators, potentiating business opportunities for both buyers and sellers.

E-business represents potential and opens opportunities to foster competitiveness, but brings in operational, tactical, and strategic challenges for small and medium enterprises (SME). This topic is gaining an increasingly relevant strategic impact on global business and the world economy, and organizations of all sort are undergoing hard investments (in cost and effort) in search of the rewarding benefits of efficiency and effectiveness that this range of solutions promise. But as we all know this is not an easy task; it is not only a matter of financial investment. It is much more, as the book will show.

Responsiveness, flexibility, agility, and business alignment are requirements of competitiveness that enterprises search for. And we hope that the models, proposals, and studies presented and discussed in this book can contribute to highlight new ways to identify opportunities and overtake trends and challenges of e-business adoption and exploitation, in particular targeting SME.

The book project was born under the intention to collect the most recent developments on the organizational, technological, and legal dimensions of electronic business, discuss its potential, impact, trends and challenges. This objective was met, due to the high adhesion of contributors and the quality and complementarity of the manuscripts proposed that allowed a comprehensive whole, addressing all the aspects initially previewed.

ORGANIZATION OF THE BOOK

This book is a compilation of 18 contributions to the discussion of the main issues, challenges, opportunities and developments related with e-business technologies and business trends, from the technological, managerial, and organizational perspectives, in a very comprehensive way, in order to disseminate current achievements and practical solutions and applications.

These 18 chapters are written by a group of 45 authors that include many internationally renowned and experienced researchers and specialists in the e-business field and a set of younger authors, showing a promising potential for research and development. Contributions came from the five continents, integrating contributions from academics, research institutions, and industry, representing a good and comprehensive representation of the state-of-the-art approaches and developments that address the several dimensions of this fast evolutionary thematic.

Innovations in SMEs and Conducting E-Business:Technologies, Trends and Solutions is organized in four sections:

- **Section 1:** "Technological and Organizational Solutions," with seven chapters, is focused in advancing solutions for the development of e-business, in particular in SME.
- **Section 2:** "Marketing Strategies" introduces new concerns of e-marketing strategies and optimization of its potential to organizations.
- **Section 3:** "Semantic Technologies" reflects the main advances in semantic technologies, ontologies, and Web services that support e-business.
- **Section 4:** "Legal and Security Aspects" discuss these issues as major concerns for e-business development.

The seven chapters in section one introduces issues in technology and organization of SMEs.

The first chapter, "*Web 2.0: An Emerging and Innovative Solution for SMEs,*" critically analyses and assesses the concept and development of Web 2.0 within SMEs. Web 2.0 is changing the way that business can be conducted, offering SMEs opportunities for developing strategies, business models, and supply chains whilst adding value and gaining competitive advantage. There are many advantages for SMEs using Web 2.0, including them being easy to use, limited skills required, and relatively low-cost; there are also a range of emerging applications in fields such as marketing, collaboration, knowledge transfer, enhancing products and services, and research. Equally, there is an array of operational and managerial challenges that need to be overcome. This chapter suggests a set of questions that SMEs may consider using as a guide if they are considering Web 2.0 as a competitive weapon for the future.

E-procurement accelerates SMEs at a reduced cost. The purpose of chapter two, "*E-Procurement System and Adoption for SMEs,*" by Bayram and Vayvay, is to show that the adoption of an e-procurement system is essential in the supply chain for SMEs and to find solutions in order to make the use of this system as easy as possible. The adoption should be considered as a re-engineering process from an innovative perspective. An adoption plan is proposed within the study, consisting of three phases: 1) identification of the e-procurement process, 2) seeking integration points with other elements of the system, and 3) IT implementation of the integration areas. The study also proposes to use business process management tools that have workflow engines and Web service implementations for integration points. Although BPM tools are seen as quite expensive to SMEs, there are also dependable free licensed ones. The chapter is concluded with a case-study that is implemented with a free-licensed BPM tool for proof-of-concepts.

In chapter three, "*Model of Functionalities for the Development of B2B E-Commerce Solutions,*" Pinto, Rodrigues, Varajão, and Gonçalves focus on business to business (B2B) e-commerce. B2B describes electronic commerce associated to operations of buying and selling products and services through the Internet or through the use of private networks shared between business partners, thus replacing the physical process around commercial transactions. The analysis of the several B2B solutions enabled the verification that there are major differences in the amount of the supported functionalities, and significant opportunities for development, with the aim of helping companies to evaluate their electronic commerce solutions and to conceive new and more complete systems. This chapter presents a new model of functionalities for the development of B2B solutions.

Chapter four, *"Cross-Site Scripting: An Overview,"* introduces a comprehensive survey on a currently relevant security threat to Web applications: cross-site scripting (XSS). The rise of reported XSS vulnerabilities has made this family of attacks an interesting area for computer security researchers. XSS consists of the injection of code in Web pages. As injected code is made up of client side scripts, it is executed at the user's Web browser. The main reason for the existence of this kind of vulnerabilities is the incorrect or insufficient handling of the input performed by Web applications. In this chapter, guidelines on proper input treatment for Web developers are offered. Additionally, existing proposals for XSS mitigations are exposed, and future lines of research are indicated to interested researchers and developers. Web applications are susceptible to including vulnerabilities that may not only disrupt the provided service, but also facilitate private and personal information to an attacker. As these applications are usually public or even publicized, attacks are expected to be more and more frequent, making it necessary to supply the means to provide an adequate level of security in the utilization of Web applications.

Chapter 5

Open Source Software (OSS) has gained a strong interest and an increased acceptance in the software industry, introducing wholly new means of software development and distribution, creating a significant impact on the evolution of numerous business processes. Chapter five, *"An Open Source E-Procurement Application Framework for B2B and G2B,"* examines the impact of the open source paradigm in the e-Procurement evolution and identifies a trend towards Open Source e-Procurement Application Frameworks (AFs) which enable the development of tailored e-Procurement Solutions. Anchored in this notion, the authors present an Open-Source e-Procurement AF with a two-phase generation procedure, combining the Model Driven Engineering (MDE) approach with the Service-Oriented Architecture (SOA) paradigm for enabling the cost-effective production of e-Procurement Solutions by facilitating integration, interoperability, easy maintenance, and management of possible changes in the European e-Procurement environment. The assessment process of the proposed AF and its resulting e-Procurement Solutions occurs in the context of G2B in the Western-Balkan European region. The evaluation yields positive results and further enhancing opportunities.

Chapter 6

Often, small and medium enterprises consider the possibility of creating their own contact centre as a tool to improve the customer service. They pose some important questions about business and technical aspects: Why should we use a contact center solution? Which technologies, architectures, and solutions are available? Which key issues should be analyzed? Rijo, in *"Contact Centers: Tool for Effective E-Business,"* provides specific information and practical guidelines about Contact Centers based on a literature review and interviews made to contact center business consultants specialized in the small and medium enterprises sector. The goal of the chapter is to help top management and Information Technology personnel in making the best technological choices and methodological approaches.

Chapter 7

Parking is costly and limited in almost every major city in the world, and misparking aggravates the competition of parking slots. Innovative parking systems for meeting near-term parking demand are needed. The chapter *"E-Parking: An Electronic Parking Service Using Wireless Networks"* proposes a novel parking system which adopts the wireless network and sensor technologies to provide an intelligent and automatic parking service, and presents the implementation and a probabilistic analysis of the new parking service. The drivers will be informed the detailed information, i.e. the vacant parking slots and the route to the slot. From the investor's view, the electronic parking system proposed in the chapter is an efficient and profitable system in utilization of slots and the maintenance cost.

The four chapters of Section 2 introduce new concerns of e-marketing strategies.

El-Gohary, in *"E-Marketing: Towards a Conceptualisation of a New Marketing Philosophy,"* aims to add to the accumulative knowledge in the field of e-marketing through conceptualising e-marketing as a new marketing philosophy. The review of the literature has revealed that one of the main obstacles to developing e-marketing potential is the absence of a clear conceptualisation of e-marketing purpose and definition. The majority of researchers within the field misuse the term e-marketing and are using the terms e-business, e-marketing, e-commerce and Internet-marketing interchangeably as if they are similar or have the same meaning, which is incorrect. The differences between these terms as well as the main components of e-marketing are illustrated and discussed in detail within the chapter towards achieving a conceptualisation of e-marketing as a new marketing philosophy and to build a ground base of understanding for these different concepts. The chapter will help researchers and scholars to have a clearer view towards this concept that in turn will contribute to the related accumulated knowledge in the field.

Chapter nine, "*Analysis of the Variables which Determine a Good E-Marketing Strategy: The Techniques Most Used During Times of Crisis,*" demonstrates how adequate planning is fundamental in a SME to increase sales. The objective is to analyze the aspects that must be taken into consideration when developing a good e-marketing strategy and to study some of the different alternatives that the Internet and e-marketing make available to us: e-mail marketing, viral e-marketing, geomarketing, and positioning within search engines. Also, the concept of Customer Relationship Management (CRM) will be analyzed. The leap into the global market is not easy and the reduction in budgets has inspired marketing professionals to adopt strategies which can be measured and the results controlled, pointing out that the online tactics and tools used by the vast majority of marketing professionals in their strategic plan are banners, search engines and e-mail.

"*Market Research 2.0: An Inclusive Approach to Understanding Customers' Needs,*" by Given and Rathi, examines the possibilities of conducting market research in Web 2.0 environments, with a focus on implications for small to medium-sized companies. The chapter discusses how companies can undertake market research using Web 2.0 platforms, explores how these tools can facilitate successful and appropriate market research design, and examines the characteristics of qualitative and quantitative "Research 2.0" techniques appropriate to a Web 2.0 environment. The chapter also presents examples of companies that are using these tools successfully for market research and discusses advantages and barriers in adopting these tools, including privacy, ethics, and legal implications of this type of research.

In chapter 11, "*E-Marketing,*" Manarte and Teixeira present e-marketing and the channels, tools and techniques that can be used by SMEs so they can optimize the benefits of an online presence. Knowing its customers is the starting point for any firm's marketing activity, so the chapter introduces concepts related to the process of gathering information about e-customers. The company website is the gateway to Internet marketing, so it is important to promote it in a variety of ways that are also explained in the chapter. Selling online can be an interesting option, but this decision should only be taken after considering the pros and cons that it involves. To conclude, the authors discuss the e-marketing plan, which should guarantee that the objectives, strategies, and actions of online marketing are coherently integrated with the offline marketing plan.

Section 3, "Semantic Technologies" describes how e-Commerce is strongly supported by advances in semantic technologies, ontologies, and Web services, as reflected in the four chapters of this section.

The purpose of Beckett, Rowland-Campbell, and Strahl in "*Critical Success Factors to Yield Business Benefits from Semantic Technologies*" is to explore opportunities offered by and issues associated with the use of emergent semantic technologies in enhancing an enterprise's business position. These technologies include a foundation level set of standards and descriptive languages supporting interpretive connections to applications. The chapter is more oriented towards applications and the human side of the human/machine interface. The authors draw on both the literature and case material available to them as active practitioners to illustrate benefits realized and potential barriers to the uptake of semantic technologies. Critical success factors are related to user learning capabilities, the establishment of trust in the technology and its providers, and factors influencing the nature of potential engagement with users and markets.

Nowadays, firms need to refocus the way they manage the knowledge generated from business processes, in order to optimize their information systems' performance. Business ontologies are an excellent tool for this. In "*The Semantic Integration of Information: A Business Ontology Proposal with Semantic Interoperability,*" Paredes-Moreno, Martínez-López, and Schwartz highlight how important is for companies to invest efforts in a closer integration of their systems, with the aim of improving their performance and cooperation. This implies moving towards more efficient systems in their knowledge management. The big challenge for firms now is the semantic integration of information. Essential questions related to this question are synthetically introduced. Then, some of the most significant initiatives and projects on semantic integration of information are presented and compared with a business ontology that authors have developed for commercial use.

With the increasing development of the Semantic Web technologies, the Semantic Web has been introduced to apply in the Web Services to integrate data across different applications. For Semantic Web Services to succeed, it is essential to maintain the security of the organizations involved. To guarantee the security of the Web Services, security measures must be considered to protect against unauthorized disclosure, transfer, modification, or destruction, whether accidental or intentional. Access control is a kind of security measurements to guarantee the service processes, which is defined to allow resource owners to define, manage, and enforce the access conditions for each resource. In "*Semantic Mapping for Access Control Model*" by Zhao and Halang, an attribute based access control model with semantic mapping (SABAC) to specify access control over attributes defined in domain ontologies is proposed. The model is built on the basis of XACML policy language. Semantic mapping process is proved to be syntactical, semantic, and structural.

Chapter 15, "*Ontological Representation of Virtual Business Communities: How to Find Right Business Partners*" by Petrič, Urbančič, and Cestnik addresses the field of efficient information retrieval and knowledge discovery from textual data. To become acquainted with a particular domain and to better understand the underlying concepts, domain knowledge can be represented by ontologies. In addition, ontologies can be used for identification of potential links in virtual business communities and for decision support when searching for right business partners, which is very relevant to small to medium-sized enterprises. Potential applications range from dynamic supply chain configuration to building consortia as quick responses to business opportunities.

Legal and security aspects are fundamentals for e-commerce, and several major concerns are introduced in section 4.

In order for a SME to conduct business electronically, that SME requires the establishment of a website. This requires agreements relating to (1) website development, (2) website hosting (3); Internet access, and (4) online content and advertising. In "*Key Contracts Needed for SMEs Conducting E-Business: A Practical Guide from a UK Law Perspective,*" Sam de Silva provides a practical guide from a UK law perspective for a SME in relation to the issues which should be considered when contracts for the above mentioned services are negotiated. The chapter does not cover the issues relating to how the SME should set up its arrangements with its own customers (for example, through website terms and conditions), nor does it consider e-commerce legislation required when conducting business on the Internet.

In cyberworld, intellectual property rights and the right to informational self determination have become two realities in tension; nevertheless, they are two main concerns of the e-commerce stakeholders. From the industry point of view, new digital technologies, left unregulated, may allow a free flow of information and unauthorized access to contents both from consumers or competitors; from the consumers' perspective, security and privacy concerns are the major barriers to contracting online. The goal of chapter 17, *"Electronic Surveillance, Privacy and Enforcement of Intellectual Property Rights: A Digital Panopticon?"* by Pedro Pina, is to understand the relationship between anti-piracy oriented private electronic surveillance and consumers' privacy. If, on the one hand, the enforcement of intellectual property is a laudable activity, on the other hand, the individual's privacy sphere is one of the most important values and personal freedoms that law, including intellectual property law, must preserve.

Nowadays, when organizations, no matter what dimension they possess, are confronted with more exigent market challenges, they must change strategies and behaviors as needed to respond according to their new business positioning. If all organizations are affected by markets instability, SMEs suffer a greater impact due to a lack of suitable resources to appropriately change business strategy or develop a new one. This reveals information and information security significance, and so the relevance of securing information systems that supports their flows through organizations. In *"SMEs E-Business Security Issues,"* Gaivéo points information security issues that are important to SMEs e-business strategies, issues which could simultaneously guarantee organizational information privacy, and Gaivéo establishes guidelines which could also be applied to SMEs, allowing information security policies definitions.

EXPECTATIONS

Along this 18 chapters, the reader is faced with discussions and confirmation of the relevance and impact of this hot topic on enterprises (and in particular SME) competitiveness; its role in the support of new organizational models (networked, collaborative, virtual, knowledge-based, ubiquitous); discussion of drivers and barriers to e-business development; and the presentation of state-of-the-art enabling technologies.

The book provides researchers, scholars, and professionals with some of the most advanced research developments, solutions, and discussions of e-business challenges, impacts, and opportunities under the social, managerial, and organizational dimensions. This way, is expected to be read by academics (teachers, researchers and students of several graduate and postgraduate courses) and by professionals of Information Technology, IT managers and responsible, Marketing experts, Enterprise managers (including top level managers), and also technology solutions developers.

Maria Manuela Cruz-Cunha
Polytechnic Insitute of Cavado and Ave, Portugal

João Varajão
University of Trás-os-Montes e Alto Douro, Portugal

Acknowledgment

Editing a book is a quite hard but compensating and enriching task, as it involves a set of different activities like contacts with authors and reviewers, discussion and exchange of ideas and experiences, process management, organization and integration of contents, and many other tasks, with the permanent objective of creating a book that meets the public expectations. And this task cannot be accomplished without a great help and support from many sources. As editors, we would like to acknowledge the help, support, and belief of all who made possible this creation.

First of all, the editing of this book would not have been possible without the ongoing professional support of the team of professionals of IGI Global. We are grateful to Dr. Mehdi Khosrow-Pour and to Ms. Jan Travers, Director of Intellectual Property and Contracts, for the opportunity and belief in this project. A very very special mention of gratitude is due to Ms. Christine Bufton, Promotions and Communications Coordinator, and to Mr. Dave DeRicco and Ms. Myla Harty, Editorial Assistants, for their professional support and friendly words of advising, encouragement, and prompt guidance. We also address our recognition and appreciation to all the staff at IGI Global, whose contributions throughout the process of production and making this book available all over the world was invaluable.

We are grateful to all the authors, for their insights and excellent contributions to this book. Also we are grateful to the authors who simultaneously served as referees for chapters written by other authors, as well as to the external referees, for their insights, valuable contributions, prompt collaboration, and constructive comments. Thank you all, authors and reviewers, you made this book! The communication and exchange of views within this truly global group of recognized individualities from the scientific domain and from industry was an enriching and exciting experience!

We are also grateful to all who made efforts to contribute to this project, some of them with high quality chapter proposals, but unfortunately, due to several constraints could not have seen their work published.

Thank you.

Maria Manuela Cruz-Cunha
Polytechnic Insitute of Cavado and Ave, Portugal

João Eduardo Varajão
University of Trás-os-Montes e Alto Douro, Portugal

Section 1
Technological and Organizational Solutions

Chapter 1
Web 2.0:
An Emerging and Innovative Solution for SMEs

Alexis Barlow
Glasgow Caledonian University, UK

Margaret McCann
Glasgow Caledonian University, UK

Anne Smith
Glasgow Caledonian University, UK

ABSTRACT

This chapter critically analyses and assesses the concept and development of Web 2.0 within small to medium sized enterprises (SMEs). Web 2.0 is changing the way that business can be conducted, offering SMEs opportunities for developing strategies, business models and supply chains whilst adding value and gaining competitive advantage. There are many advantages for SMEs using Web 2.0 including them being easy to use, limited skills required and relatively low-cost and there are a range of emerging applications in fields such as marketing, collaboration, knowledge transfer, enhancing products and services, and research. Equally, there is an array of operational and managerial challenges that need to be overcome. This chapter suggests a set of questions that SMEs may consider using as a guide if they are considering Web 2.0 as a competitive weapon for the future.

INTRODUCTION

The aim of this chapter is to critically analyse and assess the concept and development of Web 2.0 within small to medium sized enterprises (SMEs). SMEs should be continually looking at ways in

which new innovative technologies may be applied strategically. Many new innovative technologies are emerging that can be used over the Internet which have different features, applications and challenges that can be very easily used to improve the impact and performance of SMEs. In particular, the new wave of Web 2.0 technologies is facilitating interaction, socialisation, creativity,

DOI: 10.4018/978-1-60960-765-4.ch001

information sharing, and collaboration amongst users. Advances in technology, may require SMEs to consider new ways in which booking, advertising and marketing is carried out. The specific objective of the chapter is to help the readers understand Web 2.0, their particular relevance and suitability to SMEs, enable them to better exploit emerging opportunities and comprehend the challenges posed by Web 2.0.

The chapter is structured as follows. It begins by presenting the background of the chapter, through examining various definitions of Web 2.0 and identifying some of its key characteristics. Following the background, the main body of the chapter identifies the relevance and key advantages of Web 2.0 for SMEs and then explores examples of innovative applications of Web 2.0 within a SME context, using technologies such as blogs, microblogging, wikis, social networking, RSS, forums, podcasting and media sharing and software as a service. The chapter then goes on to examine the adoption and embedment of Web 2.0, issues, controversies and problems that SMEs may face in this process and then provides solutions and recommendations on how SMEs can take Web 2.0 forward and make it an integral part of their strategic direction. Finally, the chapter closes by highlighting future research directions, summarising the chapter coverage and providing some concluding remarks.

BACKGROUND

Web 2.0 is a concept which arose from a brainstorming session hosted by O'Reilly Media Inc in 2004. The term was developed to encapsulate the rapid development in the usage of the Web and associated technologies and applications, following the bursting of the dot.com bubble in the year 2000 (Sheun, 2008). Web 2.0 is the business revolution in the computer industry caused by the increasing move to the Internet as a platform but also through an attempt to understand the rules for success on that new platform (O'Reilly, 2005). The embodiment of Web 2.0 is in "building applications and services around the unique features of the Internet, as opposed to building applications and expecting the Internet to suit as a platform" (Wikipedia, 2008). A range of services, technologies and applications commonly associated with Web 2.0 are blogs, wikis, podcasts, RSS feeds, social networks, forums, multimedia sharing services, tagging and social bookmarking, text messaging and instant messaging.

Web 2.0 relates to the concept of participation and interaction with Web users connecting and sharing data, collaborating and contributing their own thoughts, ideas, experiences and knowledge. It encourages interaction amongst businesses and customers who in a traditional trading environment would be restricted by direct, 'word-of-mouth' feedback from local customers.

Nations (2009) takes a social perspective and highlights that Web 2.0 is a social web, with people connecting with other people. It encapsulates the notion of being a more socially connected society including characteristics such as openness, participation, cooperation, community and collaboration. Web 2.0 necessitates a shift in the philosophy of society to one where we aren't just using the Internet as a tool – but we are becoming part of it.

King (2006) suggests that "collaboration has come to the Web to a much greater degree than was previously feasible" (p.88). This has facilitated collaborative working practices and has allowed a range of products to be developed such as Wikipedia and Linux.

Other definitions emphasise the interactivity of the web. Over the past few years the Web has changed from a passive, read only medium to a dynamic medium where multimedia content is created and shared by many. The YouTube video, "Web 2.0: The Machine is Us/ing Us" (Wesh, 2009), explains how through using XML to separate content from form, knowledge can be exported and syndicated without complicated code. This has given to a rise in the level of uploaded user content. It is now common for existing or potential customers regardless of their location to not only place orders on-line, but also contribute their knowledge, or feedback their ideas or opinions on a business's products or services through Web technology.

IBM (2009) stress the use of Web 2.0 for taking advantage of new business opportunities and business value through: enhancing customer experience and value by innovating the way you interact with your customers; boosting the quality and speed of the decisions employees make; accelerating new business designs that are contextual and action-oriented. Web 2.0 takes a fundamentally different view of how businesses, customers, and partners interact, and in doing so, it opens up a range of different business models (Shuen, 2008). Bernoff and Li (2008) highlight five key areas of supply chain activities that Web 2.0 are being applied including: research and development; marketing; sales; customer support; and operations.

Web technologies are altering the way that business can be conducted. In particular, Web 2.0 offers tremendous potential and viable solutions for competitive SMEs. SMEs no longer need to have the same level of technical expertise as required for previous applications as Web 2.0 technologies and applications are easier to use and cost effective whilst offering SMEs the potential to compete in a global market irrespective of their location.

SMES AND ADVANTAGES OF WEB 2.0

SMEs are crucial to the global economy. In the UK economy alone they provide 59.2% of employment and 51.5% of total turnover (BERR, 2008). They are heterogeneous in the wide range of sectors they serve, as well as diverse in other factors such as size and location of business. The development of SMEs therefore requires careful consideration in relation to the markets they serve, size and growth capability, training and levels of education, and the nature of the staff involved.

It is becoming increasingly difficult for companies to develop and gain competitive advantage through traditional channels such as cost cutting or acquisitions and mergers (Robinson, 2008) and so SMEs must find other innovate ways to become and remain competitive. During the past twenty years the internet has been adopted by SMEs, at different rates, by different sectors and for different purposes.

"Businesses with fewer than 250 employees showed the largest year on year rise in the proportion selling on-line……...The Wholesale, Retail, Catering and Travel sector continued to be the sector that sold the most on-line, with £79.4bn of sales in 2007" (Office for National Statistics 2008).

However, large businesses are traditionally seen as being more innovative in the application of technology (Office for National Statistics 2008; Bughin, 2008) and reasons for this might be related to resource availability, skills and also level of business specialisation. Technology is a tool which can improve business efficiency, performance and competitiveness and may therefore be the mechanism that SMEs adopt in their fight to succeed. In particular, governments seek to encourage technology uptake in SMEs so that they can become more competitive, create more jobs and increase their economic contribution.

A business that aims to survive and grow must understand and respond to changing demands from markets, suppliers and customers. There are currently 1.6 billion internet users worldwide which accounts for 24% of world population. The number of users has grown 342% from 2000 – 2008 (Internet World Statistics, 2009). In addition from 2003 to 2009 there was an 87% growth in the number of people using Web 2.0 type applications and an 883% increase in the time users devote

Figure 1. The long tail

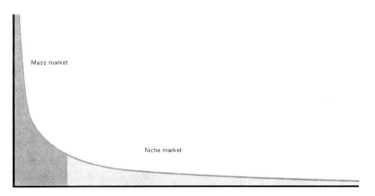

to such applications (Nielsen, 2009). Consumer purchasing behaviour has also changed rapidly and now customers want to be more connected with who supplies them, they want to be able to interact and talk about the product or the service, good and bad. Web 2.0 applications allow and encourage consumer participation and feedback.

Web 2.0 in particular offers SMEs a range of advantages and opportunities. Web 2.0 provides SMEs the potential to compete in a global market irrespective of location. Since most Web 2.0 applications can be accessed through a browser, no special equipment or software is required except for a broadband connection. Set-up costs are low, or free, for most Web 2.0 applications and they do involve a high level of skills or development time (Wagner, 2005). Therefore Web 2.0 is ideal for a SME where limited skills may exist within the company. However, if a company Web site already exists, Web 2.0 applications can be used to direct more customers to it or achieve a higher rating within search engines. Web 2.0 applications are also not as intrusive as applications such as email, as typically they are accessed in the SMEs own time.

Key advantages of Web 2.0 applications though, lie in the potential they offer for setting up and utilising business connections and collaborations. They can be used to build communities based on interest, purpose or practice between and amongst businesses and customers regard-less of location. Customer-centricity (Wagner & Majchrzak, 2007) can develop and increase as customers are encouraged to openly feedback and share thoughts, experiences and ideas while businesses can easily communicate, transfer knowledge and disseminate information to existing and potential customers. Web 2.0 can also expand and enhance business networks, their supply chains and management of their supply chains.

Web 2.0 offers a range of applications that encourage consumer participation and business collaboration and can be highly suitable for the many contexts and multiuse requirement of the diverse population of SMEs. Their operational application can not only be company specific but also service specific, customer specific and function specific.

An interesting development recently has been the creation, existence and subsequent understanding of the dynamics of the long tail (see Figure 1).

The Web offers SMEs the opportunity to connect with new customers and new markets regardless of location. The figure above illustrates the way the Web has changed traditional supply and demand for products and services and stimulated two different types of market. At the head of the curve is the mass market (mass-produced, high selling, products and services) while the tail represents a wide variety of niche products that individually do not sell massive amounts but when cumulated, represent a market to rival, or exceed, that of mass-produced products (Anderson, 2004). Consumers demand goods and services from both ends of the curve. SMEs typically fit into the long tail as they can offer niche products and services and treat customers more individually and Web 2.0 allows these smaller markets to be serviced more cost effectively (Warr, 2008). However success depends on effective marketing and, for SMEs to expand beyond their local market, the adoption and effective use of Web technology.

Before adopting such technology, an SME must better understand what Web 2.0 can offer to their business. The next section explores the range of potentially innovative applications emerging through Web 2.0 for SMEs.

INNOVATIVE APPLICATION OF WEB 2.0 ACROSS SMES

Web 2.0 applications are particularly suitable as they are easy to use and cost-effective and so can offer tremendous potential and viable solutions for SMEs who may have limited technological skills or the capital required for other effective technical solutions. As indicated by Brynjolfsson and Saunders (2010),

"Companies that don't innovate are driven out of business, but the returns to companies that do innovate are much larger than before. With each successive innovation in communication technology, the ability to reach more people easily has increased exponentially." (p. 103). Such is the imperative for the SME to consider how they use technology to develop their business. This section describes the various applications and how they can be used by SMEs, with some real-life examples.

There are a range of potential and innovative applications of Web 2.0 that could be, and have been, employed by SMEs within the public, private and voluntary sectors. This technology can be used to change their strategic direction, the way they conduct business or operate their supply chain. Applications can involve a range of technologies such as blogs, wikis, social networking, RSS, forums, podcasting and media sharing and software as a service. Key innovative applications in which Web 2.0 applications have been employed include:

- Marketing and advertising
- Collaboration and strengthening relationships with customers and suppliers
- Information and knowledge transfer
- Delivering added value to products and services
- Networking,
- Research

Blogs: Blogs are on-line journals which are used for writing short, informal communications and are one of the quickest and easiest ways for SMEs to have an online presence. Blogging software is often free and is easier to create and update than a Web site (Wyld, 2008). Entries are displayed in reverse chronological order, and readers can comment and communicate with the blog author. Blogs can be used for both internal and external communications for a wide range of information dissemination such as personal reflections, delivering news on particular topics, showcasing of products and services, sharing expert advice, opinions, frequently asked questions (FAQ) or even links to other businesses. Blogs tend to be textual but some blogs are based on photographs (photoblog), videos (vlog), music (MP3 blog), audio (podcasting), or even art (artlog) (Wyld, 2008).

Blogs are increasingly being used within a business context and their use has even been described as a paradigm shift in the way companies are interacting with customers (Stocker & Tochtermann, 2008). They are emerging as an opportunistic, external information dissemination tool for businesses to promote and personalise their brand and provide detailed information on the products and services on offer. By showcas-

Table 1.

| The Real Flower Company | This British flower company maintain a blog using photos to maximum effect to promote their products. | http://www.realflowers.co.uk/weblog |
| London Property Estate Agents | This company use their blog to promote individual properties for sale as well as provide general information on the districts properties are on offer and the current state of the property sales market. | http://www.londonpropertyadvisor.co.uk/blog/ |

ing and sharing expertise in business-to-business or business-to-customer communications, blogs can be used to gather customer feedback and to build up a loyal customer base. By providing links to other blogs or websites, a business can help promote the products and services on offer by others in their supply chain.

Anderson (2004) states that blogs are a good way to communicate with micro audiences and therefore may be particularly suitable for smaller companies. Through the blog, customers can provide vital feedback on the products or service they received for others to read. Businesses can also use blogs to gather further information about their customers through online customer registration and to develop a greater insight into their customers and the types of topics they find engaging and interesting. They can build this customer feedback into their market segmentation and product positioning process as well as into the development of future products and services.

Blogs can also be used as an internal communication tool for information dissemination on recent business activity, decisions and developments, or as a vehicle for an open staff discussion forum to help engage employees and even for employees to share passion for their work (Stocker & Tochtermann, 2008). They can be a cost-effective way to encourage staff to create and share information and best practice as well as empowering employees to get involved in decision making within the business. Many CEOs use blogging to disseminate information to their staff on recent or planned business activity.

Blogs therefore can be used by SMEs to increase their online profile. They can be used to reduce the internal communications budget, as well as promote the business to its external environment.

Examples of SME blogs are shown in Table 1.

Microblogging: A recent blogging phenomenon is microblogging which is blogging limited to a shorter message length (typically 140 characters) and typically involving mobile devices. Microblogging is becoming increasingly popular in its general use and may be useful for business updates for collaboration purposes or for the marketing of goods (Jin, 2009). It can even be used to replace radio or print advertising. The most popular microblogging tool is Twitter (http://www.twitter.com). Using Twitter, businesses can 'tweet' to raise awareness of business matters and so help branding and, since followers are encouraged to respond, can be used to gain information instantaneously for public relations and market research. Examples of SMEs that have successfully used Twitter are shown in Table 2.

Wikis: Wikis were firstly developed by Ward Cunningham in the mid-90's. Wiki are collaborative software that enable users to collaboratively create, edit, link and organise information on a website. They can facilitate cooperative work and knowledge generation (Raman, 2006) with the underlying philosophy being that all users can

Table 2.

RuhlBee supplies	A US beekeepers' supply company keep followers updated with timely tips on beekeeping and alerts for classes and other special events	http://twitter.com/ruhlbeesupply
The Real Flower Company	This company, mentioned above, also Twitter to engage with customers and promote seasonal products	http://twitter.com/realflowergirl

edit the content and style thus guiding its direction (Anderson, 2005). Moreover, they have a range of technical capabilities including quick and easy creation, collaborative authoring, the ability to link pages, content management, author tracking and locking. They can be public or private, internal or external to the business as security restrictions can be implemented to allow privileged access.

Wikis can be used socially for planning events, project management, content management systems, team agendas and meeting notes, company calendars, idea generation and discussion boards, as well as enhancing communities of practice. They can even be used within a business context replacing an intranet, for email communications or to centralise corporate documents. SMEs can therefore use wikis for document sharing and collaboration and for encouraging communication, knowledge transfer and collective intelligence between and amongst employees.

Examples of SMEs using wikis are shown in Table 3.

Social Networking: Social networking is a term which relates to people or organisations using a collection of tools to communicate, socialise and build relationships. The term can encompass applications such as instant messaging, file sharing (such as photo or video sharing), social bookmarking, and can even include blogging, discussion groups and podcasting. The following discussion relates specifically to social networking Web sites such as Facebook (http://www.facebook.com), MySpace (http://myspace.com) and LinkedIn (http://www.linkedin.com) where users create and upload relevant details onto their own page and use the network to search for and meet other members, join groups and engage with communities of interest.

Social networking has the advantage over more traditional forms of networking as they offer alternative ways to meet new people and help manage existing contacts (Enders et al, 2008). SMEs can use social networking for marketing and information dissemination as well as directing traffic to the company website or others in their supply chain.

Table 3.

Hammarskjold Information	This publishing company use wikis for the production of a bi-monthly 30 page magazine. The wiki is used by the magazine production team for everything from entering content, page layout, editing and production.	See http://twiki.org/cgi-bin/view/Main/TWikiSuccessStoryOfMagazinePublishing
LostBoys	An internet design agency with 200 employees use wikis for their internal telephone directory, information on new employees and they also host an internal company blog on their wiki.	See http://twiki.org/cgi-bin/view/Main/TWikiSuccessStoryOfLostBoys
CMed Clinical Research Organisation	This organisation have adopted wikis as their company intranet to place all of their Standard Operating Procedures and Working Practices online	See http://twiki.org/cgi-bin/view/Main/TWikiSuccessStoryOfCmed

Social networking can be particularly effective for SMEs as it can reduce feelings of isolation which might be associated with smaller firms. It can also be used to build links with other larger businesses in the supply chain as well as actively engage customers.

Facebook is the largest social networking site with over 250 million visitors (Schonfeld, 2009) and is now the 4th most popular US Web brand (Neilsen, 2009). Although initially popular with a younger generation, social networking is becoming more popular with over 35 year olds, with Facebook's fastest growing demographic being the over 55 age group (eMarketer, 2009) and overall resulting in the sites becoming more 'age neutral' (Stroud, 2007).

An excellent example of a large business using social networking is the UK retailer Marks and Spencers whose pages on Facebook reveal deep engagement with customers. They are used to adverte of new products, with links to their website, and customer feedback on the advertised products. There are other examples of engagement where customers post comments about products they like or hate (or suggestions or products they would like to see), ideas for new product lines, and even suggestions for new store locations. Such feedback provides the organisation with a wealth of information for future developments and marketing.

There are also a wide range of SMEs using social networking within business to promote their products and services, to engage with customers and others in the supply chain for B2C and B2B activities. The following can be found on Facebook (http://www.facebook.com) where membership is required:

- Social Media for Small Business by Dell (http://www.facebook.com/dellsocialmedia) is a series of guides to help small businesses use social media tools.
- Many restaurants (eg Olive Garden, BJs Restaurant and Brewhouse) have pages where they advertise the food, special offers and meal deals, include photos and invite feedback. This is an effective way to gain customer feedback on popular choices.
- Charities such as Oxfam, The Breast Cancer Site and Action Aid use Facebook to post information on their charity's work, how to get involved, advertise merchandise and generate feedback and discussion from their followers in the community.

The social networking sites *LinkedIn* and *Ecademy* are established specifically for business networking and so are used by SMEs to make business connections and engage with communities of interest (http://www.linkedin.com) and (http://ecademy.com). Since such sites are used by professionals who post their detailed employment profiles, they are commonly used by businesses looking to employ new staff.

Further examples of social networking is in photo sharing sites such as Flickr (http://www.flickr.com) and Picasa (http://picasa.google.com) where users tag and share photos, as well as social bookmarking sites such as del.icio.us (http://delicious.com), Dig (http://digg.com) and Reddit (http://reddit.com). bizSugar (http://www.bizsugar.com) is a social bookmarking and networking site specifically for small business owners and managers to share related information links with others. It also operates a voting system to allow users to see the best sites others have rated as well as links to those who voted. Users can easily submit their own content and so use bizSugar to promote stories/Web sites that they would like others to follow.

Really Simple Syndication (RSS): RSS is a technology that notifies users about changes in the content of RSS-enabled sites. Therefore there is no need to use a search engine to continually search for site updates and, instead, the updated content is sent to them, resulting in a 'live' or 'incremental' web. RSS can be used for different types of Web content such as a company Web site or a blog to keep interested parties up-to-date with company news or for marketing to existing or potential customers or suppliers.

Microsoft's small business centre offers an RSS feed specifically for small businesses to keep them up-to-date with developments in the SME marketplace. (http://www.microsoft.com/uk/smallbusiness/sbnews/rss/)

Forums: Forums or discussion boards can be used by SMEs to make business connections or share information, exchange views and seek advice on business-related matters where they may lack the expertise. There are numerous forums and discussion boards on a wide variety of topics to be found where SMEs can participate and engage with other businesses and customers. Most require registration and are governed by a moderator who is responsible for checking for unsuitable content.

Some general business forums are designed to provide small businesses and entrepreneurs with help and advice on a variety of matters such as marketing, copyright, trading & employment law, IT and accounting and bookkeeping. Examples include:

- A1 Business Forums: (http://www.a1businessforums.co.uk/forum/)
- Entrepreneur Forum: (http://entrepreneur-forum.co.uk/)

Podcasting and Media Sharing: Podcasting and media sharing sites such as YouTube (http://www.youtube.com) and GoogleVideo (http://video.google.com) are cost-effective ways for small companies to engage with others and showcase products where the cost of advertising may be prohibitive. Little technical skill is required to produce video files and use the media to market and advertise to a global market.

Business podcast directories catalogue business podcasts in one accessible site to allow users to search for information or seek advice on a variety of subjects relevant to small businesses and entrepreneurs. Examples include:

- SmallBizPod (http://www.smallbizpod.co.uk/)
- Small Business Podcast Directory (http://www.smallbusinesspodcastdirectory.com/)

Many businesses use media sharing sites such as YouTube to provide promotional video information on facilities on offer. These sites are very easy-to-use and require no great technical skill to upload content. On YouTube a business can have its own channel where it can organise its video collection. Interested followers can then subscribe to the channel and be updated when new promotional material is available.

Examples of SMEs using YouTube are shown in Table 4.

Table 4.

Estate agents can use video sharing to present detailed information on houses for sale:	Coalter's Estate Agents, York, UK Channel Singapore Property Real Estate Channel	http://www.youtube.com/user/CoaltersYork http://www.youtube.com/user/mindyyongws
Hotels can promote their facilities to potential customers	Best hotels of Malta The NEW New Yorker Hotel	http://www.youtube.com/user/HotelMalta http://www.youtube.com/watch?v=dJJ00nvkMxU)
Tourist attractions can provide detailed guides and tours of the features on offer	Warwick Castle Stonehenge	http://www.youtube.com/watch?v=5yz0xNkMm AI&feature=PlayList&p=B3AB5B D5470F8566&index=8) http://www.youtube.com/watch?v=G9zwXB9fZDU &feature=PlayList&p=B3AB5B D5470F8566&index=0

Software as a Service: The popularity of the Web is changing the way that software can be purchased and used. Software as a service is one of the fastest growing segments of the IT industry. Traditionally when businesses wanted software they either bought an application package (such as Microsoft Office) and installed it on their computer or employed a programmer to write bespoke software for the business. Software as a service is software which customers can register for and use via the internet, from any location. With on demand licensing, businesses can then use the software as needed. Since the software, and often file storage, is available over the internet, users can easily share documents and collaborate. There are many other advantages to software as a service such as lower acquisition costs for businesses. Also, since the software is automatically updated, the latest version is always available and all users will use the same version. Some software as a service such as GoogleDocs (http://docs.google.com) is free to use and designed for easy collaboration as documents can be saved locally or to a Google file server, or published online for all users to access. Therefore it can be easy to access documents from any location with Web access.

From the above examples it is clear that there is a range of Web 2.0 tools and technologies that can be employed by SMEs. These can be used to make incremental and steady changes to the way a SME does business or they can used to radically change the way a SME operates. There is therefore vast potential for SMEs to employ Web 2.0 in innovative and pioneering ways across a range of areas of business.

ADOPTING AND EMBEDDING WEB 2.0

Prior to adopting Web 2.0, SMEs must gather relevant information. This does not mean that the SME requires a high level of technical knowledge; instead they must be familiar with the wide range of tools and applications available that may suit their business needs. One of the most effective ways to gather this information is to explore how others are using the different applications or experiment with the various applications themselves. By using the applications it is likely that the SME will tacitly understand the best applications for a particular business situation. Nonako (1991) considered the activity required to create knowledge and clearly reveal that there is a process of 'internalisation'. To internalise means that the SME owner manager can really understand the potential of the applications in their vast and varied business situations (Wickert and Herschel 2001).

Some SMEs may find adopting Web 2.0 easier than others. A concept that may assist us to understand why there is so much variation is adoption theory (Rogers, 1983). The very complex nature of individual personalities, who people work with and what knowledge people possess ultimately predisposes them to react in different ways to change, and indeed anything new. Rogers (1983) suggests five categories to describe adopters of innovation. (See Table 5)

The nature of SMEs that have adopted Web 2.0 to date tend to be those in the category of Innovators and Early Adopters. Deakins and Freel (2009) acknowledge that tools such as social networking sites are increasing although it is recognised that "…the phenomenon and success of social networking websites has yet to be reduced to a generic business model." (p.165)

In Rogers's theory of adoption a critical point is the idea of being connected, so this means that Early Adopters are likely to be exposed on a daily basis to connected and collaborative activity (Bower 1998). Some examples of this exposure exist in universities and large corporations. For example students will experience the use of Web 2.0 within their programme of study and many students may later find employment within a SME which will lead to higher adoption and usage rates in the near future.

Table 5.

Innovators	Innovators are generally considered to be individuals who possess knowledge and are embedded in systems of change, are comfortable with risk and of being where new ways of doings things are normal.
Early Adopters	Considered to be in close contact with social standing and have a capacity to generate a relatively high income.
Early Majority	A group who are careful but interested to try new things.
Late Majority	This group tends to be sceptical, more risk averse than the previous category and generally not as well connected
Laggards	Considered to be older in age, less connected out with their family and friends and have less income.

In the corporate sector, organisations such as IBM and Dell have steeped their employees in a culture of Web 2.0. Their Web activity contains a rich source of collaboration and information sharing where they have created vast global communities for their employees, customers and suppliers. In a similar way SMEs can increase their adoption of Web 2.0 by creating linkages with large organisations who already embed the technology. Connections to such communities are essential for an SME adoption strategy.

Once it has been decided to adopt Web 2.0 the SME must consider how it will be embedded into work routines and practices. Embedding any new technology requires top management support, process re-engineering, good communication, training, user support and most likely a change in culture.

"A higher level of usage is found at companies that encourage it by using tactics such as integrating the tools into existing workflows, launching Web 2.0 in conjunction with other strategic initiatives, and getting senior managers to act as role models for adoption. (Bughin et al, 2009)"

Web 2.0, in particular, requires a collaborative approach in developing and using the technology as well as a change in culture to one of openness, collaboration and interactivity. Of course embedding takes time and as technologies evolve, embedding of Web 2.0 may be considered a continual process.

There are further considerations for SMEs when embedding Web 2.0. These will involve identifying the internal and external communities that will want to collaborate and interact using the technology. The internal communities may be influenced by a range of factors such as business structure, staff involved, project work, etc. External communities may be influenced by the different supply chains that the SME is involved in and are likely to involve partners, customers and suppliers. Clearly it cannot be expected that all individuals that make up a community will be at the same stage of adoption. This may mean that certain activities are more likely to be embedded at different times.

Embedding Web 2.0 should also be an opportunity for SMEs to stand back and consider what type of communication and interaction they require internally amongst employees and externally with customers, suppliers, employees and other parties. For example, a retail business has a completely different communication requirement from a manufacturing firm. There is also a need to develop an understanding about how the different parties involved will want to communicate and which are the most appropriate tools to employ. Often this understanding may be developed over time and be a continuous process. Understanding that each SME is different and that each application of Web 2.0 will be different instils concepts of creative and knowledge based approaches to usage. Furthermore all parties involved must fully understand the benefits of using Web 2.0 for interaction and collaboration.

ISSUES, CONTROVERSIES & PROBLEMS

There is a distinct requirement for SMEs to fully understand what Web 2.0 is and appreciate how they can adopt and make use of Web 2.0 to gain competitive advantage. These technologies are inherently disruptive and can challenge business operations (Chui et al, 2009). Although there are many potential opportunities for Web 2.0 applications, there are also many issues and controversies in their adoption and usage and SMEs need to be realistic and recognise these problems. Such challenges are mainly linked to the open and participative nature of Web 2.0 technologies, the level of adoption of Web 2.0, the management of Web 2.0 coupled with the security, legal and regulatory concerns regarding Web 2.0.

Web 2.0 is centred around the concepts of openness, participation and interaction. Customers are encouraged to communicate in an open manner, offer feedback on products and services and engage in discussions, through technologies such as blogs, social networks and forums. Web 2.0 technologies can add a lot of extra value to an SMEs Web presence and provide a valuable source of information. SMEs, however, will have little, if any, control over the content and Web 2.0 may create the potential for unintended uses e.g. such openness gives customers the opportunity to complain about a business in a way that the business may not expect or relish and the repercussions may be detrimental to that business.

Web 2.0 networking works best with a large and active community of users. Essentially, Web 2.0 is driven by the people who use it. It is important that people within SMEs actively embrace Web 2.0 as well as relevant people external to the SME. If there are insufficient numbers of users, or users are not particularly active, then networking

opportunities are reduced and the quality of ideas and contributions may be low (Musser & O'Reilly, 2006) as cited in Warr (2008).

Within an SME, it is often the current skill level, the type of entrepreneur leading the SME or the cultural mindset that will dictate their likely adoption of technologies. Generally, the social values of SMEs are understood to have a greater level of resistance to change and this was highlighted in an adaptation study undertaken by Schindehutte and Morris (2001) where family firms are noted as being less likely to adapt and are internally focused. Direct Line for Business identified that many SMEs are failing to give themselves the best chance to succeed as one in three do not have any online presence to support their business (Howes, 2008). The report also reveals that of those who do have a company website, a quarter have only had it for the past three years or less. The main reasons for small businesses not having an online presence were down to lack of funding (14%), time (10%) and understanding (10%) of setting up a website. SMEs need be educated on these new innovative Web 2.0 technologies which are relatively inexpensive and easy to use.

SMEs also need to carefully select appropriate tools and technologies that will generate the greatest amount of Web traffic from their customers. This will involve carefully considering the customer base that they are targeting and the likelihood of them using particular technologies. Factors such as demographics, culture and technological awareness will again be something that will have to be considered. The SME will need to promote the benefits of their Web 2.0 tools to the wider community, to gain the greatest popularity amongst their audience and the broadest range of adoption. SMEs will also have to encourage the adoption of Web 2.0 tools by suppliers and other partners for collaborating and building up communities of practice. It may be that they will have to have built up sufficient levels of trust, familiarity and identity with each other to be willing to collaborate online and share greater levels of knowledge.

The management of the Web 2.0 technologies is also a critical component. SMEs need to actively participate in Web 2.0 to keep abreast of who is talking about their business, actively listen to their users and address concerns. They should adopt a formal process to monitor and analyse what customers are saying (Hoffman, 2009; Wyld, 2008) as well as engage and participate with customers (Eikelmann et al, 2008; Boulos et al, 2006). This is an area that needs to be clearly assigned as continued active participation and monitoring is essential but also very resource intensive.

Another management issue is the continuing anxiety regarding the level of security across the Internet and using Web 2.0 technologies. According to security experts, companies looking to embrace Web 2.0 technologies could open themselves up to new forms of attack by hackers (Millman, 2007). Breach of security can cause a realm of problems such as confidential information being mishandled, wikis pages being vandalised or spamming, where people are inserting links into wiki pages to commercial or false websites in order to drive traffic (Anderson, 2005). Likewise, content in applications such as wikis may be subject to vandalism or edited in a way which affects quality or accuracy (Anderson, 2007).

There may also be copyright violations associated with content shared as users post material without permission from the copyright holder. Equally, privacy of data must be protected. Therefore Web 2.0 initiatives may be stalled by legal concerns and strict policies may be required regarding the monitoring, tracking or moderation of contributions in addition to setting up registration and editing privileges to selected users. Again, all of this can be time consuming.

SMEs can no longer afford to ignore the continued uptake of Web 2.0 technologies. They need to appreciate how customers, in particular, are increasingly using technologies such as blogs, wikis and social networking sites and they need to understand and demonstrate concern for the issues and problems that may arise. Even if they decide against implementing them specifically for their own company, customer and other key players in their supply chain may be using Web 2.0 tools that are publicly available such as Twitter, Facebook and YouTube and they may be discussing their SME in positively or negative ways!

EMERGING SOLUTIONS AND RECOMMENDATIONS

There are many driving factors pushing SMEs to use Web 2.0 including it being easy to use and cost effective but also offering an opportunity for developing strategic direction and business models and a means of competing in a global marketplace. However, there are clearly many issues and challenges, outlined in the previous section that must be addressed and overcome. Issues such as selecting appropriate technologies, application and content which will generate an appropriate level of Web traffic, as well as measures to ensure appropriate security and privacy and continued participation and monitoring need to be addressed. The following recommends a set of emerging questions that managers of SMEs could employ as a guide when embarking on Web 2.0.

Set of Questions for Managers of SMEs

Organisational:

- ○ What is the company aiming to achieve with Web 2.0?
- ○ How can Web 2.0 be used to support business strategy?
- ○ How can Web 2.0 support the marketing strategy?

Blogging:

- ○ What types of activities will blogs be used for e.g. building up customer base, gathering customer feedback?

- What type of information do you want to communicate internally, externally or both?
- What type of content should be included in the blog e.g. general information, opinions, experiences, expert advice, etc
- Who should write the blog?
- What sort of writing style should be used?
- What level of security is required/will readers need to register to contribute?
- Should it encourage interaction and comments from readers?
- If so, who will manage feedback?

Wikis:

- What types of activities will wikis be used for e.g. documentation; work in progress; project; knowledge exchange?
- How can they be used for collaborating internally and externally?
- Can anyone contribute or does there need to be different levels of privileges?
- Is there going to be an agreed code of conduct?
- How are they planning to secure the wikis?

Social Networking:

- What will social networking be used for e.g. marketing, making business connections?
- What information will be included within profile e.g. graphics?
- What sort of style should be used?
- Who will manage content e.g. keep site up to date, deal with comments from 'friends'?

Podcasting:

- What will podcasts be used for e.g. showcase products, information exchange?

- What will content be?
- What format should be used (audio/video)?
- Who will develop content?
- How will it be distributed?
- Who will keep content up-to-date?
- Who will deal with comments and feedback?

RSS:

- Who should content be pushed to?
- What content should be pushed to the various parties?
- How often?

Integration:

- How can different Web 2.0 tools and technologies be integrated as part of a cohesive Web 2.0 strategy?

Web 2.0 can be used to promote open communication and participation with customers and suppliers, gaining valuable feedback from them as well as increasing loyalty. Nonetheless, such open communication can also lead to negative feedback therefore it should be stressed that any strategy for the use of Web 2.0 must consider reputation monitoring and management. One possible way to deal with negative public communication is to ensure the SME check regularly for anything which might be negative to the business (e.g. "Google" the company name), react quickly and ensure positive (or even neutral) information is highly visible. This may involve search engine optimisation to ensure that positive Web pages are listed first in search results or create new content that is positive.

Finally SMEs need to also be careful about what they post on their websites, blogs etc to ensure that they are not breaching any copyright laws and that they are not posting anything that could be turned round to be used negatively against the company.

FURTHER RESEARCH DIRECTIONS

Further research needs to be conducted to create a developed understanding of the adoption and usage of Web 2.0 technologies in SMEs. Exploratory research could commence in the form of a questionnaire survey. The questionnaire survey should gather information on the awareness levels of Web 2.0 by SMEs and the level of usage across business operations such as advertising, customer relationship management, researching and information exchange.

Case studies could then be conducted with selected SMEs to allow more detailed investigations of Web 2.0 within particular organisational contexts, using multiple methods of data collection. Areas of particular interest would be the impact that Web 2.0 has on SMEs' future strategies, identifying the emergence of further innovative applications as the technology develops and usage grows and the development of management strategies for effectively embedding Web 2.0. A key advantage of using the case study methodology will be the ability to study the entanglement of a particular phenomenon (in this case Web 2.0) with its context and will allow focus on the different dynamics present (Hartley, 1994). These case studies will allow deeper investigation and support the development of a conceptual framework that can be used by SMEs in the future for developing Web 2.0 across their organisations.

Research could also focus on a particular industry or industry sector. Industries that may be particularly well suited to Web 2.0 are those that would welcome and could benefit from knowledge sharing, collaboration and communities of practice. For example, the Food and Drinks industry would be particularly well-suited to Web 2.0 as people enjoy discussing food and drink, it is useful to pass on experiences and provide feedback and specialised fields such as organic foods could greatly benefit from online communities.

CONCLUSION

Web 2.0 offers an innovative, collaborative and interactive approach for SMEs to incrementally or radically change the way they do business. There are many advantages in adopting Web 2.0 including low set up costs, availability of software and there being a low level of technical skills required. These advantages are particularly beneficial for SMES, coupled with opportunities for globalisation, developing communities and building collaborative partnerships across business networks. There is a gradual increase in the range of innovative applications of Web 2.0 emerging by SMEs, involving Web 2.0 tools such as blogs, microblogging, wikis, social networking, RSS, forums, podcasting and media sharing and software as a service and being employed across areas such as marketing, collaboration, knowledge transfer, enhancing products and services and research. The chapter highlights, though, how SMEs must strategically plan how they will embed Web 2.0 technology across their business and supply chain and be aware of the different issues, controversies and problems they are likely to have to tackle. The chapter closes by providing a template of recommended questions that managers should consider asking before they adopt and embed Web 2.0.

REFERENCES

Anderson, C. (2004). The long tail. *Wired, 1*(12), 10. Retrieved May 15, 2009, from http://www.wired.com/archive/12.10/tail.html

Anderson, E. (2005). Using Wikis in a corporate context. In A. Hohensyein & K. Wilbers (Eds.). *Handbuch e-learning* (pp. 8-15). Cologne, Germany: Wolters Kluwer. Retrieved September 2, 2009, from http://www.espen.com/papers/Anderson-2005-corpwiki.pdf

Anderson, P. (2007). What is Web 2.0? Ideas, technologies and implications for education. *JISC Technology and Standards Watch*. Retrieved December 12, 2007, from http://www.jisc.ac.uk/publications/publications/twweb2.aspx

Bernoff, J., & Li, C. (2008). Harnessing the power of the oh-so-social Web. *MIT Sloan Management Review*, 5(49), 36–42.

BERR. (2008). *Business enterprise and regulatory reform*. Retrieved September 1, 2009, from http://www.berr.gov.uk/whatwedo/enterprise/enterprisesmes/index.html

Boulos, M. G. K., Maramba, I., & Wheeler, S. (2006). Wikis, blogs and podcasts: A new generation of Web-based tools for virtual collaborative clinical practice and education. *BMC Medical Education*, 5(6), 41. doi:10.1186/1472-6920-6-41

Bower, D. J., Shaw, C., & Keogh, W. (1998). The process of small firms innovation in the UK oil and gas-related industry. In Oakley, R. (Ed.), *New technology-based firms in the 1990s* (pp. 138–151). London, UK: Paul Chapman Publishing.

Brynjolfsson, E., & Saunders, A. (2010). *Wired for innovation: How information technology is reshaping the economy*. Boston, MA: Massachusetts Institute of Technology.

Bughin, J. (2008). The rise of enterprise 2.0. *Journal of Direct Data and Digital Marketing Practice*, 5(9), 251–259. doi:10.1057/palgrave.dddmp.4350100

Bughin, J., Manyika, J., & Miller, A. (2008). Building the Web 2.0 enterprise: McKinsey global survey results. *The McKinsey Quarterly*, July.

Chui, M., Miller, A., & Roberts, R. P. (2009). Six ways to make Web 2.0 work. *McKinsey Quarterly*, Feb. Retrieved from www.mckinseyquarterly.com/Business_Technology/Application_Management/Six_ways_to_make_Web20_work_2294#foot2

Deakins, D., & Freel, M. (2009). *Entrepreneurship and small firms* (5th ed.). London, UK: McGraw-Hill.

Eikelmann, S., Hajj, J., & Peterson, M. (2008). Opinion piece: Web 2.0: Profiting from the threat. *Journal of Direct, Data and Digital Marketing Practice, 5*(9), 293–295. Retrieved November 27, 2008, from http://www.palgrave-journals.com/dddmp/journal/v9/n3/full/4350094a.html

eMarketer. (2009). How the old, the young and everyone in between uses social networks. *eMarketer*. Retrieved August 12, 2009, from http://www.emarketer.com/Article.aspx?R=1007202

Enders, A., Hungenberg, H., Denker, H.-P., & Mauch, S. (2008). The long tail of social networking. Revenue models of social networking sites. *European Management Journal, 5*(26), 199– 211. Retrieved November 27, 2008, from http://www.sciencedirect.com/science?_ob=ArticleURL&_udi=B6V9T- 4SJG-WTT- 2&_user=128597&_rdoc=1&_fmt=&_orig=search&_sort=d&view=c&_acct=C000010621&_version=1&_urlVersion=0&_userid=128597&md5=b2ce82b86c613a3a25eac1592aad952e

Hartley, J. F. (1994). Case studies in organizational research. In Cassell, C., & Symon, G. (Eds.), *Organizational research – a practical guide*. London, UK: Sage Publications.

Hoffman, D. L. (2009). Managing beyond Web 2.0. *The McKinsey Quarterly*, July.

Howes, G. (2008). SMEs not taking advantage of online boom. *SMEweb*. Retreived August 12, 2009, from http://www.smeweb.com/sales-and-marketing/news/smes-not-taking-advantange-of-online-boom

IBM. (2009). *Web 2.0 goes to work for business*. Retrieved September 1, 2009, from http://www-01.ibm.com/software/info/web20/

International Journal of Entrepreneurial Behaviour & Research, 3(7), 84–107.

Internet World Statistics. (2009). *Miniwatts Marketing Group.* Retreived September 13, 2009, from http://www.internetworldstats.com/stats.htm

Jin, L. (2009). Businesses using Twitter, Facebook to market goods. Retrieved August 12, 2009, from http://www.post-gazette.com/pg/09172/978727-96.stm

King, W. R. (2006). The collaborative Web. *Information Systems Management, 5*(23), 88. doi:10.1201/1078.10580530/45925.23.2.20060301/92676.9

Millman, R. (2007). Web 2.0 opens companies up to hackers. *ITPRO.* Retrieved August 12, 2009, from http://www.itpro.co.uk/108544/web-2-0-opens-companies-uo-to-hackers

Nations, D. (2009). *What is Web 2.0? How Web 2.0 is defining society.* Retrieved September 1, 2009, from http://webtrends.about.com/od/web20/a/what-is-web20.htm

Nonaka, I. (1991). The knowledge creating company. *Harvard Business Review, 5*(69), 96–104.

O'Reilly, T. (2005). What is Web 2.0: Design patterns and business models for the next generation of software. Retrieved September 1, 2009, from http://oreilly.com/web2/archive/what-is-web-20.html

Office for National Statistics E-commerce and ICT Activity. (2008). *Statistics.* Retrieved September 2, 2009, from http://www.statistics.gov.uk/pdfdir/ecom1108.pdf

Raman, M. (2006). Wiki technology as a "free" collaborative tool within an organisational setting. *Information Systems Management, 5*(23), 59–66. doi:10.1201/1078.10580530/46352.23.4.20060901/95114.8

Robinson, R. (2008). *Web 2.0 – catching a wave of business innovation.* IBM. Retrieved June 20, 2009, from http://www.ibm.com/developerworks/webservices/library/ws-enterprise1/?S_TACT=105AGX10&S_CMP=SMASH

Rogers, E. M. (1983). *Diffusions of innovations* (3rd ed.). Free Press, Macmillan Publishing.

Scheun, A. (2008). *Web 2.0: A strategy guide.* Sebastopol, CA: O'Reilly.

Schindehutte, M., & Morris, M. (2001). Understanding strategic adaption in small firms.

Schonfeld, E. (2009). Facebook is now the fourth largest site in the world. *Techcrunch.* Retrieved July 6, 2009, from http://www.techcrunch.com/2009/08/04/facebook-is-now-the-fourth-largest-site-in-the-world/

Stocker, A., & Tochtermann, K. (2008). Investigating weblogs in small and medium enterprises: An exploratory case study. *Proceedings of 11th International Conference on Business Information Management,* Innsbruck 2008.

Stroud, D. (2007). Social networking: An age-neutral commodity — social networking becomes a mature Web application. *Journal of Direct, Data and Digital Marketing Practice, 3*(9), 278–292. Retrieved November 27, 2008, from http://www.palgrave- journals.com/dddmp/journal/v9/n3/full/4350099a.html

Wagner, C., & Bolloju, N. (2005). Supporting knowledge management in organizations with conversational Ttechnologies: Discussion forums, weblogs and Wikis. *Journal of Database Management, 2*(16), 1–8.

Wagner, C., & Majchrzak, A. (2007). Enabling customer-centricity using Wikis and the Wiki way. *Journal of Management Information Systems, 3*(23), 17. doi:10.2753/MIS0742-1222230302

Warr, W. A. (2008). Social software: Fun and games, or business tools? *Journal of Information Science, 5*(34), 591-604. Retrieved November 27, 2008, from http://jis.sagepub.com/cgi/reprint/34/4/591

Wesh, M. (2009). *Web 2.0: The machine is us/ing us.* Retrieved August 15, 2009, from http://www.youtube.com/watch?v=6gmP4nk0EOE

Wickert, A., & Herschel, R. (2001). Knowledge-management issues for smaller businesses. *Journal of Knowledge Management, 4*(5), 329–337. doi:10.1108/13673270110411751

Wikipedia. (2008). *What is a Wiki?* Retrieved June 30, 2008, from http://en.wikipedia.org/wiki/

Wyld, D. C. (2008). Management 2.0: A primer on blogger for executives. *Management Research News, 6*(31), 448–483. doi:10.1108/01409170810876044

Chapter 2
E–Procurement System and Adoption for SMEs

Serdal Bayram
Siemens, Turkey

Özalp Vayvay
Marmara University, Turkey

ABSTRACT

An electronic procurement (e-procurement) system is an electronic based procurement style that facilitates effective communications along the entire supply chain. E-procurement accelerates SMEs (small and medium size enterprises) at a reduced cost. The purpose of this chapter is to show that adoption of an e-procurement system is essential in the supply chain for SMEs and to find solutions in order to make using this system as easy as possible. The adoption should be considered as a re-engineering process from an innovative perspective. An adoption plan is proposed within the study. It contains three phases: 1) identification of the e-procurement process, 2) seeking integration points with other elements of the system, and 3) IT implementation of the integration areas. The study also proposes to use business process management tools that have workflow engines and Web service implementations for integration points. Although BPM (business process management) tools are seen as quite expensive to SMEs, there are also dependable free licensed ones. The study is concluded with a case-study that is implemented with a free-licensed BPM tool for proof-of-concepts.

INTRODUCTION

The electronic procurement (e-procurement) system is a key system that facilitates effective communications between buyers and suppliers

DOI: 10.4018/978-1-60960-765-4.ch002

whilst also providing opportunities for making the system more flexible and efficient. It enhances the selection of products, and makes information more effortlessly accessible. There have been many studies on e-procurement systems. According to these studies, e-procurement allows enterprises to decentralize operational procurement processes and centralize strategic procurement processes as a result of the higher supply chain precision supplied by e-procurement systems.

The study in this chapter aims to illustrate the significant importance of e-procurement for SMEs enabling the implementation of e-procurement within an adoption plan. The plan will be illustrated in a case-study. The remainder of the chapter is organized as follows:

The first part of the chapter explains the e-procurement system and its impacts on enterprises and literatures about e-procurement systems will be addressed in this part. Since the mid-1990s, especially after the development of the internet, e-procurement has taken an important role in the supply chain. Via the Internet, communications amongst the supply chain network became much easier. The internet and aspects of it have made e-procurement enablement more viable and new concepts of communication like Business-to-Business (B2B) i.e. commerce transactions between businesses such as between a manufacturer and a wholesaler, Business-to-Consumer (B2C) i.e. activities of businesses serving end consumers with products and/or services have been encompassed in the supply chain. Today, the e-procurement system is almost crucial in the competitive market where it is necessary to be flexible in order to survive especially for SMEs. Even though there is a small cost associated with integrating the supply chain with this kind of system, the return on investment (ROI) is comparatively high.

The next part of the chapter is to propose an e-procurement adoption plan for SMEs. The adoption can be seen as an innovative strategy that begins with the identification of the process. The next step in the plan is to identify the interaction / integration points in the process. The integration point is not restricted to users but to all members of the supply chain including vendors, banks etc. The interaction points should be implemented with IT as the enabler of the innovation.

The chapter is concluded by a case study that illustrates the application of the adoption plan for a SME. It consists of a procurement process and graphical representation of the process with a BPM tool. The process also includes the web services that supply the information flow among the members. Those web services are implemented within the case study and supplies an appropriate approach to implementing an e-procurement system for SMEs. In the implementation, free licensed tools (software) are used in order to encourage SMEs to use them frequently.

BACKGROUND

E-Procurement System

In this section, the e-procurement system, its definitions, and concepts in associated literatures will be addressed in greater detail. Electronic procurement (e-procurement) has been identified as the most important element of e-business operational excellence. It has been becoming widespread throughout the business environment. According to Wyld's (2004) study, it was reported that currently almost half of all American companies use e-procurement systems. E-procurement technology is defined as any technology designed to facilitate the purchasing of goods by a commercial or a government organization over the internet. (Davilla *et al*, 2003). According to Shaoling & Yan (2008), it can be seen as the technology that opens doors to a purchasing network for suppliers and buyers, expanding the selection of products and making information more easily accessible.

Rajkumar (2001) addressed the business and technology issues for e-procurement system. The technology side is illustrated in Figure 1. It can be seen that an e-procurement system has two types of stakeholder: buyer and seller. A customer with company A (as buyer) uses the purchasing software and places an order on company B's (as seller) system over the internet. The two companies have their own internal ERP (enterprise resource planning) / DBMS (database management system).

Figure 1. A sample B2B purchasing system (Adapted from Rajkumar, 2001)

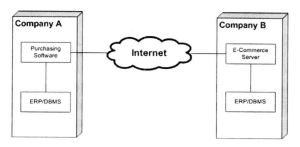

According to the study, purchasing software that is used by buyers contains e-procurement software, e-catalog, auction, marketplaces. Rajkumar also explained that defining e-procurement strategy, reengineering the procurement processes and involving key stakeholders should also be considered for the business side. According to the enterprise's competence, an appropriate procurement strategy should be identified; because the procurement process is a business process, by using electronic mediation some innovative strategies and reengineering concepts should be considered. Before an e-procurement solution can be implemented, an enterprise must go through significant procurement process re-engineering (Kalakota & Robinson, 2001).

Presutti (2003) stated that e-procurement is a technology solution that facilitates corporate buying via the internet. There is an argument that e-procurement is not new because electronic data interchange (EDI) has been used since 1980s for interconnection among buyers and suppliers. On the other hand, EDI is quite expensive to implement because it requires special infrastructure and custom integration between each pair of trading partners. For large companies, it may be affordable but for SMEs who are defined as enterprises with fewer than 250 employees and less than 20 million Euros turnover per year (Berlan & Weber, 2004), the implementation cost of EDI is not feasible. After the invention of WWW, where no special infrastructures like protocols or networks are needed for implementation; e-procurement has became the major component of the purchasing process.

Another important concept in the e-procurement system is procurement within e-catalog. E-catalogs or online catalogs are the catalogs that are provided by sellers and are usually integrated into the buyer's back-end systems (like ERP). Electronic catalogs help buyers to navigate rapidly and find the best price and fastest delivery for their requirements. They are prepared to manage a large number of goods and to order them easily for specially negotiated prices with procurement departments. They provide savings in the buying process because the procurement is automated within an online process that makes the system quicker and more efficient. Puschman & Alt (2005) reported that there are four strategies for catalog management which are listed as follows:

- **Intranet Catalog:** In this strategy, an enterprise has an internal application where vendor catalogs are hosted. These catalogs are used to pool demands. After collecting the demands, the enterprise sends a purchasing order to the vendor. It is quite feasible for large companies that have more requesters and different departments exist.
- **Punch-out:** A catalog is hosted on the supplier's server. Buyers link directly to the vendor's catalog. There is no extra pooling system needed on the buyer's side.
- **Auction:** Auctions allow buyers to compare the different supplier's products.
- **Request for Quotation** (RFQ): The purpose of an RFQ is to invite suppliers to a bidding process to bid on specific products or services in order to decrease the price.

RFQ is a document that requests a price for goods or services to solve a specific problem. It is created by the buyer and delivered to the seller. RFQ is also described as an opportunity for potential suppliers to competitively cost the final chosen solution (Mhay, nodate). RFQ is playing an important role in supplier selection. As ordering lead-time is critical for a typical manufacturing company, having the ability to respond quickly and effectively to RFQs can significantly improve the company's job capture rate and its competitive position in the market (Qian & Tan, 2008).

Neef (2001) conducted a research about e-procurement system concepts. According to that study, most good e-procurement systems encompass the following features:

- **Requisitioning:** The system should provide e-catalogs where buyers can find their requirements easily using a powerful search engine. The system should also provide product and pricing information along with request for proposals (RFPs) which is described as invitation for suppliers, often through a requesting pricing process, to submit a proposal on specific goods or services.

- **Approval Routing:** There should be an automated and e-mail based workflow within a good e-procurement system. Such an electronic approval system avoids data loses and inconsistent data, and improve data accuracy while also providing an approval tracking system. Monitoring the overall performance of the system is quite effortless and it is easy to see the bottlenecks in the system

- **Order Management:** By having such an approval system, the system also provides real time order tracking and requisition status. Both buyers and suppliers can follow the order phases easily. The system may also support the logistic services that help buyers in tracking the delivery status of their order.

- **Summary billing and consolidated reporting:** The system should be able to notify accounts payable. There is no need to create a paper-based invoice. This system might also provide an e-invoice subsystem. For some enterprises, 1000s of man-hours are spent each year tracking paper based invoices. Buyers are able to track their payments within this kind of system.

- **ERP and CMM (computerized maintenance management) systems integration:** Buyers have their own back-end system. A good procurement system should be directly integrated to the buyer system. This avoids inconsistent and which is usually down to human error.

- **Decision Support:** The e-procurement system should provide flexible reporting options that are used for decision supports such as OLAP (online analytical processing) analysis. A specialist can use reports with drill-down and drill-up options for decision making which are crucial for optimal performance. For example, In Shaoling & Yan's (2008) study, they designed an e-procurement system based on business intelligence tools namely OLAP and agent technology.

- **User-Friendly and Ergonomic:** The system should provide an ergonomic environment. It should be as simple as possible to employ a click-and-order philosophy. Bookmarking frequently purchased goods should be supported. Order tracking should be easy to understand. It enables identification of thresholds and notification of users accordingly if they are exceeded.

Benefits of E-Procurement

In this section, the benefits of e-procurement originating from publications will be addressed. Chan & Lee (2002) defined that the value of e-procurement means benefits over cost of implementing e-procurement and they formulated it as

Value of e-procurement = Price Benefits + Transaction Cost Benefits – Technology Lock-in Costs

And the parameters are as follows;

- **Price benefits:** potential price reduction off average market price
- **Transaction cost benefits:** saving in search, negotiation and contracting and co-ordination costs
- **Technology lock-in costs:** choosing and using specific procurement system, including switching costs, opportunistic behavior by contracted supplier.

According to that study, the first benefit is eliminating time zone obstacles. Communication between buyers and sellers is an important factor of procurement. The use of e-procurement saves SMEs from paying expensive communication costs. Instead of a telephone or fax service, the internet provides 24*7 communications by overcoming Geographic limitations. The next benefit is described as e-procurement makes the system a standardized business activity that is, a desired procurement process where records/information are saved in a database. This also enables tracking of procurement progress easily. The last benefit underlined in the study is that e-procurement supplies an applicable workflow enabling users of the system to reply faster via e-mail than fax.

The procurement process can be subdivided into strategic and operational procurements.

Strategic procurement is the procurement phase where long-range plans are made in order to ensure timely supply of goods and/or services that are critical to a firm's ability to meet its core business objectives. The strategic phase contains product specification, procurement planning, supplier selection, RFQ, assessment of quotation and finally negotiation. On the other hand, operative procurement is the phase where operational issues like sourcing, ordering, delivering and receiving of the goods, and verifying invoices and payments are made. For a successful procurement, the enterprises should be focused more on the strategic phase. E-procurement allows enterprises to decentralize operational functions and centralize strategic procurement functions (Puschmann & Alt, 2005). The use of the internet in procurement is aimed at realizing faster and more efficient operational procurement processes which bypass the purchasing department and enable those people to concentrate on more strategic tasks. As seen in Figure 2, e-procurement supplies an appropriate environment for the objectives. For example, request owners can directly search suppliers' e-catalogs which include the goods/services that are negotiated in strategic phase without waiting for another negotiation period.

In Rajkumar (2001) research, the long-term benefits are the "freeing of purchasing resources from transaction processing to refocus them on strategic sourcing activities."

Figure 2. Effect of e-procurement (Adapted from Puschmann & Alt, 2005)

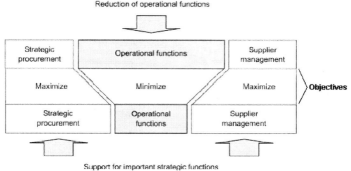

Presutti (2003) examined the economic value added factors for e-procurement. He categorized the factors in to three items:

1. Revenue (positive affect) - new products speed to market
2. Costs (negative affect) - lower purchase costs equal lower transaction costs,
3. Assets (negative affect) - inventory turns cycle time reduction.

He reported that revenue increases with an e-procurement system for example on average a reduction in time-to-market cycles of 10-15% is obtained, reduction for material costs of about between 5% and 20% is attained and a reduction of cycle-times and inventory is also achieved.

Kalakota & Robinson (2001) identified hands free procurement as the central business objective of e-procurement initiatives. They describe the main benefits as "automating the mundane, eliminating the paperwork and eliminating hidden procedures and other obstacles that keep employees from doing their real, productive jobs. Instead of dealing with the transaction process, employees can focus on their work".

They also emphasize the benefits to the CEO (chief executive officer) as;

- **Cost savings:** Well designed e-procurement software can reduce purchasing costs by nearly 90%, which translates into radically better limits for buyers. Centralizing procurement activities focuses on the total spending and improves negotiating power. As it reduces the operating resource costs, e-procurement affects the bottom line. E-procurement decreases cycle time because it provides such an automated easy to use system that avoids time-consuming, paper-based processes.
- **Improved efficiency:** By focus on strategic purchasing, a CEO can concentrate on

value-added upstream portions of the business rather than on transactional, downstream activities.

- **Control:** In an effective purchasing system, it is easy to monitor the company's total spending, including such nontraditional areas as operating resource procurement. This system also provides better inventory management by using web-based procurement which gives advantages of faster deployment to market, and uses less working capital than traditional means of procurement.

E-Procurement Adoption Plan

After a SME is motivated to adopt e-procurement into their processes, an accurate adoption plan as a road map is required. There are several published studies in the literature for examining e-procurement adoption. In Gunasekaran & Ngai's (2008) study, they proposed a theoretical framework for the implementation of e-procurement. In this study, the four items that effect the implementation were listed as; 1) perceived benefits of e-procurement, 2) perceived barriers of e-procurement, 3) critical success factors of e-procurement adoption, and 4) perceived organizational performance with e-procurement. In another study, Chan & Lee (2002) proposed a formula to evaluate the benefits (called value of e-procurement) as a summation of price and transactional benefits and then subtraction the total from technology lock-in costs and they also suggested that trust on the supplier, trust on the IT and power of the supplier play important roles in the adoption among SMEs.

Accordingly, the e-procurement adoption can be seen as an innovative process requiring IT implementation as an enabler and should contain an innovative perspective (Davenport, 1993). Using to this perspective for SMEs, this chapter proposes an adoption process in which three major steps are needed (seen on Figure 3): 1) illustrating

Figure 3. The proposed e-procurement adoption process

the procurement process, 2) seeking integration points with other parts of the supply chain and 3) having IT implement these integration points. The steps are as follows:

- **Identifying the procurement process:** In the process, the adoption starts with an applicable procurement process as a business process that contains the entire procurement members such as order requesters, vendors, procurement departments etc. This process can be varied according to the business and the enterprise. For example, in Rajkumar's (2001) study, it gives as an example from the federal government in a pilot for electronic catalogs. They developed a diagram for identifying the procurement process (seen in Figure 4). There are six steps in the process namely accessing the electronic catalog system, searching procurement vehicles, receiving evaluating search results, creating submitting order, receiving accepting items, and processing payment.

A procurement process also can be divided into sub processes. For example with respect to requested goods; some of them can be supplied directly from e-catalogs and while others can divert to the request of quotation (RFQ) phase.

All these sub processes should be considered part of a whole process. It is also of added value to illustrate the process with a BPM suite tool which makes use of graphical symbols for service activities and processes. This work also identifies opportunities to re-engineer the process. In the market, there are many BPM tools from the big software vendors like Oracle, IBM, Microsoft, and SAP amongst the others. There are also some free and open BPM tools like Intalio, jBPM (JBoss). BPM provides not only process illustration but also flexibility and agility to the process (Hayward, 2005).

As explained before, all goods may not be procured within e-catalogs; some goods are needed to be procured for specific purposes so they can not be prepared within a catalog. The procurements of these types of items may differ, and their process should also be different than e-catalogs, especially in initial phases of the process. For example, their process may start with the request for quotation which is followed by requesting, analyzing market, deciding vendor, checking offer by requester and approving order (seen in Figure 5). After order is being requested by an order requester, strategic procurement person is responsible for analyzing market and he/she is required to decide which vendors should be selected (according to vendor selection criteria), he/she submits the offers of the orders which are proposed by different vendors

Figure 4. Federal government procurement process (Adapted from Rajkumar, 2001)

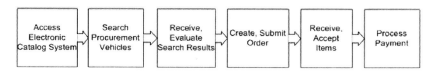

Figure 5. Request for quotation process

(in some enterprises 3 offers are required). If one of the offers is approved by requester, operational procurement person submits the order and send the procurement letter to the vendor via an electronic mediation. This process may differ according to the enterprise's business.

- **Seeking integration points:** With regards to the successful use of e-procurement, it is crucial to integrate with members of the supply chain. The next step, after identifying the process, is to look for the integration areas. When considering the information flow between buyers and suppliers, the integration points should reflect the flow of supplied goods and services from vendors and procurement orders from buyers. The above example of the federal government's procurement process, which was given in the identifying process phase, might have several integration points for the other

members. In Figure 6, the integration points are illustrated. In the sample process, there are three different sides: the request, the vendor, and the logistics sides. Four integration points place between the request and vendor sides: E-catalogs can be used within the vendors' catalog servers; order placement and management might take place in the vendor's ERP servers and payment could take place after receiving and accepting items. Logistics communication is the last point between the requestor and the logistic sides and is used for transportation the items by a third-party logistics company.

Another process which is described previously in the identification part is to procure with the request for quotation. There are additional roles in this process according to e-catalogs process like strategic procurement, operational

Figure 6. Integration areas for a federal government's procurement process

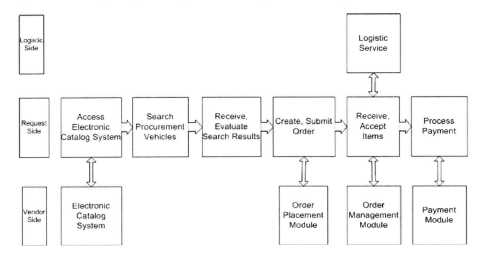

procurement. For this reason, it is more complicated and contains more integration points than e-catalog procurement. The main integration point in the RFQ process is to get offer from vendors. Offers may be sent via an electronic mediation. For example, in Qian & Tan's (2008) study, the authors propose a web-based architecture for calculating production cost estimation and providing supplier selection functionality. They conclude that using this service, "manufacturing companies become universally accessible to designers around the world. With the Web service, suppliers can collaborate with designers more quickly; win new business; and find the right work for their manufacturing capabilities. With the service, designers can find the right suppliers for their design, reduce lead-time by receiving cost estimation/quotations faster, and reduce procurement costs".

- **IT implementation of the integration:** From an innovative perspective, IT is an enabler. Thomas (1993) argues that:

"Computers have been closely tied to the way work is carried out. One might even argue that information technology began to radically alter work its location, speed, quality, and other key characteristics with the advent of the telephone. Computers and telephones clearly benefit the business processes of the companies that employ them. Telephones shrink time and distance, enabling firms, for example, to monitor field sales on a daily basis and act accordingly. Computers speed the pace of many work activities and, at the same time, drastically reduce the need for human labor. Home offices of insurance companies, for example, used to be vast halls of closely packed desks at which clerks with adding machines made actuarial or financial calculations. Today, those halls are filled by rows of mainframe computers and disk drives, and the clerks are gone."

As understood in this explanation, the IT implementation phase is a crucial part of the plan. Without trust in IT, the adoption can never been completed. After receiving the integration points of the system, the final step is to implement them. The interfaces for communications should be very obvious, and the integration should be loosely coupled, thereby reducing the degree of dependency between any two members instead of point-to-point connection. Coupling refers to the degree of dependency between any two systems (Papazoglou, 2008). A loosely coupled integration is useful in a dynamic business environment where existing requirements often change and new requirements are frequently introduced. The minimal level of coupling between the components is a real advantage in such an environment, because it provides easy maintenance and flexibility. Nowadays, in business communications between members (B2B or B2C), it is a very common trend to use web services. These services are defined as self-contained, modular applications that can be described, published, located and invoked over a network generally, the World Wide Web (Bui et al, 2006) in integration areas. For example, if necessary in the process, the communication for placing an order can take place by using an http web service (SOAP or REST standards).

In the market, there are several BPM suite tools that provide an IT environment in order to model, simulate, implement and deploy the processes which are powered by web service communications. BPM can be used not only in the identification of the process but also in the implementations of web services and workflows forms, and in deployment to the servers.

CASE STUDY FOR ADOPTION PLAN

In this section, the chapter is concluded with a case study for proof-of-concepts that illustrates the application of the adoption plan for SMEs. It consists of a procurement process and its graphical representation using a BPM tool. The process also includes the web services that supply the information flow among the members. The web services which are identified after the identification of the process will be implemented within the case study that will supply an appropriate approach to implement an e-procurement system for SMEs.

In this case study, open source and free software tools are offered for SMEs because they are available gratis (free of charge). These types of programs which are called free software can provide considerable savings for SMEs. According to Smith (2008), free software is defined as a program that offers users all of the freedoms listed below:

- *"the freedom to use the software for any purpose,*
- *the freedom to change the software to suit your needs,*
- *the freedom to share the software with your friends and neighbors, and*
- *the freedom to share the changes you make."*

Java and the Apache Software Foundation (ASF) are the leaders for open-free software as well as the leading supporters for an open-source society. The Intalio BPM Suite -Community Edition is one of the open-source and free BPM tools that has been designed and implemented by using the Java programming language and software supported by ASF (one of the components is ODE BPEL engine which ASF supports and Intalio uses). It makes use of graphical symbols for service activities and processes. Without actually writing code, the Intalio BPM Suite provides tools and techniques to develop a service-based system graphically for business process management. It also provides a human based workflow that includes human forms and web service calls. Intalio is an open-source and its community edition version is free-licensed software. It provides SMEs with important advantages to implement, create, and drive their business process within an IT context. In this case study, Intalio and free

software is used. The advantages of free software can be viewed as: 1) they are available for free or at much lower costs of software; contributing to the reduction in overall costs 2) they have necessary features that may be enough for an SME's level of operations, thus making implementation quicker and simpler.

The process modeled in the case-study is the e-catalog process (which is described briefly in the previous section of the chapter). An e-catalog or online catalog is assembled and maintained by the supplier. A catalog provides information such as descriptions, prices, availability, lead times, and discounts of the goods. They are generally automated and integrated in to the buyer's own procurement system. In the sample scenario, there are four roles namely requester, vendor, logistic and e-catalog process (as system role). The requester is the person that requests orders from e-catalogs, and tracks his/her orders. The vendor is the supplier of the goods who is responsible for preparing catalogs. The logistic is the enterprise that supplies logistical services such as transportation. The process starts with the requesting of an order by the requester. The requester prepares an order basket from catalogs, and the catalogs are directly retrieved from vendor's service. The requester submits the orders, and then tracks the order status that is supplied by the vendor's service. If the order is ready to be sent, the requester calls the logistic service for sending the goods. After receiving the items, the requester makes a payment to the vendor and the process is completed successfully. In Figure 7, the modeled process is illustrated. There are four roles (or pools) (In BPM terminology, they are called as pools). The only human side is the requester pool, which is responsible for entering forms and tracking orders. The vendor and logistics pools provide five integration areas. The e-catalog is the main process pool, which is an executable pool that generates executable processes such as business process execution language (BPEL) that is an

Figure 7. E-catalog process modeled with Intalio BPM Suite (community edition)

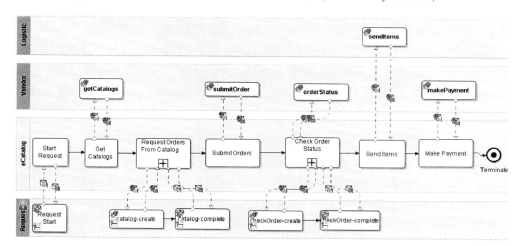

executable language for specifying interactions with web services, code in Intalio terminology.

The model and implementation contains workflow forms and web services. On the form side, the Intalio software provides human based workflow forms for system users. As the requester is the only human side, this section is the only one that has forms. There are three forms: the first two are for preparing the request and submission of the order. The third form is used by the requester to track the order status whether it is completed or not. Then after the completion of the order, he/she triggers the logistics service to transport the goods.

The Intalio BPM Suite also provides web service communications. In the case study, integration areas are implemented using the XML (extendible markup language; which provides simplicity, generality, and usability over the internet) web service technology. Service can be described as "a component capable of performing a task" (Sprott & Wilkes, 2004, p.2). The most common web service is the XML based web services. According to Erl (2004), XML web services have two of fundamental requirements: 1) it communicates via internet protocols (commonly HTTP) and 2) it sends and receives data formatted as XML documents. As XML is the most common format

and interoperable among systems, suppliers need not to be homogenous, web services are the most commonly used method for the communicating between systems, making the overall system more flexible. For example, Bui *et al* (2006) examined the functions of web services for negotiation. They proposed a topology that uses different web services which are served by different vendors (or suppliers). This topology makes the system more flexible so that the client (or supplier) can choose one of the services according to quality of services and its requirements. The implemented web services in the case can be listed as follows:

Get Catalogs: This service is served by the vendors. They prepare catalogs, catalog items, prices and other information about supplied items (such as image, color, size etc.). This service retrieves the catalog and other related information from catalog servers. A sample replied xml message after the call might be coded as;

```
<catalogs>
  <catalog name="catalog1">
    <item>
      <name> Product1 </name>
      <itemCode> P0001 </itemCode>
      <imageURL> http://....</
      imageURL>
```

```
  <price> 10 </price>
  <price_currency> EUR </price_
  currency>
  <color> BLUE </color>
  <size> 1 PACK </size>
   </item>
  </catalog>
</catalogs>
```

Submit Order: This service is again served by the vendor. Customers place orders by using this service. A sending message should contain all information about ordering (such as ordered items, amounts, delivery date etc.). A sample sending message file might be coded as,

```
<orders>
  <customerCode>C0001</customerCode>
  <!--An order -->
  <order>
   <itemCode>P0001</itemCode>
   <itemAmount>5</itemAmount>
   <deliveryDate>01.09.2009</
   deliveryDate>
  </order>
  <!--Another order-->
  <order>
   <itemCode>P0002</itemCode>
   <itemAmount>10</itemAmount>
   <deliveryDate>01.09.2009</
   deliveryDate>
  </order>
</orders>
```

The result message after execution might be coded as; `<orderNo> ON000001 </orderNo>` that simply gives the order number saved on the supplier side.

Order Status: This service is used to track the status of the order, which is submitted during the order service call. The service is served by the vendor. In submitting an order service call, the customer takes an order number. This number is used for the order status service. The sending XML message might be coded as;

```
<orderNo> ON000001 </orderNo>
```

The receiving message could be coded as (which means the order is ready to be sent)

```
<orderstatus> READY TO SEND </
orderStatus>
```

Send Items: This service is used to call the logistic vendor to transport the ordered items. Sending message should contain all information about delivery (such as sending address, destination address, delivery date, items delivered, etc.).

A sample sending XML might be coded as:

```
<sendItems>
  <sendingAdress> XXXX
  </sendingAdress>
  <destinationAdress> YYYY </
  destinationAdress>
  <deliveryDate> 01.09.2009
  </deliveryDate>
  <item>
   <itemSize> 20 </itemSize>
   <packageType> PACKAGE
   </packageType>
   <packageSize>20 KG</packageSize >
  </item>
</sendItems>
```

The received message should contain a transportation number in order to track the status of transportation and acknowledgement message. It might be coded as;

```
<transportingNo> TN00001
</transportingNo >
<acknowledgment> your goods
will be delivered on 01.09.2009
</acknowledgment>
```

Make Payment: This service is used to call the vendor to make a payment for the orders. It is also served by the vendor. Message should contain all information needed for payments such as order number, payment total, and payment account. Sample XML message sent might be coded as;

```
<payment>
  <orderNo> ON000001 </orderNo>
  <paymentTotal> 50.0000
  </paymentTotal>
  <paymentCurrency> EUR
  </paymentCurrency>
  <paymentAccount> AN000001
  </paymentAccount>
</payment>
```

Received message might be like ;

```
<paymentNo> P0000001 </paymentNo>
```

Such a system as the one is modeled within this case study has some advantages which encourage SMEs to adopt and they are as follows:

- The system provides an electronic system that collects requests from request owners. Otherwise, there may be some data loss or data integrity issues making the system inefficient and complicated.
- The system is modeled within a standard logic that is not dependent on an individual person to make the system long-lived.
- It also encourages vendors to become integrated into the process easily so they can easily publish their catalogs.
- The ordering costs are decreased because the system enables for SMEs to get rid of fax (paper), phone or another physical mediation based ordering.
- The decision process of the vendor should be within the system. When the decision procedure changes, all of the system should adopt the changes and your system

should also supply information to give an idea of which vendor is the best.

- The system offers to use free tools that can provide considerable savings for SMEs.
- The system does not require a special network like EDI because the communications are handled by using the WWW which is the global standard.
- The system makes operations (or productions) of SMEs more efficient. Efficient operations work like a competitive weapon in business (Martinich, 1997). The decreased lead time of ordered goods, enables quicker delivery to the customer.
- The organization itself might have an ERP (like SAP) system as the backend system. It is easy to integrate with such a system. ERP helps the system to get the required data within its database such as vendors, account numbers, project numbers while saving the Order to the ERP System. As mentioned above, the vendor should be integrated within the process. After approving it, is responsible for the creation and sending of the procurement order to the vendor. There should be a mechanism that automatically informs the vendor of the order like EDI.
- After procurement is completed, the procurement letter is required to be sent to the vendor. The system handles that job automatically.
- In such a system, it is easy to monitor the overall system performance. The system might have some bottlenecks. However, these bottlenecks can be easily identified.

Another point that needs to be underlined in the study is the integration between the buyers and sellers. This integration might be seen as enterprise application integration (EAI) where there is such integration an enterprise service bus (ESB) for connectivity is needed. Josuttis (2007) reported that the main purpose of ESB is to provide con-

Figure 8. Enterprise service bus for buyer and sellers

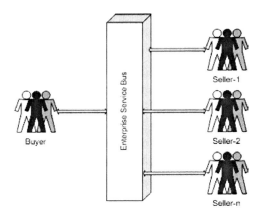

nectivity. Different senders might be connected via ESB (see Figure 8) making the system flexible and independent for individual buyers.

Not only different hardware and software platforms, but also distinct implementation of services can be connected via ESB. ESB works like a universal language in that all platforms can communicate via a standard ESB. ESB provides a loose coupling system instead of point-to-point communication where there would be tight coupling between the different parts of the system. In this system, when business conditions change, for example bankruptcy of a seller, it is very easy to change the system according to the new situation with minimal affects.

Another functionality of ESB is to route requests to the service according to predefined rules known as intelligent routing. This can include business intelligence which is described as a set of concepts, methods and processes to improve business decisions that use information from multiple sources and apply experience and assumptions to develop an accurate understanding of business dynamics (Shaoling & Yan, 2008). The highest maturity (5th level) of a process is to optimize the system continuously (Kan, 2002). In order to achieve this, business intelligence is an essential concept that ESB supplies. A service

provider can be chosen via the ESB according to the predefined rules. The past choices of ESB that made the system more efficient and better could be one rule. ESB also provides additional functionalities for security, service management, service monitoring and logging that are necessary in maintaining the system

CONCLUSION

E-procurement can be defined as the process of electronically purchasing the goods and services needed for a company's operation and is the most important element of e-business operational excellence. For SMEs, this system is required for the strong competitive environment. This study aimed to research benefits of such a system. The main advantage is that it allows enterprises to decentralize operational procurement processes where operational issues like sourcing, ordering, delivery and receipt of the goods, invoice verification and payments are made and centralize strategic procurement processes which are the procurement phase where long-range plans are made in order to ensure timely supply of goods and/or services that are critical to a firm's ability to meet its core business objectives.

Another aim of this chapter was to prepare a guide line for SMEs to implement an e-procurement system. That plan has three steps: 1) identifying the procurement processes, 2) seeking integration areas, and 3) IT implementation of the integration points. Identification of the process highlights opportunities to re-engineer the process. Integration points are the areas amongst the members like the communication point between an organization and its vendors. In the implementation phase, web services and free licensed BPM tools were offered that supply cheap, easy, and standard communications (by using XML format over HTTP) for integration.

The proof-of-concepts case study outlined a procurement process and graphical representation of the process with a BPM tool. The process included five integration points, four of which incorporate the communication between the company and vendor, and the fifth consists of the communication between the company and logistic organization.

ESB is another important concept for EAI. It supplies connectivity and loose coupled communications. Another functionality of ESB is intelligent routing which means ESB routs requests (or connections) to the service according to pre-defined rules. ESB might contain business intelligence that has the learning capability using the effectiveness of past routes. It can also support OLAP analysis so that a vendor can be chosen according to the result of the analysis. This should increase the benefits of an e-procurement system for SMEs which are very sensitive to economical conditions.

REFERENCES

Angeles, R., & Nath, R. (2007). Business-to-business e-procurement: Success factors and challenges to implementation. *Supply Chain Management: An International Journal, 12*(2), 104–115..doi:10.1108/13598540710737299

Berlak, J., & Weber, V. (2004). How to make e-procurement viable for SME suppliers. *Production Planning & Control: Management of Operations, 15*(7), 671–677..doi:10.1080/09537 280412331298139

Bui, T., Gachet, A., & Sebastion, H. J. (2006). Web services for negotiation and bargaining in electronic markets: Design requirements, proof-of-concepts, and potential applications to e-procurement. *Group Decision and Negotiation, 15*, 460–490..doi:10.1007/s10726-006-9039-5

Chan, J. K. Y., & Lee, M. K. O. (2002). SME e-procurement adoption in Hong Kong – the roles of power, trust and value. *Proceedings of the Hawaii International Conference on System Sciences, 36*, IEEE Computer Society.

Davenport, T. H. (1993). *Process innovation: Reengineering work through Information Technology*. Boston, MA: Harvard Business School Press.

Davilla, A., Gupta, & M., Palmer, R. (2003). Moving procurement systems to the Internet: The adoption and use of e-procurement technology models. *European Management Journal, 21*(1), 11-23. Elsevier Science. doi:10.1016/s0263-2373(02)00155-X

Erl, T. (2004). *Service oriented architecture: A field guide to integration XML and Web services*. Upper Saddle River, NJ: Prentice Hall.

Gunasekaran, A., & Ngai, E. W. T. (2008). Adoption of e-procurement in Hong Kong: An empirical research. [Elsevier B.V.]. *International Journal of Production Economics, 113*, 159–175. doi:10.1016/j.ijpe.2007.04.012

Hayward, S. (2005). *Service-oriented architecture adds flexibility to business processes*. Gartner Research.

Intalio. (2009). *Intalio business process management suite (BPMS)*. Retrieved on July 6, 2009, from http://community.intalio.com

Josuttis, N. M. (2007). *SOA in practice*. Sebastopol, CA: O'Reilly.

Kalakota, R., & Robinson, M. (2001). *e-Business 2.0: Roadmap for success*. Upper Saddle River, NJ: Addison-Wesley Professional.

Kan, S. H. (2002). *Metrics and models in software quality engineering* (2nd ed.). Boston, MA: Addison-Wesley Professional.

Martinich, J. S. (1997). *Production and operations management: An applied modern approach*. New York, NY: John Wiley & Sons.

Mhay, S. (n.d.). *Request for... procurement processes*. Retrieved on September 10, 2009, from http://www.negotiations.com/articles/procurement-terms/

Neef, D. (2001). *e-procurement: From strategy to implementation*. Upper Saddle River, NJ: Financial Times Prentice Hall.

Papazoglou, M. P. (2008). *Web services: Principles and technology*. Harlow, UK: Pearson Education Limited.

Presutti, W. D. (2003). Supply management and e-procurement: Creating value added in the supply chain. *Industrial Marketing Management, 32*, 219–226..doi:10.1016/S0019-8501(02)00265-1

Puschmann, T., & Alt, R. (2005). Successful use of e-procurement in supply chains. *Supply Chain Management: An International Journal, 10*(2), 122-133. Emerald Group Publishing. doi:10.1108/13598540510589197

Qian, L., & Tan, T. (2008). *Design of Web-based cost estimation and supplier selection service with Unified Modeling Language*. IEEE International Conference. Retrieved on September 10, 2009, from http://ieeexplore.ieee.org

Rajkumar, T. M. (2001). E-procurement: Business and technical issues. *Information Systems Management, 18*(4), 1-9. Taylor & Francis. doi:10.1201/1078/43198.18.4.200110901/31465.6

Shaoling, D., & Yan, L. (2008). *Design of e-procurement system based on business intelligence tools*. International Conference on Management of e-Commerce and e-Government. IEEE Computer Society. doi: 10.1109 /ICMECG.2008.73

Smith, B. *(2008)*. A quick guide to GPLv3 (free software). *Retrieved on September 5, 2009, from* http://www.gnu.org/licenses/quick-guide-gplv3.html

Sprott, D., & Wilkes, L. (2004). Understanding service-oriented architecture. *CBDI Forum*. Retrieved on October 10, 2008, from http://www.msarchitecturejournal.com/pdf/Understanding_Service-Oriented_Architecture.pdf

Wyld, D. C. (2004). *The weather report for the supply chain: A longitudinal analysis of ISM*. Hammond, LA: Department of Management, Southeastern Louisinia University.

Chapter 3
Model of Funcionalities for the Development of B2B E-Commerce Solutions

Marlene Pinto
University of Trás-os-Montes e Alto Douro, Portugal

Ana Rodrigues
University of Trás-os-Montes e Alto Douro, Portugal

João Varajão
Universidade de Trás-os-Montes e Alto Douro, Portugal

Ramiro Gonçalves
Universidade de Trás-os-Montes e Alto Douro, Portugal

ABSTRACT

The explosive growth of the Internet has revolutionized the way of conducting business in several areas, acting nowadays as an important channel of communication and for the trading of goods and services. Therefore, electronic commerce (EC), defined as the execution of transactions of goods and services which rely on computers mediated by informatics networks, assumes particular importance due to the benefits that it may imply for companies. In this chapter we focus on a particular type of electronic commerce: business to business (B2B). B2B describes electronic commerce associated to operations of buying and selling products and services through the Internet or through the use of private networks shared between business partners, thus replacing the physical process around commercial transactions. This type of EC facilitates conducting electronic transactions between companies. There are several B2B solutions that enable companies to make transactions from buying and selling goods and services, to participating in auctions. The analysis of such solutions enabled us to verify that there are big differences in the amount of the supported functionalities, and significant opportunities for development, with the aim of helping companies to evaluate their electronic commerce solutions and to conceive new and more complete systems. In this chapter, a new model of functionalities for the development of B2B EC solutions is presented.

DOI: 10.4018/978-1-60960-765-4.ch003

1. INTRODUCTION

One of the first organizations to use the term e-business (electronic business) was IBM in 1997. Up to this point, the term used was e-commerce (electronic commerce). This expansion of the terminology also necessitated a paradigm shift: until then, selling was the only experience that people could reproduce on the Web. As such, electronic business (EB), which IBM defines as "a safe, flexible and integrated proposal for distributing different business values with simplicity and range, made possible through the application of Internet technology" entails using the worldwide convenience, availability and range of the Internet to empower already existent businesses/companies or to create new businesses (Laudon & Traver, 2003). Electronic commerce (EC) becomes one of the components of EB, along with e-mailing and e-marketing, among others. Sometimes EC is understood only as "selling through the Web" or as "a company activity in which its presence is only on the Web". Nevertheless, it can also be defined as a sharing of business information, preservation of business relationships and the direction of business transactions through communication networks (Zwass, 2003). According to another definition EC entails the purchase and sale of goods and/or services through electronic networks of data such as the Internet.

As a particular case of EC, the Business-to-Business (B2B) comprises the electronic transactions made between companies and is mainly conducted in electronic markets (e-marketplaces) (Zhu & Lu, 2005). Basically it is possible to identify three big areas of B2B: e-marketplaces, e-procurement and e-distribution. In the context of the present work, the focus is on the area of e-marketplaces and of e-procurement.

B2B has a growing importance in companies and due to the great disparity in the characteristics and functionalities of solutions, there is an opportunity for contributing to its general improvement. As such, the main aim of this work is to present a model of functionalities of B2B solutions, which helps future implementations by companies of this type of EC solution. It allow companies to analyze the best way of developing a B2B solution, while also helping them to understand the advantages that solution may bring. It will help to potentiate the business, making it more profitable on a global scale, with a cost reduction in comparison to the traditional way. With this work, companies will become aware of all the electronic processes surrounding transactions between companies, from the purchase and sale of goods and products, to the exchange of information on prices.

In the next sections we review the fundamental concepts for understanding B2B and describe the process of investigation. Then, a model of functionalities for the development of B2B solutions is presented, finishing with some general conclusions.

2. CONTEXT

EC can be defined as the process of buying, selling and exchanging products, services and information, using computer networks including the Internet (Turban et al., 2002; Jennex et al., 2004). Kalakota and Whinston (1997) define EC using the perspective of an electronic data network, automated business processes, automated services and on-line buying and selling.

Nowadays it has a significant importance in the business world and it radically changes the relationship between supplier and client (Kendall et al., 2001), not only in process terms but also in the way transactions are made (Wigand, 1997; Kalakota & Whinston, 1997; Choi et al., 2006). It has the power of connecting individuals, groups and organizations worldwide and one of the differences in contrast to traditional industries is the high degree of interconnection between the several parts. It can help organizations to reduce costs, to interact directly with clients and to stay ahead of the competition (Liu & Arnett, 2000).

It is believed that EC contributes to the progress of businesses in undeveloped countries (Robey et al., 1990). This belief is derived from the potential of the Internet for reducing transaction costs, fostering some intermediary links and permitting an easier connection to the global supply chain. In order to benefit from the advantages of such potentialities, businesses should adopt EC. Nevertheless, its diffusion in undeveloped countries is still below expectations (Molla & Licker, 2005).

There are seven main characteristics of EC technology: ubiquity, global reach, universal norms, wealth, interactivity, information density and personalization (Laudon & Traver, 2003; Poong et al., 2006).

It is possible to find a wide variety of EC types and many distinguished ways of characterizing them. The present work is focused on B2B.

B2B can be considered as a form of EC oriented towards conducting business transactions between companies (Wong, 1998; Teo & Ranganathan, 2004). These transactions may be electronically conducted through Extranets, Intranets or private, between businesses or between these and other elements of the supply chain (Turban et al., 2002; Noyce, 2002). The B2B concept can be defined as a substitution of the physical processes involving commercial transactions by electronic processes.

Typical functionalities that a B2B solution offers to suppliers are the creation and maintenance of product catalogs, the reception and answer to proposal requests, ordering reception and the maintenance of the "tracking" information of orders. On the client side, the available functionalities are: the "consulting" of product catalogs and services, the possibility of placing purchasing orders, the accompaniment of the "tracking" information of the orders and also the request and reception of proposals. This way B2B solutions provide sellers and clients with a common platform, on which both can make their transactions in a perfectly integrated and compatible way.

According to a study of eMarketer in 2003, B2B EC was considered to be worth approximately ten times the value of business to consumer EC. In 2006 it was estimated that B2B could represent approximately 5 trillion USD (eMarketer, 2003). Despite the fact that B2B has already been practiced for several decades now, particularly with the use of EDI technology, it is through using the most recent technologies available that the model of B2B has been stimulating innovative forms of business cooperation, making companies increasingly competitive and helping them to face new globalization challenges (ANACOM, 2004).

There are several architectures of electronic business, including EDI, Websites, B2B hubs, e-procurement systems and Web Services that support B2B, of which some apply more than others to this type of EC (Albrecht et al., 2005).

It is foreseeable that EC B2B will exceed EC B2C (electronic commerce Business-to-Consumer) as a means of simultaneously raising sales and reducing operational costs. One of the reasons for this is that normally the biggest volume of sales occurs between business partners (more than among companies and private consumers). Furthermore, it is an opportunity to obtain efficiency in company communications while using Information Technologies (IT) that are emerging. In fact, many companies feel the need to use B2B because those competitors who use these technologies threaten to catch up on efficiency gains, jeopardizing their position in the market. To make an effective decision, it is important to estimate the benefits and understand what conditions are the most suitable when using B2B activities (Kauffman & Walden, 2001; Kaefer & Bendoly, 2004).

The process of B2B implies that the participants involved normally go through three phases such as search, negotiation and realization (Schoop et al., 2001; Quix et al., 2002), which consists of a model for business transactions:

- During the first phase, a percentage of these participants search for potential business partners. For example, a buyer may want to find relevant suppliers for the products he/she wants to obtain, or a salesman may want to find potential clients for the products that he/she supplies;

- The Second phase consists of the range of an acceptable agreement to all business partners where the details of the contract are negotiated. In this phase business partners can discuss certain important points to reach an agreement, like the prices of products, delivery dates, quality of products, etc. The goal consists of finishing the contract which specifies the business agreement;

- If negotiation occurs successfully, the completion of the contract is achieved at the third phase which will be processed by the business partners, encompassing logistics, payment, etc.

This type of EC is basically developed in three big areas: e-marketplaces, e-procurement and e-distribution. At present, a large part of B2B transactions are made through e-marketplaces and this can be defined as a business solution and cooperation of "many to many" that allows companies to buy, sell and cooperate more efficiently at a global scale. It makes the participation of sellers and buyers possible in a central market in order to exchange information about prices and offers related to the products which are most appropriate for them, facilitating the exchange of information, products, services and payments as well as supplying an infrastructure that permits the effective functioning of the market (Bakos, 1997; Bakos, 1998; Castro_Lacouture et al., 2006).

The e-procurement activity at any organization implies all the activities associated to the acquisition process of goods and services necessary for the accomplishment of the productive processes and management which will lead to the creation of added value on the products and services that are placed on the market. It involves the identification and characterization of needs, supplier's

selection, product selection, negotiation, demand, approval, order, reception, invoice and payment, and inventory, among others (Amaral et al., 2003).

E-distribution consists of electronic platforms designed to integrate companies with their distributors, branches and representatives allowing the execution of a variety of tasks from a simple search to an electronic catalog to invoice emission and goods reception (ANACOM, 2004).

3. INVESTIGATION PROCESS

In order to conceive the model of functionalities for the development of B2B solutions, we first conducted a review of the fundamental concepts for the comprehension and characterization of B2B. After a deep analysis of several B2B solutions, at a local level (Portugal) as well as internationally, some solutions were identified as the richest in terms of functionality quantity and diversity of characteristics. Three national B2B solutions were then selected: Tradecom (www.tradecom.pt), Iwaytrade (www.iwaytrade.com) and Bizdirect (www.bizdirect.pt), as well as three international solutions: Alibaba (www.alibaba.com), EC21 (www.ec21.com) and Busytrade (www.busytrade.com). A list of functionalities supported was identified for each of these solutions. Others were not studied any further seeing as the non-existence of additional characteristics was verified after a subsequent study of solutions (for example: pmelink (www.pmelink.pt), forumB2B, (www.forumb2b.com), tradekey (www.tradekey.com). Data research took place between December 2006 and January 2007.

The analysis conducted permitted the identification of multiple functionalities and characteristics that B2B solutions have. Such functionalities were organized on tables, for example in Figure 1, in order to enable an analysis related to the support of functionalities by the solutions studied.

The functionalities totally supported by the solutions (identified from P1 to P6) are signed

Figure 1. Purchase process

PURCHASE PROCESS:	P1	P2	P3	P4	P5	P6
• Make requests for proposal;	NS	S	NS	S	S	S
• Create products requests;	S	S	S	NS	NS	NS
• Approve requests;	S	S	S	NS	NS	NS
• Monitor orders;	S	S	S	NS	NS	NS
• Monitor requests, with the possibility to check the status of the request (for example: acceptance);	S	PS	S	NS	NS	NS
• Receive orders.	S	SP	S	NS	NS	NS

"S". Partially supported functionalities are signed "SP" (which means that the solution supports certain functionality but not totally). Functionalities not supported are signed "NS". When it was not possible to confirm the support (although it could be found described/explained in the solution´s information) the functionalities were signed with "PS" which means perception support.

The set of functionalities and characteristics identified over several studied solutions was essential in the creation of the functionalities model of B2B solutions, which is presented in the next section.

4. MODEL OF FUNCIONALITIES FOR THE DEVELOPMENT OF B2B ELECTRONIC COMMERCE SOLUTIONS

This section presents the identified functionalities of B2B solutions, and provides a brief description of these functionalities. Taken together they constitute the model of functionalities for the evaluation and construction of B2B e-commerce websites. For a better understanding and for consultation purposes, they were organized into different categories. Taken together they constitute a reference model for the development of B2B e-commerce solutions, as in Figure 2.

The categories of functionalities are:

- Products catalog;
- Purchase process;
- Order process;
- Payments;
- Goods dispatch;
- Used technologies;
- Information;
- Users;
- Selling mechanisms;
- Extra-company publicity;
- Announcements;
- Business reports;
- Advanced features.

The categories that are in the central part of Figure 2 are the essential functionalities for the development of a B2B website. In the following subsections the various functionalities are presented and briefly described.

Figure 2. Model of functionalities for the development of B2B electronic commerce solutions

4.1 Products Catalog

Table 1 shows the functionalities that belong to the category "Products catalog". In this category are associated functionalities related to the maintenance of the products catalog.

Create and manage products catalog: the ability to create the products catalog and the option to edit, view the status of publications and also consult the products catalog.

Publish information: the ability to publish information on sellers, buyers or companies, i.e., the publication of information on what the buyers want to buy, information on what the sellers want to sell, and information on business activities.

4.1.1 Create and Manage Products Catalog

Table 2 shows the detail of the functionality "Create and manage products catalog" of the "Products catalog" category. In general this functionality includes defining how information is presented, to search in different ways, and finally functionalities related to the process for this functionality.

View list of categories of products or services: ability to view a list of categories of products and services available on the website.

View the products catalog form: view the form with the necessary fields to create a products catalog, which may indicate the products to add to the catalog and some characteristics.

Fill member dispatch form: to make the creation of the products catalog it is necessary that the user is a member of the website, requiring him to fill out a form to become a member.

Deliver on the file to the products cataloging: after filling in the form for the products catalog, it can be delivered for cataloging.

Normalize the information: is a process of standardization of product description, or replacing abbreviations, order attributes. This process must be conducted with the monitoring of the supplier.

Sort and categorize products and services: after the standardization of information, it is possible to establish the classification and categorization of products and services, or in this case the products or services that are associated with the respective categories.

Send the file to the supplier for final validation: after the process of cataloging, the file must be sent back to the supplier to be able to validate all the information in this products catalog.

Edit on-line data catalog: ability to update the products catalog on-line.

See catalog: ability to consult the products catalog on-line, where you can view all products and services.

View the status of publications: ability to check the status of the publication of products catalogs, for example, approved and pending, among oth-

Table 1. Products catalog

Products Catalog:
• Create and manage products catalog;
• Publish information.

Table 2. Create and manage product catalog

Create and manage Products Catalog
Organization:
• View list of categories of products or services;
• View the products catalog form;
Process:
• Fill member dispatch form;
• Deliver on the file to the products cataloging;
• Normalize the information;
• Sort and categorize products and services;
• Send the file to the supplier for final validation;
• Edit on-line data catalog;
• See catalog;
• View the status of publications (for example: approved, pending).

ers, i.e., it is possible to manage the publication of products catalogs.

4.1.2 Publish Information

Table 3 shows the detail of the feature "Publish information" of the "Products catalog" category, where how information is presented, the different methods of search and, finally, the process associated with this functionality are shown.

Show form to publish information: ability to view a form with specific fields to make the publication of information about buyers, sellers and companies.

Publish information about buyers or sellers: ability to announce or publish information about a seller, indicating what he intends to sell, or about a buyer, indicating what he wants to buy.

Publish and edit the profile of a company: ability to announce and publish, or edit the profile of a company so that users can learn more about the company to decide whether they want to trade with this company. It is also possible to edit the profile of a company.

Publishing services supported by a company: ability to publish the services supported by a company.

Approve information: ability to approve the information on buyers, sellers or profile of a company, so that it can be published.

Receive notification by e-mail about the status of the publication of information: ability to receive a notification by e-mail with the status of publication of information on buyers, sellers or profile of a company.

Checking the status of publication (for example approved, pending): ability to check the status of publication of information on buyers, sellers or profile of a company, i.e., management of the publications issued.

4.2 Purchase Process

Table 4 shows the functionalities that belong to the category "Purchase process". In this category all the functionalities related to the purchase process are associated, i.e., the functionalities necessary for customers to order goods or services.

Make proposal requests: is the ability to exchange messages between buyers and sellers. Buyers can request information on products, or make a proposal request to a seller. Sellers can make a purchase request to the buyers. Proposal requests can be made from a product catalog.

Create products requests: the ability to create a new request or a request from an existing model or design. The products request is the process of ordering products from suppliers.

Table 3. Publish information

Publish information
Organization:
• Show form to publish information;
Process:
• Publish information about buyers or sellers;
• Publish and edit the profile of a company;
• Publishing services supported by a company;
• Approve information;
• Receive notification by e-mail about the status of the publication of information;
• Checking the status of publication (for example: approved, pending).

Table 4. Purchase process

Purchase process
• Make proposal requests;
• Create products requests;
• Approve requests;
• Monitor orders;
• Monitor requests, with the ability to check the status of the request (for example: acceptance);
• Receive orders.

Approve requests: after the products request their approval is required.

Monitor orders: ability to check the status of the orders made (for example: accepted or sent by the supplier), and other information related to the orders made.

Monitor requests: ability to check the status of the requests made (for example: accepted).

Receive orders: ability to check the details of the receipt of goods ordered.

4.2.1 Make Proposal Requests

Table 5 shows the detail of the functionality "Make proposal requests" of the "Purchase process" category, where how information is presented, the different methods of research and, finally, the process associated with this functionality are shown.

View categories, subcategories or a list of products or services, buyers, sellers and companies: ability to view products or services, buyers, sellers or companies through categories, subcategories or a list.

View list of keywords: ability to view a list of the most used keywords in searches.

View list of companies, buyers, sellers and products and their focus keywords: ability to view a list of companies, buyers and sellers and products in focus with the keywords.

View list of products in focus: ability to view a list of products in focus.

View list of the most visited companies: ability to view a list of the most visited company's website.

View products in focus, all products or buyers from A to Z: ability to view products in focus, all products or buyers in alphabetical order.

View list of suppliers: ability to view a list of suppliers on the website.

View list of products manufacturers: ability to view a list of manufacturers of certain products.

View list of trusted members: ability to view a list of trusted members, members who have

Table 5. Make proposal requests

Make proposal requests
Organization:
• View categories, subcategories or a list of products or services, buyers, sellers or companies;
• View list of keywords;
• View list of companies, buyers, sellers and products and their focus keywords;
• View list of products in focus;
• View list of the most visited companies;
• View products in focus, all products or buyers from A to Z;
• View list of suppliers;
• View list of products manufacturers;
• View list of trust members;
• View form for proposal request;
Search:
• Search by keyword;
• Search products or services, buyers, sellers or companies by categories, subcategories or criteria;
• Search for other products from the same supplier;
Process:
• Show details of products;
• Show details of buyers, sellers and companies;
• Consult information about suppliers;
• See similar products from other suppliers;
• Add products to cart of "proposal requests";
• Add attachments and comments;
• Submit a proposal request to suppliers;
• Consult, reply and send the response to proposal requests to customers, by suppliers;
• Receive notification to indicate the receipt of a response to a proposal request;
• Receive and respond to messages from suppliers;
• Consult and compare the responses to proposal requests;
• Make counterproposals to suppliers;
• Make an purchase offer from suppliers by e-mail;
• Consult and analyze the proposed purchase;
• Select the proposed purchase;
• Print formatted the product information;
• Add website to favorites list of the Web browser;
• Insert a keyword that is related to buyers and sellers, products or companies.

been authenticated by an external entity and that have the level of trust needed to establish business relations.

View form for proposal request: ability to verify the necessary form to complete in order to make a proposal request.

Search by keyword: ability to seek products or *services through keywords that represents the products / services.*

Search products or services, buyers, sellers or companies by categories, subcategories or criteria: ability to search by categories or subcategories, and also by certain criteria.

Search for other products from the same supplier: ability to find new products from the same supplier of the product being sought.

Show details of products: ability to see the *characteristics of the products in* detail.

Show details of buyers, sellers and companies: ability to find information relating to buyers, sellers or company in detail.

Consult information about suppliers: ability to view the contacts of suppliers and information about the companies.

See similar products from other suppliers: ability to view similar products to the research done, but that correspond to products from other suppliers.

Add products to cart of "proposal requests": to make the proposal request for more than one product or service, you can add more products or services to the cart of proposal requests.

Add attachments and comments: ability to add attachments to the proposal request and user reviews.

Submit a proposal request to suppliers: ability to submit a proposal request to their suppliers, taking into account the products or services selected.

Consult, reply and send the response to proposal requests to customers, by suppliers: capacity for suppliers to receive proposal requests, reply and send the answers.

Receive notification to indicate the receipt of a response to a proposal request: ability for the client to receive a notification that states a response to a proposal request has been received.

Receive and respond to messages from suppliers: ability for customers to respond to messages received from suppliers.

Consult and compare the responses to proposal requests: ability for customers to view and compare the responses of proposal requests in order to consider the best option for what they want to obtain.

Make counterproposals to suppliers: ability for customers to make a counterproposal to suppliers.

Make a purchase offer from suppliers by e-mail: ability of suppliers to make an offer to certain buyers in view of their purchase requirements.

Consult and analyze the proposed purchase: ability of buyers to consult and analyze the proposed purchase in order to decide on the best proposal for what they want to obtain.

Select the proposed purchase: ability to select the purchase proposal to be consulted.

Print format the product information: ability to format the print information about the products.

Add website to favorites list of the Web browser: ability to add a website to favorites list.

Insert a keyword that is related to buyers and sellers, products or companies: ability to enter a keyword and relate it to a marketing agent (buyers and sellers), or with a product or a company, to facilitate future research by keywords.

4.2.2 Create Products Requests

Table 6 shows the detail of the functionality to "Create products requests" of the "Purchase process" category, where how information is presented, the different methods of search and, finally, the process associated with this functionality are shown.

View list of categories of products or services: ability to view the categories of products and services available on the website.

Table 6. Create products requests

Create products requests
Organization:
• View list of categories of products or services;
• View list of products or services filtered according to the search criteria;
Search:
• Search in the products catalog according to certain criteria;
Process:
• Add website to favorites list of Web browser;
• Consult the characteristics of the products in detail;
• Add products to cart;
• Add comments and attachments;
• Edit requests;
• Check whether the supplier has products in stock;
• Consult information about suppliers;
• Select another supplier offering similar products;
• Add new products to the same request;
• Consult maps of requests;
• Submit request for approval.

Table 7. Approve requests

Approve requests
Organization:
• View list of requests;
Search:
• Search requests in accordance with certain criteria;
Process:
• Extract a report with a list of requests made;
• See details of requests;
• Approve the requests and enter a comment;
• Make notification of approval by e-mail, web or fax;
• Send the purchase orders to suppliers.

View list of products or services filtered according to the search criteria: after making a search the products or services related to the search are displayed.

Search in the products catalog according to certain criteria: ability to find products or services in a products catalog according to certain criteria.

Add website to favorites list of Web browser: ability to add the site to favorites.

Consult the characteristics of the products in detail: ability to see the products and check their functionalities in detail.

Add products to cart: the cart will temporarily store the products you want to order, in which the user has the ability to add products to the cart.

Add comments and attachments: ability to add comments or attachments to the request of products.

Edit requests after the creation of requests you can edit these requests, modify the desired

quantity of a product or service, or remove any unwanted product from the order.

Check whether the supplier has products in stock: ability to verify if the supplier has the required quantities of products or services that the customer is seeking.

Consult information about suppliers: ability to find information about suppliers of the desired products.

Select another supplier offering similar products: ability to select a different provider that offers products similar to those desired.

Add new products to the same request: ability to add new products to the same request where there is no limit set.

Consult maps of requests: ability to see the requests made by each user and determine who will approve the request.

Send requests for approval: to finalize the process of creating a requisition, the requisitions are sent to those responsible for making the approval.

4.2.3 Approve Requests

Table 7 shows the detail of the functionality "Approve requests" of the "Purchase process" category, where how information is presented, the different methods of search, and, finally, the process associated with this functionality are shown.

View list of requests: ability to present a list of requests that require approval.

Search requests in accordance with certain criteria: ability to search for a specific request in accordance with certain criteria.

Extract a report with a list of requests made: ability to extract a report which shows the requests made by a user.

See details of requests: ability to see the detail of the requirements and verify the products or services and the quantity that the user wants to order, among other information.

Approve requests and enter a comment: ability for those responsible to approve the requests and enter any comments.

Make notification of approval by e-mail, web or fax: ability to send the notification of approval of requests to users by e-mail, web or fax.

Send the purchase orders to suppliers: ability to send the purchase orders to their suppliers after the request is approved.

4.2.4 Monitor Orders

Table 8 shows the detail of the functionality "Monitor orders" of the "Purchase process" category, where how information is presented, the different

methods of search, as well as the process associated with this functionality are shown.

View list of orders made: ability to view a list of orders that were made.

Search orders in accordance with certain criteria: ability to search for a specific order in accordance with certain criteria.

Check status and order history: ability to check the status and history of an order, for example, check if it was accepted or sent by the supplier.

Consult orders from suppliers: ability of suppliers to check the orders received.

Accept orders: ability for suppliers to accept orders received

Send orders: ability to send orders out to customers.

Accept payment type: ability to accept the type of payment that will be used.

4.2.5 Receive Orders

Table 9 shows the detail of functionality "Receive orders" of the "Purchase process" category, where how information is presented, the different methods of search and, finally, the process associated with this functionality are shown.

View list of orders placed with the receiving state: ability to view a list of orders made and the status of the receipt.

Table 8. Monitor orders

Monitor orders
Organization:
• View list of orders made;
Search:
• Search orders in accordance with certain criteria;
Process:
• Check the status and history of the orders (for example: accepted or sent by the supplier);
• Consult orders from suppliers;
• Accept orders;
• Send orders;
• Accept payment type.

Table 9. Receive orders

Receive orders
Organization:
• View list of orders made with the receiving state;
Search:
• Search orders in accordance with certain criteria;
Process:
• Change the status of an order;
• Indicate the details of receipt of the order;
• Show details of reception;
• Confirm the receipt of goods or services ordered.

Search orders in accordance with certain criteria: ability to search for a specific order according to certain criteria.

Change the status of an order: ability to change the status of receipt of an order.

Indicate the details of receipt of the order: ability to give some details concerning the receipt of orders, such as the date of receipt, the carrier, among other.

Show details of reception: ability to check in detail the information on the order.

Confirm the receipt of goods or services ordered: ability to confirm the receipt of orders.

4.3 Order Process

Table 10 shows the functionalities that belong to the category "Order process". In this category are associated functionalities related to the order process, consisting of the functionalities that the suppliers can perform in accordance with the orders made.

Manage orders: is the receipt and verification of orders placed by customers, with the ability to perform other functions, such as reject any order, or modify the conditions of a given order.

Create invoices: ability to create a new invoice or generate an invoice from an existing document. The creation of invoices is made in accordance with the data of the associated order.

Manage invoices: ability to check the invoices created and make the necessary changes, among other functionalities.

Table 10. Order process

Order Process
• Manage orders;
• Create invoices;
• Manage invoices;
• Create dispatch note.

Create dispatch note: ability to create a new dispatch note or create one from an existing document, and consult the dispatch note.

4.3.1 Manage Orders

Table 11 shows the detail of the functionality "Manage orders" of the "Order process" category, where how information is presented, the different methods of search and, finally, the process associated with this functionality are shown.

Receive and view a list of orders: ability of suppliers to receive and view a list of orders placed.

Search orders by some criteria: ability to search for a specific order according to some criteria.

View information about the company: ability to verify information on the supplier company.

View all members by name: ability to visualize all members of the company by name.

Select and view details of an order: ability to select an order and view the details.

Table 11. Manage orders

Manage orders
Organization:
• Receive and view a list of orders;
Search:
• Search orders by some criteria;
Process:
• View information about the company;
• View all members by name;
• Select and view details of an order;
• Negotiate the terms;
• Check the capacity of delivery;
• Select payment type;
• Edit an order;
• Indicate the status of an order (for example: accepted, accepted with amendments, among others);
• Send response to buyer;
• Extracting reports.

Negotiate the terms: ability to negotiate the details of payment, terms of delivery, among other things.

Check the capacity of delivery: ability to verify if the supplier has enough in stock for the orders made, confirm the delivery date and the payment form agreed with the buyer.

Select payment type: ability to select the type of payment previously agreed with the buyer.

Edit an order: ability to make changes in orders, change prices and quantities, as well as indicate the status of the orders, for example, accepted or accepted with modifications.

Indicate the status of an order: ability to change the status of orders, for example, accepted, accepted with amendments, among others.

Send response to buyer: ability to send a response to the buyer about his order after completing all the required operations.

Extracting reports: ability to extract certain reports, such as a report of orders, orders canceled by the buyers, orders not cataloged or orders received by buyers.

4.3.2 Create Invoices

Table 12 shows the detail of the functionality "Create invoices" of the "Order process" category, where how information is presented, the different methods of search and, finally, the process associated with this functionality are shown.

View list of orders and their related characteristics: ability to view a list of orders placed and their related characteristics.

Search an order in accordance with certain criteria: ability to search an order in accordance with certain criteria.

Select an order: to associate an invoice to an order you must select the desired order.

Complete an invoice automatically according to the data of the selected order: after the order is selected, the completion of the invoice in accordance with the data of the order takes place automatically.

Edit invoice: ability to change the data of a particular invoice.

Send invoice to the buyer: after the completion of the invoice it is sent to the buyer.

4.3.3 Manage Invoices

Table 13 shows the detail of the functionality "Manage invoices" of the "Order process" category, where how information is presented, the different methods of search and, finally, the process associated with this functionality are shown.

Table 12. Create invoices

Create invoices
Organization:
• View list of orders and their related characteristics;
Search:
• Search an order in accordance with certain criteria;
Process:
• Select an order;
• Complete an invoice automatically according to the data of the selected order;
• Edit invoice;
• Send invoice to the buyer.

Table 13. Manage invoices

Manage invoices
Organization:
• View list of stored invoices and their status;
Search:
• Search the invoices according to certain criteria;
Process:
• View invoices and their status;
• Edit invoice;
• Introduce changes to pending documents;
• Print invoices;
• Download invoices;
• Delete invoices.

Table 14. Payments

Payments
• Process payments on-line;
• Making electronic notification of payment warnings;
• Use credit card for on-line payments.

View list of stored invoices and their status: ability to view the list of stored invoices and their status.

Search the invoices according to certain criteria: ability to search for a specific invoice in accordance with certain criteria.

View invoices and their status: ability to select an invoice to view its details and its status.

Edit invoice: ability to introduce some changes in the invoices.

Introduce changes to pending documents: ability to make changes in pending invoices.

Print invoices: ability to print invoices already completed formatted.

Download invoices: ability to download invoices.

Delete invoices: ability to delete invoices.

4.4 Payments

Table 14 shows the functionalities that belong to the category "Payments". In this category are associated functionalities related to the payments on-line.

Process payments on-line: is the ability to make the payment of orders through the Internet.

Making electronic notification of payment warnings: ability to receive notices of payment by customers.

Use credit card for on-line payments: is the ability to use a credit card to make the payments for the goods or services ordered.

Table 15. Goods dispatch

Goods dispatch
• Logistics.

4.5 Goods Dispatch

Table 15 shows the functionalities that belong to the category "Goods dispatch". This category refers to the functionalities related to the goods dispatch, or to the functions of logistics.

Logistics: this functionality aims to meet the diverse needs of goods dispatch from the participating companies, both nationally and internationally. With this functionality you can create requests for transport, handle those requests, simulate prices, dispatch and monitor the order.

4.5.1 Logistics

Table 16 shows the detail of the "Logistics" functionality of the "Goods dispatch" category, where how information is presented, the different methods of search and, finally, the process associated with this functionality are shown.

View list of orders accepted: ability to view a list of orders already accepted by suppliers.

View list of operators: ability to view a list of the operators belonging to the market.

View list of requests: ability to view a list of requests for transport of goods.

Search orders by some criteria: ability to search for a specific order in accordance with certain criteria.

Search requests by certain criteria: ability to search for a request for the transport of goods in accordance with certain criteria.

Table 16. Logistics

Logistics
Organization:
• View list of orders accepted;
• View list of operators;
• View list of requests;
Search:
• Search orders by some criteria;
• Search requests by certain criteria;
Process:
• Create requests for transport;
• Choose the order you want to transport and the operator;
• Make a request for transport without order;
• Enter the details of the volumes;
• Simulate prices;
• Present the estimated prices for the service;
• Dispatch;
• Choose the service;
• Complete data on the dispatch;
• Accept the conditions set by the carrier;
• Submit the request;
• Send request to the operator;
• Receive response from operator;
• Print transport guides, invoices and labels for the transport of goods;
• Send a message to explain the reason for non-acceptance;
• Track your order;
• Manage requests made by logistics operators.

Create requests for transport: ability to create a transfer request for an acquired product in an e-marketplace.

Choose the order you want to transport and the operator: to create a transfer request, if the order was made in an e-marketplace, it is necessary to select it, and also the operator.

Making a request for transport without order: if the goods were not obtained in an e-marketplace a transfer request can be made without an order, indicating the required fields on the request form.

Enter the details of the volumes: ability to indicate the contents of the volumes to be transported, the amount of goods to be transported.

Simulate prices: ability to simulate a price taking into account the goods that will be transported, or dispatch the goods directly without performing a simulation if it is not necessary.

Present the estimated prices for the service: when carrying out a price simulation, the estimated prices for the desired service are shown.

Making the dispatch:– once in accordance with the conditions proposed by the operator is made the goods dispatch.

Choose the service: to make the dispatch of the goods is necessary to choose the service.

Complete data on the dispatch: to make the dispatch of the goods is necessary to fill the dispatch details, as the company name, address, among other.

Accept the conditions set by the carrier: to make dispatch of the goods must still accept the conditions determined by the carrier.

Submit the request: to finalize the dispatch process the transfer request must be submitted.

Send request to the operator: the request is sent to the operator, but before this a screen appears to make sure that all data previously filled in are correct.

Receive response from operator: after processing the request, the operator sends the response to the request.

Print transport bills, invoices and labels for the transport of goods: in situations where the service was accepted by the operator transport guides may be printed, as well as invoices and labels for the transport of goods.

Send a message to explain the reason for non-acceptance: in situations where the service was not accepted by the operator, the system sends a message explaining the reason for non-acceptance.

Track your order: the ability to monitor the order by filling in specific fields, with the possibility of knowing the status of the order.

Table 17. Used technologies in B2B solutions

Used technologies
• Access the application by Internet / Web browser;
• Standard Really Simple Syndication (RSS);
• Develop the application in ASP mode;
• Make the electronic transfer of data through EDI.

Table 18. Information

Information
• Consult policy listing of products;
• Consult different types of information for business communities;
• Consult FAQ;
• Show terms of use;
• Show privacy policy;
• Show regulation of members;
• Show information about fraud;
• View site map.

Manage requests made by logistics operators: the ability to manage the requests made to different logistics operators.

4.6 Used Technologies

Table 17 shows the functionalities that belong to the category "Used technologies". In this category, technologies that are used on platforms in order to allow for certain functionalities are presented.

Access the application by Internet / Web browser: access the application of a B2B solution by Internet or Web browser.

Standard Really Simple Syndication (RSS): B2B solutions can support this standard, which checks for updates of information in platforms automatically and periodically.

Develop the application in ASP mode: applications can be developed using ASP technology.

Make the electronic transfer of data through EDI: ability to use the EDI standard, which allows the exchange of information or data on the Internet.

4.7 Information

Table 18 shows the functionalities that belong to the category "Information". In this category are associated functionalities that consist of a certain kind of information on a platform, which can be accessed by users.

Consult policy listing of products: ability to provide the restrictions and prohibitions related to the presentation of certain products.

Consult different types of information for business communities: ability to present information for firms.

Consult FAQ: ability to present a list of frequently asked questions and their answers.

Show terms of use: ability to view the terms and conditions that are necessary to take into account when using the functionalities supported by the website.

Show privacy policy: ability to view important information relating to privacy.

Show regulation of members: ability to visualize conditions that members must take into account.

Show information about fraud: ability to show information about fraud on the Internet to warn users.

View site map: with the site map the user can see the links of all the functionalities present on the website.

4.8 Users

Table 19 shows the functionalities that belong to the category "Users". In this category, all the associated functionalities present in the platform that are related to the users are presented.

Register users: to become a member the user is required to register in order to have access to various functionalities, depending on his/her permissions.

Table 19. Manage users

Users
• Register users;
• Recover password;
• Make login and logout;
• Edit the user information.

Table 20. Selling mechanisms of B2B solutions

Selling mechanisms
• Recommend to a friend;
• Send a comment with the user opinion;
• Receive an marketing alert by e-mail;
• Configure marketing alert;
• Create a website to promote products and services on-line of a company;

• Auctions;
  − Participate in sell auctions;
  − Participate in purchase auctions;

• Aggregations;
• Configure the products to appear at the top of the lists presented in the research of products by category or by keyword.

Recover password: ability to for users to recover their password;

Make login and logout: to be able to access the various functionalities the user must login, and when finished must logout. The user can perform some functions without logging, however, to carry out the purchase of goods and services (for example), this is required.

Edit the user information: ability to change the user registration on-line.

4.9 Selling Mechanisms

Table 20 shows the functionalities that belong to the category "Selling mechanisms". This category refers to functionalities that allow the promotion of products in the platform, so as to increase the number of sales.

Recommend to a friend: ability of the user to recommend the website by e-mail.

Send a comment with the user opinion: ability of the user to send a comment with his opinion regarding the website.

Receive an marketing alert by e-mail: ability to receive an e-mail containing information about the products or services that the user wants to know about, taking into account the configuration made.

Configure marketing alert: ability to configure a marketing alert, indicating the options concerning the information about products or services that the user wishes to receive e-mail about.

Create a website to promote a company's products and services on-line: is a tool that allows the user to quickly and easily create a website, to promote products and services of a company.

Auctions: ability to establish market prices, enabling the encounter between supply and demand in real time. There are two types of auctions, the sale auctions, where suppliers take products and services to auction and call for the participation of the purchasing companies. In the purchase auctions buyers send requests for quotations for goods and services that they are interested in buying and invite suppliers to bid on-line.

Aggregations: is the aggregation of business needs, so that placing a single order from the supplier enables the acquisition of more advantageous conditions than those that the buyer can obtain individually.

Configure the products to appear at the top of the lists presented in the research of products by category or by keyword: enables products to appear first in lists of items displayed when the user performs a search.

4.9.1 Auctions

Table 21 shows the details of the functionality "Auctions" of the "Selling mechanisms" category, where, how information is presented, the different search methods and, finally, the process associated with this functionality are shown.

Table 21. Auctions

Auctions
Organization:
• Present a form to create an auction;
• Present a registration form for the auction;
• View a list of auctions that are taking place;
• Show the "contractual conditions" on the supply of products;
• View a list of bids and functionalities;
• View graphs relating to bids;
Process:
• Promote an auction by completing a form with their parameters;
• Receive reports of activities;
• Notify potential buyers automatically by e-mail;
• Allow the participation of international companies;
• Receive confirmation of participation in the auction;
• Access the registration form at the auction and fill it;
• Automatically complete the registration form;
• Send the user a password;
• Consult the events posted on-line;
• Make and submit a bid designating specific fields;
• View the progress of the auction;
• Consult the result of the auction;
• Create and send (by e-mail) a message to the winners;
• Automatically generate purchase orders.

Present a form to create an auction: submit a form with specific fields for the creation of an auction.

Present a registration form for the auction: submit a form with specific fields to participate in an auction.

View a list of auctions that are taking place: ability to view a list of auctions that are taking place.

Show the "contractual conditions" on the supply of products: ability to query information on the conditions of the supply of products.

View a list of bids and functionalities: ability to view a list of the bids made by the participants in the auction and information regarding the bidding.

View graphs relating to bids: ability to see some graphs that represent information about the auction, such as the registration number of bids or the declining price of bids.

Promote an auction by completing a form with their parameters: in order to create an auction it is necessary to fill out a form.

Receive reports of activities: ability to receive reports, to check the activities that are taking place.

Notify potential buyers automatically by e-mail: ability to notify potential buyers to participate in auctions by e-mail.

Allow the participation of international companies: ability of international companies to participate in the auctions, in which case it would be possible to view the application in a different language.

Receive confirmation of participation in the auction: ability to receive confirmations of participation in auctions.

Access the registration form at the auction and complete it: if the auction participants are not members of the e-marketplace they have to fill out the form.

Automatically complete the registration form: if the company is a member of the e-marketplace the registration form of the auction is filled out automatically.

Send the user a password: after processing the request form of the auction the password is sent to the participants.

Consult the events posted on-line: ability to see the auctions that are taking place on-line.

Make and submit a bid designating specific fields: participants in the auctions can make and submit their bids.

View the progress of the auction: ability to view the process of auctions through the graphics present on the website.

Consult the result of the auction: ability to consult the results of the auctions on-line to see who the winners were.

Create and send (by e-mail) a message to the winners: ability to create a message for the winners of the auction, to be later sent automatically so that they can be notified of the outcome of the auction.

Automatically generate purchase orders: if the winning bidder is a member of the e-marketplace a purchase order is automatically generated.

4.9.2 Aggregations

Table 22 shows the details of the functionality "Aggregations" of the "Selling mechanisms" category, which is indicated as the information is presented, the different search methods and, finally, the process associated with this functionality.

Show ongoing purchase aggregations: ability to view a list of the aggregations that are taking place.

Show the highlights of the events on-line: ability to consult the event's highlights on-line.

Show the "general conditions of purchase" ability to find information about the purchase conditions.

Access the detail of a purchase aggregation: ability to see the detail of an aggregation submitted on-line.

Indicate the quantity of product you want to buy: ability to state the amount of product that the user wants to order.

View the chart with the state of aggregation: ability to view a chart that will indicate the fall in prices depending on the subscriptions made.

Check the purchase conditions: to subscribe the user must accept the general conditions of purchase.

Process the requests: ability to process the aggregation request, which leads to product price changes.

Automatically generate orders: when aggregations of purchase end, purchase orders are automatically generated.

Send notifications of the aggregates results by e-mail: ability to automatically send e-mail notifications to indicate the results of the aggregations.

Table 22. Aggregations

Aggregations
Organization:
• Show ongoing purchase aggregations;
• Show the highlights of the events on-line;
• Show the "general conditions of purchase";
Process:
• Access the detail of a purchase aggregation;
• Indicate the quantity of product you want to buy;
• Show graphic with the state of aggregation;
• Check the purchase conditions;
• Process the requests;
• Automatically generate orders;
• Send notifications of the aggregate results by e-mail;
• Receive notifications from buyers;
• Receive and process orders from the supplier.

Receive notifications from buyers: ability of buyers to receive the notifications sent.

Receive and process orders from the supplier: orders are received and processed by suppliers.

4.10 Extra-Company Publicity

Table 23 shows the functionalities that belong to the category "Extra-company publicity". This category refers to functionalities which permit the publicity of the products of certain vendors (extra-company), i.e., publicity that advertisers have to pay for.

Make extra-company publicity or promotion of products through banners: ability to promote products through extra-company publicity banners.

Table 23. Extra-company publicity

Extra-company publicity
• Make extra-company publicity or promotion of products through banners.

Table 24. Announcements

Announcements
• Consult and add articles;
• View news;
• Consult and search for events, conferences and tradeshows;
• Consult country profiles, services of business partners;
• Consult and participate in forums;
• Receive newsletter;
• Consult and insert success stories;

4.11 Announcements

Table 24 shows the functionalities that belong to the category "Announcements". In this category are associated functionalities that represent types of ads on this platform.

Consult and add articles: ability to check articles on the website that can be added by users.

View news: ability to view news related to the website.

Consult and search for events, conferences and tradeshows: ability to consult or research all marketing events, conferences or tradeshows that will be conducted.

Consult country profiles, services of business partners: ability to find information on the business partners' various countries and available services.

Consult and participate in forums: ability to participate and consult the forums related to the website.

Receive newsletter: ability to receive periodic information about the website, case studies, FAQs and news, among other information.

Consult and insert success stories: ability to consult and insert success stories related to their experience in using the website, and the possibility of a success.

Table 25. Business reports

Business reports
• Extracting business reports.

4.12 Business Reports

Table 25 shows the functionalities that belong to the category "Business reports". This category refers to functionalities related to obtaining reports containing information about different companies.

Extracting business reports: provides electronic commerce participants with national and international business, legal and financial information.

4.12.1 Extracting Business Reports

Table 26 shows the detail of the functionality "Extracting business reports" of the "Business reports" category, indicating how information is presented, the different search methods and, finally, the process associated with this functionality.

Table 26. Extracting business reports

Extracting business reports
Organization:
• View list of companies;
Search:
• Find a business report in accordance with certain criteria;
Process:
• Access to national and international reports;
• Accept the terms and conditions of reporting;
• View report;
• Print report.

View list of companies: ability to view a list of national or international companies.

Find a business report in accordance with certain criteria: ability to research specific companies in accordance with certain criteria.

Access to national and international reports: ability to access the report of the selected company.

Accept the terms and conditions of reporting: in order to access the reports the conditions of provision information must be accepted.

View report: ability to view the reports.

Print report: ability to print a formatted report.

4.13 Advanced Features

Table 27 shows the functionalities that belong to the category "Advanced features". This category refers to functionalities supported by the platform which stands out.

Integrating ERP systems: ability to integrate data from the platforms with ERP systems.

Support more than one language: ability of the platforms to be displayed in more than one language, i.e., the user can choose the desired language from the options presented.

Allow international transactions: ability of B2B solutions to do business with different countries.

Support different types of members: the applications can support different usage profiles, taking applications to have certain restrictions depending on the type of user.

Allow management of invoices integrated with order management: this integration allows the connection between orders placed and their bills.

Allow management of invoices integrated with existing accounting system: this allows a better performance of the system in recording all orders placed and the associated costs.

Authenticate companies by an external entity or by the e-marketplace: ability of companies (suppliers or buyers) to be authenticated in order to ensure the necessary confidence for different business partners to carry out various transactions.

Table 27. Advanced features of B2B solutions

Advanced features
• Integrate ERP systems;
• Support more than one language;
• Allow international transactions;
• Support different types of members;
• Allow management of invoices integrated with order management;
• Allow management of invoices integrated with existing accounting system;
• Authenticate companies by an external entity or by the e-marketplace;
• Perform credit evaluation;
• Establish partnerships between companies;
• Present a products catalog in the form of e-book;
• Make extra company publicity through a products catalog in video format;
• View browsing history website;
• Allow the existence of a message center;
• Indicate fraudulent firms;
• View list of fraudulent companies;
• Communicate in real time with customers and suppliers.

Perform credit evaluation: ability to allow buyers and sellers to check the veracity of the business, history and level of confidence of potential business partners or competitors.

Establish partnerships between companies: is the ability to establish partnerships between different companies and a B2B solution.

Present a products catalog in the form of an e-book: an electronic book, which allows for improved search, with good images and relevant information.

Make extra-company publicity through a products catalog in video format: opportunity for extra-company publicity for products through video.

View navigation history of the platform: as we navigate through the options in the platform a browsing history is presented, which shows where the user is and all steps taken to achieve a certain functionality.

Figure 3. Support of the functionalities by the solutions: all solutions vs. more than one solution

Allow the existence of a message center: is a functionality that allows storing, receiving and sending messages, saving the business contacts and finding a message through certain criteria, among others.

Indicate fraudulent firms: ability of the user to submit information about fraudulent companies with which they have already had some experience.

View list of fraudulent companies: ability to view a list of companies considered fraudulent by the platform.

Communicate in real time with customers and suppliers: is a tool that enables the immediate contact between buyers and sellers to search for products, vendors, shoppers and businesses, and also enables video conferencing between business partners.

This section has presented a model of functionalities of B2B EC solutions. The main virtue of this model is the ability to identify and easily understand the functionalities that a B2B solution can support. For companies, the biggest benefit of this model is that it is a useful reference for the creation or improvement of B2B solutions.

5. DISCUSSION OF THE MODEL

On the presented model in the previous section, 234 functionalities were identified, organized through 13 categories (products catalogs, purchase process, order process, payments, goods dispatch, used technologies, information, users, selling mechanisms, extra-company publicity, announce-

ments, business reports, advanced features), of which 169 of those functionalities correspond to the detail of more general functionalities (creating product requests, approving requests, monitoring orders, receiving orders, making proposal requests, publishing information, managing orders, creating invoices, managing invoices, creating and managing a products catalog, auctions, aggregations, extracting business reports, logistics).

After a deep study of the set of functionalities supported by B2B solutions, the analysis of the results allowed us to verify that 92% of the functionalities are supported by more than one solution and only 8% of the functionalities are supported by all the solutions, as we can verify in Figure 3. So we can affirm that there are few functionalities in common with the six solutions studied, which reveals not only the existence of a wide diversity of characteristics but also an opportunity for improvement of the already existing solutions.

Figure 4 reveals that 19% of the identified functionalities are supported by a single solution and 81% of the functionalities are supported by more than one solution. That is to say that 19% of the functionalities are exclusively of a single solution.

The solution that supports more features, has 62% of the features identified, as we can see in Figure 5. That is, this solution has the greatest support of features compared with other solutions.

On the other hand, the solution that supports fewer functionalities, offers 27% of the functionalities identified, as we can see in Figure 6. This

Figure 4. Support of the functionalities by the solutions: single solution vs. more than one solution

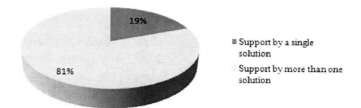

solution has the least support of the features identified.

Through the results obtained from the analysis of the features supported by several solutions, it is revealed that a model such as the one we propose is useful for evaluating existing solutions with the aim of identifying opportunities to improve them, furthermore, it might be useful for the conception of new solutions as it makes a critical evaluation of a diversified set of functionalities that solutions should support possible.

One of the restrictions of this work consists of the fact that the analysis of the survey of functionalities has only been made with six platforms.

6. CONCLUSION

Considering the extent of this work we have focused on B2B which comprises the selling and rendering of services between companies.

Despite the fact that B2B has already been practiced for several decades with the use, for example, of EDI technology, it is by applying the most recent technologies available that the B2B model has been incentivizing innovating ways of business cooperation, making companies increasingly competitive and helping them to face the new challenges of globalization (ANACOM, 2004). Thus B2B systems enable companies to

Figure 5. Solution with more supported features

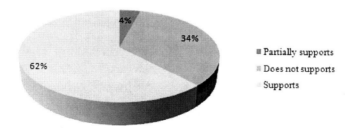

Figure 6. Solution with the lowest support of features

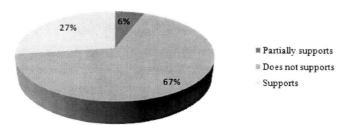

create opportunities for the expansion of markets, reduce costs, increase customers' efficiency and satisfaction and cooperate with partners as well as with competitors. In this chapter a model of functionalities was introduced for the evaluation and construction of B2B websites.

The existing B2B solutions support several of the stated functionalities presented in this chapter, however none has entirely implemented the functionalities. As such, this work becomes important in order to enable companies to improve their solutions. Through this model companies can identify certain functionalities that might be implemented in order to make business more complete and more competitive.

In this chapter a model of functionalities for B2B solutions was presented. At first, during the development process of the model, the most important aspects related to B2B were identified, including a description of the scope of all B2B. Later, through a deeper analysis of the functionalities that B2B solutions can support, research was conducted on B2B solutions presenting diverse characteristics at local (national) and international levels. Finally, the analysis of different B2B solutions allowed for the identification of different functionalities. For a better understanding and for consultation purposes, these were organized through different categories, resulting in the presented model.

The model of functionalities related to the development of B2B EC solutions contributes to the presentation of a characteristic's referential which B2B solutions may/should have, facilitating a better evaluation/selection/conception of B2B EC solutions by companies.

REFERENCES

Albrecht, C. C., Dean, D. L., & Hansen, J. V. (2005). Marketplace and technology standards for B2B e-commerce: Progress, challenges, and the state of the art. *Information & Management, 42,* 865–875. doi:10.1016/j.im.2004.09.003

Amaral, L. A., Teixeira, C., & Oliveira, J. N. (2003). *e-Procurement: Uma reflexão sobre a situação actual em Portugal.* Associação para a Promoção e Desenvolvimento da Sociedade de Informação.

ANACOM. (2004). *O comércio electrónico em Portugal - O quadro legal e o negócio.* Retrieved 15 de October, 2006, from http://www.anacom.pt

Bakos, J. Y. (1997). Reducing buyers search costs: Implications for electronic marketplaces. *Management Science, 43*(12), 1–27. doi:10.1287/mnsc.43.12.1676

Bakos, Y. (1998). The emerging role of electronic marketplaces on the Internet. *Communications of the ACM, 41*(8), 35–42. doi:10.1145/280324.280330

Bizdirect. (2007). *Website.* Retrieved December, 2006, from http://www.bizdirect.pt

Busytrade. (2007). *Website.* Retrieved January, 2007, from http://www.busytrade.com

Castro-Lacouture, D., Medaglia, A. L., & Skibniewski, M. (2006). Supply chain optimization tool for purchasing decisions in B2B construction marketplaces. *Automation in Construction.*

Choi, J. K., Park, J. S., Lee, J. H., & Ryu, K. S. (2006). *Key factors for e-commerce business success.* Paper presented at the 8th International Conference on Advanced Communication Technology, Korea.

EC21. (2007). *Website.* Retrieved January, 2007, from http://www.ec21.com

eMarketer. (2003). *E-commerce trade and B2B exchanges, April 2003.* Retrieved December, 2006, from http://www.emarketer.com

emarketservices. (2006). *Website.* Retrieved December, 2006, from http://www.emarketservices.com

Franco, L. (2004). *O case study da Tradecom.* Paper presented at the Conferência: O comércio electrónico em Portugal, Lisboa, Portugal.

Guo, J., Lam, I. H., Lei, I., Guan, X., Iong, P. H., & Ieong, M. C. (2006). *Alibaba International: Building a global electronic marketplace.* Paper presented at the IEEE International Conference on e-Business Engineering (ICEBE'06).

Jennex, M. E., Amoroso, D., & Adelakun, O. (2004). *E-commerce infrastructure success factors for small companies in developing economies* (4th ed., pp. 263–286).

Kaefer, F., & Bendoly, E. (2004). Measuring the impact of organizational constraints on the success of business-to-business e-commerce efforts: A transactional focus. *Information & Management, 41,* 529–541. doi:10.1016/S0378-7206(03)00088-0

Kalakota, R., & Whinston, A. (1997). *Electronic commerce – a manager's guide.* Massachusetts: Addison-Wesley Longman.

Kauffman, R. J., & Walden, E. A. (2001). Economics and electronic commerce: Survey and directions for research. *International Journal of Electronic Commerce, 5*(4), 5–116.

Kendall, J. D., Tung, L. L., Chua, K. H., Ng, C. H. D., & Tan, S. M. (2001). Receptivity of Singapore's SMEs to electronic commerce adoption. *The Journal of Strategic Information Systems, 10,* 223–242. doi:10.1016/S0963-8687(01)00048-8

Laudon, K., & Traver, C. (2003). *E-commerce: Business, technology, society* (2nd ed.). United States: Addison Wesley.

Liu, C., & Arnett, K. P. (2000). Exploring the factors associated with website success in the context of electronic commerce. *Information & Management, 38,* 23–33. doi:10.1016/S0378-7206(00)00049-5

Molla, A., & Licker, P. S. (2005). E-commerce adoption in developing countries: A model and instrument. *Information & Management, 42,* 877–899. doi:10.1016/j.im.2004.09.002

Noyce, D. (2002). eB2B: Analysis of business-to-business e-commerce and how research can adapt to meet future challenges. *International Journal of Market Research, 44*(1), 71–95.

PCGP. (2006). *Portal das compras públicas.* Retrieved December, 2006, from http://www.compras.gov.pt

Poong, Y., Zaman, K.-U., & Talha, D. M. (2006). *E-commerce today and tomorrow: A truly generalized and active framework for the definition of electronic commerce.* Paper presented at The Eighth International Conference on Electronic Commerce, Canada.

Quix, C., Schoop, M., & Jeusfeld, M. (2002). Business data management for business-to-business electronic commerce. *SIGMOD Record, 31*(1), 49–54. doi:10.1145/507338.507348

Robey, D., Gupta, S., & Rodriguez-Diaz, A. (1990). *Implementing information system in developing countries: organizational and cultural considerations*. Amsterdam, The Netherlands: North-Holland Publishers.

Schoop, M., Koller, J., List, T., & Quix, C. (2001). *A three-phase model of electronic marketplaces for software components in chemical engineering*. Paper presented at the Proceedings of the IFIP Conference on Towards The E-Society: E-Commerce, E-Business, E-Government Zurich, Switzerland.

Shankar, V., Urban, G., & Sultan, F. (2002). On-line trust: A stakeholder perspective, concepts, implications and future directions. *The Journal of Strategic Information Systems, 11*, 325–244. doi:10.1016/S0963-8687(02)00022-7

Teo, T. S. H., & Ranganathan, C. (2004). Adopters and non-adopters of business-to-business electronic commerce in Singapore. *Information & Management, 42*, 89–102.

Turban, E., Lee, J., Warkentin, M., & Chung, H. (2002). *Electronic commerce 2002: A managerial perspective*. Upper Saddle River & Englewood Cliffs, NJ: Prentice-Hall.

Vector21. (2006). *Website*. Retrieved December, 2006, from http://www.vector21.com

Wigand, R. (1997). Electronic commerce definition, theory, and context. *The Information Society, 13*, 1–16. doi:10.1080/019722497129241

Wong, P. K. (1998). Leveraging the global information revolution for economic development: Singapore's evolving information industry. *Information Systems Research, 9*(4), 323–341. doi:10.1287/isre.9.4.323

Zhu, Z., & Lu, T. (2005). *Pricing strategies of electronic B2B marketplaces with two-sided network externalities*. Paper presented at the Proceedings of the 7th international conference on Electronic commerce, China.

Zwass, V. (2003). Electronic commerce and organizational innovation: Aspects and opportunities. *International Journal of Electronic Commerce, 7*, 7–37.

Chapter 4
Cross—Site Scripting:
An Overview

Almudena Alcaide Raya
University Carlos III of Madrid, Spain

Jorge Blasco Alis
University Carlos III of Madrid, Spain

Eduardo Galán Herrero
University Carlos III of Madrid, Spain

Agustín Orfila Diaz-Pabón
University Carlos III of Madrid, Spain

ABSTRACT

This chapter is a comprehensive survey on a currently relevant security threat to Web applications: cross-site scripting (XSS). The rise of reported XSS vulnerabilities has made this family of attacks an interesting area for computer security researchers. XSS consists of the injection of code in Web pages. As injected code is client side scripts, it is executed at the user's Web browser. Injected script can perform unauthorized accesses, identity theft, or even cause financial loss to the attack's victim. Main reason for the existence of this kind of vulnerabilities is the incorrect or insufficient handling of the input performed by Web applications. In this chapter, guidelines on proper input treatment for Web developers are offered. Additionally, existing proposals for XSS mitigations are exposed and future lines of research are indicated to interested researchers and developers.

As any other computer program, Web applications are susceptible of including vulnerabilities that may not only disrupt the provided service, but also facilitate private and personal information to an attacker. As these applications are usually public or even publicized, attacks are expected to be more and more frequent, making it necessary to supply the means to provide an adequate level of security in the utilization of Web applications.

DOI: 10.4018/978-1-60960-765-4.ch004

INTRODUCTION

As electronic commerce is becoming a consolidated channel for businesses and costumers to perform their purchases and sales, involved Web applications get to handle an increasing volume of sensitive data concerning customer's personal information and their associated transaction records. This implies that attempts to steal and manipulate that information are expected to be more and more frequent, making it necessary to supply the means to provide an adequate level of security in the utilisation of Web applications.

Among the many threats that affect e-commerce and e-banking websites, cross-site scripting (XSS) is one of the attacks most frequently reported in well-known vulnerability lists (Stock, Williams, & Wichers, 2007) (SecurityFocus, 2009). The high number of occurrences of XSS vulnerabilities makes the problem worthy of a deep and exhaustive study in order to understand what it is, how it works and why it has become such an important issue.

The purpose of a cross-site scripting attack is the injection of arbitrary code into a Web application by an attacker. The injected code is a script or a reference to a script elaborated by the attacker. That script is intended to be executed at the Web browser of the user. The execution of those commands represents a critical security breach of a system as it could allow the execution of commands which would not be executed under normal circumstances. The danger of executing malicious injected code relies on the extremely high damage it can cause. Damage caused by code injection attacks range from quite inoffensive Web defacements to privilege escalation or even exposure, theft or corruption of sensitive information.

Globally, code injection attacks are successful because attacked applications do not validate properly all the input they receive (Su & Wassermann, 2006). This causes the system to accept injected code as correct input which will eventually be executed, as if it was a legitimate code fragment of the Web system. XSS attacks take advantage of vulnerabilities on input validation of a Web application.

There exists another variant of injection attack that also constitutes a serious threat to the security of Web applications: SQL injection. SQL (Standard Query Language) is the language used to retrieve content from a database, as well as modifying contents and structures. The purpose of an SQL Injection Attack is to execute unauthorized SQL queries through the Web application code. In this way, an attacker may be able to manipulate, steal or delete any information stored in the Web application database (from product information, to user accounts or personal data). Unlike XSS, SQL does not need a client executing the injected code, as it is executed by the Web-application itself. SQL attacks will not be subject of study in this chapter as we will be focusing on XSS attacks.

In the vast majority of the reported XSS attacks, the injected script is written in JavaScript. JavaScript is a script language designed to be embedded on HTML documents or be referenced from HTML documents. It executes in the client's side, at the Web browser and it is used to provide static Web pages with some amount of dynamism, improving interfaces and generally enhancing the navigation experience of the user.

Being the most extended mechanism for client-side Web page enriching, it is not a surprising fact that the wide majority of injected scripts are written in JavaScript. In order to prevent potential issues of code injection, JavaScript defines the same-origin policy, which prevents a document or script loaded from one origin from getting or setting properties of a document from another origin. Web Browsers which follow this policy will check that executable code that accesses or manipulates contents of a site does not come from a domain different from the site's domain. Nevertheless, XSS attacks inject JavaScript code directly into the Web application, being invulnerable to the same-origin policy, as once the code has been injected it has the same origin domain as the original Web application JavaScript.

But XSS attacks achieve their targets despite that policy. The reason is that the policy can be circumvented by an attacker who injects the script at points of the applications where the policy is not applied or is improperly applied.

The purpose of this chapter is to provide an accessible and comprehensive approach to XSS. All the different XSS threats will be exposed and described. The emphasis will be on stating the main reasons why XSS attacks are so commonly reported and successful. Finally and more importantly, we will explain, what can be done to prevent them. This chapter is addressed to any audience interested on Web application security, independently of their technical background. All the necessary concepts will be briefly introduced as and when they are needed.

The chapter is organised as follows. In Section 2, main XSS attack modalities will be described and analysed with the purpose of understanding in which different ways can these attacks take place. Section 3 shows the reason for the high diffusion of XSS attacks, why it is an important problem and will propose some basic guidelines on preventing XSS vulnerabilities to Web application developers. In Section 4, existing mechanisms that can be used to eliminate the XSS threat or at least reduce the presence and impact of these attacks will be depicted. Finally, we will finish the chapter with some conclusions and the potential future research lines on this area.

TYPES OF XSS ATTACKS

In recent years, XSS attacks have taken place in a wide variety of forms. What differences a different type of attack from other is the way in which the script is injected and how the attacker gets that script executed on the victim's Web browser.

Independently of the way employed to inject the script, XSS attacks can have a wide variety

of objectives. This is due to the fact of executing any arbitrary code is a highly desirable capacity for an attacker. On this section, the most harmful attacks will be supposed. Those attacks are the ones that have as ultimate goal identity theft and similar fraudulent actions. In consequence, we are considering that the ultimate goal of an attacker is obtaining access to personal data of an unaware user. That personal data uses to be stored at the personal accounts that users have in different Web applications and services.

To reach a better understanding of the context in which these attacks take place, it is important to define some fundamental concepts. XSS attacks happen during the use of a Web application. A Web application is a computer program that offers some functionality to the user without the need of installing any software. Instead of that, a Web application is accessed using a Web browser, through the HTTP protocol. This protocol, which is specified in RFC 2068, it is organized as follows.

A client (generally user's Web browser) sends a request to the server. Requested object can be a Webpage or some other file stored at the server. A client who was to access some resource inside the application performs a HTTP request to the Web server. This request may be just the location of the resource (URL) or it may include information such as login information, data to be uploaded to the server, etc.

When the Web server receives the request it builds a response. The content of this response usually depends on the sent data and Web server stored data. Responses include among others elements such as: HTML code (the content of the response), CSS (Cascade Style Sheets, used to tell the Web browser how to display that content), Cookies (used to track the state of the user in the site or authenticate) and scripts (to enhance the navigation experience by the user). These scripts are able to access all information on the response (HTML elements, cookies, etc.) and to communicate with other servers, that is the reason because it can be potentially dangerous the execution of unauthorized scripts.

On some occasions, it is desirable to establish that certain parts of a Website can not be accessed by every user but only by the authorized ones. Those authorized users have previously registered in the Web site in order to being easily recognized. When a user wants to interact with some Web application in which she is registered, it must prove her identity to the Web application through the submission of her username and password. After successfully identifying to the application, a user session is created. Session will be kept open until the user decides to log out or a predefined time interval passes.

Among other information included in the server response, cookies store information about the user session status. These cookies may be used, among other things to authenticate a returning user without needing to re-introduce his login or password. As this greatly improves user's browsing experience, there is an important security problem if a cookie is stolen by an attacker as the victim could be impersonated and consequently all her personal information could be stolen or manipulated or even some actions could be performed by the attacker in name of the user. In the following lines the different kinds of XSS attacks will be described considering cookie theft as the ultimate goal of an attacker, as it has the most harmful consequences for an average user.

Cross-site scripting attacks are characterized by how the code is injected and when it is executed in the client. Attending to these criteria we can consider three main attack possibilities: Reflected XSS, Stored XSS and DOM-based XSS. Each modality will be described in a detailed way, defining the key characteristics which define that specific attack type. Along with the description of the attack, real examples of each attack type are shown to help the reader understand how the attack works.

Reflected XSS

In this modality, injected script code is included in the request itself. Due to the vulnerability that the attacker is exploiting, malicious script code is transmitted unnoticed by the Web application and is included in the response to the client. In the client's browser, the script is executed without any opposition or control.

The usual scenario where this attack takes place consists of presenting the victim with a link to the attacked site. That link is sent to victims through email as in standard phishing attacks or can be sent by other means such as instant messaging, internet forums or bulletin boards. Independently of the mean it is sent through, the link is specially crafted so it exploits a vulnerability of the Web application that, through an inadequate validation of input, allows some portion of script code to be included in the response to the client. In the client's Web browser the injected code (which can be a fragment of script code or a reference to scripts stored in attacker-controlled servers) executes. It is usual that the injected script is used to send the session cookie of the user to an attacker's server with the purpose of further performing identity thefts.

Figure 1 shows a diagram of a reflected XSS attack that has the purpose of stealing the session cookie of the attacked user. The sequence of the communication between the implied parts is the following:

1. User receives a link from the attacker. It is usually received via email but can be spread through bulletin boards or similar pages. This link is specially crafted by the attacker so it contains some portion of script code.
2. User clicks on the malicious link. Malicious script code contained in the request arrives to the server and is not detected by the Web application.
3. Response is sent to the user. It contains the script code included in the request.

Figure 1. Reflected XSS

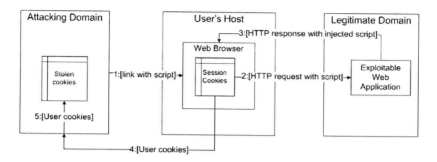

4. Injected script contained in the response from the server is executed. User's cookies are sent to the attacker's domain.

5. Attacker stores stolen cookie for future use.

This attack mode is the most frequent intuitive way of exploiting XSS vulnerabilities. The reason for this is the high speed at obtaining results and the easiness and flexibility that it offers for attackers to prepare their frauds and scams. Many relevant websites have been exposed to reflected XSS attacks. Google was affected by two cases of reflected XSS (SecuriTeam, 2005) that could be used to perform identity theft of Google services users' accounts. Those vulnerabilities affected different Google error messages such as "404 not found" error and the Google redirection script. When a page was not found or when trying to redirect to an incorrect input, Google returned an error page which displayed the URL that was not correct or was not found. If that erroneous URL was a script it would be executed by the browser. In this case, the injected script had to make use of a specific character encoding (UTF-7) which Google did not handled correctly and thus it was vulnerable to XSS attacks.

Stored XSS

In this variety of attack, script code is injected in the Web application remaining there. Usually this malicious script is inserted through a Web form which is not correctly validated. Every time a user accesses the Webpage which contains the injected script, that malicious script will be executed on the user's browser. With this attack it is enough to exploit a vulnerability of the Web application just once to affect any user visiting the page. This constitutes an easy way to perform massive and hard-to-detect attacks. Difficultness of detection of this attack is due to the fact that once the malicious script has been incorporated to the content of the Web application it is not expected to be evaluated prior to being incorporated to any HTTP responses.

This kind of attack has become frequent and highly effective with the diffusion and success of social networks and similar services. Each user has a personal profile where they can insert contents as they wish. Insufficient input validation by the Web application can allow a malicious user to incorporate to her profile some script fragments. When other users visit the page the same script will be executed.

Figure 2 illustrates a stored XSS attack whose goal is the theft of session cookies from an unaware user. The communications are the following:

1. The attacker finds some vulnerability in the Web application that allows him to insert script code. Then, the attacker exploits the vulnerability to insert the malicious script on the Web page.

Figure 2. Stored XSS

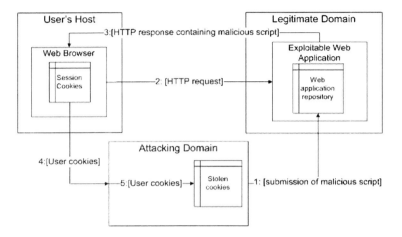

2. A user accesses the content which includes the malicious script.

3. The script is sent to the client in the payload of the HTTP response.

4. Script is executed in the context of the Web browser. It sends the session cookies to the server of the attacker.

5. Stolen cookies are stored at attacker's domain.

There have been many well-known cases of stored XSS attacks in social networks. The attack to MySpace network in 2005 managed to compromise an important amount of personal information from affected users. Additionally, the behaviour of the injected script was that of a worm (Grossman, 2006) due to the high propagation capabilities it exhibited. Injected script was inserted in the attacker's personal page making personal user information of each visitor be sent and stored in an attacker-controlled site. In addition to that, the malicious script was capable of copying itself onto the personal pages of any user that visited the originally injected page. And, again, any user who visited a profile with the injected scripts will get his personal information sent to the attacker and the malicious script inserted in her profile. This

way, propagation of the script and information theft propagated in an exponential way.

DOM-Based XSS

The DOM (Document Object Model) (Pixley & others, 2000) is a convention that establishes a tree hierarchical structure to represent the content of HTML and XML documents. This is a very useful structure for Web developers, as it allows a much easier processing of the information of Web pages. Web development languages, equally client side and server side languages, makes use of this standardized representation to manipulate that information.

This third XSS attack modality (Klein, 2007) is frequently omitted in most XSS attack classification. The reason of that fact is the relative minority of cases and the important differences with the two previous main techniques. Reflected and stored XSS attacks imply that the script must first be sent to the server and afterwards sent back to the user who made the request (as in reflected attack) or any other user (stored attack) where it is executed. By contrast, in a DOM-based XSS attack the injected script is never sent to the server. It is effective by the manipulation of the content

Figure 3. Dom-based attack

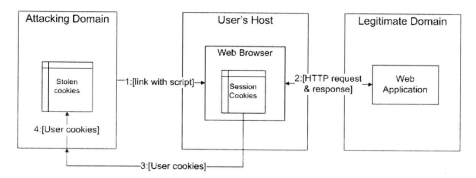

of the DOM tree of the Webpage, which can be done easily by using JavaScript.

It affects static pages, which do not contain dynamic data at all. The injected code does not need to be sent to the server and it just acts locally, in the Web browser.

In Figure 3, a potential DOM-based attack scenario is described. In this case, the attacker will steal personal information (we have supposed a session cookie) from the user through XSS by manipulating the DOM tree. The sequence of the communication between the implied parts is the following:

1. As in stored attacks, user receives a link from the attacker. It is usually received via email but can be spread through bulletin boards or similar pages. This link is specially crafted by the attacker so it contains some portion of script code.
2. User uses the malicious link. Malicious script code is not included in the request and consequently is not sent the server. Neither the request nor the response contains any script code.
3. Malicious script is executed at the client. It manipulates the content of the DOM tree to perform the theft of the cookie, which is sent to the domain of the attacker.
4. Attacker stores stolen cookie for future use.

It is important to note that this kind of attack does not exploit any vulnerability in the Web application. Instead it takes advantage from JavaScript interpreters of Web browsers that are excessively permissive in the validation of the data they receive. One representative case of this kind of attack affected the version of the Web browser Microsoft Internet Explorer, specifically its 6.0 version (Dotzler, 2005). The detected vulnerability was related the way in which error messages of the Website Bugzilla were built. They were built by using a JavaScript sentence that the browser executes. JavaScript processor of the browser did not perform the necessary validation to make sure that the data of the parameters did not include any content that could be executed.

GENERAL DEVELOPER GUIDELINES

Now that the different types of attack are known, next step is studying what can be done to prevent XSS attacks from taking place. In this chapter, that issue will be addressed to Web application developers. However, concepts and techniques exposed here can be understood by any reader who wants to learn how XSS attacks take advantage of Web application's vulnerabilities and what are the principles to apply to Web development to reduce the impact of XSS.

Previously described attacks get to be successful because they circumvent the input validation mechanisms of the Web application (if there is any). To manage that the injected code is unnoticed, it is usually necessary to apply some techniques to elude protection mechanisms of the application.

In order to successfully perform an XSS attack, there exists a vast collection of attack vectors. An attack vector is any way of exploiting some security breach of a system. In the case of XSS, attack vectors appear in the form of code fragments which are designed to be injected. These vectors are specifically crafted for the application to be attacked and its purpose is to circumvent any input validation performed by the Web application. Circumvention techniques consist of obfuscating the injected code so it can not be detected by input filters of the Web application. It is usual to input the malicious script using a different representation, like an unconventional yet valid character encoding. The differently-encoded script is treated by the application as plain text and is consequently included in the response. Web browser displays the response normally. As that response contains an unauthorised script which has been treated as valid content, it gets executed as if it were legitimate content. This way, the attacker has accomplished to inject her script and have it executed.

Web application developers can prevent the presence of XSS vulnerabilities by performing a complete input and output sanitization process. This way, attempts of injecting script code can be detected and the application performs the necessary actions such as denying the response or transforming the injected code into inoffensive content. It basically consists of two tasks:

- **Input validation:** consists of detecting in the input all potentially dangerous content. In this case, all content that could be executable in a Web browser is considered dangerous. Note that dangerous content can make use of many different representation formats in order to bypass the filters.

- **Output filtering and sanitization:** before sending data to the user, it is necessary to make sure that it can not be executed at the Web browser by any means. Data is escaped, this is transforming data into a specific representation which is not executable at all.

Exploiting Vulnerabilities

Web applications usually present XSS vulnerabilities which can be exploited through the use of specifically crafted code fragments. Those code snippets manage to elude input validation mechanisms of the application. However, unless Web application does not validate input at all, the code to be injected must be processed in order to bypass validation filters. That processing consists of modifying the script code in such a way that Web application considers it as a valid input while remains recognisable as executable code by a Web browser.

XSS attack vectors are numerous and they benefit from the wide range of encodings available for information in the Web and the permissiveness of Web browser when parsing HTML, CSS, JavaScript among others languages. That is achieved through the use of different encodings and data representations. There are XSS attack vectors catalogues (RSnake, 2009) that contain the different possibilities of encoding data which have been successful in the exploitation of XSS vulnerabilities.

Preventing Vulnerabilities

XSS vulnerabilities are frequently present in Web applications. This is the reason for the widespread occurrence of XSS attacks. The prevention of XSS vulnerabilities is not a highly complex task, as all XSS vulnerabilities exist due to errors in input validation. An exhaustive (even paranoid) input validation methodology would completely prevent all XSS attacks. (OWASP, XSS (Cross Site Scripting) Prevention Cheat Sheet, 2007)

Vulnerabilities are located at the sections of the HTML page where untrusted data is received as an input. This implies that the parts of the page that must be inspected for vulnerabilities are well known. Any script code found in that data is treated in order to make it not executable by a Web browser. This process is known as escaping. It consists of encoding the output which contains unexpected executable code into a sequence of characters that is treated by the browser as any other text. It is advisable the development of escaping or encoding APIs or the use of already existing APIs for that purpose (OWASP, OWASP Enterprise Security API, 2003), (AntiXSS, 2008) to automate this process. These APIs provide to Web developers with ready-to-use validation routines which speed up the validation of the untrusted data handled by the Web application.

Untrusted Data and Input Validation

Any data coming into the Web application such as form values, uploaded data, etc. could be used by an attacker to insert malicious code and perform an XSS attack. Therefore, all the data coming from the outside of the application must be considered untrusted data. This data can be sent by users in their request through forms, urls, etc... Prior to sending their request, depending on the data it is encoded using different schemes. Encoding is performed in order to represent that data in a way it can be transmitted through the internet without misinterpretations (i.e. all devices involved in the communication are able to transmit it correctly).

To avoid XSS attacks, the presence of untrusted data must be restricted as much as possible. Nevertheless, as dynamic Web pages need to interact with the user it will be impossible to eliminate all untrusted data vectors. Needed untrusted data fields (e.g. registration form, etc.) must undergo through the proper encoding process.

Untrusted data is encoded prior to being included in the HTML document. Depending on the ubication of the untrusted data, a different encoding will be applied.

There is a fundamental rule: disallowing the presence of untrusted data in the document with the exception of some specific ubications. Untrusted data found in those ubications must undergo through the proper encoding process.

The ubications of an HTML where untrusted data can be found to be encoded are:

- HTML elements.

```
<p> UNTRUSTED DATA </p>
<div> UNTRUSTED DATA </div>
<td> UNTRUSTED DATA </td>
```

- Value of an attribute of an HTML element.

```
<div attr=UNTRUSTED DATA>something</
div>
```

- Javascript event handlers found at various HTML elements.

```
<script> alert('UNTRUSTED DATA')>/
script>
<script> var=UNTRUSTED DATA </script>
<div onmouseclick=UNTRUSTED DATA </
div>
```

- CSS(Cascading Style Sheets) style properties.

```
<style> selector { property:
UNTRUSTED DATA ;}</style>
<style=property: UNTRUSTED
DATA;>content</style>
```

- URL attribute of the HTML document.

```
<img src=UNTRUSTED DATA />
<script src=UNTRUSTED DATA />
<a href=UNTRUSTED DATA >text </a>
```

Depending on the Web application characteristics it may not be necessary to take into account all the previously mentioned source of untrusted data. Remaining sources of untrusted data should undergo through an input validation process. Although the use of an input validation methodology does not imply high complexity in the development of the Web application, this process is overseen very frequently. Reason is the lack of minimum security awareness in the Web developers which ignore the security of the application or consider it as a secondary aspect.

Proxies

Apart from the previous considerations, developers may use other solutions such as proxies and firewalls to protect against XSS attacks. In this case, solutions have not to be deployed on the Web application but outside it.

A proxy server consists of a server that interposes between a client and one or more servers. It is usually use as an intermediary to perform tasks of caching, traffic filtering or anonymous navigation of the client among many other possibilities.

In order to protect against XSS a reverse proxy (Wurzinger, Platzer, Ludl, Kirda, & Kruegel, 2009) can be used. This kind of proxy is situated in front of a server so all traffic coming from the Internet to the server or in the opposite way must pass through the proxy. In order to work properly, this proxy must know in advance all the possible script code of the Web application. Instead of generating requests with script code, the Web application generates all the content except these pieces of script code which are replaced by reference numbers. When a server page arrives to the proxy, reference numbers are replaced by the corresponding script code, which the proxy must know in advance.

In order to generate all the numeric references and substitutions, the proxy server must pre-process the Web application before it is put in a production environment. Any further modification of the application must be notified to the proxy in order to keep up to date the repository of script code belonging to the application.

This way, any script code found by the reverse proxy will be considered as injected code since it has not been previously substituted by its reference. However, although this proposal prevents injected script from reaching the client, it does not do anything for identifying or preventing vulnerabilities in the application, it just avoids exploiting attempts.

CLASSIFICATION AND ANALYSIS OF PREVENTION AND DETECTION MECHANISMS

Important research efforts have been made in order to establish a series of mechanisms that can prevent XSS or, at least, detect when an attack is operating. Many lines of research have been followed with the purpose of stopping or at least mitigating the damage caused by XSS. Those lines will be described in this section with the intention of providing the reader with a comprehensive overview of the different ways in which XSS problem can be dealt with.

Static Analysis

These techniques address XSS problem by the exhaustive analysis of the code involved (Wassermann & Su, 2008). This can be applied either in the server side or in the client side.

When applied on the server side, static analysis is used to exhaustively examine the code of the Web application. This analysis focuses on analyzing both input and output of the Web application. Input is analyzed and sanitized in order to avoid the injection of malicious code. Output is analyzed and sanitized in case the input filter fails to avoid sending the user malicious code. When it detects some flaw in the processing of input or output it marks that as vulnerability or as potential vulnerability. Those potential vulnerabilities have to be confirmed in runtime.

Static analysis performs data-flow analysis directly on the source code (Jovanovic, Kruegel, & Kirda, 2006). It is possible to make use of data tainting. Data is marked so it can be easily tracked but, instead of being followed during the execution of a program, it is tracked in all the potential execution paths in order to identify all potential XSS vulnerabilities.

However, static analysis at server side shows an important flaw that prevents it from being a general solution against XSS. The wide range of languages and platforms available for Web development suppose that there should be static analyzers adapted to each of the languages utilised, which at the moment is unfeasible. This is due to each available platform performs its input and output processing internally on its own way.

Dynamic Analysis

This type of analysis consists of following closely all input data which is potentially unsecure during the execution of the application. Basic working of this analysis is keeping a tight control of the state of the application during its execution.

To achieve this, data that comes from non trusted sources is tainted. This data consists of all the variables of the application which value can be established by an external agent. A clear example of this would be the fields of a HTML form. In addition to this, any data derived from tainted data, gets the taint as well.

Data tainting allows to have a close watch on tainted data and be able of preventing it from perform unauthorised actions. Tainted data which is going to be outputted in the HTML response without having been properly sanitized would be detected through data tainting.

Dynamic analysis generally is not used on its own. The reason of this is the main inconvenience of this kind of analysis: as this analysis must be performed on runtime it does not constitute an efficient mechanism for extensive tests, nevertheless it is usual to utilise it to complete or verify the results obtained by static analysis.

Combined Approach: Static + Dynamic

Static and dynamic analyses have each of them its own strengths and weaknesses but joining them provides an important level of protection against XSS attacks (Huang, Yu, Hang, Tsai, Lee, & Kuo, 2004). There are many possibilities to combine both types of analysis trying to compensate the lacks of each other. Indeed, a vast majority of proposed approaches in literature use both techniques in order to achieve a satisfactory level of protection.

A possible scenario would be performing both analyses at the server. While static analysis, during the source code analysis can find errors in the input validation performed, it does not have always the means to determine if that validation flaw supposes an actual vulnerability. At runtime, by dynamic analysis (Lucca, Fasolino, Mastoianni, & Tramontana, 2004) (Balzarotti, y otros, 2008), all pages considered suspicious during static analysis are confirmed or discarded by the study of their control flow graphs.

At client side, a possible approach is the following (Vogt, Nentwich, Jovanovic, Kirda, Kruegel, & Vigna, 2007): dynamic analysis applied to every flow of sensitive (and tainted) data in the Web browser. A potentially dangerous operation with that data (such as sending it to an unknown destination) is detected as an XSS attack and consequently aborted. Static analysis component of the system is applied to execution paths that were not covered by dynamic analysis in order to make the analysis exhaustive.

Vulnerability Scanners

Another possible way of addressing XSS prevention is making use of tools that evaluate the security of Web applications against this kind of attacks (Kals, Kirda, Kruegel, & Jovanovic, 2006). Main advantage of this kind of approach is its versatility, as once developed it can be used to check any Website independently of the language program, platform, location, etc. To determine if an application presents any vulnerability, a series of attacks are crafted and launched. The availability of a complete catalogue of attack vectors is crucial for the effectiveness of these tools. Through the observation of the results of those attacks, it is possible to find all input validation flaws of a Web application in a fast and easy way without needing to have access to any source code.

However, this tool presents an important flaw: it is only capable of detecting reflected XSS vulnerabilities. The reason for this fact is the way vulnerabilities are tested: attacks are launched with the purpose of obtaining response and verifying that the attack was successful. This cannot be applied to any other attack modality than reflected XSS. In stored XSS attacks it is not possible to apply in an effective and automatic way the mechanism of testing Web applications against a set of attack vectors and in DOM-based attacks, injected script is not even sent to the server.

Firewalls

Another interesting possibility is the use of firewalls to prevent XSS attacks from causing damage to users. An application level firewall (Kirda, Kruegel, Vigna, & Jovanovic, 2006) provides an important level of security to a client. It is based on existing personal Web firewall solutions but focuses on preventing the traffic of sensitive information from the user to unknown or untrusted destinations. It does not prevent any XSS attack, only those whom purpose is to damage the user by obtaining her sensitive data in an unauthorized way.

However, this kind of firewalls is not free from aspects that need to be improved. In a system of this type, it is important to define a set of rules to specify what is considered sensitive data and what operations with that data are suspicious. This fact, though it increases the flexibility of the firewall, increases the complexity of use of this firewall, making it not suitable for an average user.

IDS (Intrusion Detection System)

Intrusion detection systems (Denning, 1987) are a consolidated type of system in the field of computer security. As its name indicates, their goal is to be capable of detecting unauthorized attempts of connection, access or modification through some kind of network, being in most cases the Internet. These systems are composed of many components: sensors, console and engine.

Sensors modules listen to the network traffic. They detect and communicate any event of the network that is considered security related. Many specialised sensors are utilised to detect a greater range of events with the adequate precision. The console is the module that receives and controls the events that are received from the different sensors. The engine is the central component that maintains a log and generates alerts by applying a set of rules to the existing security events.

According to the way they perform detection, IDS can be divided in two:

- Misuse detectors look for behaviours and traffic that fits into some of the signature of the modelled intrusions that the system have in its database. This is the way antivirus software works. Constant updating of the signature database is required to be adequately protected against new security menaces.

- Anomaly detectors act in the opposite way. The system has models of a correct and normal behaviour. In this case, any traffic that does not fit to any of the behaviour models is labelled as anomalous and is further analysed in order to determine its nature.

Anomaly detectors are better suited for the detection of XSS (Kruegel & Vigna, 2003), as this kind of attack is intrinsically ad hoc for the attacked site. A misuse detector would probably not be able to identify any possible XSS attack into any of its known intrusion signatures due to the highly changing nature of XSS.

There exist some approaches that try to assess the detection of XSS attacks by analysing exchanged traffic (Johns, Engelmann, & Posegga, 2008). Due to the nature of XSS attacks (reflected and stored) different techniques are used in each one of the cases. When detecting reflected attacks, relations between parameters in the request and the payload of the response are an important factor in the detection of XSS attacks which are taking place. To detect stored attacks, paying attention at the correlation between requests and responses would not be effective due to the different nature of the attack scenario, so it is necessary to use a different solution. The approach chosen is the use of a reverse proxy highly similar to the one introduced previously in this chapter. The system possesses a repository of valid script fragments of the protected applications. It is easy for the system to verify if all script code present in a given response is legitimate or has been injected. This proposal faces the same problem as (Wurzinger, Platzer, Ludl, Kirda, & Kruegel, 2009); as it requires to be updated each time the Web application source code changes.

Nevertheless, this proposal has a highly interesting property: detection of XSS is performed without requiring any specific configuration or adaptation from users or Web applications. This way, instead of tracking pieces of valid scripts,

it could be used to recognise patterns that adjust to XSS attacks. Those attacks can be stopped and prevented for being successful and further notified to Web application developers to put into their knowledge the existence of vulnerabilities in the application. Furthermore, the updates of this system will rely only when new attacks are discovered and not whenever the application source code changes.

CONCLUSION

Through this chapter, XSS has been thoroughly displayed. The dimension of the problem and the notorious growth it has had during the past years has been exposed. This rise in the number of reported cases of XSS attacks reveals the urgent need of applying measures that can prevent or at least mitigate the impact of this threat on Web application and their users.

Main cause of the high proliferation of this specific type of attack is the secondary role played by security in the Web application development process. Since Web applications usually require to be created and to be modified on a fast and regular basis, any aspect other than the main functionality tends to be overlooked or not even taken into account to favour availability and the inclusion of new functionalities.

Most effective way of preventing this kind of vulnerabilities is taking into consideration security aspects and a formal input filtering and validation in the development methodology of the Web application. Though this would increase development cost, it would also mean that XSS and other threats derived from a poor input validation would be effectively eliminated.

As this effort is not being frequently made, other solutions to avoid damage caused by these vulnerabilities have been designed. They are applied to currently deployed Web applications. By using different mechanisms to examine the code and the behaviour of the Web application it is possible to detect to a certain extent the presence of exploitable XSS vulnerabilities in the application.

However, none of those mechanisms is capable of resolving the issue in a satisfactory way. There are some aspects that do not get treated in a proper way. Current proposals do not achieve their goal of providing protection against these vulnerabilities. Reasons of this inability differ from one approach to another:

- A high number of solutions are oriented to an only specific type of attack (vulnerability scanners). They frequently have to be coordinated with other tools for achieving a good coverage of the different attack types. Due to insufficiently good detection rates, they constitute only a partial solution against XSS.
- Static analysis to be performed is complex and error-prone since there can be checks and validations which are overlooked.
- Static analysis of Web applications focuses on a specific language and/or platform. That fact makes it difficult to have a generic tool as there are a vast range of technologies used for Web development.
- Dynamic analysis is the most accurate way to determine if an XSS attack is taking place at run time. But it can not be applied to all traffic of the Web application as that would imply an important overhead and would damage the Website's availability. This is the reason of dynamic analysis being used as a complement and a reinforcement of static analysis.
- Client side proposals (firewalls) require a minimum deal of attention from the user, which is not usually paid. Additionally, these tools must keep their complexity to low levels to make them usable and understandable for users, implying an important decrease on the flexibility and power of the solution.

- Approaches that analyze the Web application source code (proxies and IDS) need to be updated regularly, as the Web application source code is constantly being changed and updated.

Despite of their drawbacks, all proposed anti-XSS solutions constitute an important base for solving XSS problem but all of them are ideas that have just began to be explored. Further research can improve the effectiveness of the different tools and find ways to coordinate various solutions with the last goal of designing an efficient, effective and complete anti-XSS security system.

Expanding current solutions which are effective but limited in their coverage as it is the case of vulnerability scanners to cover the detection of any kind of attack it is a promising line of research as it would contribute to have an integral solution for detecting XSS attacks without any need of integration with the protected Web applications. Another interesting line of research is the specialization of IDS in the recognition of XSS attack patterns. That would provide a highly automated and effective solution against this threat.

ACKNOWLEDGMENT

This work has been partially supported by CDTI (Ministerio de Industria, Turismo y Comercio of Spain) in collaboration with Telefónica I+D, Project SEGUR@ with reference CENIT-2007 2004

REFERENCES

AntiXSS. (2008). *Anti-XSS Library v3.0*. Retrieved from http://antixss.codeplex.com/

Balzarotti, D., Cova, M., Felmetsger, V., Jovanovic, N., Kirda, E., Kruegel, C., et al. (2008). Saner: Composing static and dynamic analysis to validate sanitization in Web applications., (pp. 387-401).

Denning, D. (1987). An intrusion-detection model. *IEEE Transactions on Software Engineering*, 222–232. doi:10.1109/TSE.1987.232894

Dotzler, A. (2005). *Bugzilla Bug 272620-XSS vulnerability in internal error messages.* Retrieved from https://bugzilla.mozilla.org/show_bug. cgi?id=272620

Grossman, J. (2006). *Cross-site scripting worms and viruses.* WhiteHat Security.

Huang, Y., Yu, F., Hang, C., Tsai, C., Lee, D., & Kuo, S. (2004). *Securing Web application code by static analysis and runtime protection* (pp. 40–52). New York, NY: ACM.

Johns, M., Engelmann, B., & Posegga, J. (2008). *XSSDS: Server-side detection of cross-site scripting attacks* (pp. 335–344). Washington, DC: IEEE Computer Society.

Jovanovic, N., Kruegel, C., & Kirda, E. (2006). *Pixy: A static analysis tool for detecting Web application vulnerabilities* (p. 6).

Kals, S., Kirda, E., Kruegel, C., & Jovanovic, N. (2006). *SecuBat: A Web vulnerability scanner* (pp. 247–256). New York, NY: ACM.

Kirda, E., Kruegel, C., Vigna, G., & Jovanovic, N. (2006). *Noxes: A client-side solution for mitigating cross-site scripting attacks* (pp. 330–337). New York, NY: ACM.

Klein, A. (2007). *DOM based cross site scripting or XSS of the third kind.* Retrieved from http://www.Webappsec.org/projects/articles/071105. html

Kruegel, C., & Vigna, G. (2003). *Anomaly detection of Web-based attacks* (pp. 251–261). New York, NY: ACM.

Lucca, G. D., Fasolino, A., Mastoianni, M., & Tramontana, P. (2004). *Identifying cross site scripting vulnerabilities in Web applications* (pp. 71–80).

OWASP. (2003). *OWASP enterprise security API.* Retrieved from http://www.owasp.org/index.php/ Category:OWASP_Enterprise_Security_API

OWASP. (2007). *XSS (cross site scripting) prevention cheat sheet.* Retrieved from http://www. owasp.org/index.php/XSS_(Cross_Site_Scripting)_Prevention_Cheat_Sheet

Pixley, T., et al. (2000). *Document Object Model (DOM) level 3 events specification.* W3C recommendation, November.

RSnake. (2009). *XSS (cross site scripting) cheat sheet.* Retrieved from http://ha.ckers.org/xss.html

SecuriTeam. (2005). *Google.com UTF-7 XSS vulnerabilities.* Retrieved from http://www.securiteam.com/securitynews/6Z00L0AEUE.html

SecurityFocus. (2009). *Bugtraq mailing lists.* Retrieved from http://www.securityfocus.com/ archive

Stock, A., Williams, J., & Wichers, D. (2007). *OWASP top 10.* Retrieved from http://www.owasp. org/index.php/Top_10_2007

Su, Z., & Wassermann, G. (2006). *The essence of command injection attacks in Web applications* (pp. 372–382). New York, NY: ACM.

Vogt, P., Nentwich, F., Jovanovic, N., Kirda, E., Kruegel, C., & Vigna, G. (2007). Cross-site scripting prevention with dynamic data tainting and static analysis. *Proceeding of the Network and Distributed System Security Symposium (NDSS'07).*

Wassermann, G., & Su, Z. (2008). *Static detection of cross-site scripting vulnerabilities* (pp. 171–180). New York, NY: ACM.

Wurzinger, P., Platzer, C., Ludl, C., Kirda, E., & Kruegel, C. (2009). SWAP: Mitigating XSS attacks using a reverse proxy. *In SESS'09: Proceedings of the 5th International Workshop on Software Engineering for Secure Systems,* Vancouver, Canada, May 2009.

Chapter 5
An Open Source E–Procurement Application Framework for B2B and G2B

Georgousopoulos Christos
INTRASOFT International S.A., Greece

Xenia Ziouvelou
Athens Information Technology, Greece

Gregory S. Yovanof
Athens Information Technology, Greece

Antonis Ramfos
INTRASOFT International S.A., Greece

ABSTRACT

Since the early 1980s, Open Source Software (OSS) has gained a strong interest and an increased acceptance in the software industry that has to date initiated a "paradigm shift" (O'Reilly, 2004). The Open Source paradigm has introduced wholly new means of software development and distribution, creating a significant impact on the evolution of numerous business processes. In this chapter we examine the impact of the open source paradigm in the e-Procurement evolution and identify a trend towards Open Source e-Procurement Application Frameworks (AFs) which enable the development of tailored e-Procurement Solutions. Anchored in this notion, we present an Open-Source e-Procurement AF with a two-phase generation procedure. The innovative aspect of the proposed model relates to the combination of the Model Driven Engineering (MDE) approach with the Service-Oriented Architecture (SOA) paradigm for enabling the cost-effective production of e-Procurement Solutions by facilitating integration, interoperability, easy maintenance, and management of possible changes in the European e-Procurement environment. The assessment process of the proposed AF and its resulting e-Procurement Solutions occurs in the context of G2B in the Western-Balkan European region. Our evaluation yields positive results and further enhancing opportunities for the proposed Open Source e-Procurement AF and its resulting e-Procurement Solutions.

DOI: 10.4018/978-1-60960-765-4.ch005

INTRODUCTION

Internet mediated purchase of goods and services has shown to contribute to increased transparency in private and public money spending, increased and open access to tendering information, faster processing of tenders, paperwork reduction, easier management of purchasing, and most importantly cost decrease of the purchased goods and services. According to market research reports e-Procurement can provide savings to the private sector (B2B) that account for 10% to 50% (Peria, 2003) where in the public sector these savings are escalated given the high purchasing volume associated with the public procurement. According to the European Commission during 2002, total public procurement (G2B) in the EU (i.e. the purchases of goods, services and public works by governments and public utilities) was estimated at about 16% of the European Union's GDP, equivalent to 1500 billion Euros (Europa, 2009).

However, although the automation, optimization and electronic mediation of the internal and external processes associated with the purchase of goods and services holds great potential both for the private (B2B) and public (G2B) sector, e-Procurement practices do not yet prevail today's economic system (Stephens, 2008). Research indicates that the expenditure related to the purchase, ownership and operation of such a system has and continues to be a key adoption barrier (Stephens, 2008; Kauffman and Mohtadi, 2004). Additionally, capital investment associated with software development has been identified as another significant barrier for the implementation of e-Procurement Solutions (Tanner et al., 2007) across B2B and G2B markets. In particular, electronic Public Procurement Solutions (ePP) in contrast to the private e-PP Solutions tend to be much more complex and advanced due to the fact that after a given procurement threshold value they must adhere to the legal and policy framework as this is defined by the European Commission (EC). This increases the required capital investment which

may be prohibiting Public Organisations with less available budget for internal development, such as local authorities, hospitals, education establishments, public museums, public agents in tourism or commerce, NGOs and other civic society associations, unless means for reducing it are found. Thus, if the capital investment associated with the development time and costs is reduced, then the production and adoption of e-Procurement Solutions would be accelerated by SMEs and Public Organisations.

Thus, could the software development process and underlying open innovation characteristics of the software technology used to deliver an e-Procurement Solution and enhance the lag in the adoption of such systems?

In this chapter we argue that both principles are critical and we propose a generic software development approach for e-Procurement practices which adopts Open Source standards and addresses the needs of the private (B2B) and the public (G2B) sector.

The remaining of this chapter is organized in seven sections. Section two describes the impact of the open source paradigm in the e-Procurement evolution, and considers the differences between e-Procurement Solutions and Application Frameworks (AF) under the open and closed source perspectives. The third section provides an overview of the traditional approaches of software development with focus to Model-Driven Engineering methodology. Section four introduces the reader to the proposed Open Source e-Procurement AF, which enables the development of Open Source e-Procurement Solutions. The fifth section provides the rational and a detailed description for the proposed AF pertinent to e-Procurement domain, following a hybrid approach of MDE, for the cost-effective and rapid development of e-Procurement Solutions. A process which entails a two-phase generation procedure is described in detail in section five. Section six presents the evaluation performed on the utilisation of the approach of software development followed by the proposed Application Framework as well as on the e-Procurement Solutions generated via the framework. The driving forces of software development evaluation were based on the software development lifecycle[3], where the evaluation of four e-Procurement Solutions generated via the proposed AF for four Western-Balkan countries was made by measuring their functionality, usability, reliability, scalability, security, and interoperability. The chapter concludes in the seventh section.

IMPACT OF OPEN SOURCE PARADIGM IN THE E-PROCUREMENT EVOLUTION

Open Source Software (OSS)[4] is considered as a disruptive technology (Jackson, 2003) that has altered the structure and the competitive landscape of the software as well the broader ICT industry. This change has emerged through the introduction of wholly new means of software development and distribution. Means that provides a unique value proposition that, aims at reaching underserved communities of users and developers of software (Ziouvelou and Yiovanof, 2008b).

In the context of e-Procurement, proprietary Solutions prevail (i.e., national and international Solutions with medium and high level of maturity, see Figure 1- Quadrant II). Although these Solutions could have been developed by utilising proprietary and company-owned (i.e., internally developed) e-Procurement Application Frameworks (Quadrant I), such practices are to date non-existent given the high development costs and system complexity involved. In recent years a trend can be observed towards the Open Source paradigm given the profound benefits that it offers to the involved stakeholders across this and other domains. The existing Open Source e-Procurement Solutions (Quadrant III) have been initiated mainly by national or European funds and reduce dramatically the capital investment required to purchase, own and operate such e-Procurement system Solutions. However, to date there is a growing need towards an Internet mediated, domain specific Open Source Application Frameworks (AFs) (Quadrant IV). Such e-Procurement AFs will support the development of Open Source e-Procurement Solutions "tailored to the needs of individual recipients with a degree of granularity not previously possible or economically viable" (Tschammer et al., 2003, p.3). The existence of such innovative AFs will allow private and

Figure 1. The e-procurement evolution (B2B & G2B) (Data sources: Ziouvelou and Yovanof, 2008a)

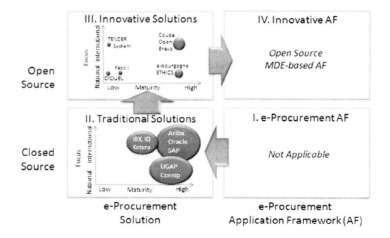

public institutions "to quickly and easily build and deploy robust, secure, scalable, manageable, interoperable, portable and lawful e-Procurement applications" (Tschammer et al., 2003, p.3).

Towards this aim an Open Source e-Procurement Application Framework (AF) would amalgamate the aforementioned benefits of an electronic purchasing system with the ones endorsed by the Open Source paradigm. Such benefits (see Table 1) would be: *(i)* supplier independence (i.e., elimination of vendor "lock-in" effects), *(ii)* improved cost effectiveness due to the absence of licensing costs, (i.e., OSS is distributed under an OSS license which mandates no license fees as opposed to proprietary software) as well as the reduction of development costs, *(iii)* technological benefits related to reduced technological risks (e.g. patches or updates to OSS subsequent to the discovery of defects are released rapidly, due to the fact that security issues tend to be resolved at a faster pace, providing this way a further independence as opposed to proprietary Solutions) and the ability to change and/or adopt the AF.

Hence, such an innovative open source e-Procurement Application Framework would enhance the adoption of web-based purchase-to-pay process technology, realizing this way the benefits of electronic procurement practices and open source paradigm while enhancing even further the competitiveness in the private and public sectors. This could be attained by capitalizing on state-of-the-art software engineering technologies, namely, Model-driven Engineering (MDE) and Service-Oriented Architecture (SOA).

MODEL-DRIVEN ENGINEERING MODEL DRIVEN AS A PREDOMINATE IN FUTURE SOFTWARE DEVELOPOPMENT

Traditional software engineering approaches are often driven by low-level design and coding (Stephen et al., 2004). A typical approach consists of a number of different phases including the conceptual and requirements gathering, analysis and functional description, design, coding, testing and deployment. However, irrespectively of the approach followed (e.g. incremental and iterative or traditional waterfall approach) documentation and diagrams produced during the first three phases rapidly lose their value as soon as the coding starts, since the connection between the diagrams and the code fades away as the coding phase progresses. This is attributed to the fact that in such approaches the code is the driving force of software development and the only phases in the development process that are really productive are coding and testing.

The gap between the documentation and code is further increased when a system is changed over time, on where amendments take place only on code level since the maintenance of documentations during development costs time and slows down the process. In this instance, during software development phases and after the delivery of a complete Solution, in relation to maintenance aspect, traditional SE methodologies lack the ability of providing support on:

- *Portability* and *reusability*: Software industry is characterized of its ever-increasing rate of new technologies that emerge. Developers need to follow these new technologies since: (i) they provide Solutions to real problems (such as XML for interchange, J2EE and.NET for platform independence), and (ii) they exhibit high level of customers demands (e.g. Web 2.0 tools and applications). The porting of a legacy system to new technologies requires extensive code-rewrites and testing. As a consequence, investment in previous technologies loose value and they may even become worthless.
- *Maintainability*: Keeping the application architecture and application code consistent is a very difficult procedure on com-

Table 1. Advantages and disadvantages of e-procurement solutions and application frameworks (AF)

		Buyer		Seller	
		Advantages	*Disadvantages*	*Advantages*	*Disadvantages*
e-Procurement Solution	*Closed Source Solutions*	- Transactional benefits (i.e., lower transaction costs resulting from e-Procurement practices, shorter supplier negotiation cycles, etc) - Monetary benefits (i.e., lower costs of goods purchased, additional sourcing capacity for highly specialised, etc) - Cost control - Management information benefits - Short-term regulatory compliance benefits	- Higher transaction and acquisition costs as opposed to an OSS alternative - Risks: (a) lock-in and internal business risks and external business risks, (b)technology risks, (c) process risk	- Transactional benefits (i.e., lower transaction costs resulting from e-Procurement practices, etc) - Monetary benefits (i.e., leverage a new sales channel and expand buyer reach, etc) - Cost control and rapid return on investment - Management information benefits (i.e., enhanced ability to forecast demand from continuous interaction, etc) - Short-term regulatory compliance benefits	- Higher transaction costs and acquisition costs as opposed to an OSS alternative - Risks: (a)lock-in and internal and external business risks, (b) technology risks, (c) process risk
	Open Source Solution	- Improved transactional benefits - Monetary benefits - Cost control - Shorter supplier negotiation cycles - Management information benefits - Short-term regulatory compliance benefits - No lock-in effects	- Risks: (a) internal (i.e., service support in-existence issues, switching costs, etc) and external business risks, (b) technology risks, (c) process risk	- Improved transactional benefits - Monetary benefits - Cost control and rapid return on investment - Management information benefits - Short-term regulatory compliance benefits	- Risks: (a) internal (i.e., service support in-existence issues, switching costs, etc) and external business risks, (b) technology risks, (c) process risk
e-Procurement Application Framework	*Closed Source AF*	- Indirect benefits (see analogous section in Closed Source Solutions)	- Indirect disadvantages (see analogous section in Closed Source Solutions)	- Indirect benefits (see analogous section in Closed Source Solutions)	- Indirect disadvantages (see analogous section in Closed Source Solutions)
	Open Source AF	- Significant transactional benefits - Monetary benefits - Cost control - Shorter supplier negotiation cycles - Management information benefits - Long-term regulatory compliance benefits (i.e., adaptive to future legal and regulatory changes) - No lock-in effects - Low development costs - Technological benefits (i.e., ability to change/adapt the AF, lower technology risks, etc)	- Risks: (a) internal (i.e., service support in-existence issues, switching costs, etc) and external business risks, (b) reduced technology risks, (c) process risk	- Significant transactional benefits - Monetary benefits - Cost control and rapid return on investment - Management information benefits - Long-term regulatory compliance benefits (i.e., adaptive to future legal and regulatory changes) - No lock-in effects - Low development costs - Technological benefits (i.e., ability to change/adapt the AF, etc)	- Risks: (a) internal (i.e., service support in-existence issues, switching costs, etc) and external business risks, (b) reduced technology risks, (c) process risk
e-Procurement Application Framework	*Closed Source AF*	- Indirect benefits (see analogous section in Closed Source Solutions)	- Indirect disadvantages (see analogous section in Closed Source Solutions)	- Indirect benefits (see analogous section in Closed Source Solutions)	- Indirect disadvantages (see analogous section in Closed Source Solutions)
	Open Source AF	- Significant transactional benefits - Monetary benefits - Cost control - Shorter supplier negotiation cycles - Management information benefits - Long-term regulatory compliance benefits (i.e., adaptive to future legal and regulatory changes) - No lock-in effects - Low development costs - Technological benefits (i.e., ability to change/adapt the AF, lower technology risks, etc)	- Risks: (a) internal (i.e., service support in-existence issues, switching costs, etc) and external business risks, (b) reduced technology risks, (c) process risk	- Significant transactional benefits - Monetary benefits - Cost control and rapid return on investment - Management information benefits - Long-term regulatory compliance benefits (i.e., adaptive to future legal and regulatory changes) - No lock-in effects - Low development costs - Technological benefits (i.e., ability to change/adapt the AF, etc)	- Risks: (a) internal (i.e., service support in-existence issues, switching costs, etc) and external business risks, (b) reduced technology risks, (c) process risk

plex large-scale systems. Developers tend to concentrate on code amendments rather than on updating appropriate architectural documentation as well. Therefore, the architectural documentation that initially forms the high-level specification of the code to be produced, as code propagates and evolves, it tends to loose its significance. Maintenance involves the customization, optimization and correction of implementation problems, where it prerequisites the identification of the specific part of the system than needs to be amended. The importance of reliable documentation lies on the fact that developers may better comprehend a system by focusing on its formal documentation (such as UML diagrams) that express the architectural structure, rather than on exploring code-segments consisted of thousand of lines.

- *Quality of code*: The quality of code produced by a developer is directly related to his expertise or his ability on choosing well-accepted programming patters on resolving specific issues. The development of a system involves the collaboration of a number of software developers of different kind of skill levels. Therefore, the quality of code cannot be guaranteed, as it is possible with model-centric approaches on where code is automatically generated based on predefined model-to-text transformation rules.

An alternative to code-centric development is the model-centric approach followed by the Model-Driven Engineering (MDE) paradigm (Schmidt, 2006; Balasubramanian, 2006). MDE is an approach to the full lifecycle integration and interoperability of enterprise systems comprised of software, hardware, humans and business practices, providing a systematic framework to understand, design, operate and evolve all aspects of such systems, using engineering technologies and tools. MDE refers to the systematic use of models as primary engineering artefacts throughout the engineering lifecycle, and therefore preserves the investment on requirements descriptions, design and analysis; which are expressed as models.

Model-Driven Development (MDD)

Despite the fact that the first tools to support MDE were the Computer-Aided Software Engineering (CASE) tools developed in the eighties (Wikipedia, 2009a), greater focus has been set in that field in the early years of the new millennium by Object Management Group (OMG[1]) with the launch of Model-Driven Development in 2001. Two popular variants of MDD are Model-Driven Architecture (MDA) and Model Integrated Computing (MIC). The main differentiation between the two standards lies on the type of formal language used to represent system elements and their relationships, as well as their transformations to platform specific artifacts. MDA uses OMG's general-purpose UML, where MIC uses Domain-Specific Modelling Languages (DSMLs) (Balasubramanian 2006).

MDD is a part of a broad effort across the industry to raise the level of abstraction in the process of system development. MDD uses modeling languages that make it possible to deliver systems at a higher level of abstraction, than it is possible using programming languages. The MDD methodology is based on the derivation of three models and appropriate model transformation rules. A representation of the MDD artifacts and their relationships is illustrated in left part of Figure 2.

Following this approach, the first model to be defined is the Computational Independent Model (CIM), usually referred to as a domain or a business model as well, that captures the system requirements of a particular business domain and identifies the key concepts or business entities and their relationships. Then the system is modeled in a formal but completely technology inde-

Figure 2. The traditional model-driven development (in left), and DSL-like (in right) workflow

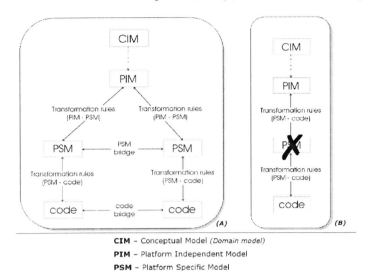

CIM – Conceptual Model *(Domain model)*
PIM – Platform Independent Model
PSM – Platform Specific Model

pendent representation within a Platform-Independent Model (PIM). Furthermore, a set of appropriate model transformation rules need to be defined in order to transform a PIM to a Platform-Specific Model (PSM). A PSM is a view of the system from the platform specific viewpoint. Typically, a PSM combines the specifications in the PIM with the details that specify the way that the system uses a particular type of platform. The final stage involves the definition of model transformation rules that aim at transforming the PSM to actual code. The shift of focus in software development from writing code to modeling, apart from raising the level of abstraction in implementing software applications, contributes also to the:

- *Improvement of productivity*: The effort required in the MDD approach on developing a system is mainly based on the modelling of the PIM and the model transformation rules. Once the rules for the transformation of PIM-to-PSM and PSM-to-code are defined, then they can be re-used and be applied to the development of other systems of relevant platform interest; increasing this way the return on technology invest-

ments. In addition, the advantage related to the developers' shift of focus from the code to PIM is twofold. Firstly, developers' work is minimised, as platform-specific details need not be designed and written down since they are already addressed in the model transformation rules. Secondly, placing more emphasis on solving the business problems at hand, rather than concentrating on code writing, results in a system that aligns much better with the needs of the end users.

- *Increase of portability across middleware vendors*: The PIM separates the specification of functionality of a system from the specification of implementation of that functionality on specific platform technology. In this instance, when there is a need to switch between middleware platforms (e.g. from J2EE to .NET), effort is only required on the definition of a new PSM, preserving this way the initial architecture of the system. The existence of a great collection of open-source MDD tools (Zhu et al., 2007) and all-ready-made customisable model transformation rules assist the transformation of a system to adhere on different middleware vendors, as well as to new emerging technologies.

- *Interoperability boost*: MDD apart from supporting the generation of multiple PSMs from a single PIM, it also enables the definition of PSM-to-PSM relationships, referred to as bridges. Bridges enable the transformation of concepts from one platform into concepts used in another platform enabling the developing of distributed systems that are made up of components running on different platforms or tiers.

- *Optimisation of maintainability, code consistency, quality and quantity*: The PIM is a high-level representation of the system. Changes made to the system will eventually be made by changing the PIM and regenerating the PSM and the code. In practice today, many of the changes are made to the PSM and code is regenerated from there. Mature tools, however, will be able to maintain the relationship between PIM and PSM, even when changes to the PSM are made. Changes in the PSM will thus be reflected in the PIM, and high-level documentation will remain consistent with the actual code. Consequently, investment on models (i.e. architectural documentation) is not lost in contrast to the code-centric approach. In addition, the quality of code produced by models is increased since to the fact that well-accepted design patters may be incorporated into model transformation rules providing developers (irrespectively of their skill level) with the ability to use the same underlying design patterns, since the code is generated in the same way every time.

- *Improvement of testing and simulation*: Enables testing and simulation at an early stage of development: since the developed models can be used to generate code, to be validated against requirements, to be tested against various infrastructures and to directly simulate the behavior of the system being designed.

Although the majority of models are expressed in XMI (XML Metadata Interchange) OMG standard, one of the limitations of MDD, and MDE in general, relates to the interchange of models between modeling tools of different vendors (i.e. lose of information during import operations). Another disadvantage lies within the scope of near-shore development where Version Control System (VCS) and Distributed Revision Control System (DRCS) applications cannot handle complex functionalities (such as "brunch and merge" on models) despite the fact that basic ones like "file locking" and "versioning" are well supported.

DSL-Like Hybrid MDD Approach

In contrast to the traditional MDD approach that requires transformations to be written between the PIM and the PSM level, a hybrid approach of MDD excludes some of the intermediate steps in the process and refines a PIM directly into code (as illustrated in the right side of Figure 2). In the DSL-like (Domain Specific Language) approach all the refinement is handled in the model-to-text transformation and consequently, a system is modeled at one level and transformed directly into code i.e. the intermediate step of PIM-to-PSM is skipped.

However, although this is a more simplistic approach, its weakness lies in the model-to-text transformations which become more complicated. Therefore, special care must be taken when they are developed, otherwise maintainability issues might emerge. In addition, intermediate abstract documentations that describe an application on a platform-specific level are reduced and focus is set to the Platform-Independent Model, where the language utilised is based on specific domain concepts that potentially simplify modeling for people working in the targeted domain.

To conclude, traditional or hybrid MDD approaches provide the means to specify systems at a higher level of abstraction. As a result there is an increase on the longevity of a system, since the business logic and architectural specifications are not tied-up with a specific technology - investment in business model is preserved even as technologies come and go. Moreover, by raising the level of abstraction quality is improved, because emphasis is given on determining the business requirements for an application rather than on the realization of the application using a particular technology standard

AN OPEN SOURCE APPLICATION FRAMEWORK FOR E-PROCUREMENT DEVELOPMENT

The Open Source Application Framework (AF) for building e-Procurement Solutions presented within this chapter follows the DSL-like approach of Model-Driven Development in where the intermediate step of generating PSMs is skipped.

MDD is highly utilized by software production lines and software factories for developing software targeting specific application domains and research has shown that the 70-80% of the required code can be automatically generated from models (Oldevik, 2006). On the other hand, the DSL-like approach (Kelly and Tolvanen, 2008) is also applied in the Microsoft Software Factories approach (Greenfield et al., 2004) and despite certain disadvantages compared to the traditional approach of MDD when it comes to documentation, it is believed that making the framework easy to use and understood will be more important in the environment that it will be applied. Nevertheless, since the majority of software developers are not familiar with model-centric approaches of software engineering, an approach which simplifies the modeling of domain concepts and realizes

the instant generation of code may considerably contribute to the adoption of the proposed AF.

In general, a development environment pertinent to a specific domain prerequisites the identification and implementation of functional and non-functional requirements, concepts, roles, and relationships of that domain, while providing the ability to easily extend and customise the end application. The realisation of such a development environment implies a high initial investment which however guarantees the cost-effective and accelerated software production line of specific application domain. To this extend, the AF offers a software development environment pertinent to e-Procurement domain which is Open Source, build with the purpose of enabling SMEs to reduce the associated development complexity, costs and time entailed by the production of complex systems such as e-Procurement Solutions.

The AF addresses all phases of phases of contract establishment process (i.e. notification, tendering, evaluation of tenders, contract conclusion) and focuses in the electronic public procurement field implying compliance to the EC legislative framework. The AF is built on top of the mature Eclipse Integrated Development Environment (Eclipse, 2009) and a number of different components are integrated to form the framework, as illustrated in Figure 3. The components include other sub-components or plug-ins that form a consistent development environment for the design of models into different types of formal modelling languages, transformation of models into code, editing of generated source code, debugging, compiling etc. The six major components identified within the architecture are the following:

- *Eclipse platform*: is the core platform that integrates all the required plug-ins for the realization of the AF.
- *Development Environment*: corresponds to the required components for the development of models and code. It comprises edi-

Figure 3. Architectural stack of e-procurement application framework

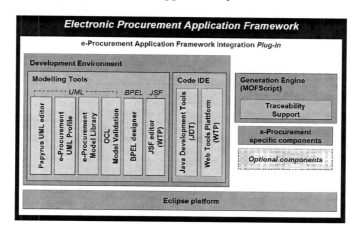

tors for UML, BPEL, JSF and JAVA languages, libraries specific to e-Procurement domain, compiler and debugging facilities.

- *Generation engine*: is responsible for the transformation of models into code. The engine bundled with the framework is a version of MOFScript (Oldevik, 2006) designed specifically for the needs of the AF.
- *e-Procurement specific components*: are components developed specifically for the Application Framework needs. These include e-Procurement model-to-text transformation rules, fixed web-services to support different security implementation schemes, conversion mechanisms of e-Procurement forms represented in XML standard into PDF/HTML documents, deployment descriptors etc.
- *Optional components*: represent a collection of components that may be optionally integrated into the AF for enhancing its operations, such as an SVN system.
- *ePP Application Framework Integration Plug-in*: is responsible for the integration of all plug-ins under the Eclipse platform.

All the components and plug-ins of the AF architecture are Open Source and can be downloaded (or updated) directly from the Vendor's official web-site. The AF is provided as a pre-configured platform of Eclipse with all the necessary plug-ins installed and it is available for public access via SourceForge.net in (SourceForge, 2009). Table 2 provides information on the required Eclipse plug-ins that constitutes each of the architecture's components, along with their dependencies.

The AF, apart from the development environment, requires and offers support for a server environment where the developed e-Procurement Solutions via the framework are deployed, as well as a testing environment where the Solutions are tested before put into operation. Although the AF is not bind to any specific server applications, the Sun GlassFish Enterprise Server 3.0 (SGES) (Sun, 2009a) and Open ESB 2.0 (OpenESB, 2009) are recommended for use with the framework due to their potential and Open Source characteristic. The SGES is an application server compatible with JAVA Enterprise Edition 5 that fully supports the EJB 3.0 (Sun, 2009b) standard for developing and delivering server side JAVA applications and Web Services; where the Open ESB is set as to the default BPEL engine due to its excellent integration with SGES.

Table 2. e-Procurement application framework eclipse plug-ins

Component	Plug-in / sub-component	Dependency	e-Procurement specific
Modelling Tool			✓/✗
	Papyrus UML editor	UML2, EMF, GEF	✗
	UML e-Procurement Profile	UML2	✓
	e-Procurement Model Library	UML e-Procurement Profile	✓
	OCL checker	UML2, EMF, OCL, LPG	✗
	Oracle BPEL editor	EMF, GEF, DTP, WTP	✗
	JSF editor	WTP	✗
Code IDE			✗
	WTP	EMF, SDO, XSD, GEF, JEM	✗
	JDT	JRE (JAVA), JDT APT, JDT Core, JDT Debug, JDT UI	✗
Generation Engine			✗
	MOFScript	AntLR, UML2, EMF	✓
	Traceability Support	MOFScript	✗
e-Procurement Application Framework Integration Plug-in			✓
	e-Procurement Application Framework Integration Plug-in	Modelling Tool, Code IDE, Generation Engine, e-Procurement specific components	✓/✗

FRAMEWORK'S DEVELOPMENT RATIONAL

The innovative aspect of the Application Framework relates to the combination of the DSL-Like approach of MDD with the Service-Oriented Architecture (SOA) paradigm for enabling the cost-effective production of e-Procurement Solutions by facilitating integration, interoperability, easy maintenance and customisation.

The guiding design rational behind an e-Procurement Solution's architecture developed via the AF is to facilitate interoperability and extensibility, as well as preserving in this sense a considerable degree of independence regarding the implementation of the end application. Key factors to achieving this objective are the adoption of widely accepted as well as emerging standards and the usage of Open Source Software. JAVA, Web standards and technologies such as JAVA EE, XML, WSDL and BPEL are utilized to bring forth the desired objective. The core implementation language utilized by the framework is the JAVA Enterprise Edition (EE) (Sun, 2009c), which is a descendant of the JAVA technology, built on the solid foundation of JAVA Standard Edition (SE). The JAVA EE is an extension to JAVA SE that allows developers to use Web technologies and develop enterprise applications. It is widely accepted as the industry standard for developing portable, robust, scalable and secure server-side JAVA applications and offers a wide range of APIs (Wikipedia, 2009b) that assist the development of SOA and next-generation Web-based applications.

An e-Procurement Solution is implemented as an annotation-based JAVA EE application on a JAVA EE platform made up of JAVA EE components which are self-contained functional software units. Application logic is divided into components according to function, and the various components may be installed on different machines depending on the tier to which the ap-

Figure 4. Overview of an electronic procurement solution's architecture

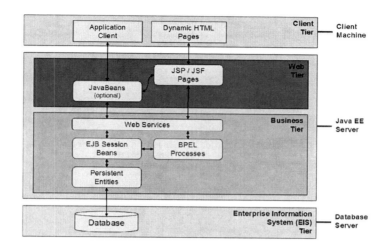

plication component belongs; though this is not always necessary. The tiers and their respective components of the distributed 4-tier application model utlised by the framework for e-Procurement Solutions are illustrated in diagram of Figure 4; where each tier offers the following:

- The *Client tier* typically contains Web clients. A Web client consists of two parts: (i) dynamic Web pages (e.g. HTML and XML), which are generated by Web components running in the Web tier, and (ii) a Web browser that accesses server-side components in the Web tier using HTTP or SHTTP and renders the pages received from the server. It is also possible to access server-side components from an application client running on the client machine. Application clients can accommodate a richer graphical user interface than what can be provided by Web browsers.

- The *Web tier* components are either servlets or pages created using JAVA Server Pages (JSP) and/or JAVA Server Faces (JSF) technologies. Servlets are JAVA programming language classes that dynamically process requests and construct responses. JSP pages are text-based documents that execute as servlets but allow a more natural approach to creating static content. JAVA Server Faces technology is built on servlets and JSP technology and provides a user interface component framework for Web applications.

- The *Business tier* contains Enterprise JAVA Beans (EJB) components that implement the e-Procurement business logic. EJB components are exposed as Web Services that use open XML-based standards and transport protocols to exchange data with calling clients. The Web Services Business Process Execution Language (BPEL) processes are used for the composition and orchestration of Web Services.

- The *Enterprise Information System tier* (EIS), (usually referred to as the persistence tier), handles EIS software and includes enterprise infrastructure systems such as Enterprise Resource Planning (ERP), mainframe transaction processing, database systems, and other legacy information systems. Resource adapters (e.g. JDBC or ODBC drivers) provide access, search and update services to databases and their data is stored in Data-Base Management Systems (DBMS).

Figure 5. The e-procurement platform independent model specifications

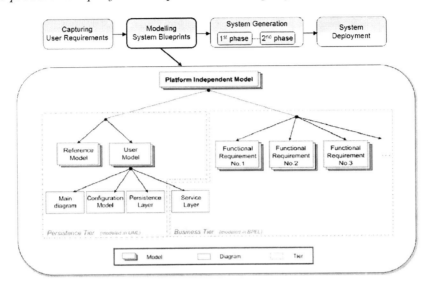

Following the DSL-Like approach of MDD, the PIM that corresponds to the blueprints of the e-Procurement Solution to be developed, is initially expressed in a formal modelling language consisted of a collection of models and diagrams. Note that a diagram may be comprehended as the building block of a model, where a model may be consisted of one or more diagrams; usually, a model's information is distributed into different diagrams for clarity purposes.

The AF provides a PIM template that corresponds to a generic implementation of an e-Procurement Solution with the basic functionality. With reference to public procurement (G2B), the AF reinforces an e-Procurement Solutions' compliance to EC legislative framework by describing the Functional Requirements for building an ePP Solution - as these are defined by IDABC (ID-ABC, 2005) - into BPEL models that correspond to the required ePP processes; of which a software developer is free to use. The specifications of the PIM template offered by the AF are illustrated in Figure 5; each of those diagrams are described in detail in the following section. In the context of PIM modeling, UML is primarily used to model the Persistence tier and part of the Business logic

of the end application, where BPEL is used specifically for the definition of e-Procurement processes that constitute the Business tier.

The advantage of the AF utilisation is that a software developer may build an e-Procurement Solution from scratch by defining his/her own model/diagrams or by using the pre-existing template model offered by the framework. In the second case, the developer's effort lies on the parameterisation of the existing model or the definition of new one based on the re-use, extension or optimisation of the pre-made PIM. Moreover, the AF offers an extensive collection of off-the-self components that may be integrated to the end application such as different types of authorisation/authentication security mechanisms (e.g. user credentials, certificates, PKI etc.), tender submission approaches (i.e. client/server-side), encryption algorithms, conversion of documents formats, multilingualism support etc. that facilitates development process.

The development of an e-Procurement Solution via the framework involves a two-phase generation. The first phase involves the generation of the Persistence tier and part of the business logic of the end application, whereas the second phase

Figure 6. Fraction of the reference model in (a), and user model in(b)

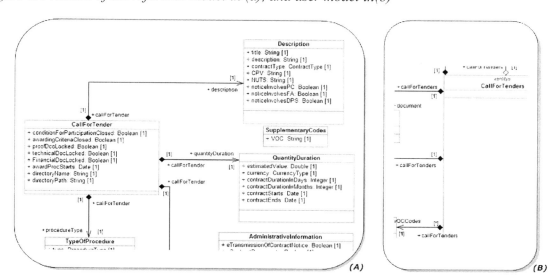

(A)   (B)

regards the generation of the Business tier and its integration with the Web tier. In essence, the first step produces persistence objects (related to e-Procurement domain) and CRUD (Create, Read, Update, and Delete) operations for managing those objects in the form of Web services, and the second step focuses on the orchestration of those Web services to form the required e-Procurement processes that are expressed as BPEL processes; along with their integration to the Web tier. No modelling is required for the Web tier as it comes off-the-self, implemented based on IDABC (IDABC, 2005) standards. Though its parameterisation is performed via UML and model-to-text transformation rules are employed for the compilation of the necessary web-pages expressed in JSF. The following two sections describe in detail the procedure of each of the two-phase generation.

First-Phase Generation

In order to simplify the modeling of the Persistence tier, the model that captures the persistence information is divided into two separate models,

namely the Reference Model (RM) and the User Model (UM).

As such, a software developer may model and make changes to the UM, but not in the RM. The RM contains specific information pertinent to e-Procurement domain of which a software developer can use in order to describe the required functionality in his/her UM and captures information from the e-Procurement UML profile constructed for the purpose of the AF modelling. RM's primarily objective is to abstract the level of complexity, and act as a reference model – no amendments are possible to be performed on this model. On one hand, from the software developer's perspective, complexity is decreased since model-to-text transformation rules use information from the RM on properties defined within the UM. On the other hand, a more abstract and simpler interface to the framework is provided. Moreover, the models are used to represent something that would normally have been specified in source code.

For instance, if a software developer designs a class in the UM and stereotypes it with the <<Entity>> stereotype of type 'CallForTender', then the code that will be generated after the model-to-text transformation rules are executed will include all

Figure 7. First-phase generation of an e-procurement solution

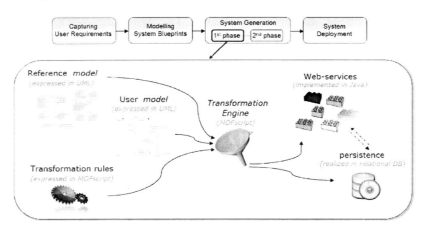

the information of the 'CallForTender' class from the RM (see Figure 6).

With reference to Figure 5, the UM is composed of the following diagrams: (a) *Main Diagram* that models the main packages of the e-Procurement Solution for placing the generated code, (b) *Persistence Layer* that models the persistence schema, (c) *Service Layer* that models the operations that manage the persistent objects defined in the Persistence Layer, and (d) *Configuration Model* that models the parameterisation of the e-Procurement Solution.

Once the design of the UM is complete, it is fed as input to the MOFScript Generation Engine along with the RM. The AF offers two types of MOFScript-specific model-to-text transformation rules. The server-side transformation rules which are utilised for the generation of the Persistence tier and part of the business logic, and the client-side transformation rules that undertake the integration of the Business with the Web tier. Consequently, during the first-phase generation, the Generation engine and the server-side transformation rules are employed for the conversion of the aforementioned models (UM and RM) into Java code. The resulting code comprises e-Procurement pertinent persistence objects and CRUD operations for managing those objects which are expressed as Web services (see Figure 7).

After the first-phase generation is complete, a software developer may manually add code into the generated Java classes.

Second-Phase Generation

Once the Persistence tier of the e-Procurement Solution is created along with the necessary operations for managing the associated persistent objects, the next step involves the definition of the Business tier of the architecture and its integration with the Web tier.

The Business tier entails the support of all e-Procurement processes required by the e-Procurement Solution to be developed, which have to formally be expressed in BPEL language according to the AF development methodology. The PIM template provided by the AF includes a collection of BPEL diagrams for the realization of the most common e-Procurement processes. Those diagrams are designed based on IDABC standards (IDABC, 2005) that describe the Functional Requirements (FR) for building an electronic Public Procurement (ePP) Solution compliant with the legislative framework of EC. Although, a non-public e-Procurement (B2B) Solution does not have to adhere to IDABC standards, the template BPEL diagrams may be applied to support most of the functionality provided by a

Figure 8. Second-phase generation of an e-procurement solution

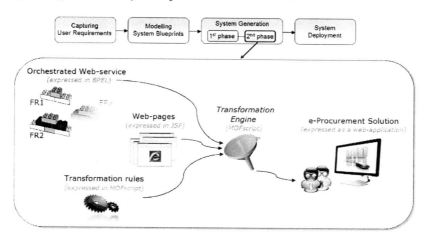

generic e-Procurement Solution. Consequently, a software developer may define his/her own BPEL diagrams from scratch to describe the required e-Procurement processes, or re-use/extend and optimise the pre-made template diagrams provided by the AF. Though, the AF prerequisites predefined interfaces for the template BPEL diagrams to enable recursion and loose coupling.

In general every FR is represented by a single BPEL diagram that describes simple ePP process such as the user authentication, or complex ones like the submission of tenders which basically involves the composition of other ePP processes. The orchestration of FRs realise a complete phase of ePP such as the notification, tendering, contract conclusion etc. From the technical point of view, a BPEL diagram orchestrates a collection of Web services in order to provide the necessary functionality of an ePP process. Those Web services involve the: (i) ones generated from the first-phase generation that manage concepts from the e-Procurement domain, (ii) other BPELs that are exposed as Web services, and/or (iii) manually implemented Web services that handle complex procedures of which are not possible to be generated via the framework.

Figure 8, provides a visualisation of the second-phase generation of an e-Procurement Solution and

illustrates how the Web services produced from the first-phase generation (drawn as Lego bricks) form the building blocks of BPEL diagrams. The BPEL designer bundled with the AF provides the necessary functionality for converting a BPEL diagrams into appropriate XML code which may be deployed on an application server.

The final step of generating an e-Procurement Solution involves the integration of the Business tier with the Web tier. More specifically, associating e-Procurement Web pages with the appropriate e-Procurement processes, which are either invoked by clicking on a Web link/button, or used for populating the content of a Web page with information retrieved/aggregated by the execution of a specific process. The AF provides a default implementation of an e-Procurement Web tier off-the-self, which shares the same look and feel as with the IDABC demonstrator (IDABC, 2009) but has been implemented with the latest JSF technology. Although, no modelling is required for the Web tier, its parameterisation is performed via the Configuration Model of UM in UML and client-server transformation rules are employed for the compilation of the distinct user interface components into the necessary Web pages that constitutes an e-Procurement Solution. Due to the fact that the interfaces of the template BPELs are predefined, the necessary code to invoke a BPEL from within a Web page is integrated within the latter.

Having specified the logic of the required BPEL diagrams (Business tier) for the corresponding Web pages (Web tier) that constitute an e-Procurement Solution, appropriate client-side transformation rules undertake the integration of the Business with the Web tier. After the completion of the second-phase generation, a software developer's effort on manually writing code which has not been automatically generated by the AF is anticipated to be the 5-15% of the total code that constitutes a complete e-Procurement Solution. Of course this is depended upon the complexity of the end application. Finally, the deployment of the end e-Procurement Solution to an application server is facilitated by the AF due to the utilization of already made deployment descriptors.

EVALUATION OF THE PROPOSED APPROACH OF SOFTWARE DEVELOPMENT

The proposed model fulfills the need for an Internet mediated, domain specific Open Source Application Framework which supports the development of Open Source e-Procurement Solutions tailored to the needs of private and public organizations. However, in order to assess it effectiveness it is critical to test and evaluate the developed Application Framework, as well as the e-Procurement Solutions generated via the utilisation of the former. In essence, to measure and compare the development effort required in terms of both time and costs on producing e-Procurement Solutions following the proposed software development approach described within this chapter in contrast with existing traditional code-centric methodologies of software development. In addition, the quality of the generated software code and the applicability of the e-Procurement Solutions (output of Application Framework) also need to

be assessed as they constitute an important aspect of the evaluation outcome. In order to ensure the scientific validity[2] of the evaluation results, the evaluation framework utilized and the conduction of the evaluation procedure itself was founded on (i) a representative sample of participants, and (ii) a number of evaluation instruments within the context of software engineering and e-Procurement domain.

The evaluation process took place in the Western-Balkan (WB) region of Europe, where four distinct electronic Public Procurement Solutions were built for the countries of Albania, Bosnia-Herzegovina, Former Yugoslav Republic of Macedonia and Republic of Serbia. Each Solution was implemented and customised by a local SME according to the special needs of the Public Procurement environment of each WB country as indicated by the representative Public Authorities. All of the four implementations covered the whole contract establishment process of Public Procurement (i.e. from Notification to Contract conclusion phase), where their development, testing and evaluation involved a number of over 50 people from both the public and private sector (i.e. software developers, Contracting Authorities and Economic Operators). The fact that the developed e-Procurement Solutions were targeting the public (G2B) sector provided the advantage of appraising the Application Framework's feature on ensuring compliance with respect to EC legislative framework; something which it is not required when implementing Solutions for the B2B sector.

The evaluation framework employed both a formative and a summative evaluation on the Application Framework and the generated (via the former) e-Procurement Solutions utilizing evaluation techniques such as quality-analysis, Goal-Question-Metric (GQM) approach, scenario-based evaluation and benchmarking. ISO standards (in specific ISO91261 and ISO/IEC9126-3) have also been considered for better assessing the technical requirements of the applied software engineering life-cycle and produced implementation. The driving forces of the proposed software development approach evaluation were based on a typical software engineering life-cycle focusing on the user requirements, analysis, design, development, integration & testing, deployment, and maintenance phases. The evaluation of the evaluation of four e-Procurement Solutions generated via the framework for four Western-Balkan countries was made by measuring their functionality, usability, reliability, scalability, security, and interoperability.

Main Findings of Application Framework Utilisation

The evaluation results indicated that the user requirements, design and analysis phase as addressed by the Application Framework met the expectations of the responders (i.e., participants of the evaluation). The framework documented well in a formal language most of the common concepts and functionalities of the e-Procurement domain, where the embedded modeling tools were found to be easy to use on creating new or modifying existing UML and BPEL diagrams. Specifically, it has been indicated that the e-Procurement UML profile, provided by the proposed framework accelerated the design and increased the clarity of UML diagrams. The rich collection of diagrams offered by the framework on describing electronic Public Procurement procedures compliant to EC directives was reported as one of its most important features. This was due to the abstraction of the legislative layer from the implementation layer, which implied that software developers did not had to be familiar with the underling legislative framework. Though, the absence of a mechanism for validating new or amended diagrams against EC-compliance was strongly recommended.

In the context of the development phase, the process of generating code from models was overall characterized as to the most simplistic procedure of the framework, involving only a few mouse clicks. Although, the realization of the

Persistence tier and the Business tier of the end application was acceptable and effortless, the Web tier was seen to deliver a fix front-end interface, and the embedded (to the framework) modeling tool for Web page component manipulation was found to be adequate. The majority of the responders reported that overall the percentage of code which was not directly generated from models was minimal, and that the developed off-the-self e-Procurement components provided by the framework contributed further to the decrease of the amount of code that had to be written manually. The code resulted from the transformation of model-to-text was evaluated positively both in terms of quality and descriptive aspect.

In relation to the integration phase of the applied software development methodology, responders expressed that the effort required for integrating the Persistent tier with the Business tier was minimal to zero. In contrast, the integration of the Business tier with the Web tier perquisites manual coding for the e-Procurement processes not described by the pre-defined diagrams or the Web components (that realize the front-end interface) offered by the framework. To this end, the responders suggested that the adoption of a wizard-like approach to easy the integration between the two tiers. With regards to the deployment of the end application to an application server, responders denoted that the framework did not provide an automated procedure to support the specific process but it generated appropriate deployment descriptors that assisted deployment; nevertheless it was indicated that this is a not a time-consuming procedure. With reference to the maintenance phase, it was concluded that the model-centric approach outperforms the bespoken development in the sense that maintainability, optimization and traceability of error tasks may be better performed on model level rather than directly on text level.

A key conclusion drawn was that the MDD approach of software development as applied to the described above Application Framework shortened the software engineering life-cycle and satisfied the needs of the parties involved in the development process. Alongside with a noticeable set of advantages, the respondents also identified a couple of issues that remain to be refined as opportunities for further improvement. Emphasis was given to the processes of electronic Public Procurement due to their peculiarity related with the compliance of EC-directives. The responders stated that the Open and Restricted procedures for awarding public contracts were well covered by the Application Framework, but indicated their desire for support of other types of procurement procedures and extensions such as the Dynamic Purchasing System, Framework Agreement and e-auction. In conclusion, the responders found really appealing the property of the Application Framework being Open Source which enables its extension and enrichment with new functionalities.

Main Findings of Generated e-Procurement Solutions

The evaluation of the four Piloting e-Procurement Solutions developed via the Application Framework provided positive results, while a number of issues were raised as opportunities for further improvement that could be exploited.

In terms of functionality and usability, the four implementations were found to be well accepted. The implementations offered a multilingual intuitive user-friendly front-end interface providing the necessary operations for the execution of the trial usage scenarios. On one hand, with respect to the back-end interface i.e. administration console, the absence of an advanced audit trailing system was found to be a limitation of the implementation with reference to security aspects. On the other hand, the authentication and authorization, the encryption, (client/server-side) secure submission and maintenance of Tender documents, as well as the opening of those documents following the 4-eye principle found to be adequate to the responders' expectations.

The process of information capturing met fully the responders' requirements due to the employment of well-structured e-Procurement forms compliant to SIMAP standards, with embedded intelligent mechanism for performing data validation activities. In addition, the use of common procurement code-lists (CPV, VOC, NUTS etc.) was found extremely helpful for descriptive purposes. The majority of the responders were not completely satisfied with the response time of the implementations and concerns were raised on how the Solution may scale when the number of Tenders increases. However, this is somehow expected due to the fact that all of the implemented e-Procurement processes are provided in the form of Web services to support loose coupling, modularity and interoperability.

CONCLUSION

Despite the significant benefits of the automation, optimisation and electronic mediation of the internal and external processes associated with the purchase of goods and services, e-Procurement practices do not yet prevail mainly due to the high capital investment associated with the development or purchase, ownership and operation of such a system.

The development of e-Procurement Solutions in Europe today is driven by low-level bespoke design and coding. Whether an incremental and iterative process or the traditional waterfall process is followed, documents and diagrams that express the specifications of the Solutions rapidly lose their value as soon as the coding starts. In contrast to code-centric development, MDE refers to the systematic use of models as primary engineering artefacts throughout the engineering lifecycle, and therefore preserves the investment on requirements descriptions, design and analysis (which are expressed as models).

However, the software development process and the underlying "paradigm shift" instigated by the Open Source have significantly impacted the e-Procurement evolution across time. Our analysis indicates that these new means of software development and distribution have created a trend towards Open Source e-Procurement Application Frameworks (AFs) which enable the development of tailored e-Procurement Solutions. Anchored in this notion, we present an Open-Source e-Procurement AF with a two-phase generation procedure, which adopts Open Source standards and addresses the needs of the private and the public sector.

The innovative aspect of the proposed Open Source e-Procurement Application Framework (AF) relates to the combination of the MDE approach with the Service-Oriented Architecture paradigm for enabling the cost-effective production of e-Procurement Solutions for B2B and G2B by facilitating integration, interoperability, easy maintenance and management of possible changes in the European ePP environment. The evaluation of the proposed framework and its derived Solutions, that took place in the context of G2B and in the Western-Balkan European region (i.e., Albania, Bosnia-Herzegovina, Former Yugoslav Republic of Macedonia and Republic of Serbia) yield positive results and further enhancing opportunities for the proposed Open Source e-Procurement AF and its resulting e-Procurement Solutions.

The study described in this chapter was limited, due to the fact that it was only evaluated in the context of G2B and within a specific geographic context. Further research could be performed in order to further assess the empirical validation of the proposed Open Source e-Procurement AF and its derived Solutions across the private sector and in the examined or new countries as well as in B2B context, which provides less legal restrictions.

ACKNOWLEDGMENT

The software development methodology applied by the Open Source Application Framework presented within this chapter for building electronic Procurement Solutions, as well as the framework itself is the result of an IST research co-funded by the European Community's Sixth Framework Programme under Contract No. 045153.

REFERENCES

Balasubramanian, K., Gokhale, A., Karsai, G., Sztipanovits, J., & Neema, S. (2006). Developing applications using model-driven design environments. *IEEE Computer Society, 39*(2), 33–40.

Eclipse. (2009). *Eclipse Foundation*. Retrieved August 25, 2009, from http://www.eclipse.org

EUROPA. (2009). *Public procurement. European Commission the EU Single Market*. Retrieved August 10, 2009, from http://ec.europa.eu/internal_market/publicprocurement/index_en.htm

Greenfield, J., Short, K., Cook, S., Kent, S., & Crupi, J. (2004). *Software factories: Assembling applications with patterns, models, frameworks and tools* (1st ed.). Wiley Publishing.

IDABC. (Interoperable Delivery of European eGovernment Services to public Administrations, Businesses and Citizens). (2005). *Functional requirements for conducting electronic public procurement under the EU framework*. Retrieved May 30, 2009, from http://ec.europa.eu/idabc/en/document/4721/5874

IDABC. (Interoperable Delivery of European eGovernment Services to public Administrations, Businesses and Citizens). (2009). *Software demonstrators for e-procurement*. Retrieved August 25, 2009, from http://ec.europa.eu/idabc/en/document/3488/5874

Jackson, J. (2003). Disruptive technologies. *Washington Technology, 17*(2). Retrieved July 30, 2009, from http://www.washingtontechnology.com/print/17_20/19859-1.html?topic=cover-stories

Kauffman, R. J., & Mohtadi, H. (2004). Proprietary and open systems adoption: A risk-augmented transactions cost perspective. *Journal of Management Information Systems, 21*(1), 137–166.

Kelly, S., & Tolvanen, J. P. (2008). *Domain-specific modeling.* Wiley-IEEE Computer Society Press. doi:10.1002/9780470249260

Oldevik, J. (2006). MOFScript Eclipse plug-in: Metamodel-based code generation. In *Proceedings of the Eclipse Technology eXchange Workshop (eTX) at the ECOOP 2006 Conference*, Nantes, France, 2006.

Oldevik, J., Solberg, A., Haugen, Ø., & Møller-Pedersen, B. (2006). Evaluation framework for model-driven product line engineering tools. In Käkölä, T., & Dueñas, J. C. (Eds.), *Software product lines: Research issues in engineering and management* (pp. 589–618). Springer.

OpenESB. (2009). *The open enterprise service bus.* Retrieved August 25, 2009, from https://open-esb.dev.Java.net

Peria, F. (2003). E-procurement can have a substantial and positive impact on your bottom line. *CIO Magazine.* Retrieved Dec, 2004, from http://www.cio.com

Schmidt, D. C. (2006). Model-driven engineering. *IEEE Computer Society, 39*(2), 25–31.

SourceForge. (2009), *ELLECTRA-WeB project.* Retrieved August 25, 2009, from http://sourceforge.net/projects/ellectra-web

Stephen, J. M., Kendall, S., Axel, U., & Dirk, W. (2004). *MDA distilled.* Addison Wesley Longman Publishing Co.

Stephens, D. (2008). Open source e-procurement software. *Open Source Business Resource* (OSBR), March. Retrieved May 15, 2009, from http://osbr.ca/ojs/index.php/osbr/article/view/536/494

Sun Microsystems. (2009a). *Sun GlassFish enterprise server.* Retrieved August 25, 2009, from http://developers.sun.com/appserver

Sun Microsystems. (2009b). *Enterprise Java-Beans technology.* Retrieved August 25, 2009, from http://Java.sun.com/products/ejb

Sun Microsystems. (2009c). *Java EE at a glance.* Retrieved August 25, 2009, from http://java.sun.com/javaee

Tanner, C., Wölfle, R., Schubert, P., & Quade, M. (2007). *Current trends and challenges in electronic procurement: An empirical study.* Paper presented in the 20th Bled eConference eMergence: Merging and Emerging Technologies, Processes, and Institutions, June 4 - 6, 2007, Bled, Slovenia.

Tschammer, V., Zinner Henriksen, H., Ramfos, A., & Renner, T. (2003). *E-procurement: Challenges and opportunities.* Paper presented in the 16th Bled eCommerce Conference eTransformation, Panel on eProcurement, June 9 - 11, 2003, Bled, Slovenia.

Wikipedia. (2009a). *Model-driven engineering.* Retrieved August 25, 2009, from http://en.wikipedia.org/wiki/Model_driven_development

Wikipedia. (2009b). *List of Java APIs.* Retrieved August 25, 2009 from http://en.wikipedia.org/wiki/List_of_Java_APIs

Zhu, L., Liu, Y., Gorton, I., & Kuz, I. (2007). *Tools for model driven development.* Paper presented in the 40th Annual Hawaii International Conference on System Sciences (HICSS'07) (p. 284).

Ziouvelou, X., & Yovanof, G. (2008a). Public procurement: A European perspective. *AIT Working Paper Series* AIT/MBIT/001 (4), July/Aug 2008, Version 1.1 (work in progress).

Ziouvelou, X., & Yovanof, G. (2008b). The state of open source software in Europe. *AIT Working Paper Series* AIT/MBIT/002 (5), Sep/Oct 2008, Version 1.1 (work in progress).

ENDNOTES

[1]   The Object Management Group (OMG) is an international, open membership, not-for-profit computer industry consortium. OMG Task Forces develop enterprise integration standards for a wide range of technologies, and an even wider range of industries, http://www.omg.org, last accessed Aug. 2009.

[2]   Scientific validity is defined as to "the applicability of a conclusion drawn in the context of a scientific experiment to the world at large", http://rationalwiki.com/wiki/Scientific_validity, last accessed Aug. 2009.

[3]   Software development lifecycle which consists on the user requirements, analysis, design, development, integration & testing, deployment, and maintenance phases.

[4]   Open Source Software is "computer software which has been developed under a open, public and collaborative mode and which provides access to the source code for use while at the same time allowing for the source code to be modified (i.e., changed and/or improved) and redistributed in compliance with the copyright license that it has been distributed" (Ziouvelou and Yovanof, 2008, p.5).

[5]   Although non-existent, a closed source Application Framework could provide advantages (e.g., (a) direct benefits: to companies that would own the proprietary AF and utilise it in order to provide (closed source) e-Procurement Solutions and (b) indirect benefits: to buyers and sellers that would adopt the output of such an AF (i.e., a closed source e-Procurement Solution)) the disadvantages would be significantly greater (e.g., (a) direct disadvantages: to companies that would incur significant costs in order to develop and resolve the system complexities of such an AF and (b) indirect disadvantages: to buyers and sellers that would adopt the derived proprietary Solution including significantly greater acquisition costs than a traditional closed source e-Procurement Solution (Quadrant II)).

Chapter 6
Contact Centers:
Tool for Effective E-Business

Rui Rijo

Institute for Systems and Computers Engineering at Coimbra & Research Center for Informatics and Communications- Polytechnic Institute of Leiria, Portugal

ABSTRACT

Often, small and medium enterprises consider the possibility of creating their own contact centre as a tool to improve the customer service. They pose some important questions about business and technical aspects: Why should we use a contact center solution? Which technologies, architectures, and solutions are available? Which key issues should be analyzed? The chapter provides specific information and practical guidelines about Contact Centers based on a literature review and interviews made to contact center business consultants specialized in the small and medium enterprises sector. The goal is to help top management and Information Technology responsible in making the best technological choices and methodological approaches.

INTRODUCTION

Most organizations, in all sectors of industry, commerce and government, are fundamentally dependent upon information systems (IS). Consequently, organizations have assumed that advances in information technology (IT) infrastructure and e-business systems will not only provide economic returns, but are an important element of business definition and competitive strategy (Bharadwaj,

2000; Johnston & Carrico, 1998; Santhanam & Hartono, 2003). However, two decades of IT performance research has shown that the link between IT investment and improved organizational performance is still elusive (Chan, 2000).

For example, 'productivity paradox' proponents claim that despite the massive investment in IT, these systems have not produced significant improvements in industrial productivity (Brynjolfsson, 1993; Thurow, 1991).

More recent reviews of IT productivity have produced encouraging results. Brynjolfsson and

DOI: 10.4018/978-1-60960-765-4.ch006

Hitt (1998) conclude that IT is valuable, even though its extent and dimension varies across organizations. The idea on IT business value can thus be summarized as follows: if the right IT is applied in the right way, improved business performance will result, conditional upon appropriate complementary investments in workplace practices and organizational structures and shaped by the competitive environment (Melville, Kraemer, & Gurbaxani, 2004; Varajão, 2002). IT and e-business are directly related. The e-business, is the use of electronic media, to review the business model, to redesign and to reposition the company and to obtain competitive advantages (Shankar, Urban, & Sultan, 2002).

Advances in e-business applications and technologies present many opportunities for contemporary businesses to redefine their strategic objectives and enhance or transform products, services, markets, work processes and business communication (Coltman, Devinney, & Midgley, 2007).

The Contact Centers are important tools that use electronic infra-structure and allow this business reformulation. A contact center covers a wide range of an organization's material and human resources with the aim to provide one or more services to users through a channel such as telephone, e-mail or the Web (Gans, Koole, & Mandelbaum, 2003; Koole & Mandelbaum, 2002).

The contact center formally appeared in the eighties (Cardoso, 2000; Gaballa & Pearce, 1979; Hawkins, Meier, Nainis, & James, 2001). At that time, the investment to start a contact center operation was only accessible to the large companies. However this situation changed. Due to its importance, contact centers play, currently, a central and decisive role for the small and medium enterprises (SME). Its growth in recent years makes them economically and socially relevant, being significant employers in several countries (Barros & Brandão, 2006; Holman, Batt, & Holtgrewe, 2007).

A contact center allows an organization to reduce costs either by reducing the need of a local presence either by improving the quality of the service. They are also a decisive tool to increase the profit by establishing a continued business relation with customers (Peppers & Rogers, 1999, 2004) in a process denominated customer relationship management (CRM).

They are considered "services factories" in a multidisciplinary area that crosses Marketing, Operational Research, Psychology, Sociology and Information Systems, among others (Gans et al., 2003). Therefore Contact Center's Information Systems projects are complex, involving a multiple kind of actors and interests.

Despite the efforts made in recent decades, information and communication technologies projects' still have modest success levels (Demarco, 1997; Ewusi-Mensah, 2003; Jones, 2004; Kappelman, McKeeman, & Zhang, 2006; Standish Group, 1996, 1998; Yetton, Martin, Sharma, & Johnston, 2000).

Thus, by its strategic, economic and social relevance, Contact Center's projects become the primary purpose of this chapter.

The main goals of the chapter are to provide insight for the top management and IT responsible in the following questions: Why should an organization use a contact center solution? Which technologies, architectures, and open-source solutions are available? Which key issues should be analyzed?

The remainder of this chapter is structured as follows: the next section gives some fundamental background for the Contact Centers and CRM understanding. The section "technologies and architectures" introduces three architectural types used in Contact Centers and emergent associated technologies. The subsequent section presents key issues that must be considered when developing a contact centre solution for a SME. The Chapter ends with considerations about issues, problems and future research directions.

BACKGROUND

Contact Centers are recent in the organizations. They formally appeared in the eighties and had a huge development in the last (almost) thirty years. The following sections make a brief historical resume and present some basic concepts about contact centers and their relation with CRM. This information is the basic block for the comprehension of the rest of the chapter and other further readings.

Contact Centres: Historical Perspective

It is possible to say that Contact Centers exist since organizations use telephones in the collaborator's desks.

The formal Call Center (predecessor of Contact Center) concept come from the eighties (Cardoso, 2000; Gaballa & Pearce, 1979; Hawkins et al., 2001). Till then the customers had always the option of calling to the organization and speak with a collaborator. At that time the telephone was the only existent technology. If the collaborator was not able to answer immediately to customer's requests then he would get customer's name and number to call back. In order to answer properly, the collaborator had to manually search records, files and other documents. Most of these elements were supported by paper. It was a very time consuming activity (Hawkins et al., 2001).

In the sixties and seventies, the advent of computers has enabled organizations to begin to improve its service to support users. Using computers, the collaborators have the means to obtain information on products, services and other issues more quickly, while talking with users. It was thus possible to reduce / eliminate the need for manual search and call back to the customer.

The Call Center then began to use switching equipment. However the firsts private branch exchanges (PBXs) were still very limited in their ability to support multiple calls and make its distribution (Koole & Mandelbaum, 2002). The PBX basically allowed a relation of one-to-one between a call and an operator.

The use of personal computers (PCs), in the eighties, simplified the control of telephone's functionality. The computers' performance made possible the management of considerable volumes of calls and their distribution to the operators of the Call Center that were (or were more) available. The development of the infrastructure and the growth of the capacity of the digital public telephone made possible the existence of first-line operators (also known as Call Center agents) accepting orders, checking inventory, processing claims and performing other operations. The organization managed to provide a complete service to its users by phone. This ability to provide a complete service through a phone call had a significant impact throughout the world on how to organize and conduct business (Hawkins et al., 2001).

The three main technological pillars of the calls centers today are the automatic call distributor (ACD), the computer telephony integration (CTI) and interactive voice response (IVR).

An ACD is a computerized phone system that responds to the caller, sometimes with a voice menu, and connects the call to the appropriate agent. It can also distribute calls equally to agents.

In the beginning of the nineties, the CTI technology arises. This technology allows a connection between the phone call and the context associated with the call, including personal data of the user, the requested service and any transactions executed during the call (Cardoso, 2000).

Developed, together with the CTI, the IVR technology enables an application to interact with a user, the automatic processing of requests, and the management of a phone call. IVR is an automated telephone that speaks to the caller with a combination of fixed voice menus and data extracted from databases in real time. The caller responds by pressing digits on the telephone, speaking words or short phrases. Applications include bank-by-phone, flight-scheduling information and automated order entry and tracking.

The ACD, the CTI, and IVR enable the distribution of hundreds of phone calls per day to specific operators, properly qualified to meet the demands of each user.

Agents' skills can be used to route calls. This routing based on agents' skills is called skills based routing (SBR) (Avramidis & L'Ecuyer, 2005; Koole & Mandelbaum, 2002). Agents can be organized upon their skills, for instance the ability to speak languages. If one call arrives and the system detects its geographical origin, it can be delivered to agents speaking the right language, providing a better service to the user.

This technology enabled the development of the concept of call center CRM, since the management of the relationship with users can be efficient and personalized regardless the number of customers that an organization have (Cardoso, 2000; Gans et al., 2003).

With the widespread use of channels of interaction beyond the phone, as e-mail, fax and web, the Call Center became Contact Center.

The concept of "waiting queue for phone calls" on the calls that were waiting to be met, was changed to a broader concept of "processing interactions queue", where this queue can have, besides calls, e-mail, Web interactions, fax, short message service (SMS), among others.

Contact Center comprehends a wide range of resources that allows the provision of services via one or more channels. This set of resources is typically made by operators that interact with users of the organization and information and communications support technology (Pichitlamken, Deslauriers, L'Ecuyer, & Avramidis, 2003).

The typical work environment of a Contact Center can be seen as a room with several cubicles in open-space in which people with headsets, the operators, are in front of computer terminals providing services through telephone, email, fax, Web, among others channels.

The need for management of interactions from different channels, its integration with existing systems in institutions and changes in strategy resulting from the interaction between technology, logistics, and human resources, has a complex set of problems associated (Adria & Chowdhury, 2004). The extension of the concept of Call Centers increases the responsiveness of organizations but it also increases the complexity of the processes, of the technology involved and the management of human resources (HR).

The Contact Center is a competitive factor in businesses since it enables (Adria & Chowdhury, 2004; Borst, Mandelbaum, & Reiman, 2004; Cardoso, 2000; Gans et al., 2003): control and costs reduction, increased efficiency and quality of service, increased productivity, make use of of customers' preferred channels in an efficient way (phone, email, fax, sms, and Web), intensive use of the phone (fixed and mobile), the retention and acquisition of new customers through CRM approaches, increase customers' loyalty, by improving the quality of service, and implementation of procedures for remote business management.

Currently, the field of Contact Centres is an industry with a growth rate of over 8% per year. It is expected to continue this way in the coming years (Aksin, Armony, & Mehrotra, 2007; Holman et al., 2007).

After this brief historical overview, the next section will introduce the main concepts and definitions to support the understanding of the rest of the chapter and other related publications.

Concepts and Definitions

The customer relationship management (CRM) is a comprehensive business and marketing strategy that integrates technology, process, and all business activities around the customer (Anton, 1996; Anton & Hoeck, 2002). It is mostly defined in terms of the acquisition and retention of customers and the resulting profitability (Nykamp, 2001).

Companies need the ability to track and manage events that may demand immediate, personalized response irrespective of conventional operating schedules. In particular, most companies are confronted with an increasingly sophisticated customer base that demands a higher level of immediate service across multiple access channels. To satisfy customer needs, companies have to maintain consistency across all interaction channels e.g. telephone, email, Web, fax, and across all areas of a company a customer interacts with, namely sales, service, and marketing.

To overcome this challenge, many organizations are considering adopting the concept of electronic Customer Relationship Management (e-CRM). This concept and practice provides the ability to capture, integrate, and distribute data gained throughout the enterprise. Contact Centres are the tool that organizations use to interact with customers. This interaction, supported by electronic means, permits the gathering of critical business data e.g. customers' preferences, trends, and new opportunities. This data can be mined and used in the definition of the company's business to offer new products, to personalized customer contact, to increase services' quality. This differentiates the company and opens the door to a continuum and profitable relationship.

The Contact Centres offer multiple services outside the organization, such as technical support, commercial support, clarification of doubts, orders registration, home-banking, medical support, emergencies services, among others. These services, where prevails the contact from outside the organization to the Contact Centre, are known as inbound services (Koole & Mandelbaum, 2002).

The Contact Centre also allows the execution of sales campaigns, products promotion, inquiries, suppliers' requests, debt collection and others. The surveys can be, for example, to check users' satisfaction, market surveys, vote intentions, or socio-economic studies. All these services, in which predominates the contact of the organization with the outside, are known as outbound services or campaigns (Pichitlamken et al., 2003).

Every contact between a user and the Contact Centre is called an interaction. Users can be, for example, customers, suppliers, and the general public, according to the characteristics of the service provided by the organization and its relationship with the user. An interaction can be inbound, if it started from the user, or outbound, if it started from the centre (Koole & Mandelbaum, 2002).

Inbound interactions are, for example, a call from a user to an organization to request the execution of an order, an e-mail to a travel agent to request a quote or a call to a bank to request help for an operation on the bank's website.

In addition to the calls from one agent to a customer, for example, to respond to a previous request made in an inbound interaction, outbound interactions are usually associated with outbound campaigns. These consist in the establishment of continuous calls to a list of users for debts collection, the conduct of an investigation, an opinion survey or a promotional campaign for a product or a service. The channel used in an interaction can be the voice (mobile or fixed phone), e-mail, fax, the Web, chat, SMS and others. The Web channel is here considered as the channel that allows the execution of requests and their processing through a website. Requests may be orders of products or services and all the processing associated with them. Therefore, the Web and chat channels are considered here as different channels.

The Web channel as well as the IVR, is a self-service channel, i.e. a channel where the user performs a set of operations ranging from the collection of information and simulation, to requests and orders without operator's intervention (Cardoso, 2000).

The phone, e-mail, fax and chat are examples of assisted channels, i.e. interaction channels that require the participation of an operator for each interaction (Demaria, 2005). The self-service channels involve an average cost per interaction from 10 to 15 times lower than the assisted ones

(Cardoso, 2000). When users move from assisted to self-service channels, organizations benefit from a considerable costs reduction.

The interactions generate large amounts of information. The information generated can be divided into three major categories (Gans et al., 2003; Koole & Mandelbaum, 2002):

- The interaction itself: when it started, which actions were taken in the IVR and how long it took each action, whether and for how long the interaction was on hold, and processed by whom;
- The business associated with the interaction: it generated a sale? It generated a new business opportunity? Became Cross-Selling/Up-Selling? Was it a complaint? Information request?
- Information of psychological type, obtained from surveys. Surveys' target may be the users, the operators and the managers. Was the customer satisfied? Did the agent "smiled" on the telephone?
- • Information on the interaction itself: when it started, what actions were taken in the IVR and how long it took each action, whether and for how long, the interaction was expected, whether and for how long, and the interaction was seen by that operator; • Information on business generated from the interaction: it was generated a sale? It generated a new business opportunity? There was cross-selling/up-selling? This was a claim? Request for information? • Information of psychological type, obtained from surveys of users, operators and managers.

This information is important (Gans et al., 2003; Koole & Mandelbaum, 2002) since it provides:

- Historical data as the main input for the resources planning;

- Real-time indicators for supervisors, making them able to react in real time with proper matching of available resources;
- Management indicators, such as whether the number of complaints increased, or which were the most profitable customers, or even which is the cost per interaction;
- MetricMM of agent's performance, and business operation of the Contact Center.

Actually, Gans and Mandelbaum (Gans et al., 2003) typically find that the Contact Centres do not store or analyze the logs of individual interactions due to the high cost of maintaining databases of large size. Another reason is that the software applications used to manage Contact Centres almost only use simple models based on the summary of statistics. Finally, this is also due to the lack of knowledge of why and how they should implement and use more detailed analysis.

The centres usually summarize the detailed information of calls from the automatic call distributor (ACD) and other related systems in averages calculated in short intervals of time (usually in periods of 30 minutes). An ACD is a computerized phone system that responds to the caller, sometimes with a voice menu, and connects the call to the appropriate agent. It can also distribute calls equally to agents. ACDs are the heart of contact centres, which are widely used in the telephone sales and service departments of all organizations. ACDs can incorporate SBR and some can also route e-mail, faxes, Web-initiated calls and callback requests.

Because the voice channel is the most widely used and because historically was the first to appear, the names and concepts of the existing indicators are closely linked to the phone. They can be extended to the other channels.

ACD's indicators, for a given period of time, are (Avramidis, N., Deslauriers, & L'Ecuyer, 2004):

- Incoming calls [Recvd], also sometimes referred to as calls offered, is the total number of calls that reached the Contact Center in the time period considered. It should be noted that the number of calls that are processed by the ACD may be substantially less than the number of calls that reach the Contact Center, as [Recvd] does not take into account the signs of busy, occurring in the telephone network (e.g. PSTN) and the PABX (when no lines available, the calls do not reach the ACD. Furthermore, in some business areas, eighty percent of the calls that reach the Contact Center are processed by IVRs;

- Answered also sometimes referred to as processed calls, is the number of calls that were answered by operators;
- Abandoned [Abn%], percentage of incoming calls that were abandoned before being answered (equal to (1 – ([Answ] ÷ [Recvd]) * 100%). [Abn%] is an average major congestion on the system;
- Average Speed of Answer [ASA], the time that calls were waiting (on hold) to be answered by an operator. As [ASA] excludes the waiting time of calls that resulted in abandoned, with the aim of having reasonable indicators of the level of congestion of a Contact Center, the values of [ASA] and

[Abn%] should both be considered average length of service [ASA4].;
- Target Service Factor [TSF], is the fraction of calls which the waiting time exceeds a specified target time. Typically the target time is 20 to 30 seconds. Some *Contact Centers* also report the maximum waiting time occurred in the range of analysis.

These concepts about contact centre data are relevant for the correct choices when designing the contact centre as explained in the further sections.

While the reports may vary from Contact Centre's ACD to Contact Centre's ACD, the reports almost always contain statistics within the four categories shown in table 1 (Gans et al., 2003):

- Number of arrivals and abandonment calls;
- Average service time;
- Time use by agents;
- Delay in the queue.

This, induces that centres can be viewed and analyzed as queuing systems.

Figure 1 is an operational diagram of a Contact Centre with only simple interactions of inbound and voice that shows the relationship between waiting queues systems and Contact Centers (Adria &

Figure 1. Contact centre as a queuing system (Source: Adapted from (Koole & Mandelbaum, 2002))

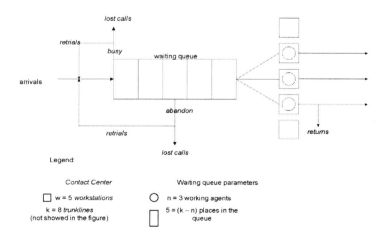

Chowdhury, 2004; Aksin & Harker, 2003; Atlason, Epelman, & Henderson, 2004; Borst et al., 2004; Pichitlamken et al., 2003).

The example discussed here can illustrate the fundamentals of Contact Centre as a queuing system. It uses the voice channel because it is the predominant channel and historically the oldest. It can be adapted to the other types of interaction.

A set of k lines (trunk lines) "offers" calls to the Contact Centre. Consider w ≤ k workstations, also referred to as positions in which a group of agents n ≤ w handles calls.

A call that arrives (inbound call) and finds all k lines busy, receive a busy signal not entering in the system. If at least one line is available, the call is "provided" to the Contact Centre occupying one of the lines that were available.

If less than n operators are busy, the call is answered immediately and processed (or served).. If, on the other hand, the system has more than n but less than k calls, the inbound call waits in queue for an available agent.

Users that become impatient abandon the queue (hang-up) before being served. For users who wait for and are attended by an operator, the order of service is first-in, first-out (FIFO).

When a call leaves the system frees the resources – the line, the workstation and the agent – making them available for other calls. Some fraction of calls that are not processed, result in new attempts (retrials) to obtain the service. The other calls, which are abandoned or blocked because there are no lines available, are lost (lost calls). Finally, users already served, may return to the system (returns). These returns may be due to a demand for new services that generate new business, and in this case can be seen as good, but on the other hand, may be due to problems with the original service, in this case are seen as bad (Gans et al., 2003).

Thus, the number of lines k acts as an upper limit on the number of calls that may exist in the system, either waiting or being processed. Similarly, the number of agents to process calls, n ≤ w, defines the maximum number of calls that can be served simultaneously. Throughout the day, the supervisors can change dynamically the number of working agents in order to match satisfactorily the number of calls that arrive.

Less often, if the technology is available, the supervisors may also vary the number of active lines to the outside.

For each fixed n it is possible to create a waiting queue model in which users are customers, agents are the servers, and the queue has the users that are waiting to be served by the agents. When n changes, the number of places in the waiting queue, (k – n), changes too.

As shown in Figure 1, the primitives of the model for this system include statistics for the arrivals of calls, their processing time and number of abandoned calls. The outputs of the model include the fraction of users who abandon the call, the distribution of waiting time in the queue, and the fraction of time that agents are busy.

These types of models are widely used in the Contact Centres management. The most used and simplest model is the waiting queue M / M / N as known as Erlang C (Koole & Mandelbaum, 2002).

In most situations, however, this model represents a simplification of reality. Looking to the Figure 1, it is easy to see that the treatment of the busy signs, the impatience of the user and the multiple visits by users are not considered (Avramidis & L'Ecuyer, 2005; Koole & Mandelbaum, 2002). They are represented only as outputs of the system and not as new entries that feed the system.

In practice, the processes of the services offered are much more complex than those presented. For example, the use of an IVR, with which users interact before joining the agents queue, establishes two in-line queues, the first is the IVR queue followed by the agents queue. Another example, the use of an information system (IS) adds a centralized resource whose capacity is shared by the set of active agents and other entities besides the Contact Centre. This can strangle the Contact Centre slowing the response time of the agents.

Figure 2. Centralized contact centre

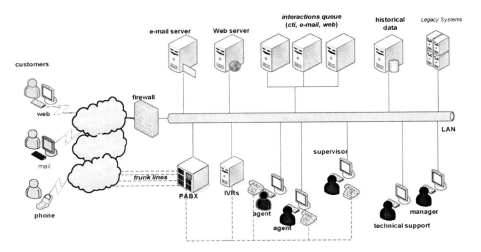

The scenario may also become more complex if we consider multiple teams of agents who are geographically dispersed over several interconnected Contact Centres with different variations of load and with different types of users. Many different technologies and architectures may be applied in the Contact Centre design. The most relevant ones are presented in the next section.

TECHNOLOGIES AND ARCHITECTURES

The Contact Centre is a powerful e-CRM tool. This section presents three main possible architectures and associated technologies.

These architectures, centralized, distributed, and hosted may be used in conjugation generating hybrid ones suiting the organization's specific requirements. Furthermore, several different technologies may be used in the architectures. There is any specific match between architecture and technology.

Centralized Contact Centre

A centralized Contact Centre, as showed in Figure 2, has a technological infrastructure based on a single server or multiple servers, from the physical point of view, but a single one from the logical point of view, and is usually supported on a local network.

The interactions, when they reach the Contact Centre, are placed in one single queue regardless of the channel (Demaria, 2005).

The system handles each interaction according to a configurable priority. For example, it is usual to treat synchronous interactions like voice and Web collaboration in real time. E-mail and fax interactions, for example, are asynchronous interactions, and may be handled offline (Koole & Mandelbaum, 2002).

Distributed Contact Centre

Distributed Contact Centre, as showed in Figure 3, represents an evolution of centralized contact centre, enabling to overcome the geographical and time zone barriers. With the Distributed Contact Centre an organization may operate in multiple geographical distinct places, sometimes with very

Figure 3. Distributed contact centre

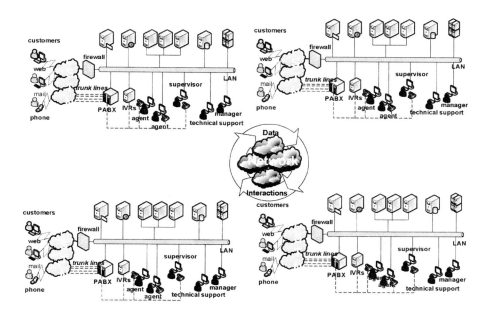

different time zones, and thus offering a service 24 hours over 24 hours. It also makes possible the load balancing (Whitt, 2005).

The basic idea of distributed contact centre is to have a set of centralized contact centres communicating and working as if they are a single one. For example, if a user tries to access the contact centre in her/his geographical area and if the centre is already closed or not responding due to an overload, then the interaction is routed to another contact centre that is available. With this architecture, the interaction can be processed by the agent with all the necessary information (Whitt, 2005). In the end, the original Contact Centre is updated with the results of the interaction thus ensuring information consistency.

Hosted Contact Center

The hosted contact centre, as showed in Figure 4, is composed of a central system responsible for the overall management of an interaction, since its entry into the system and its routing to the operator with the appropriate profile until its

finish and record of the information. This information regards the business component and the interaction component.

This central system can respond to multiple contact centres of various organizations. In figure 4, organizations A and B are supported on the same central system. Thus, organizations need only to install the agents' workstations on their side. All the processing is performed from the central system (Demaria, 2005). The control of the interactions is achieved by using session initiation protocol (SIP) and real time transport protocol (RTP). The hosted model works on an software as a service (SaaS) basis, where the computer-based service is provided to customers over a network. The organization pays a fee (usually a monthly fee) for the use of each workstation and the communications.

This model allows the organizations to overcome the problem of the initial investment, which is one of the greatest barriers to the adoption of a centre. In this way, the risk of investing in a contact centre is minimized. This model allows the adjustment of the number of agents, accord-

Figure 4. Hosted contact centre

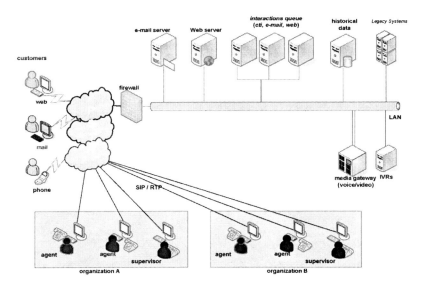

ing to the amount of work. More recently, contact centre technology is based on Voice over IP (VoIP) gateways. With VoIP and an SaaS model, the agent only needs a computer, a network connection, and a microphone to work. VoIP enables the realization of voice calls, with or without video, depending on the option. In this way the initial investment and the total cost of ownership (TCO) is reduced.

Associated and Emerging Technologies

Advances in automation technologies, such as speech recognition (SR) (Zitouni, Hong-Kwang, Kuo, & Lee, 2003) and text-to-speech (TTS) have a significant impact in the interactions design, e.g. IVR, Web and agent-customer interactions.

SR technologies enable speech recognition and their translation into manipulated symbols. It enables a human-machine interaction without any kind of keyboards (Zitouni et al., 2003).

The translation of written text in articulate speech will overcome the usual limitations of IVR where each message presented to the user

was previously recorded, reducing in this way the flexibility of the solutions.

These technologies combined with artificial intelligence systems will have a strong impact on the time needed to complete the tasks, affecting not only the effectiveness of the system but also the level of user satisfaction and even their behaviour.

Due to the proliferation of mobile phones and generalization of the messages on mobile phones (SMS), this interaction channel was included in the Contact Centers.

The VoIP technology has received much attention lately. The contact centers are beginning to migrate from PBXs based on time division multiplexing (TDM) to IP communications centers in order to save money on local and long distance calls.

Additionally, the use of VoIP permits the use of a single communications infrastructure as opposed to the traditional solution of having one network for voice and other data.

In order to monitor the quality of service and / or record excerpts of conversations when, for example, occurs the acceptance of a product by a customer, there are call recording systems that enable the recording of phone calls.

These moments are recorded and archived in a way that it is always possible, at any moment, hear the recording just searching on a database by an agent, an operator or a date / time (Demaria, 2005).

Moreover, it is sometimes important the listening of a talk by a more skilled operator helping, for example, a less skilled one. This operation is based on whispering technology.

In most existent systems, operators can make already all the phone operations using soft phones.

We are moving on a convergence of technologies. The PBX is giving its place to the communications server. This server aggregates PBX functionalities with web server, e-mail server and VoIP gateway (Demaria, 2005).

One of the most important open source projects in PBX convergence is the Asterisk. Asterisk (http://www.asterisk.org/) is an open source, converged telephony platform, originally created in 1999 by Mark Spencer of Digium (http://www.digium.com/). It is designed primarily to run on Linux. Asterisk is a robust suite of tightly integrated telecommunications applications. The power of Asterisk lies in its customizable nature, complemented by unmatched standards compliance.

Applications such as voicemail, hosted conferencing, call queuing and agents, music on hold, and call parking are all standard features built right into the software. Asterisk can also integrate with other business technologies.

Asterisk is released under a dual license model, using the GNU General Public License (GPL) as a free software license and a proprietary software license to permit licensees to distribute proprietary, unpublished system components.

Due to free licensing of the software, hundreds of community programmers have contributed features and functionality and have reported and corrected bugs. Originally designed for Linux, Asterisk now also runs on a variety of different operating systems including NetBSD, OpenBSD, FreeBSD, Mac OS X, and Solaris. A port to Microsoft Windows is known as AsteriskWin32.

A key issue when using the Asterisk is the configuration. As in most Linux environments, Asterisk is well suited to growing with organisation's needs: a small system that used to be able to handle all your call-processing and peripheral tasks can be distributed among several servers when increased demands exceed its abilities. Flexibility is a key reason why Asterisk is extremely cost-effective for rapidly growing businesses; there is no effective maximum or minimum size to consider when budgeting the initial purchase.

KEY ISSUES FOR DEVELOPING A CONTACT CENTRE SOLUTION

All interviewees are unanimous in considering that the work must start from the strategic and organizational issues to the technical ones.

The first question is: how the Contact Center will allow the company to achieve its strategic goals?

A contact center must be aligned and included in the strategy of the company. Business domain, geographical environment, and users' needs influence strategy definition. Many organizations decide to implement a contact center in order to improve their performance and competitiveness. Others, having already a contact center, decide to create or reformulate services provided by the center.

Does the company want to reduce costs using, for instance, the Contact Center as the main contact point replacing the local presence? Does it want to differentiate from the competition providing a better customer service, for instance a post-selling service? Or just to offer an internal Contact Center to support the sales force or the technical teams? Use the Contact Center to improve the performance of the sales account? Create a sales campaign? Promotional or marketing advising campaigns? Satisfaction inquiries?

The second question is related with the importance of the services/campaigns provided by the Contact Center and the company's core business. If the services represent the core business or use critical and confidential information then the Contact Center probably will be an in-house one.

The third question is to analyze the periodicity of the Contact Center's actions. Are the services permanents or periodic, in time? If the idea is to make sales or marketing campaigns or a monthly inquiry the outsourcing possibility is very strong.

If the company needs to provide a permanent set of services, the first step is to identify and document the processes that already exist and will be fully or partially supported by the Contact Center. If there is no documentation about the existent processes then it is better to use a flowchart or unified modeling language (UML) use case diagrams to document them. Each step of each process must be identified. The temporal and conditional relations between the steps, who has the responsibility, and which information is needed to achieve them must also be included in the documentation.

After this identification and documentation, the processes must be re-analyzed. They must de re-designed. It is necessary to verify which steps will be done by the Contact Center and how. In a medium sized Contact Center, this may suggest the use of skills base routing.

At this moment it is also important to select the proper interaction channels to use. The channels will influence the re-design work of the processes. Interaction channels can be classified logically as self-serviced or assisted (Cardoso, 2000). Assisted channels, such as telephone, fax, e-mail, and chat, demand agents to process the interaction. Self-service channels like IVR, wap, web site and others do not need agent intervention. Telephone and e-mail are the most considered channels. There is a growth in the use of chat and sms.

Interactions have two main components, the relational component and the transactional component. It is necessary to analyze both com-

ponents when deciding if an interaction can be automatic (e.g. using a self-service channel). Pure transactional interactions, like, for instance, a bank account transaction, tend to be supported by automatic channels. Relational transactions like, for instance, a financial investment, demand human interaction because the customers want to have an expert's opinion and more data to make a decision.

In order to reduce costs, organizations try to maximize the use of self-service channels. However, the choice of a channel must take into account the target audience. Characteristics like technology environment, user's age or culture must be analyzed. Another important issue is the use of assisted channels to conduct users, gradually, to self-service channels (Cardoso, 2000). Every time a user requests an operation that can be done automatically, the agent should teach and encourage the use of self-service channel. Last, but not least, all self-service channels must have an option to permit direct contact to an agent. A user that does not find a solution for some difficulty tends to give up and lose confidence in the service. Channel selection must take into account some factors, among others, organization strategy and image, how usually organization interacts with its users, target public profile (e.g. age, sex, culture, technological skills), and product and service characteristics like service level.

With the correct choice of channels it is possible the re-design of the processes. The new processes must also be documented using also a flowchart or UML use cases diagrams. Most of the times they become more simplified, easier to understand and with fewer steps. Based on the information needed for each step it is now possible to identify which integrations must be made between existing systems and the Contact Center. For SMEs, most of the times, the agents use existing applications with some adjustments. These adjustments include, for example, the interaction information, time, channel, duration, or number of the caller.

Another approach is to use the Contact Center application to work as an information aggregator of all existing applications. The idea is that the agent's application can use information from several existent sources, showing it in an organized way to the agent and allowing her/him to interact efficiently with the customer (internal or external). At the end of the interaction, the information gathered is stored in each source accordingly.

The join of the business information with the interaction information is the necessary data for CRM analysis. As a Contact Center generates a huge amount of information it is critical to choose which information to register and how to manipulate it. As noted in the concepts and definitions section this information provides relevant business indicators for strategy decisions.

Independently of the approach, the steps of the processes and their information constitute the skeleton of the flow of the interaction for the agents and IVRs. This flow is also called a script. This script will guide the agent in the interaction with the customer. It gives her/him information about what to do with each type of client, treating her/him in a personalized way. Agents are organizations' face to customers, so keeping and increasing the relationship between the agent and the organization is one of the most important goals of the contact center.

Another important issue is the dimensioning. Correct dimensioning is critical because the workforce represents about seventy percent of the operational cost of a contact center. Well-designed Contact Centers information systems reduce the number of necessary agents. On the other hand, the number of agents influences technology, system architecture, processes, among other relevant aspects.

Contact centers are dimensioned to answer inbound requests and to do outbound work. Dimensioning outbound is easier than dimensioning inbound work. The associated planning actions are forecasting, staffing and scheduling (Avramidis & L'Ecuyer, 2005; Gans et al., 2003).

Inbound dimensioning requires the estimation of expected volume (number of expected interactions), expected interaction durations, expected distribution by day/month/year, and target service level. This data allows the use of Erlang statistical distributions to calculate the number of necessary agents (Gans et al., 2003). Erlang distributions are also used with IVRs. IVR will deal with a certain percentage of the calls, so an Erlang distribution is used to estimate the number of calls that will be processed by IVRs, and consequently the number of necessary IVRs. Regarding the remaining calls – global volume of expected calls subtracted by the number of calls processed by IVRs – Erlang distributions allows determining how many agents are needed. The same approach is used to make skills estimations. Based on the historic of interactions, it is possible to identify the percentage of calls for each skill, and then calculate the number of necessary agents for each skill.

Outbound dimensioning requires definition of target volume, forecast of average interaction duration, and a goal for the percentage of successful contacts. This goal is a very important parameter to set the number of agents. The higher the percentage of success required, the higher the number of operation hours required. The marginal growth in percentage has a great impact. For instance, the number of agents and effort required to grow from seventy to seventy five percent is higher than to grow from ten to thirty percent. The decision about the number of agents can be done in two steps. The first step is to calculate the number of hours of operation based on the number of contacts, percentage of success wanted and average interaction duration. The second step, based on the number of hours, is to determine the number of necessary agents. That depends on the profiles of the available agents, if they are working at full-time or part-time, and others. It depends also on the schedule of projects and distribution of load along the day.

Either in inbound, outbound, or both, growth forecast for the contact center is important for dimensioning.

With the answers to the previous questions it is time to analyze the in-house or outsourcing decision. The outsourcer solution transforms the initial infrastructure investment (usually high) into operational costs, reduces setup-time and avoids a long learning curve. An outsourcer adds experience but also adds the complexity of managing a third party. This additional cost can be also a benefit, because it requires more control and attention from the organization. Organizations with in-house operations sometimes lose this control and attention. Confidentiality, control, and operation of internal resources are main reasons to implement in-house operations. An interesting solution is the mixed model, in-house and outsourcing at the same time. With this solution, it is possible to have the best of both worlds. The organization uses its business knowledge, experience and processes, and gets know-how from the contact center from the outsourcer.

Many Contact Centre initiatives often fail because implementation was limited to software installation, without providing the context, support and understanding for employees to learn, and take full advantage of the information systems. Tools for Contact Centre management should be implemented only after a well-devised strategy and operational plan are put in place.

The final step is to define a road-map with which processes, services and channels will start the operation in the contact center and the evolution and growing of the contact center in time. The learning curve in how to operate with a contact center is long, that is why the Contact Center must growth as the company gain insight.

FUTURE RESEARCH DIRECTIONS

Due to its multidisciplinary characteristic, Contact Center research crosses multiple disciplines.

In psychology some main research interests are related with the behavior of the agents and the customers. Operational Research identifies the formulas that describe the behavior of the queuing system underlying the Contact Center. Psychology, Marketing and Information Systems try to improve the techniques for a better Customer Relationship Management. In particular, the Information Systems search for the best architectures and technologies to improve agents' performance and the management of information in order to produce relevant knowledge for the companies.

In this way, the use of VoIP interactions, speech recognition, text mining, data mining represent some research lines. Another interesting trend is the use of social networks and their impact in the relation between the customer and the organization.

For the SMEs the challenges are huge. How, with limited budget, is it possible to grow in number of customers and transactions in a smoothly way? Which are the best tools, techniques and architectures to implement a strategy of sustainable growth?

Despite the effort made in the research, these questions remain and claim a persistent effort.

CONCLUSION

Contact Centers are a powerful e-business tool. For a long time this tool was inaccessible for the SMEs. This chapter provides an overview of the Contact Center area. It introduces a solid theoretical ground about the key concepts of the Contact Centers, the existing technologies, and possible architectures.

Furthermore it focuses the main issues for the SMEs, namely why and how to use the Contact Center to improve the relation between the customer and the organization. It provides a practical roadmap with the steps and questions that a SME must consider before, during, and after the implementation of the Contact Center.

As referred in the literature, the relation between the adoption of technology and productivity is not direct. The correct use of the right technology in the right time on the other hand can create a competitive advantage for an organization. This work intends to help in this challenging task of making the adequate choices for each organization when deciding to use the Contact Center as a (powerful) tool for e-business.

REFERENCES

Adria, M., & Chowdhury, S. (2004). Centralization as a design consideration for the management of call centers. *Information & Management, 41,* 497–507. doi:10.1016/S0378-7206(03)00087-9

Aksin, O. Z., Armony, M., & Mehrotra, V. (2007). (forthcoming). The modern call-center: A multi-disciplinary perspective on operations management research. *Production and Operations Management.*

Aksin, O. Z., & Harker, P. T. (2003). Capacity sizing in the presence of a common shared resource: Dimensioning an inbound call center. *European Journal of Operational Research, 147*(3), 464–483. doi:10.1016/S0377-2217(02)00274-6

Anton, J. (1996). *Customer relationship management.* New York, NY: Prentice-Hall.

Anton, J., & Hoeck, M. (2002). *E-business customer service.* Santa Monica, CA: The Anton Press.

Atlason, J., Epelman, M. A., & Henderson, S. G. (2004). Call center staffing with simulation and cutting plane methods. *Annals of Operations Research, 127,* 333–358. doi:10.1023/B:ANOR.0000019095.91642.bb

Avramidis, A. N., & L'Ecuyer, P. (2005). *Modeling and simulation of call centers.* Paper presented at the Proceedings of the 2005 Winter Simulation Conference.

Avramidis, N. A., Deslauriers, A., & L'Ecuyer, P. (2004). Modeling daily arrivals to a telephone call center. *Management Science, 50*(7), 896–908. doi:10.1287/mnsc.1040.0236

Barros, A., & Brandão, M. R. (2006). *Estudo diagnóstico e benchmarking da actividade de Contact Centers.* Lisboa, Portugal: Associação Portuguesa de Contact Centers e IZO.

Bharadwaj, A. S. (2000). A resource-based perspective on Information Technology capability and firm performance: An empirical investigation. *Management Information Systems Quarterly, 24*(1), 169–196. doi:10.2307/3250983

Borst, S., Mandelbaum, A., & Reiman, M. I. (2004). Dimensioning large call centers. *Operations Research, 52,* 17–34. doi:10.1287/opre.1030.0081

Brynjolfsson, E. (1993). The productivity paradox of Information Technology. *Communications of the ACM, 36*(12), 67–77. doi:10.1145/163298.163309

Brynjolfsson, E., & Hitt, L. M. (1998). Beyond the productivity paradox. *Communications of the ACM, 41*(8), 49–55. doi:10.1145/280324.280332

Cardoso, J. (2000). *Unified customer interaction™: Gestão do relacionamento num Ambiente Misto de Interacção Self e Assistida.* Lisboa: Centro Atlântico.

Chan, Y. E. (2000). IT value: The great divide between qualitative and quantitative and individual and organizational measures. *Journal of Management Information Systems, 16*(4), 225–261.

Coltman, T. R., Devinney, T. M., & Midgley, D. F. (2007). E-business strategy and firm performance: a latent class assessment of the drivers and impediments to success. *Journal of Information Technology, 27,* 87–101. doi:10.1057/palgrave.jit.2000073

Demarco, T. (1997). *The deadline.* New York, NY: Dorset House Publishing.

Demaria, M. J. (2005). IP: Right call for the contact center, RFI analysis. *Network Computing, 16*, 41–57.

Ewusi-Mensah, K. (2003). *Software development failures*. Cambridge, MA: MIT Press.

Gaballa, A., & Pearce, W. (1979). Telephone sales manpower planning at Qantas. *Interfaces, 9*(3), 1–9. doi:10.1287/inte.9.3.1

Gans, N., Koole, G., & Mandelbaum, A. (2003). Telephone call centers: Tutorial, review and research prospects. *Manufacturing & Service Operations Management, 5*(2), 79–141. doi:10.1287/msom.5.2.79.16071

Hawkins, L., Meier, T., Nainis, W. S., & James, H. M. (2001). *The evolution of the call center to customer contact center*. ITSC - Information Technology Support Center.

Holman, D., Batt, R., & Holtgrewe, U. (2007). *The global contact center report: International perspectives on management and employment*.

Johnston, R. H., & Carrico, S. R. (1998). Developing capabilities to use information strategically. *Management Information Systems Quarterly, 12*(1), 37–47. doi:10.2307/248801

Jones, C. (2004). Software project management practices: Failure versus success. *CrossTalk: The Journal of Defense Software Engineering*, 5-9.

Kappelman, L. A., McKeeman, R., & Zhang, L. (2006). Early warnings signs of IT project failure: The dominant dozen. *Information Systems Management*. Retrieved at February 9 2008, from http://www.ism-journal.com/ITToday/projectfailure.pdf

Koole, G., & Mandelbaum, A. (2002). Queueing models of call centers: An introduction. *Annals of Operations Research, 113*, 41–59. doi:10.1023/A:1020949626017

Melville, N., Kraemer, K., & Gurbaxani, V. (2004). Information Technology and organizational performance: An integrative model of IT business value. *Management Information Systems Quarterly, 28*(2), 283–322.

Nykamp, M. (2001). *The customer differential: The complete guide to implementing customer relationship management*. New York, NY: American Management Association.

Peppers, D., & Rogers, M. (1999). *Enterprise one to one*. Currency.

Peppers, D., & Rogers, M. (2004). *Managing customer relationships: A strategic framework*. John Wiley & Sons.

Pichitlamken, J., Deslauriers, A., L'Ecuyer, P., & Avramidis, A. N. (2003). *Modelling and simulation of a telephone call center*. Paper presented at the 2003 Winter Simulation Conference.

Santhanam, R., & Hartono, E. (2003). Issues in linking IT capability to firm performance. *Management Information Systems Quarterly, 27*(1), 125–153.

Shankar, V., Urban, G., & Sultan, F. (2002). Online trust: A stakeholder perspective, concepts, implications and future directions. *The Journal of Strategic Information Systems, 11*, 325–344. doi:10.1016/S0963-8687(02)00022-7

Standish Group. (1996). *Unfinished voyages*. Retrieved July 20, 2009, from http://www.standishgroup.com/sample_research/unfinished_voyages_1.php

Standish Group. (1998). *Chaos: A recipe for success*. Retrieved July 20 2009, from http://www.standishgroup.com/sample_research/PDFpages/chaos1998.pdf

Thurow, L. C. (1991). Foreword. In Scott-Morton, M. (Ed.), *The corporation of 1990's: Information Technology and organizational transformation* (pp. v–vii). New York, NY: Oxford University Press.

Varajão, J. E. Q. (2002). *Função de Sistemas de Informação - Contributos para a melhoria do sucesso da adopção de tecnologias de informação e desenvolvimento de sistemas de informação nas organizações*. Unpublished doctoral dissertation, Universidade do Minho, Guimarães.

Whitt, W. (2005). Engineering solution of basic call center model. *Management Science, 51*(2), 221–235. doi:10.1287/mnsc.1040.0302

Yetton, P., Martin, A., Sharma, R., & Johnston, K. (2000). A model of Information Systems project performance. *Information Systems Journal, 10*, 263–289. doi:10.1046/j.1365-2575.2000.00088.x

Zitouni, I., Hong-Kwang, Kuo, J., & Lee, C. H. (2003). Boosting and combination of classifiers for natural language call routing systems. *Speech Communication, 41*, 647–661. doi:10.1016/S0167-6393(03)00103-1

Chapter 7
E–Parking:
An Electronic Parking Service Using Wireless Networks

Gongjun Yan
Indiana University, USA

Stephan Olariu
Old Dominion University, USA

Weiming Yang
Old Dominion University, USA

Danda B. Rawat
Old Dominion University, USA

ABSTRACT

Parking is costly and limited in almost every major city in the world. The misparking aggravates the competition of parking slots. Innovative parking systems for meeting near-term parking demand are needed. We propose a novel parking system which adopts the wireless network and sensor technologies to provide an intelligent and automatic parking service. The implementation and a probabilistic analysis of the new parking service are presented as well.

The advantage of this parking system, from the drivers' point of view, is the best quality of service. The drivers will be informed the detailed information, i.e. the vacant parking slots and the route to the slot. The drivers can park without searching slots. The parking process is a non-stop experience. From the investor's view, the electronic parking system proposed in the chapter is an efficient system in utilization of slots and the maintenance cost. More importantly, it is more profitable.

1. INTRODUCTION

Parking is limited and challenging in many big cities. For example, the Manhattan Central Business District (CBD) has 109,222 off-street public parking spots, for a ratio of approximately one off-street public spot for every 16 CBD workers. Yet, often parking spots are wasted. In large parking lots, a driver may exit the lot without knowing about new spots that have just become vacant. It is a common experience that finding

DOI: 10.4018/978-1-60960-765-4.ch007

a parking slot in a busy airport may take half an hour or even more than one hour of time searing a vacant parking slot.

Parking is a common business in the world since vehicles are invented. In the cybertimes, the parking service can be turned into an electronic parking service (E-Parking) and a wireless network aided intelligent service. It is network based system because the vacancy of the slots can be transmitted thousands miles away from the actual parking lot. It is also an intelligent system because the drivers can be informed the best match of their need, for example, the cheapest slots in the lot or the closest lot to a shopping center. Traditional parking system is basically a blind try to the vacancy of the parking lot because drivers do not know the vacancy of the parking lot. The very first parking model is the Rényi's parking (Finch, 2003) where vehicles can randomly park along the street, no slot no restriction. A more advanced parking system is a slotted parking system where vehicles have to park in a slot. With electronic devices, parking lot can use counters and electronic screen to show passing-by drivers how many vacant slots left in the parking lot.

In this chapter, we will address a novel electronic and intelligent parking system. The advantage of this parking system, from the drivers' point of view, is the best quality of service. The drivers will be informed the detailed information, such as the distribution of vacant parking slots and the route of how to reach the slot. The drivers will save time to straight head the slot. The parking process is a non-stop experience. From the investor's view, the electronic parking system proposed in the chapter is an efficient system in utilization of slots and the maintenance cost. More importantly, it is more profitable.

To illustrate the advantages of the proposed electronic parking system, we will analyze all sorts of parking services. The simplest is a random parking service where vehicles can randomly park along street in Rényi's parking. The slotted parking service, the second parking service, improves

the parking utilization comparing with the Rényi's random parking service. But the parking spots are still wasted because drivers do not know about new spots that have just become vacant. Drivers are frustrated to search for an available spot in a large parking area. Therefore the slotted parking service assigns each spot a unique number. Drivers can reserve the parking spot. Since some drivers will mispark the reserved spot, a chain of misparking may happen. The misparking will greatly affect the parking quality. We address the probability of a driver that cannot find the reserved spot because of misparking of a previous driver. To short the chain of misparking, therefore, intelligent parking services are needed to improve parking space utilization and to improve the drivers' parking experience. With the help of wireless networks and sensor technologies, we proposed an intelligent parking service. The parking spots are embedded with sensors and wireless transceivers. These devices can talk to each other and create a wireless network which can dynamically manage the vacant parking spot and provide the intelligent parking service. The customers will be pleased because they can obtain non-stop, intelligent and customized parking services. The investor will be pleased because the parking services are automatically managed.

2. RELATED WORK

Cassady et al. address strategies for selecting a "good" parking space (Cassady & Kobza, 1998). A "good" parking space is defined in three aspects: the walking time of a driver, the driving time, and the time to reach the front door. A probabilistic approach is used to evaluate the three "good" performance metrics. This method used in this chapter does not help to reduce slot searching time and the slot utilization on a macro-level. Besides, Cassady assumes the drivers' knowledge of space availability. This assumption is strong in a conventional parking system. In our proposal, a probabilistic approach is used to evaluate the misparking behavior. Then we proposed a new parking system that can eliminate the misparking.

Caliskan et al. (2006) proposes a parking system in which parking automats are the producers of resource reports. The infrastructure uses IEEE 802.11 to broadcast these reports as raw text packets. Received reports are integrated into a vehicle's cache. These reports are aggregated and disseminated among vehicles. The decision strategy of which parking lot is used is based on two influencing parameters: the age of a resource and the distance to a resource. But the detail of detect vehicles is not stated. In literature, several approaches are employed to detect reliable information. First wired sensors are widely used (Mimbela & Klein, 2000): 1) inductive loops, 2) pneumatic road tubes, 3) magnetic sensors, 4) piezoelectric sensors, 5) weigh-in-motion systems. Wolff et al. (2006) use the Earth's magnetic field to detect parking spaces. These devices or sensors are physically wired to the control computers. One shortcoming of the wired sensor systems is that long and complicated wiring is required from parking lots to the central control unit. Therefore some wireless sensors can be applied to the parking space detection. Tang et al. (2006) developed such a system using Crossbow Mote products and the extended Crossbow XMesh network architecture. Benson et al. (2006) propose RF transceiver and antenna with an ATMega 128L micro-controller system. Third, image processing is applied to detect the vehicles (Takizawa et al., 2004; Zhu et al., 2007). Funck et al. uses images to detect the parking space (Funck et al., 2004). However these methods may incorrectly detect parking vehicles. One example is that a vehicle temporally uses one slot to park in another slot, or that a vehicle just happens to be in the intersection of these sensors. Panayappan et al. (2007) propose a parking system in VANET to locate the available parking lots and spots. This system uses roadside units to relay parking messages and GPS to locate vehicle position. Roadside units maintain the security certificates

and parking information. The greedy drivers are prevented from gaining more advantage from the system by lying. But it is not always working. For example, a roadside attacker pretending to be a vehicle can reserve as many slots as he wishes. In our system, all the communications are triggered by physical pressure on belts and are enabled by short range signals.

3. RÉNYI PARKING SERVICE

The first model is Rényi parking service (Finch, 2003), vehicles can randomly park on the interval of parking area which is shown in Figure 1. Consider the one-dimensional interval [0, x] with x>1. Imagine it to be a street for which parking is permitted on one side. Cars of unit length are one-by-one parked completely at random on the street and obviously no overlap is allowed with cars already in place. Figure 1 shows a big area which includes streets of several blocks. Of interest is the utilization of the parking area, i.e. the density of vehicles.

Lemma 1. *Cars of unit length are randomly parking on each street. The street parking spaces are one-dimensional intervals. The length of street x_r The density of parked vehicles is a constant.*

Proof. Consider n points, 1, 2,.., n on real axis where the total length is x_r. Therefore n the integral part of x_r, i.e. $n = [x_r]$. An arriving car "parks" if both points i and $i+1$ are unoccupied, otherwise, the car moves off. The process ends when no space left to park. Let Xn be the random variable that that counts the number of unoccupied points when the process terminates. Of interest is the "utilization factor", $1 - \frac{E[x_n]}{n}$. Let $A(i, n)$, $(1 \le i \le n)$, be the event that point i is left unoccupied. By symmetry, it is clear that $Pr[A(1, n)] = Pr[A(n, n)]$. Fairly devious logic shows that $Pr[A(i, n)] = Pr[A(i, i) \cap A(n - i + 1, n - i + 1)]$. This is because $A(i, n)$ occurs if and only if both $A(i, i)$ and $A(n$

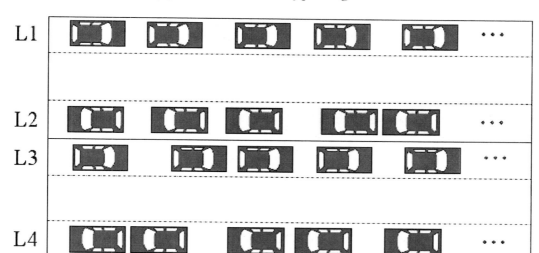

Figure 1. Vehicles can randomly park on the interval of parking area

- $i + 1$, $n - i + 1$) occur. Also, importantly, $A(i, i)$ and $A(n - i + 1, n - i + 1)$ are independent. it follows that $Pr[A(i, n)] = Pr[A(i, i)] \cdot Pr[A(n - i + 1, n - i + 1)]$.

The notation is clumsy: write $p_{i,n} = Pr[A(i, n)]$ and write $q_i = p_{i,i}$. In this notation, $\forall i$, $(1 \leq i \leq n)$, $p_{i,n} = q_i q_{n-i+1}$, observe that $q_0 = 0$, $q_1 = 1$, $q_2 = 0$ and that $\forall n$, $p_{2,n} = p_{n-1,n} = 0$. Let M_i be the event that the first car has parked at $(i, i+1)$; it is clear that $\forall i$, $(1 \leq i \leq n-1)$, $\Pr[M_i] = \dfrac{1}{n-1}$. We write $\bigcup_{i=1}^{n-1} M_i = \Omega$.

By the Law of Total Probability

$$q_n = \sum_{i=1}^{n-1} \Pr[q_n \mid M_i] \cdot \Pr[M_i]$$
$$= \frac{1}{n-1} \sum_{i=1}^{n-1} q_{n-i+1}$$
$$= \frac{1}{n-1} \sum_{j=0}^{n-1} q_j$$
$$= \frac{1}{n-1} \sum_{j=1}^{n-1} q_j$$

Thus, we are lead to the recurrence

$$q_n = \begin{cases} 1, & n = 1 \\ 0, & n = 2 \\ \dfrac{1}{n-1} \sum_{j=1}^{n-2} q_i, & n > 2 \end{cases}$$

Standard manipulations reveal that $\forall n \geq 3$,
$q_n = \dfrac{1}{2!} - \dfrac{1}{3!} + \cdots + \dfrac{(-1)^{n-1}}{(n-1)!}$. This can also be written as $q_n = \displaystyle\sum_{i=0}^{n-1} \dfrac{(-1)^i}{i!}$. Thus,

$$p_{i,n} = \begin{cases} \displaystyle\sum_{i=0}^{n-1} \frac{(-1)^i}{i!}, & i = 1, n \\ 0, & i = 2, n-1 \\ \left(\displaystyle\sum_{j=0}^{i-1} \frac{(-1)^j}{j!} q_j\right) \cdot \left(\displaystyle\sum_{j=i}^{n-1} \frac{(-1)^j}{j!} q_j\right), & 2 < i < n-1 \end{cases}$$

It is clear that the expected number of unoccupied points is $E\left[X_n\right] = \displaystyle\sum_{i=1}^{n} 1 \cdot p_{i,n} = \sum_{i=1}^{n} p_{i,n}$. For "larger" n, we have

$$\begin{cases} p_{1,n} = p_{n,n} = e^{-1} \\ p_{i,n} \approx e^{-2}, \qquad (3 \le i \le n-2) \end{cases}$$

Thus $E\left[X_n\right] = \sum_{i=1}^{n} p_{i,n} \approx \dfrac{2}{e} + \dfrac{n-4}{e^2}$.

Consider k, ≥ 1 street. Street parking spaces are one-dimensional intervals. The length of street one $x_1 > 1$, the length of street two $x_2 > 1$, and so on. Cars of unit length are randomly parking on each street. It is easy to see that the density of parked vehicles of all these streets is a constant.

4. SLOTTED PARKING SERVICE

Although Rényi's parking problem (Finch, 2003) states a random parking service, current parking lot is often slotted and each vehicle can park only on one slot. Figure 3 shows a structure of a parking site which includes several lots. Each slot is assigned to one vehicle. Drivers can park at any slots. The slotted parking site will help the increment of vehicle density. In an ideal situation, the waste of parking slots can be small (but not 0%). In reality, this strategy will cause several problems.

First, parking spots are wasted. In large parking lots, a driver may exit the lot without knowing about new spots that have just become vacant. Second, finding an empty parking spot may also lead to driver frustration if another car takes the spot before the driver can reach it. One scenario is shown in Figure 2. Vehicle F is searching a parking slot. F passes the slot E without knowing E just has become vacant.

Therefore, reserving a numbered slot can be a solution, like parking reservation for football games. We assume each vehicle can park at an assigned slot which is reserved before the driver's arrival. Although rare, there usually are some drivers who will take a wrong slot (mispark) under certain circumstances. The misparking of one driver will cause other drivers' misparking behavior. We model the misparking through a probabilistic approach.

4.1. Analysis of Misparking

Since misparking is often a small probability event, we present a probabilistic approach to analyze the effect caused by one misparking. This analysis is addressed in the chapter (Yan et al., 2009). We assume that each driver is assigned a

Figure 2. Parking area with slots

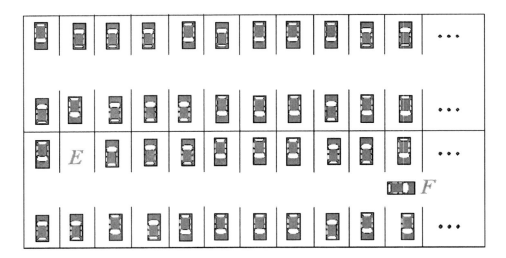

Figure 3. Parking area with numbered slots

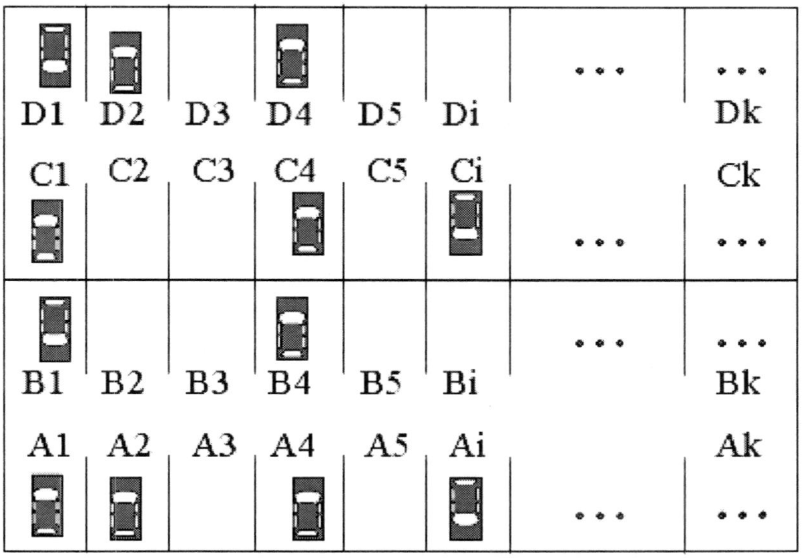

parking slot. There is a parking lot of capacity n where one of the customers misparks. Of interest is the probability that the last driver finds his assigned parking spot available. Let the n, ($n \geq 2$), drivers be P_1, P_2,..., P_n. Let B_k, ($1 \geq k \geq n - 1$), be the event that P_k is the first driver who takes a wrong slot. We assume that $\Pr[B_k] = \dfrac{1}{n-1}$ independent of k. Let A be the event that the last driver finds the assigned slot available. By the Law of Total Probability

$$\Pr[A] = \sum_{i=1}^{n-1} \Pr[A|B_k] \cdot \Pr[B_k] = \frac{1}{n-1} \sum_{i=1}^{n-1} \Pr[A|B_k] \tag{1}$$

To find the probability of Pr[A], we will start a simpler problem which is stated in the lemma 2.

Lemma 2. n, ($n \geq 2$), drivers park at a parking lot with capacity of n. Each driver is assigned a parking slot. The first driver takes the wrong slot. Subsequent drivers take their assigned slot if available; otherwise take an available slot at random. The probability that the last driver finds the assigned slot available is

$$1 - \frac{H_n - 1}{n-1}$$

Proof. Assume without loss of generality that the fist passenger P_1, with assigned slot i, takes slot j instead.

For $2 \geq k \geq n$, let S_k be the event that driver P_k is assigned slot j. Let A be the event that P_n finds her assigned slot available. Clearly

$$\Pr[A] = \sum_{k=2}^{n} \Pr[A|S_k] \cdot \Pr[S_k] = \frac{1}{n-1} \sum_{k=2}^{n} \Pr[A|S_k]$$

For $2 \geq k \geq n$, write $q_k = Pr[A|S_k]$; our goal now become to find a closed form for q_k.

Notice that $q_n = 0$ and, more generally, for $2 \geq k \geq n-1$, $q_k = \dfrac{1}{n-k+1} \cdot 1 + \dfrac{n-k}{n-k+1} \cdot q_{k+1}$. An easy inductive argument confirms that for $2 \geq k \geq$ n, $q_k = \dfrac{n-k}{n-k+1}$, as shown in lemma 4.

It follows that

$$
\begin{aligned}
\Pr[A] &= \frac{1}{n-1}\sum_{k=2}^{n}\Pr[A \mid S_k] \\
&= \frac{1}{n-1}\sum_{k=2}^{n}\frac{n-k}{n-k+1} \\
&= \frac{1}{n-1}\sum_{k=2}^{n}\left(1-\frac{1}{n-k+1}\right) \\
&= 1 - \frac{1}{n-1}\sum_{k=2}^{n}\frac{1}{n-k+1} \\
&= 1 - \frac{H_n - 1}{n-1}
\end{aligned}
$$

The probability that the last driver finds her assigned slot available is $1 - \dfrac{H_n - 1}{n-1}$.

Lemma 3. $q_n = 0$ *and, more generally, for* $2 \geq k \geq n-1$, $q_k = \dfrac{1}{n-k+1}\cdot 1 + \dfrac{n-k}{n-k+1}\cdot q_{k+1}$.

$$q_k = \frac{n-k}{n-k+1}$$

Proof. The proof is by induction on k. Basis step, $k = 2$, $q_2 = \dfrac{n-2}{n-1}$ because there are only n-2 possible correct slots can be taken by the last driver from the rest of n-1 untaken slots.

Inductive step, assume that $2 \geq k \geq n$, $q_k = \dfrac{n-k}{n-k+1}$. For $2 \geq k \geq n-1$,

$$q_k = \frac{1}{n-k+1}\cdot 1 + \frac{n-k}{n-k+1}\cdot q_{k+1}$$

$$\frac{n-k}{n-k+1} = \frac{1}{n-k+1}\cdot 1 + \frac{n-k}{n-k+1}\cdot q_{k+1}$$

$$q_{k+1} = \frac{n-k}{n-k+1}$$

From the first principle of induction, we show that for $2 \geq k \geq n$, $q_{k+1} = \dfrac{n-k}{n-k+1}$

Lemma 4. n, (n≥2), drivers park at a parking lot with capacity of *n*. Each driver is assigned a parking slot. The *k*-th driver takes the wrong slot. Subsequent drivers take their assigned slots if the slots are available; otherwise take an available slot at random. The probability that the last driver finds the assigned slot available is

$$1 - \frac{1}{2(n-1)}\left[H_{n-1}^2 + \sum_{k=1}^{n-1}\frac{1}{k^2}\right]$$

Proof. Recall that B_k is the event that P_k is the first driver who takes a wrong slot. In fact, what we have computed in the previous lemma 2 was $Pr[A|B_1]$. Now assume that B_k, $k > 1$, holds; this implies that the previous drivers $P_1, P_2, .., P_{k-1}$ took their assigned slots. We are faced with an instance of problem $\prod(n-k)$. Reasoning as in the previous slide, we obtain $\Pr\left[A|B_k\right] = 1 - \dfrac{H_n - 1}{n-1}$.

Thus,

$$
\begin{aligned}
\Pr\left[A\right] &= \frac{1}{n-1}\sum_{k=1}^{n-1}\Pr\left[A|B_k\right] \\
&= \frac{1}{n-1}\sum_{k=1}^{n-1}\left(1 - \frac{H_{n-k}}{n-k}\right) \\
&= 1 - \frac{1}{n-1}\sum_{k=1}^{n-1}\frac{H_{n-k}}{n-k} \\
&= 1 - \frac{1}{n-1}\sum_{k=1}^{n-1}\frac{H_k}{k} \\
&= 1 - \frac{1}{2(n-1)}\left[H_{n-1}^2 + \sum_{k=1}^{n-1}\frac{1}{k^2}\right]
\end{aligned}
$$

It is clear that $n \to \infty$ implies $Pr[A] \to 1$. In term of our parking lot problem, as long as the parking lot is large, one misparked user has virtually no effect. We plot the two probability formulas in Figure 4. We notice that there is a gap between curves. The is because $Pr[A]$ 2 of the lemma 4 is an instance of problem $\prod(n - k)$ which is k-slots less than the $Pr[A]$ 1 of lemma 2. The number of parking capacity n is the only parameter of $Pr[A]$. If the parking capacity decreases, the probability $Pr[A]$ decreases. If $n \to \infty$, $Pr[A] \to 1$.

Lemma 5. $Pr[A \mid B_k] = 1 - \dfrac{H_n - 1}{n - 1}$

Proof. Now assume that B_k, $k > 1$, holds; this implies that the previous drivers $P_1, P_2, ..., P_{k-1}$ took their assigned slots. We are faced with an instance of problem $\prod(n - k)$. We can map the $(n - k + 1)$-th slot as the first slots in the problem $\prod(n - k)$. Therefore, we can get this lemma by substituting n in lemma 2 with $(n - k)$.

5. INTELLIGENT PARKING SERVICE

We will introduce an intelligent parking service, SmartParking (Yan et al., 2009) which is an intelligent parking system. The parking spots are embedded with sensors and wireless transceivers. These devices can talk each other and create a wireless network which can dynamically manage the vacant parking spot and provide the intelligent parking service.

5.1. An Overview

As an overview, Figure 5 shows the scheme of the intelligent parking service, E-Parking. We deploy several transceivers along the road and one at the parking site (Yan et al., 2008). The transceiver at the parking site is called the *base station,* because it is the center of the transaction. The ones on the roadside connect to belts. They can communicate with each other. The transceiver and the belt shown as S_i and B_i in Figure 5, which first meet the oncoming traffic from right to left are called a *publisher station.* The advertisements sent by

Figure 4. The probability that the last driver finds the assigned slot available in a parking slot with n slots. Pr[A]1 is from lemma 2, Pr[A]k is from lemma 4.

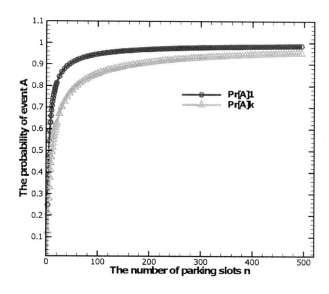

the base station are picked up by vehicles from this station. The transceiver and the belt shown as S_{i+1} and B_{i+1} in Figure 5, which meet the oncoming traffic after publisher station, is called *order station*. The spot reservation orders are collected from vehicles and transmitted to the base station from this station. There are three order stations S_{i+1} - B_{i+1}, S_{i+2} - B_{i+2} and S_{i+3} - B_{i+3} in Figure 5. The confirmation of order will be sent to the last orders station S_{i+3} - B_{i+3} and carried back to the other order station where the order maker can pick it up.

The process of advertisement publishing is the following: the computer center frequently feeds the up-to-date parking capacity information to the base station. The base station then transmits the parking information to the publisher station. Vehicles pass this belt at publisher station and receive a copy of the parking advertisement by communication with the belt. The advertisement includes the parking site location, the capacity of the empty spots, and the layout of empty spots.

5.2. Reserve Parking Spot

User terminals (e.g. PDAs, cell phones, vehicle display, and laptops) can read the output of the TRD. The received advertisement information is stored in the TRD to prevent modification of the parking information by attackers. Maps of parking sites can be preloaded/downloaded into the user terminals. The format of the software interface is the Extensible Markup Language (XML). These terminals can display the empty spots in a user-friendly manner. An example interface of the parking spots is shown in Figure 6 (Yan et al., 2008).

The process of a reservation order will be described using Figure 5. A vehicle e_3 passes the blet B_i at publisher station (S_i - B_i). It picks up an advertisement. If e_3 selects one of the parking spots, for instance $L3$-4, the user terminal/client program will send a reservation request and make a reservation order which includes the vehicle's Electronic License Plate ID(ELP-ID) and the selected parking spot number. Suppose e_3 selects the spot before it passes belt B_{i+1}. When e_3 passes B_{i+1}, the transceiver will drop the reservation order

Figure 5. Intelligent parking scheme

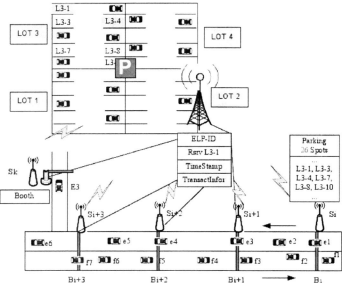

to belt B_{i+1}. The belt will generate a timestamp and transaction expire time information. The information will be appended to the reservation order message and form a new complete reservation order. The new reservation order is sent to the base station by order station S_{i+1} - B_{i+1} and processed by computer center. The feedback of this order is sent back to the last order station S_{i+3} - B_{i+3}. The vehicles in opposite traffic of e_3 will mule the encrypted feedback message to the order station S_{i+2} - B_{i+2} by picking and dropping this message on belts. Therefore e_3 can get this feedback message either on belt B_{i+2} or B_{i+3}. Since the belts are 1km apart from each other, the travel time from one belt to another belt is about

Figure 6. SmartParking User Interface. A user can view the empty spots and reserve one spot. The reserved spot in this figure is at lot 3 number 4 spot: L3-4

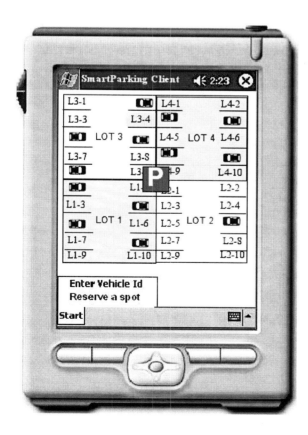

$1000(m)/31(m/s)=32(seconds)$ if the average speed of vehicles is 70 miles/hour (i.e. about 31m/s). This travel time is good enough to cover the reservation order processing time, transmission delay, etc.

Each reservation order consists of a vehicle's ELP-ID, the reserved parking spot number, a timestamp, and *transaction expiration time* information. The *transaction expiration time* is the maximum time to drive from the belt where the order is generated to the parking site. If the vehicle orders a spot but does not show up before the transaction expiration time, the reserved spot is freed and the vehicle has to reserve another parking spot.

If a vehicle does not reserve any parking spots and drives directly to the parking lot, the parking entry booth will randomly pick an empty spot for the vehicle. If several reservations collide, new randomly selected parking spots are picked from the empty spots to solve the collision. If the collided spot is the last spot, the spot will be given to the vehicle with the earlier timestamp. Other vehicles will be informed that the spot is not available anymore.

5.3. Cancel Transaction

If a driver decides to cancel a parking reservation, the cancelation process is similar to the reservation process. A cancel order is dropped to the order belt and transmitted to the base station where the cancel order is processed. Feedback is sent back to the last order station and is carried by opposite traffic until the order maker picks it up at an order station belt.

In some special scenarios, a driver might not cancel the transaction. For example, the driver changes his mind and continues to drive instead of parking and he forgets to cancel the reserved slot. The slot reserved by this driver will be freed when the transaction expiration time is past. To prevent this scenario, a fine can be charged because this driver has held parking resources for a period of time.

5.4. Wireless Communications

The infrastructure includes an E-Parking server, n parking slots, n infrared scanners and notice lights, n sensor belts. As shown in Figure 7, each slot embeds a sensor belt and an infrared pole. Pressure sensors are embedded inside the sensor belt. An infrared pole has a scanner which can scan the parking card inside the vehicle. If the scanner did not detect the parking card, an alarming light/voice can remind the user to place the parking card at the proper place inside the vehicle.

5.5. Vehicle-Belt Handshaking

5.5.1 Slot to Vehicle

The communication between slot and vehicles is shown in Figure 8 When a vehicle's wheels press on the sensor belt, the sensor belt will be activated and a send signal to the infrared pole. The pole will turn on the infrared scanner to detect the parking card. After the authentication, the infrared pole

will read the parking information: a temporal card ID, the reserved slot, a reservation timestamp, and transaction information. The temporal card ID is a random unique number of the card. The reserved slot and reservation timestamp are used for the reservation of a parking spot because the reservations from different places and users may collide. The transaction information indicates the fee, discount, payment, etc.

If the scanner does not read the parking card, an alarming light and voice will turn on to indicate the user to place the parking card in the correct place where the scanner can read it. If the parking card is read but the parking information is wrong, the alarming light and voice will inform the user about the misparking. If the user ignores the alarming information, a message will be reported to maintenance people and the vehicle of the user will be towed away by maintenance people. In this way, we prevent misparking in our system.

5.5.2. Slot to Server

Drivers usually want to reserve a parking slot before they arrive at the parking lot. They even can book a parking slot while they are heading

Figure 7. Parking spots in detail

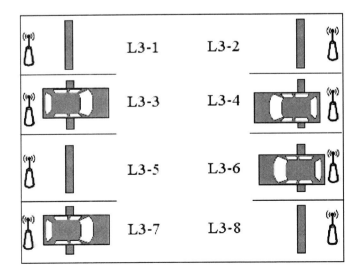

Figure 8. Parking spot detail

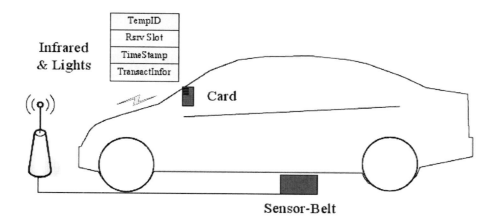

to the parking lot. To provide parking reservation service, we need to collect the empty slots. By using a wireless network, each infrared pole can report to the server that its slot is taken or not. The server will update its parking table and figure out the empty parking slots.

5.5.3. Server to Booth

When vehicles check in, the parking lot booth will assign vehicles parking slots. If a vehicle reserves a slot before arriving, the vehicle will be assigned with the reserved slot. If a vehicle does not reserve a slot before arriving, the vehicle will be assigned with a random empty slot. Therefore, the booth needs the synchronized parking capacity from the server. The communication between the server and the booth is based on a wireless network.

5.5.4. Server to Vehicle

To inform vehicles near the parking lot, the server will broadcast parking capacity through a wireless network or wireless radio. Vehicles can reserve a parking slot through their terminal devices. The terminal devices can be personal computer, laptop, PDA, cell phone, telephones, etc.

5.6. Misparking Prevention

Suppose vehicle *a* is assigned a parking slot *s* at the parking booth. A misparking vehicle *b* takes the parking slot *s*. The sensor will detect the misparking event and report to the maintenance team. The misparking vehicle *b* will be towed away immediately. The towed vehicles will be placed in an acclaim area. The misparking driver can claim the towed vehicles at the acclaim area. At the same time, the message that the slot *s* is occupied by a misparking will be synchronized to booths, servers, and vehicles inside the parking site. If *a* is inside the parking site, the announcement message of the misparking will reach *a*. The announcement message includes two options for the driver *a*. One is to wait until the misparked vehicle is towed away. Another is to park at a new assigned slot. Whichever option the driver *a* selects is companied with a discount offer on the parking fee, for example, 20% off. If *a* is not checked in the parking site yet, *a* will not be affected by the misparking because vehicles are supposed to receive a randomly assigned slot at the booth.

5.7. Maintenance Time

The parking maintenance work includes the routine check on electronics, clearance of mispaking vehicles, etc.

Suppose the vehicles arrival rate to the parking site is λ. Before maintaining the parking lot, we wait until we find no vehicles will come in next *T* time units. Of interest is the expected time we have to wait before the maintenance work can start.

Assume we start to count vehicles at time 0 and let $X_1, X_2,..$ the vehicle inter-arrival times. Let, further, *W* be the random variable that counts the vehicles that will come before we can start the maintenance work. We model this problem as geometric distribution of Bernoulli trials: find the first *T* which is larger than vehicle inter-arrival time. We write what is shown in box 1.

Thus, the expected number of vehicles that come before we can start maintenance is

$$E[W] = \sum_{K \geq 0} k \left(1 - e^{-\lambda T}\right)^k e^{-\lambda T}$$
$$= \left(1 - e^{-\lambda T}\right) e^{-\lambda T} \sum_{K \geq 0} k \left(1 - e^{-\lambda T}\right)^{k-1}$$
$$= \left(1 - e^{-\lambda T}\right) e^{-\lambda T} e^{2\lambda T}$$
$$= e^{-\lambda T} - 1$$

Finally, the expected time that we have to wait until we can start maintenance work is

$$E[W] E[X] = \frac{e^{-\lambda T} - 1}{\lambda} \qquad (2)$$

Therefore, the expected time we have to wait before the maintenance work can start is (2).

6. SIMULATION RESULTS

In the simulation, we compare two scenarios. In scenario one, drivers randomly select a parking spot. The parking spot is based on first-come-first-serve. The process that drivers arrive at or exit to the parking lot is a Poisson Process. If they move around the parking area and cannot find a parking spot, they turn around. If they turn around 3 times, they exit. In scenario two, drivers reserve a parking spot. The process that drivers arrive at or exit to the parking lot is the same Poisson Process. We assume 1% of drivers will disobey the reservation and take somebody else's parking spot for their own convenience. The remaining 99% of drivers obey the reservation. We compare the parking utilization and average waiting time for drivers. The parking capacity is 1000 parking spots. The average arrival rate is 0.5 vehicle/min (Asakura & Kashiwadani, 1994). The simulation parameters and values are listed in Table 1.

We compared the conventional parking system with the proposed parking system. We varied the number of slots from 100 to 1000 in three comparisons: slot searching time, lot utilization, and average number of the misparked vehicles. Of interest first is the parking searching time because it is frustrating that we spend a lot of time searching for a parking slot in real life. We start to count the time spent in searching slot until a slot is found. As shown in Figure 9(a), the proposed system

Box 1.

$$\Pr\left[\{W = K\}\right] = \Pr\left[\{X_1 < T\} \cap \{X_2 < T\} \cap \cdots \{X_k < T\} \cap \{X_{k+1} \geq T\}\right]$$
$$= \Pr[\{X_1 < T\} \cdot \Pr[\{X_2 < T\}] \cdot \ldots \cdot \Pr[\{X_k < T\}] \cdot \Pr[\{X_{k+1} \geq T\}]$$
$$= \left(1 - e^{-\lambda T}\right)^k e^{-\lambda T}$$

Table 1. Parameters and values

Parameters	Values
Exit booth service rate	5 vehicles/min
Entry booth service rate	20 vehicles/min
Number of exit booths	5
Number of entry booths	1
Average speed	10 km/h
Average arrival rate	0.5 vehicle/min
Average exit rate	0.5 vehicle/min
Average parking time	1.5 hour

spends much less time than the conventional system; this is because the proposed system assigns each vehicle a slot when the vehicle checks in. Vehicles directly head to the slot. We also investigated the parking utilization. After the parking system becomes stable (the number of vacant slots stays in a stable status), we count the number of vacant slots. We get the slot utilization by calculating the percentage of vacant slots. As shown in Figure 9(b), the conventional system has lower slot utilization than the proposed system. There are some vacant slots but vehicles do not find them. In the proposed system, the service server knows the vacant slots which can be assigned to next coming vehicles. Moreover, we

compared the average misparked vehicles. We collected the mispark vehicles every 30 minutes. The comparison result is shown in Figure 9(c). As expected, the proposed system almost reduces the number of misparked vehicles to zero. But the conventional system obtains more misparked vehicles while the number of slots increases.

We examined our analysis of maintenance time as well. Three metrics are examined. They are the expected waiting time, the expected waiting number of vehicles, and the probability of finding the first maintenance time. We varied the maintenance time T from 1 to 3 hours. We collected the average waiting number of vehicles, the average waiting time, and the k-th vehicle after which we found the maintenance time. The result is shown in Figure 10(a), 10(b) and 10(c). The relationship among the three figures matches with the probability analysis shown in section 5.7.

7. CONCLUSION

In the digital age and cybertimes, wireless networks and sensors are applied to the traditional parking system. We present a novel parking system built on the sensors and wireless networks. From

Figure 9. Comparisons between the conventional and the proposed parking system

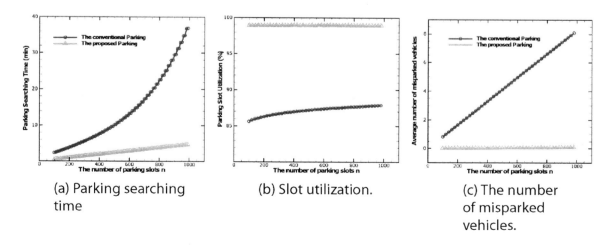

(a) Parking searching time

(b) Slot utilization.

(c) The number of misparked vehicles.

Figure 10. Comparisons of simulation results

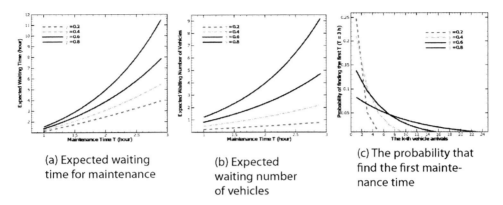

(a) Expected waiting time for maintenance

(b) Expected waiting number of vehicles

(c) The probability that find the first maintenance time

the user's point of view, the proposed system can provide high quality of service, such as saving slot finding time, reserving a parking slot before arrival, nonstop parking experience, and intelligent slot allocation, etc. From the investor's point of view, the parking system is efficient in slot utilization, intelligent management and cost-saving in maintenance. We presented probabilistic approaches and associated techniques for current parking services. Starting from the simplest parking service, we reach an intelligent parking service with the help of wireless networks and sensor technologies. Key properties of the electronic and intelligent parking services are used to please both the customers and the investors by providing a non-stop, intelligent, and customized parking service.

REFERENCES

Asakura, Y., & Kashiwadani, M. (1994). Effects of parking availability information on system performance: a simulation model approach. In *Proceedings of Vehicle Navigation and Information Systems Conference*, (pp. 251–254). Dearborn, MI.

Benson, J. P., O'Donovan, T., O'Sullivan, P., Roedig, U., & Sreenan, C. (2006). Car-park management using wireless sensor networks. In *Proceedings of 31st IEEE Conf. Local Computer Networks*, (pp. 588–595). Tampa.

Caliskan, M., Graupner, D., & Mauve, M. (2006). Decentralized discovery of free parking places. In *VANET '06: Proceedings of the 3rd international workshop on Vehicular ad hoc networks*, (pp. 30–39). New York, NY, USA.

Cassady, C. R., & Kobza, J. E. (1998). A probabilistic approach to evaluate strategies for selecting a parking space. *Transportation Science*, *32*(1), 30–42. doi:10.1287/trsc.32.1.30

Finch, S. R. (2003). *R'enyi's Parking Constant*. Cambridge, England: Cambridge University Press.

Funck, S., Mohler, N., & Oertel, W. (2004). Determining car-park occupancy from single images. In *Proceedings of International Symposium on Intelligent Vehicles (IVS04)*, (pp. 325–328). Parma, Italy.

Mimbela, L. E. Y., & Klein, L. A. (2000). A summary of vehicle detection and surveillance technologies used in intelligent transportation systems.

Panayappan, R., Trivedi, J. M., Studer, A., & Perrig, A. (2007). Vanet-based approach for parking space availability. In *VANET '07: Proceedings of the fourth ACM international workshop on Vehicular ad hoc networks*, (pp. 75–76). New York, NY, USA.

Takizawa, H., Yamada, K., & Ito, T. (2004). Vehicles detection using sensor fusion. In *Proceedings of International Symposium on Intelligent Vehicles (IVS04)*, (pp. 238–243). Parma, Italy.

Tang, V., Zheng, Y., & Cao, J. (2006). An intelligent car park management system based on wireless sensor networks. In *Proceedings Int* (pp. 65–70). Urumqi: Sym. Pervasive Computing and Applications.

Wolff, J., Heuer, T., Gao, H., Weinmann, M., Voit, S., & Hartmann, U. (2006). Parking monitor system based on magnetic field sensors. In *Proceedings IEEE Conf. Intelligent Transportation Systems*, (pp. 1275–1279). Toronto, CA.

Yan, G., Olariu, S., Weigle, M. C., & Abuelela, M. (2008). Smartparking: A secure and intelligent parking system using NOTICE. In *Proceedings of the International IEEE Conference on Intelligent Transportation Systems*, (pp. 569–574). Beijing, China.

Yan, G., Weigle, M. C., & Olariu, S. (2009). A novel parking service using wireless networks. In *Proceedings of the IEEE International Conference on Service Operations, Logistics and Informatics*. Chicago. Best Student Paper Award.

Zhu, Z. F., Zhao, Y., & Lu, H. Q. (2007). Sequential architecture for efficient car detection. In *Proceedings of IEEE Computer Society Conference on Computer Vision and Pattern Recognition (CVPR 2007)*, (pp. 1–8). Minneapolis.

Section 2
Marketing Strategies

Chapter 8
E-Marketing:
Towards a Conceptualisation of a New Marketing Philosophy

Hatem El-Gohary
Birmingham City University Business School, UK

ABSTRACT

This chapter aims to add to the accumulative knowledge in the field of e-marketing through conceptualising e-marketing as a new marketing philosophy. The review of the literature has revealed that one of the main obstacles to developing e-marketing potential is the absence of a clear conceptualisation of e-marketing purpose and definition. The majority of researchers within the field misuse the term e-marketing and are using the terms e-business, e-marketing, e-commerce and Internet-marketing interchangeably as if they are similar or have the same meaning, which is incorrect. For example, e-marketing is broader in scope than Internet marketing since it refers not only to digital media such as the Web, e-mail, and wireless media, but also includes electronic customer relationship management systems and the management of digital customer data, etc. In contrast, e-commerce and e-business have a wider and broader scope than e-marketing. The differences between these terms as well as the main components of e-marketing are illustrated and discussed in detail within the chapter towards achieving a conceptualisation of e-marketing as a new marketing philosophy and to build a ground base of understanding for these different concepts.

The chapter will help researchers and scholars in the field of e-marketing to have a clearer view towards its concept that in turn will contribute to the related accumulated knowledge in the field.

INTRODUCTION

The recent revolution in computer science, the Internet, information technology (IT), media and communications has changed the nature of business and marketing practices. A growing numbers of companies and enterprises use the Internet and other electronic tools to communicate with suppliers, business customers and end users of their products and services. New forms of marketing

DOI: 10.4018/978-1-60960-765-4.ch008

have presented an opportunity for all kinds of enterprises to grow in a dramatic and dynamic way.

This research argues that the adoption of Electronic Marketing (e-marketing) by enterprise, regardless of size, can change the shape and nature of its business all over the world. The fast propagation of the Internet, the World Wide Web (WWW), information technologies (IT), communication technologies and computer sciences has created dynamic new electronic channels for marketing, and most companies today find it essential to have an online presence (Liang and Huang, 1998). But alongside these opportunities there are problems associated with the dynamics of this new interactive media. These problems are exacerbated by the fact that much previous research has misused the term e-marketing and are using the terms E-business, e-marketing, E-Commerce and Internet-marketing interchangeably as if they are similar or have the same meaning, which is incorrect (El-Gohary, 2009). Consequently, this research aims to add to the accumulative body of knowledge in the fields of e-marketing by attempting to conceptualise e-marketing as a new marketing philosophy.

This chapter provides a comprehensive illustration of the differences between the concepts of e-marketing, Internet Marketing, E-Commerce and E-Business to build a ground base of understanding for these different concepts. This understanding will provide benefits for entrepreneurs, policy makers, students, practitioners, researchers, and educators though providing a clearer view and deep complete understanding for all the aspects related to e-marketing. The chapter also provide a detailed discussion for the main commonly used e-marketing components

BACKGROUND

Electronic Marketing (E-Marketing)

Electronic Marketing (e-marketing) can be viewed as a modern business practice associated with buying and selling goods, services, information and ideas via the Internet and other electronic means. A review of relevant literature and published research reveals that the definitions of e-marketing vary according to each researcher's point of view, background and specialization. While Chaffey (2007) defines it as:

Achieving marketing objectives through use of electronic communications technology (Chaffey, 2007, P: 339)

McDonald and Wilson (1999) define it as:

Any use of technology to achieve marketing objectives (McDonald and Wilson, 1999, P: 29)

On the other hand, Reedy and Schullo (2004) define it as:

The process aimed at facilitating and conducting of business communication and transactions over networks (Reedy and Schullo, 2004, p: 16)

Smith and Chaffey (2005) define it as:

Achieving marketing objectives through applying digital technologies (Smith and Chaffey, 2005. p: 11)

Strauss and Frost (2001) define it as:

The use of electronic data and applications for planning and executing the conception, distribution and pricing of ideas, goods and services to create exchanges that satisfy individual and organizational objectives (Strauss and Frost, 2001, p: 454)

For the purpose of conducting this research, the Strauss and Frost (2001) definition will be used to define e-marketing because it takes into consideration the main elements of e-marketing as well as all types of products, it illustrates the main objectives of E-marking which is mainly the creating of exchanges that satisfy both customer and organisational needs and it is the definition adopted by the American e-marketing Association (eMA).

Based on this definition, e-marketing includes any use of electronic data or electronic applications for conducting company marketing activities. As a result, e-marketing includes Internet Marketing, E-Mail marketing, Intranet Marketing, Extranet Marketing, Mobile Marketing, Tele Marketing, Electronic Data Interchange (EDI) for marketing activities, Customer Relationship Management (CRM) and more. In fact a review of the literature reveals that the most commonly used tools of e-marketing are: Internet Marketing, E-Mail marketing, Intranet Marketing, Mobile Marketing

and Extranet Marketing (El-Gohary et al., 2008a and 2008b; Paul, 1996; Hofacker, 1999 and 2001; Evans and King, 1999; Eid 2003; Eid and Trueman, 2004 and Chaffey et al., 2000). Consequently this research will investigate these five main tools of e-marketing that create exchanges and satisfaction for customers (Figure 1). However, in order to understand the dynamics of each of these five marketing tools, a conceptual review of the internet, its history, origins, growth and usage in marketing activities is presented in the next part of the chapter. A conceptual review of the major e-marketing tools will then be discussed.

The Internet

The Internet is one of the major components of e-marketing. In the last two decades the Internet has changed the nature and characteristics of the media and communications world in very unique ways that have never happened before. The Internet has transformed Marshall McLuhan (1911-1980)

Figure 1. E-Marketing concept

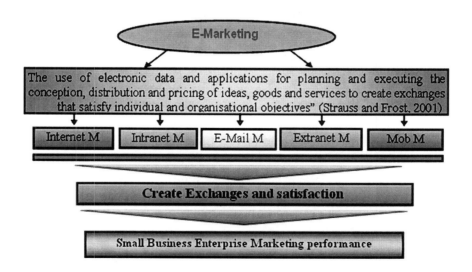

expression "Global Village" (McLuhan, 2009) into realty. In very few years, the Internet has gained an enormous recognition as a very dominant platform that has changed and restructured the way we conduct business and the way we communicate. The Internet, like no other mean, has set a global dimension to the business world and has become a unique universal source of information.

Currently, with low investments, companies owners can potentially have a web site or a web page and can reach directly a large number of markets both fast and economically. Moreover, with low investments almost any person who can read and write can have access to the World Wide Web. Nowadays, millions of people are connected to the Internet to get the latest news from around the world, search for information and purchase goods. Consequently the nature of business in all countries is changing not only fast but also dramatically. On the other hand, there are some problems associated with the dynamics of this new interactive media (such as security and privacy issues, technological problems, lack of trust, lack of face to face communications, etc). Regardless of such problems, unquestionably the Internet and electronic communication is rapidly changing traditional marketing practices and techniques (Hoffman and Novak, 1997, 1996; Kiani, 1998 and Quelch and Klein 1996) providing e-marketing with the chance to have a considerable impact on customer and business market behaviours.

History and Growth of the Internet

From a marketing perspective, the Internet can be defined as "an enabling technology and a powerful set of tools that can be used, wisely or unwisely, in almost any industry and as part of almost any strategy" (Porter, 2001; P: 64). The word itself simply means a "network of networks". The Internet can therefore be considered as a global network of interconnected computers and servers operating by a standard protocol, or as a worldwide system of interconnected networks and comput-

ers, which allows data to be transferred between the different nodes of this network (The Internet Society - IS, 2009).

The first known explanation of social communications conducted through networking was a series of memos written by J.C.R. Licklider of MIT in August 1962 discussing his "Galactic Network" concept (Leiner et al, 2006). However, the beginning of the Internet goes back to the late 1960's and early 1970's when the United States Defence Department established the ARPA Network (the Advanced Research Project Agency net) to link a variety of military and research institutions within the USA (The Internet Society, 2009). Although the first users of the Internet were mainly governmental departments or university researchers, starting from the early 1990s the Internet was opened up to other groups of public including individuals and companies (Hamill and Gregory, 1997; P: 10). This period was known as the: text-based era because the Internet participants was depending on a text interfaces.

But with the launch of the World Wide Web in 1993, with its graphical user interfaces (often known as web browsers), the internet offered huge opportunities for both individuals and organisations which were beyond belief during the text-based era of the Internet.

Since 1993 the Internet has grown in a tremendous way. Every day the number of people using the Internet is increasing in a dramatic way creating new opportunities for its users and turning the world into a global village. Within this context, the number of Internet users increased from 16 million (with a percentage of 0.4% of the world population) in December 1995 to 1,650 million (with a percentage of 24.2% of the world population) in June 2009 (Internet World Stats, 2009). Today, Internet users include individuals, companies, governments, universities, researchers and many others. However, with this increasing use there is also increasing potential for companies to communicate with their target audience and build productive relationships that will enhance their business.

The Internet and Marketing

The Internet has not only changed the way businesses interact and deal with their customers and clients but it has also changed ways of conducting business. Within this context, marketing activities on the Internet are no longer limited to the use of plain text messages. Today, the WWW allows interactive marketing because the user is actively involved in responding to vendors' promotion campaigns (Gogan, 1997; P: 93; Poon and Jevons, 1997; P: 29). This interactivity is not usually found in traditional marketing techniques that use broadcast and print media. Whereas the most recent developments of the Internet and the WWW allow full multimedia interactive animations to carry out marketing activities on the Internet almost instantly and offers great potential for direct marketing and early stage marketing (Berthon et al., 1996a, 1996b).

On the other hand, use of the Internet for commercial communications such as sharing business information, maintaining business relationships and conducting business transactions plays a very important role in today's marketing practices. According to Coppel (2002) Internet marketing applications can be classified according to three dimensions: government, business and consumer.

In other words the Internet offers the possibility for companies to communicate and conduct business at a number of different levels. There are also opportunities for companies in developing as well as developed countries to do business and enhance their marketing techniques.

E-Marketing Tools Used in this Research

As discussed earlier, for the purpose of conducting this study; the five main tools of e-marketing will be investigated. These tools are: Internet Marketing, E-Mail marketing, Intranet Marketing, Extranet Marketing and Mobile Marketing. The following parts of the chapter discuss these tools.

Internet Marketing

According to Chaffey (2007) Internet Marketing is: "*Achieving marketing objectives through applying digital technologies of the Internet*" (Chaffey, 2007, p: 1). On the other hand, according to eBusiness Connection (2008), Internet marketing is: "*The component of marketing that deals with the planning, pricing, promotion, and distribution of products and services online*" (eBusiness Connection, 2008, p: 2). They also argue that good Internet marketing strategies clearly communicate a firm's unique selling proposition, or the unique collection of benefits that creates value for its customers. Moreover, Eid (2003) defined Internet Marketing as: "*The use of the Internet to achieve marketing objectives and support marketing activities*" (Eid, 2003; P: 5)

The possibility of using the Internet as an instrument for conducting marketing, commercial and business activities has been widely investigated and recognised in marketing literature [see: Mc-Cole and Ramsey (2004), Oliva (2004), Chaston and Mangles (2003), Siddiqui et al (2003), Martin and Matlay (2003), Collins, et al (2003), Adam and Deans (2001), McGowan, et al (2001), Poon and Swatman (1996), (1997a) and (1997b), Chaffey et al., (2000), Wilson and Abel, (2002) and Kiang et al., (2000)]. This recognition of the potential of the Internet as a marketing tool rose from the great benefits that any company regardless of its size can gain from using the Internet in conducting its marketing activities. Within this context, the adoption of the Internet as a commercial intermediate and marketing tool has provided some companies with pioneering ways of marketing products in an intensively competitive environment. On the other hand, Berezai (2000) argues that companies have been forced to consider the Internet as a business and marketing tool in response to the growth in customers' usage of the Internet for almost every day to day activity. This is probably the case for companies in their dealing with large companies who may be suppliers or customers.

In fact, the revolutionary developments in IT, computer science and communications have expanded the role of the Internet beyond its simple use as a communication tool to become a unique and extremely important means for communicating with customers, providing services on a 24/7 bases, entering new markets, reducing costs and increasing sales. Moreover, one of the main characteristics of the Internet is its ability to be used both as a direct sales channel and as an interactive communications tool. Consequently the Internet can affect company marketing performance in two different ways, directly through increasing direct sales and indirectly by providing higher level of customer satisfaction. This improves relationships with customers as well as productivity.

According to Panazoglou and Tsalgatidou (2000) Internet Marketing involves more than simple online transactions. They argue that Internet Marketing facilitates activities such as market research, identifying opportunities and partners, cultivation of relationships with customers and suppliers, document exchanges and providing a facility for joint design (Panazoglou and Tsalgatidou, 2000; P: 301). Also, Greene (2009) demonstrates that the Internet provides a lot of benefits for any company in terms of marketing activities. According to him, the benefits of Internet Marketing include low start-up costs, low operating costs, cheap and free resources, time freedom and high profit margin. Moreover, Epsilon (2009) states that Internet Marketing reimbursement includes a 24/7 presence as well as convenience, added value and satisfaction, the ability to standardise sales performance, improved credibility, promotion of brick and mortar presence, growth opportunity, two-way communicative marketing, cheap market research and flexibility. Within the same line, Ghosh (1998) illustrates that the Internet can widen markets, increase efficiencies and lower costs by bringing

companies and customers together (Ghosh, 1998; P: 125). In more detail Gogan (1997) argues that the expected benefits for most companies includes improving seller competitive position, adding new markets, reducing seller costs, improving seller capabilities and improving customer service and relationship (Gogan, 1997; P: 96).

Additionally, Skinner (2000) argues that the Internet provides four different types of opportunities for different firms. According to his arguments, the Internet can establish a direct link among companies and customers to complete transactions or trade information more easily, lets companies avoid other parties in its value chain through selling directly to customers, helps the business to develop and deliver new products and services for current and prospective customers and finally allows companies to possibly use the Internet to become the main leader in a specific industry or segment and to set new business rules (Skinner, 2000; P:127).

Moreover, Lancioni (2000) argues that continual growth of Internet usage has provided businesses with a lot of important opportunities for reducing costs and improving it services. This can be achieved through the unique characteristics of the Internet which allow enterprises to keep track of different customer preferences and enables them to adapt these preferences into enterprise marketing activities such as advertising and promotions to satisfy these preferences and needs. This in turn will lead to increasing marketing productivity through the linking of enterprise expenditures with its results.

With regards to the benefits of the Internet for companies, Poon and Swatman (1999a) state that the Internet has direct and indirect marketing benefits and grouped them into short and long-term categories. They illustrate that the potential benefits of using the Internet in conducting marketing activities by small businesses increases as they extend their Internet-to-internal application integration. Within this context the more Internet-to-internal application integration the small enterprise has the more the benefit they will gain from using the Internet in conducting marketing activities. They argue that this Internet-to-internal application integration can be classified into three main levels: minimum, limited and full Internet-to-internal application integration.

On the other hand, the use of the Internet for conducting marketing activities is associated with some problems. Panazoglou and Tsalgatidou (2000) observe that these problems include only partial solutions for company needs, some rigid requirements, a limited interoperability, and most importantly insufficient trust and security as well as a lack of integration with existing business models (Panazoglou and Tsalgatidou, 2000; P: 303). Soh et al. (1997) find that the main problems facing the effective use of the Internet are difficulty in locating the right information, a rising user cost and issues related to security and data protection.

E-Mail Marketing

E-mail marketing is a format of an E-mail-based marketing activity in which advertisements, promotional and marketing activities are conducted through sending E-mails to a targeted list of recipients (usually current or perspective customers). The E-mail message (which may be a text, HTML, or rich media message) is more like a Web-based advertisement than a typical e-mail message. According to Galgano and La Mesa (2006) E-mail Marketing refers to developing marketing strategies that use electronic mail to communicate with current and prospects customers.

Moreover, Chaffey (2007) distinguish between two different types of E-Mail Marketing namely Outbound E-Mail marketing and Inbound E-Mail marketing. According to him Outbound E-Mail marketing can be defined as: "*E-Mails campaigns used as a form of direct marketing where E-mails are sent to customers and prospects from an organization*" (Chaffey, 2007, P: 421). He also defines Inbound E-Mail marketing as: "*The management of E-mails from customers by an organization*"

(Chaffey, 2007, P: 421). On the other hand, Carlton (2009) defines E-Mail marketing as: "*Sending out newsletters or e-magazines to subscribers list*" (Carlton, 2009, P: 1).

The concept behind E-mail marketing is that it makes more sense to send attractive, professional, and convincing advertisements and marketing activities to a smaller group of recipients that might be actually interested in receiving such marketing messages instead of sending the same marketing messages to a larger group that does not have much interest in receiving it. On the other hand, E-mail marketing is generally a permission-based process and depends on the willingness of the recipient to receive advertising information and other marketing information, rather than un-solicited commercial e-mail (UCE) which is often referred to as SPAM. Accordingly, it is important to emphasise that E-mail Marketing is not spamming which refers to indiscriminately sending an enormous number of e-mails and/or newsletters to the recipients without gaining their consent beforehand.

Today, most E-Mail Marketing messages include some mechanisms to provide the company (the sender) with useful feedback on the effectiveness and efficiency of its e-mail marketing campaign, such mechanisms make it possible for the marketer to track the e-mail marketing campaign through some performance measures:-

- Tracking the number of messages that were opened from the total number of messages sent.
- The total number of clicks that were generated from each message of these messages.
- The total number of e-mail recipients that asked to be removed from the company e-mail list, and finally
- The total number of messages that were blocked by the receiver server and considered as SPAM.

Moreover, the marketer (sender) may use customer segmentation techniques to ensure that the message is appropriate for the group it's sent to, and use personalisation techniques so the recipient is addressed as an individual with his/her own name, which in turn will increase the effectiveness and efficiency of E-mail Marketing.

There are a lot of reimbursements linked to the use of E-Mail Marketing. Carlton (2009) illustrates that these benefits include: e-mails are a cost-effective marketing tool, it helps build good relationships with customers, it provides useful information for customers and finally can provide instant feedback on the marketing campaign effectiveness. As a result of all these benefits associated with the use of E-Mail Marketing, a growing number of businesses are depending on it to conduct their marketing activities. According to the American e-marketing Association - eMA (2009c), the volume of promotional e-mails sent by American retailers accelerated in October 2008 and increased dramatically in December 2008 when retailers sent their consumers a monthly average of 14.6 e-mails.

On the other hand, there are some problems associated with the use of E-Mail Marketing such as SPAM reports. When conducting an E-Mail Marketing campaign, if any of the customers and/or receivers indicates that the received e-mail is a SPAM for his/her Internet service provider (ISP) the ISP will automatically generate an abuse report which can be a serious problem. Such an abuse report will result in prevention of all e-mails generated and sent from the company e-mail address from being delivered to any e-mail address through the Internet service provider. This in turn may unfavourably affect the deliverability of company e-mails to this ISP if they do not make all the needed corrective actions to avoid that. There is also a risk that SPAM mail can alienate customers.

Intranet Marketing

According to Chaffey (2007), the Intranet can be defined as: *"A private network within a single company using Internet standards to enable employees to share information using e-mail and web publishing"* (Chaffey, 2007; P: 421). Often people get confused when talking about Intranets and mix it up with the Internet. While there are a lot of similarities between the Internet and Intranets, the most noticeable difference is the facility to make internal company communications and information secure through an Intranet. Within this context, while the Internet is accessible to the global World Wide Web, whereas the Intranet is a private net operating within a company. Although both of them use some similar features like E-mail and typical World Wide Web standards, there are three main differences between them: -

- An Intranet is a closed accessed net and only authorised users of this Intranet can get access to it.
- The Intranet user can get onto the Internet while global Internet users cannot get onto an Intranet.
- An Intranet can be run without an Internet connection or link.

The most well-liked Intranet application is inter-office e-mail, but there are some other applications which include Web publishing of the corporate documents, Web-to-database links that allow users to access company information and newsletters, historical data, catalogs, price lists, information on competitors' products and customer service data. Overall this is not only a means of sharing knowledge with employees but also a way of protecting the intellectual property of the company. This research argues that an Intranet can be a key marketing tool for a company. Since the Intranet is a useful method for employees' communications, it can help to increase marketing performance through increasing the levels of coordination within the marketing department. It is also a very useful tool in conducting Internal Marketing that can help to overcome any resistance to change within the firm by informing and involving all the staff of new initiatives and strategies. In this way, company employees are more likely to understand and be committed to the value proposition of the organisation and its brands. In this way it allows companies to realise their full marketing potential.

Extranet Marketing

An Extranet is an aspect of a corporation Intranet that can be accessed by some users outside the company itself. Vlosky, Fontenot and Blalock (2000) define Extranet as: "*A network that links business partners to one another over the Internet*" (Vlosky, Fontenot and Blalock, 2000; P: 3). External stakeholders such as customers, vendors, suppliers and business partners are examples of the types of people who can benefit from Extranets as a type of private networks. These external stakeholders can exchange huge amounts of data using Electronic Data Interchange (EDI), share exclusive information, cooperate with each other on joint business ventures, contribute to training programs and share services between different companies or enterprises. Based on that, an Extranet is more likely to act as a way of communicating and sharing business information securely without facing the worries related to security, or being intercepted, over the Internet. Extra security and privacy can be achieved with the Extranet by including firewalls and requiring usernames and passwords. Vlosky, Fontenot and Blalock (2000) found that Extranets have some general uses which include conducting electronic communications, allowing contacts with customer and vendors, enabling sales to customers and purchases from suppliers, and finally product and service promotion.

This research argues that an Extranet in an effective tool for secure information sharing, cost reduction, customer services, order processing and distribution as well as building good business relationships. Accordingly, Extranets has a high potential to enhance marketing activities as well as performance of companies. Table 1 illustrate similarities and differences between Internet, Intranets, and Extranets

Mobile Marketing

Mobile Marketing is a more recent form of e-marketing based on the explosive growth of mobile technology (particularly popular in emerging economies such as Egypt). According to Norcross (2008) Mobile Marketing is: "*The systematic planning, implementing and control of a mix of business activities intended to bring together buyers and sellers for the mutually advantageous exchange or transfer of products where the primary point of contact with the consumer is via their mobile device*" (Norcross, 2008; p: 2). Based on the previous definitions, Mobile Marketing can be conducted through: SMS (Short

Table 1. Similarities and differences between the Internet, Intranets, and Extranets

Element	Internet	Intranets	Extranets
Meaning	The information Super-highway.	The use of Internet technology within a company or organisation.	A network that uses the Internet to link company Intranets in order to enhance B2B relationships.
Access	Open	Private	By agreement only
Users	Public	Organisation members	Business partners
Information	General	Proprietary	Selective

Source: Adopted from Vlosky et al (2000), Baker (1997) and SharWest Inc. (1997)

Message Service), MMS (Multimedia Messaging Service), WAP (Wireless Application Protocol) banner advertisements, mobile TV and Bluetooth. On the other hand, the use of mobile phones as well as its applications such as text messages or SMS messages is increasing at an enormous rate. Within this respect, according to the Mobile Data Association - MDA (2009) the number of text messages in the UK in December 2008 reached 7710 Millions.

One of the primary reasons behind this growth is that mobile phones and text messaging have become increasingly used as a business tool. Text messaging enables information to be sent to groups of customers quickly and conveniently in much the same way as e-mail, making it an increasing popular e-marketing channel. Moreover, the development and growth of Third Generation (3G) mobile phones had led to superior connection speeds, Wi-Fi connectivity and the increase of mobile Internet browsing by users all over the world. Overall, customers today have better quality mobile phones, improved high quality mobile networks and a very good price plans. All these elements provide a very good base for the use of mobile phone as a tool for conducting marketing activities. According to the American e-marketing association - eMA (2009a), US mobile advertising spending will increase from \$648 million in 2008 to \$3.3 billion in 2013.

SMS marketing is one of the main elements of Mobile Marketing. There are some advantages associated with this method:-

- The nature of mobile phones as a means of communications, which is very personal, makes SMS marketing a very powerful marketing tool.
- Nearly all company customers will carry mobile phone everywhere and for most of the day giving SMS marketing the chance to be effective for time sensitive marketing messages.

- SMS marketing provides companies with the ability to use text and photo marketing messages which can satisfy the different needs of the company customers and provide an attractive marketing tool.
- The majority of customers tend to read every single text they receive unlike other marketing messages that are considered to be junk mail, e.g. SPAM or even advertisements which can be ignored.

As a result, and according to the American e-marketing association - eMA (2009b), almost three quarters of the world's digital messages (74%) were sent through a mobile device in January 2009, with a 15% increase over the previous year (2008). Moreover, UK mobile users alone sent around 25 million text messages every day in 2008 (American e-marketing association – eMA, 2009d).

On the other hand, there are some disadvantages of using SMS marketing. These disadvantages include the relatively limited space of the message; the fact that a lot of customers might respond negatively to unwanted messages; some customers may be worried about responding to SMS messages due to security reasons; the increase in fraudulent messages; and (in most cases) the company needs to employ a mobile phone agency to send out the texts which can put the marketing activities at risk of being known by competitors.

DIFFERENCES BETWEEN E-MARKETING, E-COMMERCE, E-BUSINESS AND INTERNET-MARKETING

The review of the literature has revealed that one of the main obstacles to developing e-marketing potential is the absence of a clear conceptualisation of e-marketing purpose and definition. The majority of researchers within the field misuse the term e-marketing and are using the terms

E-business, e-marketing, E-Commerce and Internet-marketing interchangeably as if they are similar or have the same meaning, which is incorrect. For example, e-marketing is broader in scope than Internet Marketing since it refers not only to digital media such as the Web, e-mail and wireless media, but also includes electronic customer relationship management systems and the management of digital customer data, etc. In contrast, E-Commerce and E-business have a wider and broader scope than e-marketing. The differences between these terms will be illustrated and discussed in the following part of the chapter. As Internet Marketing has been discussed in the previous part of the chapter, the following parts of the chapter will discuss the remaining terms.

Electronic Commerce

It is difficult to find an accepted definition of E-Commerce (Duffy and Dale 2002), since its definitions vary according to interpretation and use. For example Kim and Moon, 1998 define Electronic Commerce (EC) as: *"The delivery of information, products and services, or payments via telephone lines, computer networks or any other electronic means"* (Kim and Moon, 1998, p: 2).

Zwass (1996) considers E-Commerce to be an administrative and communications tool and define it as: *"The sharing of business information, maintaining business relationships, and conducting business transactions by means of telecommunications networks"* (Zwass, 1996, P: 3). Whereas Treese and Stewart (1998) see E-Commerce as an opportunity in: *"The use of the global Internet for purchase and sale of goods and services, including services and support after the sale"* (Treese and Stewart, 1998, p: 5)

Baourakis, et al. (2002) define it as: *"The trading of goods and information through the Internet"* (Baourakis, et al., 2002; P: 581). On the other hand, Chaffey (2007) interpret E-Commerce as a means to exchange information: *"All electronically mediated information exchanges between*

an organization and its external stakeholders" (Chaffey, 2007, P: 8). In addition, according to some scholars, E-Commerce can take a variety of forms which include electronic data exchange (EDI), mobile telephone, direct links-up with suppliers, Internet, Intranet, Extranet, electronic catalogue ordering, and e-mail (Quayle 2002, P:1149).

According to Tetteh and Burn (2001), regardless of how E-Commerce is defined, the main purpose of E-Commerce is to facilitate the exchange of information and conduction of transactions. They also argue that E-Commerce presents many opportunities for businesses regardless of their size to improve its performance. It is commonly recognised that E-Commerce is equivalent to online buying and selling of products and services. In the narrow terms, E-Commerce focuses on conducting online transactions between different parties over the Internet. According to Canadian eBC (2006) E-Commerce is a term that describes a focus on buying and selling products and services on the Internet. Although Perry and Schneider (2000), as cited in Holsapple and Singh (2000), mentioned that this view is quite narrow and preclude other important non-commercial transactions, information exchanges, and intraorganisational activities" (Perry and Schneider, 2000, P: 152). The view of E-Commerce as a phenomena focusing on buying and selling activities is still one of the most accepted views about E-Commerce among marketers, scholars and practitioners.

However, E-Commerce does play a major role in today's marketing and business worlds. Within this context, UK retail E-Commerce is expected to reach 25.5 billion pounds in 2009 (with an increase of 8.6% from 2008) and expected to reach 44.9 billion pounds by 2012. Moreover, according to the American e-marketing association - eMA (2008) UK B2C E-Commerce is expected to reach 94.2 billion pounds by 2012.

Electronic Business

The concept of Electronic Business (E-Business) has gained a lot of interest from researchers and practitioners over the last decade. Although one of the foremost users of the term E-Business was IBM in 1997 (Alexandrou, 2009 and Chaffey, 2007), at present many companies all over the world are trying to use E-Business in conducting its activities. As much as E-Commerce, the concept of E-Business and its definition has created arguments among researchers and there is a no single or unique accepted definition of E-Business (Searle, 2001; Rodgers et al., 2002 and Martin and Matlay, 2003). Within this context, Harrison and Van Hoek (2005) defined E-Business as: *"Trading with an organization's suppliers and business customers, by electronic means"* (Harrison and Van Hoek, 2005: P: 284). However, Chen (2001) define E-Business as: *"The conduct of business on the Internet, not only buying and selling but also servicing customers and collaborating with business partners"* (Chen, 2001: 2).

The Australian Department for Environment and Resource Management-ADERM (2009) defined E-Business as: *"The use of computer-mediated networks to conduct the normal business of government and encompasses electronic service delivery and e-procurement"* (ADERM, 2009; P: 1). Moreover, the Australian state of Environment – ASE (2009) define E-Business as: *"Business transactions and affairs conducted electronically"* (ASE, 2009; P: 2). Jelassi and Enders (2008) defined E-Business as: *"The use of electronic means to conduct an organisation business internally and/or externally"* (Jelassi and Enders, 2008; P: 41). Finally, Alexandrou (2009) defines it as: *"The conduct of business on the Internet"* (Alexandrou, 2009; P: 1).

Alexandrou (2009) also argue that E-Business as a term is broader than E-Commerce since it does not refer only to buying and selling (as in E-Commerce) but also refers to servicing customers and collaborating with business partners. This is in line with the roots of the concept of E-Business. By tracing the first known definition of E-Business provided by IBM in 1997 it was found that IBM defined E-Business as: *"The transformation of key business organisational processes through the use of Internet technologies"* (IBM, 2009; P: 1). According to Chaffey (2007), the key business processes referred to in the IBM definition for E-Business are the main organisational process within any organisation (e.g. research and development, marketing, production and logistics).

CONCLUSION

The review of the related literature exposes that one of the main obstacles in the literature is the unclear way of dealing with the concept and definition of E-Business as well as e-marketing, E-Commerce and Internet Marketing. Within this context the majority of researchers within the field misuse the term E-Business, the mainstream of researchers are using the terms: E-Business and E-Commerce as equivalents or a different wording for the same meaning, which is incorrect because these terms are different. For most of the researchers, the term E-Business is generally regarded as the application of information technologies (IT) into business processes.

For example, Sheikh (2009) conducted a study to examine conversion rate problems of SMEs in Internet Marketing in Pakistan. By investigating the study it is found that Sheikh (2009) presented the concept of E-Commerce as an equivalent to e-marketing. Within the same line, Juena and Mirz (2008) conducted a study to investigate the utilisation of mobile advertising in B2C marketing. Instead of considering mobile advertising as an element of e-marketing, they considered it as a part of Mobile Commerce. Moreover, Ngai (2003) conducted a review of the literature related to Internet Marketing research for the period from 1987 to 2000. Within his study Ngai (2003) reviewed not only Internet Marketing but also e-marketing, E-Commerce and E-Business based on the argument that these entire three concepts are similar to each other. Moreover, Svedic (2004) conducted a study to investigate e-marketing strategies for E-business. Although the study was mainly related to e-marketing, Svedic (2004) considered e-marketing and E-Business as equivalents. Also, Fiore (2001) work on e-marketing strategies was entirely related to E-Business instead of e-marketing.

What has been discussed by Sheikh (2009), Juena and Mirz (2008), Svedic (2004), Fiore (2001) and Ngai (2003) is also true for a lot of researchers and scholars in the field of e-marketing.

This research argues (based on the various definitions for E-Commerce and E-Business illustrated and discussed within this chapter) that the concept of E-Business goes beyond the narrow understanding associated with the term E-Commerce. Within this context, E-Commerce characteristically relates to the process of buying and selling products, services and information through the use of the Internet and/or computer networks (Chaffey, 2007; Lesjak and Vehovar, 2005; Laudon and Laudon, 2004; Greenstein and Feinman, 2000 and Turban et al., 2004). Moreover, according to the arguments of Rodgers et al.

(2002), E-Commerce principally focuses on the organisation customers while E-Business expands the connectivity of the organisation to include not only its customers but also the organisation suppliers, employees and business partners.

Accordingly, E-Commerce and E-Business are not only two different concepts but also E-Commerce is a subset of E-Business, in line with the findings of Dalton (1999), Kalakota and Robinson (1999), Chaffey (2007), Lesjak and Vehovar (2005), Laudon and Laudon (2004), Jelassi and Enders (2008), Greenstein and Feinman (2000) and Turban et al. (2004). Table 2 illustrates some of the similarities and dissimilarities between E-Commerce and E-Business based on both the various definitions as well as the previous discussion within this chapter

Based on the previous discussion, it is clear that E-Business, e-marketing, E-Commerce and Internet Marketing are not equivalents or a different wording for the same meaning as observed in the literature, where there is a blurring of the distinction between the terms. Within this context, e-marketing is broader in scope than Internet Marketing since it refers not only to digital media such as the web, e-mail and wireless media, but also includes the management of digital cus-

Table 2. Similarities and dissimilarities between E-Commerce and E-Business

Similarities	- Both of the concepts depend on web technology - Both of the concepts integrated new web technology into organisational and business processes. - Both of the concepts aims to increase effectiveness and improve efficiency of the organisations	
Dissimilarities	**E-Commerce**	**E-Business**
	Principally focuses on the organisation customers	Expands the connectivity of the organisation to include not only its customer but also the organisation suppliers, employees and business partners.
	Characteristically relates to the process of buying and selling products, services and information through the use of the Internet and/or computer networks	Characteristically relates to all the key business processes within the organisation (e.g. research and development, marketing, production and logistics).
	Depend mainly on web technology	Technology employed is normally more advanced than that one used in E-Commerce. Depend mainly on web technology, Enterprise Resource Planning systems (ERP), Material Requirements Planning (MRP) and Customer Relationship Management(CRM)

Figure 2. Differences between Internet marketing, e-marketing, E-Commerce and E-Business

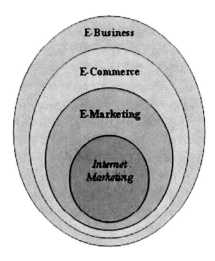

tomer data, Mobile Marketing, Intranet Marketing, Extranet Marketing and electronic customer relationship management systems. In contrast, E-Commerce and E-Business have a wider and broader scope than e-marketing. These differences can be illustrated in Figure 2.

FUTURE RESEARCH DIRECTIONS

There are few numbers of studies that have investigated the correct concept of e-marketing; consequently there is a need to conduct more research to investigate this concept in different contexts. On the other hand, there are few numbers of studies that have investigated the impact/effect of entrepreneurial skills and top management support, organisational culture and international orientation of the firm on the adoption of new technologies, such as e-marketing, E-commerce and E-business; consequently there is a need to conduct more research to investigate this impact in an e-marketing context. This will lead to a greater and deep understanding of e-marketing

as well as the impact of its adoption by different enterprises and will add to the accumulated knowledge in the field.

REFERENCES

Adam, S., & Deans, K. R. (2001). *Inter-study comparisons of small business Internet use in Australia and New Zealand.*

ADERM. (2009). *The Australian Department for Environment and Resource Management-ADERM, E-Business definition.* Retrieved May 20, 2009, from www.nrw.qld.gov.au/about/policy/documents/33/definitions.html

Alexandrou, M. (2009). *E-business.* Retrieved May 21, 2009, from http://www.mariosalexandrou.com /definition/ebusiness.asp

ASE. (2009). *The Australian state of environment – ASE, E-business definition.* Retrieved May 20, 2009, from http://www.environment.gov.au /soe/2001/publications /theme-reports/ settlements/ glossary.html

Baker, R. H. (1997). *Extranets: The complete sourcebook.* Hightstown, NJ: McGraw-Hill, Inc.

Baourakis, G., Kourgiantakis, M., & Migdalas, A. (2002). The impact of e- commerce on agro-food marketing: The case of agricultural cooperatives, firms and consumers in Crete. *British Food Journal, 104*(8), 580–590. doi:10.1108/00070700210425976

Berezai, P. (2000). *B-2-B on the Internet: 2000-2005.* London, UK: Datamonitor PLC.

Berthon, P., Pitt, L., & Watson, R. T. (1996a). Marketing communication and the World Wide Web. *Business Horizons, 39*(5), 24–32. doi:10.1016/S0007-6813(96)90063-4

Berthon, P., Pitt, L., & Watson, R. T. (1996b). Re-surfing W3: Research perspectives on marketing communication and buyer behaviour on the World Wide Web. *International Journal of Advertising, 15*(4), 287–301.

Canadian-Small-Business-Financing-Act. (2006). *Consolidated statutes and regulations of Canada, Canada small business financing regulations (SOR/99-141)*. Retrieved October 14, 2006, from http://lois.justice.gc.ca/ en/C-10.2/SOR-99-141/ index.html

Carlton, J. (2009). *The benefits of email marketing*. Retrieved June 10, 2009, from http://www.opt-in-email- marketing.org/benefits-of -email-marketing.html

Chaffey, D. (2007). *E-business and e-commerce management: Strategy, implementation and practice*. Financial Times/Prentice Hall.

Chaffey, D., Ellis-Chadwick, F., Mayer, R., & Johnston, K. (2000). *Internet marketing: Strategy, implementation and practice*. Prentice Hall.

Chaston, I., & Mangles, T. (2003). Relationship marketing in online business-to-business markets: A pilot investigation of small UK manufacturing firms. *European Journal of Marketing, 37*(5/6), 753–773. doi:10.1108/03090560310465134

Chen, S. (2001). *Strategic management of e-business*. New York, NY: John Wiley & Sons, Inc.

Collins, C., Buhalis, D., & Peters, M. (2003). Enhancing SMTEs' business performance through the Internet and e-learning platforms. *Education+Training, 45*(8/9), 483-494.

Coppel, J. (2002). *E-commerce: Impacts and policy challenges*. Paris, France: Organisation for Economic, Co-operation and Development.

Dalton, G. (1999). E-business evolution. *Information Week, 7*(37), 50–66.

Duffy, G., & Dale, B. G. (2002). E-commerce processes: A study of criticality. *Industrial Management & Data Systems, 102*(8), 432–441. doi:10.1108/02635570210445862

eBusiness-Connection. (2008). *Internet marketing*. Retrieved November 2, 2008, from http://www.e-bc.ca/

Eid, R. (2003). *Business-to-business international internet marketing: adoption, implementation and implications, an empirical study of UK companies*. Bradford, UK: Bradford University.

Eid, R., & Trueman, M. (2004). Factors affecting the success of business-to-business international internet marketing (B-to-B IIM): An empirical study of UK companies. *Industrial Management & Data Systems, 104*, 16–30. doi:10.1108/02635570410514061

El-Gohary, H. (2009). *The impact of e-marketing practices on marketing performance of small business enterprises: An empirical investigation*. Bradford, UK: Bradford University.

El-Gohary, H., Trueman, M., & Fukukawa, K. (2008a). *E-marketing and small business enterprises: A review of the literature from 2003-2008*. Paper presented at the Institute for Small Business & Entrepreneurship 2008 Conference (ISBE 2008), Belfast, N. Ireland.

El-Gohary, H., Trueman, M., & Fukukawa, K. (2008b). E-marketing and small business enterprises: A review of the methodologies. *Journal of Business & Public Policy, 2*(2), 64–93.

eMA. (2008). *American e-marketing association (eMA) - The UK B2C E-Commerce*.

eMA. (2009a). *American e-marketing association (eMA) - US mobile advertising spending from 2008–2013*. Retrieved May 12, 2009, from http://www.emarketer.com /Article.aspx?R=1007007 eMA. (2009b). *American e-marketing association (eMA) - three-quarters of the world's messages sent by mobile.* Retrieved May 12, 2009, from http://www.emarketer.com /Article.aspx?R=1006995

eMA. (2009c). *American e-marketing association (eMA) - why retail loves e-mail.* Retrieved March 24, 2009, from http://www.emarketer.com/Article.aspx?R=1006919

eMA. (2009d). *American e-marketing association (eMA) - mobile messaging in Western Europe.* Retrieved January 5, 2009, from http://www.emarketer.com /Article.aspx?R=1006842

Epsilon, C. (2009). *The benefits of Internet marketing.* Retrieved June 1, 2009, from http://www.epsilonconcepts.com/ upload/file/The%20 Benefits %20Of%20Internet%20 Marketing.pdf

Evans, J. R., & King, V. E. (1999). Business-to-business marketing and the World Wide Web planning, managing, and assessing websites. *Industrial Marketing Management, 28*(4), 343–358. doi:10.1016/S0019-8501(98)00013-3

Fiore, F. (2001). *E-marketing strategies: The hows and whys of driving sales through e-commerce: Sell anything, anywhere, any way, anytime, at any price.* Que.

Galgano, A., & La Mesa, E. (2006). *Email marketing: Salesware, IT ASP solutions for e-mail marketing.*

Ghosh, S. (1998). Making business sense of the Internet. *Harvard Business Review, 26*(2), 127–135.

Gogan, J. L. (1997). The Web's impact on selling techniques: Historical perspective and early observations. *International Journal of Electronic Commerce, 1*(2), 89–108.

Greene, S. (2009). *The 13 hidden treasures of Internet marketing.* Retrieved June 2, 2009, from http://www.sitepronews.com/ archives/2002/oct /11.html

Greenstein, M., & Feinman, T. M. (2000). *Electronic commerce: Security, risk management and control.* Irwin/McGraw-Hill.

Hamill, J., & Gregory, K. (1997). Internet marketing in the internationalisation of UK SMEs. *Journal of Marketing Management, 13*, 9–28. doi:10.1080/0267257X.1997.9964456

Harrison, A., & van Hoek, R. I. (2005). *Logistics management and strategy.* Financial Times/Prentice Hall.

Hofacker, C. F. (1999). *Internet marketing.* Digital Springs, Incorporated.

Hofacker, C. F. (2001). *Internet marketing* (3rd ed.). New York, NY: John Wiley & Sons, Inc.

Hoffman, D. L., & Novak, T. P. (1996). Marketing in hypermedia computer-mediated environments: Conceptual foundations. *Journal of Marketing,* 50–68. doi:10.2307/1251841

Hoffman, D. L., & Novak, T. P. (1997). A new marketing paradigm for electronic commerce. *The Information Society, 13*, 43–54. doi:10.1080/019722497129278

Holsapple, C. W., & Singh, M. (2000). Electronic commerce: From a definitional taxonomy toward a knowledge-management view. *Journal of Organizational Computing and Electronic Commerce, 10*(3), 149–170. doi:10.1207/S15327744JOCE1003_01

IBM. (2009). *E-business definition* Retrieved May 21, 2009, from www.ibm.com/ e-business

IS. (2009). *The Internet society (IS) - history of the Internet.* Retrieved March 1, 2009, from http://www.isoc.org/

IWS. (2009). *Internet world stats - Internet users in the world from 1995 - 2009.* Retrieved June 10, 2009, from http://www.internet worldstats.com / emarketing.htm

Jelassi, T., & Enders, A. (2008). Mobile advertising: A European perspective. *Selected Readings on Telecommunication and Networking*, 41.

Juena, S. S., & Mirza, K. (2008). *Utilization of mobile advertising in B2C marketing.* Porsön, Sweden: Luleå tekniska universitet.

Kalakota, R., & Whinston, A. B. (1999). *Electronic commerce: A manager's guide.* Addison-Wesley Professional.

Kiang, M. Y., Raghu, T. S., & Shang, K. H. M. (2000). Marketing on the Internet—who can benefit from an online marketing approach? *Decision Support Systems, 27*(4), 383–393. doi:10.1016/S0167-9236(99)00062-7

Kiani, G. R. (1998). Marketing opportunities in the digital world. *Internet Research: Electronic Networking Applications and Policy, 8*(2), 185–194. doi:10.1108/10662249810211656

Kim, J., & Moon, J. Y. (1998). Designing towards emotional usability in customer interfaces-trustworthiness of cyber-banking system interfaces. *Interacting with Computers, 10*(1), 1–29. doi:10.1016/S0953-5438(97)00037-4

Lancioni, R. A., Smith, M. F., & Oliva, T. A. (2000). The role of the internet in supply chain management. *Industrial Marketing Management, 29*(1), 45–56. doi:10.1016/S0019-8501(99)00111-X

Laudon, K. C., Laudon, J. P., & Filip, F. G. (2004). Management information systems: Managing the digital firm. *New Jersey, 8.*

Lesjak, D., & Vehovar, V. (2005). Factors affecting evaluation of e-business projects. *Industrial Management & Data Systems, 105*(4), 409–428. doi:10.1108/02635570510592334

Liang, T. P., & Huang, J. S. (1998). An empirical study on consumer acceptance of products in electronic markets: A transaction cost model. *Decision Support Systems, 24*(1), 29–43. doi:10.1016/S0167-9236(98)00061-X

Martin, L., & Matlay, H. (2003). Innovative use of the Internet in established small firms: The impact of knowledge management and organisational learning in accessing new opportunities. *Qualitative Market Research: An International Journal, 6*(1), 18–26. doi:10.1108/13522750310457348

McCole, P., & Ramsey, E. (2004). Internet-enabled technology in knowledge-intensive business services: A comparison of Northern Ireland, the Republic of Ireland and New Zealand. *Marketing Intelligence, 22*(7), 761–779. doi:10.1108/02634500410568

McDonald, M., & Wilson, H. (1999). *E-marketing improving marketing effectiveness in a digital world.*

McGowan, P., Durkin, M. G., Allen, L., Dougan, C., & Nixon, S. (2001). Developing competencies in the entrepreneurial small firm for use of the Internet in the management of customer relationships. *Journal of European Industrial Training, 25*(2/4), 126–136. doi:10.1108/EUM0000000005443

McLuhan, M. (2009). *Marshall McLuhan quotations.* Retrieved February 15, 2009, from http://www.marshallmcluhan.com /main.html

MDA. (2009). *Mobile Data Association - text message figures in the UK.* Retrieved March 21, 2009, from http://www.text.it/mediacentre / sms_figures.cfm

Ngai, E. W. T. (2003). Internet marketing research (1987-2000): A literature review and classification. *European Journal of Marketing, 37*(1/2), 24–49. doi:10.1108/03090560310453894

Norcross, T. (2008). *What is mobile marketing?* Retrieved December 20, 2008, from http://www.mobilemarketing magazine.co.uk /2005/10/ what_is_ mobile_.html

Oliva, R. A. (2004). B2B for sale. *Marketing Management, 13*(5), 48–49.

Papazoglou, M. P., & Tsalgatidou, A. (2000). Business to business electronic commerce issues and solutions. *Decision Support Systems, 29*(4), 301–304. doi:10.1016/S0167-9236(00)00079-8

Paul, P. (1996). Marketing on the Internet. *Journal of Consumer Marketing, 13*(4), 27–39. doi:10.1108/07363769610124528

Perry, J., & Schneider, G. P. (2000). *Electronic commerce*.

Poon, S., & Jevons, C. (1997). Internet-enabled international marketing: A small business network perspective. *Journal of Marketing Management, 13*, 29–41. doi:10.1080/0267257X.1997.9964457

Poon, S., & Swatman, P. (1999a). A longitudinal study of expectations in small business Internet commerce. *International Journal of Electronic Commerce, 3*, 21–34.

Poon, S., & Swatman, P. M. C. (1996). Small business alliances: Internet-enabled strategic advantage. *Monash University Department of Information Systems Working Paper 25/95*: Citeseer.

Poon, S., & Swatman, P. M. C. (1997a). Small business use of the Internet. *International Marketing Review, 14*(5), 385–402. doi:10.1108/02651339710184343

Poon, S., & Swatman, P. M. C. (1997b). Internet-based small business communication: Seven Australian cases. *Electronic Markets, 7*(2), 15–21. doi:10.1080/10196789700000019

Poon, S., & Swatman, P. M. C. (1999b). An exploratory study of small business Internet commerce issues. *Information & Management, 35*(1), 9–18. doi:10.1016/S0378-7206(98)00079-2

Porter, M. E. (2001). Strategy and the Internet. *Harvard Business Review, 79*(3), 62–79.

Quayle, M. (2002). E-commerce: The challenge for UK SMEs in the twenty-first century. *International Journal of Operations & Production Management, 22*(9/10), 1148–1161. doi:10.1108/01443570210446351

Quelch, J. A., & Klein, L. R. (1996). The Internet and international marketing. *Sloan Management Review, 37*(3), 60.

Reedy, J., & Schullo, S. (2004). *Electronic marketing – integrating electronic resources into the marketing process* (2ed ed.). Cincinnati, OH: Thomson South-Western.

Rodgers, J. A., Yen, D. C., & Chou, D. C. (2002). Developing e-business: A strategic approach. *Information Management & Computer Security, 10*(4), 184–192. doi:10.1108/09685220210436985

Searle, J. (2001). *UK online for business*. Retrieved September 9, 2008, from www.ncc.co.uk/ncc/Jenny_Searle.pdf

SharWestInc. (1997). *Productivity and customer satisfaction: Internet, Intranet, and Extranet as tools*. Retrieved from http//www.sharwest.com

Sheikh, M. A. (2009). *Conversion rate problem of SMEs in Internet marketing - a developing country perspective*. Karlskrona, Sweden: Blekinge Institute of Technology.

Siddiqui, N., Omalley, A., Mccoll, J., & Birtwistle, G. (2003). Retailer and consumer perceptions of online fashion retailers: Website design issues. *Journal of Fashion Marketing and Management, 7*(4), 345–355. doi:10.1108/13612020310496949

Skinner, S. (2000). *Business-to-business e-commerce: Investment perspective*. London, UK: Durlacher Research.

Smith, P. R., & Chaffey, D. (2005). *E-marketing excellence: At the heart of e-business* (2nd ed.). Oxford, UK: Butterworth Heinemann.

Soh, C., Mah, Q. Y., Gan, F. J., Chew, D., & Reid, E. (1997). The use of the Internet for business: The experience of early adopters in Singapore. *Internet Research: Electronic Networking Applications and Policy, 7*(3), 217–228. doi:10.1108/10662249710171869

Strauss, J., & Frost, R. (2001). *E-marketing*. NJ, USA: Prentice Hall.

Svedic, Z. (2004). *E-marketing strategies for e-business*. Simon Fraser University.

Tetteh, E., & Burn, J. (2001). Global strategies for SME-business: Applying the SMALL framework. *Logistics Information Management, 14*(1/2), 171–180. doi:10.1108/09576050110363202

Treese, G. W., & Stewart, L. C. (1998). *Designing systems for Internet commerce*. Boston, MA: Addison-Wesley Longman Publishing Co.

Turban, E., Lee, J. K., & Viehland, D. (2004). *Electronic commerce 2004: A managerial perspective*. Pearson Education.

Vlosky, R. P., Fontenot, R., & Blalock, L. (2000). Extranets: Impacts on business practices and relationships. *Journal of Business and Industrial Marketing, 15*(6), 438–457. doi:10.1108/08858620010349510

Wilson, S. G., & Abel, I. (2002). So you want to get involved in e-commerce. *Industrial Marketing Management, 31*(2), 85–94. doi:10.1016/S0019-8501(01)00188-2

Zwass, V. (1996). Electronic commerce: Structures and issues. *International Journal of Electronic Commerce, 1*, 3–24.

Chapter 9
Analysis of the Variables which Determine a Good E–Marketing Strategy:
The Techniques Most Used During Times of Crisis

Beatriz Sainz de Abajo
University of Valladolid, Spain

Isabel de la Torre Díez
University of Valladolid, Spain

Miguel López Coronado
University of Valladolid, Spain

Carlos de Castro Lozano
University of Córdoba, Spain

ABSTRACT

Internet marketing covers all aspects related to the promotion and sale of a product or service through the Internet. This chapter demonstrates how adequate planning is fundamental in a Small and Medium-sized Enterprise (SME) to increase sales. The objective is to analyze the aspects which must be taken into consideration when developing a good e-marketing strategy and to study some of the different alternatives that the Internet and e-marketing make available to us: e-mail marketing, viral e-marketing, geomarketing, and positioning within search engines. Also the concept of Customer Relationship Management (CRM) will be analyzed. The leap into the global market is not easy and the reduction in budgets has inspired marketing professionals to adopt strategies which can be measured and the results controlled, pointing out that the online tactics and tools used by the vast majority of marketing professionals in their strategic plan are banners, search engines, and e-mail.

DOI: 10.4018/978-1-60960-765-4.ch009

INTRODUCTION

E-commerce is linked to e-marketing or on-line marketing. Just as in traditional marketing, marketing on the Internet is the coming together of techniques and operations which allow us to contribute to the development and increase in sales. However it differs from traditional marketing in that we use the tools and techniques that the Internet makes available to us (Sainz, *et al.*, 2010).

This includes all activities carried out from the point when we decide to sell a product up to the after-sales or customer service. However e-marketing is not limited to the study of various forms of promotion or publicity. It involves a broader concept that brings together all the sales operations, even though the publicity is the most attractive and popular side.

The study of the market, the products to be sold, pricing, competition, publicity, discounts and the various forms of distribution also form a part of marketing and equally must be taken into account with Internet marketing. All this information allows us to best define the design of the website according to the visitors (what is it that they are looking for in the site), whether they find it (how do they arrive at the site) and finally their level of satisfaction.

The objective of this chapter is to analyze the aspects which must be taken into consideration when developing a good e-marketing strategy such as the administration of virtual shops, the creation of automatic mailing lists, the creation of newsletters, the profile of the consumer, swift and easy access, empathy, confidence and personalized treatment amongst other things.

Once the variables with which one can "play" when developing an e-marketing strategy have been analyzed, some of the alternatives that the Internet and e-marketing present us with are studied. Of these, there are four which are of most interest and on which we will focus, being those that are most readily accepted by businesses and end-users: e-mail marketing, viral e-marketing,

geomarketing and finally positioning in search engines.

Also in this chapter the concept of Customer Relationship Management (CRM) will be analyzed. More than a novelty it is the natural evolution of another highly accepted concept within the marketing world: relational marketing. CRM is an important commercial strategy, as much for e-business as for traditional firms, when it comes to facing up to a market which is increasingly competitive and demanding. The objective must be based on providing a series of processes aimed at the client through different departments and channels, in order to be able to attract and retain customers.

Finally the current economic situation is analyzed and how the reduction in budgets has inspired marketing professionals to adopt strategies which can be measured and the results controlled. In 2009, positioning in the search engines, e-mail marketing, social networks and pay-per-click campaigns will take centre stage.

A PRIMARY APPROACH TO THE CONCEPT OF E-MARKETING

In 1973, Dr. Peter Drucker (1910-2005), perhaps the greatest business consultant that the world has known, and the creator of modern Management, said: "The purpose of Marketing involves making the sale easy, or rather knowing and understanding the client so well that the product or service satisfies their needs and sells itself, practically without promotion or publicity".

The origins of e-marketing are found at the beginning of the ´90s in the form of simple web sites, which only contained text, and which offered information on products. Later came publicity banners complete with graphics. The most recent step in this evolution has been the creation of entire businesses which operate through the Internet in order to promote and sell their products and services.

As Paul Fleming commented, the 4 Fs of e-marketing are as follows (Fleming, P.):

- Flow. This is the mental state into which an Internet user enters upon immersion in a website which offers an experience full of interactivity and added value.
- Functionality. If the client has entered into the state of flow, they are on the road to being won over. So that the flow of the relationship is not broken, one must provide the website with functionality, that is to say, construct pages taking into account the limitations of technology. This refers to an attractive homepage, with clear and useful information for the user.
- Feedback. Once the relationship has started to be built, the most must be made of the information from what the user knows. The Internet gives one the opportunity to ask the customer what they like and what they would like to improve. In short, to engage in conversation with the customer in order to know them better and construct a relationship based on their needs. In this way it is possible to personalize the website following each contact.
- Loyalty. The Internet offers the possibility of creating customer communities which create content. A personalized dialogue is set up with the clients which in turn leads to customer loyalty.

E-Marketing Strategies

It is obvious that it is difficult to stand out from the crowd. One must have a competitive and effective site. It is for this reason that a website is only the first step towards success in e-commerce. Almost all companies, and some households, have their own website (more or less elaborate). But simply having a website does not automatically lead to success. Taking a serious business into the virtual world requires the scrutiny of a broad range of factors which begin with the identification of the competitive and comparative advantages of the business (Ngai, E.W.T., 2003).

The principal objective of a good e-marketing strategy is to reduce costs and increase the functionality of the resources (Sainz, B., de la Torre, I. & Lopez, M., 2009). In order to achieve this, the Internet has eliminated frontiers and distances, speeding up transactions in order to offer customer satisfaction. In short, the strategy of electronic commerce should be focused on satisfying the needs of the customer (Kalyanam & McIntyre, 2002).

To be a success, it must be based on the experience of the customer, their needs and principal requirements. Techniques such as Brainstorming and Benchmarking may be used, as well as constructing a working group which takes on the role of the customer during modelization, in this way shaping a development orientated towards selling in the way that the real or potential customer desires (Sainz, B. *et al.*, 2009).

The next step is to analyze a series of aspects which must be taken into account when designing a good e-marketing strategy:

- Management of virtual shops.
- Creation of automatic mailing lists.
- Creation of newsletters.
- Staying one step ahead.
- Customer profile.
- Easy and swift access.
- Empathy and confidence.
- Personalized treatment.

Management of Virtual Shops

The running of a website involves operating with a multidimensional vision for it to be a success. That is to say, an e-marketing dimension must be added to the business and technological dimensions, which aims to generate long term project support. Only by taking into account these three dimensions can we triumph.

Creation of Automatic Mailing Lists

E-mail is the most important electronic marketing tool which exists today. It is vital to build and keep up to date a database of contacts and customers.

Creation of Newsletters

The newsletter is a communication tool of enormous value and utility in the Internet. However, frequently the newsletter is only built in HTML format, that is to say, with photos, graphics and sometimes with Flash applications which in most cases ordinary users cannot see, creating an initial frustration and in the long term the loss of an opportunity. To counteract this, one must always develop two versions: the so-called "pure text" version which can be received by all internet users without a problem, but to which can be added links to the "HTML version". The first leads to the second, which, being housed in the Internet, at the same time allows the visitors access to the website.

Staying One Step Ahead

It is possible to stay one step ahead of their needs, providing more detailed information on the products, their uses and history, or how to make the most out them by using other complementary products. One must point out to the customer the advantages of having them, help them chose the right moment and let them know that the company is always available to give advice and keep the customer up-to-date with new products.

One of the things that the purchaser values most is having made the right decision, that they have not been cheated and that the company, as well as having a legitimate interest in selling a product, really knows and is worried about their needs.

If the company is honest with its customers, they in turn will have to be so with the company, and clear communication is the best way of ensuring that what might otherwise be a simply

transaction becomes a relationship. And between the two extremes there are limitless possibilities which may be productive and satisfactory as much for the seller as for the buyer.

Customer Profile

The online consumer looks for data, information and price comparison of products and services in the Internet. The dialogue which is set up between the user and potential buyer must be supplemented by something which is of fundamental importance: the experience of navigating the website. This factor is decisive when it comes to converting the user into a buyer, and also when it comes to making clients move over from the offline to online platform. Therefore this will be one of the determining factors which make a website profitable.

But what exactly is "the experience of navigating the website"? A good navigating and buying experience in a virtual site says everything about the business it represents. There is no better way of keeping away customers than an unpleasant buying experience, a poorly navigable site or a policy which is not obvious to the customer.

The best way of generating confidence in the internet user is by having a commercial website which is easy to use, with speedy navigation, with clear and honest information, and where the interest which the company has for the customer is obvious. All of this is fundamental to convince the customer that behind the brand there is more than great design or a fancy name.

Easy and Swift Access

One of the main preoccupations of internet users is time. Not only for the cost of navigating, but also because above all the web imposes the rhythm. It is possible that the internet user only visits the company website for a few seconds, and in this short space of time one must present oneself, show one's products and leave the user with the need to visit the page again. For this it is vitally important that the virtual site is clear and easy to navigate, and that the contents are arranged with considerable logic and empathy towards the user.

If a customer has to spend too much time in a website in order to find what they are looking or to make a transaction, this may be the sign that something is not right. It might be advisable to go over the metrics concerning the number of visits to the site made by the same user in relation to the number of purchases made, also in relation to the evolution of the value of these purchases, and try to see what would happen if the time needed to complete the process within the website were reduced.

Empathy and Confidence

Confidence is a crucial factor in electronic commerce (Lowry, P.B. *et al.*, 2008). The simplicity of communication and the clarity of information are essential for achieving this objective. The website must be useful in order to help the user overcome their doubts and leave the way clear to making a purchase. The user must perceive this sensation anytime they decide to visit the virtual site, and equally with respect to any of the products and services that are offered.

Given the competition that exists in the net, one must ensure that clarity, transparency and simplicity of use are the distinctive features of the brand. One must be prepared in order to give a dynamic response, adapted to each user. In other words, learn to converse with the clients and let them know that the main interest of the company is contributing to make their life easier (Ren & Yuan, 2007).

Personalized Treatment

The customers will feel uncomfortable if they sense, in a second or third visit, that the treatment they receive is not personalized. The foundation of the commercial memory of a website is the data and the profiles of the users, as well as the

follow-up. There are various sources of back-up which contribute to personalized treatment, such as e-mail, call centres, conventional mail, personalized offers, etc.

Although the availability of this "commercial memory" obviously has to do with the technical resources of the website, the skill of those running the company when it comes to interacting with the clients is also a determining factor. It is not easy, indeed it is sometimes impossible, to give specific treatment to each customer. However, it is possible to make the client feel that, as their importance to the company grows, they will be better remembered and will receive an ever more personalized treatment. Making the most of this advantage can awaken in the client a desire to remain loyal to the company. But first one must gain their confidence, accompanying them and explaining clearly everything about the product, the purchasing process and the aspects of the company which might be relevant to the client.

E-MARKETING TECHNIQUES

Once the variables which come into play when designing an e-marketing strategy have been analyzed, it is time to study some of the different alternatives that the Internet and e-marketing make available to us. Of these, there are four with characteristics which make them more interesting both for the customer and the company (Liu, Y. *et al.*, 2006).

E-Mail Marketing

This involves sending e-mails for publicity or commercial purposes. The Internet is becoming the most suitable medium for this type of send-out, because it reduces costs and is quick.

Whilst it is an efficient system, focusing our campaign using e-mail which imitates traditional mailing campaigns will not give good results.

The key factor to the success of this technique is based on selecting the right target group. One must spare no effort in selecting the target group for the message. A list must be made up which fits with the profile of public to be aimed at, with one choosing from two types of list:

- Opt-in email lists: these are e-mail databases made up from e-mail holders who have agreed to receive messages from the sender. The e-mail holder agrees to receive messages basically for 3 reasons:
- In exchange for money they will be paid for receiving advertising messages.
- In exchange for information which they may consider useful.
- They belong to a second list. For example, they wish to receive information about the stock-exchange and have agreed that, as well as information about that which interests them, they will receive a few advertising messages related to the same theme.
- SPAM: sending out e-mailings using e-mail databases obtained without the consent or the knowledge of the e-mail holder. Often they are gathered through chat-rooms, fora, notice boards, collected from the Web, etc. In this case the e-mail holder has not authorized anybody to use their e-mail for commercial ends. This type of undesired mail is bad practice in the Internet, and it is punishable as well as generating a poor image in the short and long term.

It has been shown that more than 30% of people who voluntarily receive a newsletter visit the website and end up using their services. And they recommend it. On the contrary, spam generates bad feeling and repulsion in 80% of those who receive it against their will (iWorld, 2003).

The next question which arises is how to obtain these lists (Savaris, 2009):

- Making up your own opt-in email lists. This may be through subscription to an electronic newsletter related to the products and / or services. Equally the customers may have given their e-mail in order to stay in contact with the company. One's own list is the first option to consider. It is a slow process but very effective.
- Contracting the services of companies specialized in "permission marketing" and massive send-outs of e-mails through opt-in lists or newsletters.
- Buying e-mail lists from companies dedicated to collecting and filtering databases of this type.

The other type of e-mail marketing is the use of an e-Newsletter. These can be divided into two types:

- E-Newsletter in text format: the body of the e-Newsletter consists of brief descriptions of contents with links.
- E-Newsletter in HTML format: the HTML messages provide a better response when they are more eye-catching and attractive, and allow for a distinction to be made between the contents. They have the added advantage of allowing for a detailed analysis of the behaviour of the subscriber. For example, if it is opened, which articles are read, if it is sent on to other people, etc. None of this is possible in e-Newsletters produced in simple text. Therefore, HTML allows us to collect more information and carry out more detailed analyses.

Finally, one must not neglect the subject matter of the e-mail being sent. One must choose between a descriptive and a suggestive approach. As a general rule, e-Newsletters with a commercial end opt for suggestive headings and those of an informative nature, for descriptive headings. This is the general trend.

Viral E-Marketing

Viral marketing or viral advertising are terms used to describe marketing techniques which try to make the most of pre-existing social networks, to bring about exponential increases in Brand Awareness, using a viral self-replicating process similar to the spread of a computer virus. It tends to be based on word of mouth by means of electronic media. It uses the effect of the "social network" created by the Internet or the modern services of mobile phones to reach a large number of people rapidly.

The term viral marketing is also used to describe veiled marketing campaigns based in the Internet, including the use of blogs and apparently amateur sites, designed in reality to spark word of mouth for a new product or service.

But how does viral marketing work? Viral marketing is part of a marketing strategy used to achieve fixed objectives. It describes a strategy which encourages a person to send a marketing message to other people, generating the ideal setting for an exponential increase in exposure to the said message. This means that the message as with viruses, is multiplied rapidly, giving feedback, converting one thousand messages into two thousand, and two thousand into four thousand, and so on and so forth.

Various studies show that when a person has a good experience online, they recommend it to at least 12 other people. But watch out! Does the same thing happen if they have a bad experience?

This is the basic dynamic of viral marketing. Marketing professionals must be conscious of the fact that the Internet is different, it is a global and chaotic medium and for this reason one must develop strategies which are effective in this new medium.

This method is generally well-received. We put our trust in the recommendations of our friends. In fact, a large percentage of sales are made thanks to the recommendations of friends.

Ralph Wilson, an American consultant who specialized in Marketing, carried out the following analysis of which are the elements that must be included to enforce this strategy. Wilson recognized six elements (Wilson, R. F., 2000):

- Offer a product or service of value to the user. The idea is to attract them with something free, then later offer products which must be paid for.
- Provide an easy form of diffusion. Viruses spread when they are easily passed on. The medium which carries the message must be easy to pass on and replicate. This might be an e-mail, a website, graphics, or the download of software.
- The service must be such that it can be rapidly scaled up.
- Exploit human motivation and behaviour. Knowing how to exploit human motivation is vital for any viral marketing plan. If the spread of the service can make the most of feelings of belonging, status and popularity, it will have achieved its objective.
- Use existing networks of communication. The human being is a social animal. It has been calculated that one person moves within a circle of 8 to 12 people, such as friends, family, associates, etc. However, according to their social position, this network may be hundreds or thousands of people. The same thing happens with Internet users surrounded by a circle of friends who may be many. Social networks are demonstrating this fact.
- Take advantage of the resources of others. The authors who allow their articles to be published free of charge in other sites are trying to position themselves by making the most of the audience already in place. A press release can be picked up by hundreds of journalists who will use the access they have to the public to do the work of creating the viral marketing campaign. These resources will therefore be used to the benefit of the "virus spreader".

Geomarketing

Geomarketing can reply to questions such as "What is the business potential for my company in a particular place?", "Where should we be directing our efforts?", "How do we identify the business opportunities?", "How do we define the most profitable areas?", "To which demographic group should we be directing our online advertising?"

In the last few years, the proliferation of free services has led companies dedicated to geomarketing to offer personalized products with defined characteristics, competing in this way with the big boys of the Internet such as Google Maps or Google Earth (CECARM, 2009).

Companies tend to have clear and concise studies carried out, or personalized representations of the possibilities of success of the company or business model in a determined geographical area. Undoubtedly, the companies which operate in extended geographical markets are the main users of this type of solution, such as financial bodies, commercial enterprises, distribution chains, agency networks, etc. Depending on the level of detail employed, studies may be at the level of micromarketing (if we use segmentation by portal for example) or on the macro level, such as municipal or provincial. It is obvious that the more detail we can use (it is not easy finding reliable databases with much detail), the better we can manage the levels of detail, since the macro levels are simply an accumulation of the micro levels.

Currently the SME are a great source for carrying out this type of study, since the price reduction in the past ten years has been dramatic, which is why these studies are not so costly to undertake.

Amongst the most important benefits, the following stand out:

- Optimization of the investment in marketing operations.
- Analysis of the market potential, households per income band, etc.
- Better market knowledge and the ability to focus efforts in specific sectors of the market.
- Identification of points of sale, offices, subsidiaries, distributors or the competition.
- Location of nearest offices, analysis of the best routes and alternatives.
- Fixing of the area of influence in order to establish the population being covered.

Positioning within Search Engines

In recent times, positioning has become one of the most sought-after tools for any website, even more so for ones dedicated to electronic commerce. Appearing in the first few positions in a search engine is indispensable if a Webmaster wants to generate traffic going to his own site. Therefore, good positioning can become the most efficient advertising for an electronic company.

Although there are various search engines such as Yahoo or Live Search, Google covers the greatest majority of searches carried out on the Web. For this reason, the study is centred on this search engine, even though many of the issues looked at are common to all of them.

A realized study using Eye Tracking tool show that the three first results in Google are read by just about everybody who carries out a search (Sherman, 2005). Interest falls away rapidly after the first page, with only 10% of users exploring beyond the third page of results.

In the same way as happens in the physical world, it is very important to carry out market analysis to know the clients as well as the competitors. In this way, the company is defining the segment of the market at which they are aiming and the niche market in which they find themselves. Companies normally only compete with a maximum number of thirty different businesses, in most cases no more than ten. This phenomenon is as true for the virtual world as it is for the physical world.

The objective must be to be placed amongst the top ten results in the search engine, at least in those pages which respond to the search criteria of the potential customers who are looking for this type of company. Getting one's link into the top ten results in Google is the obsession of any Web administrator. With Google which generates around 85% of all the traffic which goes through search engines, to make it to one of these privileged spots can mean the difference between success and failure in the Internet. One must take into account the following points when identifying the area on which the company must focus (Maciá, F., 2005):

- Precise identification of the niche market into which the company fits.
- Identification of the key search phrases of the company.
- Optimization of the management of information from the corporate web.
- Analysis of the customers who visit the website.
- Knowledge of the importance of key words.
- Concentration of key words.

Precise Identification of the Niche Market into which the Company Fits

Knowing which type of customer one should be aiming at, who they are, where they are and how they look for products and services is basic. In reality, the majority of searches are made using search phrases composed of two or three words, however the trend is that the more one uses the search engines, more specific tend to be the search phrases used. When the phrase does not give the required results, the search turns back to earlier attempts but with a more specific and focused use of words.

Identification of the Key Search Phrases of the Company

These must be related to the niche market, the geographical origin of the potential clients and the type of product offered.

For example, a company in Murcia dedicated to selling fruit mainly in the Anglo-Saxon market must have search phrases in English which are restricted to the product. That is to say that the company cannot choose a search phrase such as *"fruta de España"* if they want to be among the first few results found by the search engine. Rather they should opt for something like "fruit from Murcia".

Optimization of the Management of Information from the Corporate Web

But, how does one classify a surfer? In the same way that a person looks at the information from any object or concept.

For example, when a student thinks about buying a book they pay attention to the following: the title and the cover in general, the summary on the back cover, the index and possibly the titles of some of the chapters. Google is no different. When it comes to classifying a website, it looks at the title and the default description of the page, as well as in the contents of the home page. Following on, it starts navigating and goes from one link to another for the different parts of the website.

In addition, the student pays attention to the advice given by their classmates when it comes to opting for a book. Google does the same thing. It takes into account the pages which indicate the company, putting it in a higher position according to how prestigious the said pages are. That is to say, for an export company from Murcia it is not the same thing having a link in the personal page of an old friend as in that of a prestigious national newspaper.

Analysis of the Customers Who Visit the Website

It is important to know how many visits the website receives, where the visitors go within the site, from which country they come, which key words they use to get there from the search engine or how much time they stay.

Knowledge of the Importance of Key Words

Within the structure of the website, it is important to know how to situate the key words that the searcher will use. The reason for this is that Google attaches more importance to these words depending on where they are found. The most important part is the URL, followed by the title and the headers. The importance of adding the URL in adverts has been demonstrated by a study carried out in China (in the provinces of Beijing, Guangzhou and Shanghai), the results of which show how the inclusion of the URL in the advert increases the probability that the consumers will visit the website (Maddox & Gong, 2005).

At a lower level, links to other pages are found, and finally the text. At the final stage, those parts highlighted in black or in italics are more interesting.

Concentration of Key Words

The different search engines function by density and not by absolute values. That is to say that they compare the number of characters of the search criteria which coincide with the URL. For this reason it is important that the number of characters is not too high.

Actions to Achieve Better Positioning in the Search Engine

Once the preliminary general criteria have been taken into account, the study bases itself in con-

Figure 1. Actions to achieve better positioning

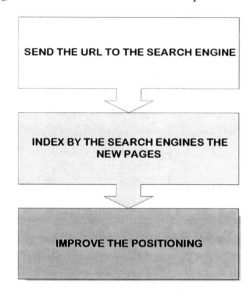

crete actions which must be undertaken to achieve better positioning in the search engine. Steps to follow (see Figure 1):

- Send the URL of the commercial website to the search engine.
- Make sure that all of the pages of the website are indexed by the search engines.
- Improve the positioning in the main screen of the search engine.

Firstly: Send the URL of the Commercial Website to the Search Engine

In the case of Google this is not strictly necessary, given that it is a search engine based on trawling links, so that if another website indicates the company, it will appear in the search results. In any case, one can always suggest a URL to Google. This does not guarantee when it will appear on the website, or if it will appear, independently of the number of times it is sent. When a URL is suggested, the system memorizes it so that it can look for it the next time it trawls. This can take a long time, sometimes weeks. If for any reason the website is not available when "Googlebot" passes, this is not a problem. It will try a few times and, if there are various links pointing to the website, it will pass again a few days later.

Secondly: Make Sure that all of the Pages of the Website are Indexed by the Search Engines

As well as being indexed by the search engines, it is also important that when we add a new page to the website, this is indexed as quickly as possible. This is where the construction of site maps comes into play. These files are an XML listing of the pages of the website, which tells the search engine where they are and some of their characteristics (such as the modification date) so that it finds them more easily and indexes them. Once this has happened, the XML file is uploaded and validated by the search engine. To validate a sitemap in Google, one must have a user account, for which a free gmail account will do, then enter into the Google Webmaster tools page and put in the URL of the sitemap.

Previously we have looked at the importance of keywords in order to have good positioning, however there has been no mention of how to reflect this in the construction of the website. This is where the so-called HTML labels come into play.

This type of label is not essential to be able to visualize the virtual sales space, it simply provides information about the page:

- The author of the document.
- When it is updated.
- The contents of the page.
- Keywords which represent the contents of the page.

Many search engines use this information to create their indexes. The most important "metas" for these engines are the Meta Keywords and the Meta Description. In both cases it is essential to use words which describe the contents of the page. In

this case it is a good thing not to cheat by adding words to try and increase your ranking, because currently the search engines have functions in place to detect this type of fraud.

Finally, and with respect to the Meta Keywords, it is a good thing to use a maximum of 5 keywords. Otherwise the search engines may think that the keywords are spam and therefore not list your page (Muller, 2002).

Thirdly: Improve the Positioning In the Main Screen of the Search Engine

Those criteria mentioned up to now refer to obtaining good positioning in the main screen of Google, where the search engine does not accept money to improve the position. However, there is another way of appearing in Google in exchange for payment: Adwords. In this case, the user creates an advert and chooses the keywords on the basis of which it will appear on the right-hand side of the results screen of the search engine (Adwords, 2009).

The cost of this service may be fixed by the company looking to promote itself. In order to do this, they may fix a maximum daily budget or a sum per click made to the advert. In this case it is worth pointing out that according to the money the company pays for each click, they will obtain a better position or on the contrary they may not even appear. On top of this, this ranking varies continually depending on the money paid by other companies with the same keywords. Because of this is it a good idea on the one hand to create a balance between the budget available for this activity and the position one wishes to occupy, and on the other hand to undertake a periodic study of the position obtained in relation to the money spent. Depending on the results of this analysis, the company must decide whether to modify or not the budget dedicated to improving its position.

Client Management

At the beginning of the year 2000 a new concept appeared that rapidly became fashionable: CRM. However, this concept is more than a novelty. It is a natural evolution from another well-accepted concept in the marketing world: relational marketing (Chalmeta, R., 2000).

The sophistication of the technology dedicated to the storing and analysis of customer data has enormously helped this evolution, undoubtedly given a boost by new technology (Gummesson, E., 2004).

However we must not confuse nor identify CRM with technology. Unquestionably technology has played an important part in shaping CRM, but it is not the only thing. CRM is above all a marketing strategy aimed at proactively constructing a preference in the consumers for a specific company, which logically leads to greater loyalty and as a consequence better profits (McKim, B., 2002).

In the end, the main objective of CRM is to construct long-term relationships through understanding the needs and individual preferences, in this way adding value both to the company and the client. The objective is customer loyalty. This presupposes knowing them, knowing who they are, what their tastes are, their preferences, in order to be able to offer them what they want, when they want it and how they want it.

CRM is an important business strategy, as much for e-businesses as for traditional companies, when it comes to facing up to an ever more competitive and demanding market. The evolution of the Internet offers infinite opportunities to businesses, but it has also opened a new world to customers. Now it is easier for them to handle more sophisticated services, which has led to them being better informed about what is around. The aim must be to focus on providing a series of processes orientated towards the customer through different departments and channels, which enables the company to attract and retain customers (Peppard, J., 2000).

A broad range of CRM solutions has been developed which provide companies with the necessary information and the best routes to make the most of their commercial strategies.

For this reason, CRM presupposes a strategic orientation of the company towards the customer. It does not involve the putting in place of specific technology, nor the creation of a department to deal with it, rather it implies that each one of the company employees carries it out irrespective of their role. This orientation completely centred on the customer is supported by three fundamental pillars: technology, processes and human resources.

Technology

CRM technology must be able to collect all of the information which comes from the relationship with the customer, irrespective of the channel through which it comes:

* E-mail
* Internet
* Telephone, etc.

and analyze it to be able to understand their needs and hence satisfy them. Although there are various tools which form a part of the technological solution, two are of vital importance: Data Warehouse and Data Mining. The Data Warehouse is a store where all of the internal and external information about the customer is kept. It is the ideal technological solution for collecting and treating the operative information necessary about the customers with the goal of developing marketing campaigns. The information is organized historically and is designed to help those enquiries orientated towards the needs of the business.

One must take into account that to get the best out of the Data Warehouse it needs to create information models. In this way, it establishes causal relationships between the information and a predetermined business objective. One of the most efficient technological tools, and that which brings much added value, is the Data Mining. This technology is based on the application of analytical techniques and statistics to a specific area of data registered in the Data Warehouse. The aim of Data Mining is to obtain patterns of behaviour using specific areas of information about the customers. Amongst other things, we can forecast demand, analyze the portfolio of products, undertake a simulation of prices / discounts or campaigns, or investigate and segment markets.

Processes

The processes must also be orientated towards satisfying as quickly as possible the needs of the customer. This implies in the majority of cases changing them, that is to say, modifying the way of doing things with the aim of improving the service to the customer.

Human Resources

The people in the company are the key to any CRM strategy. This is what dictates success or failure and their value cannot therefore be understated. It is fundamental that they know the project, that their fears and doubts are resolved before it is put in place. We must make them see its importance, but above all, educate them in this new culture of customer service (Park & Kim, 2003).

These three areas (technology, processes and human resources) form the basis of any CRM strategy. If, whilst we are setting it up, we forget any one of these, we are destined to fail.

However, CRM can become a double-edged sword. Lack of experience in selecting tools is one of the major causes of failure of CRM. It is essential to be able to count upon the necessary resources for the education of the employees, and aim the CRM strategy at the entire organization. As well as the support of management and employees,

one equally important factor of success is to have a clear definition of what the CRM objectives are (Payne & Frow, 2005).

Amongst the first companies who adopted CRM, there were many who were carried along by euphoria without knowing exactly why they needed CRM. The other common mistake is trying to do too much in one go. Companies with little experience in CRM are open to risk. Whenever businesses have a simple corporate CRM strategy, they can put it in place successfully in a department (van Bentum & Stone, 2005; Wilson, H., *et al.*, 2002).

Having a simple system, integrated with back- and front- office functionality is a fundamental part of having a unique and integrated vision. If the CRM is integrated with the back-office, the flow of the business processes will be more transparent, which should then give better customer service, the key factor for better profitability. What is more, integrated solutions offer all the possible functionality of a seller, and are cheaper and easier to maintain, to learn and to update. This makes them the most appropriate solutions for the majority of companies that are looking for tactical advantages and value based on the return of investment (Plakoyiannaki & Tzokas, 2002).

The Reality of E-Marketing

Studies undertaken annually by the company Alterian amongst more than 1,500 professionals from agencies, consultancies and marketing departments, spread across Europe, the United States and Asia, reflect a significant increase in investment in online marketing strategies looking to 2009. (Sanchez, P., 2009)

Let us highlight the most interesting results:

- 62% of those interviewed will increase their investment in online marketing, principally in SEO Marketing (Search Engine Optimization), e-mail marketing, in social networks and pay-per-click campaigns.

Figure 2. The importance of Websites

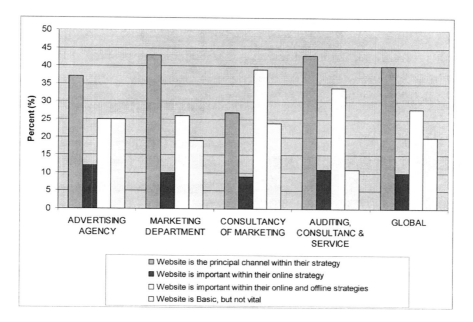

- Failure to analyze: less than 50% of companies analyze the results of their marketing campaigns, although given the economic situation a turn-around is expected in 2009. The fact is that only 47% of professionals analyze the data received from the marketing campaigns they undertake.

- The Web is important, but not that important. Although it is considered a basic aspect of business activity, it is still not vital for survival, a fact which contrasts with the use of the online channel in marketing strategies. Less than 50% of professionals consider the Internet to be a principal channel within their strategy (see Figure 2), (Alterian, 2009).

- The percentage who show an increase in investment, in contrast to that of 2006 and 2007 (85% and 84% respectively), is lower. That said, it continues to be one of the main areas of growth in this sector since the study began in 2003.

- On the contrary, the investment in offline marketing (known generally as traditional marketing) forecast a substantial drop in the coming months, a trend which started in 2005. The increase in investment in offline marketing has gone from 63% en 2005 to 38% in 2008. The reduction in budget has gone from 5% in 2005 to 19% in 2008.

The need for analyses which prevails in the marketing world, and the role of the Web as a support for online marketing strategies, are considered less important in the majority of cases than might be imagined.

The information extracted from the study is conclusive. Only 6% forecast a drop in investment in marketing in the next 12 months. 62% will increase the budget for those strategies aimed at the field of direct marketing online. The remaining 26% aim to maintain their current level of investment (Sanchez, P., 2009).

The current economic situation and subsequent reduction in budget has encouraged marketing professionals to adopt strategies for which the results can be measured and controlled. Working on this premise, it can be seen that up until now the tactics and online tools used by the vast majority of marketing professionals in their strategic mix have been banners, search engines and e-mail.

It is during this current year 2009 that search engine positioning, e-mail marketing, social networks and pay-per-click campaigns will have top priority.

FUTURE RESEARCH DIRECTIONS

The user dedicates 20% of their time to living on the Internet (Alterian, 2009). In the future, the main motivations for the use of search engine, e-mail marketing, social networks and pay-per-click campaigns will be the low cost, control and the ability to measure the evolution of the process, the speed with which new campaigns can be generated and put in place, with new messages and offers (directed at a new public) and the ability to segment immediately and with an extreme level of detail. To these reasons could be added the need to adapt to the new habits of consumers.

CONCLUSION

In this chapter the aspects to consider when developing an e-marketing strategy have been analyzed. Once the analysis of these variables has been undertaken, some of the different alternatives are studied which the Internet and e-marketing put at our disposal, such as e-mail marketing, viral e-marketing, geomarketing and search engine positioning.

Also in this chapter the concept of CRM as a business strategy has been analyzed, as much for the e-business companies as for traditional businesses, which allows them to attract and retain customers.

During 2009, studies have shown the importance of strategies such as search engine positioning, e-mail marketing, social networks and pay-per-click campaigns, whose motivation is the low cost, control and the ability to measure the evolution of the process. Only time will tell if these strategies so well-suited to lean years will maintain their position in the near future.

REFERENCES

Adwords. (2009). *Google Web page*. Retrieved July 26, 2009 from https://adwords.google.com

Alterian. (2009). *Web page*. Retrieved July 24, 2009 from http://www.alterian.com/

CECARM Web page. (2009). *Portal de negocio electrónico. Geomarketing*. Retrieved July 20, 2009, from http://www.cecarm.com/servlet/s.Sl ?METHOD=DETALLEGUIAS&id=2253&&s it=c,732

Chalmeta, R. (2006). Methodology for customer relationship management. *Journal of Systems and Software*, *49*(7), 1015–1024. doi:10.1016/j. jss.2005.10.018

Fleming, P. (2009). *Hablemos de la Mercadotecnia Interactiva*. Retrieved July 23, 2009, from http://es.wikipedia.org/wiki/Marketing_en_ Internet#Las_4_F.27s_del_Marketing_Online

Gummesson, E. (2002). Relationship marketing in the new economy. *Journal of Relationship Marketing*, *1*(1), 37–57. doi:10.1300/J366v01n01_04

Gummesson, E. (2004). Return on relationships (ROR): The value of relationship marketing and CRM in business-to-business contexts. *Journal of Business and Industrial Marketing*, *19*(2), 136–148. doi:10.1108/08858620410524016

iWorld. (2003). Las ventajas del e-marketing. *La revista de la tecnología y estrategia de negocio en Internet, 58*. Retrieved July 14, 2009, from http://www.idg.es/iworld/articulo.asp?id=146565

Kalyanam, K., & McIntyre, S. (2002). The e-marketing mix: A contribution of the e-tailing wars. *Journal of the Academy of Marketing Science*. Springer Netherlands.

Liu, Y., Zhou, C. F., & Chen, Y. W. (2006). *Determinants of E-CRM in influencing customer satisfaction. Lecture Notes in Computer Science, 4099*. Berlin/Heidelberg, Germany: Springer.

Lowry, P. B., Vance, A., Moody, G., Beckman, B., & Read, A. (2008). Explaining and predicting the impact of branding alliances and website quality on initial consumer trust of e-commerce websites. *Journal of Management Information Systems, 24*(4), 199–224. doi:10.2753/MIS0742-1222240408

Maciá, F. (2005). ¿Cabemos todos en los diez primeros puestos de Google? *Human Level Communications*. Retrieved July 25, 2009, from http://www.humanlevel.com/recursos.asp?IdNoticia=19

Maddox, L. M., & Gong, W. (2005). Effects of URLs in traditional media advertising in China. *International Marketing Review, 22*(6), 673–692. doi:10.1108/02651330510630285

McKim, B. (2002). The differences between CRM and database marketing. *Journal of Database Marketing, 9*, 371–375. doi:10.1057/palgrave.jdm.3240086

Muller, F. (2002). *Buen uso de las etiquetas Meta*. Retrieved July 25, 2009, from http://www.webexperto.com

Ngai, E. W. T. (2003). Internet marketing research (1987-2000): A literature review and classification. *European Journal of Marketing, 37*(1-2), 24–49. doi:10.1108/03090560310453894

Park, C. H., & Kim, Y. G. (2003). A framework of dynamic CRM: Linking marketing with information strategy. *Business Process Management Journal, 9*(5), 652–671. doi:10.1108/14637150310496749

Payne, A., & Frow, P. (2005). A strategic framework for customer relationship management. *Journal of Marketing, 69*(4), 167–176. doi:10.1509/jmkg.2005.69.4.167

Peppard, J. (2000). Customer Relationship Management (CRM) in financial services. *European Management Journal, 18*(3), 312–327. doi:10.1016/S0263-2373(00)00013-X

Plakoyiannaki, E., & Tzokas, N. [REMOVED HYPERLINK FIELD]. (2002). Customer relationship management: A capabilities portfolio perspective. *Journal of Database Marketing, 9*, 228–237. doi:10.1057/palgrave.jdm.3240004

Ren, L. C., & Yuan, L. J. (2007). *Analysis on influential factors of network brand in electronic commerce*. 1st International Conference on Management Innovation, JUN 04-06, 2007 Shanghai, P R China. International Conference on Management Innovation, Vols 1 and 2, (pp. 602-608).

Sainz, B., de la Torre, I., & López, M. (2009). *Soluciones de hardware y software para el desarrollo de teleservicios*. Madrid, España: Creaciones Copyright.

Sainz, B., de la Torre, I., & López, M. (2010). Analysis of benefits and risks of e-commerce. Practical study of Spanish SME. In Portela, I. M., & Cruz-Cunha, M. M. (Eds.), *Information communication technology law, protection and access rights*. Hershey, PA: IGI Global Publishing. doi:10.4018/9781615209750.ch014

Sanchez, P. (2009). *Análisis dinámico de datos. Marketing Online, rey de la estrategia de marketing en 2009*. Retrieved July 10, 2009, from http://www.slideshare.net/paula.sanchez/el-marketing-online-rey-de-la-estrategia-de-marketing-en-2009

Savaris, C. (2009). *E-mail marketing directo-vender por mail. Una poderosa arma de ventas*. Retrieved July 11, 2009, from http://www.continentalmarket.com/boletin/e-mail-marketing-directo.htm

Sherman, C. (2005). A new f-word for Google search results. *Search Engine Watch.* Retrieved July 12, 2009, from http://searchenginewatch.com/3488076

van Bentum, R., & Stone, M. (2005). Customer relationship management and the impact of corporate culture - a European study. *Journal of Database Marketing & Customer Strategy Management, 13*, 28–54. doi:10.1057/palgrave.dbm.3240277

Wilson, H., Daniel, E., & McDonald, M. (2002). Factors for success in Customer Relationship Management (CRM) Systems. *Journal of Marketing Management, 18*(1-2), 193–219. doi:10.1362/0267257022775918

Wilson, R. F. (2000). The six simple principles of viral marketing. Retrieved July 15, 2009, from http://www.wilsonweb.com/wmt5/viral-principles.htm

Chapter 10
Market Research 2.0:
An Inclusive Approach to Understanding Customers' Needs

Lisa M. Given
Charles Sturt University, Australia

Dinesh Rathi
University of Alberta, Canada

ABSTRACT

This chapter examines the possibilities of conducting market research in Web 2.0 environments, with a focus on implications for small to medium-sized companies. The chapter discusses how companies can undertake market research using Web 2.0 platforms, explores how these tools can facilitate successful and appropriate market research design, and examines the characteristics of qualitative and quantitative "Research 2.0" techniques appropriate to a Web 2.0 environment. The chapter also presents examples of companies that are using these tools successfully for market research and discusses advantages and barriers in adopting these tools, including privacy, ethics, and legal implications of this type of research.

INTRODUCTION

The explosive growth of Web 2.0 platforms in the internet environment, such as blogs and online social networks (Cooke and Buckley, 2008; Cooke, 2008), has caught the imagination of consumers, media, businesses and researchers alike. Web 2.0 has increased sharing, collaboration and openness among users in various settings. Individuals are using Web 2.0 tools including social tagging and social networking to collaborate and create new content, tools and technologies, with implications for e-businesses in the coming decades. In addition, in virtual worlds such as Second Life, avatars and online communities are now being used as tools for participation and collaboration; these virtual worlds are helping organizations to engage customers in more interactive dialogue,

DOI: 10.4018/978-1-60960-765-4.ch010

moving from being simply "buyers" of products to being "collaborators" or "innovators" in product design and assessment. However, the implications of these new platforms and tools for small to medium-sized enterprises (SMEs) have not been fully explored in the e-business literature. At the same time, the adoption of Web 2.0 technologies is challenging traditional approaches to conducting qualitative and quantitative research, with implications for market research and other forms of social science research. Web 2.0 and virtual worlds have opened new avenues for innovation in business practices and the development of new theories, methods, tools and techniques to advance research methods; however, researchers must also address challenges vis-à-vis privacy, legal and ethical issues in conducting research in Web 2.0 environments. This chapter examines the possibilities for conducting effective market research in a Web 2.0 environment, with a focus on strategies that can best inform the e-business practices of small to medium-sized organizations.

BACKGROUND

In the literature, the differences between large firms and SMEs have been highlighted; a few of the key differences will be discussed here, to provide some context for the implications of Web 2.0 technologies for market research. SMEs are in a resource deficit position as compared to large firms (Mosey, 2005); this special condition was termed *resource poverty* by Welsh and White (1981; as presented in Cassell et al., 2002, p.61), which has an impact on the operations of small enterprises. A few resource characteristics of SMEs (especially very small firms) include: generally having a smaller number of products in the portfolio; a lower technological base; limited financial strengths; lacking quality human resources with limited technical expertise; hiring generalist (rather than specialist) employees, who multitask across job roles; time constraints

for staff as they focus on day-to-day operational work (Tödtling and Kaufmann, 2001; Rostro and Grudzewski, 2008; Mosey, 2005; Pelham and Wilson, 1996; Hamill, 1997; Urwin, 2000; Harker and Akkeren, 2002; Hill and Wright, 2001). All of these issues affect the functioning of SMEs. For example, SMEs typically have reduced capabilities to gather information or conduct research (Pelham and Wilson, 1996; Tödtling and Kaufmann, 2001; Goodman, 1999); thus, an SME is likely to have an approach to marketing which is *haphazard, informal, loose, unstructured, spontaneous, reactive, built upon and conforming to industry norms*"(Gilmore et al., 2001, p. 6). However, the information needs for SMEs, in principle, are similar to large firms; these needs include purchasing statistics, economic trends, buyer behavior, new government policies and new products from competitors (Urwin, 2000). Both large and small firms need information to make decisions for competitive advantages. With increased competition due to adoption of the internet by a large number of companies for online commerce, SMEs need to "*be better informed than ever, if [a] company is to survive and prosper*" (Urwin, 2000, p. 132). According to Urwin (2000) the internet is providing opportunities to SMEs to use valuable information sources to which access can be quick and cheap (Riquelme, 2002); this can lead to a competitive advantage (Porter and Miller, 1985 and Turbin *et al.*, 1996 as presented in Riquelme, 2002) for SMEs so that they can "*compete with big business on a much more level playing field*" (p. 130).

The objective of undertaking market research is to help organizations in understanding consumers' (i.e., the market's) needs and to facilitate the organization in making decisions; also, this guides an organization in strategies to provide consumers with products and services that best suit their needs. Market research involves methodical and organized approaches to the collection and analysis of information that can aid the organization in making informed decisions (Pelham and

Wilson, 1996; Keegan, 2008). There are many definitions of market research including one proposed by Green et al. (1988): *"the systematic and objective search for and analysis of information relevant to the identification and solution of any problem in the field of marketing"* (p. 2). A general perception about market research is that it is focused on studying the needs of consumers (i.e., mass population) for fast moving consumer goods (FMCGs); however, market research is also concerned with understanding buyers' (or markets') need (Rostro and Grudzewski, 2008) in *"any type of market* (e.g. B2C [Business to Consumers], B2B [Business to Business], C2C or P2P [Consumer to Consumer or Peer to Peer], G2C [Government to Consumers/Citizens]) *where buyers and sellers come together to exchange"* (Hague and Jackson, 1999, p. 13-14) products, services or even information.

Market research is done for a variety of reasons, such as analyzing the market (e.g., size and share, segmentation, trends, key players, etc.), understanding one's consumers (e.g., needs, perceptions, etc.), assessing products (e.g., new product development, consumption, gap analysis, branding, etc.), examining distribution (e.g., distributors' needs, retail sales, etc.), analyzing pricing (e.g., trends, sensitivity, competitor analysis, etc.), and promotion of products and services (e.g., evaluation, campaign planning, etc.) (Hague and Jackson, 1999; Green et al., 1988; McFadden, 1986; Kohli, and Jaworski, 1990; Brooksbank, Kirby and Wright, 1992). However, a majority of market research activities involve studying *"market potential, market share, market sales, market characteristics, and business trends and perform sales analyses"* (Green et al., 1988, p. 4; Keegan, 2008). The market research process involves various steps such as problem formulation, research method and design, data collection (including technique and sample design), analysis and interpretation of data and writing research reports (Green et al., 1988, Hague, 2002; Rostro

and Grudzewski, 2008; Deshpande and Zaltman, 1982; Keegan, 2008).

In the traditional model of market research, the roles of the researcher(s) and the participants (i.e., consumers) have been implicitly outlined. The participants' role in market research has been typically restricted to the data collection process (or a particular step in that process), long after the project is conceptualized and designed. Companies undertaking market research generally have used different data collection techniques (either individually or in combination), such as: interviews (face to face and telephone); ethnography (field observations); questionnaires (administered either face-to-face or by post mail); in-person focus groups; projective interviewing (word association, analogy, role plays, etc.); laboratory experiments and simulations; field experiments and tests; and using case studies (Keegan, 2008; Schensul, 2008; Hague and Jackson, 1999; Bonoma, 1985). In addition, secondary data sources like government data, external reports and published case studies (Rostro and Grudzewski, 2008; Deshpande and Zaltman, 1982; Bonoma, 1985) can also inform market research practices.

Traditional approaches to data collection involved face-to-face, post mail and telephone strategies. As time progressed, the internet emerged as a new channel of communication and brought another wave of evolution to market research. In addition to using email as a tool to conduct interviews and administer surveys (Meho, 2006), a large number of online survey tools such as 'Survey Monkey' emerged (Murthy, 2008); these tools started to supplement traditional approaches to data collection like face-to-face and telephone surveys. Some of the advantages of online surveys include online storage (of both questionnaire instruments and collected data), compatibility with qualitative and quantitative data analysis packages, reductions in survey costs and time to administer, the possibility of reaching a very large number of respondents and the ability to design adaptive questionnaires (Murthy, 2008; van Selm and

Jankowski, 2006). Parise and Guinan (2008), for example, noted a number of these benefits in their project, stating that "*Web-based customer communities provided us with 50% faster turnaround time and cost reduction in obtaining effective product ideas and feedback when compared to traditional market surveys and focus groups we had used exclusively in the past*" (p. 2).

More recently, many new trends in internet technology have emerged, which may herald a new evolution in approaches to market research. These new trends include the advent of many Web 2.0 technologies, as well as the Open Source Software (OSS) movement, which are challenging traditional modes of conducting market research. These new trends can also be used in conjunction with more traditionally (e.g., face-to-face) methods of conducting market research. For example, in-person focus groups could be conducted to identify those social media that are the best for targeting specific consumer groups; additional research could then be conducted online using those media. The concept of Web 2.0 was coined by O'Reilly in 2005 and is defined as:

Web 2.0 is the network as platform, spanning all connected devices; Web 2.0 applications are those that make the most of the intrinsic advantages of that platform: delivering software as a continually-updated service that gets better the more people use it, consuming and remixing data from multiple sources, including individual users, while providing their own data and services in a form that allows remixing by others, creating network effects through an "architecture of participation," and going beyond the page metaphor of Web 1.0 to deliver rich user experiences (O'Reilly, 2007, p. 17).

The promise that Web 2.0 technologies hold for market research is embedded in the notion that these technologies are designed for "*harnessing collective intelligence*", (O'Reilly, 2007, p.22) through an "*architecture of participation*" where

the internet serves as a platform for all activities, including research design, data collection, and engaging users' (or consumers') in the web-based environment. Web 2.0 is all about participation, sharing, discussion, openness, community, and networked. von Hippel (2001) proposed the idea of community-based innovation and researchers and practitioners argue that the "*online consumer group represents a large pool of product know-how*" (Füller et al., 2006, p. 57) and that online communities can be a "*promising source of innovation*" (p. 57). For example, Linux, an open source operating system initially developed by Linus Torvalds, was enhanced and further refined by the users (community) of that system. Linux is now considered a robust and stable operating system and a formidable competitor to Microsoft operating systems.

In the literature some of the Web 2.0 tools and technologies that have been identified include blogs (e.g., wordpress), wikis (e.g., pbwiki, mediawiki, Wikipedia), social bookmarking (e.g., del.icio.us, digg.com, citeulike.com), social tagging (i.e., folksonomies), social networking (e.g., facebook.com, myspace.com, linkedin.com), podcasting, image (e.g., flickr.com, photobuket.com) and video sharing tools (e.g., youtube.com, myspace.com, hulu.com), RSS (Really Simple Syndication or Rich Site Summary) feeds, internet virtual worlds (e.g., *Second Life*), and content aggregators (e.g., Google Mashup, Yahoo pipes) (Black, 2007; McNutt, 2008; O'Reilly, 2007). These new developments are bringing changes in many businesses, educational and social domains, including market research. Increasing adoption of Web 2.0 tools and technologies, the use of virtual worlds, and the design of OSS products are now opening new avenues of research (e.g., to consumers around the globe) and new ways of conducting that research. However, they are also bringing new challenges, vis-à-vis privacy, legal and ethical issues in conducting market research, which will be discussed later in the chapter.

EMERGENCE OF MARKET RESEARCH 2.0

The Web 2.0 environment is altering current research approaches, moving from a closed, 'cathedral' style of working (i.e., the iconic image of the academic working in an 'ivory tower' that is isolated from lay persons) to a 'bazaar' style that involves open, community participation (Raymond, 1999). Today, consumers are not only buying products online but are also recommending products to other consumers, sharing and posting reviews on blogs, online forums and in social networks about products and suppliers and engaging with businesses in newer ways (Leitner and Grechenig, 2008). All this has been due to social media (i.e., Web 2.0 tools and technologies), which facilitate peer-to-peer communication and interaction.

Many large corporations are using Web 2.0 tools such as social networking, virtual worlds and blogs to conduct market intelligence (Pühringer and Taylor, 2008). The emergence of new trends in the online world is changing the way market research has been conducted so far. For example, researchers are shifting from an individual 'consumer focus' to a 'network focus' (Cooke 2008) and researchers in the future can focus on understanding how consumers interact in an online social environment (Cooke and Buckley, 2008; Cooke, 2008). In addition, the Web 2.0 environment is fostering increased collaboration among (and between) researchers and consumers. Researchers can collaborate with consumers and with other researchers to share resources. For example, if researchers wanted to study consumers' reactions to fire hazard material, they could use available web-based simulation tools such as "Fire Dynamics Simulator Demonstrator" (Curry et al. 2008); this system uses Facebook as an interactive environment in conducting simulation exercises and, at the same time, utilizes Facebook capabilities (such as the interface and blogging capability) to allow users to view the results and engage in discussion. Thus, this new medium is opening new avenues of collaboration and active participation with a large number of distributed participants which were out of reach for market researchers in earlier times by reducing temporal, spatial and interactive barriers. Also, tools like RSS feeds allow researchers to keep track, automatically, of the latest developments or new additions on a company's website (i.e., blogs, wikis, videos, etc.) without logging or visiting those sites regularly. An RSS feed is a 'pull' technology (i.e., unlike email subscription), which empowers researchers to pull updates and data from multiple sites with one click. These tools can help researchers to manage their projects effectively, by minimizing the time spent on checking for latest updates for the new data on website(s).

Another interesting example could be the use of podcasting and vodcasting in market research. Podcasting is *"a digital recording of a radio broadcast or similar program, made available on the internet for downloading to a personal audio player"* (Kretz, 2007, p. 36) and Vodcasting is podcasting with video capabilities. Podcasting, a Web 2.0 tool, is easy to create and share (as podcasts can be broadcasted via the web) and can be played within the internet browser; there is no need for an expensive gadget to play the podcast programs (Kretz, 2007; Potter, 2006; O'Reilly, 2007). Podcasting could be used not only to educate consumers on the proposed research project but also to provide low cost options to create programs to support controlled research experiments which often require participants to respond to product stimuli to emotion emotions. The findings from the thesis work of Johnson (2007), for example, show that a podcast program can be used to stimulate consumers as *"listeners do tend to visualize podcast programs"* (p. 53) and podcast programs create *"an array of emotional responses"* (p. 53).

In Web 2.0, consumers are not only consuming the data (e.g., reading online book reviews at Amazon.com to seek other consumers' viewpoints on products, services and information offered by the company), but they are also producing the data (i.e., submitting their own reviews or adding comments to previously submitted reviews to enhance content or make corrections). Data generated in a Web 2.0 environment occur in real time, from real users; these projects are often inclusive in their design, given the broad customer base that can be reached in the online world. These environments also offer many possibilities for ongoing data collection, beyond what can be gathered using traditional research methods. Small and medium-sized companies can exploit a competitive advantage by collecting and analyzing user-generated data created using different social media to improve their services and products. The market research domain can "*benefit from incorporating Web 2.0 tools to: get real-time feedback on existing products or new product ideas/concepts, build "community" among consumers around their goods, services or brand, leverage customer self-service, and have consumers collaborate on developing future product strategies*" (Parise and Guinan, 2008, p. 1). The objective of market research is not only to collect quantitative data (such as market share and size) but also to collect qualitative data, to have a better understanding of consumers' mindset and behavioral aspects (i.e., to seek answers to questions like why, how, etc.). Social media can be key destinations for market researchers to gather a large amount of qualitative data contributed by the consumers themselves. For example, Cooke (2006) noted,

Web 2.0 gives us a new window into the consumer mindset: how consumers 'tag' their photos on Flickr.com; what videos they post on YouTube. com; their favourite websites on del.icio.us; what content they choose to post and rate on digg.com, or how they describe themselves and their favourite things in their MySpace profile. This new type of data allows us to go beyond the traditional models created using group discussions and cluster analysis, and look at the ways that the population

is building its own world and how it is referencing it via the 'folksonamy' that it is using, rather than through our labels. This new window is the dataset of a 'virtual ethnography' waiting for us to tap into it (Cooke, 2006, p. 646).

The following sub-sections outline the potential avenues for incorporating Web 2.0 technologies at various stages in the research process, with a focus on mechanisms and tools for involving consumers as active participants in the design and implementation of market research projects.

Research Problem Formulation

According to the literature on market research, problem formulation is the "*heart of the research process*" (Green et al., 1988, p. 31) as it requires converting organizational requirements (i.e., the reasons for undertaking market research) into a coherent research statement that will guide the design and implementation of the project. Problem formulation is an iterative process that requires close interaction and coordination among managers (who have initiated the research), the researcher(s) and the participants; at this stage, "*researchers must engage managers and customers more actively in the research undertaking by enabling them to represent fully their thinking*" (Zaltman, 1997; p. 424). Green et al. (1988) and Chen and Hinton (1999) note that focus groups are popular in market research; this method is often used in the early stages of the research to define a problem and to generate hypotheses. Unfortunately, focus groups are quite expensive (due to room costs, participants' transportation, food and lodging costs) as compared to other instruments, such as questionnaires (Chen and Hinton, 1999). Hence conducting focus groups or other types of in-person survey methods at the preliminary stage of the market research could be cost prohibitive for SMEs. Web 2.0 tools and technologies such as blogs and community forums could facilitate the process of conducting focus groups and administering surveys online. For example, Gray (2007) highlighted the use of online media to conduct focus groups online and found that "*contacting people using this method is far cheaper than physically getting them all in a room*" (p. 104).

In the literature, several advantages for involving all stakeholders in the research have been identified, including: research participants have the right to exercise control over problems; research can stay on track, given the ease of contact with all groups; there is a better response to questions within a social situation by participants themselves; researchers can gain insider perspectives from the participants; and, this can demonstrate a democratic equity in the research design (Finley, 2008; Boylorn, 2008). Web 2.0 tools such as Wikis and/or project blogs (Grudin, 2006; Parise and Guinan, 2008; Godwin-Jones, 2003) can be used to facilitate collaboration among different research stakeholders in this stage of the research. The research problem formulation process could also involve a few members from the consumer group under study to develop the research statement and Web 2.0 tools could easily facilitate that type of interactive dialogue. There are other advantages of using such tools; for example, the use of wikis in this phase of the market research will maintain a temporal database for all the changes done in the project proposal. This leads to enhanced version control and safeguards against vandalism, while enabling collaborative authorship and concurrent editing. This can also support database searching (Boulos, et. al., 2006; Wagner and Prasarnphanich, 2007; Boeninger, 2007; Grudin, 2006) and reduces both the temporal and spatial barriers among participants (Rathi and Given, 2010 [in press]). One example of this strategy, used successfully, is the use of a blog for an ethnographic study by anthropologists working for Microsoft (Grudin, 2006). However there might be challenges for participants (and researchers) who do not have strong technical skills (i.e., one of resource poverty issues in SMEs) and who might be required to spend extra time to learn about browsing through the wiki and understanding key features such as "*the authorship or currency of material*" (Grudin, 2006, p.8).

Research Design and Implementation

This phase of the research is about detailing the methods and procedures to be used to obtain information to address the problem; this is the overall framework of the research that provide guidelines on the research process including information source identification and collection (Green et al., 1988). In traditional market research, this was done by researchers alone (i.e., consumers were not involved in this process except in the data collection stage); however, in a Web 2.0 environment, social media have created new opportunities to involve and use the collective intelligence of consumers, i.e., crowdsourcing (Howe, 2006), in developing methods and procedures for conducting market research. Crowdsourcing has created a new way of working and has "*triggered a dramatic shift in the way work is organized, talent is employed, research is conducted, and products are made and marketed*" (p. http://www.randomhouse.com/catalog/display.pperl?isbn=9780307396204). The researchers could collaborate with the consumer participants (i.e., crowdsource) and other researchers to conduct market research. An interesting example of crowdsourcing is the design of mini polls by consumers (themselves) at social shopping websites, like Kaboodle.com, to meet their individual fashion needs. Green et al. (1988) note that in this stage of research design, particularly in exploratory research, input from subject experts "*is a natural complement to the use of secondary information*" (p. 98). The identification of such experts might be a challenge; but in the networked world, consumers and other research stakeholders could help in the identification of the subject experts from their social network or point to other communities where such expertise might be available. The social network has also helped companies to identify experts within their own organization. For example, one of the authors of this chapter worked in an international trading firm which had offices located in multiple locations in the domestic market and in over 15 other countries, along with associates in group companies. Many times, the author was not even aware if there was an expert on a particular domain within the organization or in the group of companies. However, when the organization implemented an online system, one of the features (similar to a social networking website) was the ability to locate subject experts within the organization, as well as external experts with the help of in-house referrals. This helped the author in many ways, especially in the market research studies undertaken to explore new export markets or import sources from other countries; the country experts provide valuable implicit knowledge which helped in market/source selection and business strategies.

Pilot Testing Data Collection Strategies

It is also important to note the value of crowdsourcing and other social techniques for pretesting and pilot testing research strategies. Pilot testing of research instruments, recruiting strategies, recording techniques, and other elements of data collection (in any study) is an important step to enhance the validity and reliability of data collection tools. In a Web 2.0 environment, pretesting is vital, especially for researchers and participants who are not familiar with specific tools and technologies, or where data recording strategies are being used for the first time. Although, traditionally, researchers conducted pilot tests by locating members of the target group to test the wording on a questionnaire or to ensure that a digital recorder worked well, researchers can now use Web 2.0 technologies to reach a broader pilot testing audience. This will help to test procedures across time zones (e.g., to ensure that servers are working 24/7), to test wording of questionnaires with a broader, global

audience (e.g., to eliminate problems raised by the use of local terminology), or to create specialized help guides for researchers and participants who may need specialized instruction in using the data collection tools.

Sampling and Recruitment

Web 2.0 has created an environment that supports consumers' participation (Cooke and Buckley, 2008) in different steps of the research process, including sample design and data collection. Consumers can collaborate more intensely with researchers to develop a sampling plan and guide them in data collection processes, as consumers may have different insights into the data to be gathered. For example, many times researchers are not aware of additional data sources which might help them in conducting their research. Researchers could collaborate with consumers, to identify potential additional data sources such as blogs, online databanks provided by companies like Compustat by Standard and Poor (www.compustat.com), and to share data owned by the participants themselves. Social media are not only about the availability of the data created by the consumers but are also useful for identifying participants from online communities and social networking websites (e.g., facebook, orkut, linkden) who could be part of the research. Social media, such as blogs, and social networking websites, are *"virtual 'gatekeepers' with chains of 'friends' who are potential research respondents"* (Murthy, 2008 p. 845). For example; Kim and Chung (2007) identified blogs that are related cancer, which were used to identify the users and to invite members of the blog to become participants in their research. Microsoft recruited users using a survey on the Live Space Site to understand the users of Windows Live Spaces; participants were from the UK, France, Brazil, the US, Canada and China. Similarly market research done by Wrigley (manufacturers of chewing-gum) used an online environment to discuss a research problem with geographically-dispersed experts from different domains such as journalism, sociology and branding (Gray, 2007). Thus the Web 2.0 environment not only facilitates participant recruitment but also reduces spatial barriers, allowing companies to increase the sample size diversity for the study. One of the key challenges in data collection is to minimize errors. The use of blog data could possibly reduce certain sampling errors as the consumers are *"not a 'respondent' reacting to our stimulus, but rather a willing participant on a journey of discovery"* (Cooke, 2006, p. 646). Ochoa and Duval (2008) present a few interesting examples on the process of data collection, which reflect the fact that sequential sampling (i.e., setting up an advance rule for inclusion based on certain criteria (Green et al., 1988) instead of have fixed-size sampling in which the size of data collection) is possible when Web 2.0 tools are used for recruiting purposes. For example (from Ochoa and Duval, 2008): researchers could select 3500 of the 'most recent contributions' on a social bookmarking site for the study; they could also select users who had 'at least 10 book reviews' on amazon.com; and, they could evaluate users' contributions by selecting stories contributed on digg.com during the 'last month'.

Data Collection

The data collection phase of market research is considered as one of the most expensive steps in terms of financial costs and staff time. Researchers decide on the sampling design by balancing the minimum responses (or data) required to have a valid study, and the cost (and time) required to collect those responses (Green et al. 1988). Web 2.0 is making its impact felt on market research by providing opportunities to market researchers to collect relatively inexpensive datasets, such as reviews from online resources (e.g., blogs, online forums, and product reviews on e-business sites like amazon.com), while increasing consumers' participation in a study (Gray, 2007). In the

1990s, researchers wanting to use online media to administer surveys to gather data for research had to create their own web design and write their own program code; however, today, there are a large number of online resources and service providers such as Survey Monkey, kwiksurveys, and Vizu that provide services and resources (such as pre-designed templates, sample questions, and automated distribution via email) either free or for a small fee (Murthy, 2008). Web 2.0 tools have further added to the data collection capabilities beyond online text-based survey tools. For example, domains like YouTube and Hulu provide avenues for participants to upload video data, a new dimension to data collection, which prior to Web 2.0 was a challenge for researchers. Now, researchers are not required to ship special multimedia equipment to participants to record an event. Consumers are widely using commonly available tools like webcams and cellphones to create multimedia (video) data, which they are able to upload on the internet on sites such YouTube, Hulu, Myspace and various blogs. Then, market researchers can view the multimedia data in the browsers and download for future research analysis.

In traditional market research models, companies often undertake surveys following product (or service) launch to document consumers' opinions and then use those data to improve the offerings. Today, market researchers do not have to explicitly design studies to identify the problems in products or undertake market research post-launch to improve the product offering. The consumers are themselves (without being part of the research) providing valuable data to the organizations on their perceptions about the company's products and services on various forums, blogs, miniblogs, etc. in real time. According to (Cooke, 2006), there are over 70 million blogs and it is estimated that around 75,000 new blogs are created every day. Blogs offers opportunities to collect publicly available data at a relatively low cost; according to Hookway (2008) *"the majority of blog content management systems include a search feature, which allows readers to find bloggers according to demographic information such as age and location as well as interests and hobbies"* (p. 99), an important data for market researchers. For example, Green et al. (1988) presented an example of undertaking a descriptive study in which one of the research questions was to identify the demographic and socioeconomic characteristics of the primary members of a specific organization (for which the study was conducted). As the project was conducted in the pre-Web 2.0 era, this information was collected through primary, original research using traditional research methods. However, if this project was conducted today, it is likely that this could be done by analyzing data from a social networking website where these primary members were part of a community. This information can be a valuable source of data for companies engaging in market research; previously, this type of data might be available in limited capacities (e.g., through letters written to newspaper editors or to a customer service unit of an organization), or not at all outside of original data gathering. Similarly, Murthy (2008), for example, in a study on South Asian music, collected data from discussion threads, audio, video and images of musicians and bands available on social networking sites MySpace and Facebook. Hence, social media are providing market researchers with the ability to utilize these resources to have a better understanding of consumer decision making.

The feedback given by the consumer (outside of a formal study) in public internet spaces is available free of charge to the companies providing those products and services. The companies can analyze these online data to find out what consumers are saying about their services and products and devise their business strategies accordingly. For example, Dell and Kryptonite bicycle locks were recalled after consumers' blogged about the problems they experienced with the products (Constantinides and Fountain, 2008). Pan et al. (2006) used the data on the blogs to analyze *"what bloggers were*

communicating about their travel experiences" (p. 35). Avis UK (http://wetryharder.co.uk/), an auto rental company, is the first to use blogs on its website to enable consumers to comment on their services and car fleets, to share their experience of driving a particular model with other users. This information is not only helping Avis UK to upgrade their service quality but also make decisions about which different types of cars to purchase to meet consumers' needs. As noted on the Avis website:

Today, we know you have more choice than ever . . . That's why we want to know what you really think about our service and what's important to you when you hire a car. . . . this past year we've been monitoring what's said about us online. That feedback has been helping us to improve the service we offer you. . . . We'd like you to use this blog to share your experiences, tips for other travellers, feedback and questions about anything that confuses you (p. http://wetryharder. co.uk/?page_id=2).

In addition, companies such as Comcast, Dell, General Motors, H&R Block, Kodak, and Whole Foods Market are even using microblogging sites such as Twitter (twitter.com) not only to serve their customers but also to "burnish brands" (King, 2008, p. technology/content/sep2008/tc2008095_320491.htm) by analyzing consumers' postings (known as 'tweets') about companies' products and services (King, 2008; Reisner, 2009). Gartner termed the use of data from Twitter as *"Inbound Signalling"* (http://www.gartner.com/it/page.jsp?id=920813), who notes that Twitter is an avenue for *"rich source of information about what customers, competitors and others are saying about a company"* (p. http://www.gartner.com/it/page.jsp?id=920813). More detail on the number of companies using twitter for market research of these types is available at http://blog.fluentsimplicity.com/2008/04/07/connecting-with-customers-twitter/.

Finally, Web 2.0 tools have added new types of data for researchers to collect which was previously unavailable for market research. One interesting aspect of this is that the data do not require direct participation of consumers; rather, their online visits leave a trail that can be mined by companies. Market researchers are able to collect these 'consumer trails' to analyze for better website traffic management, online sales, time spent by the consumers on the website, pages clicked, returning vs. new consumers, location identification by IP address and analysis of referring websites. All of these new data sources are changing the landscape of market research in today's internet-based economy.

Analysis and Interpretation of Data

A large number of the current online tools which are used by researchers to collect data also have some basic analysis capabilities (e.g., Survey Monkey provides a quick quantitative overview of the responses by presenting them graphically like bar chart). These tools can also export data in the format accepted by other, off-the-shelf analysis packages such as SPSS and NVivo (Murthy, 2008). According to Green et al. (1988), the analysis phase of any research project requires: both an art and science acumen on the part of the researcher; intuition and informal insight; the ability to handle and code data appropriately; knowledge of the research problem context; and the use of different tools. In traditional models of market research, the researcher who collected the data would complete the analysis without much involvement from participants. However, in a Web 2.0 domain, researchers are now starting to collaborate with participants in coding and analysing data. The open source model of the 'bazaar' (Raymond, 1999) has opened new avenues to crowdsource different aspects of the data analysis, like managing the collected data in a single repository and coding of the data collectively. For example, Alonso et al. (2008) adopted a crowdsourcing strategy in data coding where the researchers used online users drawn from a large community to make relevance judgments for each query-result pair. Interestingly, the human resources the researchers' used in their work (i.e., for coding the data) was through a crowdsourcing service called 'Amazon's Mechanical Turk' (www.mturk.com) provided by Amazon Web Services (AWS). Amazon's Mechanical Turk is a marketplace for work which provide businesses access to an on demand and scalable workforce (www.mturk.com); AWS is a web-based service platform which provides IT infrastructure services (in a web cloud) including access to computational power, storage and a large number of software products (http://aws.amazon.com/what-is-aws/) on demand.

In addition, qualitative data collected from blogs, online forums, and other web sources used to gain more detailed insight into consumers' behaviour can be too large to analyze in its original form, or may include information that is not relevant to the research project. Often, these datasets require some sort of filtering to remove unwanted data and to develop coding schema to generate themes from the data. The coding of a large amount of qualitative data is difficult and expensive. Web 2.0 tools such as wikis, which support collaborative activity, can allow researchers to collaborate with participants and other users in the community to code the data. The coded data (e.g., tagged using XML tags) can be extracted using simple program codes and then can be used for further analysis.

The community members are also collaborating in developing newer tools and technologies for analysis of data and presenting an alternate to expensive analysis tools available in the market. For example, statistical tools such as 'R', which is an OSS product for statistical computing and graphics (www.r-project.org) is an alternate to expensive statistics tools likes SPSS; visualization tools such as gapminder (http://www.gapminder.org) and graphviz (http://www.graphviz.org) offer alternatives to traditional analysis output models; other data analysis tools have both statistical capabilities and visualization capabilities are also available, such as Zherlock, an open source software data analysis tools with 2-D and 3-D visualization capabilities (Alsberg, 2003); finally, open source data analysis tools (e.g., to handle interview transcripts, written texts and field notes) are now available, such as Weft QDA (http://www.pressure.to/qda), which is an alternative to expensive, proprietary tools, such as NVivo.

In addition, the OSS community (of which consumers are a large part) has developed newer web analytics tools that serve as alternatives to Google analytics tools and fee-based website data tracking tools like sitemeter (www.sitemeter.com). These include Piwik (http://piwik.org) and AWStats, a free real-time logfile analyzer to get advanced statistics (http://awstats.sourceforge.net) from the website. The web analytics tools which are used to analyze web traffic and related data can provide insight on consumers on a real-time basis in comparison to past practices when such data were either not available or were not used in analysis.

In the following section, the paper will present a few examples where consumers are interacting and collaborating with each other and at the same time are providing the organization with valuable inputs (or data).

Discussion and Examples

Social media are providing companies with an environment with the potential to further increase the productivity level, lower data collection costs and time required for research, and increase collaboration with consumers, which was missing in earlier models of market research. A large number of online businesses are working towards enhancing users' shopping experience, for example, and adding some Web 2.0 tools on their websites. The inclusion of Web 2.0 tools such as blogs, polling options, wikis and tagging have led to the new phenomenon of "social shopping" (Leitner and Grechenig, 2008). Social shopping is a new way of enhancing the e-business experience of consumers as it *"tries to combine two favorite online activities: shopping and social networking"*. (Tedeschi, 2006). This relates to crowdsourcing, or the idea of soliciting the shopping trends and seeking opinion from peers on their purchasing decisions. Social Shopping provides a channel for online retailers to engage consumers in a low-cost, word-of-mouth marketing approach (Leitner and Grechenig, 2008; Tedeschi, 2006). A few examples of online retailers that provide support for social shopping include kaboodle.com, myitthings.com, zebo.com, productwiki.com and shopstyle.com (http://www.webtrends.about.com). This is an interesting phenomenon which has emerged due to the popularity of Web 2.0 tools and technologies and one that can also form the basis for a market research plan. This phenomenon assumes important significance for market research as it would provide readily available data to analyze consumers' choices, behavior, and emerging trends among consumers. These data are voluntarily created by consumers to maintain their profile in social shopping services by creating their own shopping page. Also, social shopping websites are providing additional features, like blogs (for discussion among consumers on new trends, products, promotions, sales and reviews), tagging (for allowing users to name the products they like) and RSS feed (for allowing consumers to get regular updates on new developments in their community). For example, Kaboodle.com connects a buyer with other buyers, features product reviews on its blogs and consumers can bookmark their own products and share these with other consumers (http://www.webtrends.about.com). All these features, in return, are providing companies access to valuable data like spotting 'influential customers' who might be involved in marketing plans, market research, and product testing. *"If you're the go-to guy for buying Kona coffee, I want to find you, not a generalist"* as pointed out by Gordon Gould, Chief Executive, ThisNext (Tedeschi, 2006).

In the past, conducting surveys or opinion polls was, exclusively, the market researchers' domain; however, now consumers are creating their own mini-surveys to seek opinions from their fellow consumers on product selection. For example, online retailers such as Kaboodle.com allow consumers to create what we call 'micro-surveys' to seek help from other shoppers. The sample poll welcome note on Kaboodle says, "*Help your fellow Kaboodlers choose the best products! Vote on Help Me Choose polls and make your opinion count. Click 'Choose This' to vote and add a comment or click on an image to find out more about that item*" (http://www.kaboodle.com/za/fun-polls). Similarly, Zebo.com has created an environment where consumers can chat, get tips and browse products; as well, the system allows consumers to conduct polls and post pictures to seek other consumers' opinions (e.g., which necklace goes best with which dress?) (http://www.webtrends. about.com). These micro-surveys track not only ranked opinions but also provide space for open comments (i.e., qualitative data) which help consumers to make purchase decisions and help companies to understand emerging trends. In this way, companies are getting both quantitative and qualitative data from these micro-surveys, which are created by consumers. The data can be used by the companies to develop new business strategies (like promotional activities) and seek influential customers to support successful implementation. In addition, this saves companies from conducting large-scale market research, a time consuming process; instead these micro-surveys can provide quick and real-time feedback to the companies. However, companies cannot use these exclusively, as consumers' preferences for poll questions may not always match an organization's information (i.e., research) needs. Through these processes, consumers are creating data for their own needs and they are adding value to companies who can plan their sales promotion and advertisement strategies

according to these feedback mechanisms. This is a true architecture of participation and crowdsourcing of the market research to understand consumer needs and perceptions, market trends and sales promotion effectiveness (i.e., a few reasons why companies conduct market research).

Challenges and Issues

One of the key challenges, however, for all researchers engaged in internet-based research, is in finding a balance between gathering available data and protecting participants' privacy. Increasingly, individuals are becoming savvier about managing the personal information they provide online – and are being encouraged to do so, in light of identity fraud and other worries about online security (Miyazaki, A. D. and Fernandez, A., 2000; Smith and Lias, Allen, 2005). Unfortunately, consumers may not be aware of the ways that organizations are using social media as data collection tools (as well as providing these as services to their consumers), which can result in a loss of trust with the company if users view the organization as making inappropriate use of their voluntarily provided opinions, ratings, and web traffic statistics. This can lead to not only loss of research participants but also loss in online business for the organization. For example, it is estimated that around US \$15 billion business opportunity was lost due to individuals' privacy concerns (Forrester Research report as cited by Power et al., 2002). Organizations must find ways to involve consumers in discussions about the use of their data for research purposes, so that individuals' desire for privacy (in certain circumstances) is respected (Powers, et al., 2002). Open dialogue about how web postings or web analytic data are to be used by the company is one way to ensure that consumers are, truly, participating in a voluntary manner when they engage with social media on an organization's website.

Similarly, researchers who are contracted with companies to conduct market research on their behalf (e.g., university scholars) may need to undergo ethics review at their home institutions, prior to engaging in data collection activities. The ethics review process may require particular modes of engagement with participants to ensure that (e.g.) informed consent and confidentiality provisions are maintained (Powers, et al., 2002), according to the guidelines published by the countries in which the data will be collected. For example, in Canada, universities are bound by the *Tri-Council Policy Statement, Ethical Conduct for Research Involving Humans* (www.pre.ethics.gc.ca). Also, researchers and participants will need to negotiate intellectual property issues that arise in cases where participants are involved in the design and development of products resulting from collaborative research. This negotiation is best handled at the outset of the project, as part of the consent process.

In addition, researchers must also consider relevant legislation governing the protection of privacy for individuals engaging with social media. Some national/federal governments have created policies that are intended to protect the use of individuals' personal information, including disclosure policies related to photographs, addresses, and other personal data (e.g., Canada's *Personal Information Protection and Electronic Documents Act* and the *Privacy Act*). In other cases, policies have been created at a state/provincial level (e.g., Alberta's *Freedom of Information and Protection of Privacy* legislation – see http://foip.alberta.ca/). Organizations must ensure that their market research practices and use of Web 2.0 technologies abide by the appropriate legislation for the jurisdictions in which they work.

CONCLUSION

The social media or Web 2.0 environment has created an unprecedented opportunity for organizations and market researchers to undertake research activities by including consumers and other stakeholders in every stage of the research.

This has created options particularly for small (including online startups) and medium-sized companies who may have limited budgets to undertake market research through traditional means. The new mantra for market researchers is focused on an architecture of participation, to engage with consumers in ways that have not been fully utilized by in the past. In the future, researchers wil certainly need to learn ways to engage consumers to co-create and co-analyze data for better understanding of the market and consumers' needs and perceptions. With the progression of time, researchers will be required to understand consumers' needs and demands on a real-time basis; otherwise, market researchers might become *"blogging irrelevant"* (Cooke, 2006, p. 646). According to Schillewaert, et al. (2009) who noted that *"while traditional research will not cease to exist, we will move from 'rather accurate information two months late' to more fuzzy immediate insights"* (p. 24). To conclude, we would like to quote Cooke and Buckley (2008), *"Market research is no longer a small decentralised profession. It has become so rationalised that, in David Morrison's (1998) words, 'one can refer to the production of knowledge within market research as the industrialisation of knowledge"* (p. 268).

REFERENCES

Alonso, O., Rose, D. E., & Stewart, B. (2008). Crowdsourcing for relevance evaluation. *ACM SIGIR Forum, 42*(2), 9–15. doi:10.1145/1480506.1480508

Alsberg, B. K., Kirkhus, L., Hagen, R., Knudsen, O., Tangstad, T., & Anderssen, E. (2003). Zherlock: An open source data analysis software. [from http://www.ncbi.nlm.nih.gov/sites/entrez]. *SAR and QSAR in Environmental Research, 14*(5-6), 349–360. Retrieved on September 11, 2009. doi:10.1080/1062936031000l623944

Black, E. L. (2007). Web 2.0 and library 2.0: What librarians need to know. In Courtney, N. (Ed.), *Library and 2.0 and beyond: Innovative technologies and tomorrow's user* (pp. 1–14). Westport, CT: Libraries Unlimited.

Boeninger, C. F. (2007). In Courtney, N. (Ed.), *Library and 2.0 and Beyond: Innovative technologies and tomorrow's user* (pp. 25–33). Westport, CT: Libraries Unlimited.

Bonoma, T. V. (1985). Case research in marketing: Opportunities, problems, and a process. *JMR, Journal of Marketing Research, 22*(2), 199–208. doi:10.2307/3151365

Boulos, M. N. K., Maramba, I., & Wheeler, S. (2006). Wikis, blogs and podcasts: A new generation of Web-based tools for virtual collaborative clinical practice and education. *BMC Medical Education, 6*(41). Retrieved from http://www.biomedcentral.com /1472-6920/6/41.

Boylorn, R. M. (2008). Participants as co-researchers. In Given, L. M. (Ed.), *The Sage encyclopedia of qualitative research methods* (pp. 599–601). Thousand Oaks, CA: Sage Publications.

Brooksbank, R., Kirby, D. A., & Wright, G. (1992). Marketing and company performance: An examination of medium sized manufacturing firms in Britain. *Small Business Economics, 4*, 221–236. doi:10.1007/BF00389477

Cassell, C., Nadin, S., Gray, M., & Clegg, C. (2002). Exploring human resource management practices in small and medium sized enterprises. *Personnel Review, 31*(6), 671–692. doi:10.1108/00483480210445962

Chen, P., & Hinton, S. M. (1999). Realtime interviewing using the World Wide Web. *Sociological Research Online, 4*(3). Retrieved on May 3, 2009 from http://www.socresonline.org.uk /4/3/chen.html

Cooke, M. (2006). Viewpoint: The importance of blogging. *International Journal of Market Research, 48*(6), 645–646.

Cooke, M. (2008). The new world of Web 2.0 research. *International Journal of Market Research, 50*(2), 569–572. doi:10.2501/S147078530820002X

Cooke, M., & Buckley, N. (2008). Web 2.0, social networks and the future of market research. *International Journal of Market Research, 50*(2), 267–292.

Curry, R., Kiddle, C., Markatchev, N., Simmonds, R., Tan, T., Arlitt, M., & Walker, B. (2008). *Facebook meets the virtualized enterprise.* (Technical Report 2008-907-20), Department of Computer Science, University of Calgary, June 18, 2008. Retrieved on September 1, 2009 from http://grid.ucalgary.ca/ documents/Curry KiMaSi08c2.pdf

Deshpande, R., & Zaltman, G. (1982). Factors affecting the use of market research information: A path analysis. *JMR, Journal of Marketing Research*, 14–31. doi:10.2307/3151527

Finley, S. (2008). Community-based research. In Given, L. M. (Ed.), *The Sage encyclopedia of qualitative research methods* (pp. 501–502). Thousand Oaks, CA: Sage Publications.

Füller, J., Bartl, M., Ernst, H., & Mühlbacher, H. (2006). Community based innovation: How to integrate members of virtual communities into new product development. *Journal of Electronic Commerce Research, 6*, 57–73. doi:10.1007/s10660-006-5988-7

Gilmore, A., Carson, D., & Grant, K. (2001). SME marketing in practice. *Marketing Intelligence & Planning, 19*(1), 6–11. doi:10.1108/02634500110363583

Godwin-Jones, R. (2003). Emerging technologies: Blogs and Wikis environments for online collaboration. *Language Learning & Technology, 7*(2), 12–16.

Goodman, M. R. V. (1999). The pursuit of value through qualitative market research. *Qualitative Market Research: An International Journal, 2*(2), 111–120. doi:10.1108/13522759910270025

Gray, R. (2007). Market research: Age of the 2.0 focus group. *Marketing,* 104.

Green, P. E., Tull, D. S., & Albaum, G. (1988). *Research for marketing decisions* (5th ed.). Englewood Cliffs, NJ: Prentice Hall.

Grudin, J. (2006). Enterprise knowledge management and emerging technologies. *Proceedings of the 39th Annual Hawaii International Conference on System Sciences* (HICSS-39), 3, 57a (pp. 1-10).

Hague, P., & Jackson, P. (2002). *Market research: A guide to planning, methodology and evaluation* (3rd ed.). London, UK: Kogan Page.

Hamill, J. (1997). The Internet and international marketing. *International Marketing Review, 14*(5), 300–323. doi:10.1108/02651339710184280

Harker, D., & Akkeren, J. V. (2002). Exploring the needs of SMEs for mobile data technologies: The role of qualitative research techniques. *Qualitative Market Research: An International Journal, 5*(3), 199–209. doi:10.1108/13522750210432002

Hill, J., & Wright, L. T. (2001). A qualitative research agenda for small to medium-sized enterprises. *Marketing Intelligence & Planning, 19*(6), 432–443. doi:10.1108/EUM0000000006111

Hookway, N. (2008). Entering the blogosphere: Some strategies for using blogs in social research. *Qualitative Research, 8,* 91–113. doi:10.1177/1468794107085298

Howe, J. (2006) Crowdsourcing: A definition. *Wired Blog Network: Crowdsourcing,* 2006. As assessed on May 20, 2009 from http://crowd sourcing.typepad.com/ cs/2006/06/ crowdsourcing_a. html

Johnson, K. (2007). *Imagine this: Radio revisited through podcasting.* Master's Thesis. Retrieved on September 11, 2009, from http://etd.tcu.edu/ etdfiles/available/ etd-08102007-105646/ unrestricted/Johnson.pdf

Keegan, S. (2008). Market research. In Given, L. M. (Ed.), *The Sage encyclopedia of qualitative research methods* (pp. 501–502). Thousand Oaks, CA: Sage Publications.

Kim, S., & Chung, D. S. (2007). Characteristics of cancer blog users. *Journal of the Medical Library Association, 95*(4), 445–450. doi:10.3163/1536-5050.95.4.445

King, R. (2008). How companies use Twitter to bolster their brands. Retrieved on September 11, 2009, from http://www.businessweek.com /technology/content/ sep2008/tc2008095_320491.htm

Kohli, A. K., & Jaworski, B. J. (1990). Market orientation: The construct, research propositions, and managerial implications. *Journal of Marketing, 54*(2), 1–18. doi:10.2307/1251866

Kretz, C. (2007). Podcasting in libraries. In Courtney, N. (Ed.), *Library 2.0 and beyond: Innovative technologies and tomorrow's user* (pp. 35–48). Westport, CT: Libraries Unlimited.

Leitner, P., & Grechenig, T. (2008). *Collaborative shopping networks: Sharing the wisdom of crowds in e-commerce environments.* 21st Bled eConference eCollaboration: Overcoming Boundaries through Multi-Channel Interactions, June 15-18. Retrieved May 15, 2009 from http:// domino.fov.uni-mb.si/proceedings.nsf /Proceedings/ 824F8A6AC21D3F 99C125748100440406 /$File/25Leitner.pdf

McFadden, D. (1986). The choice theory approach to market research. *Marketing Science, 5*(4), 275–297. doi:10.1287/mksc.5.4.275

McNutt, J. G. (2008). Web 2.0 tools for policy research and advocacy. *Journal of Policy Practice, 7*(1), 81–85. doi:10.1080/15588740801909994

Meho, L. I. (2006). E-mail interviewing in qualitative research: A methodological discussion. *Journal of the American Society for Information Science and Technology, 57*(10), 1284–1295. doi:10.1002/asi.20416

Miyazaki, A. D., & Fernandez, A. (2000). Internet privacy and security: An examination of online retailer disclosures. *Journal of Public Policy and Marketing (Privacy and Ethical Issues in Database/Interactive Marketing and Public Policy), 19*(1), 54-61.

Mosey, S. (2005). Understanding new-to-market product development in SMEs. *International Journal of Operations & Production Management, 25*(2), 114–130. doi:10.1108/01443570510576994

Murthy, D. (2008). Digital ethnography: An examination of the use of new technologies for social research. *Sociology, 42*(5), 837–855. doi:10.1177/0038038508094565

O' Reilly, T. (2007). What is Web 2.0: Design patterns and business models for the next generation of software. *Communications & Strategies, 1*, 17-37. Retrieved on September 10, 2009 from http://ssrn.com/abstract=1008839

O'Reilly, T. (2005). What is Web 2.0: Design patterns and business models for the next generation of software, 2005. Retrieved on June 14, 2009, from http://oreilly.com/pub/a/ oreilly /tim/news/2005/09/30/ what-is-web-20.html

Ochoa, X., & Duval, E. (2008). Quantitative analysis of user-generated content on the Web. *Proceedings of WebEvolve 2008: Web Science Workshop at WWW'08.*

Pan, B., MacLaurin, T., & Crotts, J. C. (2007). Travel blogs and the implication for destination marketing. *Journal of Travel Research, 46*, 35–45. doi:10.1177/0047287507302378

Parise, S., & Guinan, P. J. (2008). Marketing using Web 2.0. *Proceedings of the 41ˢᵗ Hawaii International Conference on System Sciences* (HICSS-41), 2008.

Pelham, A. M., & Wilson, D. T. (1996). A longitudinal study of the impact of market structure, firm structure, strategy, and market orientation culture on dimensions of small-firm performance. *Journal of the Academy of Marketing Science, 24*(1), 27–43. doi:10.1007/BF02893935

Potter, D. (2006). Ipod, you pod, we all pod. *American Journalism Review, 28*(1), 64.

Powers, C. S., Ashley, P., & Schunter, M. (2002). Privacy promises, access control, and privacy management. *Proceedings of the 3rd International Symposium on Electronic Commerce* (ISEC'02).

Pühringer, S., & Taylor, A. (2008). A practitioner's report on blogs as a potential source of destination marketing intelligence. *Journal of Vacation Marketing, 14*(2), 177–187. doi:10.1177/1356766707087524

Rathi, D., & Given, L. M. (2010). Research 2.0: A framework for qualitative and quantitative research in Web 2.0 environments. *Proceedings of the 43ʳᵈ Hawaii International Conference in System Science* (HICSS-43).

Raymond, E. (1999). The cathedral and the bazaar. *Knowledge, Technology, and Policy, 12*(3), 23–49. doi:10.1007/s12130-999-1026-0

Reisner, R. (2009). Comcast's Twitter man. Retrieved on September 11, 2009 from http://www.businessweek.com/ managing/content/ jan2009/ca20090113 _373506.htm

Riquelme, H. (2002). Commercial Internet adoption in China: Comparing the experience of small, medium and large businesses. *Internet Research: Electronic Networking Applications and Policy, 12*(3), 276–286. doi:10.1108/10662240210430946

Rostro, F. R., & Grudzewski, W. M. (2008). Marketing strategic planning as a source of competitive advantage for Mexican SMEs. *Institute of Organization and Management in Industry, 1*(1), 19–26.

Schensul, J. J. (2008). Methods. In Given, L. M. (Ed.), *The Sage encyclopedia of qualitative research methods* (pp. 501–502). Thousand Oaks, CA: Sage Publications.

Schillewaert, N., De Ruyck, T., & Verhaeghe, A. (2009). Connected research: How market research can get the most out of Semantic Web waves. *International Journal of Market Research, 51*(1), 11–27. doi:10.2501/S1470785308200286

Smith, A. D., & Lias, A. R. (2005). Identity theft and e-fraud as critical CRM concerns. *International Journal of Enterprise Information Systems, 1*(2), 17–36. doi:10.4018/jeis.2005040102

Tedeschi, E. (2006). Like shopping? Social networking? Try social shopping. *E-Commerce Report on The New York Times*. Retrieved on September 11, 2009 from www.nytimes.com/2006/09/11/technology/11ecom.html

Tödtling, F., & Kaufmann, A. (2001). The role of the region for innovation activities for SMEs. *European Urban and Regional Studies, 8*(3), 203–215. doi:10.1177/096977640100800303

Urwin, S. (2000). The Internet as an information solution for the small and medium sized business. *Business Information Review, 17*(3), 130–137. doi:10.1177/0266382004237647

van Selm, M., & Jankowski, N. W. (2006). Conducting online surveys. *Quality & Quantity, 40*(3), 435–456. doi:10.1007/s11135-005-8081-8

von Hippel, E. (2001). Innovation by user communities: Learning from open-source software. *MIT Sloan Management Review, 42*(4), 82.

Wagner, C., & Prasarnphanich, P. (2007). Innovating collaborative content creation: The role of Altruism and Wiki technology. *Proceedings of the 40th Hawaii International Conference on System Sciences* (HICSS-40).

Zaltman, G. (1997). Rethinking market research: Putting people back in. *JMR, Journal of Marketing Research, 34*(4), 424–437. doi:10.2307/3151962

Chapter 11
E–Marketing

Nuno Manarte
University of Trás-os-Montes e Alto Douro

Mário Sérgio Teixeira
University of Trás-os-Montes e Alto Douro

ABSTRACT

In this chapter, we will present e-marketing and the channels, tools, and techniques that can be used by Small and Medium Enterprises (SMEs), so that they can optimize the benefits of an online presence.

Knowing its customers is the starting point for any firm's marketing activity, so we will start by presenting some concepts that are related to the process of gathering information about e-customers.

The company website is the gateway to Internet marketing, so it is important to promote it in a variety of ways that will be explained later. Selling online can be an interesting option, but this decision should only be taken after considering the pros and cons that it involves. To conclude, we will talk about the e-marketing plan, which should guarantee that the objectives, strategies, and actions of online marketing are coherently integrated with the offline marketing plan.

INTRODUCTION

E-marketing can be defined as "achieving marketing objectives through use of electronic communications technology" (Chaffey & Smith, 2008, p. 489). In this day and age, electronic marketing is mainstream marketing (Hughes, 2006) and even SMEs should be involved.

The company website can be used as a customer information source, as a communication and promotion medium and/or as a sales and distribution channel for its products and services. It may also allow firms to reach new and broader markets, in a faster and cheaper way than through traditional means, something of particular importance for SMEs.

The internet is a level playing field for companies of all sizes, giving SMEs the chance to

DOI: 10.4018/978-1-60960-765-4.ch011

compete globally. One of the reasons for this is that large corporations cannot use their budgets to prevent small firms from having a relevant share of voice. In fact, online customers control communication and target companies, as opposed to more traditional channels in which these roles are reversed.

Throughout the chapter we will present the website's role in the company's e-marketing strategy. In order to fulfill its potential there is a range of options a SME can implement, which we will explore in some detail. As more and more people use smart phones and other mobile phones with internet capability, it is also important to prepare websites for compatibility with these handheld devices.

Knowing e-customers, their needs, perceptions, behaviors and profile, is the first step to prepare an e-marketing program. The conception of an e-marketing plan will involve a number of actions that must be integrated in a way that enables them to exploit synergies and ensure the plan's global consistency.

Promoting SMEs online presence is an e-marketing imperative, which requires the use of several techniques.

Selling online can be an option for firms to explore new markets and reduce distribution costs that can be implemented in a variety of ways.

These are some of the subjects that will be approached in this chapter. There are entire books written on some of the subjects that will be addressed, so the reader is not expected to get an in depth knowledge of all of them. Many of the subjects had to be simplified so that a larger number of concepts could be explained within the confines of one chapter. The goal of this chapter is to provide a broad understanding of key internet marketing concepts and to present the company website as a marketing tool, in a way that can be used by SMEs to improve their online marketing effectiveness.

THE WEBSITE AS A MARKETING TOOL

A website can be created to fulfill many different functions, supporting communication, sales and other kinds of customer interaction, such as (Carrera, 2009):

- **Institutional communication:** It's a website used by almost every company aimed at presenting the company and what it can do. It also works as a business card and an online communication tool;
- **Selling products and services:** the website can also enable e-commerce by creating an online shop which sells products and services using different means of payment.
- **Other types of customer interaction:** the website can also permit other types of customer interaction such as technical and commercial support.

Online registry of customers into a database gives firms the chance to know the history of interactions with customers, which can be very useful in understanding customer behavior and defining the customer's profile, both individually and by customer segment. Whether they are creating a site for business-to-business (B2B) or business-to-consumer (B2C), or both, companies should build it based on their customers' needs and not on what they want to sell. Some firms even have different websites for different kinds of customers.

This enables the use of one-to-one marketing techniques that allow individual marketing actions according to a customer's shopping behavior or search for information in the company's website.

On the other hand, with the Web 2.0 and collaborative content creation, the company's website can be built with the help of its users who can also be responsible for the creation of new content and functionalities. This proximity between customers and company helps strengthen the bonds between them, but it also demands a continuous management of the website and flexibility of the company's organizational structure, in order to maximize the advantages of that close relationship. The opportunity of creating or adjusting products and services to the dynamic needs of current or potential customers is one of the possible advantages.

The creation of information, emotional or entertainment features on the website, among other things, can increase the level of involvement of current or potential customers with the website and, in addition, with the company or brand because it creates a stimulus for customers to keep visiting the website and to reinforce the brand's values in the online world. A stock market ticker, fitness exercises that can be performed in front of the computer or a daily calorie calculator are examples of these elements.

KNOWING THE E-CUSTOMER

Motivations and Expectations of Online Customers

In an era of continuous change and of regular paradigm shifts, it is essential for companies to keep up with the evolution of their customers' needs and perceptions on a regular basis, trying to learn and listen to them, adjusting marketing actions and strategies accordingly.

With the Web 2.0 and an increasingly active customer online participation, continuous customer monitoring becomes paramount, and companies must respond swiftly in order to ensure their complete satisfaction. Customer dissatisfaction should, by all means, be avoided, because its effects on the company's image or the brand can be very penalizing, as customers spread their displeasure online, damaging the company's reputation and sales.

There are several places on the web where consumers create content about products and

services. This information is usually in third party sites, like www.epinions.com, that should be monitored by firms to identify negative feelings from their customers and use this feedback to improve their products or services accordingly.

Customers are ever less tolerant with companies that provide poor quality services. In 2007, 80% of consumers stated that they wouldn't buy again from a company with which they had a bad experience, up from 68% the year before (Harris Interactive, 2007 in Chaffey & Smith, 2008). Furthermore, customers tend to share those bad experiences with other consumers by publishing web content about those companies or brands in blogs, social network sites and other online media, in a way that cannot be controlled by companies or brands.

Online customers' satisfaction is strongly related to how firms manage their expectations when they visit a website. These expectations are related to a number of variables, such as service, speed of delivery or competitive prices, among others. Customers mainly want everything to work and expect to find and/or buy what they're looking for easily and quickly.

Chaffey & Smith (2008) consider that the most significant expectations are related to customer service, which means that it is important to work on every interaction between the firm and the customer, before, during and after the buying process.

Customer satisfaction shouldn't be seen as the evaluation of a single buy or specific transaction, but as a cumulative process. In this sense, satisfaction represents a global assessment based on the overall experience that the customer has had with the company over time. (Johnson *et al.*, 1995)

On the other hand, the satisfaction level of customers depends not only on the adequacy of the features of a product or service to their needs, but also on their expectations of the overall performance of that product or service (Pires & Santos, 1996). Thus, it is important to manage expectations adequately, so that they are close, but preferably lower than what can be achieved.

Creating expectations that can't be achieved or even exceeded, causes customer dissatisfaction, even when the features of a product or service are adequate to their needs.

For online customer expectations to be met, or even exceeded, a company should (Chaffey &Smith, 2008):

- Understand e-customers' expectations for service levels and identify possible gaps with current delivery, using customer research and site benchmarking;
- Set and communicate the service promise on security, delivery, price and customer service response time through informal or formal agreement;
- Deliver the service promise through perfect fulfillment and excellent customer service.

Customers' motivations to access the internet can be very different depending on whether they are B2C or B2B customers. While B2C customers' motivations are related to socialization, shopping and entertainment, B2B customers are more concerned with cost savings and the speed of the transaction process.

Many models of online customer motivations have been delineated to help define the online value proposition, such as Chaffey's (2004), which identifies the 6Cs of customer motivations:

- **Content:** Online content must provide information to support the buying process or product usage, in a way that is adequate to the target segment;
- **Customization:** The content must be tailored according to individuals or groups, so that everyone can view personalized content in web pages or e-mail messages;
- **Community:** Brand communities, social networks, or review sites have information, generated by their audiences, that is important to determine the customer perception of brands;

- **Convenience:** Online customers can easily find, select, purchase or even use products and services, from their PC;
- **Choice:** The internet allows a wider choice of products and services than traditional channels;
- **Cost reduction:** Because of the reduction of intermediaries in the sales process, or the automation of the administrative process associated with sales, the internet is usually seen as a low-cost channel.

Segmentation of E-Customers

Segmentation consists of subdividing the market into homogeneous subgroups of customers, so that the company can adapt its marketing policy to each of these segments (Lindon *et al.*, 2004; Kotler, 2005).

According to Myers (1996), companies develop segmentation processes for their current or potential markets, in order to identify individual or business customers that need products or services with similar features, which are different from those needed by other market segments.

In order to define market segments, one must decide what criteria to use for segmentation, which can be geographic, socio-demographic, psychographic, behavioral or other (Dionísio *et al.*, 2009).

Markets are not homogeneous when it comes to wanted benefits, purchase rates, and price and promotion elasticity, which means that their response to products and services or to a firm's marketing decisions differs (Walker *et al.*, 1992).

By treating different customer groups differently, a firm can present a unique value proposition that is more suitable to each segment, thus increasing their satisfaction level.

Ultimately, each customer can be treated as unique. Online segmentation lets you do this dynamically, by processing real time information about customers, like, their individual characteristics, and their purchase or search behavior, defining the individual profile of each e-customer. This allows us to develop an adequate online value proposition (Dionísio *et al.*, 2009).

To perform online segmentation, one needs to know which channels customers can access, which channels influence them or where they buy (Chaffey & Smith, 2008).

Online segmentation differs from traditional offline segmentation on the following aspects (Dionísio *et al.*, 2009; Pal & Rangaswamy, 2003):

- It is centered on the consumer (not the company), because customers identify the segment they belong to when they specify features and indicate their interests relative to products or services, price or other marketing elements;
- Several criteria can be used for segmentation simultaneously and the boundaries are blurry, since one individual can belong to several segments at different times, depending on behavior;
- It is dynamic and used in real time in the relationship with the customer. This means that changes in behavior result in the redesign of marketing strategies and actions and their value propositions, which should be adjusted according to the changes in customer needs;
- Each customer can be treated as being part of a segment or individually (one-to-one marketing). In any case, treatment should be differentiated and the marketer's job is setting the rules that automatically generate online value propositions, according to customer behavior.

Online segmentation can be carried out using several information sources, such as (Dionísio *et al.*, 2009):

- **Clickstream:** the path a visitor takes in a website or application, i.e., the pages a user visits;

- **RFM analysis (Recency, Frequency, Monetary):** a customer's potential is determined based on transaction history, using the date of latest purchase (recency), the time between transactions (frequency) and the value of each transaction (monetary);
- **E-mails sent to the customers:** to determine response, open and conversion rates;
- **Information from cookies or forms:** to know the user's path on the web or the website (cookies), or to ask for information directly (forms), such as personal or demographic.

Database Marketing

Database Marketing (DBM) is the use of a database for marketing activities (Drozdenko & Drake, 2002). Database Marketing allows us to recognize customers across different channels and track their behavior. The use of a database and data mining tools lets us find patterns, trends or unexpected changes in consumer behavior that would, otherwise, be very difficult or take too long to discover. Data mining is the discovery of knowledge (actionable information) in data, in other words it is turning information into knowledge. This is where many organizations fail in their attempt to implement a DBM program. They think about collecting information and how to store it, but forget about turning information into knowledge and knowledge into action.

Many firms use separate databases for different channels. Sometimes these databases are even incompatible, making it impossible to combine their information. Research shows that a firm's most valuable customers are multi-channel buyers. With database marketing we can segment customers according to profitability and according to behavior, but in order to do that well we need to be able to recognize and track them across all channels. A firm may have a customer that is not profitable in one channel but is highly profitable in another, if that information is not integrated it runs the risk of losing a good customer because it treated her or him as expendable. If we want to build a relationship with customers, we have to recognize them across all channels and remember their preferences and previous communications. The marketing database is the corporate memory. As Hughes (2006) puts it, DBM lets big corporations build relationships and engage in dialogue with their customers in the same way the old corner grocer used to do.

On the internet, the use of DBM and cookies allows us to greet customers by name when they come back to a website. Amazon not only greets its customers by name, but also changes its front-page to display the products they believe the customer is interested in, based on past purchases and the behavior of customers with similar interests. As consumers are getting more knowledgeable, they become increasingly protective of their privacy. An increasing number of consumers are expressing concern about receiving targeted offers, ads or messages based on their past behavior, especially if they know the kind of data that is being monitored. There are also strict privacy laws that must be respected. We argue that firms should let their customers know what kind of information they are collecting and why they need it. The reasons they provide should be clearly related to customers' needs and service level expectations. Companies should also reassure them that they will never sell or share their personal data with other organizations. Then, they should let customers decide whether they want to have access to the full customer experience, with customized treatment, or if they want to be treated anonymously, without anyone monitoring their behavior.

Database marketing is expensive and therefore not appropriate for all businesses. With a few exceptions DBM is not viable in low margin businesses. In B2B, because of the higher value of individual transactions, DBM is always recommended. In a B2B relationship it is likely that more than one employee will contact a different number of people in the client organization. The

use of a marketing database will keep track of all these communications and allow employees to always have access to the latest information, preventing them from asking the same questions over and over again.

E-CRM

E-CRM is the use of electronic tools, or information technology, such as the internet and mobile phones for Customer Relationship Management, which can be defined as "the strategic process of selecting the customers a firm can most profitably serve and of shaping the interactions between a company and these customers. The goal is to optimize the current and future value of the customers for the company" (Kumar & Reinartz, 2006, p. 6). The use of a marketing database, data mining techniques and the integration of data from multiple channels are essential to effective e-CRM.

In addition, e-CRM should be fully integrated with offline CRM. A firm has to recognize its customers and remember their preferences whether they buy online, by phone, or postal order. In some cases, this is even possible at bricks and mortar stores that, due to the nature of their business, require customers to identify themselves, or through the use of loyalty cards.

Companies can also use electronic tools to enhance customer service levels offline. Some fast food chains are using smartphone apps to let their customers order in advance and pick up their meal at the chosen store a few minutes later. In New York, food trucks use Twitter to let their customers know where they are parked. With the use of a database you can create automatically generated messages that remind your customers of an important birthday or anniversary, or thank them for achieving a certain milestone with the company.

E-mail and SMS or MMS messaging are powerful e-CRM tools. A good CRM strategy should state the frequency of contact, preferred channel and type of message for each customer. One can determine which customers should get messages to promote up-selling (sale of premium products or services), cross-selling (sale of products or services from a different range), increased consumption, or simply retention messages (designed to increase customer loyalty).

One common mistake businesses of all sizes make, is assuming that once they buy and install CRM software, their work is done. Building, maintaining and enhancing relationships with customers is not something that can be achieved by software alone. The organization as a whole has to become customer centric and this may involve changing its culture and business processes.

The barriers to customer defection are even less online and information about competitors' offers is easily available, which means that customers can change suppliers with only a few clicks. If a firm truly engages its customers, they will share more and more information with it. This allows it to provide better service levels with each interaction, making their life easier and their decision making process faster. Ultimately the perceived cost of changing suppliers will be so great that it can afford to charge higher prices than the competition. E-customers are usually affluent and busy people who place a high value on their time. They are more than willing to pay a premium for service that makes their lives easier.

A good company website with lots of support information can help reduce the number of calls to a customer support line. Many people prefer to find the information they need online, because it is available 24/7 and they never get put on hold. This improves the perceived service quality, making customers happier and, as an added bonus, it also costs less money.

The metrics of e-CRM and DBM are similar, we need to measure the effects our actions have on customer loyalty, or the opposite metric customer churn rate (the percentage of customers who abandon a company). We can also calculate customer lifetime value, i.e., the net present value of the profit an average customer will generate in a given number of years. Customer profitability can be monitored to determine who the most profitable customers are and what effects our actions are having on their profitability. In order to correctly monitor the effects of our actions we need to have control groups and, preferably, test different alternatives, before large scale implementation.

Social Media

Social media is the new hype in marketing. When most firms were struggling to start a dialogue with their customers, the web 2.0 and social media changed the rules again and turned dialogue into trialogue. This means that consumers communicate among themselves, as well as with companies. Consumers have always communicated among themselves, but now the internet gives consumer generated content, levels of reach that were only available to large corporations. In addition, consumers trust the opinion of other consumers a lot more than they trust any marketing message. Social media includes blogs, microblogging (Twitter), social networks, social bookmarking and photo and video sharing sites.

Even though blogs and social networks can be used as ways of promoting an online presence or brand, we argue that their main purpose is relationship building and so we decided to include them in this section. In fact, firms that have used social media purely for the transmission of commercial messages have failed in mobilizing a significant community. In some cumbersome attempts, they even generated strong negative reactions. Community is the operative word in social media and what marketers need to understand is that they don't have a community, they belong to a community. They may own the infrastructure, but they will never own the community, so they have to give as much as they get. Companies need to learn to share their brand with their customers, because it is no longer possible for a marketer to control all the content associated with it.

A brand community may be created by the company or by its customers, on the company website or on an independent site. Many times it is created by a group of consumers, who take advantage of the brand without any previous authorization (brandjacking). Some authors state that it is advisable to maintain independence from these communities, mostly because of the risk of strong criticism towards the company, which shouldn't appear on the company's website, and also because the company's involvement may limit the participation of some consumers. On the other hand, it is essential that the company that owns the brand monitors all these websites (Dionísio *et al*, 2009), so that it can be aware of the community's perceptions and experiences with the brand.

Blogs are a great way to add frequently updated content to a website. We can use blogs to establish some employees as experts in their field, or as a way of showing how to get the most out of the company's products. By adding a comments section we can get instant feedback from customers.

Twitter is a micro blogging site in which each post, or tweet, is limited to 140 characters. Oddly enough, this limit is working rather well for both marketers and consumers. Because we only have 140 characters or less, we have to get straight to the point, which means we have to eliminate all the superfluous marketing speak. When time is our most precious resource and people are constantly bombarded with information, it is also good news for the consumers to be able to quickly read a message and decide whether they're interested or not. If they want to know more, additional information is usually just one click away. SMEs can benefit from Twitter because with 140 characters or less they don't really need a marketing department or a copywriter to create their messages. In addition, they can react more quickly than large corporations and come across more natural, because their messages don't have to be approved by several layers of management plus the legal department. This doesn't mean we should use Twitter purely

for commercial messages. We can use it to provide customer support and to know more about customers and how people view a brand, a company and its competitors. We can use twitter's real time search feature to see every tweet related to a query or we can go to www.tweetfeel.com and see if comments about a brand, company or product are mainly positive or negative. Twitter is also a very good way to get instant feedback from customers.

Social networks allow people with common interests to get together online and discuss different topics, share articles, videos or photos, or provide support for each other in solving different problems. Some social networks are more business oriented like LinkedIn and others like Facebook, Hi5 or MySpace tend to be for personal use.

The number of users and the time spent on social networks is increasing and, with it, so are the advertising budgets for social networking sites. At the time of writing this chapter, Facebook has over 500 million users, up from 200 in a little over one year. Firms can create their own Facebook pages and let their customers become fans. Once customers are fans, we should reward them with exclusive content and exclusive promotions to make them feel special. We should also use this opportunity to get feedback from them and learn about their needs and motivations. Negative feedback must also be seen as an opportunity to learn and improve, if it is unfair, the company's fans will be the first to defend it. If it is fair, the company should show genuine interest in trying to understand and solve the problem. Firms should resist the urge to censor negative feedback. Censorship should be reserved for offensive content or spam.

Wherever feedback comes from, it should have an impact on business decisions. If online communities see that a company takes all their feedback and puts it in the trash bin, the reaction may be more negative than if no feedback was requested at all.

One of the reasons some companies are shying away from social media is the difficulty in measuring the results of their actions. Calculating the effects of social media efforts can be a daunting task. Once again SMEs have an advantage, because they can more easily identify the reasons for the changes in sales, or lead generation. The metrics to monitor depend on the objectives of the social media program. If the objective is generating website traffic, we can use different URLs for different media and monitor their relative performance. The number of followers or fans is easy to monitor, but translating that into business results is an entirely different matter.

PROMOTING AN ONLINE PRESENCE

The internet is typically a pull medium. This means that users actively seek information, as opposed to passively receiving it like they do on other media such as television, which is mainly a push medium. There are some push communications on the internet, as well as there is some pull on television, mostly due to the advent of interactive TV and the spread of digital video recorders. However, we maintain that the internet is, for the most part, a pull medium. The point is that internet users control their online experience. They decide what to see, when and where to see it.

Setting up a website and expecting visitors to come pouring in without any further effort, can be compared to baking cookies in our kitchen and wondering why people aren't coming in by the dozens to buy them. We have to help them find it. Ironically, research shows that offline communications have a significant role to play in helping customers and prospects find firms online. A 2007 study, published by iProspect.com, showed that 67% of search engine users in the United States had performed a search on a search engine due to exposure to offline marketing communications. Therefore, the synergies between offline and online communications are far from negligible and must be exploited through an integrated approach.

Search Engine Marketing

Search Engine Marketing (SEM) is probably the most important thing we can do to help people find our website. Studies show that a significant percentage of people who do not respond directly to an advertisement, be it on or offline, will eventually use a search engine to try to discover more information about that company or product. The last thing we want is for the search engine result pages (SERPs) to be filled with offers from our competition, while we are nowhere to be found.

In addition, an increasing number of people are using the internet to research products or services before they buy them. Unless we have a very strong brand and an easy to remember web address, it is safe to assume that a large portion, if not the majority, of traffic to our website will come from search engines.

SEM can be divided into two main components: Search Engine Optimization (SEO) and paid search.

Search Engine Optimization

SEO is a set of techniques used to improve a website's ranking in search engines' organic results for certain keywords or key phrases (the set of words that users type into the search box). Placement in organic results is free and results are ordered according to relevance. We cannot buy the top places in organic results, all we can do is make our website more search engine friendly.

The first step is to let the search engines know we exist. Search engines have automatic programs called bots, spiders or crawlers that scour the web in search of new websites or changes made to existing ones. If a site is new, it may take a while for search engines to find it, so in order to speed up the process, we can submit our URL. Google is the world leader in search, so we should definitely make sure our site is registered with them, and monitor its ranking. In an effort to challenge Google's leadership, Microsoft launched Bing with an unprecedented marketing budget. They also signed a deal with Yahoo that will make Bing the search technology provider for Yahoo sites. All this and some interesting new features have made Bing's share of search show an interesting growth rate in the United States. To submit an URL to Google go to www.google.com/addurl; for Bing go to www.bing.com/docs/submit.aspx. If there are local search engines that are very popular in a country that is important to a company, it should also register with them and monitor its rankings.

Location is the name of the game when it comes to SEO and the place to be is among the top three organic results in SERPs. Ideally, everyone would like to hold the top spot, and the minimum we have to achieve is a place in the first page for the keywords or phrases that are most relevant to our business. If we can't appear in the first results page through SEO, we should seriously consider using paid search.

Search engines rank results according to complex algorithms that are always being refined and upgraded, so SEO is a very technical activity that requires constant monitoring. Ideally, SEO principles should be taken into consideration from the early stages of conception of a website.

There are a few basic principles that can improve the ranking of a particular website:

- Search engines love relevant, frequently updated content;
- If we have fresh relevant content, chances are people will link to our site, which is something search engines value as well;
- They also pay attention to keyword or key phrase density, i.e. the number of times a key phrase is used throughout the webpage, but here there is a danger of overdoing it, which will get a site excluded from SERPs for search engine spam. Companies can use their market knowledge, or a free tool like Google Analytics to determine which key phrases are used by customers to find their website;

- If we use HTML code wisely, especially title tags, headings and link anchor text (the text in hyperlinks) that can also help improve our ranking;
- One thing search engines don't like is sites they cannot "read", so sites with heavy use of flash and java tend to rank poorly.

Even if we don't have the budget to do anything else, we should at least follow these basic principles.

When it comes to SEO, there is no quick fix and no one can guarantee a top spot in SERPs. In fact, SEO changes may take months before they impact a site's ranking and those effects are very hard to predict.

Paid Search

With paid search we bid for certain keywords or phrases in order to appear on the sponsored links section of the SERPs. Paid search is also called pay-per-click (PPC), because the amount we bid is the cost-per-click (CPC) of every user who clicks on an ad and we only have to pay if users actually click on it. The search engine will then rank the ad according to the bid amount and a number of factors to assess relevance and relative performance. Therefore, being the highest bidder will not guarantee the first place on the list, it may not even guarantee a place on the list at all, depending on the assessed relevance of the ad. Click fraud is an issue in PPC advertising. Click fraud occurs when someone clicks on an ad repeatedly. This usually happens for one of two reasons: a website owner clicks on ads in order to increase his or her income; or someone clicks on an ad in order to hamper the effectiveness of a competitor's paid search campaigns. Estimates of fraudulent clicks vary from under 10% to close to 30%, depending on the source. Search engines are taking this matter seriously and have taken several measures to prevent it, but although it is getting harder, click fraud is still far from impossible.

Paid search also includes contextual ads displayed in a search engine's ad network, which places ads in third party sites. Contextual ads are displayed if they are relevant to the content on a given web page. These ads can be placed on a cost-per click (CPC), cost-per-thousand (CPM) or cost-per-action (CPA) basis. With CPM we pay a certain amount for a thousand ad impressions (ad impressions are the number of times an ad is displayed). With CPA we only pay if a predetermined action is taken by the visitor. This action can be filling in a contact form, asking for a price quote, or making a purchase.

It is recommended that after clicking on the ad, visitors are directed to a landing page closely related to the offer. The landing page and the text in the ad should also have a clear call to action. One should also test combinations of ad copy and landing pages to determine which combinations produce the best results. If we're generating plenty of traffic, but have a high bounce rate, the problem is probably in the landing page (assuming there's nothing wrong with the product or service). If we have a low click-through rate and a high conversion rate, we should make changes in our ad copy. Let us explain some of the metrics we just mentioned. Bounce rate is the percentage of visitors that leave the site after viewing only one page. The click-through rate gives us the percentage of people who respond to an ad by clicking on it. The importance of the click-through rate as a standalone metric is now being questioned, as research shows that a high percentage of the people who respond to an ad, do not click on the ad itself. Many respondents prefer to search for information about the offer or type the URL of the firm directly into their browser. The conversion rate shows the percentage of visitors who complete the desired process, e.g., become leads (by filling in a form) or customers (by completing a sale).

One thing to remember about search engine marketing and paid search in particular, is that we need to plan our budget in order to maintain a constant presence in the SERPs, as opposed to traditional advertising in which we maximize impact by concentrating our budget in shorter time periods. One very important metric to monitor in SEM, as in any other aspect of business, is the return on investment (ROI).

Affiliate Marketing

Chaffey *et al.* (2009) define affiliate marketing as "a commission based arrangement where the merchant only pays when they make the sale or get a lead" (p. 535). When visitors come in to a site from an affiliate website, a cookie is placed on their computer. The cookie is valid for a certain period of time during which a sale or a lead generated from that visitor will be credited to the affiliate. During that period, several affiliates may have referred the same visitor to the website, so we must be able to tell which one is the last referrer, which is usually credited with the sale.

The commission can be based on a percentage or a fixed amount per sale. It is similar to search engine marketing's CPA because we only pay if a certain action is taken by the visitor, although sometimes there may be a pay-per-click arrangement. The obvious advantage is that if no sales or leads are generated, affiliate marketing won't cost us a cent.

Affiliates can drive significant traffic to a website and help improve its search engine visibility, but we have to be careful not to destroy our profit margin when deciding how much commission to pay. Firms that don't do their math correctly may end up generating a loss with every sale.

Affiliate marketing is not easy to manage and requires a lot of time and skill, so most companies resort to affiliate networks or affiliate agencies that will manage the affiliate program for a percentage of the commissions. Using an affiliate network means that offers may be placed in sites that companies do not want to be associated with, so they may need to establish, beforehand, the kind of sites that are deemed unsuitable.

Some companies with stronger brands question the usefulness of an affiliate marketing program, because they feel that commissions are paid for sales that would happen even without affiliate referral.

Online Display Advertising

Many people claim that online display advertising is dead because of banner blindness. They say that people look at the parts of the websites they are interested in and simply ignore the banner ads around them.

However, in a recent study, published by iProspect.com, online display advertising showed surprising levels of effectiveness with a 52% response rate among internet users, even though only 31% of them clicked on the ad itself. The rest either search for information about the product or service, or type the URL of the company directly into their browser. What this means is that the performance of an online display advertising campaign has to be measured more carefully than simply calculating click-through rates, because a substantial part of its impact cannot be measured directly. These numbers are also a good argument for the integration of search engine marketing with display advertising campaigns.

There are ways of improving the effectiveness of display ads. Ads placed in the middle of content tend to perform better than those placed on top or on the right side of a page. When feasible, we should also try to adapt the copy of the ads to the page in which they are going to be placed, in order to make them more relevant and less intrusive. Display ads should also have a clear call to action. A call to action is what we want people to do. A call to action shouldn't be "Click here" or "Click now!", it should be related to our offer. If we were advertising a subscription for a magazine or a newspaper, our call to action should be something like "Subscribe today!" or "Subscribe today and get one year free!". With display advertising, as in paid search, we should also optimize the landing page. Testing is also very important. If an ad isn't performing, we should test alternatives.

With online display advertising we can monitor the click-through rate, with the care of using other metrics as well, such as brand awareness. We can also monitor the conversion rates of different copy, the value and profitability of the sales it generated, and ROI.

E-Mail Marketing

Sending e-mail is so cheap that the ROI for e-mail marketing is unrivalled by that of any other online marketing activity. This is why there is so much spam, even if only a small number of people respond it is still worth it. Spam is unsolicited e-mail sent indiscriminately. Spam is not only illegal in some countries, but it will also generate negative feelings towards the sender. In addition, Internet Service Providers (ISPs) are monitoring the open rates of e-mail and using them to categorize spam even if people don't click the "report spam" button. So, if content is not seen as relevant and enough e-mail recipients don't open our messages, they may soon be marked as spam. This is why we shouldn't think that e-mail is so cheap that we can send it to every address on the database.

E-mail marketing can be both inbound and outbound. Most organizations only plan and prepare for outbound e-mail marketing, but failing to respond to inbound e-mail in a timely and satisfactory manner will have a negative impact on an organization's image. We should answer an e-mail within one business day, or at least acknowledge that the situation is being looked at, when the case in hand requires further investigation.

Outbound e-mail marketing can be used for customer acquisition and for customer retention. Even though the effectiveness of e-mail as a customer acquisition medium is diminishing, mainly because of spam, it is still a good option, especially if prospects give us permission to contact them. We should always try to get permission to send e-mails and once we get permission we should treasure it. If people give us permission to send them e-mails, it means that they want to know what we have to offer. Thus, our messages are more likely to be read and the predisposition to respond to our offers is also higher. We should only send relevant, personalized, value added offers. E-mail is probably the cheapest medium to personalize. This means that instead of sending the same offer to everyone, based on what we want to sell, we can send an offer that a customer or prospect is most likely interested in. That's why e-mail is most effective as a customer retention tool. As we get to know customers better, we can target e-mails more effectively. The low cost of personalization and delivery of e-mail makes testing inexpensive, which means that we can test the effects of different copy writing and design, different offers and the effects that non-commercial messages, such as a simple thank you, can have on customer loyalty.

We can also enhance our service levels with e-mails that let people know that their order has been shipped and when it is expected to arrive. The most common metrics used to evaluate the performance of e-mail marketing are the delivery, open and click-through rates, and, of course, ROI. The delivery rate gives us the percentage of e-mails that were delivered and the open rate gives us the percentage of e-mails that were viewed.

Viral Marketing

According to the American Marketing Association, viral marketing is "a marketing phenomenon that facilitates and encourages people to pass along a marketing message". It is called "viral because the number of people exposed to a message mimics the process of passing a virus or disease from one person to another". Viral marketing is also called online word of mouth or word of mouse, because the internet is where viral messages spread more quickly.

Why do people pass along a marketing message? They pass it along because they think it's funny, startling and/or controversial, and want to

share it. They pass it along because it makes them feel good. If enough people share the message, it can have a tremendous impact, reaching millions of people in a relatively short period of time.

The most appealing factor of viral marketing is that with a relatively short budget and a healthy dose of talent and creativity, we can have a big impact. In order to succeed, we should tone down our message, making it more entertaining and less commercial. Kirby (2006) states that viral marketing should have an effect on the bottom line and questions the effectiveness of campaigns that succeed from a viral perspective (are viewed by a lot of people), but fail from a marketing perspective (have little impact in sales, brand awareness or brand favorability). There is a delicate balance to manage between a message that is too commercial and therefore will not be passed along, and a message that can hardly be associated with our brand or product.

SELLING ONLINE

Selling online is no longer something reserved for large companies or internet startups. Nowadays, e-commerce solutions are relatively easy to set up and free open source alternatives are readily available. Selling online may be the only way SMEs can truly compete globally, without the need for international intermediaries or physical facilities. In some cases, such as the software industry, the need for physical distribution channels has almost been eliminated by the spread of broadband. This lets companies that used to rely on intermediaries, sell directly to their customers, with savings in packaging and distribution costs.

Nevertheless, there is more to e-commerce than setting up a website and starting to take orders. The company's business processes must also be adjusted in order to adapt to the new requirements.

Before deciding to sell online, we must determine if it is a viable solution:

- Can our products or services be sold online?
- Are there any legal barriers to selling our products/services online?
- Do we have the ability to deliver them to customers in a timely manner?
- Can our products/services be delivered digitally?
- Are we prepared to accept online payments?
- Can we offer secure payment options?
- Can we protect our customers' private and financial data?
- Are current invoicing and inventory systems prepared for e-commerce?
- Are there any legal barriers to selling internationally?
- Are we prepared to cope with international taxation and customs?

Then we must determine if our customers are both willing and able to buy online, and what benefits can they get from it:

- Are our target customers comfortable buying online?
- Is buying online cheaper/faster/easier? What can customers gain from it?
- Is it a pleasant experience?
- Can customers find what they want and pay for it in a simple manner?
- Is it important to have physical contact with the products before buying?

Once the decision to sell online has been made, we have to decide what to sell online. We can replicate our offline offers; we may decide to have exclusive online offers, or a combination of both. Some companies that do not sell directly to consumers, offline, can do so online. This decision must not be taken lightly, since it can endanger the relationship with offline distributors and retailers. The opposite is also true; firms that sell directly offline may use one or more levels of intermediaries online. Infomediaries are a new kind of intermediary that gather large chunks of information and organize it in a way that is easy to understand by consumers, saving them time and helping them make their decisions. E-marketplaces are electronic platforms that gather B2B buyers and vendors, allowing them to interact (Dionísio *et al.*, 2009).

Some of these new intermediaries share their negotiation power with consumers, making it cheaper to buy through an intermediary, than buying directly.

The most relevant metrics in online selling are: the number of buyers and transactions; the number, value and profitability of transactions per buyer; the global profit margin and average profit per transaction and buyer; the total sales and average sales per buyer and transaction. We can also monitor entry pages and referring sites, the percentage of abandoned shopping carts and global conversion rates.

CREATING AN E-MARKETING PLAN

The e-marketing plan should be integrated into the business planning system, together with other plans the company may have, like the strategic plan, business plan, offline marketing plan, etc.

Integrating online and offline marketing strategies and actions is a complex challenge for both marketers and the firm's information systems. This integrated approach of on and offline markets enables the real time customization of offers, just like what can be done for exclusively online approaches, it also enables (Dionísio *et al.*, 2009):

- The multi-channel tracking of customers;
- The detections of differences between online and offline customer behavior;
- The customization of more complex value propositions that require a cross-channel approach;

- The analysis of the impact of traditional media campaigns in the firm's customer base.

However, this integrated approach isn't possible in companies that do not keep individual customer level information, such as companies without a CRM solution for on and/or offline markets. If this information is available, the company can create its e-marketing plan based on solid foundations.

The analysis of information about the company's e-market, its customers, competitors and intermediaries, as well as the information about its external environment, is the starting point for the creation of the e-marketing plan. Together with information retrieved from the internal analysis of the firm, which will show us the amount of available resources and its strengths and weaknesses. This provides an analytical framework that supports the setting of marketing objectives, as well as strategies, actions and resources that make its successful implementation possible.

According to Chaffey & Smith (2008), there are five broad benefits, reasons or objectives of e-marketing that can be summarized as the 5Ss:

- **Sell – Grow Sales:** Through wider distribution, promotion and sales to customers that you can't service offline;
- **Serve – Add Value:** Giving customers extra benefits online or develop the product or service in response to online feedback;
- **Speak – Get closer to customers:** Creating a two-way dialogue through formal (surveys, polls and forms) and informal (monitoring chat rooms, for example) online market research;
- **Save – Save Costs:** Using internet to reduce transaction, promotion and distribution costs, enabling you to cut prices and generate greater market share and therefore make online sales more profitable;

- **Sizzle – Extend the brand online:** Reinforce brand awareness and values in a new medium like the web.

Once the objectives are defined, one must establish the strategy to reach them. Defining the online value proposition is an essential aspect of that strategy. This proposition can be undifferentiated, when the company presents the same proposition to its customers and prospects.

However, if the company possesses a CRM solution and analysis tools that allow it to gather individual customer information and segment its customers in real time, it can create segmented or individual online value propositions. In the first case, a value proposition is created for each previously identified segment; in the latter, the proposition is also generated automatically and in real time for each customer, according to profile and behavior.

In order to create online value propositions differentiated by segment or customer, a company must be able to (Dionísio *et al.*, 2009):

- **Gather and process information about its customers:** This information, that must be gathered for both customers and prospects, will enable us to identify the needs and desires of customers, based on their search and/or buying behavior in the company website, through time;
- **Create and offer differentiated online value propositions:** These propositions, differentiated by segment or individual, must be defined according to the marketing-mix variables – product, price, promotion and place. They should also be actionable with the information that is gathered and generate a profit.

To implement the e-marketing plan, one must define the actions and resources that are needed for its execution. It is thus necessary to produce a project action plan that delineates the actions to be taken and the necessary resources, in terms of people, money and time, for its execution. Project management skills allow us to plan and control the correct and timely execution of these actions.

The control process of the e-marketing plan uses a set of metrics that allow us to assess its performance and, if necessary, take corrective action, by developing a new e-marketing plan or by reforming it.

You must use a set of metrics that measure performance on three levels: business measures, marketing measures and specific internet marketing measures (Chaffey *et al.*, 2009). These metrics should give you a global picture of your performance from tactical to strategic level.

There are other metrics that can help understand why you succeeded or failed in achieving your goals, so it is important to identify which metrics let you know if you're moving in the right direction and which variables can help to explain it. These metrics can and should change with different kinds of activities, campaigns or businesses and some of them are given by web analytics tools.

The internet lets you measure almost everything with very little cost. This provides internet marketing with a level of accountability far greater than that of most offline marketing activities. However, when the cost of measuring a few variables is the same as the cost of measuring many variables, people have a tendency to try to monitor all metrics. This can lead to an information overload, when there is so much information available that people can't process it in its entirety.

CONCLUSION

In the customer centric company, marketing plays a pivotal role, as it is essential in providing the necessary intelligence for the design, planning and implementation of the business strategy. Consumers are spending more and more time online at the expense of other media, so companies need to adjust to this new reality. E-marketing responds to this need by taking advantage of new information technologies and is growing in importance when compared to offline marketing. Companies in general and SMEs in particular, need to be aware of e-marketing's tools and techniques, and monitor their evolution in order to choose which ones they can use in their marketing activities.

As more and more people research online before buying products or services, the company website is the first thing that many prospects will see. Therefore, it is not only important to make a good first impression, but also to make sure that the website is easy to find. Search engine marketing, affiliate marketing, online display advertising and viral marketing are ways of promoting the company website.

The website and other online resources can be used to gather information about customers' needs and motivations. This information can be turned into knowledge and then into action with data mining, database marketing and customer relationship management. All this actionable knowledge lets firms create online value propositions that can be tailored to the needs of different segments or even individual customers, which are an important part of an e-marketing plan. In this plan, we set the objectives that will shape the company's e-marketing strategies and actions, and make sure they are integrated with the offline marketing plan.

E-marketing can have different levels of complexity and requires some adjustment for SMEs to be able to respond to its demands. Theoretically, e-marketing is a relatively recent subject where new developments are always occurring, as the internet and new digital media evolve at a dizzying rate.

REFERENCES

Carrera, F. (2009). *Marketing digital na versão 2.0 – o que não pode ignorar*. Lisboa, Portugal: Edições Sílabo.

Chaffey, D. (2004). Online value proposition. *CIM: What's New in Marketing?* Retrieved August 5, 2009 from http://www.davechaffey.com /E-marketing-Insights/ Customer-experience -management/ Online-customer -value-proposition/

Chaffey, D., Ellis-Chadwick, F., Mayer, R., & Johnston, K. (2009). *Internet marketing: Strategy, implementation and practice*. Essex, England: Pearson Education.

Chaffey, D., & Smith, P. R. (2008). *eMarketing eXcellence* (3rd ed.). Oxford, UK: Butterworth-Heinemann.

Dionísio, P., Rodrigues, J. V., Faria, H., Canhoto, R., & Nunes, R. C. (2009). *Blended marketing*. Lisboa, Portugal: Publicações Dom Quixote.

Drozdenko, R. G., & Drake, P. D. (2002). *Optimal database marketing: Strategy, development and data mining*. Thousand Oaks, CA: Sage Publications.

Hughes, A. M. (2006). *Strategic database marketing* (3rd ed.). New York, NY: McGraw-Hill.

iProspect. (2007). *Offline channel influence on online search behavior study*. Retrieved August 20, 2009, from http://www.iprospect.com/ about/researchstudy_2007 _offlinechannelinfluence.htm

iProspect. (2009). *Search engine marketing and online display advertising integration study*. Retrieved August 20, 2009, from http://iprospect.com/abou t/researchstudy_2009_ searchand-display.htm

Johnson, M. D., Anderson, E. W., & Forrel, C. (1995). Rational and adaptive performance expectations in a customer satisfaction framework. *The Journal of Consumer Research, 21*, 695–707. doi:10.1086/209428

Kirby, J. (2006). Viral marketing. In Kirby, J., & Marsden, P. (Eds.), *Connected marketing: The viral, buzz and word of mouth revolution* (pp. 87–106). Oxford, UK: Butterworth-Heinemann.

Kotler, P. (2005). *Marketing management – analysis, planning, implementation and control* (12th ed.). London, UK: Prentice Hall.

Kumar, V., & Reinartz, W. J. (2006). *Customer relationship management: A database approach*. Hoboken, NJ: John Wiley & Sons.

Lindon, D., Lendrevie, J., Rodrigues, J. V., & Dionísio, P. (2004). *Mercator XXI*. Lisboa, Portugal: Publicações Dom Quixote.

Myers, J. H. (1996). *Segmentation and positioning for strategic marketing decisions*. Chicago, IL: American Marketing Association.

Pal, N., & Rangaswamy, A. (2003). *The power of one: Gaining business value from personalization technologies*. Victoria, Canada: Trafford Publishing.

Pires, A., & Santos, A. P. (1996). *Satisfação dos clientes – um objectivo estratégico de gestão*. Lisboa, Portugal: Texto Editora.

Viral marketing. (n.d.). In *AMA dictionary*. Retrieved August 20, 2009, from http://www.marketingpower.com /_layouts/Dictionary.aspx

Walker, O. C., Boyd, M. W., & Larréché, J. C. (1992). *Marketing strategy: Planning and implementation*. USA: Richard D. Irwin.

Section 3
Semantic Technologies

Chapter 12
Critical Success Factors to Yield Business Benefits from Semantic Technologies

Ronald C Beckett
University of Western Sydney, Australia

Anni Rowland-Campbell
Semantic Transformations Pty Ltd, Australia

Paul Strahl
Semantic Transformations Pty Ltd, Australia

ABSTRACT

The purpose of this chapter is to explore opportunities offered by and issues associated with the use of emergent semantic technologies in enhancing an enterprise's business position. These technologies include a foundation level set of standards and descriptive languages supporting interpretive connections to applications. The chapter is more oriented towards applications and the human side of the human/machine interface. We draw on both the literature and case material available to us as active practitioners to illustrate benefits realized and potential barriers to the uptake of semantic technologies. Critical success factors are related to user learning capabilities, the establishment of trust in the technology and its providers, and factors influencing the nature of potential engagement with users and markets.

INTRODUCTION

The word *semantic* relates to the meaning of words, or more broadly to philosophy concerned with meaning. Meaning can be context-specific. For example the word 'field' can have a variety of lay-person and professional community mean-ings, depending on the context in which it is used (e.g. agriculture, sport, or IT usage). The internet provides a fast communication pathway to large volumes of information, but it is up to the user to decide what information is relevant and how it might be interpreted and used – matters of context. The concept of a *semantic web* involves making this information understandable by computers (linked via the internet) in a generic way so rel-

DOI: 10.4018/978-1-60960-765-4.ch012

evant data sub-sets can be rapidly found, shared and combined in an appropriate context.

At a conceptual level, the possibilities offered by the semantic web are not new – we already use some relatively simple ideas to access large amounts of data. Here are some examples.

Consider a street directory where a relatively small number of icons having specific meanings are used to map a vast amount of information on to a grid to form a map. The information can be presented at higher or lower levels of detail and when specific instances of an icon or region are named, they can be linked to a key-word search facility. Other information such as height contours can be added to the grid. Google maps provide an on-line version. Combining machine-readable versions of the information with satellite navigation data has resulted in a new family of sat-nav products. Another example - libraries round the world use a common categorisation system to help store and find books and articles. One can search for a book by author, by name, or simply browse around one part of the library. In a similar way, Tufts University is using software called VUE (Visual Understanding Environment) to map key concepts and linkages between them to connect with vast amounts of multi-media data used in teaching (http://vue.tufts.edu/about/index.cfm). Going in the other direction, social scientists are using Leximancer software to scan substantial bodies of text and rapidly consolidate it into meaningful 'Themes', 'Concepts' and their associated relationships (http://leximancer.com). A common requirement is an ability to navigate a journey to new places in a complex data environment. Imagine having a "map" of some important aspect of a business that is easily interpreted and automatically updated.

Consider the data-bus technology being used on modern aircraft. A relatively simple but dynamically changing data set managed by on-board computers is accessed by many functional devices via a communication system. Redundancy in the data and the communication pathways plus data interrogation by the data bus management system assure the availability and quality of data. Connected functional devices draw data off the bus and update some of the data in real time. As long as the data exchange protocols are honored each device can be independently changed. Imagine if, in an analogous way, semantic technologies could be used to link together disparate data-bases, and kept up-to-date through RSS feeds uniquely specified by individual users.

The ability to work with large volumes of data is becoming increasingly important as enterprises become more information and knowledge driven. Current internet search tools use key words to assemble a sub-set of information that may be useful in a particular context, but there may still be a large volume of information to sort through manually. In addition, the nature of the subset obtained depends on the search strategy adopted. In other words, there is know-how associated with the use of the tool, and we have to think about the best way to characterize what we are searching for. Analogous practices have emerged in the world of semantic technologies.

In this chapter we draw on the functional level (as compared with foundation level) concepts behind semantic technologies to frame ways in which people can beneficially use them without getting into matters of data interface standards, particular ontology languages and the like. Our objective is, through the use of case examples, to illustrate some of the benefits obtained using this approach and some of the potential barriers to utilization of the concept of the semantic web. As well as considering opportunities associated with semantic technologies, we also consider some critical success factors supporting their adoption. We draw on ideas from the organizational learning, technology diffusion, and market characterization literature on the basis that one must firstly understand what is on offer and its significance, then be able to use it within the enterprise and/or to better access market opportunities. Our objective is to provide insights that will stimulate the informed utilization of semantic technologies.

BACKGROUND

The World of Knowledge and Communication

Knowledge, according to Peter Drucker, is "the basic economic resource - the means of production … is no longer 'capital', nor natural resources … nor 'labor'. It is and will be knowledge." (Drucker 1993).

When humans describe ideas, concepts and things, they do so using the richness of language combined with an innate sense of cultural experience and knowledge. This knowledge is built upon data and information (Davenport and Prusak 1998) and in order to fully appreciate and understand knowledge we need to understand the relationship between the two.

Data may be described as "a discrete set of objective facts about events, specifically in organisations being structured records of transactions." Information is that data which is "contextualised, categorised, calculated and condensed". It is about "informing", has a sender and a receiver, and is meant to change the way the receiver perceives "something" and therefore can have an impact on judgment and behaviour. (Davenport and Prusak 1998). From data and information can be gleaned "knowledge" which may be described as "an extension of human experience and values, which uses these human attributes and contextualised information to interpret the message and define decisions and action. It is the capacity to act. It is dynamic and is constantly being updated and made obsolete" (Sveiby 1997).

The Impact of Digital Technologies

Digital technologies have radically changed the way we manage data, information and knowledge.

In work done over the past twenty years Professor Shoshana Zuboff has investigated the impact of the computer on the workplace (Zuboff 1988; Zuboff and Maxmin 2002) and identified that digital technologies change the paradigm within which humans operate. Being able to capture and store data in vast quantities does not necessarily help us make better decisions, and according to Gartner (Gartner 2009) "through 2012, more than 35 per cent of the top 5,000 global companies will regularly fail to make insightful decisions about significant changes in their business and markets." Why? Because of the lack of intelligence which leads to knowledge, and the overwhelm of the amount of data that is increasingly being generated (http://news.netcraft.com/archives/web_server_survey.html, viewed 14th September, 2009).

The challenge is that unless we can actually harness and understand that data within a context, we are limited in our ability to fully utilise it, and, in fact, the "overwhelm" of data can sometimes be downright disadvantageous (Wurman 2001). Hence the current focus on "business intelligence" (Gartner 2009).

The Promise of "Semantic" Technologies

Semantic technologies have been described as bringing together technology, politics, psychology and philosophy (Cregan 2009) because the aim is to enable humans and machines to inter-operate more effectively, and for humans to leverage machine technologies to deal with vast arrays of complex information and data. The primary vehicle for doing this is the web-based interface, but the delivery mechanism will be independent of particular devices, will be largely mobile, and will evolve as the ability to visualise data evolves.

The concept of a "universal medium for data, information and knowledge exchange" was envisaged by Tim Berners-Lee who saw a way that humans could harness the power of computers which would be "capable of analysing all the data on the Web – the content, links, and transactions between people and computers ... and where the day-to-day mechanisms of trade, bureaucracy and our daily lives will be handled by machines talking to machines." The main obstacle to this vision, and to the realisation of the ultimate potential of the Web, is the inability of machines to make sense of the vast quantities of data that humans publish, because web pages are designed to be read by people, not machines, and thus they rely on the ability of humans to contextualise the information they present.

The approach of traditional information technologies is to "hard wire" meanings and relationships into data formats; in contcept, the idea of semantic technologies is to encode relationships and meanings separately from data and content files, and separately from the application code itself (Berners-Lee, Hendler et al. 2001). There are a range of disciplines which make up "semantic technologies' which include natural language processing, discourse analysis and machine learning, all of which attempt to bring together the human and machine interface, with the ultimate aim of enabling machines to make contextual connections around the information that humans publish.

According to The Economist the interest in and focus on semantic technologies is because of their promise to bring together the quantitative and qualitative data that now exists within databases and published on the web, and thus is a powerful solution to the problem of dealing with vast quantities of information both in real time and from multiple sources (Ilube 2009).

Extracting Value from Semantic Technologies

Presented with an opportunity to embrace a new technology or practice such as e-business, an enterprise may reject the idea, explore the idea, embrace the idea and extract value from the idea. Starting at the opportunity end, the motivation to learn more may come from an individual's initiative and interest; from some incentive to consider the idea such as a financial reward or a pronouncement by a visionary CEO; or as a matter of survival when competitors or clients have already embraced the idea or when completely new ways of doing business are sought. An up-front strategic decision may be taken to embrace the idea, appreciating that there may be a lot to learn in implementing it. Two points to be made here are that having an end-point in mind is beneficial and that the nature of the starting point influences the dynamics of the journey. Both of these matters may require significant changes in current thinking.

People Learning about New Things

Some literature on adult learning (e.g. Jarvis, 1987), organisational learning (e.g. Senge et al, 1999) and technology diffusion (e.g. Cohen and Levinthal, 1990) indicates the rejection or ineffective uptake of a new idea may result from:

- A poor understanding of the idea – it may be couched in unfamiliar language or the relevance of the idea may not be apparent, for example if the recipient has no prior knowledge of the concept or technology on offer
- The idea is not seen as something new, or is considered unlikely to add value
- The idea is incompatible with personal or enterprise values. For example working over the Internet may be seen as conflicting with an ambition to provide personal services.

Outcomes from responding to a learning opportunity may be that:

- Non-reflective learning takes place. What is learned may be stored in memory for potential future use, a current practice may be incrementally enhanced, or current knowledge or practice may be legitimized

- Reflective learning takes place. This may result in an altered set of values, adoption of new practices or the verification of some hypothesis about how things work

Following this logic we can understand some people issues associated with the diffusion of semantic technologies.

People Utilising New Ideas

Learning from a new idea is one thing; doing something with it is another. E-business opportunities may deliver value by enhancing the internal practices of an enterprise and/or by enhancing its market engagement. This may be achieved via new personal or inter-enterprise linkages, through facilitating market-related activities or by accessing new resources. An international group of marketing management researchers, the IMP group (www.impgroup.org) have found it convenient to study market dynamics in terms of the intersecting networks of actors, activities and resources involved. It has been observed that each of these three networks do not change that fast, but changing linkages between actors, activities and resources can result in apparent rapid change. In an analogous way, other researchers have observed that financial transactions, may be linked to resources, events and agents in a shared data environment (REA accounting model: McCarthy, 1982) and are using an adaptation of this idea to develop an enterprise economic ontology (Geerts and McCarthy, 2000, 2002). In the context of semantic technologies, we suggest:

- Significant kinds of actors/agents that influence e-business markets are technology developers, technology users (enterprise, partners and clients) and regulators
- E-business activities and associated events primarily relate to innovation, marketing/sales, operations/delivery and life-cycle support

- Networks of resources drawn on to support e-business initiatives are enterprise infrastructure, linking infrastructure and application tools

We will use this networked view of markets to provide a case study analysis framework. For example, we have observed differences in language and mental models between technology developers and technology users that can lead to dysfunctional actor network operation.

The internal operations of an enterprise can also be viewed as intersecting networks of actors, activities and resources, but these are controlled within the enterprise. E-business involves some interdependency on external autonomous agents, and issues of reliability and trust can arise (e.g. McGuiness et al, 2006). Can an enterprise and a client trust the linking infrastructure? Can data obtained from the Internet be confidently used? Can a client buying a physical product over the Internet be confident of its delivery and performance? Trust is related to personal belief systems; it is built over time but may rapidly dissipate if something goes wrong. In assigning trust, it is assumed there is a low risk that anticipated outcomes will not be realized. From this point of view, trust is a risky business, and in this paper we will consider matters of potential risk in the use of semantic technologies as a proxy for trust to help identify the challenges in embracing those technologies.

Combining the ideas presented above, we can start to work backwards from our desired future state by asking some key questions. How can we improve our competitiveness through increasing revenue, reducing costs and/or improving asset utilization using semantic technologies? What networks of activities will be involved – innovation, marketing/sales, operations/delivery and/or life-cycle support? Which technology developers, regulators and users will be involved? What resource networks will be involved? What risks are associated with each network entity and the connections between them? What do we have to learn to extract value from the application of semantic technologies?

Some International Experience to Date

Let us consider some recent observations relating to the diffusion of semantic technologies. An international consortium (W3C) was established in the late 1990s to identify appropriate standards and practices, and presented their ideas in a hierarchical scheme sometimes referred to as the "semantic web stack". Various standards for tagging and linking data form the foundation layer, followed by structured ways of interpreting this data that are consistent with how people think and make sense of the world. At the top level there are rules that are concerned with verifying the validity of the data for the intended purpose and building trust in its quality and security. Collectively these elements are referred to as *Semantic Technologies*. By the mid 2000's, these technologies were being used in real-world applications by early adopters, and those people and enterprises involved to date suggest that the use of such technologies will become dominant within the next ten years.

A W3C Education and Outreach Special Interest Group (Pollock, 2001) has considered the business case for adopting these technologies. In broad terms, they see these technologies to be an enabler that will "Empower, directly and indirectly, new business capabilities; throttle back IT expenditures within medium and large businesses; and transform the foundation of enterprise software, and data interpretation in particular." Drawing on the expertise of about forty research, government and industry contributors, they examined the benefits of semantic technologies in terms of three selection criteria that commonly influence new practice adoption decisions. These were – identification of the lowest risk option, selection for tactical fit (making a difference NOW), and

choosing the right partner – where ties between a customer and vendor matter.

Some risks associated with the adoption of semantic technologies in 2008 were seen as:

- Minimal large-vendor support for development tools
- Expensive, hard-to-find skill sets to hire
- Few proven reference implementations in the public domain
- The need for a very real paradigm shift in modeling, design and declarative programming

However, the Special Interest Group felt that these considerations had to be balanced against the risk of not beginning to engage with the new technologies.

In terms of tactical fit, the Special Interest Group argued that for "information-centric operations --- it is hard to beat the power of the Semantic Web data specifications". This is on the basis of superior data flexibility, audit-ability and data re-use. In particular, Semantic Web technologies were expected to excel in the:

- Specification of computationally sound business information models
- Specification of linking and relationship (meta) data across physical data locations
- Specification of dynamic structural logic and rules that are part of the data realm
- Specification of a federation approach for geographically separate data records.

The Special Interest Group observed that enterprises commonly partnered with technology providers they had successfully worked with in the past, building on the social capital (e.g. connections, mutual understandings and trust) that had been established. This was seen as reducing the risks involved, but unless these trusted technology providers are also innovative, the outcomes may be disappointing.

SME ADOPTION OF SEMANTIC TECHNOLOGIES

The experience with semantic technologies described in the preceding section primarily related to larger enterprises. In the following sections we will draw on the operational experience of the authors in dealing with both large and small individual enterprises.

Some Barriers

We have observed that SMEs and in fact all businesses find it difficult to exploit the full power of semantic technologies for the following reasons:

- The mindset required to grasp and implement these technologies is very different from the way traditional business operates (i.e. It is not such a linear, incremental progression, but one that adapts to dynamic change)

- To fully exploit the new technologies, new skills are required, which are generally not held by existing employees. For instance, if one was to implement an "automated chat bot" to replace a livechat operator, the existing livechat staff would not be able to train and maintain: the "bot". Instead, the existing staff would have to be replaced by and someone with a "blended multidisciplinary skill-set – this person would need to blend natural language, sales process, product knowledge and business process, with some basic IT understanding. From our observations, the best way of developing these sorts of people is to take clever graduates and train them in house.

- Businesses are generally not aware of emerging technologies - they are used to being served by technology vendors who offer them a suite of offerings, generally in the context of current paradigms.

- There is (from our observations) faulty thinking around new technologies, of "well that's all very well, but how does that make me, or save me money". The truth is that of and by themselves, they don't! However, if they are used as the "glue" to stitch together a brand new business model, they certainly can save or make money.

- We observe most businesses have difficulty in grasping new business model concepts or in seeing their potential. Nor can they accommodate the new employee skill sets required to run them.

- Introducing these new technologies cuts across many established centres of power and influence – they "threaten" the established positions of IT departments, marketing and sales professionals, analysts, process engineers, etc Who wants to investigate a new technology which reduces the significance of their role and potentially makes their role obsolete??

- Even when new technologies do not require radical change, but simply make a task easier or more efficient, there is still the linking of humans and data to successfully address. This has been seen in one of our case studies: a small Sydney charity - a non profit organisation with about 5 employees. They email a database of around 700+ members through Microsoft Outlook. They have now been introduced to an email marketing system, which will cost them roughly $10/month and save them hours of tedious labour. However, they need to learn how to use it, how to get their data in there, how to set it up, etc. Unless someone who is good at both people skills and IT is present, the change will fail.

- Further, individuals often don't know what to do with the potential opportunities the technology presents. For instance, an Australian not for profit organisation has

1700 unique visitors to their website every week, or roughly 80,000 unique visitors per year. Drill down into the data, and they have a "bounce" rate of 20%. What's going on there? They don't know what people are doing on their site, or why they are coming. As an organisation, they are starved for funds. Better mining of their data, and understanding their client base, would provide the blueprint for an ongoing membership/supporter drive, which could go a long way to bringing in extra funds. However, no one sees the potential – all they see is the static number of 1700 unique visits per week - "oh, isn't that interesting, now let's move to the next item on the agenda..."

• Because new technologies are evaluated from the paradigm of the existing IT department, their benefits may be missed and their adoption can be seen as potentially risky. They are run through the traditional "how will they be supported, what other clients are they selling to, our department is java focussed, so we only operate in an J2EE environment and eliminate everything else" etc The problem with this is that the new technologies don't work in the same way. Take, for example open source – if you try to support open source in house, it will generally be very costly, because the chances of hiring someone with the specific knowledge are low, and the open source software keeps evolving...a traditional employee will simply not keep up. Instead, different models of support emerge. One such proposed model is to have a general IT person who can understand the fundamentals of different kinds of open source software. Back them up with low cost annual support packages provided by open source support companies, so that as soon as something is out of their grasp, a guaranteed answer is simply four hours away. The key ability then becomes not so much the hard skills of coding, but rather the ability to keep evolving and be able to find solutions by communicating with others. As an aside, we have observed that generation 'Y' programmers are really comfortable with this, but others seem to struggle.

Working with Immature Technologies

New technologies are often a little less efficient than the existing technologies when they are first launched so are dismissed as being inferior, or trivial compared with highly developed applications. Take for example Webex (www.webex.com) vs. Dim Dim (www.dimdim.com) communication tools. When evaluating a solution for a larger enterprise, it became apparent that people wanted to connect easily with others, and were also very sensitive about budgets. The IT department simply signed up with Webex, and passed costs onto the cost centre managers. This detracted from the usage, as the costs were very high. The alternative is Dim Dim, a "disruptive innovator" in the Webex space. Their enterprise edition would provide an 80% saving when compared to Webex, if implementing a company wide web meeting solution. Dim Dim is also more user-friendly in that no software download is required, and scheduling meetings is very easy. However, because Dim Dim used VOIP from each person's computer rather than the phone line, their voice quality was not as good. BUT, as with any emerging technology, the quality gets better and better. A year later the sound quality was significantly improved. Also, additional features were added, which were not available in Webex. The question is, can an organisation tolerate the year of lower but ever increasing quality? The payoff is that everyone can suddenly use web meetings at any time, without charge and without having to "book" it in through the IT department. Also, a huge saving of 80% is involved. Do you wait until the quality tipping point is reached, and then implement? These are very different models of

Figure 1. An overview of critical success factors

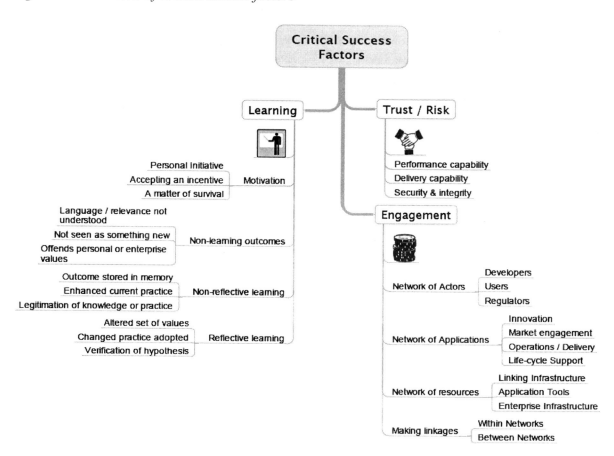

evaluation, which some IT departments are not familiar with, so they may simply dismiss them and go with an existing well understood approach.

Identifying Critical Success Factors

Our earlier discussion regarding learning about and utilizing new technologies based on the literature, plus observations from experience to date is summarized in Figure 1 under three headings: matters relating to learning, matters relating to trust and risk, and matters relating to engagement.

Apart from the need to be able to understand the jargon and concepts associated with semantic technologies, we see the most significant success factor as being able to work with new ideas and

data combined with an ability to imagine different futures in a reflective learning environment (e.g. Pollock, 2001). This may require external facilitation and the establishment of a team separated from day-to-day activities.

Matters of trust relate to both the technology and the people supporting it. Will the technology perform as claimed? Can it actually be delivered for use with minimal disruption? Is our data secure? (e.g. McGuinness et al, 2006)

When and how to engage are both important considerations. For SMEs with limited resources, choosing the right time to act is just as important as choosing to act. When action is taken, who will be involved, what will be the focus of the initiative, and what resources will be needed? Expectations and the mental models of developers and users need to be surfaced and the need for learning by both parties accepted. Depending on the nature of the data and how it is handled, regulators may be involved, for example in relation to privacy and intellectual property matters. Again, external facilitation may be needed to support SME engagement.

Another important success factor is the alignment of the application to be developed with the firm's strategic needs. A suitable application may, for example support an open innovation strategy. Interpretation of customer data may give deeper insight into their unmet needs (e.g. Silva, Soares and Simoes, 2006). Operations and delivery performance may be more accurately assessed (e.g.Zdravkovic et al, 2009), and life-cycle support may be improved by accumulating knowledge about problems and solutions e.g. Christl et al, 2008). The point to be made here is that semantic technologies facilitate other things happening, so choose the area with the largest long-term impact as the application focus.

The network(s) of resources used to deliver value from the use of semantic technologies may be within the firm or external to it. As semantic technologies become transparently embedded in web-based applications, they may be accessed through the Internet or set up within a firm. Different combinations of actor networks and resource networks may suit particular applications.

Working from the End Customer Back

As stated earlier, using semantic technologies involves a blend of philosophy, psychology, politics and technology. The promise of "semantics" brings together natural language, discourse analysis, machine learning, and artificial intelligence. And the "semantic wave" is building, at least in terms of "hype".

It is the authors' view that a semantic approach to technology application in human-oriented sys-

tems is the most effective way in which to really enable authentic conversations, to empower end users, and to harness the power of information and communications technologies to really enable knowledge work In our experience, web-based technologies increasingly occupy a foundational position within an organisation's information and knowledge paradigm, and are central to both its day-to-day activities as well as its ability to communicate with key stakeholders. The socio-technical environment is complex, fragile and often ambiguous, and any changes that are made may impact on entire organisation, not just the division or business unit that is specifically affected.

Our philosophy is to view any system within the context of those who use it. All too often-new technologies or "clever solutions" are implemented without this in mind, with a reliance on training programmes, mandated practices and reward programmes to generate buy-in and encourage participation. Our preference is to focus on individual work practices together with realistic organisational outcomes in order to bring together systems and processes that reflect how people actually work, recognising that each and every one of them undertakes different tasks, has different needs, and works in a unique way, which may differ from hour to hour and day to day. Therefore we always deliberately take a holistic view of how any such system, and the accompanying cultural and business processes, does and could fit in with the customer environment. This means that regardless of the specific project that we might be engaged to undertake we will always assess other ICT projects that are being undertaken, both past and present, and try at all times to see the complete picture of how people need to use data, information and knowledge to do their work. Our primary focus is on activity networks and actor networks.

We have also observed that the introduction of a new technology tool or system in an enterprise resource network will not solve the majority of problems in the medium or longer term. All organisations have a number of incumbent technologies which have functioned perfectly well for many years, and which, if they can be linked and given a more "user friendly" face, could well continue to serve the organisation well into the future. New technologies are continually emerging which are challenging the role of proprietary technologies and "out of the box" solutions, and it is our intent to always assess these technologies and match them to a client organisation's readiness to embrace them should that be deemed appropriate. This perspective is necessarily long term, and, through as wide a consultation as possible, we suggest options to be considered covering the short, medium and longer terms.

Strategies for Dealing with Organizational and Cultural Aspects

The W3C Education and Outreach special interest group (Pollock, 2001) suggests four actions to help diffuse semantic web concepts within an organization. Firstly, "invest in training and skills development now". Secondly, "prototype a solution and explore some new tools now". Thirdly, "probe your software vendors about their semantic technology roadmap now". And fourthly, "compel your enterprise architects to formulate a multi-year metadata strategy now". The authors suggest that current operations need to be sustained while new approaches are being developed, and have observed several different approaches that integrate learning and change, considering both people and technology factors:

1. Develop a skunkworks group, with a sole mission of finding better, faster, more economical ways of doing things in the organisation. Because this group is exploratory, it needs to be driven by "ideals and zeal", and made up of a mix of innovators, implementers, and maintainers. The key is to have this group close enough to the business so they can see the issues at hand, but not too close, so that they become tainted with "the existing ways." The challenge for this group is "re-entry" of the new developments into the existing organisation...to arrive at its findings; the group has necessarily been through a journey of trial and error, discovery and rediscovery. To simply "tell" the organisation that this is the way to go, without the organisation having been through its own journey, can result in skepticism and disbelief.

2. Develop a big vision, and then look at the existing people in the organisation. Chances are they cannot achieve the new vision, as they do not have the necessary skills and mindset. So, bring in new people, who are hired specifically to achieve the vision. But, the proviso to this is that it is done all at once if wishing to bring about rapid change. If bringing about slow and gradual change, then bringing in "fresh" people is good, but the risk is that these people cannot tolerate the slowness of the rest of the organisation, nor can they work with the ambiguity for an extended period of time. Simply bringing new people into the mix creates a "buzz", but doesn't necessarily fundamentally change anything. One example is an Australian B2B supplier. After several years of declining revenue and profits, a new GM was brought in. He made his mission super clear from day one – it's about raising revenue and margin, and cutting costs. Within the first three months, all people who could potentially roadblock it were either dismissed, or put in new positions with a mandate to perform. The web was an emerging technology, and a specialist marketer from outside the company was brought in to "research" for one year prior to commencing a build. The existing IT group did a good job of telling the GM why he couldn't get what he wanted with the web, and they were summarily outcast and "encouraged to leave." A debate was held

at MD level as to whether this non technical GM could run the web development using an external specialist company, or whether the in house head office IT department got to run it. The MD at the time was extremely wise, and awarded the control to the GM, stating that he had the most vested interest in the project succeeding. Along with that control came "enough rope" - at various stages small wins needed to be achieved in order for the project to get the full funding it required. The full control with accountability and "enough rope" became the guiding mantra for success – in the final stages of development, an e-Business manager was appointed, with the job of refining the development to meet the market, get the user adoption, integrate with the sales and marketing processes, etc Any roadblocks/resistances which were encountered, the GM "bulldozed" for him. Essentially, an emerging business was being built, with a whole new business model – it wasn't so much a case of integrating in to the existing organisational structure as it was demanding it in.

3. Put the whole thing outside of the organisation, and have the group "sell" hosted solutions back into the organisation. This way, the IT department and business managers are simply evaluating a product in much the same way they would any other offering. The trouble with this approach is that the evaluation framework often misses the true benefit of the implementation, because to truly realise its benefits a new business model is required with new skill-sets of its people.

OUR OWN RESEARCH INTO "SEMANTICS"

In 2006 we began a research project, jointly funded by Fuji Xerox Australia, RMIT University and the Australian Government through and Australian Research Council (ARC) Linkage Grant, into the impact of semantic technologies on the printing and publishing industries. This research focused on the impact these technologies were beginning to have on organisations large and small, government, non-profit and commercial. Early findings in 2008 revealed that there was a great deal of research under way globally, that the technologies themselves were evolving rapidly, and that there were many small pockets emerging within a wide range of organisations who understood the value of utilising a semantic technology approach to the management of data and information. This value comes from the fact that semantic technologies allows an unparalleled transparency in the analysis of data from a disparate range of sources, and, coupled with web access and mobile technologies, this can be both dynamic and real-time.

At the International Metadata Forum held in Sydney in 2008, the Metadata Seminar held in Canberra in 2009, and the Semantic Technologies Conference held in San Jose in 2009, it was abundantly clear that the need to "link data" was increasing, and that a "semantic approach" to data management was emerging beyond just the research community. This is demonstrated by a number of examples which include work being undertaken by the CSIRO (http://www.csiro.au/science/Information-engineering.html), the LIXI project in Australia (http://www.lixi.org.au/), Thompson Reuters' "Calais" initiative (http://www.opencalais.com/), and the declared intention of both the US and UK governments to open up their data (www.data.gov; http://www.number10.gov.uk/Page19579). As of mid 2009 the launch of both Wolfram Alpha (http://www.wolframalpha.com/) and Microsoft's "Bing" search engine (largely built on technologies developed from Fuji Xerox Palo Alto Labs and Xerox PARC) brought semantic search to the broader community and, as the Harvard Business Review stated in February 2009, semantics is constituting a "quite revolution that will radically change the way the internet works" (Ilube 2009).

Differing Approaches

There seem to be two different approaches to the concept of "semantics". The conceptual nature of the technologies themselves, and the difficulty of clearly articulating the business value, has meant that champions, such as Tim Berners-Lee, have launched initiatives such as "Linked Data" (http://www.ted.com/talks/tim_berners_lee_on_the_next_web.html) in an effort to both make the concept simpler, and to enlist support. The promise of the "semantic web" can only be realised if data is made available via the web, and for that data to be linked.

The first approach is what we are terming the "bottom up". This is largely the work being done in academic environments and research institutions, and builds upon the basic components of semantic technologies themselves, as defined by the World Wide Web Consortium (W3C). These components, entitled the "Semantic Web Stack" (Berners-Lee, http://www.w3.org/2000/Talks/1206-xml2k-tbl/slide10-0.html), provide a technical framework upon which each of the elements is being built.

An alternative approach, which we are terming the "top down", is where there is a development of a set of industry standards and terminologies, which are then cascaded down to provide a framework within which the semantic approach can be developed. This is what has been driving initiatives in the financial industry, such as LIXI (http://www.lixi.org.au/), much of the work within the pharmaceuticals industries, and other industry driven initiatives such as Thompson Reuters' Open Calais (www.opencalais.com).

Whilst both approaches have their advantages and disadvantages our research suggests that the "top down" is gaining more traction, particularly in concert with the development of Web 2.0 technologies and social networking sites.

Applications to Business

Social networking is almost by definition "semantic" because it operates through the linkage of data and information through social connections. In fact, one easy way to understand the concept of semantic technologies is through the social networking approach, where the "friend of a friend" network enables data and information to be exchanged, enriched and utilised. In particular some sites such as ensembli (http://ensembli.com/), ning (http://www.ning.com/) and twine (http://www.twine.com/) operate on "semantic" principles, where individuals share their own data and that of others, connected through common themes and interests. Therefore all of the data gathered becomes information because it is contextualised, and from a "trusted" source.

Above all social networks are about connecting people, and, with semantic technologies underpinning these networks, new opportunities to develop relationships within the "B2C" and "B2C2B" worlds are fast becoming a reality. This is also influencing the value network which is no longer linear but more kaleidoscopic (Allee 2000; Zuboff and Maxmin 2002) and less something based on the industrial age mentality of manufacturing but rather being redefined by the currency of knowledge.

For all businesses this is now a new world in terms of how to engage, understand and provide value to customers. Customers are increasingly empowered with information, and this information is rapidly becoming more valuable as it is contextualised into knowledge. For many years the mantra was that "the customer is King"; with the emerging technologies of the twenty first century this is now a reality, which any business ignores at its peril.

Making a Compelling Business Case

So, what makes new technology in organisations work? We need to first identify or create a significant need for change that can be supported by semantic technologies. The extent to which the technology delivers value to the enterprise and its employees needs to be measured and related to expectations of that technology. Measuring the impact of enabling technologies such as semantics can be difficult as they facilitate improved performance in other areas. One way around this is to set demanding targets that cannot be met by conventional means. For instance, an Admin manager who is told to cut his costs by 50% within one year, will have to operate outside the current paradigm to do so, and is forced to create a new business model. On the other hand, an Admin manager who is told to simply "take a look" at a new technology, but is otherwise told everything is going OK in the division, will not make the same exertion.

In the Australian B2B supplier example mentioned earlier, the KPI was "reduce customer service headcount by 70% within 12 months". Another KPI was double the size of sales territory a single person could cover, with 24 months. The implication of not achieving this was that the business would operate at a loss, compare with making a significant profit.

In our earlier Sydney charity example where additional sources of income were needed, there is no such compelling measure to stimulate people to think differently.

Some change-driven examples involving new online marketing approaches, and advanced data analytics techniques are provided by a Sydney consultant, who utilises sophisticated data analytics to ramp up marketing returns. His core market is not the large corporates one would expect – there are too many politics, no clear compelling KPIs, and instead he spends his time justifying his techniques which are continuously brought into question. The ready and willing market he has discovered is smaller organisations, with a leader who has a KPI to achieve. Examples of such clients are: a start up telecommunications company in the USA, which needed to compete effectively against larger firms, but with very small budget. User adoption was the key. Advanced analytics tied directly into achieving the bottom line of one client; a start up NZ based home shopping company entering Australia, and competing against an established player. Another client was a charity whose donor bequest that had supported it for approx 20 years was coming to an end – a crisis would emerge if the charity did not find other means of generating revenue.

WHAT THE NEW MARKETSPACE LEADERS SAY

In this section, we present some practical examples of semantic technology usage by SMEs. In doing this, in the context of the emergent nature of these technologies, we have found it helpful to make reference to the technological positioning associated with an application as represented in Figure 2.

Based on our research, and observations within the Australian market-space, SME adoption of semantics tends to be limited, and currently sits within the level of "Syntactic interoperability", we suggest for two reasons:

- Building an initial taxonomy for an organisation is a time consuming task, requiring a "librarian" type approach, which is a skill not present within most SMEs; and
- There is presently no clear business case for an individual SME to move into the level of structural or semantic interoperability. Whilst large organisations can derive process efficiencies, it is unlikely that the variables within the SME business model will achieve a positive ROI on such an exercise.

Figure 2. Technological positioning in a semantics environment

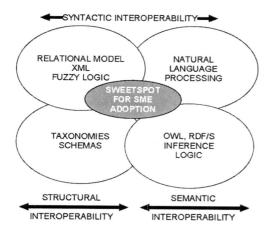

None-the-less, SMEs can presently derive exceptionally strong business benefits by focusing on the level of syntactic interoperability. Following are real world examples.

Example 1: A Reseller of Printing Equipment

This business has an arduous task of processing orders, which it is contracted to make through a corporate supplier. The current process is to accept an order from a customer, enter it into the company CRM, then log on to the corporate portal, and re enter the order. The business is currently in negotiations with the corporate supplier, to enable an XML feed to be sent from its CRM directly into the portal, thus saving the time of double entry and eliminating the possibility for human data entry error. Although technically feasible, the corporate has concerns...the field mapping and business rules need to be carefully constructed, which is a time consuming collaborative process. Further, if this were the start of an emerging trend for supply chain connectivity between large corporate and small reseller, would not a more efficient approach be to publish to all resellers a set of APIs. This would eliminate the need for the corporate and reseller to collaborate each time a connectivity solution was required, as each reseller will have a different CRM and different ordering terminologies.

Another application the business wishes to build will lead to exceptional process efficiencies, and a leading sales edge. This involves the stitching together of two disparate applications:

- A commercially available "Smart device" which can simply be plugged into a prospect's network, and quickly extracts the pertinent data associated with each printing device across the organisation
- An analytics engine, which calculates print volumes against associated leasing information of each printing device, and can produce clear recommendations as to where newer printing devices will produce cost savings for the organisation

Current implementation of this process involves a lengthy manual step between these two applications. The data retrieved from the smart device needs to be manually mapped and entered into the analytics engine. An ontology approach, with complete mappings in place, would potentially save up to 8 hours of analysis for a large organisation, and enable a salesperson to produce an "on the spot" savings indicator.

Example 2: A Quasi-Government Organisation with Many Disparate Customer Databases

This organisation is facing the reality of having up to 20 disparate databases holding information on its constituents. This currently makes it difficult to gain an accurate view of a constituent, which has negative flow on effects on outgoing communications, which have poor contextual relevance. Also, in light of tightening Privacy Legislation, the data collection and data maintenance tasks will become near impossible to adhere to.

The traditional approach to this issue would be to amalgamate all data sources in a data warehouse. However, semantic technologies operating within the syntactic level offer a far simpler, faster and more cost effective solution.

Firstly, all disparate databases are left in their separate states, rather than being amalgamated.

Next, a "fuzzy matching" engine is built, capable of extracting information from all databases on demand, and providing a user all likely matches across all data sources, for each record searched. This provides a single customer view, and also enables a user to update any or all data sources through the one interface.

Example 3: An Australian Organics B2C Firm

A business providing home delivery of organic fruit and vegetables to consumers has a vision of enabling their customers to order exactly what items they require, in the exact quantities they require them. There are several key variables which make this a challenging exercise – market pricing varies day-by-day, item availability changes with season and with short term supply fluctuations, items may be unavailable from one market supplier yet simultaneously available from another, and there are often minimum purchase requirements of particular items. All of this information is kept by the different market suppliers on different databases or spreadsheets, and much of it changes on a daily basis.

The business has tried to tackle the problem with a database holding per unit pricing and seasonal availability which can be updated manually. It then enables customers to order online, displaying available stock. However, it does run into problems with quick price fluctuations, minimum order requirements from suppliers and unexpected out of stocks, which require quick substitution decisions on the part of the business.

A proposed solution is to build a web based upload facility for suppliers to use on a daily

basis. (NB – the ideal solution would be to use APIs to access supplier data, but most suppliers are not sufficiently enabled in their systems for this). The uploaded information would then be mapped using a predefined ontology. This would then dynamically generate a web page for customer ordering, based on business rules, which decide what products to display, and dynamically adjust the display based on availability, optimal profitability, and minimum supplier order targets being reached.

This approach would not only enable the business to reach optimal efficiencies, it also provides a readily scalable model which could be used in locations across Australia.

Example 4: Online Survey Company

Online monitoring of media and social networking sites can provide laser-focused opportunity for SMEs. One such organisation appears to monitor the web for mentions of its competitor "Survey Monkey". When a mention is made by an individual on a social networking site, a message is sent advising of their alternative product. If "sentiment analysis" was to be added to the monitoring process, messages could be automatically sent according to context. To illustrate, a disgruntled mention of Survey Monkey could produce a message highlighting the "more reliable, service oriented" competitor. Alternatively, a positive mention could produce a message focusing on "same features, lower cost, free trial offer". When the costs of traditional approaches to online and offline marketing are considered, this emerging approach is most likely significantly less expensive, and has the added benefit of targeting prospects at the "right time" in their lifecycle.

Example 5: Automated Chat Bot

An Australian company has developed an "Automated chat bot" which utilises natural language processing to enable fluid, human like livechat.

Already in use by several large corporates, it is an expensive solution which only a corporate budget could accommodate. There is however, a simpler version aimed at SMEs, with a pricing model of free set up and 80 cents per chat.

This has strong potential to enable SMEs to provide real time online answers to prospects and existing customers, increasing customer satisfaction levels and simultaneously reducing their cost of servicing clients. The set up interface has been made extremely simple, so that no specialist technical or linguistic knowledge is required by the SME.

FUTURE RESEARCH DIRECTIONS

The World-wide-web Consortium (W3C) suggests research is being carried out on four intersecting fronts: networking (e.g. semantic web, grid and p2p), content (e.g. knowledge extraction, semantic enhancement, executable content, semantic search), services (e.g. composite applications, semantic web services), and cognition (e.g. semantic User Interface, knowledge computing, intelligent agents.

There is a keen interest in ontologies as frameworks for sense-making and the foundation standards that have been established (e.g. Colomb, 2007). Other work is oriented towards discourse analysis techniques (e.g. Buitelarr et al, 2005). Our current applications research looks at applying semantics to the challenge of sustainability reporting. In the context of SME technology uptake, we see opportunities for action research projects using our critical success factors view (Figure 1) as a framework.

CONCLUSION

We see that semantic technologies may enable enhanced performance in a number of different business functions: in innovation, in market engagement, in operations/delivery and in product life-cycle support.

Semantic technologies help provide meaning and context to large amounts of information. The general idea has been in use for a long time, as illustrated in our parallels with a street directory and the integrating utility of data-bus technologies. The current tool development initiatives have been stimulated by a vision of their application to the world-wide-web and the access it provides to an unprecedented volume of data. The tools - software standards and methodologies, are a means of providing more explicit meaning to data we can access. Capabilities for intelligent search, retrieval, discovery of relevant information, question-answering, and autonomous action are at various stages of the development cycle. We observe that most SME applications are at the earlier stages of this continuum.

We have identified three kinds of critical success factor in the diffusion of semantic technologies:

- The first is accepting the challenge of imagining a "street directory" that may help a particular enterprise find a way to new, more competitive places or in envisaging the kind of "data-bus" that will help us make better use of information we can potentially access. This may require the adoption of a different mind-set and reflective learning practices.

- Semantic technologies are in the early stage of maturity in the technology lifecycle and rely on strong Internet and intranet connectivity. Trust in the technology may be a concern. So the second success factor is being able to find and access the expertise, technology and resources to realize the enterprise vision.

- The third success factor is in stimulating and implementing change to deliver benefits associated with our vision and associated with working in new ways. We have suggested that the targeted change be somewhat radical and measurable. Apart from the first two challenges, it is our view that this is a people problem rather than a specific technology problem. Advice from the literature on organization change suggests we should consider matters of motivation, psychological and physical learning space, the use of temporary support, and maintaining a focus on the desired future state (e.g. Smid and Beckett, 2004). We should also recognize that there will be phases in implementing sustainable change, and that different support arrangements will be appropriate to each phase. In the context of making a paradigm shift, Dunphy, Griffith and Benn (2003) suggest characteristic phases are: Rejection (of the whole idea). Non-responsiveness (as a form of resistance), Compliance (but not necessarily acceptance), Efficiency (acceptance of short-term benefits), Strategic proactivity (obtaining leverage from the technology), and the Sustaining organization (where the technology is transparently embedded)

We suggest that mapping the status quo in terms of these three factors and comparing with a desired future state will identify suitable transition pathways, and that implementation may require a team to work in parallel with the current organisation.

REFERENCES

Berners-Lee, T., & Hendler, J. (2001). The Semantic Web: A new form of Web content that is meaningful to computers. *Scientific American*, 34–43. doi:10.1038/scientificamerican0501-34

Buitelaar, P., Cimiano, P., & Magnini, B. (Eds.). (2005). *Ontology learning from text: Methods, evaluation and applications. Frontiers in artificial intelligence and applications*, vol 123. Amsterdam, The Netherlands: IOS Press. ISSN 0922-6389

Christl, C., Ghidini, C., Guss, J., Lindsaedt, S., Pammer, V., Scheir, P., & Serafini, L. (2008). *Deploying Semantic Web technologies for work integrated learning in industry. A comparison: SME and large-sized company.* ISWC 7th International semantic web conference, October 26-30, Karlsruhre, Germany

Cohen, W. M., & Levinthal, D. A. (1990). Absorptive capacity: A new perspective on learning and innovation. *Administrative Science Quarterly*, *35*(1), 128–152. doi:10.2307/2393553

Colomb, R. M. (2007). *Ontology and the Semantic Web. Frontiers in artificial intelligence and applications,* vol 156. Amsterdam, The Netherlands: IOS Press. ISSN 0922-6389

Cregan, A. (2009). *Weaving the Semantic Web: Contributions and insights* (p. 234). Sydney, Australia: University of New South Wales.

Davenport, T. H., & Prusak, L. (1998). *Working knowledge - how organisations manage what they know*. Boston, MA: Harvard Business Press.

Drucker, P. (1993). *Post-capitalist society*. Oxford, UK: Butterworth Heinemann.

Dunphy, D., Griffith, A., & Benn, S. (2003). *Organizational change for corporate sustainability: A guide for leaders and change agents of the future*. London, UK: Routledge.

Gartner. (2009). Gartner reveals five business intelligence predictions for 2009 and beyond. Retrieved 14th September, 2009, from http://www.gartner.com/it /page.jsp?id=856714

Ilube, T. (2009). What you need to know about the Semantic Web. *Harvard Business Review.*

Jarvis, P. (1987). *Adult learning in the social context*. New York, NY: Croon Helm.

Mc Guinness, D. L., Zeng, H., da Silva, P. P., Ding, L., Narayanan, D., & Bhaowal, M. (2006). Investigations into trust for collaborative repositories: A Wikipedia case study. [Edinburgh, UK.]. *Proc, WWW2006*(May), 22–26.

Mosca, A., Palmonari, M., & Sartori, F. (2009). An upper-level functional design ontology to support knowledge management in SME-based E-manufacturing of mechanical products. *The Knowledge Engineering Review, 24*, 265–285. doi:10.1017/S0269888909990063

Pollock, J. (2001). *A Semantic Web business case*. Presented on behalf of the W3C Semantic Web Education and Outreach interest group. Retrieved December, 2009, from http://www.x3.org/2001 / sw/sweo/public/BusinessCase /Business Case. PDF

Senge, P., Kleiner, A., Roberts, C., Ross, R., Roth, G., & Smith, B. (1999). *The dance of change: The challenges of maintaining momentum in learning organizations*. London, UK: Nicholas Brearley Publishing.

Silva, M. M., Soares, A. L., & Simoes, D. (2006). *Integrating semantic resources to support knowledge communities*. INCOM06 12th IFAC Symposium on information control problems in manufacturing, 17-19 May, Saint-Etienne, France.

Smid, G., & Beckett, R. (2004). Learning and sustainable change: Designing learning spaces. In Boonstra, J. J. (Ed.), *Dynamics of organizational change and learning* (pp. 403–428). Chichester, UK: John Wiley & Sons. doi:10.1002/9780470753408.ch20

Sveiby, K. E. (1997). *The new organisational wealth*. San Francisco, CA: Berrett-Koehler Publishers Inc.

Wurman, R. S. (2001). *Information anxiety,* vol 2. Indianapolis, IN: Que.

Zdravkovic, M., Panetto, H., & Trajanovic, M. (2009). *Concept of semantic information pool for manufacturing supply networks*. 5th international working Conference on Total Quality Management - advanced and intelligent approaches. 1-4 June, Belgrade, Serbia.

Zuboff, S. (1988). *In the age of the smart machine: The future of work and power*. USA: Basic Books.

Zuboff, S., & Maxmin, J. (2002). *The support economy: Why corporations are failing individuals and the next episode of capitalism*. New York, NY: Viking, Penguin Books.

ADDITIONAL READING

Abdoullev, A. (2008) *Reality, Universal Ontology and Knowledge Systems: Towards the Intelligent World* IRM Press (ISBN 878-1-59904-966-3)

Chapter 13

The Semantic Integration of Information:
A Business Ontology Proposal with Semantic Interoperability

Antonio Paredes-Moreno
University of Seville, Spain

Francisco J. Martínez-López
University of Granada, Spain

David G. Schwartz
Bar-Ilan University, Israel

ABSTRACT

Nowadays, firms need to refocus the way they manage the knowledge generated from business processes in order to optimize their Information Systems' performance. Business ontologies are an excellent tool for this. In this chapter, we briefly treat and highlight how important is companies invest efforts in a closer integration of their systems, with the aim of improving their performance and cooperation. This implies moving towards more efficient systems in their knowledge management. The big challenge for firms now is the semantic integration of information. Essential questions related to this question are synthetically introduced. Then, some of the most significant initiatives and projects on semantic integration of information are presented and compared with a business ontology we have developed for commercial use.

INTRODUCTION

With the first phase of Web connectivity infrastructure consolidation over, the development of electronic commerce is now immersed in a process of vast expansion. Many companies are making economies of scale in order to justify investment, and they demand improved information integration processes. So, the need for process optimization is urgent. More information is required, and more rapidly, to gain better quality knowledge. That is, we are in a phase that requires closer integration

DOI: 10.4018/978-1-60960-765-4.ch013

of business information systems to make better use of the enormous quantity of data, by means of an improved and more accurate interpretation of those data. Undoubtedly, this will bring a stark improvement in companies' knowledge generation capabilities (Kambhampati & Knoblock, 2003). Our proposal is based on years of experience around commercial enterprises, with access to their databases, as well as on the analysis of how companies in different branches of industry use Internet (design, electronic commerce, production, electronic administration, integration with clients, suppliers, employees, etc).

In recent years, two facts or situations of great importance have become clear. One, companies increasingly want their information systems to perform better (e.g.: Deveraj & Kohli, 2003). Two, these systems are prone to error, redundancies and even semantic failures, which result in lower quality knowledge (e.g.: Fan et al., 2001). Company data are often scattered over different areas, formats and systems. Such data must be managed by means of processes that are more centralized and sophisticated to exploit their information more effectively and profitably (Lytras & Athanasia, 2006). Therefore, a transition is needed towards systems that are more efficient in their knowledge management.

Many companies that previously used database management systems available in the market in the form of individual software applications have come to manage their information resources via their local networks or the Internet itself by means of the so-called shared environment Intranets, or even sharing information with other companies (associates, clients, suppliers) through Extranets. Today, companies want to grow towards more powerful database management systems able to manage information from the Web, within centralized environments and with the need to integrate as much as possible (e.g.: Su et al., 2006). It is also known that companies see information as a highly valuable asset. To keep this information from its various sources and between companies fresh and integrated is of the utmost importance today. Therefore, applications created especially for working in these environments are necessary, as is a data vision that is new and integrative.

Likewise, companies need to optimize the internal management processes of their resources, which normally leads to changes in the structures of information and the applications used. This involves making databases, tables, attributes, restrictions, etc, compatible. The need for the integration and reorganization of data sources is also evident (de Bruijn, 2004) in the case of the adoption of solutions developed by third parties, for example, SAP, Navision, etc.

The main contribution of this paper is the development of an ontology from a set of company databases to integrate information sources for the companies and to contribute to the logical treatment and strengthening of current databases. The ontology fits between commercial and managerial. This ontology has a series of characteristics that make it highly appropriate for solving current problems of homogenization and integration revealed by the Semantic Web project. The ontology contributes solidity to the renewal processes through which the company modernizes its information systems at the same time that it integrates its various sources into an information model that is coherent, consistent and shared with the other associated companies and with clients and suppliers.

The paper is structured as follows: first, we present various questions related to the background on which our proposal is based, that is: the Semantic Web, the semantic interoperability needed for the integration of information between systems, as well as the role of the ontologies in this process. Then, in section 3, the business ontology we have developed is presented in full. In section 4, we compare our ontology with other important business ontologies. Finally, we present our conclusions and plans for further research.

BACKGROUND

The New Context of the Semantic Web

The Semantic Web (Berners-Lee, Hendler & Lassila, 2001) is a new area of investigation built on Web fundamentals. Its main objective is to give formal meaning to Web contents that are often scattered, disparate and semi-structured. This enables us to know the contents and also deduce new information from what already exists. The Semantic Web is developed from languages arising from HTML, such as (Antoniu & van Harmelen, 2004): XML (e*Xtensible Markup Language*; e.g.: W3C Consortium, 1997)[1], RDF[2] (*Resource Description Framework*; e.g.: Lassila & Swick, 1999), OWL[3] (*Ontology Web Language*; e.g.: Dean & Schreiber, 2004; Smith, Welty and McGuinness, 2004; Mitra & Wiederhold, 2004,), which allow the incorporation of more semantic elements into the documents as well as tools capable of integrating, structuring and processing data in order to reason and infer new knowledge.

As a consequence of the continued expansion of Information & Communication Technologies, the business world sees the possibility of optimizing its information resources by making the most of these technologies to extract from its systems information that is the fastest, the most refined and accurate possible, to act as the basis for correct and effective decision-making, and with minimal risk. Alongside the new technological environment, we see the unstoppable process of globalization; in business terms, this process is of vital importance. Companies undergo association and absorption processes, businesses jump country and continental barriers. All this, together with greater profit demands, makes them very aware of the added value of the correct integration of information and its sharing with partners, shareholders, clients and suppliers, etc, (see, as e.g.: Schwartz, 2008; Siau, 2003)

From all this, we deduce the need to initiate or continue renewal processes not only in operative fields but also, and fundamentally, in applications capable of integrating and sharing resources and information. In the main, this leads to a renewal of and migration away from obsolete management databases towards more modern, powerful and reliable managers.

In the Semantic Web, the recent investigation into ontologies (see Sivashanmugam, 2004) is now of vital importance in terms of the business problem we have so far elaborated. Traditionally, ontology refers to the philosophical concept in Metaphysics that studies the being, that is to say, the definition of all that it is, how it is and how it is possible, and it describes the basic categories and relationships of existing beings or entities. These existing entities or beings are the objects, people, concepts, ideas, in other words, the things. The ontology models what we know about a domain or part of reality by means of concepts and relationships. The ontologies are represented by classes (categories), properties and class attributes.

Although there is no universally accepted definition, it could be said synthetically that "*an ontology is an explicit specification of a conceptualization*" (Gruber, 1995), "conceptualization" meaning an abstract model of some phenomena in the world; the concepts identify these phenomena; "explicit" means that the concepts used and the restrictions for their use are explicitly defined. In Artificial Intelligence, ontology refers to a document or file that contains formal definitions of the concepts and relationships between them in a specific knowledge domain. An ontology basically contains a set of classes (relational taxonomy of concepts and roles) and a group of axioms that enable new knowledge to be deduced.

SEMANTIC INTEROPERABILITY: THE NEW CHALLENGE FOR FIRMS' INTEGRATION OF INFORMATION

At the start of this paper, we emphasize the growing need for companies, and organizations in general, to work within business environments that allow their information to be integrated. Firstly, competitive collaboration systems are the most reasonable formula not only for firms to subsist in an economic sector but to do so successfully. The time when a company's ability to compete was based exclusively on its individual strengths is over (Bendoly, Soni & Venkataramanan, 2004). On the contrary, sectors are now made up of value constellations that compete among each other.

Obviously, understanding between companies that collaborate within the same specific value network is critical, as its nonexistence would lead to competitive inefficiency (see Kogut, 2000). Secondly, we must not forget that the diversity of economic agents in the world business environment beyond the value systems is increasingly interconnected thanks to Internet and the generalized use of e-business applications. This means that firms must work with Information Systems that use languages that are compatible, homogenous and universal in meaning. This involves resolving interoperability between systems and, specifically, semantic interoperability (see Schwartz, 2008). In fact today, the search for systems' semantic interoperability is so crucial as to be a key aspect of investigation and technical challenge (see March, Hevner and Ram, 2000). This is relevant for companies using e-business applications intensively for process management, and for electronic commerce in particular.

Something simple but which needs to be kept clearly in mind is that the problem of interoperability is not new, neither for systems technicians nor for users. Totally solving interoperability involves crossing three dimensions of lesser to greater complexity: technical, syntactical and semantic. Today, technical interoperability associated to the systems' capacity to exchange signals is solved. The same cannot be said of the two other dimensions, especially the semantic. The existence of syntactic interoperability supposes the capability of diverse systems or software components to interpret the syntax of data with the same form. This interoperability definitively enables cooperation between systems even when they differ in language, interface and execution platform (Ram, Park and Lee, 1999); i.e. syntactic compatibility between systems. Nevertheless, as we have pointed out, complete interoperability will not exist until the semantic is guaranteed; that is, the scenario in which semantic meanings are shared in each terminology used (Chen and Vernadat, 2003). Currently, semantic heterogeneity is broad, which assumes that considerable effort is needed to integrate information. So, the development of business environments that enable the semantic management of information is recommended, as suggested by Schwartz (2008).

Diverse types of approaches are evident with regard to the semantic management of information integration (see, as e.g., for more detail: Park and Ram, 2004): (1) the mapping-based approach. This is based on correspondence or mapping from local data sources onto a global diagram; (2) the intermediary-based approach, based on the use of intermediary mechanisms (mediators, agents, ontologies, etc.), and (3) the query-oriented approach, based on interoperable languages (SQL), logic-based languages.

As is detailed in section 3, we pose a hybrid approach that, although we are based mainly on the use of ontologies, is particularly interesting for the resolution of the problem of semantic interoperability (see, as e.g.: Obrst, 2003; Yang et al., 2007; Yang and Zhang, 2006)

PREVIOUS PROJECTS ON INFORMATION INTEGRATION – A SHORT REVIEW

There are many projects that investigate the integration, mixing and articulation of information through ontologies. What follows is a brief description of the most important.

The project whose methodology most closely fits the work in this paper is that of Fensel et al. (2005). These authors elaborate the *Corporate Ontology Grid* (COG) project undertaken by Fiat (Italy), Unicorn (Israel) and LogicDIS (Greece), with the Institute of Computational Sciences of the University of Innsbruck (Austria) acting as consultant. The COG project investigated the problem of semantic heterogeneity among the data sources of the Fiat automobile company, and how it could be overcome by integrating these sources using a central information model, that is, an ontology.

The problems of integration were solved by the application of the information semantic via a Unicorn Workbench tool. This tool was used to create an ontology based on schemas collected from the sources under study. These schemes were mapped onto an information model (ontology) to make the meaning of the concepts explicit and to relate them, thus creating an information architecture that made for a unified vision of the organization's data sources.

MOMIS (*Mediator environment for Multiple Information Sources*) (Beneventano et al., 2002), developed at the universities of Módena, Reggio Emilia and Milano, is a framework project that pursues the extraction and integration of information from structured and semi-structured sources.

InfoSleuth (Fowler, 1999; Infosleuth, 2001) is a multi-agent system for semantic interoperability on heterogonous data sources. It supports the construction of complex ontologies from small ontologies.

OBSERVER (MENA et al., 1996) is defined as a system based on ontologies perfected by re-lationships for the resolution of the heterogeneity of vocabulary.

KRAFT (*Knowledge Reuse & Fusion / Transformation*), (Gray et al., 1997) was set up by the universities of Aberdeen, Cardiff and Liverpool in collaboration with British Telecom. Its main proposal is to research the possibility of sharing and reusing information contained in databases and heterogonous knowledge systems.

Chimaera (McGuinness et al., 2000a and 2000b) is a Web-based tool used to mix and diagnose ontologies. It was developed by Stanford University's Knowledge Systems Laboratory (KSL).

ONION (*ONtology CompositION*), (Mitra et al., 1999, 2000 and 2001) is a system centred on a secure formalism that allows the support of a working framework capable of scaling the interoperability of ontologies. ONION uses rules that cover the semantic voids by creating an articulation between systems.

A NEW BUSINESS ONTOLOGY PROPOSAL WITH SEMANTIC INTER-OPERABILITY CAPACITIES

The methodology we propose enables the development of a business ontology to consolidate business processes, modernize information systems and at the same time integrate varied sources into an information model that is coherent, consistent and shared with other companies. It is specific ontology that has highly applicable to medium-sized and large commercial companies.

The case study we present, and on which the ontology is based, originates in the business system of companies that trade energy-related products in their various forms. This information system contains subsystems for offers, sales, warehousing, invoicing, accounts and treasury. Its sources follow the relational model. The information model has tables, queries and sets of logical rules as well as norms and restrictions specific to the company (see Figures 2 and 3).

In terms of semantic interoperability, our approach applies the information semantic in the following way. In the first phase, we analyse the metadata and schemas of the databases in the case study. With this knowledge, we fix a partial map of concepts to a newly created ontology. This first phase sees the generation of a hierarchy of classes, properties and restrictions out of the semantic structure of the company's schemas and norms in the mapped sources. The map is partial because it was necessary to reinterpret many schemas in order to provide the ontology with a well-organized logical structure. In addition to mapping from the schema sources, we also drew on the help of experts in the domain during the creation of the taxonomy. In the second phase, we filled the ontology with real requests from the databases. We used our own *ad hoc* creation, (GOWL). This tool consists of an SQL query manager that produces OWL format code containing both the individuals and the relationships with other individuals via their properties and restrictions.

As it is seen, our methodology is centred on the three aforementioned approaches – mapping the databases, the construction of a global ontology and the use of logic-based languages in its development. Definitively, unlike integration projects based solely on one of the approaches mentioned in Section 2.2, this hybrid formula allows the exploitation of the advantages of the approach based on ontologies, offsetting some of their inconveniences with the strengths of other approaches (for a deeper discussion, see: Park and Ram, 2004).

The ontology incorporates all the characteristics of the conceptual model of the data, both those related to the concepts, or TBox (schemas, integrity restrictions and company rules) and those related to the individuals with their relationships (ABox), as the data are imported from the tables. Likewise, the ontology expands and improves the expressivity of the firms' databases. This improvement, together with the solidity that the logic provides, converts the ontology into a useful platform and a starting-off point for the development of future applications to new information models. This (future) process of returning to a new model of information from the ontology will see databases treated and enriched semantically thanks to the fundamental contribution of the ontology.

We have used the OWL DL (*Ontology Web Language Description Logic*), based on descriptive logic (see Baader et al., 2003). Descriptive logics are a family of knowledge representation languages. They have a formal semantic based on the logic of predicates and they represent an excellent jumping-off point for defining languages that can construct ontologies. These logics aid the reasoning tasks needed to support the construction, integration and evolution of ontologies. The ontology has been edited by Protégé[4] (Knublauch et al., 2004) and Swoop[5], and treated by the RacerPro[6] and Pellet[7] reasoning services.

STAGES OF THE METHODOLOGY

We have constructed our own methodology for the development of the ontology. Its stages are the following (see Figure 1):

1. Shared analysis of requirements. Fixing the range of the project, its starting-off point, aims to be fulfilled and method used for the construction.
2. Collection and cataloguing of metadata from an exhaustive analysis of the relevant sources: schemas, restrictions, company rules or norms, procedures, uses or performance modes when faced with the varied circumstances associated to specific practice, etc
3. Construction of the ontology: that is, the development of a new information model

Figure 1. Steps in the construction of the ontology

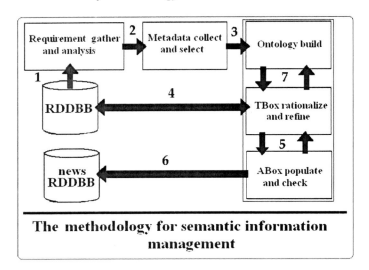

from existing ones, following these two steps:

a) Modelling the taxonomy of classes, properties and restrictions (TBox). Figure 6 shows "commercial.owl", the ontology's collapsed tree. Its class root is "Managing Trading", from which all other branches or classes derive.

b) Populating the ontology with class queries (ABox). This is done by means of a tool created ad hoc that makes the process automatic, importing data from the table registers.

4. Rationalizing and refining the ontology, extracting the semantic from the sources and mapping it onto the ontology. The steps are:

a) Checking the taxonomy: to find the ontology's incoherencies or contradictions via the most up-to-date automatic reasoners already mentioned.

b) Checking and treating of the individuals to find axiomatic inconsistencies and make the necessary corrections to achieve consistency.

5. Comparison of our ontology with other business-type ontologies such as *TOVE, REA, EO, BMO* and *e³ value*, that already exist on the Web, highlighting differences, mutual deficiencies and contributions.

6. Collection of teaching experiences and selection of the best practices in integration, correction of possible errors and projections on future lines of investigation in order to make the most of our research.

By checking the ontology with logical reasoners, a solid consistent ontology with future projection perspectives is arrived at, using the model created as the basis for new applications. These are its most important aspects: (1) The ontology as repository of business knowledge. That is, we have a specific ontology that describes the commercial concepts used by the companies, both in terms of the classes and the properties or relationships between them. Also described are the restrictions imposed not only from the metadata but also from other data arising from daily use and practice that report what we could call "the company's behavioural philosophy"; (2) The ontology as basis for new information systems, as it has all the expressivity of its sources. In addition, it is enriched by the incorporation of company rules and restrictions and, given its basis in logic, we

Figure 2. The commercial information system

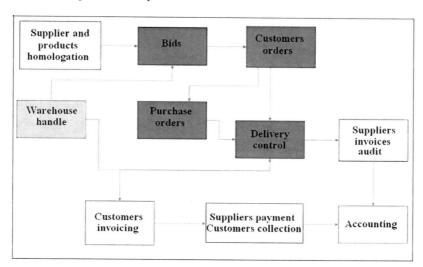

can assure that it is guaranteed for the modernization of information systems.

EMPIRICAL APPLICATION: A CASE STUDY

Our case study is based on the information system of a company involved in the large-scale trade of energy products in their various forms and which belongs to an industrial group that is leader in the field of new technologies. Its trading volume is over 500€ million per year. It sells products in telecommunications, energy transport, solar energy and supplies' management. Figure 2 illustrates the structure of its commercial information system.

All these elements make up the universe of discourse, subdivided into domains (semantic classes or tables) in which are defined the relationships whose extension takes in subsets of explicit elemental facts (literal, records, registers, queries) and general laws normally represented by rules of integrity or inference.

Figure 3 shows some of the more important tables. Their sources follow the relational model and are implemented on the databases in MSAccess.

MODELLING THE ONTOLOGY (TBOX)

The semantic management of information gives us a methodology for the modelling of the ontology, based on the very semantic of the data sources. We have taken into account the various integration methods of the projects previously mentioned, comparing their methods with the ones applied in our investigation, but with this criterion uppermost: applicability to the integration of data schemas. The main characteristics of our methodology (see Figure 4) are the following:

1. The integration paradigm of our methodology consists of the construction of a central ontology (with possible future links to more generic ontologies) starting from an exhaustive analysis of the metadata collected from business databases, and setting up a correspondence between schemas towards the concept hierarchy.

2. Following on, we could say that the correspondence pattern (mapping) between sources and ontology is very close to one-to-one correspondence. However, it needs to be said that although the ontology's concepts are coherent, this is not the case with all its corresponding concepts in the databases.

Figure 3. Tables and database relationships

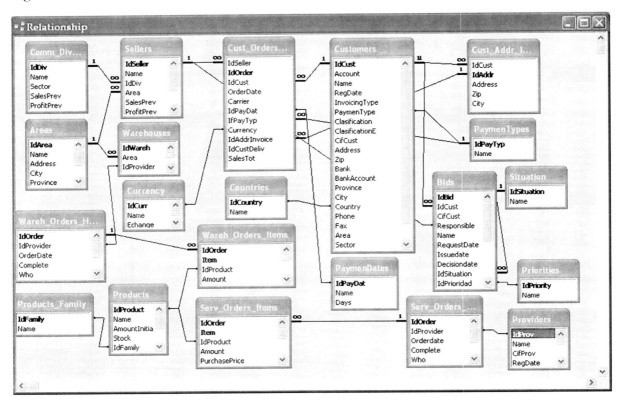

Figure 4. The semantic management of information

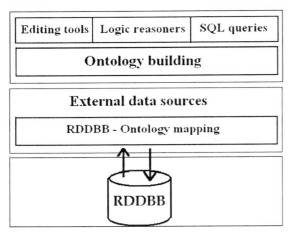

3. Our methodology supports a partial mapping at class level, and a total mapping at property, individual, axiom and restriction levels.

4. Our methodology's degree of automation fits between semi-automatic and interactive. The taxonomy's creation process is manual, with the use of the Protégé tool, but the integration process of queries is automated by our own ad hoc application, in which a series of SQL enquiries integrated into codified events in the application is defined. When these events are executed automatically, they generate OWL code files that are totally compatible and integrable with the ontology in Protégé.

5. Regarding interoperability, we need to state that the ontology supports the semantic interoperability, being implemented by the standard OWL language (which, as we know, is based on descriptive logic), having past the logical reasonability test (RacerPro, Pellet).

6. The mapping tool's visualizing interface is made up of graphic forms in VBasic on Access. The ontology can be seen and edited using various tools, for example, Protégé, Swoop, Eclipse, etc.

Figure 5. Taxonomy of commercial.owl (upper level)

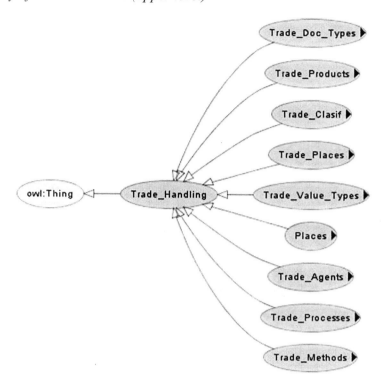

7.   The maturity of this methodology with its tools makes it the basis for new applications. In fact, it is being used for building new business databases on the SQL Server.

The semantic management of information as reported by our methodology contains the following layers:

The external data sources' layer lies within the block at the bottom of the figure. It describes the place and origin of the data and metadata. In our case study, these sources are databases in a relational format (RDDBB). This layer includes correspondences between the ontology's sources and concepts. The block at the top contains the tools and ontology construction layers. The latter describes the meaning of the data, that is, the information model.

The ontology built with this methodology is made up of the following elements:

1.   **The hierarchy of classes.** The concepts are set in a hierarchy of classes. The classes, as mentioned before, basically come from metadata schemas collected from databases. In the ontology, each element (classes, properties, individuals) is given its own name that should be as expressive as possible. The names of the subclasses and subproperties have prefixes that indicate their origin immediately above them. The names of individuals are imported from the corresponding tables and, to avoid duplication, they are given a prefix indicating the class to which they belong (see Figure 5).

2.   **The properties of the classes.** The roles or properties of the classes, that is, their relationships, are taken and organized into a hierarchy. These can be two types:

a.   **Object property:** are those that relate an individual of a class to an individual

Figure 6. Partial taxonomy of the ontology (agents' branch)

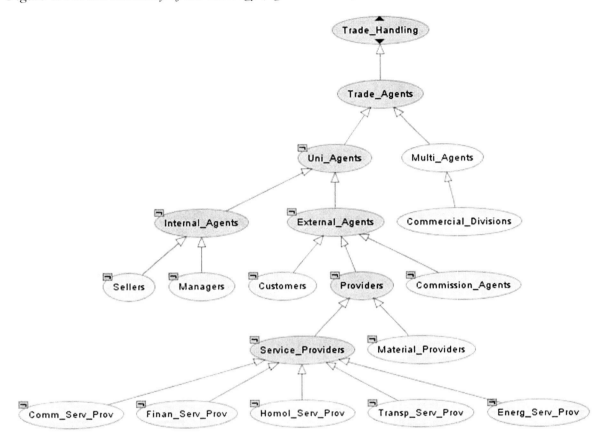

of another class, or, whose domain and range are classes. In the methodology, different types of object property are considered (functional, inverse functional, symmetric and transitive), and these are applied to each property that forms part of the ontology's hierarchy. For example, the *"have_payment"* property means: The payment of invoices to the supplier is done by a payment order at a bank or financial company. The domain of the property is *"supplier_invoices"*, and its range is *"payment_order"*.

b. **Data-type Property:** those that relate individuals of a class to some type of value; their domain are the classes but their range is a type of fixed value data. The ontology only accepts the creation of object properties. The reason (of a technical nature) is that the reasoners do not currently consider this type of property, which makes it impossible to check the ontology. To get around this problem, the values of number and date are represented by a chain format in the ontology.

3. **Company rules and restrictions.** Next, the specific conditions imposed on the classes are generated, with the aim of modelling their meaning within the company environment (for example, suppliers' invoices are to be paid after a certain number of days, or the profit made on each sale cannot be less than

Algorithm 1.

```
SELECT
        "<Clientsdf:ID="+'"Cli_'+[NomCli]+'"'+">"+"
              <have_country>
                    < Countryrdf:ID="+'"Ct_'+Clients.CountryCli+'"'+"/>"+"
              </have_country>"+"
        </Clients>"
FROM Clients;
```

a set percentage). The conditions restricting the classes can be either *necessary* or *necessary and sufficient.*

4. **Descriptions and notes.** In addition to their formal description, notes or comments can added to the classes and properties in natural language in order to make their meaning more intelligible.

MODELLING THE ONTOLOGY (ABOX)

Once the taxonomy and all its elements are created, the *entities or individuals* are inserted and each one matched to its corresponding class with its properties. Then the relationships between individuals are generated and the properties that affect them are applied to each one. In order to automate the process of mapping and integration of the sources' individuals, we have constructed a software tool, codified in Vbasic, whose main content is a series of SQL enquiries capable of translating the data in the MsAccess registers into OWL and integrating them into the body of the ontology. The following SQL enquiry extracts each client from the database with th[8]e "have_country" attribute and converts them into OWL code (see Algorithm 1).

The result for each client from the database is shown in Algorithm 2.

The ontology constructed with this methodology possesses the characteristics of the domains and subdomains of the sources in the case study. In this context, we could say that ours is a standard ontology as it aims to take in the entire terminology used by companies trading products related to energy, engineering and telecommunications. Therefore, we have taken into account the very experience of the development of the databases, the applications and their maintenance in working companies.

TREATING THE ONTOLOGY

In order to guarantee the logical coherence and solidity of the ontology, our methodology incorporates treatment and repairing processes of possible errors (Kalyanpur, 2006). The RacerPro 1.9 and

Algorithm 2.

```
<Clientsrdf:ID="Cli_InstalacionesyMontajesS.A.">
        < have_country >
              <Countryrdf:ID="Ct_Spain"/>
        < have_country >
</Clientes>
```

Pellet 1.5. logical reasoners are used for this in the computational logic field. These carry out a complete check of the class and property hierarchy, and of the individuals and their relationships. It is important to point out that the resulting ontology is totally coherent from the logic viewpoint, which means that it is free of contradictions. This coherence is necessary when recovering information or when serving as a base for new databases or applications.

Regarding expressivity, the ontology has all the expressive power of the OWL-DL language based on descriptive logic. It formalizes the data source elements and even takes on new elements drawn from the experience and reflections of experts and users. The level of expressivity it reaches is "*SHOIN(D)*" in terms of descriptive logic. This assumes that the ontology has most of the features of descriptive logic (see, for an in-depth review: Baader et al., 2003), of which we emphasize its capacity to: formalize concepts, attributes, roles and complements, and structure them in a hierarchy; integrate database queries (individuals); incorporate negative properties and qualified restrictions; and admit various types of data.

A COMPARATIVE ANALYSIS WITH OTHER BUSIESS ONTOLOGIES

An Introduction to the Most Significant Business Ontologies

Following the construction of our ontology, it is a useful and interesting exercise to match it to other existing business ontologies whose domains are similar or close to ours, contrast focus and components, and reveal similarities and differences. We have selected the business world's most representative ontologies currently available, and we describe synthetically the main ideas put forward by their investigators:

BMO*(Business Management Ontology)*. The BMO (Jenz & Partner GMBH, 2004) ontology,

or set of ontologies, represents an integrated information model which, along with the design of the business processes, incorporates project management, requirements and performances to make up the fundamentals of a company management knowledge base. Its main users are business analysts, but it has also been taken up by information technology (IT) experts to establish correspondences with related software deficiencies such as business focus and the description of Web services. It enables the definition of the private and public processes of companies, entities and business focus, as well as the services implemented by the processes of activity. It follows the European Union's UN/CEFACT methodology. The BMO currently contains 40 ontologies that define some 650 classes belonging to various domains within the business environment. BMO characteristics include: a) linking ontologies to produce a single general vision; b) multiple ontologies can exist in parallel to supply many organizations or industries. Each ontology specific to an industry integrates and extends the ontologies of the companies' generic domain ontologies; c) it associates the company's fundamental process concepts to generic business concepts such as properties, company rules and documents, etc,; and d) it contains technically oriented ontologies like the ontology of business focuses.

REA (*The ResourceEventAgent*). This is a business domain ontology originally created to define and develop accounting systems. Like its data semantic model, the REA business model is based on the Entity-Relationship metamodel but contains additional primitive ontologies, axioms and guidelines associated to the model that help construct and validate the conceptual models of the information systems belonging to the accounting systems. The REA was initially created by McCarthy (1982 and 2003) mainly to model accounting systems. However, it was found to be very useful and intuitive as it brought a greater understanding of company processes, and became one of the best frameworks both for traditional companies and electronic commerce systems. It has been extended in order to provide concepts of greater use in understanding aspects of processing as well as economic aspects (economic exchanges). For almost 20 years, the REA model has been widely used as an instrument for teaching business students how to design accounting databases (McCarthy, 1999). However, few companies use it for systems development practice. Recently, researchers and professionals have renewed their interest in this model for two reasons (see O'Leary, 2004):

a. The developers of the REA model have signed up to the ISO OpenEDI initiative, UN/CEFACT, OAG, eBTWG. Their participation has resulted in the adoption of the REA model as a business ontology in the UMM [UN/03] methodology and the ECIMF system, as indicated in the ECIMF Project Group of 2003.

b. The REA model has been proposed as the theoretical foundation for the basic models of ERP (*Enterprise Resource Planning*) systems.

The architecture of the REA business ontology has three levels or layers representing economic activity, three classes of elements that can be identified in each economic exchange or conversion process: economic resources, economic events and economic agents. Each economic resource is linked to an economic event that causes its entry and exit flows (stock flow). In addition, each economic event that results in a resources entry (a purchase, for example) is necessarily paired to an exit event (a payment), and vice versa (duality). The participative relationship describes the agents involved in an economic event.

This simple ontological pattern is the basis of the REA ontology, and it comes from McCarthy's original model (Geerts and McCarthy, 1997). The economic events are performed within a chain or ordered sequence of actions called business processes. We refer to the architecture on three levels (chain value, business processes and economic events). With advances in technology and specification methods, the applicability of the REA conceptual model has also changed. Works by Geerts and McCarthy (2002) have widened its basic framework several times over recent years. The REA changes the direction of the transaction model in two ways: removing it from the traditional vision inherited from the subject matter based on finance and the single company, and directing it towards big business with the new perspective of the modern ERPs and the information systems of the varied types of electronic commerce. With the entry of commercial partners and long-term relationships, there is a need for more reliable and predictable structures in which both parts formalize their exchange contracts.

The REA ontology answers this need by adding classes such as economic commitment, economic contract, agreement, etc. The REA establishes correspondences with one of the ontologies from the IEEE Standard Upper Ontology Working Group, called SUMO (*Suggested Upper Merged Ontology)*, which is on a superior level.

EO (*Enterprise Ontology*): The Enterprise Ontology (Uschold et al., 1998) has been developed as part of the Enterprise project by the University of Edinburgh's Institute of Artificial Intelligence Applications, together with IBM, Lloyd's Register, Logica UK Limited and Unilever. The project has been backed by the UK's Department of Trade and Industry within its Intelligent Systems Integration programme (IED4/8032). Its business modelling aims to achieve a global vision of the organization such that it can be used as a basis for decision-making. It is not a traditional organizational vision but a vision that comprises the subject matter or domain of the organization's functioning. To achieve this aim, strong flexible tools are needed to support integration and communication.

During the EO development process, the aim was to embrace those concepts that were widely accepted in the business world, presenting their definitions in natural language. It begins with basic concepts (activity, relationship, actor, for example). These are used to define the main body of the terms, which is divided into the following areas or sections: activities and processes, organization, strategy and marketing.

TOVE (*TOronto Virtual Enterprise*). The TOVE project aims to develop an integrated set of ontologies for public and private company modelling, with the following features (Fadel, Fox & Grüninger, 1994):

a. To provide a terminology that companies can share so that each agent can use and understand it.
b. To define the meaning of each (semantic) term as precisely as possible. Implementing the semantic within a set of axioms will give TOVE the ability to automatically deduce most common-sense questions about the company.
c. To define a group of symbols to graphically represent a term or the concept built from it.

A series of ontologies have been developed in the TOVE (T.O.V.E., 1997) framework that comprises various aspects of the business environment. These ontologies have recently been structured on three levels:

a. Foundation ontologies, which among others include ontologies on activities (Gruninger & Pinto, 1995), resources (Fadel, Fox & Grüninger, 1994), and organization (Fox, Burbuceanu & Gruninger, 1996).
b. Derived ontologies, which include among others ontologies on quality management (Kim et al., 1995), product design (Lin, Fox & Bilgic, 1996), and costs (Tham, Fox & Gruninger, 1994).
c. Business ontologies, which include ontologies on company design, flow of materials, projects and business processes.

e³_value. With the new information technologies, business models based on e-business have an increasingly wide field of development and their share of all business transactions grows daily. This ontology edges closer to a more rigorous conceptualization of business modelling. The e³_value ontology's main feature is its basis in value (see Gordijn and Akkermans, 2001). The e³_value ontology consists of a conceptual approach whose objective is the representation of business models. The notion of value, and how the objects are created, exchanged and consumed in a multi-agent network, is the central theme of this ontology. It enables the representation and analysis of many non-trivial ideas on business domains, even processes and mechanisms that are important to the company such as the causality of income flows, client property, the ability to fix prices and chose alternative agents to deliver objects of value and company business. Based on the notion of value, as a foundation of electronic commerce modelling, the concepts are defined as: Agent, Activity of the Value, Object of the Value, Port of the Value, Interface of the Value, Exchange of the Value and Offer of the Value. The benefits of this ontology oriented towards value are two (Gordijn and Akkermans, 2001): better communication between those who must make decisions on the essential points of the model and the shareholders; a greater and more complete understanding of the operations of electronic commerce and its requirements.

COMPARISON

Comparison Criteria

To compare our ontology with the others, a true understanding of these ontologies is necessary together with a pattern that establishes the elements on which the comparison is based. Taking works by Pateli, and Giaglis (2003) and Jasper and Uschold (1999), we have fixed a comparative framework whose main elements are as follows:

1. Purpose of the ontology. Motives or reasons that justify the existence of the ontology (achieving better communication, interoperability, reliability, specification, representation and knowledge, etc).
2. Focus of the ontology. The focus of attention differs from model to model. Some centre on one company, others look to a variety of companies. Some are based on strategy, others on operational aspects. Some focus specifically on technology, while others turn their attention to innovation or work on both simultaneously.
3. Components of the ontology. This refers to the concepts, relationships or properties, rules and axioms that the ontology uses to represent the business model.
4. The role of the ontology. Whether it contains operational data or is made up of concepts, relationships and axioms in order to contain operational data, or whether it is a language that expresses ontologies on the two previous levels.
5. Ontological representation. The degree of meaning that an ontology represents. This varies greatly from one to another. The simplest ontologies are a simple collection of terms. The meaning grasped by an ontology varies according to the quantity of the data represented and the representation's degree of formality. According to the quantity of data, there are lightweight ontologies (a limited number of concepts, relationships and axioms) and heavyweight ontologies (a greater number of concepts, relationships and axioms). According to the degree of formality, they move between "highly informal" and "strictly formal".

Similarities and Differences

Starting from the previous parameters, we make a comparison between our ontology (Commercial. owl) and the business ontologies just described in which we highlight similarities, differences, deficiencies and contributions. We will also analyse the possibilities of aligning our ontology developed for a specific company with these others which are much more generic.

1.- Purpose of the ontology. Both Commercial. owl and BMO aim to improve the various forms communication by means of the business model's representation and shared knowledge. BMO. Both provide high levels with the possibility of defining processes and objects - Commercial. owl for a more specific level - generalizing the knowledge of the databases that are its base, and providing a semantic step for the future integration of the information models at company group level. Commercial.owl shows how to improve interoperability between companies enabling them to work together in a network, jointly offering products and services. BMO reflects this in the way the concepts are associated in its ontologies. For Commercial.owl, the creation and maintenance of the information model between companies is of utmost importance. In terms of reliability, Commercial.owl has passed all the current reasoning tests, with its TBox coherent and ABox consistent. The Pellet test on BMO showed inconsistencies in some queries although the taxonomy was deemed coherent.

REA was initially created to add semantic content to accounting systems' modelling mainly at academic level. Commercial.owl, however, is totally oriented to the business world. REA and Commercial.owl both aim to provide a theoretical framework for a business information model; Commercial.owl is based on the modelling of specific companies in transition and REA has a more traditional vision and tends towards information systems for big business (ERP) and electronic commerce.

The Semantic Integration of Information

The EO ontology was developed by a group of organizations to provide a methodology and software tools for business modelling in a changing environment that would serve as a basis for decision-making. In general, Commercial.owl has the same aims, only that it is developed in a more specific environment and its aims are less generalized. The TOVE project is an integrated set of ontologies that models for public and private enterprises. Commercial.owl is a single ontology whose aim is modelling for a specific company or companies. Obviously, it needs to have a terminology that can be shared and a well-grounded semantic. Their aims are similar but differ in the general and specific.

The objective of the e³_value ontology is to define concepts from the value perspective, describing how economic value is created and its various occurrences within the network of agents and elements with which it relates. Although it coincides with certain Commercial.owl concepts, its focus is different.

2.- Focus of the ontology. While the BMO is made up of a set of ontologies, Commercial.owl is a single ontology specific to a group of companies. In this sense, it could be another BMO ontology. For that to be so, there would have to be a correspondence between the concepts in both. On the one hand, Commercial.owl's contribution would enable this correspondence to enrich the semantic of BMO definitions; on the other, Commercial.owl would be semantically covered as a branch of the BMO tree.. REA focuses on the business process in terms of the "economic events" aggregate that relates resources and agents. Each economic resource is linked to an event through the merchandise flow. Each event is paired to the intrinsic duality (entry/exit) typical of accounting movements. The agents participate by controlling the processes. Commercial.owl's focal point is in the specification of all the elements of a company, or companies, of a particular type (i.e. commercial). You only need to check Commercial.owl's taxonomic tree to see that the

three concepts (Resources, Events, Agents) are defined. Commercial.owl's scope is substantially broader than the REA's in this area.

The EO ontology attends to those concepts that are widely accepted in the business world, from which it presents its definitions for the areas of activity and processes of the company (activity, agent), organization (legal entity, organizational unit), business strategy (planning, decision, risk) and marketing (sales, market). Commercial.owl's focus is more specific, as can be seen from previous comparisons.

As regards the ontologies in TOVE, it is necessary to state that the fundamentals present theoretical models on the company. Only a few of the so-called company ontologies or derived ontologies can compare to Commercial.owl when defining elements specific to the business environment.

In terms of e³_value, we shall say that its focus is more generic than Commercial.owl's.

3.- Components of the ontology. Commercial.owl's conceptualization is organized into a tree with nine classes or branches whose root is Trade_Handling, with its properties and restrictions. These basic classes are conceptualized as follows:

a. Agent with type varieties (clients, suppliers, company personnel, banks, commission agent, etc).

b. Classification, broken down into different sub-classifications.

c. Document with different types (offers, orders, invoices, etc.) BMO also defines this concept but gives it a different meaning.

d. Location, which takes in temporary aspects and modals, both geographic and virtual.

e. Existing entities such as company local offices or warehouses.

f. Commercial focus in its product and service aspects.

g. Commercial modalities that define concepts such as invoice types, etc.

h. Process in its commercial and economic aspects.

i. Value types in its various meanings, always within the commercial environment, like prices, expenditure, financial values, etc.

BMO includes areas of interest modelled on the ontology as value-related elements, client segments, distribution channels, relationship mechanisms, basic resources and capacities, etc., as well as the relationship between these elements.

REA's elements deal with concepts and properties related to economic transactions. However, Commercial.owl has many more elements because this ontology's model is more specific.

EO defines the concepts of Activity, Organization, Strategy, Marketing, Time, etc. As mentioned above, TOVE consists of three blocks of ontologies, each ontology defining the terms that are specific to its domain of interest. From an economic perspective, e^3_value defines a series of elements and relationships within the following concepts of its business model: actors, objects, ports and interfaces of value, activities and exchanges of value. Also, the ontology models relationships of dependence, connection, stimulus and the AND/OR connectors between the previous elements.

4.- The ontological role. Commercial.owl and the other ontologies are made up of concepts, relationships and axioms to have operational data to express their business model.

5.- Ontological representation. Commercial.owl can be classified as middleweight or heavyweight in terms of the data of its metric: named classes, 136; unnamed classes (restrictions), 178 (existential 174, universal 2, maxcardinality 2); Properties, 106. With specified domain 73, with specified rank 100, with specified inverse 10; Annotations, 28; Individuals: 13,475. Its expressivity level is SHOIN(D) and it is written in OWL.

BMO, on the other hand, is a lighter ontology with its limited number of concepts, relationships and axioms. Version 11 (September 2004) is constituted by 12 partial ontologies with 47

classes and 121 properties and 124 individuals. Its format is OWL.

The accessed version of REA has 12 classes, 19 properties and 27 individuals. It is formatted in RDF. However, REA links up with a higher-level ontology, SUMO, which has 630 classes, 239 properties and 435 individuals defined.

The most recent version of EO consulted is in KSL. It has 92 classes, 62 relationships, 7 functions, 10 individuals and no axioms. Its levels of generality and maturity are moderate. Its edition format is Ontolingua and its source code is in Lisp.

FUTURE RESEARCH

Given that the ontology is created from local sources, the quality of the global model depends mainly on the quality of the local model. In our case, the ontology has been refined in two ways: avoiding inclusion of the databases' errors and incoherencies; and not adding concepts that were not in the databases. Another quality element has been the interaction with experts and users drawing lessons from their work in practice. Thus we can state that the ontology reflects the knowledge of the company.

In terms of the future, and leading on from our research and the experience gained, we consider it necessary to investigate along these lines:

- The possibilities of alignment or mixing of specific ontologies such as the one we have presented with others which are more general.

- The development of reasoners with greater checking capacity would be of great importance, not only in terms of memory use but above all for their capacity to reason and explain errors.

- We also believe it is vitally important to develop projects that investigate and produce software applications capable of using ontologies directly from the network in order to convert their enormous quantities of data into information and productive knowledge.

CONCLUSION

Beyond specific questions detailed earlier, this comparison leads us to the following conclusions:

- Commercial.owl is an ontology whose business model is applicable to a specific company sector (commercial), and for this field it is quite complete as, apart from the metadata, it integrates the entire semantic support of the uses, habits, norms and ways of understanding a specific domain.
- The models represented by the other ontologies are much more generic. In ours, concepts exist that could be easily integrated within the models represented by the majority of ontologies described. However, we believe it would be very difficult to align them. Without doubt, these ontologies would provide Commercial.owl with many enriching concepts, in particular those economic and business concepts whose rigorous definitions could complete the meaning of Commercial.owl's concepts. On the other hand, our ontology could provide all these business ontologies with the richness offered by specific knowledge directly extracted from real companies and fully treated from the formal logic point of view.

REFERENCES

W3C Consortium. (1997). *Extensible markup language (XML)*. Retrieved from http://www.w3.org/XML/

Antoniu, G., & van Harmelen, F. (2004). *A Semantic Web primer*. Cambridge, MA & London, UK: The MIT Press.

Baader, F., Calvanese, D., McGuinness, D., Nardi, D., & Patel-Schneider, P. F. (Eds.). (2003). *The description logic handbook: Theory, implementation, and applications*. Cambridge University Press.

Bendoly, E., Soni, A., & Venkataramanan, M. A. (2004). Value chain resource planning: Adding value with systems beyond the enterprise. *Business Horizons*, *47*(2), 79–86. doi:10.1016/j.bushor.2003.08.004

Beneventano, D., Bergamaschi, S., Bianco, D., Guerra, F., & Vincini, M. (2002). *"SI-Web: A Web based interface for the MOMIS project*. Demo Session, Convegno su Sistemi Evoluti per Basi di Dati (SEBD02).

Berners-Lee, T., Hendler, L., & Lassila, J. (2001). The Semantic web. *Scientific American*, *284*, 34–43. doi:10.1038/scientificamerican0501-34

Chen, D., & Vernadat, F. B. (2003). Enterprise interoperability: A standardized view. In Kosanke, K. (Eds.), *IFIP series* (*Vol. 108*, pp. 273–282). Kluwer Academic Publishers.

de Bruijn, J. (2004). Semantic integration of disparate data sources in the COG project. In *Proceedings of the 6th International Conference on Enterprise Information Systems (ICEIS2004)*, Porto, Portugal, ICEIS Press.

Dean, M., & Schreiber, G. (Eds.). (2004). *OWL Web Ontology Language reference*. World Wide Web Consortium recommendation (REC-owl-ref-20040210).

Deveraj, S., & Kohli, R. (2003). Performance impacts of information technology: Is actual usage the missing link? *Management Science*, *49*(3), 273–289. doi:10.1287/mnsc.49.3.273.12736

ECIMF Project Group. (2003). *E-commerce integration meta–framework.* Final draft. Technical report.

Fadel, F., Fox, M. S., & Grüninger, M. (1994). A generic enterprise resource ontology. In *Proceedings of the Third Workshop on Enabling Technologies – Infrastructures for Collaborative Enterprises.* West Virginia University.

Fan, W., Lu, H., Madnick, S. E., & Cheung, D. (2001). Discovering and reconciling value conflicts for numerical data integration. *Information Systems, 26*(8), 635–656. doi:10.1016/S0306-4379(01)00043-6

Fensel, D. (2003). *Ontologies: Silver bullet for knowledge management of electronic commerce* (2nd ed.). Berlin, Germany: Springer.

Fensel, D. (2005). *Information integration with ontologies, experiences form an industrial showcase.* John Wiley & Sons Ltd.

Fowler, J. (1999). Agent based semantic interoperability in infosleuth. *SIGMOD Record, 28*(1), 60–67. doi:10.1145/309844.310060

Fox, M. S., Burbuceanu, M., & Gruninger, M. (1996). An organization ontology for enterprise modelling: Preliminary concepts for linking structure and behaviour. *Computers in Industry, 29,* 123–134. doi:10.1016/0166-3615(95)00079-8

Geerts, G. L., & McCarthy, W. (1997). Modeling business enterprises as value-added process hierarchies with resource-event-agent object templates. In Sutherland, J., & Patel, D. (Eds.), *Business object design and implementation* (pp. 113–128). Springer-Verlag.

Geerts, G. L., & McCarthy, W. (2002). An ontological analysis of the primitives of the extended-REA enterprise information architecture. *International Journal of Accounting Information Systems, 3,* 1–16. doi:10.1016/S1467-0895(01)00020-3

Gordijn, J., & Akkermans, H. (2001). E³-value: Design and evaluation of e-business models. *IEEE Intelligent Systems, 16*(4), 11–17. doi:10.1109/5254.941353

Gray, P. M. D., Preece, A., Fiddian, N. J., Gray, W. A., Bench-Capon, T. J. M., Shave, M. J. R., et al. Wiegand, M. (1997). KRAFT: Knowledge fusion from distributed databases and knowledge bases. In R. R. Wagner (Ed.), *Eighth International Workshop on Database and Expert System Applications* (DEXA-97), (pp. 682-691). New York, NY: IEEE Press.

Gruber, T. R. (1995). Toward principles for the design of ontologies used for knowledge sharing. *International Journal of Human-Computer Studies, 43*(5-6), 907–928. doi:10.1006/ijhc.1995.1081

Gruninger, M., & Pinto, J. A. (1995). A theory of complex actions for enterprise modelling. Working Notes AAAI Spring Symposium Series 1995: Extending Theories of Action: Formal Theory and Practical Applications, Stanford.

Jasper, R., & Uschold, M. (1999). *A framework for understanding and classifying ontology applications.* 12th Workshop on Knowledge Acquisition Modeling and Management KAW'99.

Jenz & Partner GmbH. (2004). *Business management ontology* (BMO) version 1.0 (release notes). Technical report.

Kalyanpur, A. (2006). *Debugging and repair of OWL ontologies.* PhD. Dissertation, University of Maryland.

Kambhampati, S., & Knoblock, C. A. (2003). Information integration on the Web: A view from AI and databases. *SIGMOD Record, 32*(4), 122–123. doi:10.1145/959060.959086

Kim, H., Fox, M. S., & Gruninger, M. (1995). An ontology of quality for enterprise modelling. *Proceedings of the Fourth Workshop on Enabling Technologies: Infrastructure for Collaborative Enterprises* (pp. 105-116). IEEE Computer Society Press.

Knublauch, H., Fergerson, R., Noy, N. F., & Musen, M. A. (2004). The protégé OWL plugin: An open development environment for Semantic Web applications. In S. A. McIlraith, D. Plexousakis, & F. van Harmelen (Eds.), *Proceedings of the International Semantic Web Conference (ISWC): Third International Semantic Web Conference, Hiroshima, Japan. Volume 3298 of Lecture Notes in Computer Science*, (pp. 229–243). Springer.

Kogut, B. (2000). The network as knowledge: Generative rules and the emergence of structure. *Strategic Management Journal,21*(3),405–425.doi:10.1002/(SICI)1097-0266(200003)21:3<405::AID-SMJ103>3.0.CO;2-5

Lassila, O., & Swick, R. R. (Eds.). (1999). *Resource description framework (RDF) model and syntax specification*. W3C Recommendation. Retrieved from http://www.w3.org/TR/ REC-rdf-syntax/

Lin, J., Fox, M. S., & Bilgic, T. (1996). A requirement ontology for engineering design. *Proceedings of the Third International Conference on Concurrent Engineering*, (pp. 343-351).

Lytras, M. D., & Athanasia, P. (2006). Towards the development of a novel taxonomy of knowledge management systems from a learning perspective: An integrated approach to learning and knowledge infrastructures. *Journal of Knowledge Management, 10*(6), 64–80. doi:10.1108/13673270610709224

March, S. T., Hevner, A., & Ram, S. (2000). Research commentary: An agenda for Information Technology research in heterogeneous and distributed environments. *Information Systems Research, 11*(4), 327–341. doi:10.1287/isre.11.4.327.11873

McCarthy, W. E. (1982). The REA accounting model: A generalized framework for accounting systems in a shared data environment. *Accounting Review, 57*(3), 554–578.

McCarthy, W. E. (1999). Semantic modeling in accounting education, practice, and research: Some progress and impediments. In Thalheim, B., Akoka, J., & Kangassalo, H. (Eds.), *Conceptual modeling: Current issues and future directions* (pp. 144–153). Springer.

McCarthy, W. E. (2003). The REA modelling approach to teaching accounting information systems. *Issues in Accounting Education, 18*(4), 427–441. doi:10.2308/iace.2003.18.4.427

McGuinness, D. L., Fikes, R., Rice, J., & Wilder, S. (2000a). An environment for merging and testing large ontologies. In [Morgan Kaufmann.]. *Proceedings of KR, 2000*, 483–493.

McGuinness, D. L., Fikes, R., Rice, J., & Wilder, S. (2000b). The chimaera ontology environment. In *Proceedings of the 7th Conference on Artificial Intelligence (AAAI00) and of the 12th Conference on Innovative Applications of Artificial Intelligence* (IAAI00), (pp. 1123–1124). AAAI Press.

McGuinness, D. L., & van Harmelen, F. (2004). *OWL Web ontology language overview*. W3C recommendation. Retrieved from http://www. w3.org/ TR/owlfeatures/

Mena, E., et al. (1996). *OBSERVER: An approach for query processing in global information systems based on interoperation across preexisting ontologies* (pp. 14–25).

Mitra, P., Jannink, J., & Wiederhold, G. (1999). Semiautomatic integration of knowledge sources. In *Proceedings of Fusion '99*. Sunnyvale, USA.

Mitra, P., & Wiederhold, G. (2001). *An algebra for semantic interoperability of information sources* (pp. 174–182). In BIBE.

Mitra, P., & Wiederhold, G. (2004). An ontology composition algebra. In Staab, S., & Studer, R. (Eds.), *Handbook on ontologies, international handbooks on Information Systems* (pp. 93–116). Springer.

Mitra, P., Wiederhold, G., & Kersten, M. (2000). A graph oriented model for articulation of ontology interdependencies. *Proceedings of the 7th International Conference on Extending Database Technology: Advances in Database Technology*, (pp. 86-100).

O'Leary, D. E. (2004). On the relationship between REA and SAP. *International Journal of Accounting Information Systems*, *5*, 65–81. doi:10.1016/j.accinf.2004.02.004

Obrst, L. (2003). Ontologies for semantically interoperable systems. *Proceedings of the International Conference on Information and Knowledge Management*, (pp. 366-369).

Park, J., & Ram, S. (2004). Information Systems interoperability: What lies beneath? *ACM Transactions on Information Systems*, *22*(4), 595–632. doi:10.1145/1028099.1028103

Pateli, A., & Giaglis, G. M. (2003). A framework for understanding and analysing e-business models. *BLED 2003 Proceedings*. Retrieved from http://ais.bepress.com/bled2003/4

Ram, S., Park, J., & Lee, D. (1999). Digital libraries for the next millennium: Challenges and research directions. *Information Systems Frontiers*, *1*(1), 75–94. doi:10.1023/A:1010021029890

RIDE Consortium. (2006). A roadmap for interoperability of e-health system in support of com 356 with special emphasis in semantic interoperability.

Schwartz, D. G. (2008). Semantic information management and e-business: Towards more transparent value chains. *International Journal of Business Environment*, *2*(2), 168–187. doi:10.1504/IJBE.2008.019510

Siau, K. (2003). Interorganizational systems and competitive advantages - lessons from history. *Journal of Computer Information Systems*, *44*(1), 33–39.

Sivashanmugam, K., Miller, J. A., Sheth, A. P., & Verma, K. (2004). Framework for Semantic Web process composition. *International Journal of Electronic Commerce*, *9*(2), 71–106.

Smith, M., Welty, C., & McGuinness, D. (Eds.). (2004). *OWL Web ontology language guide*. Recommendation, W3C.

Su, K., Huang, H., Wu, X., & Zhang, S. (2006). A logical framework for identifying quality knowledge from different data sources. *Decision Support Systems*, *42*(3), 1673–1683. doi:10.1016/j.dss.2006.02.012

Tham, D., Fox, M. S., & Gruninger, M. (1994). *A cost ontology for enterprise modelling*. Third Workshop on Enabling Technologies-Infrastructures for Collaborative Enterprises, West Virginia University.

T.O.V.E. (1997). *TOVE ontologies*: Technology research in heterogeneous and distributed environment. *Information Systems Research*, *11*(4), 327–341. Retrieved from http://www.eil.utoronto.ca/ tove/toveont.html.

Uschold, M., King, M., Moralee, S., & Yannis, Z. (1998). The enterprise ontology. *The Knowledge Engineering Review*, *13*(1), 31–89. doi:10.1017/S0269888998001088

Yang, Q. Z., & Zhang, Y. (2006). Semantic interoperability in building design: Methods and tools. *Computer Aided Design*, *38*, 1099–1112. doi:10.1016/j.cad.2006.06.003

Yang, X., He, N., Wu, L., & Liu, J. (2007). Ontology based approach of semantic information integration. *Journal of Southeast University*, *23*(3), 338–342.

ENDNOTES

[1] XML is a metalanguage extending from labels developed by the World Wide Web Consortium (W3C).

[2] RDF is a description language developed by the W3C.

[3] OWL is a labelling language, built on RDF and codified in XML. Developed by the W3C.

[4] http://protege.stanford.edu/.

[5] http://www.mindswap.org/2004/SWOOP/.

[6] http://www.racer-systems.com/.

[7] http://www.mindswap.org/2003/pellet/ moved to http://pellet.owldl.com

Chapter 14
Semantic Mapping for Access Control Model

Yi Zhao
Lehrgebiet Informationstechnik, Germany

Wolfgang A. Halang
Lehrgebiet Informationstechnik, Germany

ABSTRACT

With the increasing development of the Semantic Web technologies, the Semantic Web has been introduced to apply in the Web Services to integrate data across different applications. For the Semantic Web Services to succeed it is essential to maintain the security of the organizations involved. Security is a crucial concern for commercial and mission critical applications in Web-based environments. To guarantee the security of the Web Services, security measures must be considered to protect against unauthorized disclosure, transfer, modification, or destruction, whether accidental or intentional. Access control is a kind of security measurements to guarantee the service processes, which is defined to allow resource owners to define, manage, and enforce the access conditions for each resource. In this chapter, an attribute based access control model with semantic mapping (SABAC, for short) is proposed to specify access control over attributes defined in domain ontologies. The model is built on the basis of XACML policy language. Semantic mapping process is proved to be syntactical, semantic, and structural. Our SABAC model between the service requester and service provider can make the access to the Semantic Web Services secure.

1. INTRODUCTION

With the increasing development of the Semantic Web technologies and the increasing need for

information systems integration in organizations, the Semantic Web has been introduced to apply in the Web Services to help integrate data across different applications, which causes a security problem. Hence, for the Semantic Web Services

DOI: 10.4018/978-1-60960-765-4.ch014

to succeed it is essential to maintain the security of the organizations involved.

Security is a crucial concern for commercial and mission critical applications in Web-based environments. To guarantee the security of the Web Services, security measures must be considered to protect against unauthorized disclosure, transfer, modification, or destruction, whether accidental or intentional. Access control is a kind of security measurements to guarantee the service processes, which is defined as the mechanism that allows resource owners to define, manage, and enforce the access conditions for each resource (Samarati, 2001). Up to now, there are a lot of access control models have been proposed such as the mandatory access control (MAC), the discretionary access control (DAC), role-based access control (RBAC) (Sandhu, 2000), attribute-based access control (ABAC) (Priebe, 2004), and context-based access control (CBAC) (Corradi, 2004). A major drawback of the approaches mentioned above is that they do not exploit the rich semantic interrelationships in the data model. The relative complement is the semantic-aware access control model which contains semantic-based access control (SBAC) (Javanmardi, 2006), and semantic context-aware access control (SCAC) (Ko, 2008). These two models support making more precise decisions regarding authorization and inference rules. They fetch users' context and ontology from middleware, with which context hierarchies are built. However, the semantic relationships between the contexts, authorizations and inference rules are not considered.

Web Services are defined as small units of functionality, which are made available by service providers for use in larger applications. The intention to develop Web Services was to reduce the overhead needed to integrate functionality from multiple providers. However, extensive human interaction is still required in the process. Semantically enabled Web Services are forming the research area known as Semantic Web Services (SWS) (Payne, 2004). Semantic Web Services are kind of Web Services whose descriptions are annotated by machine-interpretable ontologies, so that other software agents can use them without having any prior knowledge about how to invoke them. Since Web Services are mainly designed for the purpose of integration of different applications and platforms, it is very important to find a convenient access control mechanism which can interoperate easily with any information system.

In this chapter, an attribute based access control model with semantic mapping (SABAC, for short) is proposed to specify access control over concepts defined in ontologies. The model is built on the basis of XACML (Moses, 2005) policy language with the application of semantic mapping. The semantic mapping is realized between the attributes of the service requester and the service provider. The mapping result can be kept in a mapping base for reuse, and similarly, the generated access control policies can be saved for future reuse. All of these can make the access to the Semantic Web Services secure.

The whole chapter is organized as follows. The preliminaries relevant to the Semantic Web, ontology, Semantic Web Services, access control models, as well as the architecture of the XACML model, are given in Section 2. In Section 3, some currently used Semantic Web based access control approaches are investigated, and the motivation of our access control model is presented; The architecture of the proposed semantic mapping based access control model SABAC, and its performance principle which includes the semantic mapping method, the policy reuse are also described in Section 3. Section 4 gives the authors' some future research work. Section 5 concludes this paper.

2. BACKGROUND

The Semantic Web (Berners-Lee, 2001) is a universal medium to exchange data, information and knowledge. It suggests annotating web resources with machine-processable metadata. The emerging Semantic Web integrates logical inference, knowledge representation, and technologies of intelligent software agents. With the increasing interest in Semantic Web Services, the relative security control methods, like access control method, have to be developed to secure the whole service process.

In this section, first, some fundamental knowledge of Semantic Web, ontology, Semantic Web Services, and access control based security method will be given. Then, some currently used access control models like mandatory access control, discretionary access control, attribute based access control, role based access control, and some other models will be reviewed. And then, the basic architecture of a kind of attribute based access control model – XACML, upon which our access control is designed, -- will be introduced. Furthermore, the access control policy will be explained.

2.1 Semantic Web and Ontology

Ontologies can be seen as the key to realize the vision of the Semantic Web, which includes raising the level of specification of knowledge by incorporating semantics into the data, and promoting knowledge exchange in an explicitly understandable form. The term ontology is borrowed from philosophy, where it refers to a systematic account of what can exist in the world. In the fields of artificial intelligence and knowledge representation the term refers to the construction of knowledge models that specify a set of concepts, their attributes, and the relationships between them. Ontologies are defined as "explicit conceptualization(s) of a domain" (Gruber, 1993), in which concepts, attributes and the relationships between them are defined as a set of representational terms, enabling knowledge to be shared and re-used.

Many formal languages for representing ontologies in the Semantic Web were proposed, such as XML Schema, RDF1, RDFS2, DAML-ONT (DAML Ontology)3, OIL (the Ontology Inference

Layer)4, etc. RDFS in particular is recognised as an ontology representation language, talking about classes and properties, range and domain constraints, and subclass and sub-property (subsumption) relations. RDFS is a very primitive language, and more expressive power would clearly be necessary in order to describe resources in sufficient detail and to determine the semantic relationship between syntactically different terms. The OIL is proposed for a web-based representation and inference layer for ontologies, which combines the modeling primitives from frame-based languages with the formal semantics and reasoning services provided by description logics. It is compatible with RDFS, and includes a precise semantics for describing term meanings.

2.2 Semantic Web Services

Web Services are defined as small units of functionality, which are made available by service providers for use in larger applications. The intention to develop Web Services was to reduce the overhead needed to integrate functionality from multiple providers. Communication with Web Services is usually achieved using the SOAP (Simple Object Access Protocol) (Gugdin, 2003). SOAP is an XML-based protocol for communication between distributed environments. Descriptions of the interfaces of the web services are formulated using the Web Service Description Language (WSDL) (Christensen, 2001). WSDL documents are generally stored in a Universal Description Discovery and Integration (UDDI) repository where services can be discovered by end-users.

While Web Services have indeed reduced the overhead needed to integrate functionality from multiple providers, extensive human interaction is still required in the process. Semantically enabled Web Services are forming the research area known as Semantic Web Services (SWS). Semantic Web Services (Payne, 2004) can be defined as Web Services whose descriptions are annotated by machine-interpretable ontologies, so that other software agents can use them without having any prior 'built-in' knowledge about how to invoke them. Semantic Web Services complement standards around Web Services Description Language (WSDL), SOAP and UDDI which aim to enable total or partial automation of tasks such as discovery, selection, composition, mediation, invocation, and monitoring of services. The research on Semantic Web Services addresses definition and development of concepts, ontologies, languages, and technologies for SWSs.

Developers of Semantic Web and Semantic Web Service applications are inclined to use their own domain ontologies in defining services even for the same subjects. Such kind of heterogeneous service ontologies cause problems of interoperation for reasons of mismatches or misunderstandings between ontological concepts. Ontology matching, or ontology mapping, is then used to acquire the relationships holding between the entities of two ontologies. Matching results can be used for various purposes such as ontology integration, information retrieval, or query mediation.

2.3 Security & Access Control Models

To guarantee semantic interoperation, security measures must be considered to protect against unauthorized disclosure, transfer, modification, or destruction, whether they are accidental or intentional. To realize these, proper identity must reliably be established by employing authentication techniques, and confidential data must be encrypted during semantic interoperation. The requirements of security include authentication, authorization, integrity, confidentiality, privacy, trust and reputation, where confidentiality is generally associated with encryption technologies; Privacy is closely related to security. Some portions of a document (XML, RDF, or ontology) may set to be private, so that they are invisible during interoperation, while certain other portions

may set to be public or semi-private; and trust and reputation are also related to security. Trust exerts an enormous impact on decisions whether to believe or disbelieve information asserted by peers (Ziegler, 2004). Security and confidentiality are the key points for the success of Electronic Commerce (E-Commerce). Suppose two organizations want to carry out a transaction, they may both use a variety of information interoperation tools to exchange data and information. Various access control and usage control policies must be applied to ensure that the users can carry out the operations and access the data. Safeguarding Web Service systems also requires the development of access control models for themselves.

Authentication, authorization and access control are terms often mistakenly interchanged. Authentication determines the identity or role of a party attempting to perform some action such as accessing a resource or participating in a transaction. Authorization is the act of checking to see if a user has the proper permission to access a particular file or perform a particular action, assuming that user has been identified. Authorization is dependent upon specific rules and access control lists, which are preset by the data owners. Access control mechanisms are considered as a necessary and crucial design element to any application's security. Access control is a much more general way of talking about controlling access, than both authentication and authorization, to a web resource. Access can be granted or denied based on a wide variety of criteria.

Access control is the process that evaluates resource access. Resources can represent software applications, web services and even facility access. An effective access control model should be capable of evaluating resource access based on user characteristics and environmentals. Currently, access control lists (ACL) (Prud'hommeaux, 2001) and groups represent static listings of individual names allowed access to resources. This per person approach of establishing resource access becomes unmanageable as the number of users requiring resources access grows. Traditional access control models like mandatory access control (MAC), discretionary access control (DAC), attribute-based access control (ABAC), role based access control (RBAC), and context-based access control (CBAC) fail to address these issues since they do not consider the rich semantic relations in the data model under the Semantic Web.

2.3.1 Mandatory Access Control MAC & Discretionary Access Control DAC

Access control is originally divided to mandatory access control (MAC) and discretionary access control (DAC). Mandatory access control is a set of procedures on which the user cannot affect.

MAC refers to a kind of access control by which the operating system constrains the ability of a subject to access or perform a sort of operation on an object based on fixed security attributes. Whenever a subject attempts to access an object, an authorization rule enforced by the operating system kernel examines these security attributes and decides whether the access can take place. Any operation by any subject on any object will be tested against the set of authorization rules to determine if the operation is allowed. The access control rule cannot be modified by users or their programs. MAC is widely used in government systems.

Discretionary access control is a means of restricting access to objects based on the identity of subjects, and process. The controls are discretionary in the sense that a subject with certain access permission has the capability to pass that permission on to any other subject. DAC is also called Identity-based access control (IBAC).

With MAC, the security policy is centrally controlled by a security policy administrator. Users are not able to override the policy and, for instance, grant access to files that would be restricted. By contrast, DAC, which also governs the ability of subjects to access objects, allows users to be able to make policy decisions and/or assign security

attributes. DAC is commonly defined in opposition to MAC. A system is seldom considered to have (purely) discretionary access control as a way of saying that the system lacks mandatory access control. On the other side, MAC and DAC can be implemented in conjunction in a system simultaneously, where DAC refers to a category of access controls that subjects can transfer between each other, and MAC refers to a second category of access controls that imposes constraints.

2.3.2 Role-Based Access Control RBAC

RBAC (Sandhu, 1996) uses roles as a basis for access control decisions and access permissions are based on the roles a subject is performing. RBAC allows the specification of security roles that map naturally to an organization's authorization structures. This kind of access control is commonly used in enterprise. In RBAC, role is an abstract description of behavior and collaborative relation with others in an organization, and permission is an access authorization to an object, which is assigned to role instead as to an individual user to simplify security administration.

Dynamic Role Based Access Control model (DRBAC) (Zhang, 2003) is an extension of the traditional role based access control model to use dynamic information while making access control decision. Specifically, DRBAC addresses two key requirements: (1) A user's access privileges must change when the user's context changes; and (2) a resource must adjust its access permission when its system information (e.g., network bandwidth, CPU usage, memory usage) changes.

2.3.3 Attribute-Based Access Control ABAC

As RBAC is not flexible to be used in large open systems, where the number of potential users is very high and most users will not be known beforehand, attribute-based access control (ABAC) (Yuan, 2005) model has been introduced.

The basic idea of attribute-based access control (ABAC) (Priebe, 2004) is not to define permissions directly between subjects and objects, but instead to compare values of selected object attributes and object attributes as the basis for authorizations. Attributes describe the characteristics of the requester, and may be a combination of identity and role. Attributes may be subject attributes, resource attributes or environment attributes.

The RBAC and ABAC have something in common, that is, they both provide ways to include contextual information (Huselbosch, 2005).

2.3.3 Context-Based Access Control CBAC

Context-based access control is described by access control rules, which specify access privileges of an entity in a context. CBAC is described by adaptation rules, which specify an action to perform when a condition becomes satisfied in a dynamic context.

CBAC is used for intranets, extranets and internets, to intelligently filter TCP and UDP packets based on application layer protocol session information. CBAC can be configured to permit specified TCP and UDP traffic through a firewall only when the connection within the network needs protection. CBAC inspects traffic that travels through the firewall to discover and manage state information for TCP and UDP sessions. This state information is used to create temporary openings in the firewall's access lists to allow return traffic and additional data connections for permissible sessions.

2.3.5 Semantic-Based Access Control SBAC

A major drawback of the previous approaches mentioned above does not exploit the semantic information of context. The Semantic-Based Access Control (SBAC, Javanmardi, 2006) model is based on the semantic properties of the resources to be controlled, properties of the clients that request access to them, semantics about the context and finally, semantics about the attribute certificates trusted by the access control system. It is based on the OWL ontology language and considers the semantic relationships in the domains of subjects, objects, and actions to make decision about an access request. SBAC consists of three basic components: Ontology Base, Authorization Base, and Operations. Ontology Base is a set of ontologies: Subjects–Ontology (SO), Objects–Ontology (OO), and Actions–Ontology (AO). By modeling the access control domains using ontologies, SBAC aims at considering semantic relationships in different levels of ontology to perform inferences to make decision about an access request. Authorization Base is a set of authorization rules. In the other words, a rule determines whether a subject which presents a credential s can have the access right a on object o or not. The main feature of the model is reduction of semantic relationships in ontologies to subsumption relation.

2.4 The XACML Architecture

XACML stands for eXtensible Access Control Markup Language. It is recognized as an effective ABAC policy description method that can exactly describe the semantics of a policy (Lang, 2009). XACML is a declarative access control policy language implemented in XML and a processing model, describing how to interpret the policies.

Figure 1 depicts the standard XACML architecture (XACML). It illustrates the interaction between the components in the architecture. The main components of the XACML architecture as shown in Figure 1 are PDP (Policy Decision Point), PEP (Policy Enforcement Point), PAP (Policy Administration Point), and PIP (Policy Information Point), where the PDP receives an XACML request, fetches the applicable policy(s) from the policy administration point, retrieves the attribute values from the policy enforcement point, evaluates the request against the applicable

Figure 1. The XACML Architecture

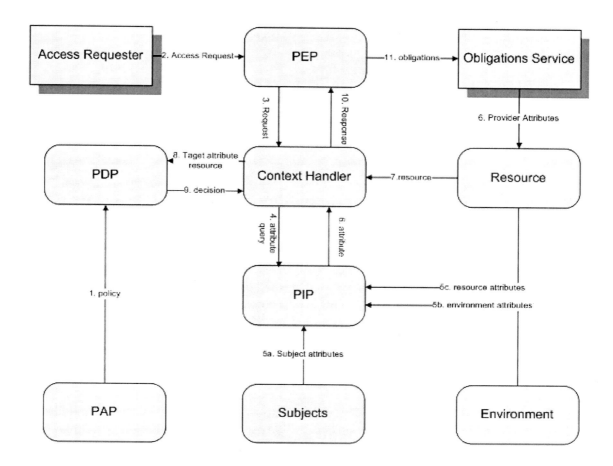

access control policies and returns an authorization decision to the PEP; The PEP receives an access request, extracts the attributes in the request, generates an XACML request and sends it to the PDP for evaluation; The PAP creates an XACML access control policy(s) and stores it in a policy database server. In addition to this, it sets a restriction in order to prevent unauthorized access to the access control policies. Beside this, it conducts a regular check in order to maintain the uniqueness of policy identifiers; The PIP is a component that acts as a directory server that stores the attribute values and makes it available to the PDP. Attribute values are the data that describe the characteristics of a subject, resource, action and environment.

The XACML architecture works as follows. A request for authorization lands at the Policy Enforcement Point (PEP). The PEP creates an XACML request and sends it to the Policy Decision Point (PDP), which evaluates the request and sends back a response. The response can be either access permitted or denied, with the appropriate obligations.

The PDP arrives at a decision after evaluating the relevant policies and the rules within them. A number of policies may be available: The PDP does not evaluate all of them; only the relevant ones are chosen for evaluation, based on the policy target. The policy target contains information about the subject, the action, and other environmental properties.

To get to the policies, the PDP uses the Policy Access Point (PAP), which writes policies and policy sets, and makes them available to the PDP. The PDP may also invoke the Policy Information Point (PIP) service to retrieve the attribute values related to the subject, the resource, or the environment. The authorization decision arrived at by the PDP is sent to the PEP. The PEP fulfills the obligations and, based on the authorization decision sent by PDP, either permits or denies access.

2.5 Access Control Policy

Access control policies provide authorization rules on controlling access to information and systems. Normally, the format of an access control policy is defined to consist of four elements: access group, action group, resource group, and relationship. Access group is the group of users to which the policy applies; Action group is a group of actions performed by the user on resources; Resource group is the group of resources controlled by the policy; Relationship, which is optional, means that each resource class can have a set of relationships associated with it, and each resource can have a set of users that fulfill each relationship.

3. MAIN FOCUS OF THIS CHAPTER

In this section, our design motivations will be presented based on the analysis of the currently available access control methods. Then, a semantic mapping based ABAC (SABAC) method will be given. The SABAC architecture is built on the XACML with the addition of the Mapping Base and Policy Reuse.

3.1. Motivations

Most of current access control schemes base their authorization approaches on locally-issued credentials that are based on user identities, but the drawback is that they are not interoperable, which

is the reason that Semantic Web based approaches to access control policies have been developed in recent years (Ferraiolo, 2001; Yagüe, 2003; Uszok, 2003; Damiani, 2004; Pan, 2006; Naumenko, 2007; Finin, 2008; Priebe, 2006; Warner, 2007).

An access control approach proposed by (Yagüe, 2003) defines an own policy language SPL (Semantic Policy Language) on the basis of XML employing Semantic Web technologies. It also allows for dynamic instantiation, i.e. querying external XML and RDF data sources for attribute values. The model is built based on the semantic properties of the resources, clients (users), contexts and attribute certificates and relies on the rich expressiveness of the attributes to create and validate access control policies. It is flexible to define access control over attributes but faces the complexity problem of the system.

The KAoS framework (Uszok, 2003) is a collection of services for distributed policy management and enforcement. It uses OWL ontologies to specify the policies themselves, which poses difficulties because the gap between specification and actual implementation of such policies cannot be coped with automatically (Tonti, 2003).

Damiani et al. (Damiani, 2004) use XACML as their policy language. They extend it with an operator to trigger requests for object metadata from a semantic environment. Subject metadata is used for the access control decision as delivered by the requester.

Pan et al. present a novel middle-ware based system (Pan, 2006) to use semantics in access control. It is based on RBAC model (Ferraiolo, 2001) with a mediator to translate the access request between organizations by replacing roles and objects with matched roles and matched objects. Semantic mapping is used for roles interoperation in order to find the similarity or separation of duties between roles in two ontologies.

In both (Finin, 2008) and (Naumenko, 2007), the access control policies are defined in terms of prohibitions or permissions for certain actors to perform certain operations. The coordination over shared resources is not dynamic, i.e. the conflicts are not resolved on per-instance basis. Rather, an agent with authority imposes some restriction on other agents' behaviors to avoid the conflicts.

Current tendency of the research of ABAC is around the application of semantic or ontologies. In (Priebe, 2006; Warner, 2007), the authors have made a try to use ontologies in the attribute-based access control. In (Priebe, 2006) an ontology-based inference engine is proposed to obtain the policies. The authors claim that it enables policy administrators to concentrate on the properties they deem necessary from their point of view; and they do not need to determine in advance which attributes a subject may use to prove these properties. While with the popularity of the Semantic Web techniques, the application of domain ontologies is becoming more and more common. The approach in (Warner, 2007) is based on determining the set of required user attributes to access a specific object in order to facilitate coalition based access control. It has four steps to realize the targets: 1) Discovering user attributes that are semantically related to object attributes; 2) Merging candidate attribute-value pair sets; 3) Pruning attribute-value pair sets by assessing significance of attribute-value pairs; and 4) Checking attribute requirements across roles. But this approach relies on identifying the necessary attributes required by external users to gain access to a specific organizational object (or service).

Semantic mapping can disclose the latent relationships between subjects and objects though they are syntactically different, and the current access control methods are either dynamically not interoperable, or the semantic based ABAC methods have also shortcomings. As RBAC is not flexible to be used in large open systems, we are highly motivated by the aforementioned problems to develop our semantic mapping based ABAC methods, aiming to realize the agent interoperation dynamically and deal with the semantic attribute mapping with the support of domain ontologies

both on service request side and service provider side. In this means, the access control is transferred to be the comparison between domain ontologies.

3.2 Architecture of the SABAC Model

Our SABAC architecture (see Figure 2) of the semantic mapping based approach is modeled based on XACML (Moses, 2003). Similar to XACML, SABAC includes the components of Application (requester), Provider, PAP, PEP, PDP, and PIP. Some other components are added to the original XACML model, which are application domain ontology, provider domain ontology, Semantic Mapping, Mapping Base, and Rule Generation. With the popularity of the use of the Semantic Web techniques, the service requester and service provider have to be strengthened with the domain ontologies. The semantic mapping component can therefore realize the mapping work with the support of the two domain ontologies.

The Mapping Base is designed, on one side, to save the mapping results; on the other side, to allow the query of source attributes' mapping result. The Rule Generation component is used to generate rules on account of the obtained similar mapping result, and transfer the rules to the format of the access control policies.

With the help of these additional components (compared to the traditional XACML model), the proposed SABAC model is more semantic and efficient. Its performance analysis will be given in the coming section.

3.3 The Performance Principle of the Architecture

Our model is built under the condition that both the application side and provider side are deployed with domain ontologies, which are designed by domain experts. The access control decision of our SABAC model is performed as follows. A PAP creates an XACML policy and provides it to the PDP. The application sends an attribute

Figure 2. Architecture of SABAC

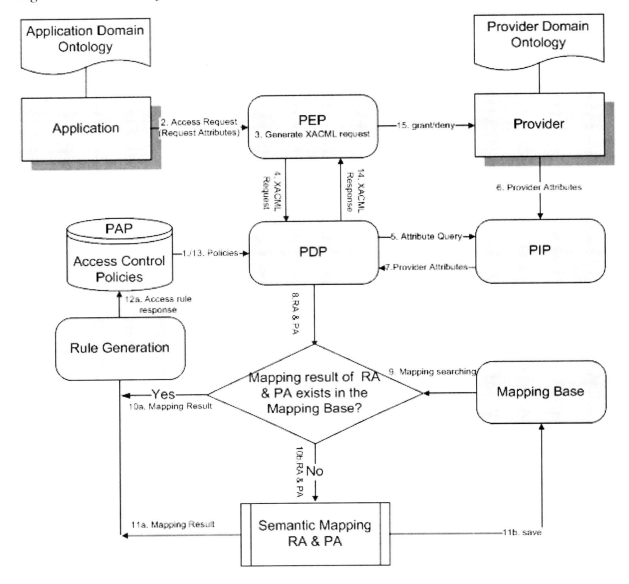

request to the PEP, the PEP forms the request as an XACML request, and forwards the request attributes (RA) to the PDP. The PDP requests those attributes from a PIP. The PIP collects the provider attributes (PA) from provider side, and delivers the attributes back to the PDP. The PDP then sends the RA and PA first to the Rule Base to check whether the mapping result has already exists. If the rule does exist, it is sent back to the PDP; otherwise, the both attributes are sent to the mapping component, where the semantic similarity between RA and PA is calculated. The generated mapping result is, on one side, sent back to the PAP to form a policy, on another side, saved in the Mapping Base for the future use. The PDP evaluates the policy and sends the response back to the native format of the PEP and forwards it. The PEP makes the decision: grant the access or

Table 1. Relationships between attributes

No	Characteristic	Rules: Given two attributes *sa* and *sb*
R1	Properties	If properties (data type property/object property $\notin$ null) of *sa* and *sb* are similar, *sa* and *sb* are also similar.
R2	Child classes	If all child classes of *sa* and *sb* are similar, *sa* and *sb* are also similar.
R3	Parent- & child-classes	If parent class & one of their child classes of *sa* and *sb* are similar, *sa* and *sb* are also similar.

deny it. If access is granted, the PEP allows access to the resource. Otherwise, access is refused.

As to the semantic similarity between request attributes and provider attributes, there have been a lot of works proposed on ontology mapping (Madhavan, 2001; Noy, 2004; Shvaiko, 2005; Sabou, 2006; Zhao, 2006). In (Madhavan, 2002), a hybrid similarity mapping algorithm has been introduced. The proposed measure integrates the linguistic and structural schema matching techniques. The matching is based primarily on schema element names, not considering their properties. In (Sabou, 2006), a mapping method with automatically selected online ontologies as background knowledge is proposed, but it faces a problem that there are currently not so many ontology resources available.

The attribute mismatches between them are mainly caused by independent development of domain ontologies. The mismatches (Zhao, 2006) can be broadly distinguished into syntactic, semantic, and structural heterogeneity. Syntactic heterogeneity denotes differences in the language primitives used to specify ontologies, semantic heterogeneity denotes differences in the way domains are conceptualised and modelled, while structural heterogeneity denotes differences in information structuring.

In our approach, we employ an algorithm combining syntactic analysis measuring the difference between request attributes and provider attributes by the edit distance, semantic analysis based on WordNet (Fellbaum, 1999) as semantic relation. Based on WordNet, the semantic relations are as follows:

- synonyms: different naming of the same content,
- hypernyms or hyponyms: different abstraction levels, generic terms vs. more specific ones (e.g., name vs. first name and last name), and,
- meronyms: different structures about the same content (separate type vs. part of a type).

When two class terms are neither syntactically similar nor semantically related, a further step is to judge their relationship with their hidden structural information, such as relative properties R1 (property of range or of domain), or with their child classes R2, or with parent-and-child classes R3according to Table 1. In Table 1., given two source attributes *sa* and *sb*, if the properties of them (either data type property or object property) are same, they are similar – R1; if all child classes of *sa* and *sb* are similar, they are also considered similar – R2; if the parent class, together with one of their child classes of *sa* and *sb* are similar, they are similar – R3. This kind of similarity measure employs the structural information of the ontology representation to get similarity value between two source attributes.

The complete mapping method here in this chapter can be described in Figure 3. The syntactic mapping on the basis of edit distance is first of all executed, if the calculated similarity measure is above a pre-defined similarity threshold, for instance, 70%, the two attributes are considered similar; otherwise, the semantic mapping is introduced in two steps: 1) mapping according to the WordNet with their semantic relations; 2)

Figure 3. Semantic Mapping Method

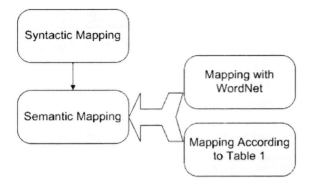

calculating the structural relations through their properties, their child classes, or their parent classes according to Table. 1. In this way, all the possible relationships between two source attributes are included, without missing results.

3.4 Rule Generation & Policy Reuse

If the two attributes from request side and provider side have the up mentioned semantic relationship, i.e. synonyms, hypernyms, meronyms, or the similarity through their ontology structures, such as their properties, child classes, or parent classes, they are considered similar. Therefore, the requester can get the access permission from the service provider. In other words, the requester can have access to the provider resources. Furthermore, the access control rule can be automatically generated according to the mapping result of the related attributes from both sides.

During the mapping process, the source attributes (request attributes and provider attributes) are first browsed in the Mapping Base to check if there already exist available mapping results. Once the mapping result does exist, it can be immediately obtained from the Mapping Base. Otherwise, the similarity measure must be calculated to put in the Mapping Base. If the similarity value between two source attributes is above a pre-defined threshold, the two attributes are considered similar.

The access control rules are then generated in the Rule Generation component according to the mapping result, with the following format:

Attributes RA and PA are similar ==> the service request is granted;

Or,

Attributes RA and PA are not similar ==> the service request is denied.

Here, "similar" means syntactically, semantically, or structurally resemble with the up mentioned methods. If the two source attributes are considered similar, the requester is granted to access the service provider and get the response; and if two source attributes are not considered similar, the service requester is then denied to get access to the service provider.

The access control policy is formed according to the generated rules, which consists of the service request attributes, action group (such as grant and deny), and the service provider attributes. If the number of request attributes and provider attributes gets rising, the management of the access control policy is worth discussing. For the policy reuse, it is closely related to the Mapping Base. When the current mapping result is already existent in the Mapping Base, the mapping result can be immediately applied to generate an access control policy. Otherwise, the similarity measure between two attributes has to be calculated. And the mapping result is then saved in the Mapping Base for the future application, while at the same time; the access control rule which is formed with respect to the mapping result is then used to get the access control policy to get saved in the PAP for future reuse. This kind of policy reuse greatly improves the efficiency of the service mapping.

4. FUTURE RESEARCH DIRECTIONS

The architecture of the access control model SA-BAC is thoroughly proposed and analyzed. Our future work is to employ the proposed architecture in an implementation of the access control system in which we can simulate the service access, i.e., defining domain ontologies for service requester and service provider, and generating access control rules.

On the other hand, we will work on the representation of the Semantic Access Control Policy Language for the policy reuse. As the sizes of the domain ontologies of service requester and service provider can be very large, the number of source attributes can also be relatively high, which causes a policy management problem. How can the access control policies be efficiently managed and reused? An access control policy ontology could be a good way to help manage, search, and reuse of the generated policies, which would be more convenient for the future reuse of policies.

5. CONCLUSION

In this chapter, an attribute based access control model with semantic mapping is proposed to specify access control over request attributes and provider attributes defined in their domain ontologies. The architecture of the model SABAC is built on XACML policy language, where the modification lies in four ways: 1) Both the Requester and Provider are strengthened with their domain ontologies; 2) The semantic mapping process between attributes is syntactical, semantic, and structural; 3) Mapping Base is designed to save the semantic mapping result. When the mapping result between two source attributes are already existent in the Mapping Base, the efficiency of the mapping is greatly improved; 4) The Policies obtained from the access control rules are saved in the PAP for future use, similar to the Mapping Base. Semantic mapping for attribute based access

control between the service requester and service provider can make the access to the Semantic Web Services secure. The performance analysis of the SABAC model shows that the proposed model is very promising. Our further work will be around a sample implantation and the semantic representation of the access control policies.

REFERENCES

Ardagna, C. A., Cremonini, M., & Damiani, E. (2006). Supporting location–based conditions in access control policies. *Proceedings of ASI-ACCS'06*, Taipei, ACM.

Berners-Lee, T., Hendler, J., & Lassila, O. (2001). The Semantic Web. *Scientific American*, (May): 28–37.

Christensen, E., Curbera, F., Meredith, G., & Weerawarana, S. (2001). *Web service description language* (WSDL) 1.1. Bericht, W3 Consortium, March 2001.

Corradi, A., Montanari, R., & Tibaldi, D. (2004). Context-based access control for ubiquitous service provisioning. *Proceedings of the 28th International Computer Software and Applications Conference* (COMPSAC'04).

Damiani, E., De Capitani di Vimercati, S., Fugazza, C., & Samarati, P. (2004). Extending policy languages to the Semantic Web. *Proc. Web Engineering - 4th International Conference* (ICWE 2004), Munich, Germany, July 2004.

Fellbaum, C. (1999). *WordNet: An electronic lexical database*. MIT press.

Fernandez, E. B., & Pernul, G. (2006). Patterns for session based access control. *Proceedings of the 2006 Conference on Pattern languages of programs*.

Ferraiolo, D. F., Sandhu, R., Gavrila, S. I., Kuhn, D. R., & Chandramouli, R. (2001). Proposed NIST standard for role based access control. *Information and System Security, 4*(3), 224–274. doi:10.1145/501978.501980

Finin, T., Joshi, A., Kagal, L., Niu, J., Sandhu, R., Winsborough, W., & Thuraisingham, B. (2008). ROWLBAC: Role based access control in OWL. *Proceedings of the ACM Symposium on Access Control Models and Technologies*, (pp. 73–82).

Gruber, T. R. (1993). *Formal ontology in conceptual analysis and knowledge representation: Toward principles for the design of ontologies used for knowledge sharing.* Kluwer Academic Publishers.

Gugdin, M., et al. (2003). *SOAP version 1.2 part 1: Messaging framework.* Retrieved from http://www.w3.org/TR/soap12-part1

Huselbosch, R. J., Salden, A. H., Bargh, M. S., Ebben, P. W. G., & Reitsma, J. (2005). Context sensitive access control. *Proceedings of SAC-MAT'05*, Stockholm, ACM.

Javanmardi, S., Amini, M., Jalili, R., & Ganji Saffar, Y. (2006). *Sbac: A semantic based access control model.* In 11th Nordic Workshop on Secure IT-systems (NordSec'06), Linkping, Sweden, 2006.

Ko, H. J., & Kang, W. (2008). Enhanced access control with semantic context hierarchy tree for ubiquitous computing. *International Journal of Computer Science and Network Security, 8*(10), 114–120.

Lang, B., Zhao, N., Ge, K., & Chen, K. (2008). *An XACML policy generating method based on policy view.* 3th International Conference on Pervasive Computing and Applications, vol. 1 (pp. 295–301). ISBN: 978-1-4244-2020-9

Madhavan, J., Bernstein, P., & Rahm, E. (2001). Generic schema matching with cupid. *Proc. VLDB* (pp. 49-58).

Madhavan, J., Bernstein, P. A., Domingos, P., & Halevy, A. (2002). Representing and reasoning about mappings between domain models. *Proceedings of the 18th National Conference on Artificial Intelligence* (AAAI'02), Edmonton, Alberta, Canada.

Moses, T. (2005). *eXtensible Access Control Markup Language (XACML) version 2.0.* OASIS Standard.

Naumenko, A. (2007). Semantics-based access control – ontologies and feasibility study of policy enforcement function. In *Proceedings of the ACM 3rd International Conference on Web Information Systems and Technologies, Volume Internet Technologies*, (pp. 150–155).

Noy, N. (2004). Semantic integration: A survey of ontology-based approaches. *SIGMOD Record, 33*(4), 65–70. doi:10.1145/1041410.1041421

Pan, C. C., Mitra, P., & Liu, P. (2006). Semantic access control for information interoperation. In *SACMAT '06: Proceedings of the 11th ACM symposium on Access control models and technologies*, (pp. 237–246). New York, NY: ACM.

Payne, T. R., & Lassila, O. (2004). Guest editors' introduction: Semantic Web services. *IEEE Intelligent Systems, 19*(4), 14–15. doi:10.1109/MIS.2004.29

Priebe, T., Dobmeier, W., & Kamprath, N. (2006). *Supporting attribute-based access control with ontologies.* First International Conference on Availability, Reliability and Security (ARES'06) (pp. 465-472). IEEE Computer Society Press. ISBN 0-7695-2567-9

Priebe, T., Fernandez, E. B., Mehlau, J. I., & Pernul, G. (2004). A pattern system for access control. *Proceedings of the 18th Annual IFIP WG 11.3 Working Conference on Data and Application Security*, Sitges, Spain.

Prud'hommeaux, E. (2001). *W3C ACL system*.

Sabou, M., d'Aquin, M., & Motta, E. (2006). Using the Semantic Web as background knowledge for ontology mapping. *Proceedings of the International Workshop on Ontology Matching (OM-2006)*, collocated with ISWC'06.

Samarati, P., & de Capitani di Vimercati, S. (2001). Access control: Policies, models, and mechanisms. [Springer.]. *Lecture Notes in Computer Science, 2171*, 137–196. doi:10.1007/3-540-45608-2_3

Sandhu, R., Coyne, E., Feinstein, H., & Youman, C. (1996). Role-based access control models. *IEEE Computer, 29*(2), 38–47.

Sandhu, R., Ferraiolo, D., & Kuhm, R. (2000). The NIST model for role-based access control: Towards a unified standard. *Proceedings of the 5th ACM workshop on Role-based access control, 2000*, (pp. 47-63).

Shvaiko, P., & Euzenat, J. (2005). A survey of schema-based matching approaches. *Journal on Data Semantics, 4*, 146–171.

Su, X. M., & Atle Gulla, J. (2006). An information retrieval approach to ontology mapping. *Data & Knowledge Engineering, 58*(1), 47–69. doi:10.1016/j.datak.2005.05.012

Tonti, G., Bradshaw, J. M., Jeffers, R., Montanari, R., Suri, N., & Uszok, A. (2003). Semantic Web languages for policy representation and reasoning: A comparison of KAoS, Rei, and Ponder. *Proceedings of the 2nd International Semantic Web Conference* (ISWC 2003), Sanibel Island, FL, October 2003.

Uszok, A., Bradshaw, J., Jeffers, R., Suri, N., Hayes, P., & Breedy, M. ... Lott, J. (2003). KAoS policy and domain services: Toward a description-logic approach to policy representation, deconfliction and enforcement. *Proceedings of the 4th IEEE International Workshop on Policies for Distributed Systems and Networks* (POLICY 2003), Comersee, Italy.

Warner, J., Atluri, V., Mukkamala, R., & Vaidya, J. (2007). Using semantics for automatic enforcement of access control policies among dynamic coalitions. In *Proceedings of SACMAT 2007*.

Yage del Valle, M. I., del Mar Gallardo, M., & Mana, A. (2005). Semantic access control model: A formal specification. In De Capitani di Vimercati, S., Syverson, P. F., & Gollmann, D. (Eds.), *ESORICS, Lecture Notes in Computer Science 3679* (pp. 24–43).

Yagüe, M., Mana, A., Lopez, L., & Troya, J. M. (2003). Applying the Semantic Web layers to access control. *Proceedings of the DEXA 2003 Workshop on Web Semantics* (WebS 2003), Prague, Czech Republic.

Zhang, G., & Parashar, M. (2003). *Dynamic context-aware access control for grid applications*. IEEE Computer Society Press, 4th International Workshop on Grid Computing (Grid 2003), (pp. 101-108). Phoenix, AZ, USA.

Zhao, Y., Wang, X., & Halang, W. A. (2006). Ontology mapping techniques in information integration. In M. M. Cunha, & G. D. (Eds.), *Putnik adaptive technologies and business integration: Social, managerial and organizational dimension*. Hershey, PA: Idea Group Reference. ISBN 1-59904-048-4

Ziegler, C., & Lausen, G. (2004). Analyzing correlation between trust and user similarity in online communities. *Proceedings of the Second International Conference on Trust Management*.

KEY TERMS AND DEFINITIONS

Access Control: Access control is a mechanism that allows resource owners to define, manage, and enforce the access conditions for any resource.

Access Control Policy: Access control policies provide authorization rules on controlling access to information and systems.

Ontology: Ontologies are defined as "explicit conceptualisation(s) of a domain" (Gruber, 1993), and are seen as a key to realise the vision of the semantic web.

Policy Administration Point (PAP): The PAP creates an XACML access control policy(s) and stores it in a policy database server. It sets a restriction in order to prevent unauthorized access to the access control policies. Beside this, it conducts a regular check in order to maintain the uniqueness of policy identifiers.

Policy Decision Point (PDP): The PDP receives an XACML request, fetches the applicable policy(s) from the policy administration point, retrieves the attribute values from the policy enforcement point, evaluates the request against the applicable access control policies and returns an authorization decision to the PEP.

Policy Enforcement Point (PEP): The PEP receives an access request, extracts the attributes in the request, generates an XACML request and sends it to the PDP for evaluation.

Policy Information Point (PIP): The PIP is a component that acts as a directory server that stores the attribute values and makes it available to the PDP.

Security: Syntax for encrypting or decrypting digital content in XML documents, in RDF triples, or in ontology representation languages.

Semantic Mapping: Semantic mapping is used to support collaboration across different enterprise systems.

Semantic Web: Envisioned by Tim Berners-Lee, the semantic web is a universal medium for data, information, and knowledge exchange. It suggests to annotate web resources with machine-processable metadata.

Semantic Web Service: Semantic Web Services are kind of Web Services whose descriptions are annotated by machine-interpretable ontologies, so that other software agents can use them without having any prior knowledge about how to invoke them.

XACML: XACML stands for eXtensible Access Control Markup Language. It is recognized as an effective ABAC policy description method that can exactly describe the semantics of a policy (Lang, 2009). XACML is a declarative access control policy language implemented in <u>XML</u> and a processing model, describing how to interpret the policies.

ENDNOTES

1. www.w3.org/RDF/
2. http://www.w3.org/TR/rdf-schema/
3. www.daml.org
4. www.ontoknowledge.org/oil/

Chapter 15
Ontological Representation of Virtual Business Communities:
How to Find Right Business Partners

Ingrid Petrič
University of Nova Gorica, Slovenia

Tanja Urbančič
Jozef Stefan Institute, Slovenia

Bojan Cestnik
Jozef Stefan Institute, Slovenia

ABSTRACT

Business knowledge that is embodied in texts such as business news and companies profiles has become widely accessible to the business community, as well as to the general public, mostly due to the growing popularity of the Internet. The field of efficient information retrieval and knowledge discovery from textual data is an increasingly important research topic driven by the Internet growth and easy access to very large business directories on the Internet. To become acquainted with a particular domain and to better understand the underlying concepts, domain knowledge can be represented by ontologies. In addition, ontologies can be used for identification of potential links in virtual business communities and for decision support when searching for right business partners, which is very relevant to small to medium-sized enterprises. Potential applications range from dynamic supply chain configuration to building consortia as quick responses to business opportunities.

INTRODUCTION

The difference between being able to use the right knowledge and not being able to do so shows most dramatically when facing difficult decisions. One

example of such decisions is how to find a right business partner for a given business idea. This has been a research issue for many years, from 1960s when it was mainly a part of the problem of supply chain management, until now, when it is mostly investigated in the context of virtual organizations. The historical span and the range

DOI: 10.4018/978-1-60960-765-4.ch015

of used methods is nicely presented in (Jarimo et al., 2008).

Interesting information about enterprises from a particular business sector can be found in various Internet business directories. They list enterprises according to different criteria (e.g. regions or company profiles) providing a broad range of information. One such directory is BizEurope. com – the European Business Directory (UGA media, 2009). It includes export and import trade leads, suppliers, importers, distributors, business resources and contacts. Besides offering payable data to BizEurope members it enables free search on various product categories and provides lists of companies and links to their websites. Internet and real-time communication provide the possibility to build virtual communities in different platforms, which can foster enormous business opportunities. Those SMEs which are able to quickly recognize potential partners' products, expertise and skills, are in advantage when developing new services, products or new ways how to produce or deliver them in a cooperative, more effective way.

Since business research is increasingly relying on the Internet as information source and communication medium, managers and experts in enterprises have to master rapidly changing Information and Communication Technology (ICT) in order to explore heterogeneous data sources that are constantly on the increase. Besides operating with collections of well structured data, they often have to deal with semi-structured text collections, too. To analyse such datasets, the use of text mining techniques is required. The principal feature of text mining is its concentration on the document collection, which can be any group of text-based documents (Feldman and Sanger, 2006). Essentially, the term text mining is used to denote the analyses of large quantities of natural language text and the detection of usage patterns with the goal to extract some useful information (Sebastiani, 2002). Having access and ability to work with the newest information that is increasingly available on internet, indeed

means great potential for experts, who can benefit from the advantages of information systems and technologies. Business informatics thus presents an essential element of business research process.

Generally, small to medium-sized enterprises (SMEs) do not possess all necessary information and knowledge that is required for business success and therefore need to acquire external knowledge through different channels of knowledge interactions. The empirical evidence collected from an investigation conducted in the United Kingdom by Chen et al. (2006) confirms the crucial importance of external knowledge for SMEs. External knowledge is often distributed in various documents from heterogeneous sources. Text mining tools make it possible to discover new knowledge through analysis of text. Extracting important information from the knowledge that is represented in digital text forms has been proved as an important opportunity for the development of solutions and novel discoveries also in the context of business. News and other information from business domains can be extracted by text mining tools and represented as ontologies in the form of a tree-based concept hierarchy. We propose the use of ontologies constructed by using information from the application domain as an important component of the knowledge base used in the research process. Such domain ontologies contain background information and define the concepts and the structure of a conceptualization of a particular target domain. As an example we examined the pump manufacturing domain.

This chapter is in particular addressing the possibilities to improve the enterprise integration and organisational capabilities using ontological representations of business information. With ontologies construction tools text documents containing business information can be automatically analysed and placed into ontologies according to their content similarity. In particular, domain ontologies can support enterprises in organising business information and finding associations among organisations and linking them through

Figure 1. Text mining process. The sequence of steps is modelled in conformity with a definition of knowledge discovery in databases (KDD) process as originally proposed by Fayyad and colleagues in (Fayyad et al., 1996).

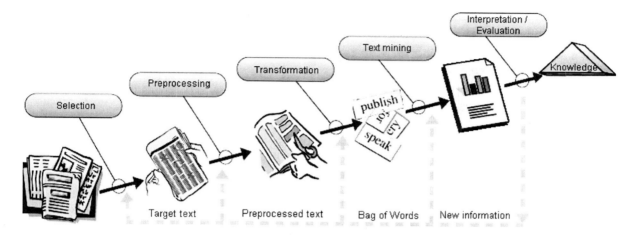

the relevant relationships by utilising textual information. Such identification of links contributes to creation of virtual communities that provide significant business opportunities for SMEs (Matlay and Westhead, 2005). In accordance with the motive of focusing on the text-based knowledge discovery, our aim was to show how to use the text mining tools to support the analysis work of researchers and experts in business domains.

BACKGROUND

While it is often easy to automatically collect data, it requires considerable effort to link and transform them into practical information that can be used by entrepreneurs and executives of small and medium-sized enterprises (SMEs). In Figure 1 we illustrate the main phases of the text mining process, where the Bag of Words approach (Sebastiani, 2002) is used for representation of collection of words. The Bag of Words is a popular method for representing words from text documents, which disregards grammar and word order. We modelled the sequence of the text mining steps according to the basic flow of knowledge discovery steps as

defined by Fayyad, Piatetsky-Shapiro and Smyth (Fayyad et al., 1996).

Knowledge discovery by combining text mining and clustering techniques plays an important role in solving this information overload problem and many researchers have attempted to build models of text mining and clustering of related information in order to improve the efficiency of knowledge discovery systems. Clustering methods can reveal the structures of implicit communities and suggest interesting points in such communications channels for knowledge sharing. It enables building up networks of interconnected subjects by exploring associations among subjects and linking them through the relevant relationships. It is also useful in trust management which is an important, although often neglected aspect in creating and functioning of virtual enterprises (Lavrač et al., 2007).

Clustering by link analysis has frequently been applied to issues such as co-citation analysis to explore relationships between authors or as co-coupling measurements to determine the similarity between documents. McCain, for example, used the author co-citation analysis to display dynamics in intellectual structure of macroeconomics by focusing on changing relationships among authors in this field of economics over time (McCain, 1984).

Clustering by link analysis has developed over the past twenty years in many different areas, from computer science and informatics to social sciences. In computer science, a number of link-based algorithms have been proposed for the web link analysis to identify web communities. The link analysis functionality was incorporated in several web information retrieval algorithms e.g., the Hypertext Induced Topic Search (HITS) algorithm that was developed by Kleinberg (1999). The HITS algorithm (Kleinberg, 1999) is a link analysis algorithm that views the web as a graph where the web pages are nodes. It ranks web pages by utilizing the hyperlink structure of the web. The ranking is based on the authority and hub value. The hub value estimates the quality of outgoing links from the page to other pages where a good hub is a page that refers to many good authority pages. The authority value is the sum of the hub values of all incoming links (i.e. of the web pages that point to the page). A good authority is a page that is pointed to by many good hubs. The authority value is thus used to estimate the value of the content of a web page.

Similarly, in information science, there is a growing interest in link analysis for studying the structure of hyperlink networks of documents (e.g., web pages), categories, and users of common interests (Thelwall, 2004). Such link analysis studies typically apply data and text mining algorithms to large collections of web data (Reid, 2003). In the field of web research, there is a particular link structure analysis called webometrics (Almind and Ingwersen, 1997). Webometrics has emerged as a research field of information science in recent years. It examines the quantitative aspects of how different users access and handle information in different contexts.

The most characteristic for the clustering by link analysis field is the category of graph representations of objects and links between them such as thematic concepts captured in ontologies. In fact, graph data structures can be widely applied to different research issues, such as network analysis. Therefore, they are often employed to investigate linking patterns in various communities and networks, including networks of communities of business with common interests. Besides, the ontology-based knowledge discovery methods for processing and analysing textual data can improve the existing methods of link discovery by providing a more intuitive search of unexplored links between information fragments.

Ontologies have been used for a long time in different sciences and fields of investigation as a means to organize information and, more importantly, to provide a common vocabulary of concepts. From this perspective, ontologies are part of the common-sense understanding of the world, which define the concepts and structures in a domain. Also entrepreneurs can benefit from an ontology representation of the focused business domain when they are analysing large information sources. Placing domain ontologies in the framework of knowledge discovery in business processes facilitates the acquisition of insight and understanding of a research domain and especially improves the communication process between domain expert and knowledge engineer.

Tools for ontology construction make use of text mining and clustering techniques to enable semi-automatic clustering of text documents and organising them into domain dependent ontologies. In information science, ontology is a data model that represents a domain and is used to reason about the objects in that domain and the relations between them. Ontologies in general with their capability to share a common understanding of domains give the ability to reason over and to analyze the information at issue (Joshi and Undercoffer, 2004). Many tools that help constructing ontologies from texts were developed and successfully used in practice (Brank et al., 2005). Among them, OntoGen (Fortuna et al., 2006), the interactive tool for semi-automatic construction of ontologies, received a remarkable attention.

Ontologies are used in information science as a form of knowledge representation of the world or some part of it. In general, ontologies include descriptions of objects, concepts, attributes and relations between objects. They integrate and conceptualize the heterogeneity of the domain terminologies that can be identified in text. Therefore, ontologies reflect the content and the structure of the knowledge as it can be recognized through the use of terms in the inspected collection of texts. The data that is utilised in the construction of topic ontologies must be carefully selected before it is processed and considered for analyses.

Ontologies define the concepts and the structure of a conceptualization on the basis of the business texts collections that contain information about a target business sector. This can be exploited in knowledge management needed to increase the ability of an organization to promptly react to business opportunities in virtual enterprises, where good knowledge repositories can ease decision making about potential partnerships (Jermol et al., 2004). Another potentially important application area can be found in various e-government applications like described in (Cestnik et al., 2007; 2008). The use of ontologies for business research include also configuration of dynamic SME supply chains (Blomqvist et al., 2005) and acceleration of innovation projects (Bullinger et al., 2005).

For this chapter purposes, we choose the pump manufacturing domain as an illustrative example. This domain draw our attention through a North American pump systems educational initiative *Pump Systems Matter* aimed at improving the energy effiency of pumping systems (Tutterow et al., 2006a). As stated in (Tutterow et al., 2006b), there is a significant lack of understanding regarding the proper application and operation of pumps which leads to excessive operating costs. As pumps are among the most widely used machines and the market is huge, there is a lot of potential for optimizations from which manufacturers as well as users could benefit.

ONTOLOGIES FOR ENHANCING COMPREHENSION OF BUSINESS-RELATED DOCUMENTS

Issues, Controversies, Problems

Incorporating ontologies in the decision process can help SMEs to bridge the knowledge gaps by providing integrated views and facilitating information exchange. In such way ontologies can help domain experts in their cognitive processes to properly model the conceptual understanding of the domain under investigation. For that reason, ontologies are often used to provide an integrated view over knowledge fragments that otherwise would remain known only to individuals within a particular disciplinary community. Therefore, we propose to include ontologies in knowledge discovery frameworks for facilitating communication among interdisciplinary groups of experts.

One of the most common problems SME's are facing is the lack of formalised knowledge needed for effective functioning of the enterprise. There is a trade-of between agility, which is often regarded as a strong virtue of SME's, and high ceremony of process and knowledge formalisation that is necessary in larger enterprises. Ontologies are knowledge formalizations by their nature. Therefore, they can be used as an effective form to represent the derived knowledge. Besides better formality, ontologies often improve the knowledge fragmentation providing more unified view on the domain under investigation.

In order to obtain an improved insight into a business domain structure and to make valuable new discoveries about pump manufacturers, which were analyzed in our case study, we decided to examine the professional profiles of pump manufacturers that are collected and publicly accessible on the World Wide Web in the BizEurope company directory (UGA media, 2009).

Ontologies might come in handy when sharing information across different contexts. When a knowledge engineer captures domain knowledge into ontology, the role of a domain expert is crucial in the process. The domain expert can help by identifying some specific knowledge concepts that fall within a certain scope of interest. Moreover, ontologies can also be used to facilitate communication between knowledge engineers and domain experts. Therefore, they can make the understanding and interpretation of the domain structure easier. In particular, ontologies help exchanging views between knowledge engineers and domain experts and are thus substantial parts of the process of verification the comprehension of the domain knowledge. In the case of SME's, such representation can be used to increase the formality of the documented knowledge and can be viewed also as a way towards knowledge preservation.

Data mining enables us to discover new knowledge. This knowledge, once put together, might describe the still unknown connections among phenomena and point towards potential networks and thus contribute to the recognition of new business opportunities. Also, connectivity and computer-supported analysis of numerous large data sets, may contribute, in a methodological sense, to the development of e-business. Namely, information that is related across different contexts is difficult to identify with conventional associative approaches. The creative computer-supported analysis of such data, however, is often needed for innovative discoveries.

Automated knowledge discovery based on text data sets in the field of business is an intriguing challenge as it requires intensive involvement of business domain experts during the processes of both domain-specific text analysis and evaluation. Hence an interactive approach is recommended when text mining and decision support are combined. Also, it is beneficial to apply efficient methods of text mining when searching for indirect connections and for knowledge discovery from large amounts of business data.

The major aim here is to unravel the potential relations among business entities. In the process,

use of appropriate visualization on the part of the experts is desirable as it supports knowledge discovery and interpretation of results.

Solutions and Recommendations

Until recently, the practice of ontology construction has relied mostly on the manual extraction of interesting concepts from data and their organisation in a suitable hierarchy. Nowadays, the largely increased amount of data requires automated support for such a task. With new knowledge technologies, the ontologies can be constructed semi-automatically, and therefore, the process of ontology construction can be made more effective and feasible in practice. Thus, ontologies are particularly important when the process of knowledge acquisition embraces insight and understanding of a specific domain. Ontologies actually can help to integrate and understand the complex and heterogeneous spectre of information about a specific business sector.

In the continuation, a case study of finding potential virtual communities in a mechanical business sector is conducted by ontology construction and concepts visualization. The process is schematically presented in Figure 2. Note that the main added value of the presented study lies in the efficient transformation of knowledge dispersed in the collection of raw documents to a form of ontology that can be operationally used for supporting business decisions.

To represent the specific domain of pump manufacturing in an organized manner we performed semi-automatic construction of domain ontologies, as an example shown in Figure 3. This domain ontology was constructed based on the business profiles information. We collected professional descriptions of pump manufacturers from the BizEurope company directory (UGA media, 2009) and in the first place examined their business profiles by the construction of domain ontologies. To this end, we used OntoGen (Fortuna et al., 2006), the interactive tool for semi-

Figure 2. The process of constructing ontology from a collection of documents for generating operational knowledge in mechanical business sector

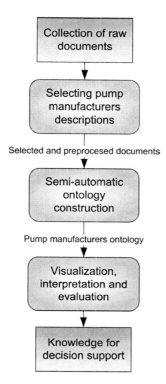

automatic construction of ontologies. The main concepts of the pump manufacturing domain as they result from the first level of our ontology models are:

- *submersible pumps and electric motors,*
- *positive displacement blowers and vacuum pumps,*
- *centrifugal pumps for industrial applications,*
- *air and gas pumps,*
- *hydraulic and pneumatic components.*

OntoGen automatically generates 3 keywords, which constitute the semantic description of companies' profiles that are mapped to a particular concept. As advocated by OntoGen's literature (Fortuna et al., 2006), we renamed the concepts accordingly, based on the suggested keywords.

Each company profile can only be mapped to one concept. However, different keywords may appear in a concept description according to different approach to constructing ontologies. In our experimental study, the distribution of companies' profiles among 5 concepts of the pump manufacturers' ontology is rather uniform. However, as intuitively expected, it can be observed that the major sub-concept of pump manufacturers' profiles from the BizEurope company directory deals with centrifugal pumps for industrial applications and that another important group describes submersible pumps and electric motors. The information about the major sub-concepts within ontologies can be easily obtained by observing the number of instances in each concept of ontology.

The main motivation for using OntoGen was to gain a quick insight into a given domain, which is particularly relevant for SME's. By semi-automatic generation of ontologies from the domain's texts (e.g. from the companies profiles) we can construct models of business networks and obtain knowledge about potential virtual communities. The semi-automatic ontology construction method implemented in OntoGen incorporates basic text mining principles. The input for the tool is a collection of texts, which are then represented as vectors and together often referred to as a vector space model. Using this representation, similarities between texts can be defined as the cosine of the angles between the corresponding vector representations. When suggesting domain concepts, OntoGen utilizes a K-Means clustering technique (Jain et al., 1999) and a keyword extraction method using Support Vector Machine (Brank et al., 2002).

To automatically process news and other information from large databases, it is very practical if the documents are available in XML or text format. The material for our case study was a textual collection of business information from the business directory BizEurope.com – the Eu-

Figure 3. Top- and second-level ontology concepts from pump manufacturers' profiles. Concepts were renamed based on descriptions (three for each concept) that were automatically suggested by OntoGen.

ropean Business Directory (UGA media, 2009). In the business directory BizEurope.com there were descriptions of profiles of 483 enterprises manufacturing pumps at the end of June 2009. A sample profile is given for the manufacturer ABS Pumps:

"Manufacturer of pumps, mixers and aerators for wastewater and water applications. Production facilities in Sweden, Germany, Ireland and Brazil. World-wide sales and service network. Features document bank with manuals and CAD drawings as well as life cycle cost calculator."

For the experiments with HTML or PDF formats of documents, it should be noted that the pre-processing of such documents is necessary by converting the HTML and PDF papers to text, and by deleting graphics, paragraph marks, and manual line breaks from the original text versions, so that each document occupies one record in the input file. Obtaining and handling of such documents formats requires extra time in terms of locating and converting them into a plain text format. However, documents in HTML and PDF format may contain an abundance of data and if user could capture important information from them, it is worth spending additional time on obtaining and processing such text.

Semi-Automatic Construction of Potential Business Community Ontology

Traditionally, ontologies for a given domain are constructed manually using some sort of language or representation and rely on the manual extraction of common-sense knowledge from various sources. Recently, several programs that support manual ontology construction have been developed, such as Protégé (Gennari et al., 2002). Since manual ontology construction is a complex and demanding process, there is a strong tendency to provide a computerised support for the task. Based on text mining techniques that have already proven successful for the task, OntoGen is a tool that enables the interactive construction of ontologies from text in a selected domain. A user can create concepts, organise them into topics and also assign documents to concepts. With the use of machine learning techniques, OntoGen supports individual phases of ontology construction by suggesting concepts and their names, by defining relations between them and by the automatic assignment of text to the concepts (Fortuna et al., 2006). It is available as a free download from http://ontogen.ijs.si/.

For our case study we used one input text file of 483 lines of texts about pump manufacturers that we obtained by our search in the BizEurope directory. In the process of semi-automatic ontology construction, we used OntoGen to construct several top-level ontology concepts and describe them with suggested keywords.

Using OntoGen we displayed sub-concepts of pump manufacturing domain as suggested by its clustering algorithm, and described them with their main keywords extracted from companies' profiles texts. The keywords that we used for concepts description were calculated both according to the concept centroid vector, and by the Support Vector Machine based linear model (Fortuna et al., 2006). In fact, ontoGen implements two keyword extraction techniques. The first one, results in keywords extracted from the concept's centroid vector. The second one extracts keywords from the concept's Support Vector Machine linear model by dividing documents within the concept from the neighbouring documents and thus takes into account the context of the topic. However, when describing concepts of pump manufacturers' ontologies we used the first method (i.e. the concept's centroid vector), because we were basically focused on finding only the most important words within the concepts that served as keywords. The system also displayed the current coverage of each concept by the number of companies' profiles that it positively classified into the concept and the inner-cluster similarity measures.

Finally, we compared the locations of a particular company profile within ontologies and performed an analysis on how the variation of parameter k impacts the positioning of a company in the ontology sub-concepts. We experimented with various values of the parameter k used by OntoGen's K-means clustering algorithm. Clustering algorithms, such as K-means clustering, are useful tools for data mining; however, when we have to cluster datasets, it is not always clear which is the most appropriate number of clusters (parameter k) to use (Jain et al., 1999). Therefore, it is generally recommended to experiment also with various other values of k in order to determine the best result for the domain under investigation. In fact, determining the proper number of top-level concepts (the value of parameter k) for a specific domain is very important when constructing ontologies in a semi-automatic way. Besides, experimenting with other values of k may also reveal some interesting domain properties of the single level ontology concepts within the domain.

This observation suggested that different number of sub-concepts affects also the positioning of a particular company profile in a semantic space. As a consequence, the pump manufacturers' ontologies were built with parameter k=5 that experimentally turned out to be a well-balanced trade-off between the complexity and comprehensibility in building a domain model (Petrič et al., 2006). Although the concepts generated with other values of k also revealed some interesting domain properties, they were either too broad when k was small or too narrow when k was large. The resultant ontology concepts are illustrated by example ontology in Figure 3.

In the ontology construction process we performed also a more focused investigation of the contextual links between instances (i.e. the manufacturers' profiles) of the ontology concepts by searching for clusters of pump manufacturers. This investigation was done by concentrating on neighbouring manufacturers in the concept visualisation of pump manufacturers' ontology. The clustering of pump manufacturers was performed and visualized with OntoGen (Figure 4) on the collection of same descriptions of pump manufacturers from the BizEurope company directory as used for ontology construction.

A screenshot of OntoGen version 2.0.0.0 showing the concept visualisation of pump manufacturers' ontology is presented in Figure 4. Each company's profile is treated as one instance to be clustered. The instances are presented as named points on a map. Instances are positioned in the two dimensional space so that the distance between two instances (i.e. between two companies' profiles) corresponds to the content similarity between them. In this manner, instances with similar or related meanings are represented closed in the two dimensional space, while less-similar instances are located more distant. Therefore, such visualization can assist the user when searching for groups of companies which share similar words in their company profile's descriptions.

FUTURE RESEARCH DIRECTIONS

The main direction of further work is to construct new tools that integrate ontologies for more focused and efficient information retrieval, tailored to meet requirements of executives and experts in business. Such tools should support knowledge management and decision-making of SME managers by focusing on most relevant information, with good visualisation capabilities and possibilities of interactive guidance provided by the user. There is a lot of potential for enhancement by including analysis of existing links in projects, business associations and other types of cooperation. A well-established field of social networks analysis provides some solutions for trust modelling which should be incorporated when making decisions about partners for future projects, collaborative networks and consortia.

We also intend to apply a literature-based knowledge discovery tool RaJoLink (Petric et al., 2009), currently used in biomedical domains, to the domain of business-related textual databases. The tool supports open discovery of hidden relations that might reveal new hypotheses connecting concepts across different disciplines. We believe that this may serve as a basis for suggesting virtual communities in a new, broader way as it could break conventional boundaries of fields and disciplines, thus indicating potential for new, maybe unexpected connections in search for innovative products and services.

Figure 4. Screenshot of OntoGen, version 2.0.0.0 (Fortuna et al., 2006) showing concept visualisation of pump manufacturers ontology. An instance (marked by increased font size, yellow font colour) in the similarity map represents a particular pump manufacturer. The instances (i.e. the manufacturers) are grouped into clusters of pump manufacturers according to the similarities between the companies' profiles.

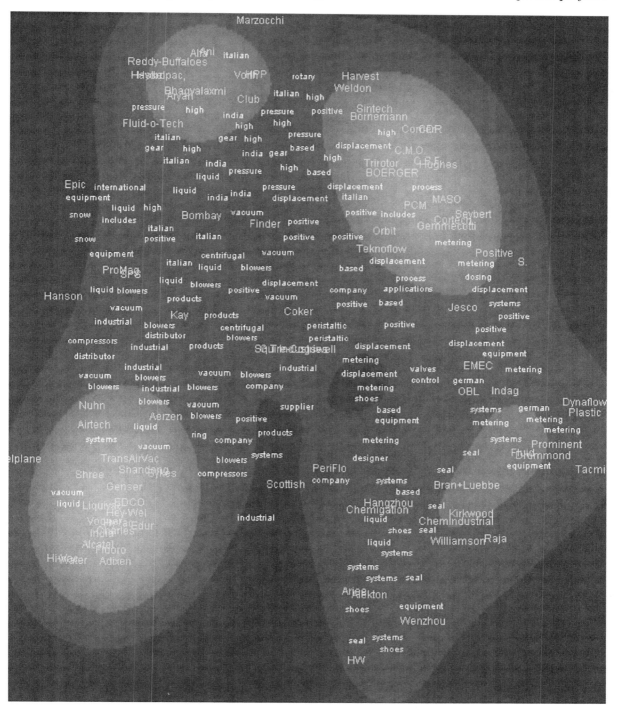

CONCLUSION

In this chapter, we describe the organizational aspect of modelling the possibilities of enterprise integration. In particular, we examine the visualization of potential business networks for the development of SMEs virtual communities. In order to exploit existing but often overlooked knowledge that is hidden in business information we investigated the potential of two information science disciplines, namely the text mining and clustering methods. The computational dimension of the chapter proposal addresses the information integration in business domain ontologies and their visualization through the similarity maps. The ontologies were constructed using descriptions of company profiles of the pump manufacturing enterprises, which was done semi-automatically with the computational support of OntoGen version 2.0.0.0 (Fortuna et al., 2006). The use of OntoGen enables a quick insight into a given domain by semi-automatically generating the main ontology concepts from the domain's documents.

Our observations show that ontologies help gaining understanding in a given subject area. Therefore, using tools for semi-automatic ontology construction from textual data can significantly speed up the process of becoming acquainted with the domain of interest. Instead of reading an extra load of information, researchers can first generate top-level domain ontology concepts and thus obtain a general overview and understanding of the domain. After that, a detailed study of the concepts of interest might be in order. In such a way, semi-automatically constructed ontologies actually helped us to review and understand the spectrum of companies' profiles that belong to the pump manufacturers' domain. In particular, the proposed text mining approach based on ontologies will be of significant help to small and medium-sized companies in finding suitable business partners to expand their business and enter into new business networks of mutual interest and support.

REFERENCES

Almind, T. C., & Ingwersen, P. (1997). Informetric analyses on the World Wide Web: Methodological approaches to "Webometrics.". *The Journal of Documentation*, *53*(4), 404–426. doi:10.1108/EUM0000000007205

BizEurope.com. (2009). *European business directory*. Retrieved May 11, 2009, from http://www.bizeurope.com

Blomqvist, E., Levashova, T., Ohgren, A., Sandkuhl, K., Smirnov, A., & Tarassov, V. (2005). Configuration of dynamic SME supply chains based on ontologies. In Marik, V., Brennan, R. W., & Pechouček, M. (Eds.), *HOLOMAS 2005, LNAI 3593* (pp. 246–256). Berlin/Heidelberg, Germany: Springer-Verlag.

Brank, J., Grobelnik, M., Milić-Frayling, N., & Mladenić, D. (2002). Feature selection using support vector machines. In Zanisi, A., Brebbia, C. A., Ebecken, N. F. F. E., & Melli, P. (Eds.), *Data mining III* (pp. 261–273). Southampton, Boston, MA: WIT Press.

Brank, J., Grobelnik, M., & Mladenić, D. (2005). A survey of ontology evaluation techniques. In O. Markič, M. Gams, U. Kordeš, M. Heričko, D. Mladenić, M. Grobelnik,... M. Bohanec (Eds.), *Proceedings of the 8th International Multiconference Information Society IS 2005* (pp. 166-169). Ljubljana, Slovenia.

Bullinger, H., Warschat, J., Schumacher, O., Slama, A., & Ohlhausen, P. (2005). Ontology-based project management for acceleration of innovation projects. In Hemmje, M. (Eds.), *E.J. Neuhold Festschrift, LNCS 3379* (pp. 280–288). Berlin/Heidelberg, Germany: Springer-Verlag.

Cestnik, B., Kern, A., & Modrijan, H. (2007). The housing lottery in Slovenia: E-government perspective. In: A. Groenlund, H. J. Scholl & M. A. Wimmer (Eds.), *Electronic Government. 6th International Conference, EGOV 2007, Proceedings of ongoing research, project contributions and workshops*. Linz, Austria: Trauner Verlag.

Cestnik, B., Kern, A., & Modrijan, H. (2008). Semi-automatic ontology construction for improving comprehension of legal documents. In M. A. Wimmer, H. J. Scholl & E. Ferro (Eds.), *Electronic Government. 7th International Conference, EGOV 2008, Lecture Notes in Computer Science* (pp. 328-339). Torino, Italy: Springer.

Chen, S., Duan, Y., Edwards, J. S., & Lehaney, B. (2006). Toward understanding inter-organizational knowledge transfer needs in SMEs: Insight from a UK investigation. *Journal of Knowledge Management, 10*(3), 6–23. doi:10.1108/13673270610670821

Fayyad, U., Piatetsky-Shapiro, G., & Smyth, P. (1996). From data mining to knowledge discovery in databases. *AI Magazine, 17*(3), 37–54.

Feldman, R., & Sanger, J. (2006). *The text mining handbook: Advanced approaches in analyzing unstructured data*. Cambridge University Press. doi:10.1017/CBO9780511546914

Fortuna, B., Grobelnik, M., & Mladenić, D. (2006). Semi-automatic data-driven ontology construction system. In: M. Bohanec, M. Gams, V. Rajkovič, T. Urbančič, M. Bernik, D. Mladenić, ... B. Novak Škarja (Eds), *IS-2006. Proceedings of the 9th International multi-conference Information Society* (pp 223-226). Ljubljana, Slovenia.

Gennari, J., Musen, M. A., Fergerson, R. W., Grosso, W. E., Crubezy, M., Eriksson, H., et al. Tu, S.W. (2002). *The evolution of Protégé: An environment for knowledge-based systems development*. Retrieved December, 2006, from http://smi.stanford.edu/smi-web/reports/SMI-2002-0943.pdf

Jain, A. K., Murty, M. N., & Flynn, P. J. (1999). Data clustering: A review. *ACM Computing Surveys, 31*(3), 264–323. doi:10.1145/331499.331504

Jarimo, T., Ljubič, P., Hodik, J., Salkari, I., Bihanec, M., & Lavrač, N. (2008). Multi-criteria partner selection in virtual organizations. In Putnik, G. D., & Cunha, M. M. (Eds.), *Encyclopedia of networked and virtual organizations* (pp. 964–970). doi:10.4018/978-1-59904-885-7.ch127

Jermol, M., Lavrač, N., & Urbančič, T. (2004). Managing business intelligence in a virtual enterprise: A case study and knowledge management lessons learned. *Journal of Intelligent and Fuzzy Systems, 14*(3), 121–136.

Joshi, A., & Undercoffer, J. L. (2004). On data mining, semantics, and intrusion detection. What to dig for and where to find It. In Kargupta, H., Joshi, A., Sivakumar, K., & Yesha, Y. (Eds.), *Data mining. Next generation challenges and future directions* (pp. 437–460). Menlo Park, California.

Kleinberg, J. M. (1999). Authoritative sources in a hyperlinked environment. *Journal of the ACM, 46*(5), 604–632. doi:10.1145/324133.324140

Lavrač, N., Ljubič, P., Urbančič, T., Papa, G., Jermol, M., & Bollhalter, S. (2007). Trust modeling for networked organizations using reputation and collaboration estimates. *IEEE Transactions on Systems, Man and Cybernetics. Part C, Applications and Reviews, 37*(3), 429–439. doi:10.1109/TSMCC.2006.889531

Matlay, H., & Westhead, P. (2005). Virtual teams and the rise of e-entrepreneurship in Europe. *International Small Business Journal, 23*(3), 279–302. doi:10.1177/0266242605052074

Petrič, I., Urbančič, T., & Cestnik, B. (2006). Comparison of ontologies built on titles, abstracts and entire texts of articles. In M. Bohanec, M. Gams, V. Rajkovič, T. Urbančič, M. Bernik, D. Mladenić, ... B. Novak Škarja (Eds), *IS-2006. Proceedings of the 9th International multi-conference Information Society* (pp. 227-230). Ljubljana, Slovenia.

Petrič, I., Urbančič, T., Cestnik, B., & Macedoni-Lukšič, M. (2009). Literature mining method RaJoLink for uncovering relations between biomedical concepts. *Journal of Biomedical Informatics, 42*(2), 219–227. doi:10.1016/j.jbi.2008.08.004

Reid, E. (2003). Using Web link analysis to detect and analyze hidden Web communities. In Vriens, D. (Ed.), *Information and communications technology for competitive intelligence* (pp. 57–84). Hilliard, OH: Ideal Group Inc.

Sebastiani, F. (2002). Machine learning in automated text categorization. *ACM Computing Surveys, 34*(1), 1–47. doi:10.1145/505282.505283

Thelwall, M. (2004). *Link analysis: An Information Science approach.* Amsterdam, The Netherlands: Elsevier Academic Press.

Tutterow, V., Asdal, R., & McKane, A. T. (2006a). Pump systems matter – part 1. *World Pumps, 481,* 44–66.

Tutterow, V., Asdal, R., & McKane, A. T. (2006b). Pump systems matter – part 2. *World Pumps, 482,* 28–31.

ADDITIONAL READING

Barabási, A.-L. (2002). *Linked: The New Science of Networks.* Cambridge, MA: Perseus Publishing.

Berry, M. (Ed.). (2003). *Survey of Text Mining: Clustering, Classification, and Retrieval.* New York: Springer-Verlag.

Camarinha-Matos, L., & Afsarmanesh, H. (2005). Collaborative networks: A new scientific discipline. *Journal of Intelligent Manufacturing, 16*(4), 439–452. doi:10.1007/s10845-005-1656-3

Cimiano, P. (2006). *Ontology learning and population from text: Algorithms, evaluation and applications.* New York, NY: Springer-Verlag.

Davies, J., Grobelnik, M., & Mladenić, D. (Eds.). (2009). *Semantic Knowledge Management: Integrating Ontology Management, Knowledge Discovery, and Human Language Technologies.* Berlin, Heidelberg: Springer.

Fensel, D. (2001). *Ontologies: Silver Bullet for Knowledge Management and Electronic Commerce.* Heidelberg: Springer-Verlag.

Fortuna, B., Grobelnik, M., & Mladenić, D. (2005). Visualization of Text Document Corpus. *Informatica, 29,* 497–502.

Fortuna, B., Grobelnik, M., & Mladenić, D. (2006). Background Knowledge for Ontology Construction. In L. A. Carr, D. C. De Roure, A. Iyengar, C. A. Goble, & M. Dahlin (Eds.), *Proceedings of the 15th International World Wide Web Conference* (pp. 949-950). Edinburgh, UK: ACM Press.

Franke, U. (2000). The knowledge-based view (KBV) of the virtual web, the virtual corporation, and the net-broker. In Malhotra, Y. (Ed.), *Knowledge Management in Virtual Organizations* (pp. 20–41). Hershey, PA; London, UK: Idea group publishing.

Fridman-Noy, N., & Hafner, C. D. (1997). The State of the Art in Ontology Design. *AI Magazine, 18*(3), 53–74.

Gomez-Perez, A., Fernandez-Lopez, M., & Corcho, O. (2004). *Ontological Engineering.* London, UK; New York, NY: Springer.

Grobelnik, M., & Mladenic, D. (2002). Efficient visualization of large text corpora. In *Proceedings of the 7th TELRI seminar*. Dubrovnik, Croatia.

Gruber, T. R. (1991). The Role of Common Ontology in Achieving Sharable, Reusable Knowledge Bases. In J. A. Allen, R. Fikes, & E. Sandewall (Eds.), *Principles of Knowledge Representation and Reasoning: Proceedings of the Second International Conference* (pp. 601-602). Cambridge, MA: Morgan Kaufmann.

Gruber, T. R. (1993). A translation approach to portable ontologies. *Knowledge Acquisition, 5*(2), 199–220. doi:10.1006/knac.1993.1008

Hardwick, M., Spooner, D., Rando, T., & Morris, K. (1996). Sharing manufacturing information in virtual enterprises. *Communications of the ACM, 39*(2), 46–54. doi:10.1145/230798.230803

Joachims, T. (2002). *Learning to Classify Text Using Support Vector Machines: Methods, Theory, and Algorithms*. Boston: Kluwer Academic Publishers.

Khan, L., & Luo, F. (2002). Ontology construction for information selection. In *Proceedings of the 14th IEEE International Conference on Tools with Artificial Intelligence (ICTAI 2002), 4-6 November 2002* (pp.122-127). Washington, DC.

Ljubič, P., Lavrač, N., Mladenić, D., Plisson, J., & Mozetič, I. (2006). Automated structuring of company profiles. *Metodološki zvezki 3*(2), 369-380.

Ljubič, P., Lavrač, N., Plisson, J., Mladenić, D., Bollhalter, S., & Jermol, M. (2005). Automated structuring of company competencies in virtual organizations. In O. Markič, M. Gams, U. Kordeš, M. Heričko, D. Mladenić, M. Grobelnik, I. Rozman, V. Rajkovič, T. Urbančič, M. Bernik, & M. Bohanec (Eds.), *Proceedings of the 8th International Multiconference Information Society IS 2005* (pp.190-193). Ljubljana, Slovenia.

Maedche, A., & Staab, S. (2000). Discovering Conceptual Relations from Text. In W. Horn (Ed.) *Proceedings of the 14th European Conference on Artificial Intelligence (ECAI 2000), Berlin, 21-25 August 2000.* Amsterdam: IOS Press.

McGuinness, D. L., & van Harmelen, F. (2004). OWL Web Ontology LanguageOverview. *W3C recommendation* retrieved from http://www.w3.org/TR/owl-features

Mladenić, D., Lavrač, N., Bohanec, M., & Moyle, S. (Eds.). (2003). *Data Mining and Decision Support: Integration and Collaboration*. London: Kluwer Academic Publishers.

Noy, N. F., & McGuinness, D. L. (2001). Ontology Development 101: A Guide to Creating Your First Ontology. *Stanford Knowledge Systems Laboratory Technical Report KSL-01-05*. Stanford, CA: Stanford University.

Staab, S., & Studer, R. (Eds.). (2004). *Handbook on Ontologies, International Handbooks on Information Systems*. Heidelberg: Springer-Verlag.

Steinbach, M., Karypis, G., & Kumar, V. (2000). A comparison of document clustering techniques. In *Proceedings of KDD Workshop on Text Mining, at the 6th ACM SIGKDD International Conference on Knowledge Discovery and Data Mining* (pp. 109-110). Boston, MA.

Uschold, M., & Gruninger, M. (1996). Ontologies: Principles, methods and applications. *The Knowledge Engineering Review, 11*(2), 93–136. doi:10.1017/S0269888900007797

Uschold, M., King, M., Moralee, S., & Zorgios, Y. (1998). The enterprise ontology. *Knowledge Engineering Review. Special Issue on Putting Ontologies to Use, 13*(1), 31–89.

Zhao, Y., & Karypis, G. (2005). Hierarchical clustering algorithms for document datasets. *Data Mining and Knowledge Discovery, 10*(2), 141–168. doi:10.1007/s10618-005-0361-3

Section 4
Legal and Security Aspects

Chapter 16
Key Contracts Needed for SMEs Conducting E-Business:
A Practical Guide from a UK Law Perspective

Sam De Silva
Taylor Walton LLP, UK

ABSTRACT

In order for a small to medium enterprise (SME) to conduct business electronically, that SME requires the establishment of a website. This requires agreements relating to (1) website development, (2) website hosting (3), Internet access, and (4) online content and advertising. The chapter will provide a practical guide from a UK law perspective for a SME in relation to the issues which should be considered when contracts for the above mentioned services are negotiated. The chapter does not cover the issues relating to how the SME should set up its arrangements with its own customers (for example, through website terms and conditions) nor does it consider e-commerce legislation required when conducting business on the Internet.

INTRODUCTION

Increasing use of the Internet as a business medium has created the need for new service and supply agreements to facilitate that business to emerge. Any small to medium enterprise (SME) wanting to establish an online business presence requires agreements relating to some or all of the following:

- website development;
- website hosting;
- Internet access; and
- online content and advertising.

The next sections in this chapter provide a practical guide from a UK law perspective for a SME in relation to the issues which should be considered when contracts for the above mentioned services are negotiated. Even though such agreements were unheard of before the advent of the Internet, it is important to remember that the general principles of contract law apply in the same manner as for other conventional contractual arrangements.

DOI: 10.4018/978-1-60960-765-4.ch016

It should be noted that this chapter focuses on the contracts related to the establishment of the website and does not cover the issues relating to how the SME should set up its arrangements with its own customers (for example, through website terms and conditions) nor does it consider the various e-commerce legislation required when conducting business on the Internet.

DEFINITIONS

There is no one definition for a SME. According to a study conducted by the International Labour Organisation, more than 50 definitions were identified in 75 countries with considerable ambiguity in the terminology used (Pobobsky 1992). In the UK the most widely used definition of an SME is that of a firm with 0-250 employees (DTI 2007).

The distinction between e-commerce and e-business is not entirely clear and frequently the terms are used interchangeably. Davydov (2000) defines e-business as:

"an all encompassing concept of enabling the exchange of information and automation of commercial transactions over the Internet."

For the purposes of this chapter, the definitions of SME and e-business as outlined above will be used.

THE NEED FOR THIS GUIDE

Whilst there have been various checklists on a number of different types of website agreements as well as various articles and books on such contracts, to date as far as the author is aware, there has been no collective "guide" on the contractual issues related to the specific contracts needed by SMEs to conduct e-business. One reason for this may be that although e-business has spread rapidly

throughout large firms, its growth amongst SMEs has been much less pervasive (Poole 2006).

This chapter attempts to provide such a guide for the benefit of SMEs.

WEBSITE DEVELOPMENT AGREEMENTS

Background

The Internet allows users to search for and retrieve information stored in remote computers. Any person or organisation with Internet access can "publish" information on the Internet. To create a presence on the Internet, a website (comprising one or more web pages) is required. The forms and functions of websites have evolved remarkably in recent years, from allowing the supply of static information consisting of text only, to billboard type websites, to those that constitute fully interactive, e-commerce enabled marketplaces (Chong 2009).

Initial Considerations

The appointment of an appropriate website developer and host is the first key decision for a SME wishing to establish an Internet presence (Bode 2001). The following are some initial considerations that should be taken into account. The extent to which these issues need to be addressed depends on the complexity of the proposed website and the underlying business.

Does the SME Need a Website Developer, or can the SME do this Itself?

The SME needs to consider whether it has the in house resources to develop the website. In determining this, the SME needs to take into account the level of functionality required for the website. It is generally recognised that website development requires specialist skills and resources. Whilst it is possible to develop a website using easy to use software packages and even have the website hosted for free, the functions that can be performed by such a website and the options available are limited. Therefore, in practice, website development and website hosting are outsourced by most SMEs (Falkenstein 1996).

Does the SME Need One Service Provider or Two?

It is relatively common for a single service provider to offer both website development and website hosting services. However, there is no overriding reason why one service provider should supply both services. This decision may be determined primarily by the choice of website developer. If a particular developer is favoured because of the services it provides and that developer does not provide website hosting services, then a separate website host will be needed. Alternatively, if the necessary developments and hosting services can be as easily provided by a single service developer, it may be easier to appoint just one service provider.

Will the Service Provider Offer all the Services the SME Needs?

Other services that are usually required when establishing a website include:

- Domain name registration: The service provider will need to register the SME's domain name with the relevant registration body. The relevant registration body depends on the suffix of the domain name being registered. For example, for ".uk", in the UK the registration body is Nominet and for ".com" or ".net" it is VeriSign.
- Search engine registration: The service provider will register the website URLs with various search engines to ensure the website is indexed.

- Online promotion: Promotional activities to promote the website or build an online image.

It is possible for the SME to attend to these matters. Alternatively, the ability of a proposed website developer or website host to offer these services as part of a package may be a persuasive factor in the selection of that service provider (Gable 1991).

Once a suitable service provider has been identified, it is necessary to agree on the terms on which the services will be provided.

What is a Website Development Agreement?

A website development agreement covers the supply of design, programming, and other related skills necessary for website creation. Issues the SME should consider when negotiating a website development agreement include (Raysman 1996):

- design;
- specifications;
- development;
- project plan;
- scope of the services;
- implementation;
- acceptance testing;
- support and maintenance;
- training; and
- general contractual issues.

Design

Before a SME talks to a website developer, the SME should have developed a clear picture of what it wants to achieve with the website and what use it expects to be made of the website. This picture is often recorded in the form of the initial website design. The initial website design provides a very basic outline of the SME's requirements. If the design is straightforward (as with a billboard type website) or the SME has adequate resources, the initial design can be carried out by the SME. If the design is more complicated, it is perhaps more efficient that the design is carried out by a website developer.

Specifications

Once the initial website design is decided on, it is usually recorded in more detail in the form of specifications. Specifications are important, as they provide the blueprint for how the website will appear and operate. Therefore, these specifications should be included in the website development agreement (Goodman 1996). Website specifications can range from the high level to the very detailed. Often, a website developer is required to produce detailed specifications based on the SME's initial high level requirements. Generally, the more detailed the specifications, the less confusion, delay, and cost to the SME. This is because there will be less scope for misunderstanding between the SME and website developer as to what is required.

Requirements that should be covered in the specifications include:

- Content: What will the website look like? What will be displayed on the front pages? Will the website be interactive?
- System specifications: What are the minimum specifications for the Internet browser and desktop?
- Capacity: How many users can the website accommodate concurrently? What bandwidth is required?
- Scalability: As use of the website increases, will the website be able to handle the increased use without its performance being affected?
- Compatibility: Will the website operate for all types of Internet browser?

- Security: What security measures are required to prevent hackers exploiting the website?
- Responsiveness and performance: What is the required download time for the website's pages?
- Compliance with relevant legislation: The website needs to comply with relevant legislation. In the UK such legislation includes the Consumer Protection (Distance Selling) Regulations 2000, the Electronic Commerce (EC Directive) Regulations 2002, the Data Protection Act 1998 and sector specific regulations (for example, if the website was offering financial services, there will be numerous financial services regulations that need to be complied with). See also below under the heading titled "Website design & accessibility". It is beyond the scope of this chapter to provide detailed analysis on legislation with which a SME is required to comply with in order to do e-business.

The developer and SME should always keep in mind the particular audience to which the website is aimed and keep the design relevant to that audience. They also need to consider the latest industry standards of design technology and whether the specifications meet those standards.

If changes are required to the specifications, these should be recorded in writing. While the design of the specifications should involve both parties, the SME should have final sign off before more involved development begins.

If not restricted by contract to do so, it is always open to a SME to not use the developer who created the specifications. A SME may instead consider seeking competitive bids for the final development work for the website. In this situation, the SME will need to ensure it has ownership of (or at least wide rights to use) the rights in the specifications, and the contract should provide for termination and transition to another service provider.

DEVELOPMENT

Once the specifications are agreed, the next stage is the development of the website. The website developer constructs the website by developing the software applications that comprise the website.

Project Plan

Like any software development project, website development should follow a detailed project plan (Gussis 1998). The project plan should be included as part of the website development agreement. The project plan should contain a commencement date and end date for the development of the website. The project plan should also record key milestones in the development process. These milestones may trigger events such as testing, acceptance procedures and partial payment. If timing is a critical issue, the website development agreement may set out appropriate remedies if a relevant milestone is not met on time. In some circumstances, it may be necessary to provide for termination of the agreement if a crucial milestone is not met on time.

Scope of the Services

The website development agreement should set out the nature and scope of the rest of the services to be provided after design and specifications have been created (Goodman 1996). These services should be listed in sufficient detail so that the services to be provided to the SME are clear. However, the website development agreement should also contemplate and allow any changes in the services being provided to be made.

Implementation

Issues in relation to the implementation of the developed website in the website host's environment and performance testing the website should be addressed.

Acceptance Testing

Acceptance testing is a critical part of website implementation. Acceptance testing is the process to ensure the website meets the specifications that were recorded as part of the design services (Gussis 1998). Acceptance of the website can have an effect on a number of provisions in a website development agreement. For example, acceptance of the website could affect the transfer of risk and title in the website, or the commencement and end of any warranty period, and may trigger one or more payment milestones.

Whilst the SME relies on the website developer to provide technical acumen, acceptance testing allows the SME to test what has been produced against the particular requirements the SME has specified to ensure that in practice the website provides the SME with the required functionality. Best practice suggests that a SME should be able to decide what qualifies as conforming with the relevant acceptance test and what needs to be fixed.

The website development agreement should include an acceptance testing procedure. An outline of a commonly followed acceptance testing procedure is:

- The SME determines the criteria for what constitutes acceptance. Ideally, the criteria include the original website design and specifications.
- When the website developer believes the website is fully operational, it notifies the SME that the website is ready for testing.
- Acceptance tests are carried out, often by the developer, in the presence of the SME. The SME either provides an acceptance certificate (if the website passes the acceptance test) or notifies the website developer that the website does not pass the acceptance test. If the website fails the acceptance test, there is an opportunity for the developer to correct the failure and retest.

Not all bugs in a website will be found straight-away. It is a good idea for testing to be over an extended period, with final acceptance testing conducted at some period after the "go live" date. If this is done, it is necessary to ensure the testing is not prejudiced by operation of the website. Six months is generally considered sufficient to find most bugs. The acceptance testing procedure should also provide for website redesign, re-specification, and retesting.

The types of acceptance test used should reflect the unique aspects and complexity of the website development. The tests should assess:

- website performance when it is accessed using different browsers, including earlier versions of those browsers;
- different hardware platforms and different Internet connection speeds;
- availability of the website content during peak and off peak times and when other users are accessing the website;
- security of the website from unauthorised access;
- download speed of the web pages; and
- ease of navigation and use.

Support

The developer and the SME should discuss the support services needed to maintain the website and/or train the SME's personnel. These support services are usually optional but are often included in the website development agreement. However, support services for a website can also be provided by the website host, a third party, or the SME.

Maintenance

Internet users are becoming more demanding and their expectations are growing. An out of date website (in terms of content, industry standards, or design technology) does not reflect well on a business. In addition, faults in a website need to

be corrected as soon as possible. As a result, the issues of who maintains a website and how it is maintained are critical to the website's ongoing life. If the developer is to maintain the website, the website development agreement will need to include details on:

- the period over which support is to be provided;
- who has the ability to add, change or delete content on the website; and
- a timetable for how long maintenance will be carried out.

If maintenance is to be performed by a third party, this needs to be reflected in the agreement, and appropriate licences need to be granted for third party maintenance.

If maintenance services are to be performed by the website developer, ideally, maintenance charges should be recorded in the website development agreement.

Training

Depending on the type of website and the services provided by the developer, training on how to use the website may be necessary. For example, a SME may need to instruct its staff on how to use its new website to gather relevant sales information. If the SME is going to maintain the website in house, then it may need to train its technical staff. Any training requirements need to be reflected in the website development agreement.

Website Design and Accessibility

The profile of "accessibility" has received particular attention recently, with publicity through surveys and "naming and shaming" of large companies (Disability Rights Commission 2004). The relevant legislation in the UK is the Equality Act 2010 (formerly, the provisions were contained in the Disability Discrimination Act 1995), and in the context of the Internet, the issue has been to make website pages accessible to those suffering from disabilities. The inherent requirement therefore consists of having alternative interfaces available to those with disabilities. However, this gives rise to some issues in itself, namely:

- the level of awareness amongst website developers about the mechanisms which need to be incorporated to address accessibility requirements; and
- the lack of any prescribed standard for website accessibility.

With regard to the first issue, this is something that a SME should discuss with a website developer prior to entering into a contract in order to check that the website developer is aware of what needs to be implemented to address this legislation. If the website developer cannot provide sufficient comfort, then the SME should either consider an alternative designer, or face the risk that the website which will be designed and developed, will not be compliant with legislative requirements. With regard to the second issue, guidance has been provided in the form of the World Wide Web Consortium's Content Accessibility Guidelines, but the Disability Rights Commission has called for these to be updated, and for a standard to be prescribed, so this is still something which is an evolving process (Disability Rights Commission 2004).

GENERAL ISSUES

The following are provisions that are common in most service agreements, but which have a number of unique issues in the context of website development.

Payment

It is common for the payment terms for website development to consist of:

- an initial payment on commencement of the agreement;
- periodic payments tied to the achievement of key milestones; and
- a final payment, kept "in reserve", to be paid to the website developer on final acceptance of the website.

This allows a website developer to meet its initial set up and labour costs for what is often a labour intensive process. It also allows the SME to retain an element of control to ensure that the website developer keeps to the milestones. In particular, the final payment is a valuable negotiation tool to ensure the website meets all the SME's requirements.

Change Management Procedure

Website development is a dynamic and ongoing process. Not every aspect required for the website is likely to have been considered. A SME is likely to expect its website to change in accordance with its needs and its target market's needs. For example, a website may provide only information when it is first developed, but it may become evident that the website should enable SMEs to sell goods and services online. It is useful for a website development agreement to have a change management procedure that deals with changes to the scope of the services needed for the website during the term.

Intellectual Property

The development and creation of a website involve a number of intellectual property rights. The developer and the SME need to consider who will own the visual appearance, methodologies, software, templates, and future developments for the website.

In the absence of an agreement to the contrary, section 11 of the Copyright, Designs and Patents Act 1988 provides certain rules in relation to who owns copyright in an original work, such as a website. The general rule is that the person who is an author of a work is the owner of that work. This means that in a situation where a SME commissions and pays the website developer to create a website on its behalf, the website developer (and not the SME) owns the copyright in the graphic works and software that make up the website, even though the SME has commissioned and paid for the development. For this reason if the SME wishes to own the intellectual property it is important that the default position is varied by appropriate contractual provisions in the website development agreement.

Pre-Existing Intellectual Property

The website developer and the SME each provide their own pre-existing intellectual property for the creation of a website. A website developer often provides the underlying methodology and technology. It is in the best interests of the website developer to retain ownership of its pre-existing intellectual property as the underlying technology and methodologies are the tools of the developer's trade and can often be recycled for a number of SMEs. The benefit to the SME in having the website developer maintain ownership of the rights in its underlying methodologies and technology is that by recycling these tools, the developer can keep its development costs down and pass the savings on to the SME.

The SME often provides website's content, including any data or branding, and will want to ensure it maintains ownership of this data or branding.

New Intellectual Property

One of the most contentious and difficult areas of intellectual property ownership for any software development project (including website development) is the commissioning of a unique feature or function that provides the SME with a competitive advantage. Having commissioned the unique feature or function and based on the fact that it gives the SME a competitive advantage, the SME will want ownership to control the use that can be made of it. The website developer is also likely to want ownership of the rights in any feature that can be recycled and included as part of the website developer's tools of trade.

Whilst the feature may be unique when commissioned, in the fast paced world of the Internet, unique features rapidly become industry standards. However, the SME will want to retain any competitive advantage for as long as possible. In this situation both parties need to be clear on exactly what constitutes the feature that provides the competitive advantage. It may be possible, by negotiation, to limit any restriction to a certain period, location, or industry.

Third Party Intellectual Property

The development of a website often involves use of third party intellectual property. Where third party intellectual property is provided by the website developer, the SME should ensure it is granted appropriate rights (ideally for a perpetual term and free of all royalties) for its current and future use of that third party intellectual property.

Neither the SME nor the developer wants to be sued by a third party for infringement of a third party's intellectual property rights. The SME and website developer should provide warranties to each other that the materials that each party provides do not infringe any third party intellectual property rights, supported by an indemnity against claims of third party infringement.

Other IP issues relate to meta-tags and image, texts and designs as set out below.

Meta-Tags

Meta-tags are "invisible" keywords inserted into website pages, so that they can be used by search engines to index and locate website pages. Although the concept for the inclusion of meta-tags is sound, their use has been open to abuse. The abuse arises from website developers using the names or trademarks of other organisations as meta-tags. For example, if Ford used the key-word "Toyota" in their meta-tag, certain search engines might show the listing for Ford when a user entered a search for "Toyota". This form of unlawful activity has already received the attention of the Courts, initially in the USA, but also subsequently in the UK, and the clear message from the Courts is that such use of terms in meta-tags will not be tolerated (Murray 2000).

Although a SME might decide against use of such prohibited keywords in its meta-tags, an over-zealous website developer might unknowingly to the SME include such very terms without appreciating the consequences of the designer's actions. This therefore needs to be guarded against both in the contract, through intellectual property rights' warranties and indemnities, and also from a practical perspective by discussing with the website developer which terms have been included in the meta-tags of the website pages.

Images, Texts and Designs

Images, text and designs are the common aspects of website pages that come to mind when one thinks of intellectual property rights. However, it is important to ensure that the website developer has the rights to use in particular, any third party stock photos or clip art which have been included in the website pages.

Although from a legal perspective this can again be guarded to some extent by the contract, from a practical perspective it might be worth investigating the source of any third party images and checking or obtaining confirmation that the third party is authorised to provide such stock photos, particularly if the stock photographs are going to be used in a parallel print marketing campaign by the SME.

Warranties

Warranties should be sought by a SME from a website developer. Examples of warranties that are often included in a website development agreement are:

- The website complies with the specifications provided.
- The website remains operational and accessible for a certain period.
- Intellectual property provided by the website developer does not infringe any third party intellectual property rights. (In circumstances where the SME is providing content, the website developer may seek a similar warranty from the SME.)
- The website is scalable and can handle any increased use without any adverse effect on its performance.
- The website is easily transferred to another service provider.

Some of these warranties will be resisted by website developers on the basis that once a website has "gone live", the developer cannot control and be responsible for interference or modifications to the website by parties accessing, using, or maintaining the website. Although working out what caused a problem can sometimes be complex, exceptions to the warranties for specific events can be included.

Subcontracting

Not every website developer has all the in house skills or tools to create every aspect of every website. Subcontracting specialist functions may be necessary. It is generally in the interests of the SME and the website developer that the original website developer remains primarily responsible for the provision of all goods and services, including subcontracted services.

Legal Review

It is advisable to allow for a legal review of the website's content (similar to one that would be conducted for an advertisement). This reduces the potential exposure of the developer and the SME to liability. Either party may require this review.

Reference Website

The website developer may want to use the SME's website as a reference website. If so, this should be covered in the website development agreement. It is also common for a website to acknowledge the website developer.

Termination and Portability

The parties have the right to terminate the agreement on the occurrence of certain events. Requiring the website to be portable to another service provider and that the website developer provides adequate documentation for the website will assist in transition to a new service provider. It is likely the SME will need some assistance from the original website developer with the transition and implementation of its website and this should be covered in the website development agreement.

If the website development agreement is being terminated because of a breach by the website developer, the website developer should provide such assistance at no cost to the SME. However, if the agreement is being terminated "at will" by the SME (i.e. for no fault), it is reasonable that the website developer will charge a fee for this assistance.

Termination of the website development agreement should deal with the return of each party's intellectual property, data, and confidential information.

WEBSITE HOSTING AGREEMENTS

Once the website is developed, it must be "hosted" so that it can be accessed on the Internet. There is no point in having a great website if the SME's target market cannot access it. The costs for website hosting services range from free to hundreds of thousands of dollars. Thorough research of the most appropriate option is needed before that option, and the associated rights and obligations of the parties, can be adequately captured in a website hosting agreement.

There are generally four basic options for website hosting (Gussus 1998):

- virtual website hosting;
- virtual server hosting;
- dedicated server hosting; and
- co-location.

Virtual Website Hosting

Virtual website hosting is generally the cheapest of the four options. A SME's website sits among several hundreds of others on one server using one copy of the server's software. Every website hosted has the same access to the one server and competes for the use of system features and resources with the other websites being hosted. For a sophisticated website with new tools or ongoing development work, this type of hosting is not suitable.

The main advantage to a SME is ease of use, and the SME does not have to purchase and maintain its own server and Internet connections. The disadvantages of virtual website hosting include limited flexibility over the tools that can be used on the website, limited services that can be offered and the website address.

Typically, in the case of virtual website hosting the website host's domain name forms part of the address for any website that it hosts. This means the website address is often lengthy and harder for potential users to find. This can be a disadvantage if a SME wants a website that is easily accessible and a potential competitor is only a click away.

Virtual Server Hosting

Virtual server hosting is a "middle of the road" website hosting option in terms of costs and flexibility. The main advantage is that it allows the SME to have greater website customisation.

Typically, this hosting arrangement involves approximately 30 to 50 websites being hosted on one server. Each SME has its own copy of the server's software. However, the SME does not have to manage the server hardware. The reason this is a more expensive option than virtual website hosting is that there are fewer SMEs on any one server and more copies of the server's software are provided.

Further advantages to the SME include the SME being able to modify:

- its settings for downloading;
- the types of file being used;
- passwords; and
- account maintenance.

Another advantage is that the SME can have its own domain name.

Dedicated Server Hosting

Dedicated server hosting involves rental and exclusive use by a SME of a server, related software, and Internet connection. This server is housed at the website host's premises. The server typically provides a stated amount of memory, hard disk space and bandwidth. Use of a dedicated server is most appropriate in situations where a website attracts a lot of traffic, usually millions of hits per day.

Advantages include the increased flexibility and customisation that is available for the website. By hosting the website in this way there are savings for the SME in terms of router, interconnection, security, and network administration costs.

Potential disadvantages include the SME being restricted in the type of computer system that can be used.

Co-Location

Co-location is the most expensive option for website hosting. The SME purchases the hardware and software needed and sets up the server, and the website host provides the network connection to the Internet. This requires large set up costs on behalf of the SME. As in the case of dedicated server hosting, co location is most suited to large, sophisticated SMEs who expect to attract millions of hits a day to their websites.

The website host is essentially providing the space for the website hosting hardware and monitors and maintains the equipment to the level set out in the website hosting agreement.

Co-location is preferable to dedicated server hosting when a SME wants to maintain control over the equipment used but wants to rely on the website host's specialist skills for website hosting.

OTHER KEY ISSUES TO CONSIDER FOR WEBSITE HOSTING AGREEMENTS

Once the most suitable option in respect of website hosting for the SME is decided, the following issues need to be considered and negotiated in the website hosting agreement.

Specifications

As in the case of website development, the website hosting agreement must set out the relevant requirements for hosting the website. The agreement should include a full and detailed description of the scope of the services provided. Requirements that should be considered and covered in the specifications include:

- Exclusive server space: How much server space does the website need? This depends on the website hosting option chosen by the SME.
- Bandwidth: How fast does the data travel to and from the SME's website?
- Server response and throughput capacity: How long does it take a user to access the website?
- System redundancy: Does the SME require mirror servers and back up connections to other Internet Service Providers (ISPs) to reduce the likelihood of unscheduled downtime?
- Security: What security measures, for both the physical and computer environment, does the website host provide?
- Environment: Does the SME require that the physical location has adequate air conditioning and back-up generators? What restrictions are placed on physical access to the building that houses the server?
- Availability: What are the SME's requirements for availability of the server to provide access to the website? Is additional capacity required for peak traffic flows to the SME's website? Depending on the website hosting option, is it necessary to allocate priority for server space when there are competing websites?
- SME support: In the case of problems, how does the SME contact the host? What is the process for resolving problems? What are the time frames for the resolution of those problems?

Service Levels

From the SME's perspective, one of the most important provisions in a website hosting agreement deals with the levels of service being provided. The performance obligations that create the service levels need to be tied to the specifications and should be clear, measurable, and objective.

The SME needs to consider what appropriate remedies or service rebates (i.e. "service credits") it requires if its website is not available to the level set out in the specifications. This depends on the type of website being hosted. For example, in the case of an e-commerce enabled website for the sale of goods or services, it is more vital to the SME that the website is available 24 hours a day, 7 days a week than it would be for a website that provides only information. Typically, a website host would offer service credits for not meeting service levels.

Service Credits

Service credits are an attempt to incentivise the service provider and compensate the SME in a pre-agreed manner for levels of performance which are not perfect but not disastrous either. Service credits are by no means appropriate for all degrees of failure.

The SME needs to decide whether it favours a service credit regime and, if so, how extensive it should ideally be. Of course, it will always have to be negotiated and agreed with the service provider. Service credit regimes have the advantages to both the SME and service provider of certainty and of keeping risk to identifiable and manageable levels. Pre-agreed service credits also avoid disputes about applicable compensation occurring on an ongoing basis. Service credits are also useful where it is particularly difficult to quantify the loss which has been suffered as a result of specific breaches.

In order to be enforceable, service credits must be a genuine pre-estimate of loss. They must also not be unduly "oppressive". If they are a penalty they will be unenforceable in their entirety. A recent English case, *McAlpine v Tilebox* suggests that a court will be slow to interfere with a liquidated damages clause negotiated at arms' length between commercial parties. In that case even though the liquidated damages amount was quite significant (£45,000 per week), it was still not held to be a penalty. In practice, circumstances in which a SME could negotiate a regime which amounts to a penalty are likely to be quite rare. The English courts have certainly begun to incorporate this requirement for a liquidated damages clause to amount to "oppression" before it would be unenforceable in a contract negotiated between commercial entities.

Nevertheless, from a practical perspective, when negotiating the amount of service credits it is prudent for the customer to retain evidence indicating how the predetermined sum was calculated and any evidence demonstrating how that sum was negotiated. This is particularly important if it is difficult to calculate likely losses with precision.

Intellectual Property

The hosting of a website involves a number of intellectual property rights. These are similar to the intellectual property issues that arise in the context of website development. Both parties will need to ensure:

- they each have adequate intellectual property rights to perform their respective obligations under the website hosting agreement;
- they do not infringe third party intellectual property rights; and
- ownership of existing and new intellectual property is covered in the agreement.

Third Party Intellectual Property

Where the website host provides third party intellectual property, it should grant the SME an appropriate licence for the SME's use. The website host should also provide an indemnity to the SME that any intellectual property it provides does not infringe any third party intellectual property rights.

The website host may also set out, in its acceptable use policy (see below under the heading titled "Acceptable use policy"), the type of content that is acceptable for display on the SME's website. This is likely to include a restriction on content that infringes any third party intellectual property rights or breaches legislative restrictions. In addition, the website host often seeks indemnity from the SME that the website content does not infringe any such third party intellectual property rights.

Data and Privacy

If any data (including personal information) is collected or transferred through the SME's website, the website hosting agreement needs to specify who owns this data and who is responsible for complying with any legal requirements in obtaining and using the data.

Domain Names

If the website host is registering the domain names for the SME's website, it is in the SME's interests to ensure it owns or, where the particular item cannot be owned, has the exclusive right to use all domain names and an Internet Protocol (IP) addresses in connection with its website. This helps avoid unnecessary disputes if the website is transferred to another website host. At a practical level, if the website is registering a domain name on the SME's behalf, the SME should insist that it is listed as the contact for domain name purposes.

Often the domain name registry responds only to the listed contact person. In addition, the SME should hold the relevant name-holder identification and authentication keys. If the SME is a company, measures should be put in place to ensure safe custody of these keys and continued access to them if there are staff changes.

Liability and Indemnity

The Internet is a network of millions of computers, so a website's ability to provide all the information that it is intended to provide and for it to be accessed on the Internet depends on a number of factors and various service providers (such as telecommunication providers) over which the website host has no control. A website host often seeks a disclaimer that a SME's website is not guaranteed continuous access to the Internet.

As with any services agreement, the obligations of either party to protect the other from certain types of liability should be set out. A website host should seek to avoid any liability if a SME's website cannot be accessed due to factors such as computer malfunction, maintenance, or upgrades that are beyond the host's control.

Reporting

The website host maintains logs of information about the website and its hosting. This means the website host can provide valuable information to the SME. The SME should consider requiring the host to provide the following types of reports and information:

- number of hits on the website;
- amount of use of the website;
- availability of the website;
- amount of downtime of the website; and
- number of attempted security breaches of the website.

Pricing

The website hosting agreement needs to record the chosen method of charging. Ideally, all charges should be agreed in advance and recorded. Charges for all services should be itemised separately for transparency, including any extra charges (for example, if the website exceeds a certain amount of hits). Options usually include a charge per usage or a flat rate. The website hosting agreement should include the ability to change these rates where necessary. There may be a number of changes made to a website over time. The agreement should address whether there will be any additional charges for changes to the website.

Force Majeure

"Force majeure" deals with events that are beyond the reasonable control of a party, such as earthquakes, wars, and sometimes fires. The force majeure clause should be reviewed to ensure the definition of a force majeure event is appropriate. For example, it may not be acceptable for electrical power failure or fluctuations to be considered a force majeure event if it is an obligation of the website host to provide adequate power back-ups.

In any event, the website hosting agreement should specify the obligations of the parties to work around any force majeure event and provide for either party to have a right to terminate the website hosting agreement should the force majeure event continue beyond a certain period.

Access

As stated at the beginning of this section, the website developer and website host may be different parties. The website hosting agreement should include consideration of who is likely to make changes to the website. If the website developer (or SME) is to make the changes, the website agreement should provide for the website developer (or SME) to have suitable access to the website host's physical site if this is necessary to effect these changes.

Acceptable Use Policy

It is common for website hosts to incorporate acceptable use policies ("AUPs") into the website hosting agreement. These AUPs are usually posted on the website host's site. The AUP sets out the requirements for those websites that are hosted by the website host. It is likely to prohibit websites transmitting any material that is obscene, threatening, abusive, or defamatory, or that encourages conduct that would give rise to a criminal offence. The AUP may also cover the SME's obligations for copyright infringement, network security, the observance of "netiquette", and advertising. The SME needs to be clear on the intended use of its website and ensure such use does not conflict with any AUP. If the staff of the SME maintains or provide material for the website, they should be made aware of any website host AUP, and the SME should consider whether it is necessary to have a back to back AUP of its own.

Termination and Portability

Post termination services can be critical. The SME is likely to want to transfer the website to a different website host as fast as possible. If the transition is not handled properly, the SME will require assistance from the website host whose services are being terminated, so this should also be covered in the website hosting agreement. Other issues regarding termination of hosting services will be similar to those raised for the termination of website development services.

INTERNET ACCESS AGREEMENTS

A SME seeking access to the Internet does so through an Internet service provider ("ISP"). An ISP provides a gateway service, connecting SMEs to the Internet through the ISP's network. Additional services usually offered by an ISP include e-mail accounts and website hosting.

Terms and Conditions

The terms and conditions for a SME's Internet access are set out in the ISP's Internet access agreement. As in the case of website hosting, the Internet access agreement may also incorporate directly or by reference an AUP. The AUP in relation to Internet access usually states the ISP's ethics policy and the SME's usage conditions. The ISP's Internet access agreement and AUP are commonly found on the ISP's website.

Generally, any ISP Internet access agreement is a standard form and is often said to be non-negotiable. As such, the terms usually favour the ISP. However, depending on bargaining leverage, the SME may be able to get some concessions from the ISP.

Gatekeeper

It must be remembered that the ISP's role is Internet gatekeeper. The ISP does not have control over, or ownership of, all the facilities and communication lines necessary for access to all websites or over the content that is accessible on different websites on the Internet. Similarly, the ISP has little control over the use that its SMEs make of the Internet. On this basis, one of the main concerns of the ISP is to limit its liability as to the ability of a SME to access the Internet. The ISP will also seek to disclaim any responsibility for supervising, controlling, or editing any content that is provided by or accessed by a SME.

KEY ISSUES

Some of the key issues typically dealt with in an Internet access agreement are outlined below.

Services

The services and service levels provided by the ISP need to be defined. What is the extent of

Internet access provided by the ISP? Will the services include e mail, chat facilities, or website hosting? For the services provided, the parties need to negotiate how reliable the access will be in terms of downtime and how fast the SME can access the Internet. The speed of access depends on the ISP's equipment and on its use of techniques, such as caching. It will also depend on the SME's equipment, such as its modem speed.

SME Use

The SME's obligations in relation to the services provided by the ISP are contained in the Internet access agreement or AUP. An ISP often reserves the right to terminate the Internet access agreement with a SME should that SME breach any of its obligations for usage. Conditions that are commonly imposed include:

- Use of "netiquette": The SME is expected to be familiar with and to practise netiquette.
- Hacking: The SME is expected to not engage in activity such as seeking unauthorised access to other users' accounts (hacking), circulating unsolicited advertising (spamming), insulting other Internet users online (flaming), or knowingly spreading viruses, Trojan horses, or worms.
- Intellectual property infringement: The SME will not infringe any third party intellectual property rights.
- No unlawful acts: The SME will not engage in any unlawful acts, such as defamation or distribution of objectionable material.
- Use of ISP services: The SME is expected to use the services it is provided with appropriately. For example, if a SME has an account that provides for dial up access to the Internet only, the ISP may prohibit the SME from providing its ISP services to others using this account. If the ISP is providing an e mail account, then there may be

limits on the amount of server space that is allocated for that SME's e mail.

Payment

The ISP often provides various payment options for its services. Mechanisms most favoured by ISPs are:

- Prepaid amounts: The SME pays a set amount that entitles it to a certain amount of access time.
- Hourly or per minute rates: The SME is charged for the actual amount of time it accesses the Internet.
- Flat rate: The SME usually pays an amount each month and has unlimited access for that month.

Careful consideration of the implications of the different payment options and the SME's intended use is needed. For example, with the flat rate option, it is common for the ISP to prohibit SMEs from maintaining a permanent connection to the Internet. This may mean the SME is disconnected from the Internet every few hours.

Limitation of Liability

Much of the data that flows through the Internet is beyond the control of the ISP. Therefore, the ISP attempts to limit its liability. Apart from the usual exclusions or limitations (such as exclusion of liability for consequential losses and warranties that can be contracted out of), the ISP is also likely to seek to exclude or limit its liability for Internet specific issues. Examples of such issues include:

- privacy and security of SME information that is accessed or made available over the Internet;
- compatibility of any software provided by the ISP that is used for access to the Internet with the SME's equipment;

- viruses, worms, and Trojan horses that are transmitted over the Internet; and
- guarantees that SME Internet access will be uninterrupted or error free.

Security

An Internet access agreement often specifies the security obligations with which the SME is expected to comply. Examples of security obligations include:

- not sharing passwords or Internet access accounts;
- changing passwords on a regular basis or ad hoc, as required by the ISP; and
- using anti-virus software.

The level of security provided by the ISP is an area that a SME needs to look at closely. The ISP is unlikely to provide any warranty to the SME that it will provide adequate security measures for the protection of SME information.

Equipment to be Provided by the SME

An Internet access agreement will commonly state the equipment that is required for access and which party is expected to provide it. The SME is usually expected to provide:

- a telephone line;
- a modem; and
- computer hardware.

The ISP usually provides everything else that is required for a SME to access the Internet.

Variations

The terms and conditions for Internet access are often simply posted on the ISP's home website. It is common for the ISP to state in the agreement that it has the ability to modify any of the terms and conditions at any time at its sole discretion. This should be resisted by the SME.

Termination

Internet access agreements are typically easy to get into and out of for the SME and the ISP. The ISP often states in the agreement that it can terminate any of its services without notice or liability to the SME if the SME breaches any of the agreement's terms and conditions. Once again, the SME should be careful that its use will not provide grounds for the ISP to terminate the Internet access agreement.

CONTENT AND ADVERTISING AGREEMENTS

In the age of the Internet, content is very important. The content on a website is what differentiates one from another. One of the main reasons for the Internet's popularity is that it provides access to vast amounts of information and is an effective tool for gathering and providing information. With increasing bandwidth has come the ability to provide increasingly diversified forms of content for a website. Examples of the types of content that can now be provided on a website include text, music, sound, graphics, and video streaming.

The convergence of the telecommunications, broadcasting, media and information technology industries increases marketplace competition and creates innovation opportunities. One such opportunity is the development of strategic alliances with media companies, resulting in websites that use content from a number of different providers.

Providing Website Content

The main aim of the website is to attract potential customers. As SMEs have become more sophisticated, the type and form of the content available on the website can be what makes one business stand out from all the others.

The website's purpose also needs consideration. There is little point in having a sophisticated e-commerce enabled website if all the website does is provide information. The content must suit the potential market.

The three main ways a business can build website content are:

- create and provide the content itself;
- copy the content from other sources; and
- have third parties provide the content.

Providing Content in House

While content can be created in house, this can be time consuming and expensive.

Copying Content from Other Sources

If the content that is being copied is not in the public domain or has not been authorised (and is still within its period of copyright protection), this is infringement of another party's copyright.

Having Third Parties Provide Content

If a third party is going to provide content for a website then a content agreement is necessary to set out the rights and obligations of the content user and content provider. However, it should be kept in mind that the issues that arise for provision of content for the Internet are similar to those that arise for "bricks and mortar" business, such as magazine publishers, that use or provide content.

Advertising

Advertising is a form of content that populates many websites. As in the case of most paper based magazines, website advertising provides a useful source of revenue or is a useful medium to provide information about the goods or services offered by

a business. Although advertising has its particular issues, an advertising agreement is similar in a lot of respects to other content agreements. Although the Internet has created its own unique forms of advertising (for example, banner advertising that can be clicked on to take a user to the advertiser's website), many of the advertising issues are the same as if the advertising was not online.

There are also a number of websites that act as intermediaries between advertisers and website publishers. Advertisements are selected and placed on websites publishing the types of advertisement being offered.

KEY ISSUES: CONTENT AND ADVERTISING AGREEMENTS

Some of the key issues that need to be considered in relation to content and advertising agreements are set out below.

Form of Content

Before launching into a discussion with a content provider or advertiser, the following issues should be considered:

- What is the purpose of the website?
- Does the SME want a streamlined look to its website or a busy one full of content and advertising?
- What type of content suits the needs of the SME's target audience?
- Will advertising assist or detract from the website's purpose?

Once the SME has considered these issues, it is time to commence discussions with a content provider and/or an advertiser as to the terms and conditions of a suitable agreement.

Use of Content

The SME will need to consider why the content is being provided and the extent to which the Internet user is able to manipulate the content:

- Does the content need to be displayed in a particular form?
- Can the content on the website be combined with content provided by another content provider?

There is a need to state clearly in the content agreement exactly which types of media the content can be displayed on. Issues to be considered are:

- From where will the SME be getting the content?
- Can that content be displayed on the Internet?
- Which party bears the risk if there is a claim about misuse of the content?
- Is there a limit on the extent to which parties will be liable?

The list of questions and issues to consider depends on the SME's particular circumstances.

The content agreement should also contemplate the different platforms that can access content on the Internet. Although the Internet is mainly accessed over a wired platform consisting of many networks that are physically linked, it is possible to access the Internet over a wireless platform. Will the content agreement for display of content on the Internet cover the display of content to a mobile phone using WAP technology?

Exclusivity

The exclusivity of the arrangement will depend on whether a party wishes to limit the extent to which other content users can use the same content provided by the SME. Exclusivity can work both ways. Often a content provider wants exclusivity for a certain category of content; for example, a content provider who gives financial information to a content user may want to restrict the ability of competitors to provide information to the same content user. Conversely, the SME can enter into an exclusive arrangement with the content provider under which it is the only person with access to the content.

Intellectual Property

The use or provision of content is effectively the use or provision of intellectual property. Therefore, careful consideration needs to be given to intellectual property issues in the agreement. These include:

- ownership of pre-existing intellectual property;
- ownership of modifications to the content; and
- indemnities for third party intellectual property infringement.

These provisions need to be examined in the particular context of the use or provision of content and/or advertising in the agreement.

Look and Feel

The content agreement should cover:

- how the content is presented on the website;
- who is responsible for making sure the content is presented in the desired way;
- what brand or brands will appear and how; and
- whose brand will be associated with the content.

Delivery of Content

The content agreement should also set out the particular form or manner in which the content is to be delivered to the user.

Indemnity and Liability

What indemnities are provided by the content provider or advertiser? Who is liable if an action is brought in relation to the content? These are particularly relevant in the context of advertising when a company advertising on a website makes misleading statements or infringes intellectual property rights, or where content contains defamatory statements. Which party runs the risk of litigation? These issues need to be thought out and included in the agreement clearly.

Updates

The content agreement should state clearly:

- which party updates the content being provided; and
- how frequently those updates will occur.

The requirements for updating content are critical, because the Internet has resulted in much shorter time-frames for information provision, meaning that content can date quickly.

Quality Control

Most Internet users are subject to acceptable use policies (either from their ISP or their workplace). These content rules need to be adhered to. The rules are set up to ensure inappropriate, objectionable, or poor-quality material is not included in the content provided. While a content provider should be subject to general obligations regarding the content's suitability (such as acceptable use policies), the SME may wish to also have the explicit right to remove any material it considers offensive or objectionable.

Linking and Framing

If someone else's content is being used, linking and framing to other websites are key ways to build up the website's substance. The ability to link or frame to and from the website raises a number of legal issues that may need to be covered in a content agreement (for example, copyright infringement and trademark infringement). A discussion of these issues is beyond the scope of this chapter.

Compliance with Law

The parties to an agreement need to consider who is responsible for ensuring the content complies with any legal requirements. Given that some types of Internet banner advertising are dynamic, so constantly changing, this becomes an important issue. Although a website allocates a particular space to banner advertising, the same advertisement will not necessarily appear every time the website is accessed. In these situations, it is the advertiser, not the website owner, who should be responsible for ensuring the advertisement complies with all relevant legal requirements.

Advertisers should also be aware of various advertising guidelines contained in codes of conduct issued by the Advertising Standards Authority (ASA) and the Direct Marketing Association (DMA). These are voluntary codes that ASA and DMA members agree to abide by.

Term of Agreement

Parties need to agree on the appropriate lifespan for any content agreement. Most content agreements have a limited term, reflecting the rapid rate of change in what is being offered over the Internet. If the agreement is for a limited term, the parties should consider whether it will be subject to renewal and which party has the right of renewal.

SUMMARY AND OVERALL RECOMMENDATIONS

Any SME wanting to establish an online business presence requires agreements relating to some or all of the following: (1) website development; (2) website hosting; (3) Internet access; and (4) online content and advertising. A number of key issues arise across all these types of agreements and these include ensuring that the SME has certainty over the scope of the services and has agreed specifications in place. Other contractual issues common to the above-mentioned contracts include intellectual property rights, payment terms, liability and indemnities and termination and portability.

Specifically in relation to website development agreements, the SME needs to initially consider the following questions:

- Does the SME need a website developer, or can the SME do this itself?
- Does the SME need one service provider or two?
- Will the service provider offer all the services the SME needs?

After the SME has made a decision in respect of the questions above it needs to consider issues related to:

- design;
- development;
- project plan;
- implementation;
- acceptance testing;
- support and maintenance;
- training; and
- general contractual issues, change management procedure, warranties, subcontracting, legal review and use of a reference website.

In relation to website hosting agreements, the SME needs to initially consider which website hosting option to adopt. After this decision is made the SME needs to ensure that the issues specifically related to the website hosting agreement are addressed, including service levels, service credits, data and privacy, domain names, reporting, pricing, force majeure, access and acceptable use policies.

Specifically in respect of Internet access agreements, the SME needs to address its rights of use and security.

Finally, in relation to online content and advertising agreements the SME should initially consider how it intends to develop its website content. After this decision is made the SME should address specific issues arising from online content and advertising agreements such as the form and use of content, exclusivity, look and feel, delivery of content, updates, quality control, linking and framing and compliance with law.

REFERENCES

Alfred McAlpine Capital Projects Ltd v Tilebox Ltd, EWHC 281. (TCC 2005).

Bode, S., & Burn, J. (2001). *Consultancy engagement and e-business development: A case analysis of Australian SMEs*. A paper presented at the Global Co-Operation in the New Millennium, the 9th European Conference on Information Systems, Bled, Slovenia.

Chong, W., & Shafaghi, M. (2009). Performances of B2B e-marketplace for SMEs. *The Research Methods and Survey Results Communications of the IBIMA, 9*, 185–192.

Davydov, M. M. (2000). *E-commerce solutions for business and IT managers. Corporate portals and e-business integration.* New York, NY: McGraw Hill.

Disability Rights Commission. (2004). *The Web access and inclusion for disabled people a formal investigation conducted by Disability Rights Commission 2004.* Retrieved September 22, 2009, from http://83.137.212.42/sitearchive/drc/PDF/2.pdf

DTI (Department of Trade and Industry). (2009). *Website*. Retrieved September 22, 2009, from http://www.dti.gov.uk

Falkenstein, S. (1996). Why you should outsource the creation of your website. *Pennsylvania Certified Public Accounting Journal, December*, 9-12.

Gable, G. G. (1991). Consultant engagement for computer system selection: A pro-active client role in small businesses. *Information & Management, 20*, 83–93. doi:10.1016/0378-7206(91)90046-5

Goodman, P. & Zizmor, A. (1996). What to consider when a web site contract hits your desk: Aesthetics, ownership and portability are important issues. *Corp. Legal Times*, 30.

Gussis, G. (1998). Website development agreements: A guide to planning and drafting. *Washington University Law Quarterly, 76*(72), 721–757.

Murray, A. (2000). The use of trade marks as meta tags: Defining the boundaries. *International Journal of Law and Information Technology, 8*(3), 263–284. doi:10.1093/ijlit/8.3.263

Pobobsky, G. (1992). Small and medium enterprises and labour law. *International Labour Review, 131*(6).

Pool, P. W., Parnell, J. A., Spillan, J. E., Carraher, S., & Lester, D. L. (2006). Are SMEs meeting the challenge of integrating e-commerce into their businesses? A review of the development, challenges and opportunities. *International Journal of Information Technology and Management, 5*(2/3), 97–113.

Raysman, R., & Brown, P. (1996). Key issues in website development agreements. *New York Legal Journal*, 3.

UK Government. (1988). *Copyright.* Designs and Patent Act.

UK Government (1995). *Disability Discrimination Act.*

UK Government (1998). *Data Protection Act.*

UK Government. (2000). *Consumer protection (distance selling) regulations.*

UK Government (2002). Electronic commerce (EC directive) regulations.

Chapter 17
Electronic Surveillance, Privacy and Enforcement of Intellectual Property Rights:
A Digital Panopticon?

Pedro Pina
Polytechnic Institute of Coimbra, Portugal

ABSTRACT

In cyberworld, intellectual property rights and the right to informational self determination have become two realities in tension. Nevertheless, they are two main concerns of the e-commerce stakeholders. From the industry point of view, new digital technologies, left unregulated, may allow a free flow of information and unauthorized access to contents both from consumers or competitors; from the consumers' perspective, security and privacy concerns are the major barriers to contracting on-line. The goal of the present chapter is to understand the relationship between anti-piracy oriented private electronic surveillance and consumers' privacy. If, on the one hand, the enforcement of intellectual property is a laudable activity – since the recognition of economic exclusive rights is an incentive to artistic or scientific creation and the protection of the investments is an ICT industry's legitimate interest –, on the other hand, the individual's privacy sphere is one of the most important values and personal freedoms that law, including intellectual property law, must preserve.

INTRODUCTION

In the last years, with the emergence of information and communication technologies (ICT), digital contents have been assuming a preeminent role within the context of the knowledge economy, in general, and of the e-commerce, in particular. Nevertheless, the growth and the competitiveness

of the digital content based informational economy have been facing several obstacles: from the industry point of view, new digital technologies, left unregulated, may allow a free flow of information and unauthorized access to contents both from consumers or competitors; from the consumers' perspective, security and privacy concerns are the major barriers to contracting on-line.

However, the protection of both focuses of interests may rely on conflicting goals, which is

DOI: 10.4018/978-1-60960-765-4.ch017

perfectly drawn in the field of digital intellectual property enforcement, specifically in the cases of the on-line market of digital music, movies or software.

Intellectual property law, including patent and copyright law, was one of the bodies of law called to protect the ICT industries' legitimate interests, since a large part of digital contents like music, films, software or data bases were copyrightable or patentable. Intellectual property was seen by the industry as an adequate tool to control access to contents, since it gives the rights holders the exclusive right to use or to explore the work, excluding others from using it without authorization. But, considering the proliferation of peer-to-peer (P2P) file-sharing technology permitting the exchange of digital files and contents, and the economic loss that it causes to rights' holders, the need to preventively control access to those contents can easily be regarded as one of the main vectors of the competitiveness in the sector.

In this context, the use of tracking software or other technological measures to identify unauthorized and non-paying users of protected works or to restrict unauthorized usages has been increasing.

Undoubtedly, controlling the access to or the usages of protected contents is a right of the rights' holders and, in an economic perspective, a factor of security and of competiveness advantage. However, the use of technological protection measures (TPM) may have serious impacts on users' privacy. In fact, amongst other powers, digital rights management (DRM) systems give the rights' holders the power to control access to protected works, to restrict unauthorised reproduction and possibly other usages of such works, to identify the works, the relevant rights' holders or even some of the users' identification data.

This means that the holders of rights over digital content protected under intellectual property laws may electronically survey users' behaviors and invade their privacy.

The collision between digital intellectual property and privacy is a reality, which is to say that, considering the constitutional basis of both rights, industry's and consumers' concerns need to achieve a balanced but not a manichean answer.

In fact, if, on the one hand, the enforcement of intellectual property is a praiseworthy activity – since the recognition of economic exclusive rights is an incentive to artistic or scientific creation and the protection of the investments is an ICT industry's legitimate interest –, on the other hand, the individual's privacy sphere is one of the most important values and personal freedoms that law, including intellectual property law, must preserve.

The goal of the present chapter is to understand the relationship between anti-piracy oriented private electronic surveillance and consumers' privacy, to analyze the most important case law and court decisions on the matter and to describe some future trends regarding the need to conciliate both fundamental rights.

PRIVATE AND ANTI-PIRACY ELECTRONIC SURVEILLANCE:

Toward a Digital *Panopticon*?

Generally, intellectual property law gives rights' holders the exclusive rights to use and to explore their works, excluding others from its unauthorized consumption or exploitation. Traditionally, in cases of intellectual property infringement, rights' holders have the right to sue infringers in public courts. This protection is reactive and localized, since national courts' jurisdiction and competence are territorially confined and limited by territorial sovereignty.

If the shortly described public enforcement mechanism is acceptable in the analogical world, it seems feeble in a digital context. In fact, digital technologies allow not only to make perfect copies of works massively but also to disseminate them world widely through the internet. Consequently, digitization had an inevitable impact on intellectual property.

Initially, from the users' perspective, the cyber world seemed to be totally independent from the analogical world. According to Boyle (1997),

"[f]or a long time, the Internet's enthusiasts have believed that it would be largely immune from state regulation. It was not so much that nation states would not want to regulate the Net, it was that they would be unable to do so; forestalled by the technology of the medium, the geographical distribution of its users and the nature of its content. This tripartite immunity came to be a kind of Internet Holy Trinity, faith in it was a condition of acceptance into the community".

Consequently, in this libertarian context and perspective, concepts like property or regulation were dimmed. Since information seemed to flow freely throughout the internet, consumers of digital works may possibly act as free riders, choosing neither to pay nor to contribute for their production. That is to say that, from an economic point of view, digital contents, as informational and immaterial goods, are public goods. In fact, the consumption of an informational good by one person doesn't exclude the possibility of consumption by others, which means that they are non-rivaled goods; and, without regulation, no one can be excluded from using the good, which means that they are non-excludable goods. These characteristics are emphasized in the digital world as the positive externalities created by the free flow of copyrighted content information increase disproportionately, to the disadvantage of creators and rights' holders. That is the general justification for public regulation of the intellectual creations' market where intellectual property law is presented as an instrument used to create scarcity, since it gives the rights' holders the economic exclusive of the works' exploitation, excluding others from it without proper authorization. But, as it had to adapt to the challenges revealed by successive technological developments, whether we are referring to the invention of the printing press,

audio or video-recorders or the internet, today intellectual property also needs to be adjusted to the new forms of digital usages and infractions. In the first times of the digital challenge, taking into account the amount of uncontrolled, unauthorized and globally disseminated illegal utilizations, intellectual property law and public judiciary enforcement seemed to be an anachronic and inefficient framework to protect the interests of the rights' holders. For that reason, TPM started being developed to digitally control access to works and to enclosure information, but soon circumvention devices showed the insufficiency of electronic fences. As so, ICT industrial sector needed to find a new robust and harmonized legal framework that could protect its activity and investments and, at the same time, that could be combined with TPM; which is to say that traditional intellectual property law, created to protect works in an analogical and localized world, had to be re-invented so that, in the first place, it could be combined with the use of TPM and DRM, and, secondly, it could be a harmonized regulation all over the world. With these purposes, the industry started lobbying toward a strengthened, expanded and harmonized intellectual property framework. It achieved its intents as, at the international level, the Agreement on Trade Related Aspects of Intellectual Property Rights (TRIPS), the World Intellectual Property Organization (WIPO) Copyright Treaty and the WIPO Performances and Phonograms Treaty came into force, or, at the regional or national levels, the Digital Millennium Copyright Act (DMCA), in the USA, or the Information Society Directive (InfoSoc Directive), in the European Union. In all the mentioned legal texts, the use of TPM is recognized as a means to the potentiate DRM. This means that the law recognizes private enforcement and self-help systems based on TPM. Furthermore, circumvention acts, the creation or dissemination of circumvention devices are forbidden and punished as criminal offenses. As Werra (2001) states, *"copyright owners have three levels of cumulative protection: the first is the legal protection by copyright. The second level is the technical protection of works through measures protection techniques. The third level is the new legal protection against circumvention of technological protection measures introduced by the WIPO Treaties"* (p. 77).

If the use of TPM and DRM is acceptable considering the losses of the industry, nonetheless they have a potential intrusive effect on the users' private sphere.

In fact, as Cohen (1997) warns,

"Leading recent surveys of developments in the field of "rights management" describe the capabilities of an ideal system as follows: detecting, preventing, and counting a wide range of operations, including open, print, export, copying, modifying, excerpting, and so on; maintaining records indicating which permissions have actually been granted and to whom; capturing a record of what the user actually looked at, copied or printed; and sending this usage record to the clearinghouse when the user seeks additional access, at the end of a billing period or whenever the user runs out of credit. In addition, the system operator could manipulate this acquired data to generate predictive profiles of particular consumers for use in future marketing activities, or for sale to other vendors" (pp. 186-187).

Given the structure of the Internet and the World Wide Web (WWW), all the navigation leaves a digital track that can be used to reconstitute the actions of the users (without his/her knowledge or consent), like the sites he/she has visited, the downloads or uploads that have been made, the e-mail messages that were sent and received, amongst other actions.

Taking those technologic possibilities into account, several authors have pointed out that the architecture of cyberspace - especially of the

peer-to-peer (P2P) structures - closely resembles the *Panopticon* imagined by Bentham and recovered by Michel Foucault.

Even though Foucault did not directly addressed the subject, his writings on the disciplinary society have been used as a major reference for the study of electronic control and surveillance in the digital environment.

The *Panopticon* was an ideal type of a prison imagined by the English utilitarian philosopher Jeremy Bentham. According to him, the panoptic structure is based on a central watchtower encircled by a peripheral ring divided into cells facing the centre. As the cells were backlit from the outside, all the prisoners could be seen by those standing in the watchtower. However, the guards in the centre couldn't be seen because of the use of venetian blinds on the towers' windows. This way, in the ring, one is totally seen; at the same time, in the watchtower, one is never seen. By dissociating the see/being seen binomial, this scenario creates in the prisoners' minds the feeling of being permanently controlled even when the guards are actually standing in the tower.

From the Bentham's proposal, Foucault conceptualized the disciplinary society based on the panopticism. According to him,

"disciplinary power [...] is exercised through its invisibility; at the same time it imposes on those whom it subjects a principle of compulsory visibility. In discipline, it is the subjects who have to be seen. Their visibility assures the hold of the power that is exercised over them. It is the fact of being constantly seen, of being able always to be seen, that maintains the disciplined individual in his subjection" (Foucault, 1977, p. 187).

On a digital environment, a panoptic structure is perfectly achievable. Particularly in the cases of digital intellectual property infringements, it should be noted that they occur mainly in P2P networks. The technology and the architecture of these networks clearly permit the adoption of a panoptic surveillance and control mechanism. P2P software enables a computer to find files directly on the hard drive of another network connected device without the need for central servers. This way, each user can be a consumer and a supplier at the same time. In a decentralized network like this, the boundaries between what is public and what is private grow fainter given the consented access to the hard disk of the computer, and, therefore, the number of potential invasions increases rapidly.

As in the Panopticon, on an online environment, specifically in a P2P network, one user cannot or may not know when another one is accessing to the contents stored on his/her computer. The digital panopticism is thus a behaviors detection system mediated by the use of digital technology, primarily on an online environment, characterized by the fact that there might have been not just a hyper-vigilant (a role that, traditionally, fits the government and that, in Orwell's novel *1984*, is personalized in the Big Brother), but many Little Brothers, individuals or private entities, peers of the observed user, moved by curiosity or by the defense of their material interests.

In this context, given the extent of illegal file-sharing of copyrighted or patented works and the inefficient reaction of public enforcement mechanisms, the private enforcement technology-based strategy turned very attractive for rights' holders.

However, what could be justified as a defensive mechanism, revealed itself an intrusive and, sometimes, disproportioned means. As Katyal (2004a) states,

"the problem of piracy has led some private entities to respond even more forcefully than necessary, seeking to destroy not only the peer-to-peer networks that have sprouted across the Internet, but the very boundaries of privacy, anonymity, and autonomy in cyberspace".

TPM and DRM may, in fact, enable right's holders to trace and to monitor internet users whether they are infringers or no. Though copyright is currently considered a human right, its exercise is not absolute, since it must respect other rights of similar importance or at the same hierarchical level. The balance between intellectual property enforcement and the respect for online users' privacy is precisely one of the issues that need a proper and broad discussion.

The Right to Privacy and to Informational Self-Determination

The development of ICT has promoted a cornucopia of data digital transmission and communication that can be easily observed, collected and controlled, considering the electronic trail that online users leave.

Consequently, as Canotilho & Moreira (2007) state,

"safeguards against the treatment and misuse of computerized personal data are becoming increasingly important [since] their tense relationship with various fundamental rights, freedoms and guarantees (development of the personality, personal dignity, private life) is unquestionable" (pp. 550-551).

In this sense, some Constitutions have been predicting the right to communicational and informational self-determination as a fundamental right with a larger scope of protection than the right to privacy. The term was first used in December of 1983 by the Germany Federal Constitutional Court (BVerfGE, 1983) ruling that

"in the context of modern data processing, the protection of the individual against unlimited collection, storage, use and disclosure of his/her personal data is encompassed by the general personal rights constitutional provisions. This basic right warrants in this respect the capacity of the individual to determine in principle the disclosure and use of his/her personal data";

and defining it as "the authority of the individual to decide himself, on the basis of the idea of self-determination, when and within what limits information about his private life should be communicated to others".

This right is, thus, conceptualized not only as a mere guarantee of the right to privacy, but as a true fundamental right with an independent meaning, conceived

"for the protection of new facets of personality – it is a right of personality – and consisting in the recognition of the freedom to control the use of information respecting to it (if it is personal), and in the protection against attacks arising from the use of such information" (Castro, 2005, pp. 65 ss).

The right to communicational and informational self-determination displays two intrinsically linked dimensions. The first one, with a defensive nature, just like the guarantee for the secrecy of correspondence and of other means of private communication, is built as a negative right, protecting the holder against interference by the State and by individuals who are responsible for processing digital or analogical data or others. The second dimension shows a positive right and a true fundamental freedom, "a right to dispose of your own personal information, a power of controlling it and from which exercise you may determine what others can, at every moment, know about your respect" (Castro, 2006, p. 16).

This conception goes beyond the traditional United States law understanding of the right to privacy as "the right to be left alone" (Warren & Brandeis, 1890), imposing opacity to the others. As a consequence, in the American conception of privacy, an individual only has a right to action in cases of commitment of tortious acts. As Garcia (2005) summarizes, in face of the Restatement (second) of torts § 652a (1977),

"This invasion of privacy is generally understood to mean one of four invasions: «(a) unreasonable intrusion upon the seclusion of another, . . . (b) appropriation of the other's name or likeness, . . . (c) unreasonable publicity given to the other's private false light before the public»" (pp. 1238-1239).

This solution is clearly satisfactory for those who defend a market regulation of privacy. In the USA, where that conception prevails, apart from the government regulation of specific sectors like the protection of children online, all the procedures for collecting, keeping or transferring consumer's data are left to the industry self-regulation. The Federal Trade Commission (FTC), an independent agency of the USA government, whose main mission is the promotion of consumer protection, has an important role on promoting fair privacy policies. Besides that, the FCT only has the power

"to prosecute firms whose practices are at variance with their policy disclosures for engaging in a deceptive trade practice. However, Web sites are not required to post any disclosures, and without a posted privacy policy, the FTC has no basis for acting under its current authority" (Culnan, 2000, p. 25).

In the aforementioned conception of privacy, in the absence of public regulation imposing duties to the industry, online consumers may not have the information or the powers to control what personal information is collected, how it is collected, how it will be used, if it will be disclosed or transferred to third parties, amongst other usages.

On the contrary, the right to communicational and informational self-determination gives an individual the power to control all the possible usages of his/her personal data.

That right is recognized in the European Union (EU) as a true fundamental right, connected to the development of the personality of each individual, in article 8 of the EU Charter of Fundamental rights, where it is foreseen that:

1. *Everyone has the right to the protection of personal data concerning him or her.*
2. *Such data must be processed fairly for specified purposes and on the basis of the consent of the person concerned or some other legitimate basis laid down by law. Everyone has the right of access to data which has been collected concerning him or her, and the right to have it rectified.*
3. *Compliance with these rules shall be subject to control by an independent authority.*

The Charter was influenced by the European Convention on Human Rights and by the jurisprudence from the European Court of Human Rights. In fact, as Rouvroy & Poullet (2007) state,

"[a]ccording to the Strasbourg jurisprudence the State is not merely under the obligation to abstain from interfering with individuals' privacy, but also to provide individuals with the material conditions needed to allow them to effectively implement their right to private and family life. In other words, [...] States are under the obligation to take all appropriate measures in order to protect fundamental rights of the individuals including against infringements by other non-state parties" (pp. 20-21).

On the EU derivative law level, three directives can be highlighted: 1) Directive 95/46/EC of the European Parliament and of the Council of 24 October 1995 on the protection of individuals with regard to the processing of personal data and on the free movement of such data; 2) Directive 2002/58/EC of the European Parliament and of the Council of 12 July 2002 concerning the processing of personal data and the protection of privacy in the electronic communications sector (Directive on privacy and electronic communications); and 3) Directive 2000/31/EC of the European Parlia-

ment and of the Council of 8 June 2000 on certain legal aspects of information society services, in particular electronic commerce, in the Internal Market ('Directive on electronic commerce).

From the above mentioned directives, it can be concluded that, in the European Union, the activity of electronic collecting and computer processing of personal data is regulated according to standards that embody the following principles: (a) the principle of lawful collecting, according to which collecting and processing of data constitute a restriction on the holder's informational self-determination and are only permitted within the parameters of the law and, particularly, with the holder's knowledge and consent, (b); the finality principle, meaning that the data collection and the data processing can only be made with a clear, specific and socially acceptable finality that must be identifiable right at the moment of the gathering; (c) the principle of objective limitation, as the use of the collected data must be restricted to the purposes that were communicated to the holder in the moment of the collection, and must respect the ideas of proportionality, necessity and adequacy, (d) the principle of temporal limitation, meaning that data shall not be kept by more than the time needed to achieve the justificative finality (e) the principle of data quality, according to which the collected data must be correct and up to date, (f) the principle of the free access to data by its subject, who must be able to know the existence of the collection and the storage of his/her personal data and to rectify, erasure or block the information if incomplete and inaccurate; and (g) the security principle, under which the controller must implement appropriate technical and organizational measures to protect personal data against accidental or unlawful destruction or accidental loss, alteration, unauthorized disclosure or access, in particular where the processing involves the transmission of data over a network.

IDENTIFYING ONLINE INFRINGERS:

A Cat and Mouse Game

The online digital communication is based on codes and protocols. Thereby, even when intrusive tracking software is spread through the network and a digital trail left by a user, alleged intellectual property infringer, is found, the watcher can only, at the most, identify an IP address. The identification of the user can only be made through the Internet service providers (ISP). These are the ones who, given the contractual relationships established with the users, are in a better position to give a name to the user behind the IP address. In fact,

"ISPs have developed into a relatively new form of governance in cyberspace because they maintain a substantial amount of private, consumer information regarding users' online activities, and because they often control the transmission and distribution of requested information. For these reasons, many consider the ISP the principal repository for all identifying information regarding individual users and their Web activities" (Katyal, 2004a, p. 311).

Some laws related to e-commerce or other online activities tend to assign an important role to ISPs. A good example of the mentioned solution is the Directive 2001/29/EC of the European Parliament and of the Council of 22 May 2001 on the harmonisation of certain aspects of copyright and related rights in the information society (InfoSoc Directive). On its recital (59), it is declared that

"[i]n the digital environment, in particular, the services of intermediaries may increasingly be used by third parties for infringing activities. In many cases such intermediaries are best placed to bring such infringing activities to an end. Therefore, without prejudice to any other sanctions and remedies available, rightholders should have the possibility of applying for an injunction against an
intermediary who carries a third party's infringement of a protected work or other subject-matter in a network".

Considering the above mentioned, rights' holders depend on the ISPs to act against online infringers. Nevertheless, ISPs didn't have a collaborative reaction, keeping the anonymity of its clients. As a consequence, the industry started looking for possible means to hold ISPs responsible for intellectual property infringements and to oblige them to survey and monitor their clients' behaviors.

In the United States of America, the Congress, by the 1998's Online Copyright Infringement Liability Limitation Act (corresponding to the Title II of the DMCA added to the Copyright Act, Section 512), established the possibility of ISPs' and others online service providers (OSP) being liable for copyright infringing acts of their clients. However, foresees that liability may be excluded in the next four cases, commonly known as safe harbors: (1) transmitting, routing, and providing connections to infringing material; (2) system caching; (3) storing infringing material at the direction of a user; and (4) linking or referring users to infringing material. But, to apply for the referred exemptions, OSPs, including ISPs, must follow notice and take down procedures that provide that when a copyright owner becomes aware of infringing material or infringing activity residing or taking place on a service provider's system or network that copyright owner may notify the service provider of the infringement and require the service provider remove or disable access to the infringing material or activity (Oktay & Wrenn, 1999, p. 6).

Consequently, if OSPs and ISPs want to be exempted from liability, they will have, in the first place, to survey the contents that were uploaded or transmitted by their customers, whether those are legitimate or not. However, considering the architecture of P2P networks, specially the fact that unauthorized storage of digital works is made on the users' computers rather than on ISPs' servers, their liability turned a controversial issue even outside the safe harbors provisions.

In 2005, in *MGM Studios, Inc. vs. Grokster, Ltd.*, the US Supreme Court decided that Grokster and Streamcast, both P2P file sharing companies, could be liable for inducing copyright infringements.

Although the defendants proved that the file-sharing technology permitted legitimate uses - particularly in the cases when one shares non-copyrighted content – invoking *Sony Betamax* case decision, the Court held inapplicable the alleged precedent, and considered the existence of inducement or incitement to breach of copyright, "holding that one who distributes a device with the object of promoting its use to infringe copyright, as shown by clear expression or other affirmative steps taken to foster infringement, is liable for the resulting acts of infringement by third parties"(545 U.S. 913, 2005).

In the end, the Supreme Court did not give an answer the fundamental question of controversy, clinging to the fact that, in this case, Grokster attracted customers by presenting itself as the successor to Napster - the until then most popular network of illegal file sharing, though this one didn't use P2P software, storing the files in a central server from where they could be downloaded - but making use of new technology (P2P) allegedly not illegal. Therefore, it remained to future clarification the issue concerning the application of traditional doctrines of indirect liability - the vicarious liability and contributory infringement - in the field of P2P, which has caused, so far, uncertainty and insecurity in copyright's enforcement. Because of that, for caution, some ISPs started to implement technological measures so that they could filter and control users' files containing unauthorized works; and other ISPs started making themselves digital contents available after agreements with rights' holders.

After the decision, Grokster stopped offering its peer-to-peer file sharing service and displayed the following message in its website (www.grokster.com): "The United States Supreme Court unanimously confirmed that using this service to trade copyrighted material is illegal. Copying copyrighted motion picture and music files using unauthorized peer-to-peer services is illegal and is prosecuted by copyright owners. [...] Your IP address is [...] and has been logged. Don't think you can't get caught. You are not anonymous".

Furthermore, considering that the industry itself had been using tracking software and web crawlers to identify IP addresses' of potential infringers, it started suing ISPs based on Section 512(h) do Copyright Act, where it is foreseen that "[a] copyright owner or a person authorized to act on the owner's behalf may request the clerk of any United States district court to issue a subpoena to a service provider for identification of an alleged infringer in accordance with this subsection".

RIAA vs. Verizon was a leading case on this matter. In 2002, The Recording Industry Association of America (RIAA) asked Verizon, an ISP, to reveal the identity of one of its subscribers who allegedly made available online through the P2P file-sharing network Kazaa more than 600 copyrighted music files.

Verizon refused to identify the user, alleging that the disclosure of personal data would violate the subscriber's privacy. Moreover, according to Verizon's understanding the subpoena covered only the cases where files were stored in its central servers and not in their clients' personal computers. As Katyal (2004b) observed,

"[g]iven the fact that almost everyone can be a copyright owner in cyberspace, Verizon contended that the RIAA's construction would result in a world where anyone who wants to assert copyright infringements may do so and obtain the identity of another person through the DMCA's subpoena power. The result would potentially expose the identity of anyone in cyberspace" (p.283)

Nevertheless, RIAA had an initial victory as the D. C. Circuit Court granted RIAA's motion to enforce its subpoena, and ordered Verizon to comply with it and to disclosure the users' identities.

Afterward, the D. C. Circuit of Appeals overruled that decision and vacated the order enforcing the subpoena, considering that the DMCA did not provide for the disclosure of information stored in the subscribers' computers and that, consequently, the only measure that could be adopted by Verizon was suspending the internet service for the internet connection. However, such solution was not provided by the Copyright Act.

According to the Electronic Frontier Foundation, during the period between the two decisions, the RIIA notified several ISPs for more than 3000 times, which resulted in more than 400 prosecutions against the revealed subscribers.

It turns out that, among those who had their identities revealed and their files surveyed by private entities, some were online users and file-sharers acting legitimately. The Sara Ward's case became famous. This sexagenarian woman, after being incorrectly identified, was sued by Sony Music Entertainment, Inc., BMG Music, Virgin Records America, Inc., Interscope Records, Atlantic Recording Corporation, Warner Brothers Records, Inc., and Arista Records, Inc., for the illegal sharing of more than 2000 songs, seeking a compensation of U.S. $ 150 000 per work, though she had never downloaded or shared files on the Internet. Although subsequently the lawsuit was withdrawn, the right to informational self determination of Sara Ward was clearly violated in face of the disproportionate law enforcement strategy.

In the EU, the Article 8, paragraph 1, of the Directive 2004/48/EC of the European Parliament and the Council of 29 April 2004 on the enforcement of intellectual property rights ("Enforcement" Directive) is particularly relevant in this matter, as it states that

"Member States shall ensure that, in the context of proceedings concerning an infringement of an intellectual property right and in response to a justified and proportionate request of the claimant, the competent judicial authorities may order that information on the origin and distribution networks of the goods or services which infringe an intellectual property right be provided by the infringer and/or any other person who:

(a) was found in possession of the infringing goods on a commercial scale;

(b) was found to be using the infringing services on a commercial scale;

(c) was found to be providing on a commercial scale services used in infringing activities; or

(d) was indicated by the person referred to in point (a), (b) or (c) as being involved in the production, manufacture or distribution of the goods or the provision of the services".

This right to information is essential to ensure the high level of protection of intellectual property that was the purpose of the Directive, and is absolutely necessary to identify the infringer. This right is not unlimited however: in paragraph 3 of that same article it is foreseen, amongst other circumstances, the possibility of liability for abuse of the right to information (c) or the protection of confidentiality of information sources or the processing of personal data (e). Actually, the concern that the EU has about the protection of personal data is clearly manifested in recital 2 of the "Enforcement" Directive, where it is assumed that although the protection of intellectual property should allow the inventor or creator to derive a legitimate profit from his invention or creation and to allow the widest possible dissemination of works, ideas and new know-how, "[a]t the same time, it should not hamper freedom of expression, the free movement of information, or the protection of personal data".

If the main principle is categorically recognized, its concretization is an open task left to national legislators. Those are the ones who need to find the delicate balance between intellectual property enforcement and the right to informational self determination.

Moreover, the Infosoc Directive provides in Article 8, paragraph 3, that "Member States shall ensure that rightholders are in a position to apply for an injunction against intermediaries whose services are used by a third party to infringe a copyright or related right".

In face of such legislation, the industry in the EU has been using methods similar to those used by the RIAA. National courts diverge, however, over the boundaries of their conduct's legality and the extent of admissible enforcement measures.

In Italy, the German record company Peppermint Jaw hired the Swiss firm Logistep to develop a tracking software able to identify the IP addresses of copyright infringers. It managed identify the IP address of 3636 suspects of illegal file sharing of music from the repertoire of Peppermint. Initially, the Court of Rome addressed an injunction to the ISP identify the subscribers in question. With such support, Peppermint notified the identified users, asking them to pay € 330 for each shared work. Nevertheless, in 2007, in a similar case, the Court of Rome decided in the opposite way and stated that the disclosure of users' personal data would result in the violation of their right to privacy in communications, and argued that the enforcement of copyright is not strong enough to sacrifice that fundamental right.

In the Republic of Ireland, in 07.06.2007, the High Court, deciding a civil injunction process, ordered 6 ISPs, Digiweb, Smart Telecom, Irish Broadband, NTL, Eircom and Imagine, to reveal the names and addresses of 23 people whose IPs the Irish Recorded Music Association (IRMA) investigated.

In France, in 23.05.2007 the *Conseil d'État* revoked a decision from the *Commission Nationale de l'Informatique et des Libertés* (CNIL), according to which this commission had refused to give an authorization to four collective management societies for the use of digital devices that could automatically detect breaches of the *Code de la*

Propriété Intellectuelle and forward messages to Internet users. The CNIL understood that those devices constituted disproportional measures considering the pursued goals:

"They are not designed just to implement occasional actions strictly limited to the specific needs of the fight against counterfeiting; they may lead to a massive collection of personal data; they provide an exhaustive and continuous surveillance over the P2P networks" (2005).

The *Conseil d'État* has modified that decision, affirming that the CNIL had erred in assessing the applicable law, including the weighting of proportionality, considering on the one hand, the quantitative dimension of copyright infringements on the Internet, and, on the other hand, that the survey related only to users who shared or provided copyrighted works up from a certain number. Later on, the *Cour d'appel* de Paris held that IP addresses should not be qualified as personal data and, consequently, they were not protected under the right to privacy or to informational self-determination, personal as, *per se*, they don't identify the person behind them.

This understanding clearly diverges from the generalized idea that IP addresses must be considered personal data. In this matter, it is highly recommendable the Opinion 4/2007 on the concept of personal data, from the Working Party set up under Article 29 of Directive 95/46/EC:

"[t]he Working Party has considered IP addresses as data relating to an identifiable person. It has stated that "Internet access providers and managers of local area networks can, using reasonable means, identify Internet users to whom they have attributed IP addresses as they normally systematically "log" in a file the date, time, duration and dynamic IP address given to the Internet user. The same can be said about Internet Service Providers that keep a logbook on the HTTP server. In these cases there is no doubt about the fact that one can

talk about personal data in the sense of Article 2 a) of the Directive. Especially in those cases where the processing of IP addresses is carried out with the purpose of identifying the users of the computer (for instance, by Copyright holders in order to prosecute computer users for violation of intellectual property rights), the controller anticipates that the "means likely reasonably to be used" to identify the persons will be available e.g. through the courts appealed to (otherwise the collection of the information makes no sense), and therefore the information should be considered as personal data" (Article 29 data protection working party, 2007, p. 16).

In the Netherlands, a high court acquitted an ISP from an injunction requested by BREIN, an association representing the dutch recording industry and movie studios, to disclosure the identity of an alleged infringer. The court began by declaring the BREIN's private research mechanism, based on a computer program created by U.S. firm Media-Sentry, unreliable, inaccurate and intrusive, as it sought personal files on users' computers by name and not by its content, disregarding the existence of suspicions of infringement. It therefore ruled that this practice did not comply with legislation designed to protect the researched personal data.

The question of ISP filtering on P2P traffic has also jurisprudential reflexes. In Belgium, the *Sabam v Scarlet* case became famous as the court held Scarlet liable for copyright infringement, because it had allowed its subscribers to share copyrighted works illegally in its P2P. Furthermore, the court ruled that Scarlet should use a software application designed by Audible Magic for the filtering of protected files.

The Court was not sensitive to the Scarlet' arguments according to which no technical measures can distinguish the legality from illegality of the work, as that activity implies a personalized normative and valorative interpretation; that the use of filters will eventually block access to legal files; and that with the imposed measure the ISPs

goes beyond the role of a mere intermediary or transporter of data. Furthermore, if, on the one hand, the Directive on privacy and electronic communications admits in its article 4, paragraph 1, the adoption of filtering measures to safeguard security of ISPs' own services, on the other hand, as it is foreseen in Article 5, confidentiality of electronic communications must be ensured, and in particular by prohibiting "listening, tapping, storage or other kinds of interception or surveillance of communications and the related traffic data by persons other than users, without the consent of the users concerned", except when those actions are legally authorized in accordance with Article 15(1)", as they are necessary for the prevention, investigation, detection and prosecution of criminal offences or of unauthorized use of the electronic communication system.

At the community judiciary level, one of the most important cases related to the discussion on the balance between intellectual property enforcement and privacy was Case C-275/06. In this case *Promusicae* asked the ISP *Telefonica de España* to reveal personal data on their users in order to enable the latter to, in the future, bring civil law charges against the detected intellectual property rights' infringers. As, under Spanish law ISPs only have to reveal personal data to state judiciary authorities in cases of criminal investigations and prosecutions, The Spanish court (*Juzgado de lo Mercantil n.º 5 de Madrid*) wanted to know from the EU Court of Justice if that material restriction is in conformity with EU law.

Advocate-General Juliane Kokott, concluded that it is compatible with Community law for Member States to exclude the communication of personal traffic data for the purpose of bringing civil proceedings against copyright infringements, and declared that

"126. Should the Community consider that more far-reaching protection of the holders of copyrights is necessary, that would require an amendment of the provisions on data protection. Up to now,

however, the legislature has not yet taken that step. On the contrary, in adopting Directives 2000/31, 2001/29 and 2004/48, it provided for the unaltered continued applicability of data protection and saw no reason, when adopting the sector-specific Directives 2002/58 and 2006/24, to introduce restrictions of data protection in favour of the protection of intellectual property.

127. Directive 2006/24 could, on the contrary, lead to a strengthening of data protection under Community law with regard to disputes concerning infringements of copyright. The question then arises, even in criminal investigations, as to the extent to which it is compatible with the fundamental right to data protection under Community law to grant aggrieved rightholders access to the results of the investigation if the latter are based on the evaluation of retained traffic data within the meaning of Directive 2006/24. Up to now that question is not affected by Community law since the Data Protection Directives do not apply to the prosecution of criminal offences" (CJEC, 2007).

In the end, the Court decided that EU law does not require the Member States to lay down, in a situation such as that *sub judice*, an obligation to communicate personal data in order to ensure effective protection of copyright in the context of civil proceedings.

Concerning the ISPs or OSPs' liability for copyright damages committed by their clients, Directive 2000/31/CE of the European Parliament and of the Council of 8 June 2000 on certain legal aspects of information society services, in particular electronic commerce, in the Internal Market (Directive on electronic commerce) though it predicts that Member States shall not impose a general obligation on providers to monitor the information which they transmit or store, nor a general obligation actively to seek facts or circumstances indicating illegal activity, foresees their liability for the transmission or the storage of illegal contents, except in cases of mere conduit,

caching or hosting, if the conditions of articles 12, 13 and 14 are respected.

Moreover, as it is recognized in recital 45,

"limitations of the liability of intermediary service providers established in this Directive do not affect the possibility of injunctions of different kinds; such injunctions can in particular consist of orders by courts or administrative authorities requiring the termination or prevention of any infringement, including the removal of illegal information or the disabling of access to it".

In fact, rights' holders have today in the EU two different legal ways to make an online infringement stop: through a court decision or through a communications regulatory authority administrative decision (with possible appeal to a court).

Whether is chosen one way or another, it is important to ensure that the weighting and the comparison between the two colliding rights is casuistically made. This way, avoiding theoretical discussions about the dignity of both rights, it will be possible to a public decisory and impartial entity to conclude about the extension of the damages that will be caused and of the sacrifices imposed upon each right.

NEW TRENDS

From the above exposed, it can be easily concluded that whether a market regulation or a state regulation perspective is adopted, the doctrine and the judicial practice have been revealing similar law application problems as both right to privacy or to informational self determination and intellectual property rights are fundamental to the development of the individuals and of the society.

If the enforcement of intellectual property rights is faced as an absolute goal, then, as Katyal (2004b) affirms, *"compared to real space, where property rights tended to serve as a shield from harm, property rights in cyberspace serve to form the basis for a host of potentially offensive strategies that have deleterious implications for privacy, anonymity, and freedom of expression" (p. 224).*

If privacy is enshrined as an absolute value, intellectual property infringements in cyberspace will remain unpunished, with clear disadvantage for creative creation, for culture diversity, for the knowledge economy and to the e-commerce that is based on digital creative and informational contents.

At least, there was one solution that seemed relatively consensual: intellectual property could only trump privacy and justify access to personal data if the infringements constituted criminal offenses.

The proposed directive on criminal measures aimed at ensuring the enforcement of intellectual property rights establishes that Member States shall consider all intentional infringements of an intellectual property right on a commercial scale as a criminal offence. According to this proposal, infringements on a commercial scale are defined as any infringement of an intellectual property right committed to obtain commercial advantage; therefore, acts committed by private users for personal and non-profitable use shall not be considered criminal offences though they may held civil liability.

Therefore, only unauthorized uses of copyrighted works that constitute criminal offences shall be sufficiently strong to base measures that may conflict with other fundamental rights such as the right to informational self-determination. This adaptation of the principle *de minimis non curat lex* seems to be the most consistent with the principle of objective limitation of personal data's collection and storage.

Nevertheless, from the right to informational self determination perspective, France has adopted recently a repressive and highly controversial

solution as the HADOPI law came into force. This law establishes a government agency called *Haute Autorité pour la Diffusion des Oeuvres et la Protection des Droits sur Internet* (Hadopi) that will have powers to order ISPs to suspend or block internet access of copyright infringers up to a year. That measure is the third of the so-called three strikes response: before it is taken, in a preventive phase, Hadopi should send two informative communications warning the infringer of its legal obligations and of the penalties for further infringements. In the original version of the Hadopi law proposal, it wasn't foreseen the possibility of appealing to a court when the suspension decision was taken. After being declared unconstitutional, that part was altered and, today, that appeal is foreseen.

The controversy around the Hadopi law has several facets related to the sanction itself has access to the internet is tended to be recognized as a fundamental right, but also related to information self determination. In fact, Hadopi will have to collect information related to all file sharing traffic in France and to ISPs subscribers' behaviors. Only after that collection – potentially done without the knowledge and the expressed consent of individuals –, data will be qualified and recorded to future actions. This means that, if in the qualification phase, the collected data is considered irrelevant for the purposes of the law, right to informational self determination will be violated for nothing. This repressive answer, though it can be efficient from an intellectual property law enforcement perspective, may however reveal disproportioned sacrifices to privacy.

There are alternative proposals to overcome the conflict between intellectual property enforcement and the right to information self determination. One of the most relevant consists in turning the problem around and is based on new business models where P2P file sharing is completely legal as users obtain a global license in exchange for a fee on broadband Internet subscriptions. It is a criticized solution as it imposes the inclusion of all works in the system, even against the will of their creator; there are no reliable methods for the distribution of the money raised to artists; internet users would have to pay the contribution even if they were not file sharers.

At the present time, there is no mature and solid legal solution able to conciliate all the interests at stake: solutions like the one established by the Hadopi law are not acceptable from a privacy concerned point of view; and a revolutionary Copernican change erasing rights' holders exclusive rights is not realistic (at least for now). The future will certainly bring clarity to the discussion.

REFERENCES

Article 29 data protection working party. (2007). *On the concept of personal data.* Retrieved September 25, 2009, from http://www.droit-technologie.org/upload/actuality/doc/1063-1.pdf

Boyle, J. (1997). *Foucault in cyberspace: Surveillance, sovereignty, and hard-wired censors.* Retrieved September 15, 2009, from http://www.law.duke.edu/boylesite/foucault.htm

Bverf, G. E. (1983). *1BVerfGE 65, 1 – Volkszählung Urteil des Ersten Senats vom 15. Dezember 1983 auf die mündliche Verhandlung vom 18. und 19. Oktober 1983 - 1 BvR 209, 269, 362, 420, 440, 484/83 in den Verfahren über die Verfassungsbeschwerden.* Retrieved September 25, 2009, from http://www.servat.unibe.ch/dfr/bv065001.html.

Canotilho, J. J. G., & Moreira, V. (2007). *Constituição da República Portuguesa anotada* (4th ed.). Coimbra: Coimbra Editora.

Castro, C. S. E. (2005). O direito à autodeterminação informativa e os novos desafios gerados pelo direito à liberdade e à segurança no pós 11 de Setembro. In *Estudos em homenagem ao Conselheiro José Manuel Cardoso da Costa* (*Vol. II*). Coimbra: Coimbra Editora.

Castro, C. S. E. (2006). *Protecção de dados pessoais na Internet. Sub Judice, 35. Abr-Jun.* Coimbra: Almedina.

CJEC. (2007). *Court of Justice of the European Communities - opinion of Advocate General Kokott) -* (Case C-275/06).

CNIL. (2005). *Délibération n°2005-235 du 18 octobre 2005.* Retrieved September 25, 2009, from http://www.legifrance.gouv.fr/affichCnil.do?oldAction=rechExpCnil&id=CNILTEXT000017652059&fastReqId=137369379&fastPos=1

Cohen, J. (1997). Some reflections on copyright management systems and laws designed to protect them. *Berkeley Technology Law Journal, 161.* Retrieved September 25, 2009, from http://www.law.berkeley.edu/journals/btlj/articles/vol12/Cohen/html/text.html

Culnan, M. J. (2000). Protecting privacy online: Is self-regulation working? *Journal of Public Policy & Marketing, 19*(1), 20–26. doi:10.1509/jppm.19.1.20.16944

de Werra, J. (2001). Le régime juridique des mesures techniques de protection des oeuvres selon les Traités de l'OMPI, le Digital Millennium Copyright Act, les Directives Européennes et d'autres legislations (Japon, Australie). *Revue Internationale du Droit d'Auteur, 189,* 66–213.

Foucault, M. (1977). *Discipline and punish: The birth of the prison* (trans. Alan Sheridan).

Garcia, F. J. (2005). Bodil Lindqvist: A Swedish churchgoer's violation of the European Union's data protection directive should be a warning to U.S. legislators. *Fordham Intellectual Property, Media, & Entertainment Law Journal, 15,* 1204.

Katyal, S. (2004a). The new surveillance. *Case Western Law Review, 54*(297). Retrieved September 25, 2009, from http://ssrn.com/abstract=527003

Katyal, S. (2004b). Privacy vs. piracy. *Yale Journal of Law & Technology, 7.* Retrieved September 25, 2009, from http://ssrn.com/abstract=722441

MGM Studios, Inc. v. Grokster, Ltd. 545 U.S. 913 (2005).

Oktay, B., & Wrenn, G. (1999). *A look back at the notice-takedown provisions of the US Digital Millennium Copyright Act.* WIPO Workshop on service provider liability, Geneva, Retrieved September 25, 2009, from www.wipo.int/edocs/mdocs/mdocs/en/osp_lia/osp_lia_2.doc

Rouvroy, A., & Poullet, Y. (2008). The right to informational self-determination and the value of self-development. Reassessing the importance of privacy for democracy. Reinventing data protection. *Proceedings of the International Conference,* Springer, Brussels, 12-13 October 2007, Retrieved September 25, 2009, from http://www.miauce.org/images/stories/paper/the%20right%20to%20informational%20self-determination%20and%20the%20value%20of%20self-development.pdf

Warren, S., & Brandeis, L. (1890). The right to privacy. *Harvard Law Review, 4*(5). Retrieved September 25, 2009, from http://www.lawrence.edu/fast/BOARDMAW/Privacy_brand_warr2.html

Chapter 18
SMEs E-Business Security Issues

José Gaivéo
Polytechnic Institute of Setubal, Portugal

ABSTRACT

Nowadays, when organizations, no matter what dimension they possess, are confronted with more exigent market challenges, they must change strategies and behaviours as needed to respond according to their new business positioning. If all organizations are affected by markets instability, small and medium enterprises (SMEs) suffer a greater impact due to a lack of suitable resources for the appropriate change of business strategy or even to develop a new strategy, which reveals information and information security significance, and so the relevance of securing Information Systems that supports their flows trough organizations. This chapter is intended to point information security issues that are important to SMEs' e-Business strategies, issues which could simultaneously guarantee organizational information privacy. Another purpose is the establishment of guidelines which could also be applied to SMEs, allowing information security policies definitions.

INTRODUCTION

In face of new markets opportunities, most part conducted by a globalization context, organizations feel constrained to carry out new activities in order to acquire the better competitive position at possible, changing in nearly all situations the way how they act in response to client desires.

Those sorts of changes are in general supported by the emergency of new information and communication technologies, which have the capability to perform new and improved functionalities, related with what is perceived as critical success factors, to deal with these innovative perspectives about business.

Supported by those technologies, and in some aspects allowed by a society where the information is a central topic, the e-Business seems to become a development factor to carry on business and

DOI: 10.4018/978-1-60960-765-4.ch018

to revolutionize the evolution of organizations to new market opportunities that affect first and foremost how they provide products and services to their customers.

This kind of environment where e-Business occurs are, for the most of its components, permitted by the diversity of communication services provided by information and communication technologies usage, allowing organizations to use those services to establish closer business relations with their customers, and even an enlargement of their business network connections.

In this perspective it could be assumed that, in general terms, information and communication technologies are recognized as a positive feature that could rise up people performance and also organizations competitiveness, allowing an optimal resources allocation to what are identified as business objectives. Nevertheless no matter what are their potential advantages, neither the ways how it can be applied; what should make the difference is the fact that sometimes it could cause adverse reactions that come from whom use it at some point in their common activities, reactions that are mainly motivated by: fears about work maintenance, employment stability, and even personal security.

The referred issues assume a wider significance, particularly when more resources are demanded, implying more costs and a larger commitment from management. A common technological approach that might solve SMEs problems is supported in by information systems and by information and communication technologies that are planned taking into account organizational strategies.

However, in this context, people and the different ways that they apply their skills and competences to carry out organizational activities can make the difference between organizational success and failure. This situation is always decisive, particularly in organizations that have limited resources, like SMEs where people assume a crucial role on organizational performance, and above all that which business are performed with

an intensive usage of information and communication technologies.

Therefore, even assuming that are several situations where information and communication technologies impacts on business activities require special attention, should be considered a particular set of issues that relates people and their usage of information and communication technologies to perform organizational requirements, what requires attention to all aspects where security of resources is a major preoccupation, above all those that imply information privacy and all implications that it could have on business activities.

Taking into consideration what potentially might occur with organizational resources protection and preservation, it's important to put in place measures to assure the security of those resources, task that could be performed by applying information security standards requirements to each case, focusing in what are mission and objectives of organization.

Situation in which, according to Barman (2002), it's necessary to identify what should be protected, namely information and communication technology resources (hardware and software), information (documents, business processes, etc.), essentially related with people's capacities to use information systems to support organizational activities.

A possible solution, perhaps the most usual, requires the application of a common and recognized standard as International Organization for Standardization (ISO)/International Electrotechnical Commission (IEC) 27000 standards series that currently represents the international references in information security terms. Considering that information, and the people that use it every day within organization, are key organizational assets that assume a crucial role in their performance and development inside the markets in which they act, it's essential to understand the interrelationship provided by those standards between people and information security in all their environment.

As previously stated, these standards are applicable to all type of organizations no matter dimensions (SMEs, corporations, etc.), activity area (grocery, technology, automobile, etc.), purpose (commercial, governmental, etc.), business channel (traditional, Internet, etc.) or nature (profit, non-profit), what allows their usage to answer to information security requests (International Organization for Standardization, 2008).

The most important purpose of the present work is to identify, understand, and structure the main potentialities of ISO/IEC 27000 standard series to support the organizational business activities, with reference to people and information as fundamental assets that information security policies must adequately protect.

In this work we would consider ISO/IEC 27001:2005 (Information Technology – Security Techniques – Information Security Management Systems – Requirements), ISO/IEC 27002:2005 (Information Technology – Security Techniques – Code of Practice for Information Security Management), and ISO/IEC 27005:2008 (Information Technology – Security Techniques – Information Security Risk Management) standards as main guidelines references to support the main security issues characterization, mostly attending to their relevance to organizational business activities, giving special attention to e-Business.

Bearing in mind the pertinence of taken option and before an entrance on the subject, should be referred that the assumption of these standards as fundamental issues in information security area relates with former standards- developed by British Standard Institution (in this case standards referred as BS 7799, parts 1, 2 and 3) - that constitutes the primary basis to its development and had been widely tested and implemented all over the world.

E-BUSINESS IN SMES

E-Business, seen as business mainly conducted through the application of electronic means, is essentially based on Internet usage, situation that brought growing preoccupations about information security, preoccupations that comes in essence from the Internet that born as an open network with universal usage, besides what control mechanisms have fewer impact, and whose efficacy depends, in most cases, of the attitudes of people that use it in business activities.

Due to its applicability to all kind of organizations, e-Business is a business solution, whose adoption by SMEs is increasing, allowing the enlargement of SMEs market positioning and consequently their competitiveness, affecting their internal structure and the relationships with their business partners.

In this domain, the creation of a reliable organizational climate is crucial to those activities, essentially in assumption of a responsibility environment that involves all actors on organizational activities, as interested parties, no matter which is their positioning, either internal or external, relatively to organization.

Any adopted solution will always have people as active parties, trying to assure that the policy to be implemented have answers to all actors needs, following organizational culture and applicable legislation.

WHY WE NEED INFORMATION

If this is a question the first answer could be because. However the current social and businesses context reports to a broader domain where information and their supports are central and their application to organizations strategies assumes a fundamental role in business strategy accomplishment. So, that seems clear that the difficulty grows when organization type is SMEs, and particularly when organizational activity is essentially based on e-Business.

The simple specification of information as an important and priceless organizational asset is a significant milestone that becomes as important as its application to organizational activities revealing their business support. To understand the value associated to information, there are some issues, like globalization or information society, about which organizations are obliged to stay alert.

Globalization and information society are new conceptual terms that involve organizational environment, implying innovative postures and attitudes to perform their business activities. Those activities should take into account people, information, information systems, information and communication technologies, and consequently their relations and dependencies, that affect all type of organizations in general and SMEs in particular.

The handling of cited organizational resources implies some options that should be placed to guarantee their protection against a wide range of threats that could affect this sort of resources. Should also be referred that the application of those resources on organizational activities is decisive to be succeeded in the information society where they compete, principally when e-Business is assumed as the preferential business option.

It's clear that this sort of concern should be applied only in the cases that the globalization and information society are understood as business opportunities, and challenges to innovate, and improve organizational competitiveness and performance. However, if those preoccupations are common in all organizations, it assumes wider significance when we are in presence of SMEs, implying proactive attitudes and business needs adequacy.

According those statements and in an business environment where SMEs are frequently understood as minor competitors, bearing in mind people as organizational resources, it's essential that top management set the mission, vision, and organizational objectives, with the identified challenges and opportunities, to support organizational needs in this evolutional context.

The SMEs e-Business activities represents a particular case of information application to business support, what clearly contributes to reinforce its importance to those type of organization, assuming the broad prevalence of people, and information and communication technologies as indispensable resources to support it. Nevertheless, what seems clear is that these types of preoccupations imply a statement of what we understand about what is this thing of information.

A common definition of information is that it is an amount of related data, interpreted according a vision or a particular objective, that make sense to someone or to fulfil a specific personal or organizational purpose. A wider vision about information is provided by Greenberg (2003) that states it as "a database, a transaction, a data file, an email message, some combination of those things while in transport, and so forth." (p. 29).

Being more assertive, Petrocelli (2006) understand information as data placed and interpreted in a specific context, mentioning also that data by itself haven't so much value. It's also referred in that context that relationships, application independence, and determined value are the most important characteristics of information.

In this particular situation, the earlier question that probably is obligatory to be formulated is about information and their organizational and personnel potential impacts. Isn't clear that information possesses the same value to all organizations or even to all people within one single organization, but what seems to be undeniable is the fact that information arise as an incontestable organizational asset.

Bearing in mind what is usual within nowadays markets, information and the ways how they support the identified organizational needs, emerge as something that all of us, as organizational actors, we must take into account when we need to carry out our organizational obligations, no matter what tasks are to performed, type of organization that we are dealing or even the organizational dimension.

However, within a SMEs business environment, according Petrocelli (2006), considering provided definition of information, the allocation of data protection resources is determined by organizational dimension, what constitutes an obstacle to SMEs set up all of resources relatively to a larger organization. Attending to this is also important to point out the fact of organizational size it can be irrelevant to business, when who is important is to protect data to minimize business losses and damages to organizational assets.

In this context and according Peltier (2001), information and communication technologies and the information that they support, are often considered as critical assets that support organization mission, assuming that their protection should be as important as the protection of other organizational resources how are the financial ones, physical assets or collaborators.

Due this, thinking about information and their significance to organizational performance leaves a particular perception that the information is bounded by cultural e social issues. Perhaps the first thing what we thought about information when someone ask us why it is so important for us or for our organizations, is their usage against us and our safety, or even our staffs.

In same sense we need information concerning to a lot of things; we need information about food, about culture, about sports, about family, about whatever we assume as significant in our life. But, above all we need safety; we need to feel comfortable about people and about things that are around us, besides we also need to fulfil our most basic necessities.

A similar situation happens when we are on an organizational context that arouses the same type of doubts and fears that could affect organizational activities, and also people expectations and his routine in the usual places of work within organizations, particularly when it seems to be a menace to organizational relationship.

This awareness about people and their organizational roles requires a closer view about what are the potential implications of its activities and, to verify people's importance in organizational activities, it's crucial to accomplish what Herold (2003) assumes as the success of information

security and protection, that requests the participation, agreement and support from people over all organization, independently of their activity and the recognition of relations within organization.

PEOPLE ON ORGANIZATIONS AND SOCIETY

When someone thinks about people in general terms, the conclusions frequently depend of personal cultural perspectives, and the way that everybody looks for this sort of subject matter. This type of circumstance leads always to some variety of restrictions that are directly related with social and personal relationships.

On the other hand all organizational partners have their single role within organization, to be precise depending of their commitment; where impact of business activities varies according the relevance that they have on the business value chain, and of their organizational activities involvement degree.

Attending that business value chain might change throughout business life cycle, the importance of individuals varies according those modifications, trying to adapt the Organization's responses to the needs of business markets. Nevertheless, people's importance varies as well with the capacities that they possess for assume new roles and challenges, mainly using their skills and competences in order to accomplish the organizational needs.

By exposed reasons, seems to be undeniable that people are the foremost important resource in any situation, no matter what kind of situation, but seem to be indelible that people are omnipresent in all society activities, whatever the context analysis.

For that, and according Greenberg (2003), people protection by itself requires an understanding about their organizational roles, and also about their information visions. However, the people's main roles are in organizations. As a result, no matter the specificity or the difficulty of the task to perform, what is important is the depth of this commitment, and as the management sees its involvement, assuming that they are critical success factors that are capable to fulfil the needs of organizational business activities.

Once people are in the front line of organization activities, the attention of top management should converge to their behaviour and performance trying to optimize their skills and knowledge in order to extract all of their potential. Taking this option as an important issue to organizational activities implies more attention to people's behaviour and obviously to perceived organizational loyalty.

Provide awareness, training, education, skills, competences, and capabilities are major aspects that can allow people contribute to organizational performance, particularly in organizations that assume the Information Society new challenges as opportunities to improve their own market position.

A complementary vision about people's value focuses on their attitudes and how they solve problems that are confronted. Attitudes that in the face of organizational needs or new information and communication technologies, may possibly make the difference between to be well succeeded or not, reinforcing the relevance of people in the organizational context.

Because of that, considering the particularities of information society, the ways how people make use of information and communication technologies are essential to assure organizational competitiveness, and simultaneously improve organization general performance. Consequently it's important to understand the relations that occur between information, people and security considering the specified organizational context.

What's New about Information, People and Security?

Think about information and their supports it's essential to a broader perception about what it means to organizations, so how is important

understand the people's roles and its application to organizational business activities, what brings to discussion the needs of a better comprehension about the relations between those assets and security.

For those reasons, a further relevant question is related with security, or more appropriately with information security and the potential impacts to social and organizational environments. With this purpose is indispensable having a closer look to a few relevant issues that might affect personal or organizational information.

Facing Information Society in the sense that is mandatory nowadays, no matter the direction of the Organization, nor what people do for them, or even how the societies realize the new challenges.

Indeed what seems to have potential to make the difference is one vision that should be proficient on gather the skills of people, their competences and know-how, and applying them to use information, and the information systems that support its use, to fulfil organizational requirements on their business activities.

This sort of attitude must be considered in conjunction with people and with organizational information security requirements, in order to keep those organizational assets away from threats, which could consequently conduct to loss or damage in organizational resources.

Today's challenges are focusing on information and also on information systems, and information and communication technologies that support their flows through organization. However, respond to any challenges related with information is always possible with people who should be having awareness, formation and education about information security and its impacts on organizational activities.

Considering people as "the single most important asset in protecting" information and communication technologies, Hansche (2003) assumes that users "who are aware of good security practices can ensure that information remains safe and available." (p. 322).

In nowadays reality the main issues are identified as information, people, and the ways how people are applying the information according organizational needs to support business activities. This situation underlies the people competences and know-how relevance to an adequate handling of information to accomplish organizational requirements.

By the other side, thinking about security leads us, initially to physical aspects, particularly those related to people and their natural fears, and subsequently to perception of environments where the focus should be the organisational aspects, including the human aspects.

This sort of vision doesn't contribute to an adequate approach to security problems, particularly to those ones that concern to assure that information, personal or organizational, remaining confidential, available and integer.

For that reason it seems clear that it's necessary to establish some rules that allow an adequate approach to organizational interests, trying to guarantee that the adopted security policy it's adequate to support the organizational business needs. Additionally, this implies that people should be aware about all security topics that are essentials to organization and to their own activities.

Usually security was something that people do not bother, unless they have problems with that and not had any solution. This type of problems seems to be greater than they really is, and this situation does not contribute to timely and adequately find the appropriate solution.

In information security matters, SMEs deal with some difficulties that are essentially related with their dimensions, fact that limits resources availability to a major involvement on security assumption as an organizational obligation. These kinds of limitation results in an implicit break to their usual business activities when a security breaches occurs, affecting normal functions and organizational performance.

To deeply understand what the dilemma is when we think about e-Business it's important to focus on a broader and holistic vision about their potentialities to organizations. First of all, be aware about information and communication technologies that potentially support the e-Business activities, secondly framing the main e-Business challenges, and finally comprehend the SMEs needs for compete on e-Business markets.

These circumstances constitute fundamental aspects in the adoption of information security measures, pointing to an adequate framing of organizational requirements that must allow business continuity without breaking down daily activities. The displayed intentions require the establishment of primary security issues and the comprehension of their interrelations applied to organizational needs and the adequate follow up of actions in order to assure security measures adequacy.

SOME INFORMATION SECURITY ISSUES

A broad understanding about information security key issues is an essential critical success factor to any study about information systems and about their usage to support organizational business activities, particularly those that are performed by the application of information and communication technologies, assuming that security is something that must be considered as fundamental issue in that context.

So, assuming that's not possible to identify all of crucial factors, we will consider as essential the following: information security (and all their components), vulnerabilities, threats, and security risks. Note that this option doesn't limit the understanding about other terms whenever needed to a better comprehension about chapter focus, namely people that are omnipresent in all of these issues.

Information Security Key Factors

Indicate information security key factors only is possible if we can understand what is it significance.

According Whitman and Mattord (2005), there are eight key concepts of information security: confidentiality (only those with adequate privileges may access to certain information); integrity (quality of being complete and uncorrupted); availability (access to information must be allowed without obstruction and in an usable format); privacy (information should only be used for purposes that are declared at the moment they are collected); identification (recognition of individual users); authentication (guarantee that a user identity is that they claim to be); authorization (user had been proper authorized, by who have authority, to dealing with information assets); accountability (control to assure that all performed activities can be associated to a specific person or automated process).

These concepts are different degrees of relevance that possibly reflect its impact on securing organizational information, and consequently the how and when of their application to business activities, affecting also people that supposed to use those information as an organizational resource.

Another perception about these concepts is brought by the assumption of the information security as the "preservation of confidentiality, integrity and availability of information", ISO/IEC 27001 provides another perspective about fundamental issues in information security where confidentiality is "the property that information is not made available or disclosed to unauthorized individuals, entities, or processes", integrity is "the property of safeguarding the accuracy and completeness of assets", and availability is "the property of being accessible and usable upon demand by an authorized entity." (International Organization for Standardization, 2005, p.2)

Previous perspectives agree in three key concepts-confidentiality, integrity, availability- that are common to all standards that constitute ISO/IEC 27000 series, reinforcing their significance on information security area.

Vulnerability, another aspect to consider, should be understood as a system failure or weakness that exposes information assets to attacks or damages (Whitman & Mattord, 2005), what allow the assumption that vulnerabilities are systems weakness, which possibly will be explored by threats materialization.

An additional point of view defines vulnerability as "a weakness in the security system" (Pflegger, 2003: p.6). We can also consider a complementary definition of vulnerability provided by Tippett (2002) as being "the likelihood of success of a particular threat category against a particular organization." (p. 54-3)

In ISO/IEC 27002 standard, threat is "a potential cause of an unwanted incident, which may result in harm to a system or organization" while vulnerability is assumed as "a weakness of an asset or group of assets that can be exploited by one or more threats." (International Organization for Standardization, 2005, p.2)

The closer relation between threat and vulnerability implies an integrated approach to their impacts on business activities, particularly in those that affect people tasks, where it's advised that the human resources should be aware about vulnerabilities and threats that menace their information, in order to they could take one or more actions to avoid or minimize the inherent risks.

According Woon and Kankanhalli (2006), the threat of computer security breaches, that could be external or internal, constitutes a great apprehension to organizations. They also refers that the security breaches occur usually in sequence of disasters in their different forms that might be naturals (earthquake, flood, lightening), or non naturals (technological, like systems failures, and human, as inappropriate access, theft and sabotage).

In this sense, information security threats are any kind of occurrence that might cause losses of organizational assets. For instance, threat is defined as "a potential cause of an unwanted incident, which may result in harm to a system or organization." (International Organization for Standardization, 2004). Another definition is presented by Tippett (2002) for whom "threat is the frequency, or occurrence rate, of potentiality adverse events." (p. 54-2)

Related with the likelihood of threats occurrence, and their consequences to organizational assets, Weaver (2007) proposes a classification to likelihood (between low and very high) and to consequences (between minimal and serious), combining both to ranking each threat.

Considering that the likelihood of a threat successfully exploiting a given vulnerability is defined by opportunity and threat source's motivation, and by methods for that exploitation. The impact of such successful exploitation is calculated through the analysis of their impacts on the confidentiality, integrity, and availability of the system and the information it processes. (Bowen et al., 2006)

As result we could conclude, with the purpose of adopting preventive attitudes in order to minimize or eradicate vulnerabilities and to keep away from breaches occurrence, that avoidance of damages to organizational assets it's a major objective which are only possible if proactive attitudes are taken.

Consequently, hiding security breaches and related problems isn't the best option to organizational information security assets. Without a doubt, no matter what is the problem type, their dimension, or even the value of potential damages, what is clear is that any kind of solution must be supported according the organizational business needs, if we want to be succeeded.

An international security standard, like ISO/IEC 27002, allows organizations have main orientations on adopting security policies, with international recognition, in order to guarantee the security resources needed to preserve information systems functionality, and consequently the business continuity.

As an indispensable milestone to be conscious about what key issues on security are, should be referred that there are no such thing of total security, and neither total effective and efficient security policies, nevertheless, their planning, implementation and regular control may contribute to use the potential of organizational information systems as an additional value to business.

Another factor closely related to relevant issues is information security policy, or briefly security policy, that is defined by Hare (2003) "as the set of practices that regulate how an organization manages, protects, and assigns resources to achieve its security objectives." (p.353)

It's also intended to set up boundaries of indispensable aspects to the definition of information security policies (mainly concerning confidentiality, integrity, and availability), to assure an effectively information safeguard, without any implication on business and their information systems that support activities, as well as guarantee the privacy of personal and business data.

In these matters, the usual attitude of looking to the other side didn't solve the problem and didn't also help to implement the necessary organizational proactive posture to reduce the wide range of common security threats. Also must be referred that in front of this type of situations, is always important to think about it and take some preventive measures in relation to usual threats.

At same sense must exist a common organizational attitude about what sort of security is needed to their business information, to allow the establishment of a security policy. This policy shall be appropriately documented and be obliged to cover up all of the most important organizational security requirements.

Within this context it's crucial an enough information assets identification to produce and implement appropriate policies to fulfil all identified security needs. Those policies ought to be clearly documented according recommended procedures of security standard.

One more key factor is security risk with reference to information and their application in organizational activities, subjects that are part of information security documents. For instance, ISO/IEC 27008 refers to information security risk as the "potential that a given threat will exploit vulnerabilities of an asset or group of assets and thereby cause harm to the organization" noting that "it is measured in terms of a combination of the likelihood of an event and its consequence". (International Organization for Standardization, 2008, p.1)

Another definition presents risk as "the possibility of damage or loss." (Weaver, 2007: p. 49) However, in Pretocelli (2006) statements, risk "is a measure of potential economic loss, lack of return on an investment or asset, or material injury", or seen as "a measure of exposure to harm".

In business terms, risk has two correlated, but individual, topics whose specification is relevant. The first one is directly related with business, and depends of its competitors and clients. The other topic relates to business support tools and activities or more precisely with risks to information security.

These needs are frequently presented as something that aren't in organizational managers attention but might, particularly whenever information are assumed as an important organizational asset, makes the difference in competitive advantages acquisition, and improve organizational development.

The actuality of organizations and societies implies new and more assertive attitudes to face their social positioning, directing the appropriated answers to business needs by organizations, essentially considering the new information and communication technologies, that by it require better and more competences from people.

All of these contexts reinforce organizational performance people's role, particularly when they are fundamental to an ample resources usage, to appropriately respond to new business requirements when confronted with larger competitive

demands, occasion where information seems to emerge, simultaneously with people, as a valuable and indispensable resource in organizational environment.

Pay attention to organizational requirements in business activities terms is only possible by covering information that are used daily in organizations, attempting to guarantee their confidentiality, integrity and availability according specific organization needs.

Besides this, as support of organizational information flows between them and their business partners, the information systems, and information and communication technologies must be placed under attention of organizational managers', including their security in all aspects to be considered in terms of organizational information security policies definition and implementation.

Gather key factors in a central idea oblige to assume that the preoccupations about information security ought to be assumed in holistic terms to incorporate their handling in organizational culture. According these thoughts, one of bigger preoccupations relates to the obligation of trying that all involved in organizational activities are aware of information security relevance to these activities.

Nevertheless is always fundamental reaffirm people's importance when it's crucial to deal with information security, applying their knowledge to treat all aspects that involve confidentiality, integrity, and availability of business information.

Following that idea, and according Dark (2006), when people are considered as the first security defence line, organizations be obliged to make available the appropriated resources to carry out their requirements about awareness, training, and education in information security area. Take into account this assumption, reinforces the people roles in information security subjects, allowing the support of most of SMEs needs related to business activities.

Even about security key factors, it should be noted that the organizational choices about

Table 1. Impact degree of threats on security

Threat	1 to 3	4	5	6	Don't Know
Virus/Trojan horses/Worms/etc.	6,25	9,38	24,11	41,07	19,20
Hackers	7,14	11,16	20,54	42,86	18,30
Information disposal	7,59	12,05	22,77	38,39	19,20
Inside unauthorized access	7,14	13,39	25,89	33,93	19,64
Information steel	8,93	14,29	21,88	36,16	18,75
e-mail interception	12,95	15,18	29,91	22,32	19,64

Table 2. Security relevant issues

Threat	1 to 3	4	5	6	Don't Know
e-mail	10,27	16,07	29,46	30,36	13,84
People	12,95	15,63	29,46	28,57	13,39
Information System Network	11,16	14,73	25,00	32,59	16,52
Internet	10,71	16,07	32,59	25,00	15,63

information security polices depend of particular environments where e-Business activities are performed, particularly for SMEs- due to its dimension and available resources, depending essentially of practical aspects.

Practical Experimental Aspects

In a former investigation about people in information security, I had the opportunity to write about a diversity of security issues where people have a huge impact. As result of those work it was developed a model with the purpose of define references that may support metrics to measure security implications related to people and their information and communication technologies usage.

During the development of that process, in which field work was supported by an inquiry-conducted in 2007- people perceptions about information security and their involvement in all related procedures, people frequently arise as an important organizational asset, indeed the most important, reinforcing their organizational roles on business performance.

As inquiry results, with 224 answers, when asked to classify from 1 (not important) to 6 (very important) the impact on security by given threats, the most cited (when the marks 5 and 6 are higher than 50%) is stated in Table 1.

In another related issue about relevant questions on security matters, with the same classification, show as results (when the marks 5 and 6 are higher than 50%), in Table 2, the most important threats.

From tables' analysis and as related aspects must have special relevance the emergence of two main tendencies that are: people, and information and communication technologies. The first one relates to collaborators and partners, and the other with the support to organization business activities.

Those aspects cover some significant issues that are related with e-Business, situation that contributes to reinforce security relevance in any circumstance that implies simultaneously people, and information and communication technologies applied on organizational business activities.

A closer analysis of results- significant level of "don't know" answers- brought to discussion the relevance measures related to people awareness, training and education that must be taking to improve their performance on organizational activities, that otherwise organizations could be confronted with adverse attitudes related to information security policies adoption.

Any situation, when organizations are confronted with new markets, namely those that force to assume e-Business challenges, requires organizational resources that must be appropriate for respond to business organization requests.

The availability of these human, technological or economical resources implies a clear management commitment with these new objectives and, particularly when people needs to be aware, trained and educated on those areas, in order to improve their knowledge and skills.

To acquire a wide vision about this sort of condition we must answer to some questions, to be precise issues concerning with information relevance, foremost people roles and expectations, or even organizations objectives and strategies, in order to establish the requirements identified with ISO/IEC 27000 standards.

Attending that the main difficulty seems to be on a framework usage to support an adequate approach to this sort of situation, the ISO/IEC 27000 Information Security Standard Series, essentially those that I had the opportunity to use, like ISO/IEC 27001 and ISO/IEC 27002, provides a most advantageous platform to establishing a workable base to allow business competitiveness.

In fact, ought to be considered that there are a strong relation between business enlargement and their information systems. The organizations strategies success is based in an easy and accurate access to information and in fast data acquisition, treatment, and distribution.

From that results a strong organizational dependence from their information systems, and information and communication technologies. That sort of dependence brought the inevitability of a security policy definition that has an effect from the conscience increasing about organizational vulnerabilities, and threats with that they are confronted.

From these situations results that is crucial thinking about information and communication technologies to allow the planning and implementation of information systems. In this sense it's hard to understand the organizational vision concerning to future and their strategy without a security policies definition, for the most part to assure business data and process privacy preservation.

In view of the reported experience, the best option to support the tasks related to information security is to choose international security standards- well tested and widely implemented- that could support the diversity of activities, and involve people in processes conception and implementation.

People on ISO/IEC 27000 Standard Series

Any selection process of security standards must be conducted taking into account its availability, business activity and, above all, having in mind what are organizational objectives and culture, trying to provide better and faster processes conception and implementation to incorporate organizational and personal contributions.

For this reason, if we want to comprehend how people are framed by these standards, and how it can be used to fulfils personal and organizational requests, we must firstly identify the main references that each one of these standards makes about people in an information security environment.

As we had previously stated, ISO/IEC 27001 (that substitutes BS 7799-part2- first published in 1998), ISO/IEC 27002 (that substitutes ISO/IEC 17799- first published in 2000, former now as BS 7799-part1- first published in 1995), and ISO/IEC 27005 (that incorporates the most concepts and guidelines of BS 7799-part3) are used to ac-

Table 3. People references in ISO/IEC 27002

Clause	Category
Security Policy	Information Security Policy
Organizing Information Security	Internal Organization
Asset Management	Responsibility for Assets
Human Resources Security	Prior to Employment
	During Employment
	Termination or Change of Employment
Communications and Operations Management	Operational Procedures and Responsibilities
	Third Party Service Delivery Management
Access Control	Business Requirement for Access Control
	User Access Management
	User Responsibilities

complish this purpose, i.e. support organizational information security definition and implementation. To obtain a comprehensible image about it, we will begin with a short resume of the purpose and objectives of each one of these standards, before the identification of the clauses related to people.

The first security standard to be used is ISO/IEC 27002 that defines appropriated guidelines to implement, maintain, and improve information security management in order to carry out organizational security needs. This International Standard provides a best practices code that is used as a practical guideline to organizational security standards development and to set up the suitable security management practices (International Organization for Standardization, 2005).

This standard has 133 security controls framed in 11 clauses (International Organization for Standardization, 2005); each one organized in categories that group the controls, which is as follow:

- Security policy;
- Organizing information security;
- Asset management;
- Human Resources security;
- Physical and environmental security;
- Communications and operations management;

- Access control;
- Information systems acquisition, development and maintenance;
- Information security incident management;
- Business continuity management;
- Compliance.

The clause presentation order hasn't any significance to their importance or in their applicability to organizational security needs; neither possesses any particular meaning to information security policies establishment.

Related with the reference of people in standard structure, should be mentioned as relevant security clauses and categories (including specific controls, their objectives and implementation guides) those that are specified in Table 3.

Related with the organizations (SMEs included), their structure and relations, and business activities (e-Business included) reference in standard structure, should be mentioned as relevant security clauses and categories (including specific controls, their objectives and implementation guides) those that are pointed in Table 4.

With reference to information systems and information and communication technologies - mainly those that are closely related with business activities- in standard structure should be men-

Table 4. Business references in ISO/IEC 27002

Clause	Category
Security Policy	Information Security Policy
Organizing Information Security	Internal Organization
	External Parties
Physical and Environmental Security	Secure Areas
Communications and Operations Management	Operational Procedures and Responsibilities
	Third Party Service Delivery Management
	Media Handling
	Exchange of Information
	Electronic Commerce Services
Access Control	Business Requirement for Access Control
	Network Access Control
	Application and Information Access Control
	Mobile Computing and Teleworking
Business Continuity Management	Information Security Aspects of Business Continuity Management
Compliance	Compliance with Legal Requirements

tioned as relevant security clauses and categories (including specific controls, their objectives and implementation guides) those that are in Table 5.

Should be noted that Tables 3, 4, and 5 point out most relevant aspects on ISO/IEC 27000 series that frame those people perceptions, what allows the statement of ISO/IEC 27002 as the most important reference on information security area.

Another of security standards is the ISO/IEC 27001 that provides a model for establish, implement, operate, monitor, review, maintain and improve an information security management system, whose adoption constitutes an organizational strategic decision. The implementation of an information security management system is done taking into account organizational needs and objectives, considering to organizational dimension and business structure (International Organization for Standardization, 2005).

The new one of this series, ISO/IEC 27005, provides rules for information security risk management, which are provided by supporting ISO/IEC 27001 general concepts, to implement

information security based on a risk management approach (International Organization for Standardization, 2008).

The appropriate handling of these security standards requires an integrated usage of all of them, where the knowledge about concepts, models, processes and terminologies of all of them are essential for a complete perception of any of them.

Should also be referred that all of these International Standards are applicable to all types of organizations (no matter what are their type or dimension), that assumes organizational information security as an important issue to their business evolution.

In ISO/IEC 27002 specifications, people are incorporated as an asset that acts with other assets but didn't posses any particular role in the information security environment; however it is an important issue to all activities related with information security policies definition and implementation.

As a result, if we intend to use those international standards to support a better understanding about people involvement on information security

Table 5. Business information and communications technologies references in ISO/IEC 27002

Claus	Category
Security Policy	**Information Security Policy**
Asset Management	Responsibility for Assets
	Information Classification
Communications and Operations Management	Protection against Malicious and Mobile Code
	Back-up
	Network Security Management
	Media Handling
Access Control	Business Requirement for Access Control
	Network Access Control
	Application and Information Access Control
	Mobile Computing and Teleworking
Information Systems Acquisition, Development and Maintenance	Security Requirements of Information Systems
	Correct Processing in Applications
	Cryptographic Controls
	Security of System Files
	Security in Development and Support Processes
	Technical Vulnerability Management

problems, is essential identify the main vulnerabilities and the threats that could explore those vulnerabilities to cause damage to people property.

WHAT E-BUSINESS INFORMATION SECURITY SOLUTIONS?

First of all, in information security matters, should be considered the fact that all of main aspects affecting or could be affected by security issues are prevalent in all organizations, being independent of dimension, market or technology.

Besides that, by definition, an information security management system- that incorporates information security policy- is an integrated part of organizational general management system, fact that allows the assumption of information security as a management process, not a technological one. Without any doubt, it's evident that information and communication technologies act only as a business tool, assuming that the main role remains in people.

Because of those circumstances, no matter how deeply the information and communication technologies goes through organizational structure to support e-Business requests or even its daily activities, what seems to make the difference are people and their knowledge, skills and competences to use it to act in response of organizational needs.

Implementing an information security management system requires a group of pertinent issues that enclose indispensable aspects that allow ISO/IEC 27002 application to carry out all process needed activities, where are relevant the following requirements:

- Ambit definition;
- Information assets identification;
- Information assets value assessment;
- Risk determination;
- Policy and controls assurance specification;

- Identify controls objectives, and controls;
- Identification of policies, standards and procedures to controls implementation;
- Conception and implementation of policies, standards and procedures;
- Information security management system finalization.

Those requirements, supported by ISO/IEC 27002, that relates with ISO/IEC 27001 and ISO/IEC 27005 in the following ways: ISO/IEC 27001 is mainly used to support the certifications processes and provides a continuous cycle of information security management system improvement based on a Plan-Do-Check-Act (PDCA) model; and ISO/IEC 27005 is applied to support all information security risk aspects that are needed to assure ISO/IEC 27002 requirements fulfilment.

Considering what was defined as fundamental requirements, and their broader application potentialities, should be noted that any e-Business information security solution is identical to any other solution, in fact the standards applicability it's equal to all organizations and it's independent of every kind of information and communication technologies compliance.

The difference between solutions is in the organizational assumptions about its mission, business specificity, market positioning, culture, and available resources. When where demand for a solution to security problems, it's advised to pay attention to management commitment, and obviously to organizational environment, in order to avoid misunderstandings and unexpected interruptions of the process.

However there are some implications of using those standards to support information security policy definition and implementation, most of them associated with the time to do this, being needed resources- usually with some relevance- to accomplish related tasks, and management commitment.

In time matters, this sort of process takes at least 12 to 18 months, affecting frequently people and business activities due to the involvement level that are required. About resources allocation and consumption, the problem it's similar, requiring financial, technological and human resources, that are both larger and more extensive are the applications of organizational security, what- as occurs with the previous implication- are a serious problem to a SME if it's intended to implement it over all organization. The other implication affects all types of organizations that chose to adopt information security policies and must be seen as a starting point of all related activities, indistinctly applied to all type of organizations.

FUTURE RESEARCH DIRECTIONS

Actually, no matter the perspective that we look to organizational, social and personal relationships, because information, their security and the people that use these information are distinct issues whose interconnection forces a synchronized action over all these issues, even if we only want to act over one single issue.

Business environments are largely conditioned by the ways how customers, partners, and competitors saw each one behaviour, circumstances that have particular evidence when markets are predominantly e-Business. Facing this situation most organizations tends to change their attitudes to "keeping the appearances". In fact, nowadays a large amount of enterprises plays this game, particularly when speaking about how secure client's information is in their hands.

Generally this is like it seems it is; only appearances, but every one of the clients didn't knew anything about what happens with their personal information. They simply believe that organizations are trusted, what put the final attitude in organizations side, in order to don't defraud customer's expectations.

However, the global reality brought to day light a cruel, hard and true reality, and for people that seem to have some difficulties to face this kind of challenges, only exist an appropriate solution that is the commitment of everyone with information protection, assuming a broad and trustable partnership.

Information systems, and information and communication technologies that support it, are always preponderant tools that amplify this problem, allowing organizations to kept appearances at a large level.

That preponderance leaves to another high point that relates to the likelihood of technologically following someone. Whenever we are or whatever we are doing in each time frame, we are always being seen. This simple fact reveals that we don't know what happens with us or with our information. Consequently there are some questions that must be placed in day order to analyze and take the appropriate preventive measures.

Security is nowadays a society common term that involves every areas where human activities take place. Emerging with special relevance when people physical security could be affected, the problematic of security seems to be profound, reflecting society insecurity impacts.

Indeed, information security requires at the present time, from managers and people, a proactive approach that involves new attitudes and a larger mutual aid that goes beyond what were the usual day to day activities.

Resuming what are the main points, information, information systems, information and communications technologies, information security management systems, risk management, and business continuity management, recurrent terms more and more integrated, are components that must be assumed as an essential support of organizational activities, satisfying business needs.

Using previous concepts, and consequently their support tools possibly will increase the business activities competitiveness, and the number of people (clients, employees, business partners, and stakeholders) involved in those activities.

As an important issue and for further needs, we must also refer that any information security approach ought to include the security of information systems, and information and communications technologies that supports that information, in order to assure business continuity, even when the case are e-Business.

At the present time, society is other of the innermost situations that organizations, particularly SMEs, are confronted. The actual economic and social crisis brought to day light a broad range of serious problems that, in reality, are already old and known but, because it's critical and difficult to solve, many decision makers don't take care about impacts in organizations.

The signs of this crisis are at very long time ago on the information systems, consequently seems to be important question why nobody saw them. Or even why nobody take care about their potential implications on society?

There are no easy answers. Politic, social, and economical interests imply various compromises, frequently unknown, that leave for "better" occasions some insignificant but precious signs that could contribute to attenuate, or even avoid, those kinds of problems. However, e-Business could be in certain extent a viable alternative to SMEs evolution.

Awareness and social responsibility are indispensable, demanding proactive attitudes and a clear commitment by all of us. Make a note of that this is precisely the time to assume information systems, and information and communication technologies as something that possibly provides a huge contribution to implement and support the measures that will be needed.

CONCLUSION

Actually, there are a strong relation between business enlargement and their information systems. The organizations strategies success is based in an easy access to information and in a fast data acquisition, as well as their treatment, safeguarding, and availability.

From that results a strong organizational dependence from their information systems and information and communication technologies. This kind of dependence brought the inevitability of the definition of an information security policy as an effect from the conscience increasing about organizational vulnerabilities.

Consequently is crucial think about information and communication technologies to allow information systems planning and implementation. In this case it's hard to understand the organizational vision concerning to future and their strategy without security policies definition, mainly to assure business data and process privacy preservation.

By the other side, in a business and information systems globalized environment, the success and organizational competitiveness, supported by information and communication technologies, must include information security policies definition in order to guarantee that the information flows intra and inter organizations in a secure way.

As indispensable milestone to be aware about what key issues on security are, should be referred that there are no such thing of total security, and neither total effective and efficient information security policies, however, their planning, implementation and regular control may contribute to use the organizational information systems potentials as an additional value to business.

Whatever solution that organizations adopt in response to their information security problems, people always remains an asset whose organizational impact should be taken into account on business activities, particularly e-Business.

Such things are usual problems that organizations are faced nowadays, but by itself people suffer equal problems, particularly because information security threats and vulnerabilities are the same, differing essentially through the resources that they have to solve or avoid this kind of problem.

Attending that information systems, and information and communication technologies are omnipresent in organizations and home places, people are constantly challenged to use it in the most various ways, transforming this relation in a partnership that forces their evolution on these areas and simultaneously implies a greater effort on education in order to acquire more and better competences.

Attending to what are identified as foremost organizational resources and assets, should be assumed that the ISO/IEC 27002 is the best option to provide, develop and implement guidance on information security policies specification. Its connection with organizational management systems, including people and technologies, reinforces the relevance of being applied for support all activities related with information security.

Clauses, categories- and related controls- specified in tables 3, 4, and 5, are relevant to frame the SMEs information security needs for their normal business activities and consequently those related with e-Business specificity, and have got to be used with this purpose. Complementarily should be used the pertinent issues previously referred that allow ISO/IEC 27002 application on information security definition and implementation.

What is here suggested doesn't avoids the total applicability of the ISO/IEC 27002 controls, however its application it's obligatory to who wishes to obtain an ISO/IEC 27000 certification, nevertheless is advised follow it in a preliminary approach of information security to e-Business on SMEs.

REFERENCES

Barman, S. (2002). *Writing information security policies*. New Riders Publishing.

Bowen, P., Hash, J., & Wilson, M. (2006). *Information security handbook: A guide for managers*. Gaithersburg, MD: National Institute of Standards and Technology, Technology Administration - U.S. Department of Commerce.

Dark, M. J. (2006). Security education, training, and awareness from a human performance technology point of view. In Whitman, M. E., & Mattord, H. J. (Eds.), *Readings and cases in the management information security* (pp. 86–104). Boston, MA: Thomson Course Technology.

Greenberg, E. (2003). *Mission-critical security planner: Creating customized strategies*. Indianapolis, IN: Wiley Publishing.

Hansche, S. D. (2003). Making security awareness happen. In Tipton, H. F., & Krause, M. (Eds.), *Information security management handbook* (4th ed., *Vol. 3*, pp. 317–335). Boca Raton, FL: Auerbach Publications.

Hare, C. (2003). Policy development. In Tipton, H. F., & Krause, M. (Eds.), *Information security management handbook* (4th ed., *Vol. 3*, pp. 353–383). Boca Raton, FL: Auerbach Publications.

Herold, R. (2003). Information protection: Organization, roles, and separation of duties. In Tipton, H. F., & Krause, M. (Eds.), *Information security management handbook* (4th ed., *Vol. 4*, pp. 415–439). Boca Raton, FL: Auerbach Publications.

International Organization for Standardization. (2004). *ISO/IEC FDIS 13335-1 – Information technology - guidelines for the management of IT security - concepts and models for information and communications technology security*.

International Organization for Standardization. (2005). *ISO/IEC 27001 – Information Technology - security techniques - information security management systems – requirements*.

International Organization for Standardization. (2005). *ISO/IEC 27002 – Information Technology - code of practice for information security management*.

International Organization for Standardization. (2008). *ISO/IEC 27005 – Information Technology - security techniques - information security risk management*.

Kaplan, R. (2003). A matter of trust. In Tipton, H. F., & Krause, M. (Eds.), *Information security management handbook* (4th ed., *Vol. 3*, pp. 385–405). Boca Raton, FL: Auerbach Publications.

Peltier, T. R. (2001). *Information security risk analysis*. Boca Raton, FL: Auerbach Publications.

Petrocelli, T. (2006). *Data protection and information lifecycle management*. New Jersey: Prentice Hall.

Pfleeger, C. P., & Pfleeger, S. L. (2003). *Security in computing* (3rd ed.). New Jersey: Prentice Hall.

Pipkin, D. L. (2006). Linking business objectives and security directions. In Whitman, M. E., & Mattord, H. J. (Eds.), *Readings and cases in the management information security* (pp. 8–16). Boston, MA: Thomson Course Technology.

Tippett, P. (2002). The future of information security. In Bosworth, S., & Kabay, M. E. (Eds.), *Computer security handbook* (4th ed., pp. 54.1–54.18). New York, NY: John Wiley & Sons.

Weaver, R. (2007). *Guide to network defense and countermeasures* (2nd ed.). Boston, MA: Thomson Course Technology.

Whitman, M. E., & Mattord, H. J. (2004). *Management of information security*. Boston, MA: Thomson Course Technology.

Whitman, M. E., & Mattord, H. J. (2005). *Principles of information security* (2nd ed.). Boston, MA: Thomson Course Technology.

Woon, I., & Kankanhalli, A. (2006). Trust, controls, and information security. In Whitman, M. E., & Mattord, H. J. (Eds.), *Readings and cases in the management information security* (pp. 120–128). Boston, MA: Thomson Course Technology.

ADDITIONAL READING

Batley, S. (2007). *Information architecture for information professionals*. Oxford: Chandos Publishing.

Bishop, M. (2002). *Computer security: Art and science*. Boston, MA: Addison-Wesley Professional.

Cassidy, A. (2005). *A practical guide to information systems strategic planning* (2nd ed.). Boca Raton, FL: Auerbach Publications. doi:10.1201/9781420031089

Chew, E., Swanson, M., Stine, K., Bartol, N., Brown, A., & Robinson, W. (2008). *Performance measurement guide for information security*. Gaithersburg, MD: National Institute of Standards and Technology, Technology Administration - U.S. Department of Commerce.

Dhillon, G. (2001). *Information security management: Global challenges in the new millennium*. Hershey: IGI Global.

Dhillon, G. (2006). *Principles of information systems security: Texts and cases*. New Jersey: John Wiley & Sons.

Halsall, F. (2005). *Computer networking and the internet* (5th ed.). New York, NY: Addison Wesley.

Herrmann, D. S. (2002). *A practical guide to security engineering and information assurance*. Boca Raton, FL: Auerbach Publications.

Herrmann, D. S. (2007). *Complete guide to security and privacy metrics: Measuring regulatory compliance, operational resilience, and ROI*. Boca Raton, FL: Auerbach Publications. doi:10.1201/9781420013283

Jaquith, A. (2007). *Security metrics: Replacing fear, uncertainty, and doubt*. New York, NY: Addison Wesley.

King, C. M., Dalton, C. E., & Osmanoglu, T. E. (2001). *Security architecture: Design, deployment & operations*. Berkeley: Osborne/McGraw-Hill.

Kurose, J. F., & Ross, K. W. (2005). *Computer networking: A top-down approach featuring the internet* (3rd ed.). Boston, MA: Addison Wesley.

Lambe, P. (2007). *Organising knowledge: Taxonomies, knowledge and organisational effectiveness*. Oxford: Chandos Publishing.

Laudon, K. C., & Laudon, J. P. (2006). *Management information systems: Management the digital firm* (10th ed.). New Jersey: Pearson International.

Layton, T. P. (2007). *Information security: Design, implementation, measurement, and compliance*. Boca Raton, FL: Auerbach Publications.

LeVeque, V. (2006). *Information security: A strategic approach*. New Jersey: John Wiley & Sons.

Mackey, D. (2003). *Web security for network and system administrators*. Boston, MA: Thomson Course Technology.

Organisation for Economic Co-operation and Development. (2002). *Guidelines for the security of information systems and networks – Towards a sulture of security*.

Osborne, M., & Summitt, P.M., (2006). *How to cheat at managing information security*. Rockland: Syngress.

Palmer, M. (2004). *Guide to operating systems security*. Boston, MA: Thomson Course Technology.

Peltier, T. R. (2002). *Information security policies, procedures, and standards*. Boca Raton, FL: Auerbach Publications.

Scarfone, K., Souppaya, M., Cody, A., & Orebaugh, A. (2008). *Technical guide to information security testing and assessment*. Gaithersburg, MD: National Institute of Standards and Technology, Technology Administration - U.S. Department of Commerce.

Stallings, W. (2003). *Network security essentials: Applications and standards* (2nd ed.). New Jersey: Pearson Education.

Taylor, L. (2007). *Knowledge, information and the business process: Revolutionary thinking or common sense?* Oxford: Chandos Publishing.

Tudor, J. K. (2001). *Information security architecture: An integrated approach to security in the organization*. Boca Raton, FL: Auerbach Publications.

Turban, E., & Volonino, L. (2010). *Information technology for management: Transforming organizations in the digital economy* (7th ed.). New Jersey: John Wiley & Sons.

Widén-Wulff, G. (2007). *The challenges of knowledge sharing in practice: A social approach.* Oxford: Chandos Publishing.

Winkler, I., (2007). *Zen and the art of information security*. Rockland: Syngress.

Compilation of References

Adam, S., & Deans, K. R. (2001). *Inter-study comparisons of small business Internet use in Australia and New Zealand.*

ADERM. (2009). *The Australian Department for Environment and Resource Management-ADERM, E-Business definition.* Retrieved May 20, 2009, from www.nrw.qld. gov.au/ about/policy/documents/ 33/definitions.html

Adria, M., & Chowdhury, S. (2004). Centralization as a design consideration for the management of call centers. *Information & Management*, *41*, 497–507. doi:10.1016/S0378-7206(03)00087-9

Adwords. (2009). *Google Web page.* Retrieved July 26, 2009 from https://adwords.google.com

Aksin, O. Z., Armony, M., & Mehrotra, V. (2007). (forthcoming). The modern call-center: A multi-disciplinary perspective on operations management research. *Production and Operations Management.*

Aksin, O. Z., & Harker, P. T. (2003). Capacity sizing in the presence of a common shared resource: Dimensioning an inbound call center. *European Journal of Operational Research*, *147*(3), 464–483. doi:10.1016/S0377-2217(02)00274-6

Alexandrou, M. (2009). *E-business.* Retrieved May 21, 2009, from http://www.mariosalexandrou.com /definition/ebusiness.asp

Alfred McAlpine Capital Projects Ltd v Tilebox Ltd, EWHC 281. (TCC 2005).

Almind, T. C., & Ingwersen, P. (1997). Informetric analyses on the World Wide Web: Methodological approaches to "Webometrics.". *The Journal of Documentation*, *53*(4), 404–426. doi:10.1108/EUM0000000007205

Alonso, O., Rose, D. E., & Stewart, B. (2008). Crowdsourcing for relevance evaluation. *ACM SIGIR Forum*, *42*(2), 9–15. doi:10.1145/1480506.1480508

Alsberg, B. K., Kirkhus, L., Hagen, R., Knudsen, O., Tangstad, T., & Anderssen, E. (2003). Zherlock: An open source data analysis software. [from http://www.ncbi.nlm. nih.gov/sites/entrez]. *SAR and QSAR in Environmental Research*, *14*(5-6), 349–360. Retrieved on September 11, 2009. doi:10.1080/10629360310001623944

Alterian. (2009). *Web page.* Retrieved July 24, 2009 from http://www.alterian.com/

Anderson, C. (2004). The long tail. *Wired*, *1*(12), 10. Retrieved May 15, 2009, from http://www.wired.com/archive/12.10/tail.html

Anderson, E. (2005). Using Wikis in a corporate context. In A. Hohensyein & K. Wilbers (Eds.). *Handbuch e-learning* (pp. 8-15). Cologne, Germany: Wolters Kluwer. Retrieved September 2, 2009, from http://www.espen.com/papers/Anderson-2005-corpwiki.pdf

Anderson, P. (2007). What is Web 2.0? Ideas, technologies and implications for education. *JISC Technology and Standards Watch.* Retrieved December 12, 2007, from http://www.jisc.ac.uk/publications/publications/twweb2.aspx

Angeles, R., & Nath, R. (2007). Business-to-business e-procurement: Success factors and challenges to implementation. *Supply Chain Management: An International Journal*, *12*(2), 104–115. doi:10.1108/13598540710737299

AntiXSS. (2008). *Anti-XSS Library v3.0.* Retrieved from http://antixss.codeplex.com/

Anton, J. (1996). *Customer relationship management.* New York, NY: Prentice-Hall.

Anton, J., & Hoeck, M. (2002). *E-business customer service*. Santa Monica, CA: The Anton Press.

Antoniu, G., & van Harmelen, F. (2004). *A Semantic Web primer*. Cambridge, MA & London, UK: The MIT Press.

Ardagna, C. A., Cremonini, M., & Damiani, E. (2006). Supporting location–based conditions in access control policies. *Proceedings of ASIACCS'06*, Taipei, ACM.

Article 29 data protection working party. (2007). *On the concept of personal data*. Retrieved September 25, 2009, from http://www.droit-technologie.org/upload/actuality/doc/1063-1.pdf

Asakura, Y., & Kashiwadani, M. (1994). Effects of parking availability information on system performance:a simulation model approach. In *Proceedings of Vehicle Navigation and Information Systems Conference*, (pp. 251–254). Dearborn, MI.

ASE. (2009). *The Australian state of environment – ASE, E-business definition*. Retrieved May 20, 2009, from http://www.environment.gov.au /soe/2001/publications /theme-reports/ settlements/ glossary.html

Atlason, J., Epelman, M. A., & Henderson, S. G. (2004). Call center staffing with simulation and cutting plane methods. *Annals of Operations Research, 127*, 333–358. doi:10.1023/B:ANOR.0000019095.91642.bb

Avramidis, N. A., Deslauriers, A., & L'Ecuyer, P. (2004). Modeling daily arrivals to a telephone call center. *Management Science, 50*(7), 896–908. doi:10.1287/mnsc.1040.0236

Avramidis, A. N., & L'Ecuyer, P. (2005). *Modeling and simulation of call centers*. Paper presented at the Proceedings of the 2005 Winter Simulation Conference.

Baader, F., Calvanese, D., McGuinness, D., Nardi, D., & Patel-Schneider, P. F. (Eds.). (2003). *The description logic handbook: Theory, implementation, and applications*. Cambridge University Press.

Baker, R. H. (1997). *Extranets: The complete sourcebook*. Hightstown, NJ: McGraw-Hill, Inc.

Balasubramanian, K., Gokhale, A., Karsai, G., Sztipanovits, J., & Neema, S. (2006). Developing applications using model-driven design environments. *IEEE Computer Society, 39*(2), 33–40.

Balzarotti, D., Cova, M., Felmetsger, V., Jovanovic, N., Kirda, E., Kruegel, C., et al. (2008). Saner: Composing static and dynamic analysis to validate sanitization in Web applications., (pp. 387-401).

Baourakis, G., Kourgiantakis, M., & Migdalas, A. (2002). The impact of e- commerce on agro-food marketing: The case of agricultural cooperatives, firms and consumers in Crete. *British Food Journal, 104*(8), 580–590. doi:10.1108/00070700210425976

Barman, S. (2002). *Writing information security policies*. New Riders Publishing.

Barros, A., & Brandão, M. R. (2006). *Estudo diagnóstico e benchmarking da actividade de Contact Centers*. Lisboa, Portugal: Associação Portuguesa de Contact Centers e IZO.

Bendoly, E., Soni, A., & Venkataramanan, M. A. (2004). Value chain resource planning: Adding value with systems beyond the enterprise. *Business Horizons, 47*(2), 79–86. doi:10.1016/j.bushor.2003.08.004

Beneventano, D., Bergamaschi, S., Bianco, D., Guerra, F., & Vincini, M. (2002). *"SI-Web: A Web based interface for the MOMIS project*. Demo Session, Convegno su Sistemi Evoluti per Basi di Dati (SEBD02).

Benson, J. P., O'Donovan, T., O'Sullivan, P., Roedig, U., & Sreenan, C. (2006). Car-park management using wireless sensor networks. In *Proceedings of 31st IEEE Conf. Local Computer Networks*, (pp. 588–595). Tampa.

Berezai, P. (2000). *B-2-B on the Internet: 2000-2005*. London, UK: Datamonitor PLC.

Berlak, J., & Weber, V. (2004). How to make e-procurement viable for SME suppliers. *Production Planning & Control: Management of Operations, 15*(7), 671–677. doi:10.1080/09537280412331298139

Berners-Lee, T., & Hendler, J. (2001). The Semantic Web: A new form of Web content that is meaningful to computers. *Scientific American*, 34–43. doi:10.1038/scientificamerican0501-34

Berners-Lee, T., Hendler, J., & Lassila, O. (2001). The Semantic Web. *Scientific American*, (May): 28–37.

Bernoff, J., & Li, C. (2008). Harnessing the power of the oh-so-social Web. *MIT Sloan Management Review*, *5*(49), 36–42.

BERR. (2008). *Business enterprise and regulatory reform*. Retrieved September 1, 2009, from http://www.berr.gov.uk/whatwedo/enterprise/enterprisesmes/index.html

Berthon, P., Pitt, L., & Watson, R. T. (1996a). Marketing communication and the World Wide Web. *Business Horizons*, *39*(5), 24–32. doi:10.1016/S0007-6813(96)90063-4

Berthon, P., Pitt, L., & Watson, R. T. (1996b). Re-surfing W3: Research perspectives on marketing communication and buyer behaviour on the World Wide Web. *International Journal of Advertising*, *15*(4), 287–301.

Bharadwaj, A. S. (2000). A resource-based perspective on Information Technology capability and firm performance: An empirical investigation. *Management Information Systems Quarterly*, *24*(1), 169–196. doi:10.2307/3250983

BizEurope.com. (2009). *European business directory*. Retrieved May 11, 2009, from http://www.bizeurope.com

Black, E. L. (2007). Web 2.0 and library 2.0: What librarians need to know. In Courtney, N. (Ed.), *Library and 2.0 and beyond: Innovative technologies and tomorrow's user* (pp. 1–14). Westport, CT: Libraries Unlimited.

Blomqvist, E., Levashova, T., Ohgren, A., Sandkuhl, K., Smirnov, A., & Tarassov, V. (2005). Configuration of dynamic SME supply chains based on ontologies. In Marik, V., Brennan, R. W., & Pechouček, M. (Eds.), *HOLOMAS 2005, LNAI 3593* (pp. 246–256). Berlin/Heidelberg, Germany: Springer-Verlag.

Bode, S., & Burn, J. (2001). *Consultancy engagement and e-business development: A case analysis of Australian SMEs*. A paper presented at the Global Co-Operation in the New Millennium, the 9th European Conference on Information Systems, Bled, Slovenia.

Boeninger, C. F. (2007). In Courtney, N. (Ed.), *Library and 2.0 and Beyond: Innovative technologies and tomorrow's user* (pp. 25–33). Westport, CT: Libraries Unlimited.

Bonoma, T. V. (1985). Case research in marketing: Opportunities, problems, and a process. *JMR, Journal of Marketing Research*, *22*(2), 199–208. doi:10.2307/3151365

Borst, S., Mandelbaum, A., & Reiman, M. I. (2004). Dimensioning large call centers. *Operations Research*, *52*, 17–34. doi:10.1287/opre.1030.0081

Boulos, M. G. K., Maramba, I., & Wheeler, S. (2006). Wikis, blogs and podcasts: A new generation of Web-based tools for virtual collaborative clinical practice and education. *BMC Medical Education*, *5*(6), 41. doi:10.1186/1472-6920-6-41

Boulos, M. N. K., Maramba, I., & Wheeler, S. (2006). Wikis, blogs and podcasts: A new generation of Web-based tools for virtual collaborative clinical practice and education. *BMC Medical Education*, *6*(41). Retrieved from http://www.biomedcentral.com /1472-6920/6/41.

Bowen, P., Hash, J., & Wilson, M. (2006). *Information security handbook: A guide for managers*. Gaithersburg, MD: National Institute of Standards and Technology, Technology Administration - U.S. Department of Commerce.

Bower, D. J., Shaw, C., & Keogh, W. (1998). The process of small firms innovation in the UK oil and gas-related industry. In Oakley, R. (Ed.), *New technology-based firms in the 1990s* (pp. 138–151). London, UK: Paul Chapman Publishing.

Boyle, J. (1997). *Foucault in cyberspace: Surveillance, sovereignty, and hard-wired censors*. Retrieved September 15, 2009, from http://www.law.duke.edu/boylesite/foucault.htm

Boylorn, R. M. (2008). Participants as co-researchers. In Given, L. M. (Ed.), *The Sage encyclopedia of qualitative research methods* (pp. 599–601). Thousand Oaks, CA: Sage Publications.

Brank, J., Grobelnik, M., Milić-Frayling, N., & Mladenić, D. (2002). Feature selection using support vector machines. In Zanisi, A., Brebbia, C. A., Ebecken, N. F. F. E., & Melli, P. (Eds.), *Data mining III* (pp. 261–273). Southampton, Boston, MA: WIT Press.

Brank, J., Grobelnik, M., & Mladenić, D. (2005). A survey of ontology evaluation techniques. In O. Markič, M. Gams, U. Kordeš, M. Heričko, D. Mladenić, M. Grobelnik, ... M. Bohanec (Eds.), *Proceedings of the 8th International Multiconference Information Society IS 2005* (pp. 166-169). Ljubljana, Slovenia.

Brooksbank, R., Kirby, D. A., & Wright, G. (1992). Marketing and company performance: An examination of medium sized manufacturing firms in Britain. *Small Business Economics, 4*, 221–236. doi:10.1007/BF00389477

Brynjolfsson, E., & Saunders, A. (2010). *Wired for innovation: How information technology is reshaping the economy.* Boston, MA: Massachusetts Institute of Technology.

Brynjolfsson, E. (1993). The productivity paradox of Information Technology. *Communications of the ACM, 36*(12), 67–77. doi:10.1145/163298.163309

Brynjolfsson, E., & Hitt, L. M. (1998). Beyond the productivity paradox. *Communications of the ACM, 41*(8), 49–55. doi:10.1145/280324.280332

Bughin, J. (2008). The rise of enterprise 2.0. *Journal of Direct Data and Digital Marketing Practice, 5*(9), 251–259. doi:10.1057/palgrave.dddmp.4350100

Bughin, J., Manyika, J., & Miller, A. (2008). Building the Web 2.0 enterprise: McKinsey global survey results. *The McKinsey Quarterly,* July.

Bui, T., Gachet, A., & Sebastion, H. J. (2006). Web services for negotiation and bargaining in electronic markets: Design requirements, proof-of-concepts, and potential applications to e-procurement. *Group Decision and Negotiation, 15*, 460–490. doi:10.1007/s10726-006-9039-5

Buitelaar, P., Cimiano, P., & Magnini, B. (Eds.). (2005). *Ontology learning from text: Methods, evaluation and applications. Frontiers in artificial intelligence and applications,* vol 123. Amsterdam, The Netherlands: IOS Press. ISSN 0922-6389

Bullinger, H., Warschat, J., Schumacher, O., Slama, A., & Ohlhausen, P. (2005). Ontology-based project management for acceleration of innovation projects. In Hemmje, M. (Eds.), *E.J. Neuhold Festschrift, LNCS 3379* (pp. 280–288). Berlin/Heidelberg, Germany: Springer-Verlag.

Bverf, G. E. (1983). *1BVerfGE 65, 1 – Volkszählung Urteil des Ersten Senats vom 15. Dezember 1983 auf die mündliche Verhandlung vom 18. und 19. Oktober 1983 - 1 BvR 209, 269, 362, 420, 440, 484/83 in den Verfahren über die Verfassungsbeschwerden.* Retrieved September 25, 2009, from http://www.servat.unibe.ch/dfr/bv065001.html.

Caliskan, M., Graupner, D., & Mauve, M. (2006). Decentralized discovery of free parking places. In *VANET '06: Proceedings of the 3rd international workshop on Vehicular ad hoc networks,* (pp. 30–39). New York, NY, USA.

Canadian-Small-Business-Financing-Act. (2006). *Consolidated statutes and regulations of Canada, Canada small business financing regulations (SOR/99-141).* Retrieved October 14, 2006, from http://lois.justice.gc.ca/en/C-10.2/SOR-99-141 /index.html

Canotilho, J. J. G., & Moreira, V. (2007). *Constituição da República Portuguesa anotada* (4th ed.). Coimbra: Coimbra Editora.

Cardoso, J. (2000). *Unified customer interaction™: Gestão do relacionamento num Ambiente Misto de Interacção Self e Assistida.* Lisboa: Centro Atlântico.

Carlton, J. (2009). *The benefits of email marketing.* Retrieved June 10, 2009, from http://www.opt-in-email-marketing.org/benefits-of -email-marketing.html

Carrera, F. (2009). *Marketing digital na versão 2.0 – o que não pode ignorar.* Lisboa, Portugal: Edições Sílabo.

Cassady, C. R., & Kobza, J. E. (1998). A probabilistic approach to evaluate strategies for selecting a parking space. *Transportation Science, 32*(1), 30–42. doi:10.1287/trsc.32.1.30

Cassell, C., Nadin, S., Gray, M., & Clegg, C. (2002). Exploring human resource management practices in small and medium sized enterprises. *Personnel Review, 31*(6), 671–692. doi:10.1108/00483480210445962

Castro, C. S. E. (2005). O direito à autodeterminação informativa e os novos desafios gerados pelo direito à liberdade e à segurança no pós 11 de Setembro. In *Estudos em homenagem ao Conselheiro José Manuel Cardoso da Costa (Vol. II).* Coimbra: Coimbra Editora.

Castro, C. S. E. (2006). *Protecção de dados pessoais na Internet. Sub Judice, 35. Abr-Jun.* Coimbra: Almedina.

CECARM Web page. (2009). *Portal de negocio electrónico. Geomarketing.* Retrieved July 20, 2009, from http://www.cecarm.com/servlet/s.Sl?METHOD=DETALLEGUIAS&id=2253&&sit=c,732

Cestnik, B., Kern, A., & Modrijan, H. (2007). The housing lottery in Slovenia: E-government perspective. In: A. Groenlund, H. J. Scholl & M. A. Wimmer (Eds.), *Electronic Government. 6th International Conference, EGOV 2007, Proceedings of ongoing research, project contributions and workshops*. Linz, Austria: Trauner Verlag.

Cestnik, B., Kern, A., & Modrijan, H. (2008). Semi-automatic ontology construction for improving comprehension of legal documents. In M. A. Wimmer, H. J. Scholl & E. Ferro (Eds.), *Electronic Government. 7th International Conference, EGOV 2008, Lecture Notes in Computer Science* (pp. 328-339). Torino, Italy: Springer.

Chaffey, D. (2007). *E-business and e-commerce management: Strategy, implementation and practice*. Financial Times/Prentice Hall.

Chaffey, D., Ellis-Chadwick, F., Mayer, R., & Johnston, K. (2009). *Internet marketing: Strategy, implementation and practice*. Essex, England: Pearson Education.

Chaffey, D. (2004). Online value proposition. *CIM: What's New in Marketing?* Retrieved August 5, 2009 from http://www.davechaffey.com/E-marketing-Insights/Customer-experience -management/ Online-customer -value-proposition/

Chaffey, D., & Smith, P. R. (2008). *eMarketing eXcellence* (3rd ed.). Oxford, UK: Butterworth-Heinemann.

Chalmeta, R. (2006). Methodology for customer relationship management. *Journal of Systems and Software, 49*(7), 1015–1024. doi:10.1016/j.jss.2005.10.018

Chan, Y. E. (2000). IT value: The great divide between qualitative and quantitative and individual and organizational measures. *Journal of Management Information Systems, 16*(4), 225–261.

Chan, J. K. Y., & Lee, M. K. O. (2002). SME e-procurement adoption in Hong Kong – the roles of power, trust and value. *Proceedings of the Hawaii International Conference on System Sciences, 36*, IEEE Computer Society.

Chaston, I., & Mangles, T. (2003). Relationship marketing in online business-to-business markets: A pilot investigation of small UK manufacturing firms. *European Journal of Marketing, 37*(5/6), 753–773. doi:10.1108/03090560310465134

Chen, S. (2001). *Strategic management of e-business*. New York, NY: John Wiley & Sons, Inc.

Chen, S., Duan, Y., Edwards, J. S., & Lehaney, B. (2006). Toward understanding inter-organizational knowledge transfer needs in SMEs: Insight from a UK investigation. *Journal of Knowledge Management, 10*(3), 6–23. doi:10.1108/13673270610670821

Chen, D., & Vernadat, F. B. (2003). Enterprise interoperability: A standardized view. In Kosanke, K. (Eds.), *IFIP series* (*Vol. 108*, pp. 273–282). Kluwer Academic Publishers.

Chen, P., & Hinton, S. M. (1999). Realtime interviewing using the World Wide Web. *Sociological Research Online, 4*(3). Retrieved on May 3, 2009 from http://www.socresonline.org.uk /4/3/chen.html

Chong, W., & Shafaghi, M. (2009). Performances of B2B e-marketplace for SMEs. *The Research Methods and Survey Results Communications of the IBIMA, 9*, 185–192.

Christensen, E., Curbera, F., Meredith, G., & Weerawarana, S. (2001). *Web service description language* (WSDL) 1.1. Bericht, W3 Consortium, March 2001.

Christl, C., Ghidini, C., Guss, J., Lindsaedt, S., Pammer, V., Scheir, P., & Serafini, L. (2008). *Deploying Semantic Web technologies for work integrated learning in industry. A comparison: SME and large-sized company*. ISWC 7th International semantic web conference, October 26-30, Karlsruhre, Germany

Chui, M., Miller, A., & Roberts, R. P. (2009). Six ways to make Web 2.0 work. *McKinsey Quarterly*, Feb. Retrieved from www.mckinseyquarterly.com/Business_Technology/Application_Management/Six_ways_to_make_Web20_work_2294#foot2

CJEC. (2007). *Court of Justice of the European Communities - opinion of Advocate General Kokott) - (Case C-275/06).*

CNIL. (2005). *Délibération n°2005-235 du 18 octobre2005*. Retrieved September 25, 2009, from http://www.legifrance.gouv.fr/affichCnil.do?oldAction=rechExpCnil&id=CNILTEXT000017652059&fastReqId=137369379&fastPos=1

Cohen, W. M., & Levinthal, D. A. (1990). Absorptive capacity: A new perspective on learning and innovation. *Administrative Science Quarterly, 35*(1), 128–152. doi:10.2307/2393553

Cohen, J. (1997). Some reflections on copyright management systems and laws designed to protect them. *Berkeley Technology Law Journal, 161*. Retrieved September 25, 2009, from http://www.law.berkeley.edu/journals/btlj/articles/vol12/Cohen/html/text.html

Collins, C., Buhalis, D., & Peters, M. (2003). Enhancing SMTEs' business performance through the Internet and e-learning platforms. *Education+ Training, 45*(8/9), 483-494.

Colomb, R. M. (2007). *Ontology and the Semantic Web. Frontiers in artificial intelligence and applications,* vol 156. Amsterdam, The Netherlands: IOS Press. ISSN 0922-6389

Coltman, T. R., Devinney, T. M., & Midgley, D. F. (2007). E-business strategy and firm performance: a latent class assessment of the drivers and impediments to success. *Journal of Information Technology, 27*, 87–101. doi:10.1057/palgrave.jit.2000073

Cooke, M. (2006). Viewpoint: The importance of blogging. *International Journal of Market Research, 48*(6), 645–646.

Cooke, M. (2008). The new world of Web 2.0 research. *International Journal of Market Research, 50*(2), 569–572. doi:10.2501/S147078530820002X

Cooke, M., & Buckley, N. (2008). Web 2.0, social networks and the future of market research. *International Journal of Market Research, 50*(2), 267–292.

Coppel, J. (2002). *E-commerce: Impacts and policy challenges.* Paris, France: Organisation for Economic, Co-operation and Development.

Corradi, A., Montanari, R., & Tibaldi, D. (2004). Context-based access control for ubiquitous service provisioning. *Proceedings of the 28ᵗʰ International Computer Software and Applications Conference* (COMPSAC'04).

Cregan, A. (2009). *Weaving the Semantic Web: Contributions and insights* (p. 234). Sydney, Australia: University of New South Wales.

Culnan, M. J. (2000). Protecting privacy online: Is self-regulation working? *Journal of Public Policy & Marketing, 19*(1), 20–26. doi:10.1509/jppm.19.1.20.16944

Curry, R., Kiddle, C., Markatchev, N., Simmonds, R., Tan, T., Arlitt, M., & Walker, B. (2008). *Facebook meets the virtualized enterprise.* (Technical Report 2008-907-20), Department of Computer Science, University of Calgary, June 18, 2008. Retrieved on September 1, 2009 from http://grid.ucalgary.ca/ documents/Curry KiMaSi08c2.pdf

Dalton, G. (1999). E-business evolution. *Information Week, 7*(37), 50–66.

Damiani, E., De Capitani di Vimercati, S., Fugazza, C., & Samarati, P. (2004). Extending policy languages to the Semantic Web. *Proc. Web Engineering - 4th International Conference* (ICWE 2004), Munich, Germany, July 2004.

Dark, M. J. (2006). Security education, training, and awareness from a human performance technology point of view. In Whitman, M. E., & Mattord, H. J. (Eds.), *Readings and cases in the management information security* (pp. 86–104). Boston, MA: Thomson Course Technology.

Davenport, T. H. (1993). *Process innovation: Reengineering work through Information Technology.* Boston, MA: Harvard Business School Press.

Davenport, T. H., & Prusak, L. (1998). *Working knowledge - how organisations manage what they know.* Boston, MA: Harvard Business Press.

Davilla, A., Gupta, & M., Palmer, R. (2003). Moving procurement systems to the Internet: The adoption and use of e-procurement technology models. *European Management Journal, 21*(1), 11-23. Elsevier Science. doi:10.1016/s0263-2373(02)00155-X

Davydov, M. M. (2000). *E-commerce solutions for business and IT managers. Corporate portals and e-business integration.* New York, NY: McGraw Hill.

de Bruijn, J. (2004). Semantic integration of disparate data sources in the COG project. In *Proceedings of the 6th International Conference on Enterprise Information Systems (ICEIS2004)*, Porto, Portugal, ICEIS Press.

de Werra, J. (2001). Le régime juridique des mesures techniques de protection des oeuvres selon les Traités de l'OMPI, le Digital Millennium Copyright Act, les Directives Européennes et d'autres legislations (Japon, Australie). *Revue Internationale du Droit d'Auteur*, *189*, 66–213.

Deakins, D., & Freel, M. (2009). *Entrepreneurship and small firms* (5th ed.). London, UK: McGraw-Hill.

Dean, M., & Schreiber, G. (Eds.). (2004). *OWL Web Ontology Language reference.* World Wide Web Consortium recommendation (REC-owl-ref-20040210).

Demarco, T. (1997). *The deadline*. New York, NY: Dorset House Publishing.

Demaria, M. J. (2005). IP: Right call for the contact center, RFI analysis. *Network Computing*, *16*, 41–57.

Denning, D. (1987). An intrusion-detection model. *IEEE Transactions on Software Engineering*, 222–232. doi:10.1109/TSE.1987.232894

Deshpande, R., & Zaltman, G. (1982). Factors affecting the use of market research information: A path analysis. *JMR, Journal of Marketing Research*, 14–31. doi:10.2307/3151527

Deveraj, S., & Kohli, R. (2003). Performance impacts of information technology: Is actual usage the missing link? *Management Science*, *49*(3), 273–289. doi:10.1287/mnsc.49.3.273.12736

Dionísio, P., Rodrigues, J. V., Faria, H., Canhoto, R., & Nunes, R. C. (2009). *Blended marketing*. Lisboa, Portugal: Publicações Dom Quixote.

Disability Rights Commission. (2004). *The Web access and inclusion for disabled people a formal investigation conducted by Disability Rights Commission* 2004. Retrieved September 22, 2009, from http://83.137.212.42/sitearchive/drc/PDF/2.pdf

Dotzler, A. (2005). *Bugzilla Bug 272620-XSS vulnerability in internal error messages*. Retrieved from https://bugzilla.mozilla.org/show_bug.cgi?id=272620

Drozdenko, R. G., & Drake, P. D. (2002). *Optimal database marketing: Strategy, development and data mining*. Thousand Oaks, CA: Sage Publications.

Drucker, P. (1993). *Post-capitalist society*. Oxford, UK: Butterworth Heinemann.

DTI (Department of Trade and Industry). (2009). *Website*. Retrieved September 22, 2009, from http://www.dti.gov.uk

Duffy, G., & Dale, B. G. (2002). E-commerce processes: A study of criticality. *Industrial Management & Data Systems*, *102*(8), 432–441. doi:10.1108/02635570210445862

Dunphy, D., Griffith, A., & Benn, S. (2003). *Organizational change for corporate sustainability: A guide for leaders and change agents of the future*. London, UK: Routledge.

eBusiness-Connection. (2008). *Internet marketing*. Retrieved November 2, 2008, from http://www.e-bc.ca/

ECIMF Project Group. (2003). *E-commerce integration meta–framework*. Final draft. Technical report.

Eclipse. (2009). *Eclipse Foundation*. Retrieved August 25, 2009, from http://www.eclipse.org

Eid, R. (2003). *Business-to-business international internet marketing: adoption, implementation and implications, an empirical study of UK companies*. Bradford, UK: Bradford University.

Eid, R., & Trueman, M. (2004). Factors affecting the success of business-to-business international internet marketing (B-to-B IIM): An empirical study of UK companies. *Industrial Management & Data Systems*, *104*, 16–30. doi:10.1108/02635570410514061

Eikelmann, S., Hajj, J., & Peterson, M. (2008). Opinion piece: Web 2.0: Profiting from the threat. *Journal of Direct, Data and Digital Marketing Practice*, *5*(9), 293–295. Retrieved November 27, 2008, from http://www.palgrave-journals.com/dddmp/journal/v9/n3/full/4350094a.html

El-Gohary, H. (2009). *The impact of e-marketing practices on marketing performance of small business enterprises: An empirical investigation*. Bradford, UK: Bradford University.

El-Gohary, H., Trueman, M., & Fukukawa, K. (2008b). E-marketing and small business enterprises: A review of the methodologies. *Journal of Business & Public Policy*, *2*(2), 64–93.

El-Gohary, H., Trueman, M., & Fukukawa, K. (2008a). *E-marketing and small business enterprises: A review of the literature from 2003-2008.* Paper presented at the Institute for Small Business & Entrepreneurship 2008 Conference (ISBE 2008), Belfast, N. Ireland.

eMA. (2008). *American e-marketing association (eMA) - The UK B2C E-Commerce.*

eMA. (2009a). *American e-marketing association (eMA) - US mobile advertising spending from 2008 – 2013.* Retrieved May 12, 2009, from http://www.emarketer. com /Article.aspx?R=1007007

eMA. (2009b). *American e-marketing association (eMA) - three-quarters of the world's messages sent by mobile.* Retrieved May 12, 2009, from http://www.emarketer.com /Article.aspx?R=1006995

eMA. (2009c). *American e-marketing association (eMA) - why retail loves e-mail.* Retrieved March 24, 2009, from http://www.emarketer.com/ Article.aspx?R=1006919

eMA. (2009d). *American e-marketing association (eMA) - mobile messaging in Western Europe.* Retrieved January 5, 2009, from http://www.emarketer.com /Article. aspx?R=1006842

eMarketer. (2009). How the old, the young and everyone in between uses social networks. *eMarketer.* Retrieved August 12, 2009, from http://www.emarketer.com/Article. aspx?R=1007202

Enders, A., Hungenberg, H., Denker, H.-P., & Mauch, S. (2008). The long tail of social networking. Revenue models of social networking sites. *European Management Journal, 5*(26), 199–211. Retrieved November 27, 2008, from http:// www.sciencedirect.com/science?_ob=ArticleURL&_ udi=B6V9T- 4SJGWTT- 2&_user=128597&_rdoc=1&_ fmt=&_orig=search&_sort=d&view=c&_acct=C0000 10621&_version=1&_urlVersion=0&_userid=128597& md5=b2ce82b86c613a3a25 eac1592aad952e

Epsilon, C. (2009). *The benefits of Internet marketing.* Retrieved June 1, 2009, from http://www.epsilonconcepts.com/ upload/file/The%20Benefits %20Of%20 Internet%20 Marketing.pdf

Erl, T. (2004). *Service oriented architecture: A field guide to integration XML and Web services.* Upper Saddle River, NJ: Prentice Hall.

EUROPA. (2009). *Public procurement. European Commission the EU Single Market.* Retrieved August 10, 2009, from http://ec.europa.eu/internal_market/publicprocurement/index_en.htm

Evans, J. R., & King, V. E. (1999). Business-to-business marketing and the World Wide Web planning, managing, and assessing websites. *Industrial Marketing Management, 28*(4), 343–358. doi:10.1016/S0019-8501(98)00013-3

Ewusi-Mensah, K. (2003). *Software development failures.* Cambridge, MA: MIT Press.

Fadel, F., Fox, M. S., & Grüninger, M. (1994). A generic enterprise resource ontology. In *Proceedings of the Third Workshop on Enabling Technologies – Infrastructures for Collaborative Enterprises.* West Virginia University.

Falkenstein, S. (1996). Why you should outsource the creation of your website. *Pennsylvania Certified Public Accounting Journal, December*, 9-12.

Fan, W., Lu, H., Madnick, S. E., & Cheung, D. (2001). Discovering and reconciling value conflicts for numerical data integration. *Information Systems, 26*(8), 635–656. doi:10.1016/S0306-4379(01)00043-6

Fayyad, U., Piatetsky-Shapiro, G., & Smyth, P. (1996). From data mining to knowledge discovery in databases. *AI Magazine, 17*(3), 37–54.

Feldman, R., & Sanger, J. (2006). *The text mining handbook: Advanced approaches in analyzing unstructured data.* Cambridge University Press. doi:10.1017/ CBO9780511546914

Fellbaum, C. (1999). *WordNet: An electronic lexical database.* MIT press.

Fensel, D. (2003). *Ontologies: Silver bullet for knowledge management of electronic commerce* (2nd ed.). Berlin, Germany: Springer.

Fensel, D. (2005). *Information integration with ontologies, experiences form an industrial showcase.* John Wiley & Sons Ltd.

Fernandez, E. B., & Pernul, G. (2006). Patterns for session based access control. *Proceedings of the 2006 Conference on Pattern languages of programs.*

Ferraiolo, D. F., Sandhu, R., Gavrila, S. I., Kuhn, D. R., & Chandramouli, R. (2001). Proposed NIST standard for role based access control. *Information and System Security*, *4*(3), 224–274. doi:10.1145/501978.501980

Finch, S. R. (2003). *R'enyi's Parking Constant.* Cambridge, England: Cambridge University Press.

Finin, T., Joshi, A., Kagal, L., Niu, J., Sandhu, R., Winsborough, W., & Thuraisingham, B. (2008). ROWLBAC: Role based access control in OWL. *Proceedings of the ACM Symposium on Access Control Models and Technologies*, (pp. 73–82).

Finley, S. (2008). Community-based research. In Given, L. M. (Ed.), *The Sage encyclopedia of qualitative research methods* (pp. 501–502). Thousand Oaks, CA: Sage Publications.

Fiore, F. (2001). *E-marketing strategies: The hows and whys of driving sales through e-commerce: Sell anything, anywhere, any way, anytime, at any price.* Que.

Fleming, P. (2009). *Hablemos de la Mercadotecnia Interactiva.* Retrieved July 23, 2009, from http://es.wikipedia.org/wiki/Marketing_en_Internet#Las_4_F.27s_del_Marketing_Online

Fortuna, B., Grobelnik, M., & Mladenić, D. (2006). Semiautomatic data-driven ontology construction system. In: M. Bohanec, M. Gams, V. Rajkovič, T. Urbančič, M. Bernik, D. Mladenić,... B. Novak Škarja (Eds), *IS-2006. Proceedings of the 9th International multi-conference Information Society* (pp 223-226). Ljubljana, Slovenia.

Foucault, M. (1977). *Discipline and punish: The birth of the prison* (trans. Alan Sheridan).

Fowler, J. (1999). Agent based semantic interoperability in infosleuth. *SIGMOD Record*, *28*(1), 60–67. doi:10.1145/309844.310060

Fox, M. S., Burbuceanu, M., & Gruninger, M. (1996). An organization ontology for enterprise modelling: Preliminary concepts for linking structure and behaviour. *Computers in Industry*, *29*, 123–134. doi:10.1016/0166-3615(95)00079-8

Füller, J., Bartl, M., Ernst, H., & Mühlbacher, H. (2006). Community based innovation: How to integrate members of virtual communities into new product development. *Journal of Electronic Commerce Research*, *6*, 57–73. doi:10.1007/s10660-006-5988-7

Funck, S., Mohler, N., & Oertel, W. (2004). Determining car-park occupancy from single images. In *Proceedings of International Symposium on Intelligent Vehicles (IVS04)*, (pp. 325–328). Parma, Italy.

Gaballa, A., & Pearce, W. (1979). Telephone sales manpower planning at Qantas. *Interfaces*, *9*(3), 1–9. doi:10.1287/inte.9.3.1

Gable, G. G. (1991). Consultant engagement for computer system selection: A pro-active client role in small businesses. *Information & Management*, *20*, 83–93. doi:10.1016/0378-7206(91)90046-5

Galgano, A., & La Mesa, E. (2006). *Email marketing: Salesware, IT ASP solutions for e-mail marketing.*

Gans, N., Koole, G., & Mandelbaum, A. (2003). Telephone call centers: Tutorial, review and research prospects. *Manufacturing & Service Operations Management*, *5*(2), 79–141. doi:10.1287/msom.5.2.79.16071

Garcia, F. J. (2005). Bodil Lindqvist: A Swedish churchgoer's violation of the European Union's data protection directive should be a warning to U.S. legislators. *Fordham Intellectual Property, Media, & Entertainment Law Journal*, *15*, 1204.

Gartner. (2009). Gartner reveals five business intelligence predictions for 2009 and beyond. Retrieved 14th September, 2009, from http://www.gartner.com/it/page.jsp?id=856714

Geerts, G. L., & McCarthy, W. (2002). An ontological analysis of the primitives of the extended-REA enterprise information architecture. *International Journal of Accounting Information Systems*, *3*, 1–16. doi:10.1016/S1467-0895(01)00020-3

Geerts, G. L., & McCarthy, W. (1997). Modeling business enterprises as value-added process hierarchies with resource-event-agent object templates. In Sutherland, J., & Patel, D. (Eds.), *Business object design and implementation* (pp. 113–128). Springer-Verlag.

Gennari, J., Musen, M. A., Fergerson, R. W., Grosso, W. E., Crubezy, M., Eriksson, H., et al. Tu, S.W. (2002). *The evolution of Protégé: An environment for knowledge-based systems development.* Retrieved December, 2006, from http://smi.stanford.edu/smi-web/reports/SMI-2002-0943.pdf

Ghosh, S. (1998). Making business sense of the Internet. *Harvard Business Review, 26*(2), 127–135.

Gilmore, A., Carson, D., & Grant, K. (2001). SME marketing in practice. *Marketing Intelligence & Planning, 19*(1), 6–11. doi:10.1108/02634500110363583

Godwin-Jones, R. (2003). Emerging technologies: Blogs and Wikis environments for online collaboration. *Language Learning & Technology, 7*(2), 12–16.

Gogan, J. L. (1997). The Web's impact on selling techniques: Historical perspective and early observations. *International Journal of Electronic Commerce, 1*(2), 89–108.

Goodman, M. R. V. (1999). The pursuit of value through qualitative market research. *Qualitative Market Research: An International Journal, 2*(2), 111–120. doi:10.1108/13522759910270025

Goodman, P. & Zizmor, A. (1996). What to consider when a web site contract hits your desk: Aesthetics, ownership and portability are important issues. *Corp. Legal Times*, 30.

Gordijn, J., & Akkermans, H. (2001). E³-value: Design and evaluation of e-business models. *IEEE Intelligent Systems, 16*(4), 11–17. doi:10.1109/5254.941353

Gray, P. M. D., Preece, A., Fiddian, N. J., Gray, W. A., Bench-Capon, T. J. M., Shave, M. J. R., et al. Wiegand, M. (1997). KRAFT: Knowledge fusion from distributed databases and knowledge bases. In R. R. Wagner (Ed.), *Eighth International Workshop on Database and Expert System Applications* (DEXA-97), (pp. 682-691). New York, NY: IEEE Press.

Gray, R. (2007). Market research: Age of the 2.0 focus group. *Marketing*, 104.

Green, P. E., Tull, D. S., & Albaum, G. (1988). *Research for marketing decisions* (5th ed.). Englewood Cliffs, NJ: Prentice Hall.

Greenberg, E. (2003). *Mission-critical security planner: Creating customized strategies.* Indianapolis, IN: Wiley Publishing.

Greene, S. (2009). *The 13 hidden treasures of Internet marketing.* Retrieved June 2, 2009, from http://www.sitepronews.com/ archives/2002/oct /11.html

Greenfield, J., Short, K., Cook, S., Kent, S., & Crupi, J. (2004). *Software factories: Assembling applications with patterns, models, frameworks and tools* (1st ed.). Wiley Publishing.

Greenstein, M., & Feinman, T. M. (2000). *Electronic commerce: Security, risk management and control.* Irwin/McGraw-Hill.

Grossman, J. (2006). *Cross-site scripting worms and viruses.* WhiteHat Security.

Gruber, T. R. (1995). Toward principles for the design of ontologies used for knowledge sharing. *International Journal of Human-Computer Studies, 43*(5-6), 907–928. doi:10.1006/ijhc.1995.1081

Gruber, T. R. (1993). *Formal ontology in conceptual analysis and knowledge representation: Toward principles for the design of ontologies used for knowledge sharing.* Kluwer Academic Publishers.

Grudin, J. (2006). Enterprise knowledge management and emerging technologies. *Proceedings of the 39th Annual Hawaii International Conference on System Sciences* (HICSS-39), 3, 57a (pp. 1-10).

Gruninger, M., & Pinto, J. A. (1995). A theory of complex actions for enterprise modelling. Working Notes AAAI Spring Symposium Series 1995: Extending Theories of Action: Formal Theory and Practical Applications, Stanford.

Gugdin, M., et al. (2003). *SOAP version 1.2 part 1: Messaging framework.* Retrieved from http://www.w3.org/TR/soap12-part1

Gummesson, E. (2002). Relationship marketing in the new economy. *Journal of Relationship Marketing, 1*(1), 37–57. doi:10.1300/J366v01n01_04

Gummesson, E. (2004). Return on relationships (ROR): The value of relationship marketing and CRM in business-to-business contexts. *Journal of Business and Industrial Marketing, 19*(2), 136–148. doi:10.1108/08858620410524016

Gunasekaran, A., & Ngai, E. W. T. (2008). Adoption of e-procurement in Hong Kong: An empirical research. [Elsevier B.V.]. *International Journal of Production Economics, 113,* 159–175. doi:10.1016/j.ijpe.2007.04.012

Gussis, G. (1998). Website development agreements: A guide to planning and drafting. *Washington University Law Quarterly, 76*(72), 721–757.

Hague, P., & Jackson, P. (2002). *Market research: A guide to planning, methodology and evaluation* (3rd ed.). London, UK: Kogan Page.

Hamill, J., & Gregory, K. (1997). Internet marketing in the internationalisation of UK SMEs. *Journal of Marketing Management, 13,* 9–28. doi:10.1080/0267257X.1997.9964456

Hamill, J. (1997). The Internet and international marketing. *International Marketing Review, 14*(5), 300–323. doi:10.1108/02651339710184280

Hansche, S. D. (2003). Making security awareness happen. In Tipton, H. F., & Krause, M. (Eds.), *Information security management handbook* (4th ed., *Vol. 3*, pp. 317–335). Boca Raton, FL: Auerbach Publications.

Hare, C. (2003). Policy development. In Tipton, H. F., & Krause, M. (Eds.), *Information security management handbook* (4th ed., *Vol. 3*, pp. 353–383). Boca Raton, FL: Auerbach Publications.

Harker, D., & Akkeren, J. V. (2002). Exploring the needs of SMEs for mobile data technologies: The role of qualitative research techniques. *Qualitative Market Research: An International Journal, 5*(3), 199–209. doi:10.1108/13522750210432002

Harrison, A., & van Hoek, R. I. (2005). *Logistics management and strategy.* Financial Times/Prentice Hall.

Hartley, J. F. (1994). Case studies in organizational research. In Cassell, C., & Symon, G. (Eds.), *Organizational research – a practical guide.* London, UK: Sage Publications.

Hawkins, L., Meier, T., Nainis, W. S., & James, H. M. (2001). *The evolution of the call center to customer contact center.* ITSC - Information Technology Support Center.

Hayward, S. (2005). *Service-oriented architecture adds flexibility to business processes.* Gartner Research.

Herold, R. (2003). Information protection: Organization, roles, and separation of duties. In Tipton, H. F., & Krause, M. (Eds.), *Information security management handbook* (4th ed., *Vol. 4*, pp. 415–439). Boca Raton, FL: Auerbach Publications.

Hill, J., & Wright, L. T. (2001). A qualitative research agenda for small to medium-sized enterprises. *Marketing Intelligence & Planning, 19*(6), 432–443. doi:10.1108/EUM0000000006111

Hofacker, C. F. (2001). *Internet marketing* (3rd ed.). New York, NY: John Wiley & Sons, Inc.

Hoffman, D. L., & Novak, T. P. (1996). Marketing in hypermedia computer-mediated environments: Conceptual foundations. *Journal of Marketing, 50*–68. doi:10.2307/1251841

Hoffman, D. L., & Novak, T. P. (1997). A new marketing paradigm for electronic commerce. *The Information Society, 13,* 43–54. doi:10.1080/019722497129278

Hoffman, D. L. (2009). Managing beyond Web 2.0. *The McKinsey Quarterly,* July.

Holman, D., Batt, R., & Holtgrewe, U. (2007). *The global contact center report: International perspectives on management and employment.*

Holsapple, C. W., & Singh, M. (2000). Electronic commerce: From a definitional taxonomy toward a knowledge-management view. *Journal of Organizational Computing and Electronic Commerce, 10*(3), 149–170. doi:10.1207/S15327744JOCE1003_01

Hookway, N. (2008). Entering the blogosphere: Some strategies for using blogs in social research. *Qualitative Research, 8,* 91–113. doi:10.1177/1468794107085298

Howe, J. (2006) Crowdsourcing: A definition. *Wired Blog Network: Crowdsourcing,* 2006. As assessed on May 20, 2009 from http://crowd sourcing.typepad.com/cs/2006/06/ crowdsourcing_a.html

Howes, G. (2008). SMEs not taking advantage of online boom. *SMEweb*. Retrieved August 12, 2009, from http://www.smeweb.com/sales-and-marketing/news/smes-not-taking-advantange-of-online-boom

Huang, Y., Yu, F., Hang, C., Tsai, C., Lee, D., & Kuo, S. (2004). *Securing Web application code by static analysis and runtime protection* (pp. 40–52). New York, NY: ACM.

Hughes, A. M. (2006). *Strategic database marketing* (3rd ed.). New York, NY: McGraw-Hill.

Huselbosch, R. J., Salden, A. H., Bargh, M. S., Ebben, P. W. G., & Reitsma, J. (2005). Context sensitive access control. *Proceedings of SACMAT'05*, Stockholm, ACM.

IBM. (2009). *E-business definition* Retrieved May 21, 2009, from www.ibm.com/ e-business

IBM. (2009). *Web 2.0 goes to work for business*. Retrieved September 1, 2009, from http://www-01.ibm.com/software/info/web20/

IDABC. (Interoperable Delivery of European eGovernment Services to public Administrations, Businesses and Citizens). (2005). *Functional requirements for conducting electronic public procurement under the EU framework*. Retrieved May 30, 2009, from http://ec.europa.eu/idabc/en/document/4721/5874

IDABC. (Interoperable Delivery of European eGovernment Services to public Administrations, Businesses and Citizens). (2009). *Software demonstrators for e-procurement*. Retrieved August 25, 2009, from http://ec.europa.eu/idabc/en/document/3488/5874

Ilube, T. (2009). What you need to know about the Semantic Web. *Harvard Business Review*.

Intalio. (2009). *Intalio business process management suite (BPMS)*. Retrieved on July 6, 2009, from http://community.intalio.com

International Journal of Entrepreneurial Behaviour & Research, 3(7), 84–107.

International Organization for Standardization. (2004). *ISO/IEC FDIS 13335-1 – Information technology - guidelines for the management of IT security - concepts and models for information and communications technology security*.

International Organization for Standardization. (2005). *ISO/IEC 27002 – Information Technology - code of practice for information security management*.

International Organization for Standardization. (2008). *ISO/IEC 27005 – Information Technology - security techniques - information security risk management*.

Internet World Statistics. (2009). *Miniwatts Marketing Group*. Retrieved September 13, 2009, from http://www.internetworldstats.com/stats.htm

iProspect. (2009). *Search engine marketing and online display advertising integration study*. Retrieved August 20, 2009, from http://iprospect.com/abou t/research-study_2009_ searchanddisplay.htm

iProspect. (2007). *Offline channel influence on online search behavior study*. Retrieved August 20, 2009, from http://www.iprospect.com/ about/researchstudy_2007 _offlinechannelinfluence.htm

IS. (2009). *The Internet society (IS) - history of the Internet*. Retrieved March 1, 2009, from http://www.isoc.org/

iWorld. (2003). Las ventajas del e-marketing. *La revista de la tecnología y estrategia de negocio en Internet, 58*. Retrieved July 14, 2009, from http://www.idg.es/iworld/articulo.asp?id=146565

IWS. (2009). *Internet world stats - Internet users in the world from 1995 - 2009*. Retrieved June 10, 2009, from http://www.internet worldstats.com /emarketing.htm

Jackson, J. (2003). Disruptive technologies. *Washington Technology, 17*(2). Retrieved July 30, 2009, from http://www.washingtontechnology.com/print/17_20/19859-1.html?topic=cover-stories

Jain, A. K., Murty, M. N., & Flynn, P. J. (1999). Data clustering: A review. *ACM Computing Surveys, 31*(3), 264–323. doi:10.1145/331499.331504

Jarimo, T., Ljubič, P., Hodik, J., Salkari, I., Bihanec, M., & Lavrač, N. (2008). Multi-criteria partner selection in virtual organizations. In Putnik, G. D., & Cunha, M. M. (Eds.), *Encyclopedia of networked and virtual organizations* (pp. 964–970). doi:10.4018/978-1-59904-885-7.ch127

Jarvis, P. (1987). *Adult learning in the social context*. New York, NY: Croon Helm.

Jasper, R., & Uschold, M. (1999). *A framework for understanding and classifying ontology applications.* 12th Workshop on Knowledge Acquisition Modeling and Management KAW'99.

Javanmardi, S., Amini, M., Jalili, R., & Ganji Saffar, Y. (2006). *Sbac: A semantic based access control model.* In 11th Nordic Workshop on Secure IT-systems (Nord-Sec'06), Linkping, Sweden, 2006.

Jelassi, T., & Enders, A. (2008). Mobile advertising: A European perspective. *Selected Readings on Telecommunication and Networking*, 41.

Jenz & Partner GmbH. (2004). *Business management ontology* (BMO) version 1.0 (release notes). Technical report.

Jermol, M., Lavrač, N., & Urbančič, T. (2004). Managing business intelligence in a virtual enterprise: A case study and knowledge management lessons learned. *Journal of Intelligent and Fuzzy Systems*, *14*(3), 121–136.

Jin, L. (2009). Businesses using Twitter, Facebook to market goods. Retrieved August 12, 2009, from http://www.post-gazette.com/pg/09172/978727-96.stm

Johns, M., Engelmann, B., & Posegga, J. (2008). *XSSDS: Server-side detection of cross-site scripting attacks* (pp. 335–344). Washington, DC: IEEE Computer Society.

Johnson, M. D., Anderson, E. W., & Forrel, C. (1995). Rational and adaptive performance expectations in a customer satisfaction framework. *The Journal of Consumer Research*, *21*, 695–707. doi:10.1086/209428

Johnson, K. (2007). *Imagine this: Radio revisited through podcasting.* Master's Thesis. Retrieved on September 11, 2009, from http://etd.tcu.edu/ etdfiles/available/ etd-08102007-105646/ unrestricted/Johnson.pdf

Johnston, R. H., & Carrico, S. R. (1998). Developing capabilities to use information strategically. *Management Information Systems Quarterly*, *12*(1), 37–47. doi:10.2307/248801

Jones, C. (2004). Software project management practices: Failure versus success. *CrossTalk: The Journal of Defense Software Engineering*, 5-9.

Joshi, A., & Undercoffer, J. L. (2004). On data mining, semantics, and intrusion detection. What to dig for and where to find It. In Kargupta, H., Joshi, A., Sivakumar, K., & Yesha, Y. (Eds.), *Data mining. Next generation challenges and future directions* (pp. 437–460). Menlo Park, California.

Josuttis, N. M. (2007). *SOA in practice.* Sebastopol, CA: O'Reilly.

Jovanovic, N., Kruegel, C., & Kirda, E. (2006). *Pixy: A static analysis tool for detecting Web application vulnerabilities* (p. 6).

Juena, S. S., & Mirza, K. (2008). *Utilization of mobile advertising in B2C marketing.* Porsön, Sweden: Luleå tekniska universitet.

Kalakota, R., & Whinston, A. B. (1999). *Electronic commerce: A manager's guide.* Addison-Wesley Professional.

Kalakota, R., & Robinson, M. (2001). *e-Business 2.0: Roadmap for success.* Upper Saddle River, NJ: Addison-Wesley Professional.

Kals, S., Kirda, E., Kruegel, C., & Jovanovic, N. (2006). *SecuBat: A Web vulnerability scanner* (pp. 247–256). New York, NY: ACM.

Kalyanam, K., & McIntyre, S. (2002). The e-marketing mix: A contribution of the e-tailing wars. *Journal of the Academy of Marketing Science.* Springer Netherlands.

Kalyanpur, A. (2006). *Debugging and repair of OWL ontologies.* PhD. Dissertation, University of Maryland.

Kambhampati, S., & Knoblock, C. A. (2003). Information integration on the Web: A view from AI and databases. *SIGMOD Record*, *32*(4), 122–123. doi:10.1145/959060.959086

Kan, S. H. (2002). *Metrics and models in software quality engineering* (2nd ed.). Boston, MA: Addison-Wesley Professional.

Kaplan, R. (2003). A matter of trust. In Tipton, H. F., & Krause, M. (Eds.), *Information security management handbook* (4th ed., Vol. 3, pp. 385–405). Boca Raton, FL: Auerbach Publications.

Kappelman, L. A., McKeeman, R., & Zhang, L. (2006). Early warnings signs of IT project failure: The dominant dozen. *Information Systems Management.* Retrieved at February 9 2008, from http://www.ism-journal.com/IT-Today/projectfailure.pdf

Katyal, S. (2004a). The new surveillance. *Case Western Law Review, 54*(297). Retrieved September 25, 2009, from http://ssrn.com/abstract=527003

Katyal, S. (2004b). Privacy vs. piracy. *Yale Journal of Law & Technology, 7.* Retrieved September 25, 2009, from http://ssrn.com/abstract=722441

Kauffman, R. J., & Mohtadi, H. (2004). Proprietary and open systems adoption: A risk-augmented transactions cost perspective. *Journal of Management Information Systems, 21*(1), 137–166.

Keegan, S. (2008). Market research. In Given, L. M. (Ed.), *The Sage encyclopedia of qualitative research methods* (pp. 501–502). Thousand Oaks, CA: Sage Publications.

Kelly, S., & Tolvanen, J. P. (2008). *Domain-specific modeling.* Wiley-IEEE Computer Society Press. doi:10.1002/9780470249260

Kiang, M. Y., Raghu, T. S., & Shang, K. H. M. (2000). Marketing on the Internet—who can benefit from an online marketing approach? *Decision Support Systems, 27*(4), 383–393. doi:10.1016/S0167-9236(99)00062-7

Kiani, G. R. (1998). Marketing opportunities in the digital world. *Internet Research: Electronic Networking Applications and Policy, 8*(2), 185–194. doi:10.1108/10662249810211656

Kim, J., & Moon, J. Y. (1998). Designing towards emotional usability in customer interfaces- trustworthiness of cyber-banking system interfaces. *Interacting with Computers, 10*(1), 1–29. doi:10.1016/S0953-5438(97)00037-4

Kim, S., & Chung, D. S. (2007). Characteristics of cancer blog users. *Journal of the Medical Library Association, 95*(4), 445–450. doi:10.3163/1536-5050.95.4.445

Kim, H., Fox, M. S., & Gruninger, M. (1995). An ontology of quality for enterprise modelling. *Proceedings of the Fourth Workshop on Enabling Technologies: Infrastructure for Collaborative Enterprises* (pp. 105-116). IEEE Computer Society Press.

King, W. R. (2006). The collaborative Web. *Information Systems Management, 5*(23), 88. doi:10.1201/1078.105 80530/45925.23.2.20060301/92676.9

King, R. (2008). How companies use Twitter to bolster their brands. Retrieved on September 11, 2009, from http://www.businessweek.com /technology/content/ sep2008/ tc2008095 _320491.htm

Kirby, J. (2006). Viral marketing. In Kirby, J., & Marsden, P. (Eds.), *Connected marketing: The viral, buzz and word of mouth revolution* (pp. 87–106). Oxford, UK: Butterworth-Heinemann.

Kirda, E., Kruegel, C., Vigna, G., & Jovanovic, N. (2006). *Noxes: A client-side solution for mitigating cross-site scripting attacks* (pp. 330–337). New York, NY: ACM.

Klein, A. (2007). *DOM based cross site scripting or XSS of the third kind.* Retrieved from http://www.Webappsec.org/projects/articles/071105.html

Kleinberg, J. M. (1999). Authoritative sources in a hyper-linked environment. *Journal of the ACM, 46*(5), 604–632. doi:10.1145/324133.324140

Knublauch, H., Fergerson, R., Noy, N. F., & Musen, M. A. (2004). The protégé OWL plugin: An open development environment for Semantic Web applications. In S. A. McIlraith, D. Plexousakis, & F. van Harmelen (Eds.), *Proceedings of the International Semantic Web Conference (ISWC): Third International Semantic Web Conference, Hiroshima, Japan. Volume 3298 of Lecture Notes in Computer Science,* (pp. 229–243). Springer.

Ko, H. J., & Kang, W. (2008). Enhanced access control with semantic context hierarchy tree for ubiquitous computing. *International Journal of Computer Science and Network Security, 8*(10), 114–120.

Kogut, B. (2000). The network as knowledge: Generative rules and the emergence of structure. *Strategic Management Journal, 21*(3), 405–425. doi:10.1002/(SICI)1097-0266(200003)21:3<405::AID-SMJ103>3.0.CO;2-5

Kohli, A. K., & Jaworski, B. J. (1990). Market orientation: The construct, research propositions, and managerial implications. *Journal of Marketing, 54*(2), 1–18. doi:10.2307/1251866

Koole, G., & Mandelbaum, A. (2002). Queueing models of call centers: An introduction. *Annals of Operations Research, 113,* 41–59. doi:10.1023/A:1020949626017

Kotler, P. (2005). *Marketing management – analysis, planning, implementation and control* (12th ed.). London, UK: Prentice Hall.

Kretz, C. (2007). Podcasting in libraries. In Courtney, N. (Ed.), *Library 2.0 and beyond: Innovative technologies and tomorrow's user* (pp. 35–48). Westport, CT: Libraries Unlimited.

Kruegel, C., & Vigna, G. (2003). *Anomaly detection of Web-based attacks* (pp. 251–261). New York, NY: ACM.

Kumar, V., & Reinartz, W. J. (2006). *Customer relationship management: A database approach.* Hoboken, NJ: John Wiley & Sons.

Lancioni, R. A., Smith, M. F., & Oliva, T. A. (2000). The role of the internet in supply chain management. *Industrial Marketing Management, 29*(1), 45–56. doi:10.1016/S0019-8501(99)00111-X

Lang, B., Zhao, N., Ge, K., & Chen, K. (2008). *An XACML policy generating method based on policy view.* 3th International Conference on Pervasive Computing and Applications, vol. 1 (pp. 295–301). ISBN: 978-1-4244-2020-9

Lassila, O., & Swick, R. R. (Eds.). (1999). *Resource description framework (RDF) model and syntax specification.* W3C Recommendation. Retrieved from http://www.w3.org/TR/ REC-rdf-syntax/

Laudon, K. C., Laudon, J. P., & Filip, F. G. (2004). Management information systems: Managing the digital firm. *New Jersey, 8.*

Lavrač, N., Ljubič, P., Urbančič, T., Papa, G., Jermol, M., & Bollhalter, S. (2007). Trust modeling for networked organizations using reputation and collaboration estimates. *IEEE Transactions on Systems, Man and Cybernetics. Part C, Applications and Reviews, 37*(3), 429–439. doi:10.1109/TSMCC.2006.889531

Leitner, P., & Grechenig, T. (2008). *Collaborative shopping networks: Sharing the wisdom of crowds in e-commerce environments.* 21st Bled eConference eCollaboration: Overcoming Boundaries through Multi-Channel Interactions, June 15-18. Retrieved May 15, 2009 from http://domino.fov.uni-mb.si/proceedings.nsf/Proceedings/ 824F8A6AC21D3F 99C125748100440406 /$File/25Leitner.pdf

Lesjak, D., & Vehovar, V. (2005). Factors affecting evaluation of e-business projects. *Industrial Management & Data Systems, 105*(4), 409–428. doi:10.1108/02635570510592334

Liang, T. P., & Huang, J. S. (1998). An empirical study on consumer acceptance of products in electronic markets: A transaction cost model. *Decision Support Systems, 24*(1), 29–43. doi:10.1016/S0167-9236(98)00061-X

Lin, J., Fox, M. S., & Bilgic, T. (1996). A requirement ontology for engineering design. *Proceedings of the Third International Conference on Concurrent Engineering,* (pp. 343-351).

Lindon, D., Lendrevie, J., Rodrigues, J. V., & Dionísio, P. (2004). *Mercator XXI.* Lisboa, Portugal: Publicações Dom Quixote.

Liu, Y., Zhou, C. F., & Chen, Y. W. (2006). *Determinants of E-CRM in influencing customer satisfaction. Lecture Notes in Computer Science, 4099.* Berlin/Heidelberg, Germany: Springer.

Lowry, P. B., Vance, A., Moody, G., Beckman, B., & Read, A. (2008). Explaining and predicting the impact of branding alliances and website quality on initial consumer trust of e-commerce websites. *Journal of Management Information Systems, 24*(4), 199–224. doi:10.2753/MIS0742-1222240408

Lucca, G. D., Fasolino, A., Mastoianni, M., & Tramontana, P. (2004). *Identifying cross site scripting vulnerabilities in Web applications* (pp. 71–80).

Lytras, M. D., & Athanasia, P. (2006). Towards the development of a novel taxonomy of knowledge management systems from a learning perspective: An integrated approach to learning and knowledge infrastructures. *Journal of Knowledge Management, 10*(6), 64–80. doi:10.1108/13673270610709224

Maciá, F. (2005). ¿Cabemos todos en los diez primeros puestos de Google? *Human Level Communications.* Retrieved July 25, 2009, from http://www.humanlevel.com/recursos.asp?IdNoticia=19

Maddox, L. M., & Gong, W. (2005). Effects of URLs in traditional media advertising in China. *International Marketing Review, 22*(6), 673–692. doi:10.1108/02651330510630285

Madhavan, J., Bernstein, P., & Rahm, E. (2001). Generic schema matching with cupid. *Proc. VLDB* (pp. 49-58).

Madhavan, J., Bernstein, P. A., Domingos, P., & Halevy, A. (2002). Representing and reasoning about mappings between domain models. *Proceedings of the 18th National Conference on Artificial Intelligence* (AAAI'02), Edmonton, Alberta, Canada.

March, S. T., Hevner, A., & Ram, S. (2000). Research commentary: An agenda for Information Technology research in heterogeneous and distributed environments. *Information Systems Research, 11*(4), 327–341. doi:10.1287/isre.11.4.327.11873

Martin, L., & Matlay, H. (2003). Innovative use of the Internet in established small firms: The impact of knowledge management and organisational learning in accessing new opportunities. *Qualitative Market Research: An International Journal, 6*(1), 18–26. doi:10.1108/13522750310457348

Martinich, J. S. (1997). *Production and operations management: An applied modern approach.* New York, NY: John Wiley & Sons.

Matlay, H., & Westhead, P. (2005). Virtual teams and the rise of e-entrepreneurship in Europe. *International Small Business Journal, 23*(3), 279–302. doi:10.1177/0266242605052074

Mc Guinness, D. L., Zeng, H., da Silva, P. P., Ding, L., Narayanan, D., & Bhaowal, M. (2006). Investigations into trust for collaborative repositories: A Wikipedia case study. [Edinburgh, UK.]. *Proc, WWW2006*(May), 22–26.

McCarthy, W. E. (1982). The REA accounting model: A generalized framework for accounting systems in a shared data environment. *Accounting Review, 57*(3), 554–578.

McCarthy, W. E. (2003). The REA modelling approach to teaching accounting information systems. *Issues in Accounting Education, 18*(4), 427–441. doi:10.2308/iace.2003.18.4.427

McCarthy, W. E. (1999). Semantic modeling in accounting education, practice, and research: Some progress and impediments. In Thalheim, B., Akoka, J., & Kangassalo, H. (Eds.), *Conceptual modeling: Current issues and future directions* (pp. 144–153). Springer.

McCole, P., & Ramsey, E. (2004). Internet-enabled technology in knowledge-intensive business services: A comparison of Northern Ireland, the Republic of Ireland and New Zealand. *Marketing Intelligence, 22*(7), 761–779. doi:10.1108/02634500410568

McDonald, M., & Wilson, H. (1999). *E-marketing improving marketing effectiveness in a digital world.*

McFadden, D. (1986). The choice theory approach to market research. *Marketing Science, 5*(4), 275–297. doi:10.1287/mksc.5.4.275

McGowan, P., Durkin, M. G., Allen, L., Dougan, C., & Nixon, S. (2001). Developing competencies in the entrepreneurial small firm for use of the Internet in the management of customer relationships. *Journal of European Industrial Training, 25*(2/4), 126–136. doi:10.1108/EUM0000000005443

McGuinness, D. L., Fikes, R., Rice, J., & Wilder, S. (2000a). An environment for merging and testing large ontologies. In [Morgan Kaufmann.]. *Proceedings of KR, 2000*, 483–493.

McGuinness, D. L., & van Harmelen, F. (2004). *OWL Web ontology language overview.* W3C recommendation. Retrieved from http://www.w3.org/TR/owlfeatures/

McGuinness, D. L., Fikes, R., Rice, J., & Wilder, S. (2000b). The chimaera ontology environment. In *Proceedings of the 7th Conference on Artificial Intelligence (AAA100) and of the 12th Conference on Innovative Applications of Artificial Intelligence* (IAAI00), (pp. 1123–1124). AAAI Press.

McKim, B. (2002). The differences between CRM and database marketing. *Journal of Database Marketing, 9*, 371–375. doi:10.1057/palgrave.jdm.3240086

McLuhan, M. (2009). *Marshall McLuhan quotations.* Retrieved February 15, 2009, from http://www.marshallmcluhan.com /main.html

McNutt, J. G. (2008). Web 2.0 tools for policy research and advocacy. *Journal of Policy Practice, 7*(1), 81–85. doi:10.1080/15588740801909994

MDA. (2009). *Mobile Data Association - text message figures in the UK.* Retrieved March 21, 2009, from http://www.text.it/mediacentre /sms_figures.cfm

Meho, L. I. (2006). E-mail interviewing in qualitative research: A methodological discussion. *Journal of the American Society for Information Science and Technology, 57*(10), 1284–1295. doi:10.1002/asi.20416

Melville, N., Kraemer, K., & Gurbaxani, V. (2004). Information Technology and organizational performance: An integrative model of IT business value. *Management Information Systems Quarterly, 28*(2), 283–322.

Mena, E., et al. (1996). *OBSERVER: An approach for query processing in global information systems based on interoperation across preexisting ontologies* (pp. 14–25).

MGM Studios, Inc. v. Grokster, Ltd. 545 U.S. 913 (2005).

Mhay, S. (n.d.). *Request for... procurement processes.* Retrieved on September 10, 2009, from http://www.negotiations.com/articles/procurement-terms/

Millman, R. (2007). Web 2.0 opens companies up to hackers. *ITPRO.* Retrieved August 12, 2009, from http://www.itpro.co.uk/108544/web-2-0-opens-companies-uo-to-hackers

Mimbela, L. E. Y., & Klein, L. A. (2000). A summary of vehicle detection and surveillance technologies used in intelligent transportation systems.

Mitra, P., & Wiederhold, G. (2001). *An algebra for semantic interoperability of information sources* (pp. 174–182). In BIBE.

Mitra, P., & Wiederhold, G. (2004). An ontology composition algebra. In Staab, S., & Studer, R. (Eds.), *Handbook on ontologies, international handbooks on Information Systems* (pp. 93–116). Springer.

Mitra, P., Jannink, J., & Wiederhold, G. (1999). Semiautomatic integration of knowledge sources. In *Proceedings of Fusion '99.* Sunnyvale, USA.

Mitra, P., Wiederhold, G., & Kersten, M. (2000). A graph oriented model for articulation of ontology interdependencies. *Proceedings of the 7th International Conference on Extending Database Technology: Advances in Database Technology,* (pp. 86-100).

Miyazaki, A. D., & Fernandez, A. (2000). Internet privacy and security: An examination of online retailer disclosures. *Journal of Public Policy and Marketing (Privacy and Ethical Issues in Database/Interactive Marketing and Public Policy), 19*(1), 54-61.

Mosca, A., Palmonari, M., & Sartori, F. (2009). An upper-level functional design ontology to support knowledge management in SME-based E-manufacturing of mechanical products. *The Knowledge Engineering Review, 24,* 265–285. doi:10.1017/S0269888909990063

Moses, T. (2005). *eXtensible Access Control Markup Language (XACML)* version 2.0. OASIS Standard.

Mosey, S. (2005). Understanding new-to-market product development in SMEs. *International Journal of Operations & Production Management, 25*(2), 114–130. doi:10.1108/01443570510576994

Muller, F. (2002). *Buen uso de las etiquetas Meta.* Retrieved July 25, 2009, from http://www.webexperto.com

Murray, A. (2000). The use of trade marks as meta tags: Defining the boundaries. *International Journal of Law and Information Technology, 8*(3), 263–284. doi:10.1093/ijlit/8.3.263

Murthy, D. (2008). Digital ethnography: An examination of the use of new technologies for social research. *Sociology, 42*(5), 837–855. doi:10.1177/0038038508094565

Myers, J. H. (1996). *Segmentation and positioning for strategic marketing decisions.* Chicago, IL: American Marketing Association.

Nations, D. (2009). *What is Web 2.0? How Web 2.0 is defining society.* Retrieved September 1, 2009, from http://webtrends.about.com/od/web20/a/what-is-web20.htm

Naumenko, A. (2007). Semantics-based access control – ontologies and feasibility study of policy enforcement function. In *Proceedings of the ACM 3rd International Conference on Web Information Systems and Technologies, Volume Internet Technologies,* (pp. 150–155).

Neef, D. (2001). *e-procurement: From strategy to implementation*. Upper Saddle River, NJ: Financial Times Prentice Hall.

Ngai, E. W. T. (2003). Internet marketing research (1987-2000): A literature review and classification. *European Journal of Marketing*, *37*(1-2), 24–49. doi:10.1108/03090560310453894

Nonaka, I. (1991). The knowledge creating company. *Harvard Business Review*, *5*(69), 96–104.

Norcross, T. (2008). *What is mobile marketing?* Retrieved December 20, 2008, from http://www.mobilemarketing magazine.co.uk /2005/10/what_is_ mobile_.html

Noy, N. (2004). Semantic integration: A survey of ontology-based approaches. *SIGMOD Record*, *33*(4), 65–70. doi:10.1145/1041410.1041421

Nykamp, M. (2001). *The customer differential: The complete guide to implementing customer relationship management*. New York, NY: American Management Association.

O' Reilly, T. (2007). What is Web 2.0: Design patterns and business models for the next generation of software. *Communications & Strategies*, *1*, 17-37. Retrieved on September 10, 2009 from http://ssrn.com/abstract=1008839

O'Leary, D. E. (2004). On the relationship between REA and SAP. *International Journal of Accounting Information Systems*, *5*, 65–81. doi:10.1016/j.accinf.2004.02.004

O'Reilly, T. (2005). What is Web 2.0: Design patterns and business models for the next generation of software, 2005. Retrieved on June 14, 2009, from http://oreilly.com/pub/a/oreilly /tim/news/ 2005/09/30/ what-is-web-20.html

Obrst, L. (2003). Ontologies for semantically interoperable systems. *Proceedings of the International Conference on Information and Knowledge Management*, (pp. 366-369).

Ochoa, X., & Duval, E. (2008). Quantitative analysis of user-generated content on the Web. *Proceedings of WebEvolve 2008: Web Science Workshop at WWW '08*.

Office for National Statistics E-commerce and ICT Activity. (2008). *Statistics*. Retrieved September 2, 2009, from http://www.statistics.gov.uk/pdfdir/ecom1108.pdf

Oktay, B., & Wrenn, G. (1999). *A look back at the notice-takedown provisions of the US Digital Millennium Copyright Act*. WIPO Workshop on service provider liability, Geneva, Retrieved September 25, 2009, from www.wipo.int/edocs/mdocs/mdocs/en/osp_lia/osp_lia_2.doc

Oldevik, J., Solberg, A., Haugen, Ø., & Møller-Pedersen, B. (2006). Evaluation framework for model-driven product line engineering tools. In Käkölä, T., & Dueñas, J. C. (Eds.), *Software product lines: Research issues in engineering and management* (pp. 589–618). Springer.

Oldevik, J. (2006). MOFScript Eclipse plug-in: Metamodel-based code generation. In *Proceedings of the Eclipse Technology eXchange Workshop (eTX) at the ECOOP 2006 Conference*, Nantes, France, 2006.

Oliva, R. A. (2004). B2B for sale. *Marketing Management*, *13*(5), 48–49.

OpenESB. (2009). *The open enterprise service bus*. Retrieved August 25, 2009, from https://open-esb.dev.Java.net

OWASP. (2003). *OWASP enterprise security API*. Retrieved from http://www.owasp.org/index.php/Category:OWASP_Enterprise_Security_API

OWASP. (2007). *XSS (cross site scripting) prevention cheat sheet*. Retrieved from http://www.owasp.org/index.php/XSS_(Cross_Site_Scripting)_Prevention_Cheat_Sheet

Pal, N., & Rangaswamy, A. (2003). *The power of one: Gaining business value from personalization technologies*. Victoria, Canada: Trafford Publishing.

Pan, B., MacLaurin, T., & Crotts, J. C. (2007). Travel blogs and the implication for destination marketing. *Journal of Travel Research*, *46*, 35–45. doi:10.1177/0047287507302378

Pan, C. C., Mitra, P., & Liu, P. (2006). Semantic access control for information interoperation. In *SACMAT '06: Proceedings of the 11th ACM symposium on Access control models and technologies*, (pp. 237–246). New York, NY: ACM.

Panayappan, R., Trivedi, J. M., Studer, A., & Perrig, A. (2007).Vanet-based approach for parking space availability. In *VANET '07: Proceedings of the fourth ACM international workshop on Vehicular ad hoc networks*, (pp. 75–76). New York, NY, USA.

Papazoglou, M. P. (2008). *Web services: Principles and technology*. Harlow, UK: Pearson Education Limited.

Papazoglou, M. P., & Tsalgatidou, A. (2000). Business to business electronic commerce issues and solutions. *Decision Support Systems*, *29*(4), 301–304. doi:10.1016/S0167-9236(00)00079-8

Parise, S., & Guinan, P. J. (2008). Marketing using Web 2.0. *Proceedings of the 41ˢᵗ Hawaii International Conference on System Sciences* (HICSS-41), 2008.

Park, C. H., & Kim, Y. G. (2003). A framework of dynamic CRM: Linking marketing with information strategy. *Business Process Management Journal*, *9*(5), 652–671. doi:10.1108/14637150310496749

Park, J., & Ram, S. (2004). Information Systems interoperability: What lies beneath? *ACM Transactions on Information Systems*, *22*(4), 595–632. doi:10.1145/1028099.1028103

Pateli, A., & Giaglis, G. M. (2003). A framework for understanding and analysing e-business models. *BLED 2003 Proceedings*. Retrieved from http://ais.bepress.com/bled2003/4

Paul, P. (1996). Marketing on the Internet. *Journal of Consumer Marketing*, *13*(4), 27–39. doi:10.1108/07363769610124528

Payne, A., & Frow, P. (2005). A strategic framework for customer relationship management. *Journal of Marketing*, *69*(4), 167–176. doi:10.1509/jmkg.2005.69.4.167

Payne, T. R., & Lassila, O. (2004). Guest editors' introduction: Semantic Web services. *IEEE Intelligent Systems*, *19*(4), 14–15. doi:10.1109/MIS.2004.29

Pelham, A. M., & Wilson, D. T. (1996). A longitudinal study of the impact of market structure, firm structure, strategy, and market orientation culture on dimensions of small-firm performance. *Journal of the Academy of Marketing Science*, *24*(1), 27–43. doi:10.1007/BF02893935

Peltier, T. R. (2001). *Information security risk analysis*. Boca Raton, FL: Auerbach Publications.

Peppard, J. (2000). Customer Relationship Management (CRM) in financial services. *European Management Journal*, *18*(3), 312–327. doi:10.1016/S0263-2373(00)00013-X

Peppers, D., & Rogers, M. (1999). *Enterprise one to one*. Currency.

Peppers, D., & Rogers, M. (2004). *Managing customer relationships: A strategic framework*. John Wiley & Sons.

Peria, F. (2003). E-procurement can have a substantial and positive impact on your bottom line. *CIO Magazine*. Retrieved Dec, 2004, from http://www.cio.com

Perry, J., & Schneider, G. P. (2000). *Electronic commerce*.

Petrič, I., Urbančič, T., Cestnik, B., & Macedoni-Lukšič, M. (2009). Literature mining method RaJoLink for uncovering relations between biomedical concepts. *Journal of Biomedical Informatics*, *42*(2), 219–227. doi:10.1016/j.jbi.2008.08.004

Petrič, I., Urbančič, T., & Cestnik, B. (2006).Comparison of ontologies built on titles, abstracts and entire texts of articles. In M. Bohanec, M. Gams, V. Rajkovič, T. Urbančič, M. Bernik, D. Mladenić, ... B. Novak Škarja (Eds), *IS-2006. Proceedings of the 9th International multi-conference Information Society* (pp. 227-230). Ljubljana, Slovenia.

Petrocelli, T. (2006). *Data protection and information lifecycle management*. New Jersey: Prentice Hall.

Pfleeger, C. P., & Pfleeger, S. L. (2003). *Security in computing* (3rd ed.). New Jersey: Prentice Hall.

Pichitlamken, J., Deslauriers, A., L'Ecuyer, P., & Avramidis, A. N. (2003). *Modelling and simulation of a telephone call center*. Paper presented at the 2003 Winter Simulation Conference.

Pipkin, D. L. (2006). Linking business objectives and security directions. In Whitman, M. E., & Mattord, H. J. (Eds.), *Readings and cases in the management information security* (pp. 8–16). Boston, MA: Thomson Course Technology.

Pires, A., & Santos, A. P. (1996). *Satisfação dos clientes – um objectivo estratégico de gestão*. Lisboa, Portugal: Texto Editora.

Pixley, T., et al. (2000). *Document Object Model (DOM) level 3 events specification*. W3C recommendation, November.

Plakoyiannaki, E., & Tzokas, N. [REMOVED HYPER-LINK FIELD]. (2002). Customer relationship management: A capabilities portfolio perspective. *Journal of Database Marketing, 9*, 228–237. doi:10.1057/palgrave.jdm.3240004

Pobobsky, G. (1992). Small and medium enterprises and labour law. *International Labour Review, 131*(6).

Pollock, J. (2001). *A Semantic Web business case.* Presented on behalf of the W3C Semantic Web Education and Outreach interest group. Retrieved December, 2009, from http://www.x3.org/2001/sw/sweo/public/BusinessCase/Business Case. PDF

Pool, P. W., Parnell, J. A., Spillan, J. E., Carraher, S., & Lester, D. L. (2006). Are SMEs meeting the challenge of integrating e-commerce into their businesses? A review of the development, challenges and opportunities. *International Journal of Information Technology and Management, 5*(2/3), 97–113.

Poon, S., & Jevons, C. (1997). Internet-enabled international marketing: A small business network perspective. *Journal of Marketing Management, 13*, 29–41. doi:10.1080/0267257X.1997.9964457

Poon, S., & Swatman, P. (1999a). A longitudinal study of expectations in small business Internet commerce. *International Journal of Electronic Commerce, 3*, 21–34.

Poon, S., & Swatman, P. M. C. (1997a). Small business use of the Internet. *International Marketing Review, 14*(5), 385–402. doi:10.1108/02651339710184343

Poon, S., & Swatman, P. M. C. (1997b). Internet-based small business communication: Seven Australian cases. *Electronic Markets, 7*(2), 15–21. doi:10.1080/10196789700000019

Poon, S., & Swatman, P. M. C. (1999b). An exploratory study of small business Internet commerce issues. *Information & Management, 35*(1), 9–18. doi:10.1016/S0378-7206(98)00079-2

Poon, S., & Swatman, P. M. C. (1996). Small business alliances: Internet-enabled strategic advantage. *Monash University Department of Information Systems Working Paper 25/95*: Citeseer.

Porter, M. E. (2001). Strategy and the Internet. *Harvard Business Review, 79*(3), 62–79.

Potter, D. (2006). Ipod, you pod, we all pod. *American Journalism Review, 28*(1), 64.

Powers, C. S., Ashley, P., & Schunter, M. (2002). Privacy promises, access control, and privacy management. *Proceedings of the 3rd International Symposium on Electronic Commerce* (ISEC'02).

Presutti, W. D. (2003). Supply management and e-procurement: Creating value added in the supply chain. *Industrial Marketing Management, 32*, 219–226. doi:10.1016/S0019-8501(02)00265-1

Priebe, T., Dobmeier, W., & Kamprath, N. (2006). *Supporting attribute-based access control with ontologies.* First International Conference on Availability, Reliability and Security (ARES'06) (pp. 465-472). IEEE Computer Society Press. ISBN 0-7695-2567-9

Priebe, T., Fernandez, E. B., Mehlau, J. I., & Pernul, G. (2004). A pattern system for access control. *Proceedings of the 18th Annual IFIP WG 11.3 Working Conference on Data and Application Security*, Sitges, Spain.

Prud'hommeaux, E. (2001). *W3C ACL system.*

Pühringer, S., & Taylor, A. (2008). A practitioner's report on blogs as a potential source of destination marketing intelligence. *Journal of Vacation Marketing, 14*(2), 177–187. doi:10.1177/1356766707087524

Puschmann, T., & Alt, R. (2005). Successful use of e-procurement in supply chains. *Supply Chain Management: An International Journal, 10*(2), 122-133. Emerald Group Publishing. doi:10.1108/13598540510589197

Qian, L., & Tan, T. (2008). *Design of Web-based cost estimation and supplier selection service with Unified Modeling Language.* IEEE International Conference. Retrieved on September 10, 2009, from http://ieeexplore.ieee.org

Quayle, M. (2002). E-commerce: The challenge for UK SMEs in the twenty-first century. *International Journal of Operations & Production Management, 22*(9/10), 1148–1161. doi:10.1108/01443570210446351

Quelch, J. A., & Klein, L. R. (1996). The Internet and international marketing. *Sloan Management Review, 37*(3), 60.

Rajkumar, T. M. (2001). E-procurement: Business and technical issues. *Information Systems Management, 18*(4), 1-9. Taylor & Francis. doi:10.1201/1078/43198.18.4.20 0110901/31465.6

Ram, S., Park, J., & Lee, D. (1999). Digital libraries for the next millennium: Challenges and research directions. *Information Systems Frontiers, 1*(1), 75–94. doi:10.1023/A:1010021029890

Raman, M. (2006). Wiki technology as a "free" collaborative tool within an organisational setting. *Information Systems Management, 5*(23), 59–66. doi:10.1201/1078.1 0580530/46352.23.4.20060901/95114.8

Rathi, D., & Given, L. M. (2010). Research 2.0: A framework for qualitative and quantitative research in Web 2.0 environments. *Proceedings of the 43rd Hawaii International Conference in System Science* (HICSS-43).

Raymond, E. (1999). The cathedral and the bazaar. *Knowledge, Technology, and Policy, 12*(3), 23–49. doi:10.1007/s12130-999-1026-0

Raysman, R., & Brown, P. (1996). Key issues in website development agreements. *New York Legal Journal, 3*.

Reedy, J., & Schullo, S. (2004). *Electronic marketing – integrating electronic resources into the marketing process* (2ed ed.). Cincinnati, OH: Thomson South-Western.

Reid, E. (2003). Using Web link analysis to detect and analyze hidden Web communities. In Vriens, D. (Ed.), *Information and communications technology for competitive intelligence* (pp. 57–84). Hilliard, OH: Ideal Group Inc.

Reisner, R. (2009). Comcast's Twitter man. Retrieved on September 11, 2009 from http://www.businessweek.com/managing/content/ jan2009/ ca20090113 _373506.htm

Ren, L. C., & Yuan, L. J. (2007). *Analysis on influential factors of network brand in electronic commerce*. 1st International Conference on Management Innovation, JUN 04-06, 2007 Shanghai, P R China. International Conference on Management Innovation, Vols 1 and 2, (pp. 602-608).

RIDE Consortium. (2006). A roadmap for interoperability of e-health system in support of com 356 with special emphasis in semantic interoperability.

Riquelme, H. (2002). Commercial Internet adoption in China: Comparing the experience of small, medium and large businesses. *Internet Research: Electronic Networking Applications and Policy, 12*(3), 276–286. doi:10.1108/10662240210430946

Robinson, R. (2008). *Web 2.0 – catching a wave of business innovation*. IBM. Retrieved June 20, 2009, from http://www.ibm.com/developerworks/webservices/library/ws-enterprise1/?S_TACT=105AGX10&S_CMP=SMASH

Rodgers, J. A., Yen, D. C., & Chou, D. C. (2002). Developing e-business: A strategic approach. *Information Management & Computer Security, 10*(4), 184–192. doi:10.1108/09685220210436985

Rogers, E. M. (1983). *Diffusions of innovations* (3rd ed.). Free Press, Macmillan Publishing.

Rostro, F. R., & Grudzewski, W. M. (2008). Marketing strategic planning as a source of competitive advantage for Mexican SMEs. *Institute of Organization and Management in Industry, 1*(1), 19–26.

Rouvroy, A., & Poullet, Y. (2008). The right to informational self-determination and the value of self-development. Reassessing the importance of privacy for democracy. Reinventing data protection. *Proceedings of the International Conference*, Springer, Brussels, 12-13 October 2007, Retrieved September 25, 2009, from http://www.miauce.org/images/stories/paper/the%20right%20to%20informational%20self-determination%20and%20the%20value%20of%20self-development.pdf

RSnake. (2009). *XSS (cross site scripting) cheat sheet*. Retrieved from http://ha.ckers.org/xss.html

Sabou, M., d'Aquin, M., & Motta, E. (2006). Using the Semantic Web as background knowledge for ontology mapping. *Proceedings of the International Workshop on Ontology Matching (OM-2006)*, collocated with ISWC'06.

Sainz, B., de la Torre, I., & López, M. (2010). Analysis of benefits and risks of e-commerce. Practical study of Spanish SME. In Portela, I. M., & Cruz-Cunha, M. M. (Eds.), *Information communication technology law, protection and access rights*. Hershey, PA: IGI Global Publishing. doi:10.4018/9781615209750.ch014

Sainz, B., de la Torre, I., & López, M. (2009). *Soluciones de hardware y software para el desarrollo de teleservicios.* Madrid, España: Creaciones Copyright.

Samarati, P., & de Capitani di Vimercati, S. (2001). Access control: Policies, models, and mechanisms. [Springer.]. *Lecture Notes in Computer Science, 2171,* 137–196. doi:10.1007/3-540-45608-2_3

Sanchez, P. (2009). *Análisis dinámico de datos. Marketing Online, rey de la estrategia de marketing en 2009.* Retrieved July 10, 2009, from http://www.slideshare.net/paula.sanchez/el-marketing-online-rey-de-la-estrategia-de-marketing-en-2009

Sandhu, R., Coyne, E., Feinstein, H., & Youman, C. (1996). Role-based access control models. *IEEE Computer, 29*(2), 38–47.

Sandhu, R., Ferraiolo, D., & Kuhm, R. (2000). The NIST model for role-based access control: Towards a unified standard. *Proceedings of the 5th ACM workshop on Role-based access control, 2000,* (pp. 47-63).

Santhanam, R., & Hartono, E. (2003). Issues in linking IT capability to firm performance. *Management Information Systems Quarterly, 27*(1), 125–153.

Savaris, C. (2009). *E-mail marketing directo-vender por mail. Una poderosa arma de ventas.* Retrieved July 11, 2009, from http://www.continentalmarket.com/boletin/e-mail-marketing-directo.htm

Schensul, J. J. (2008). Methods. In Given, L. M. (Ed.), *The Sage encyclopedia of qualitative research methods* (pp. 501–502). Thousand Oaks, CA: Sage Publications.

Scheun, A. (2008). *Web 2.0: A strategy guide.* Sebastopol, CA: O'Reilly.

Schillewaert, N., De Ruyck, T., & Verhaeghe, A. (2009). Connected research: How market research can get the most out of Semantic Web waves. *International Journal of Market Research, 51*(1), 11–27. doi:10.2501/S1470785308200286

Schindehutte, M., & Morris, M. (2001). Understanding strategic adaption in small firms.

Schmidt, D. C. (2006). Model-driven engineering. *IEEE Computer Society, 39*(2), 25–31.

Schonfeld, E. (2009). Facebook is now the fourth largest site in the world. *Techcrunch.* Retrieved July 6, 2009, from http://www.techcrunch.com/2009/08/04/facebook-is-now-the-fourth-largest-site-in-the-world/

Schwartz, D. G. (2008). Semantic information management and e-business: Towards more transparent value chains. *International Journal of Business Environment, 2*(2), 168–187. doi:10.1504/IJBE.2008.019510

Searle, J. (2001). *UK online for business.* Retrieved September 9, 2008, from www.ncc.co.uk/ncc/ Jenny_Searle.pdf

Sebastiani, F. (2002). Machine learning in automated text categorization. *ACM Computing Surveys, 34*(1), 1–47. doi:10.1145/505282.505283

SecuriTeam. (2005). *Google.com UTF-7 XSS vulnerabilities.* Retrieved from http://www.securiteam.com/securitynews/6Z00L0AEUE.html

SecurityFocus. (2009). *Bugtraq mailing lists.* Retrieved from http://www.securityfocus.com/archive

Senge, P., Kleiner, A., Roberts, C., Ross, R., Roth, G., & Smith, B. (1999). *The dance of change: The challenges of maintaining momentum in learning organizations.* London, UK: Nicholas Brearley Publishing.

Shankar, V., Urban, G., & Sultan, F. (2002). Online trust: A stakeholder perspective, concepts, implications and future directions. *The Journal of Strategic Information Systems, 11,* 325–344. doi:10.1016/S0963-8687(02)00022-7

Shaoling, D., & Yan, L. (2008). *Design of e-procurement system based on business intelligence tools.* International Conference on Management of e-Commerce and e-Government. IEEE Computer Society. doi: 10.1109 / ICMECG.2008.73

SharWestInc. (1997). *Productivity and customer satisfaction: Internet, Intranet, and Extranet as tools.* Retrieved from http//www.sharwest.com

Sheikh, M. A. (2009). *Conversion rate problem of SMEs in Internet marketing - a developing country perspective.* Karlskrona, Sweden: Blekinge Institute of Technology.

Sherman, C. (2005). A new f-word for Google search results. *Search Engine Watch.* Retrieved July 12, 2009, from http://searchenginewatch.com/3488076

Shvaiko, P., & Euzenat, J. (2005). A survey of schema-based matching approaches. *Journal on Data Semantics, 4*, 146–171.

Siau, K. (2003). Interorganizational systems and competitive advantages - lessons from history. *Journal of Computer Information Systems, 44*(1), 33–39.

Siddiqui, N., Omalley, A., Mccoll, J., & Birtwistle, G. (2003). Retailer and consumer perceptions of online fashion retailers: Website design issues. *Journal of Fashion Marketing and Management, 7*(4), 345–355. doi:10.1108/13612020310496949

Silva, M. M., Soares, A. L., & Simoes, D. (2006). *Integrating semantic resources to support knowledge communities.* INCOM06 12th IFAC Symposium on information control problems in manufacturing, 17-19 May, Saint-Etienne, France.

Sivashanmugam, K., Miller, J. A., Sheth, A. P., & Verma, K. (2004). Framework for Semantic Web process composition. *International Journal of Electronic Commerce, 9*(2), 71–106.

Skinner, S. (2000). *Business-to-business e-commerce: Investment perspective.* London, UK: Durlacher Research.

Smid, G., & Beckett, R. (2004). Learning and sustainable change: Designing learning spaces. In Boonstra, J. J. (Ed.), *Dynamics of organizational change and learning* (pp. 403–428). Chichester, UK: John Wiley & Sons. doi:10.1002/9780470753408.ch20

Smith, P. R., & Chaffey, D. (2005). *E-marketing excellence: At the heart of e-business* (2nd ed.). Oxford, UK: Butterworth Heinemann.

Smith, A. D., & Lias, A. R. (2005). Identity theft and e-fraud as critical CRM concerns. *International Journal of Enterprise Information Systems, 1*(2), 17–36. doi:10.4018/jeis.2005040102

Smith, B. *(2008).* A quick guide to GPLv3 (free software). *Retrieved on September 5, 2009, from* http://www.gnu.org/licenses/quick-guide-gplv3.html

Smith, M., Welty, C., & McGuinness, D. (Eds.). (2004). *OWL Web ontology language guide.* Recommendation, W3C.

Soh, C., Mah, Q. Y., Gan, F. J., Chew, D., & Reid, E. (1997). The use of the Internet for business: The experience of early adopters in Singapore. *Internet Research: Electronic Networking Applications and Policy, 7*(3), 217–228. doi:10.1108/10662249710171869

SourceForge. (2009), *ELLECTRA-WeB project.* Retrieved August 25, 2009, from http://sourceforge.net/projects/ellectra-web

Sprott, D., & Wilkes, L. (2004). Understanding service-oriented architecture. *CBDI Forum.* Retrieved on October 10, 2008, from http://www.msarchitecturejournal.com/pdf/Understanding_Service-Oriented_Architecture.pdf

Standish Group. (1996). *Unfinished voyages.* Retrieved July 20, 2009, from http://www.standishgroup.com/sample_research/unfinished_voyages_1.php

Standish Group. (1998). *Chaos: A recipe for success.* Retrieved July 20 2009, from http://www.standishgroup.com/sample_research/PDFpages/chaos1998.pdf

Stephen, J. M., Kendall, S., Axel, U., & Dirk, W. (2004). *MDA distilled.* Addison Wesley Longman Publishing Co.

Stephens, D. (2008). Open source e-procurement software. *Open Source Business Resource* (OSBR), March. Retrieved May 15, 2009, from http://osbr.ca/ojs/index.php/osbr/article/view/536/494

Stock, A., Williams, J., & Wichers, D. (2007). *OWASP top 10.* Retrieved from http://www.owasp.org/index.php/Top_10_2007

Stocker, A., & Tochtermann, K. (2008). Investigating weblogs in small and medium enterprises: An exploratory case study. *Proceedings of 11th International Conference on Business Information Management,* Innsbruck 2008.

Strauss, J., & Frost, R. (2001). *E-marketing.* NJ, USA: Prentice Hall.

Stroud, D. (2007). Social networking: An age-neutral commodity — social networking becomes a mature Web application. *Journal of Direct, Data and Digital Marketing Practice, 3*(9), 278–292. Retrieved November 27, 2008, from http://www.palgrave-journals.com/dddmp/journal/v9/n3/full/4350099a.html

Su, Z., & Wassermann, G. (2006). *The essence of command injection attacks in Web applications* (pp. 372–382). New York, NY: ACM.

Su, K., Huang, H., Wu, X., & Zhang, S. (2006). A logical framework for identifying quality knowledge from different data sources. *Decision Support Systems, 42*(3), 1673–1683. doi:10.1016/j.dss.2006.02.012

Su, X. M., & Atle Gulla, J. (2006). An information retrieval approach to ontology mapping. *Data & Knowledge Engineering, 58*(1), 47–69. doi:10.1016/j.datak.2005.05.012

Sun Microsystems. (2009a). *Sun GlassFish enterprise server.* Retrieved August 25, 2009, from http://developers.sun.com/appserver

Sun Microsystems. (2009b). *Enterprise JavaBeans technology.* Retrieved August 25, 2009, from http://Java.sun.com/products/ejb

Sun Microsystems. (2009c). *Java EE at a glance.* Retrieved August 25, 2009, from http://java.sun.com/javaee

Svedic, Z. (2004). *E-marketing strategies for e-business.* Simon Fraser University.

Sveiby, K. E. (1997). *The new organisational wealth.* San Francisco, CA: Berrett-Koehler Publishers Inc.

T.O.V.E. (1997). *TOVE ontologies*: Technology research in heterogeneous and distributed environment. *Information Systems Research, 11*(4), 327–341. Retrieved from http://www.eil.utoronto.ca/ tove/toveont.html.

Takizawa, H., Yamada, K., & Ito, T. (2004). Vehicles detection using sensor fusion. In *Proceedings of International Symposium on Intelligent Vehicles (IVS04),* (pp. 238–243). Parma, Italy.

Tang, V., Zheng, Y., & Cao, J. (2006). An intelligent car park management system based on wireless sensor networks. In *Proceedings Int* (pp. 65–70). Urumqi: Sym. Pervasive Computing and Applications.

Tanner, C., Wölfle, R., Schubert, P., & Quade, M. (2007). *Current trends and challenges in electronic procurement: An empirical study.* Paper presented in the 20th Bled eConference eMergence: Merging and Emerging Technologies, Processes, and Institutions, June 4 - 6, 2007, Bled, Slovenia.

Tedeschi, E. (2006). Like shopping? Social networking? Try social shopping. *E-Commerce Report on The New York Times.* Retrieved on September 11, 2009 from www.nytimes.com/ 2006/09/11/technology/ 11ecom.html

Tetteh, E., & Burn, J. (2001). Global strategies for SME-business: Applying the SMALL framework. *Logistics Information Management, 14*(1/2), 171–180. doi:10.1108/09576050110363202

Tham, D., Fox, M. S., & Gruninger, M. (1994). *A cost ontology for enterprise modelling.* Third Workshop on Enabling Technologies-Infrastructures for Collaborative Enterprises, West Virginia University.

Thelwall, M. (2004). *Link analysis: An Information Science approach.* Amsterdam, The Netherlands: Elsevier Academic Press.

Thurow, L. C. (1991). Foreword. In Scott-Morton, M. (Ed.), *The corporation of 1990's: Information Technology and organizational transformation* (pp. v–vii). New York, NY: Oxford University Press.

Tippett, P. (2002). The future of information security. In Bosworth, S., & Kabay, M. E. (Eds.), *Computer security handbook* (4th ed., pp. 54.1–54.18). New York, NY: John Wiley & Sons.

Tödtling, F., & Kaufmann, A. (2001). The role of the region for innovation activities for SMEs. *European Urban and Regional Studies, 8*(3), 203–215. doi:10.1177/096977640100800303

Tonti, G., Bradshaw, J. M., Jeffers, R., Montanari, R., Suri, N., & Uszok, A. (2003). Semantic Web languages for policy representation and reasoning: A comparison of KAoS, Rei, and Ponder. *Proceedings of the 2nd International Semantic Web Conference* (ISWC 2003), Sanibel Island, FL, October 2003.

Treese, G. W., & Stewart, L. C. (1998). *Designing systems for Internet commerce.* Boston, MA: Addison-Wesley Longman Publishing Co.

Tschammer, V., Zinner Henriksen, H., Ramfos, A., & Renner, T. (2003). *E-procurement: Challenges and opportunities.* Paper presented in the 16th Bled eCommerce Conference eTransformation, Panel on eProcurement, June 9 - 11, 2003, Bled, Slovenia.

Turban, E., Lee, J. K., & Viehland, D. (2004). *Electronic commerce 2004: A managerial perspective*. Pearson Education.

Tutterow, V., Asdal, R., & McKane, A. T. (2006a). Pump systems matter – part 1. *World Pumps, 481*, 44–66.

Tutterow, V., Asdal, R., & McKane, A. T. (2006b). Pump systems matter – part 2. *World Pumps, 482*, 28–31.

UK Government (1995). *Disability Discrimination Act.*

UK Government (1998). *Data Protection Act.*

UK Government (2002). Electronic commerce (EC directive) regulations.

UK Government. (1988). *Copyright*. Designs and Patent Act.

UK Government. (2000). *Consumer protection (distance selling) regulations.*

Urwin, S. (2000). The Internet as an information solution for the small and medium sized business. *Business Information Review, 17*(3), 130–137. doi:10.1177/0266382004237647

Uschold, M., King, M., Moralee, S., & Yannis, Z. (1998). The enterprise ontology. *The Knowledge Engineering Review, 13*(1), 31–89. doi:10.1017/S0269888998001088

Uszok, A., Bradshaw, J., Jeffers, R., Suri, N., Hayes, P., & Breedy, M. … Lott, J. (2003). KAoS policy and domain services: Toward a description-logic approach to policy representation, deconfliction and enforcement. *Proceedings of the 4ᵗʰ IEEE International Workshop on Policies for Distributed Systems and Networks* (POLICY 2003), Comersee, Italy.

van Bentum, R., & Stone, M. (2005). Customer relationship management and the impact of corporate culture - a European study. *Journal of Database Marketing & Customer Strategy Management, 13*, 28–54. doi:10.1057/palgrave.dbm.3240277

van Selm, M., & Jankowski, N. W. (2006). Conducting online surveys. *Quality & Quantity, 40*(3), 435–456. doi:10.1007/s11135-005-8081-8

Varajão, J. E. Q. (2002). *Função de Sistemas de Informação - Contributos para a melhoria do sucesso da adopção de tecnologias de informação e desenvolvimento de sistemas de informação nas organizações*. Unpublished doctoral dissertation, Universidade do Minho, Guimarães.

Viral marketing. (n.d.). In *AMA dictionary*. Retrieved August 20, 2009, from http://www.marketingpower.com /_layouts/Dictionary.aspx

Vlosky, R. P., Fontenot, R., & Blalock, L. (2000). Extranets: Impacts on business practices and relationships. *Journal of Business and Industrial Marketing, 15*(6), 438–457. doi:10.1108/08858620010349510

Vogt, P., Nentwich, F., Jovanovic, N., Kirda, E., Kruegel, C., & Vigna, G. (2007). Cross-site scripting prevention with dynamic data tainting and static analysis. *Proceeding of the Network and Distributed System Security Symposium (NDSS'07).*

von Hippel, E. (2001). Innovation by user communities: Learning from open-source software. *MIT Sloan Management Review, 42*(4), 82.

W3C Consortium. (1997). *Extensible markup language (XML)*. Retrieved from http://www.w3.org/XML/

Wagner, C., & Bolloju, N. (2005). Supporting knowledge management in organizations with conversational Ttechnologies: Discussion forums, weblogs and Wikis. *Journal of Database Management, 2*(16), 1–8.

Wagner, C., & Majchrzak, A. (2007). Enabling customer-centricity using Wikis and the Wiki way. *Journal of Management Information Systems, 3*(23), 17. doi:10.2753/MIS0742-1222230302

Wagner, C., & Prasarnphanich, P. (2007). Innovating collaborative content creation: The role of Altruism and Wiki technology. *Proceedings of the 40th Hawaii International Conference on System Sciences* (HICSS-40).

Walker, O. C., Boyd, M. W., & Larréché, J. C. (1992). *Marketing strategy: Planning and implementation*. USA: Richard D. Irwin.

Warner, J., Atluri, V., Mukkamala, R., & Vaidya, J. (2007). Using semantics for automatic enforcement of access control policies among dynamic coalitions. In *Proceedings of SACMAT 2007.*

Warr, W. A. (2008). Social software: Fun and games, or business tools? *Journal of Information Science, 5*(34), 591-604. Retrieved November 27, 2008, from http://jis.sagepub.com/cgi/reprint/34/4/591

Warren, S., & Brandeis, L. (1890). The right to privacy. *Harvard Law Review, 4*(5). Retrieved September 25, 2009, from http://www.lawrence.edu/fast/BOARDMAW/Privacy_brand_warr2.html

Wassermann, G., & Su, Z. (2008). *Static detection of cross-site scripting vulnerabilities* (pp. 171–180). New York, NY: ACM.

Weaver, R. (2007). *Guide to network defense and countermeasures* (2nd ed.). Boston, MA: Thomson Course Technology.

Wesh, M. (2009). *Web 2.0: The machine is us/ing us.* Retrieved August 15, 2009, from http://www.youtube.com/watch?v=6gmP4nk0EOE

Whitman, M. E., & Mattord, H. J. (2004). *Management of information security*. Boston, MA: Thomson Course Technology.

Whitman, M. E., & Mattord, H. J. (2005). *Principles of information security* (2nd ed.). Boston, MA: Thomson Course Technology.

Whitt, W. (2005). Engineering solution of basic call center model. *Management Science, 51*(2), 221–235. doi:10.1287/mnsc.1040.0302

Wickert, A., & Herschel, R. (2001). Knowledge-management issues for smaller businesses. *Journal of Knowledge Management, 4*(5), 329–337. doi:10.1108/13673270110411751

Wikipedia. (2008). *What is a Wiki?* Retrieved June 30, 2008, from http://en.wikipedia.org/wiki/

Wikipedia. (2009a). *Model-driven engineering.* Retrieved August 25, 2009, from http://en.wikipedia.org/wiki/Model_driven_development

Wikipedia. (2009b). *List of Java APIs.* Retrieved August 25, 2009 from http://en.wikipedia.org/wiki/List_of_Java_APIs

Wilson, S. G., & Abel, I. (2002). So you want to get involved in e-commerce. *Industrial Marketing Management, 31*(2), 85–94. doi:10.1016/S0019-8501(01)00188-2

Wilson, H., Daniel, E., & McDonald, M. (2002). Factors for success in Customer Relationship Management (CRM) Systems. *Journal of Marketing Management, 18*(1-2), 193–219. doi:10.1362/0267257022775918

Wilson, R. F. (2000). The six simple principles of viral marketing. Retrieved July 15, 2009, from http://www.wilsonweb.com/wmt5/viral-principles.htm

Wolff, J., Heuer, T., Gao, H., Weinmann, M., Voit, S., & Hartmann, U. (2006). Parking monitor system based on magnetic field sensors. In *Proceedings IEEE Conf. Intelligent Transportation Systems*, (pp. 1275–1279). Toronto, CA.

Woon, I., & Kankanhalli, A. (2006). Trust, controls, and information security. In Whitman, M. E., & Mattord, H. J. (Eds.), *Readings and cases in the management information security* (pp. 120–128). Boston, MA: Thomson Course Technology.

Wurman, R. S. (2001). *Information anxiety, vol 2.* Indianapolis, IN: Que.

Wurzinger, P., Platzer, C., Ludl, C., Kirda, E., & Kruegel, C. (2009). SWAP: Mitigating XSS attacks using a reverse proxy. *In SESS'09: Proceedings of the 5th International Workshop on Software Engineering for Secure Systems,* Vancouver, Canada, May 2009.

Wyld, D. C. (2008). Management 2.0: A primer on blogger for executives. *Management Research News, 6*(31), 448–483. doi:10.1108/01409170810876044

Wyld, D. C. (2004). *The weather report for the supply chain: A longitudinal analysis of ISM.* Hammond, LA: Department of Management, Southeastern Louisinia University.

Yage del Valle, M. I., del Mar Gallardo, M., & Mana, A. (2005). Semantic access control model: A formal specification. In De Capitani di Vimercati, S., Syverson, P. F., & Gollmann, D. (Eds.), *ESORICS, Lecture Notes in Computer Science 3679* (pp. 24–43).

Yagüe, M., Mana, A., Lopez, L., & Troya, J. M. (2003). Applying the Semantic Web layers to access control. *Proceedings of the DEXA 2003 Workshop on Web Semantics* (WebS 2003), Prague, Czech Republic.

Yan, G., Olariu, S., Weigle, M. C., & Abuelela, M. (2008). Smartparking: A secure and intelligent parking system using NOTICE. In *Proceedings of the International IEEE Conference on Intelligent Transportation Systems*, (pp. 569–574). Beijing, China.

Yan, G., Weigle, M. C., & Olariu, S. (2009). A novel parking service using wireless networks. In *Proceedings of the IEEE International Conference on Service Operations, Logistics and Informatics*. Chicago. Best Student Paper Award.

Yang, Q. Z., & Zhang, Y. (2006). Semantic interoperability in building design: Methods and tools. *Computer Aided Design, 38*, 1099–1112. doi:10.1016/j.cad.2006.06.003

Yang, X., He, N., Wu, L., & Liu, J. (2007). Ontology based approach of semantic information integration. *Journal of Southeast University, 23*(3), 338–342.

Yetton, P., Martin, A., Sharma, R., & Johnston, K. (2000). A model of Information Systems project performance. *Information Systems Journal, 10*, 263–289. doi:10.1046/j.1365-2575.2000.00088.x

Zaltman, G. (1997). Rethinking market research: Putting people back in. *JMR, Journal of Marketing Research, 34*(4), 424–437. doi:10.2307/3151962

Zdravkovic, M., Panetto, H., & Trajanovic, M. (2009). *Concept of semantic information pool for manufacturing supply networks*. 5th international working Conference on Total Quality Management - advanced and intelligent approaches. 1-4 June, Belgrade, Serbia.

Zhang, G., & Parashar, M. (2003). *Dynamic context-aware access control for grid applications*. IEEE Computer Society Press, 4th International Workshop on Grid Computing (Grid 2003), (pp. 101-108). Phoenix, AZ, USA.

Zhao, Y., Wang, X., & Halang, W. A. (2006). Ontology mapping techniques in information integration. In M. M. Cunha, & G. D. (Eds.), *Putnik adaptive technologies and business integration: Social, managerial and organizational dimension*. Hershey, PA: Idea Group Reference. ISBN 1-59904-048-4

Zhu, L., Liu, Y., Gorton, I., & Kuz, I. (2007). *Tools for model driven development*. Paper presented in the 40th Annual Hawaii International Conference on System Sciences (HICSS'07) (p. 284).

Zhu, Z. F., Zhao, Y., & Lu, H. Q. (2007). Sequential architecture for efficient car detection. In *Proceedings of IEEE Computer Society Conference on Computer Vision and Pattern Recognition (CVPR 2007)*, (pp. 1–8). Minneapolis.

Ziegler, C., & Lausen, G. (2004). Analyzing correlation between trust and user similarity in online communities. *Proceedings of the Second International Conference on Trust Management*.

Ziouvelou, X., & Yovanof, G. (2008a). Public procurement: A European perspective. *AIT Working Paper Series* AIT/MBIT/001 (4), July/Aug 2008, Version 1.1 (work in progress).

Ziouvelou, X., & Yovanof, G. (2008b). The state of open source software in Europe. *AIT Working Paper Series* AIT/MBIT/002 (5), Sep/Oct 2008, Version 1.1 (work in progress).

Zitouni, I., Hong-Kwang, Kuo, J., & Lee, C. H. (2003). Boosting and combination of classifiers for natural language call routing systems. *Speech Communication, 41*, 647–661. doi:10.1016/S0167-6393(03)00103-1

Zuboff, S. (1988). *In the age of the smart machine: The future of work and power*. USA: Basic Books.

Zuboff, S., & Maxmin, J. (2002). *The support economy: Why corporations are failing individuals and the next episode of capitalism*. New York, NY: Viking, Penguin Books.

Zwass, V. (1996). Electronic commerce: Structures and issues. *International Journal of Electronic Commerce, 1*, 3–24.

About the Contributors

Maria Manuela Cruz-Cunha is currently an Associate Professor in the School of Technology at the Polytechnic Institute of Cavado and Ave, Portugal. She holds a Dipl. Eng. in the field of Systems and Informatics Engineering, an M.Sci. in the field of Information Society and a Dr.Sci in the field of Virtual Enterprises, all from the University of Minho (Portugal). She teaches subjects related with Information Systems, Information Technologies, and Organizational Models to undergraduate and post-graduate students. She supervises several PhD projects in the domain of Virtual Enterprises and Information Systems and Technologies. She regularly publishes in international peer-reviewed journals and participates on international scientific conferences. She serves as a member of Editorial Board and Associate Editor for several International Journals and for several Scientific Committees of International Conferences. She has authored and edited several books, and her work appears in more than 70 papers published in journals, book chapters, and conference proceedings. She is the co-founder and co-chair of CENTERIS – Conference on ENTERprise Information Systems.

João Eduardo Varajão is Professor of Information Systems Management and Software Engineering at the University of Trás-os-Montes e Alto Douro and visiting professor at EGP – University of Porto Business School. He graduated in 1995, received his Master's degree in Computer Science in 1997 and, in 2003, received his PhD in Technologies and Information Systems, from University of Minho (Portugal). He currently supervises several Msc and PhD theses in the Information Systems field. His current research includes Information Systems management, project management and enterprise Information Systems. He has over one hundred publications, including books, book chapters, refereed publications, and communications at international conferences. He serves as associate editor and member of editorial board for international journals and has served in several committees of international conferences. He is the co-founder and co-chair of CENTERIS – Conference on ENTERprise Information Systems. He is also a member of AIS, IEICE and APSI.

* * *

Agustín Orfila is an Associate Professor at the Computer Science Department of the Universidad Carlos III de Madrid and a member of the Information Security Group of this department. He has a Bachelor's degree in Physics from Universidad Complutense de Madrid and he obtained his Ph.D degree in Computer Science from Universidad Carlos III de Madrid in 2005. Dr. Orfila has several publications both in international conference proceedings and journals, and he acts as a reviewer of different ISI journals. His interests are mainly focused on the security in Information Technologies, particularly on RFID and intrusion detection systems.

Alexis Barlow is a lecturer at Glasgow Caledonian University. Her teaching and research interests are in the field of Information Systems, e-business, and supply chains. She is currently involved in teaching on a range of programmes including the BA (Hons) Management, Technology & Enterprise, MsC in Management of Information Systems, and the Master of Business Administration. Alexis is a member of the Higher Education Academy, British Academy of Management (BAM), e-business research network, and has served as track chair for the E-Business and E-Government track at the BAM conference. Alexis is currently leading a Greater Glasgow Articulation Partnership project examining student transition from college to university and is an external examiner for University of West of Scotland. She has recent publications in journals such as the International Journal of Business Science & Applied Management, International Journal of Information Technology and Management, and Electronic Commerce Research and Applications, as well as a range of book chapters.

Almudena Alcaide received a degree in (Mathematics) at Complutense University of Madrid, obtained her M. Sc. in Advanced Computing at Kings College University of London and got her PhD in Computer Science and Technology at Carlos III University of Madrid. Currently, she is a Teaching Assistant at the same University in the Computer Science Department. Her areas of interest are focused in the design and formal validation of cryptographic protocols, having several publications in conference proceedings, journals, and books. Specifically, her most recent research area is comprised into the field of Rational Cryptography, where results obtained from Games Theory are applied to the formal analysis of safe exchange protocols.

Ana Rodrigues has a Degree in Informatics and a Masters in Informatics, both from the University of Trás-os-Montes e Alto Douro. Currently Ana has the position of informatics technician at the City of Vila Pouca de Aguiar, Portugal. She also has experience in Information Technology training. She has some publications in international conferences.

Anne Smith, lectures in entrepreneurship at Glasgow Caledonian University. Anne is third generation family business and so survival, success and growth of the SME are the foundation of her research. She has over a number of years created a portfolio of companies from the old and new economy, which form the basis of longitudinal research studies. Within the portfolio are sector clusters, which include packaging, agribusiness, construction and social firms. Anne was involved at inception with the Royal Society of Edinburgh fellowships for technology transfer, through design and provision of a commercialisation programme. She is very keen to integrate this work with the old economy firms and is currently researching connectivity of these firms with Scotland's innovation system. Finally, an action research approach with her SME portfolio has developed pedagogical thinking in learning environments and is manifested in creative and innovative developments for entrepreneurship education.

Anni Rowland-Campbell has been leading Fuji Xerox Australia's ARC funded research in semantics for the past four years, and through that has developed networks with research organisations around the world involved in the development of semantic technologies. She has worked in a number of government and non-profit roles and is currently undertaking a PhD focusing on the impact of globalisation and semantic technologies on multinational organisations and their local operating companies in Australia. Anni is also a member of a multidisciplinary team at Semantic Transformations Pty Ltd.

Antonio Paredes is a lecturer in commercial Information Systems at the Financial Economy and Operations Research, University of Seville, Spain. He earned Bachelor degrees of Philosophy and Theology, and his Ms.C. and Ph.D. in Artificial Intelligence and Computational Logic. Most part of his professional career has worked in the design and supervision of commercial databases and Information Systems for the Spanish firms Abencor and Nicsa. His main research interests are business ontologies and the Semantic Web.

Antonis Ramfos joined INTRASOFT International SA in 1997 and is currently the Research and Innovation Department Manager. Dr. Ramfos has gained considerable experience in managing R&D projects and exploiting R&D results through his participation in numerous research projects. Dr. Ramfos has several publications in journals, conferences, and books. He holds a BSc in Mathematics from the University of Sussex, UK, (1983), an MSc in Computing and Statistics from the University of Wales, College of Cardiff, UK, (1985), and a PhD in the area of Distributed Heterogeneous Databases from the University of Wales, College of Cardiff, (1991).

Beatriz Sainz de Abajo is a young telecommunications researcher in the University of Valladolid (Spain). She received the Engineer degree in telecommunications engineering from the University of Valladolid (Spain) in 2001, and has a PhD from the University of Cordoba (Spain). She has devoted all her professional life to the investigation around telecommunication regulation matters and novel telecommunication systems. Her future research interests are e-commerce, e- marketing, e-government, telecommunications policy, and also digital contents, both from the user's standpoint, and from the competitive market vision.

Bojan Cestnik is the general manager of the software company Temida and a researcher at the Department of Knowledge Technologies at the Jožef Stefan Institute in Ljubljana, Slovenia. He obtained his PhD in Computer Science at the Faculty of Electrical Engineering and Computer Science, University of Ljubljana. His professional and research interests include knowledge-based Information Systems and machine learning. His research work has been presented at several international conferences. He has been involved in several large-scale software development and maintenance projects.

Carlos de Castro Lozano has a PhD in Sciences from the University of Cordoba (Spain). Professor of the department of Computer Science, he is the person in charge of the subjects "Interaction Person - Computer and Systems Multimedia." Director of the group of Research EATCO (Education and Learning for Technologies of the Communication), he coordinates the Network EVA (Virtual Spaces of Learning) of the International University of Andalusia (UNIA). President of the Foundation FREE and president of AETAP (Association of Entities for the Technologies of Support for the Personal Autonomy).

Danda B. Rawat received the Bachelors of Engineering in Computer Engineering in 2002 and the Masters of Science in Information and Communication Engineering (with First class, first with distinction) in 2005 from Tribhuvan University, Kathmandu, Nepal. He worked as an instructor (assistant lecturer) in Institute of Engineering, Tribhuvan University from 2002 to 2006 and worked as a Network Engineer at Center for Information Technology, Institute of Engineering from June 2003 to July 2004. He also worked as an ICT (Information and Communication Technology) officer for Government of

Nepal from January 2004 to December 2006. He is currently working toward the PhD degree with the Department of Electrical and Computer Engineering, Old Dominion University, Norfolk, VA, USA. He has published more than 20 journal papers, book chapters, and conference papers. He has been serving as a reviewer for several IEEE conferences and manuscripts. His research interests are in the areas of wireless communications, wireless cellular/ad-hoc networks, and vehicular communications. He is the recipient of Outstanding PhD Researcher of the Year Award 2009 given by the Department of Electrical and Computer Engineering, Old Dominion University, Norfolk, VA, USA.

David G. Schwartz is a senior lecturer at the Graduate School of Business Administration at Bar-Ilan University, Israel. His main research interests are Knowledge Management, Ontology, Internet-based Systems, and Computer-mediated Communications. Since 1998 he has served as Editor of the journal Internet Research. Dr. Schwartz's research has appeared in publications such as IEEE Intelligent Systems, International Journal of Human-Computer Studies, IEEE Transactions on Professional Communications, Advances in Management Information Systems, and the Journal of Organizational Behavior. His books include Cooperating Heterogeneous Systems, Internet-Based Knowledge Management and Organizational Memory, and the Encyclopedia of Knowledge Management. He has been a visiting scholar at Columbia University, Department of Biomedical Informatics (New York, USA) and Monash University, Faculty of Information Technology (Melbourne, Australia). Dr. Schwartz received his Ph.D. from Case Western Reserve University; MBA from McMaster University; and B.Sc. from the University of Toronto, Canada.

Dinesh Rathi is Assistant Professor in the School of Library and Information Studies at the University of Alberta. His research interests are in the area of Web 2.0, knowledge management, e-marketing, human computer interaction, text mining, email-based customer support, and help desk systems. Dinesh has an MS in Finance and a Ph.D. from the University of Illinois at Urbana-Champaign, Illinois, USA. Dinesh also has a Post-graduate Diploma in Business Administration (PGDBA) with a major in Marketing and International Business and an undergraduate degree in Mechanical Engineering. Dinesh has over five years of corporate experience. He worked with TATA International Limited, Mumbai, India for over three years in the area of international business and with Kirloskar Electric Company, Bangalore, India in the area of automation and process re-engineering.

Eduardo Galan is a Research Technician at the Security Group of the Computer Science Department of the Carlos III University of Madrid. He obtained his Computer Engineer Degree at Carlos III University of Madrid and received his M. Sc. in Computer Science and Technology from the same University. His main areas of interest are the prevention of phishing and other modalities of online fraud and the analysis of the security of Web applications and the attacks which can affect them.

Francisco J. Martínez-López, MSc in Marketing, European PhD in Business Administration, is an Associate Professor in Marketing at the University of Granada (Spain) and Assistant Professor in Marketing at the Open University of Catalonia, Barcelona (Spain). Among his main areas of interest are consumer behavior on the Internet, e-marketing, marketing channels, and KDD methodologies for marketing. He has authored academic books, chapters of academic books, and contributions to international conferences and international journals, such as Int. J. of Electronic Marketing and Retailing, Internet Research, Industrial Marketing Management, Int. J. of Management Reviews, Computers &

Education, Int. J. of Services Technology and Management, Expert Systems with Applications, Int. J. of Business Environment, and Journal of Internet Business, among others.

Christos Georgousopoulos joined INTRASOFT International S.A. in 2006 and is currently an ICT Specialist in the department of Research and Innovation Development. He holds an H.N.D. (1997) in Computer Science from British-Hellenic College, Athens, a B.Sc. (1999), and a Ph.D. (2005) in Computer Science from University of Wales, Cardiff. From 2000 to 2010 he published more than 15 research papers in journals and conferences, and contributed in the authoring of newspaper and magazine articles. His current research interests entail software engineering and innovative software development techniques, cloud-computing, and service-oriented architectures.

Gongjun Yan received his MS in Computer Science from University of Electronics Science and Technology of China in 2004 and BS in Mechanical Engineering in Sichuan Institute of Technology in 1999. Currently, he is a Ph.D candidate in Computer Science at Old Dominion University. His main research areas include wireless security and Intelligent Transportation Systems. In the area of security Gongjun is mostly interested in location security, confidentiality, and availability (the so-called CIA model). He has published about 18 papers and journals and 5 book chapters during his Ph.D research.

Gregory S. Yovanof is an Associate Professor at Athens Information Technology (AIT) and an adjunct professor at Carnegie Mellon University. He currently serves as the Graduate Program Director of the "Management of Business, Innovation and Technology" program at AIT. In April 2008, Dr. Yovanof was elected member of the BoD of Hellas-On-Line. Before joining AIT in 2002, he worked as a staff scientist at Eastman Kodak Research Labs and Hewlett-Packard Laboratories, engaged over a period of nine years in multimedia signal processing for computer peripheral devices. He has also led the development of several award-winning ICs for the DVD market as a co-founder and an executive manager at two start-up companies in Silicon Valley. Dr. Yovanof received a Ph.D degree in Communications from the University of Southern California, Los Angeles, in 1988. A holder of four patents on imaging systems, Dr. Yovanof is a senior member of the IEEE.

Hatem El-Gohary is a Senior Lecturer in Marketing at Birmingham City University Business School (Birmingham, West Midlands, UK) and Marketing Researcher at Cairo University Business School (Cairo, Egypt). He has more than 15 years of experience in academia and worked as the marketing director of a multinational company, a general manager for Egyptian company and a marketing consultant for a number on national and multinational companies. His research interest include: Electronic Marketing, Electronic Business, Electronic Commerce, Internet Marketing, and Small Business Enterprises. He has published in journals such as Journal of Business and Public Policy, Journal of International Business and Finance, International Business & Technology Review and Int. Journal of Business Science and Applied Management.

Ingrid Petrič is researcher at the Centre of Systems and Information Technologies at the University of Nova Gorica, Slovenia. She received her MSc in Information Management at the Faculty of Economics, University of Ljubljana in 2004. During her Master's studies, she worked for a software company specializing in business software development. In 2006, she enrolled at the PhD program New Media and E-science at the Jožef Stefan International Postgraduate School and received her PhD in 2009. As a researcher at the Centre of Systems and Information Technologies, she investigates available data about autism spectrum disorders. Her research interests include database systems, data and text mining, knowledge discovery, business informatics, and bioinformatics.

Isabel de la Torre Diez was born in Zamora, Spain, in 1979. She received the Engineer degree in telecommunications engineering from the University of Valladolid (Spain) in 2003. Currently, she is an assistant professor in the Department of Signal Theory and Communications at the University of Valladolid, where she is working towards the Ph.D. degree. Her research has been mainly focused in development of telemedicine applications, EHRs (Electronic Health Records) standards in Ophthalmology, e- learning, and e-commerce applications.

Jorge Blasco is a Teaching Assistant member of the Information Security Research Group at the Computer Science Department of the Carlos III University of Madrid. He obtained his Computer Engineer degree at University Carlos III of Madrid. He also received his M. Sc. in Computer Science and Technology from the same University where he is currently a PhD candidate. Blasco has published several research papers on international conferences proceedings. His main research interests are data leakage protection technologies and steganography.

José Manuel Gaivéo is Adjunct Professor on Department of Information Systems of School of Business Administration, Polytechnic Institute of Setubal, since 1998, teaching Information Security, Systems Analysis, Data Modeling, and Business Intelligence. Dr. Gaiveo is the coordinator of Department of Information Systems. Holds a PhD degree in Informatics, by Open University of Lisbon with a doctoral thesis named "People on Information Security Management Systems," a Master of Sciences degree in Organizations and Information Systems, by University of Evora, and a Licentiate's degree in Computers and Electronics Engineering by of School of Technology, Polytechnic Institute of Setubal. Has successfully completed a Lead Auditor Course of ISO 27001:2005, and passed the examination.

Lisa M. Given, Ph.D., is Professor of Information Studies in the School of Information Studies (Faculty of Education), Charles Sturt University, Australia. Lisa is also an Adjunct Professor in Humanities Computing (Faculty of Arts) and Educational Policy Studies (Faculty of Education) at the University of Alberta. A former Director of the International Institute for Qualitative Methodology, Lisa has received numerous research grants and awards and has published widely on topics related to individuals' information behaviours and qualitative inquiry. Her research interests include the social construction of knowledge, web usability, spatial analysis, information literacy, research methods, and information issues in the context of higher education. Lisa is Editor of the 2-volume set, *The Sage Encyclopedia of Qualitative Research Methods* (2008).

Margaret McCann is a lecturer in the Department of Strategy, Innovation and Enterprise, Glasgow Caledonian University. In her 20 years at the University she has taught predominantly within the field of Information Technology/Information Systems and how businesses can successfully exploit technology. Her current main research interests are in e-learning as well as business uses of Web 2.0 technology, and she has published several articles and book chapters in these areas. She is currently undertaking a research project on easing the transition for college students entering university, as well as researching the use of plagiarism detection software to improve academic writing. Margaret is also a validator for the Scottish Qualification Agency and an advisor for the Scottish Information Literacy Framework.

Mário Sérgio Carvalho Teixeira is Assistant Professor at UTAD – University of Trás-os-Montes and Alto Douro. PhD in Management, UTAD. MSc and MBA, with specialisation in Marketing, Portuguese Catholic University. Post Graduate Course in Marketing Research, INDEG/ISCTE. BSc in Economics, ISEG/UTL. Teacher in MSc and BSc Degrees Courses of Marketing, Marketing Research, Entrepreneurship, Strategic Management and other Business areas. Former Director of Master in Entrepreneurship and Assistant Director of CETRAD – Center of Transdisciplinary Studies for Development. Coordination or participation in several national and international studies and research projects, such as: "National Market Study and Definition of a Marketing Strategy for Douro Wines"; "Tourism Market Research for the Douro and Trás-os-Montes Regions".

Marlene Pinto has a Degree in Informatics and a Masters in Informatics, both from the University of Trás-os-Montes and Alto Douro, Portugal. Currently is a consultant in Business Intelligence at ADP Dealer Services Portugal. Between 2007 to 2008, she worked as a technical training specialist at the University of Trás-os-Montes and Alto Douro. She has some publications in electronic commerce area.

Miguel López Coronado is a telecommunications professor in the University of Valladolid (Spain). He was born in Barcelona, Spain; in 1950. He has a PhD in Telecommunications Engineering from the Polytechnic University of Madrid, in 1982. Since 1991 he has been devoted to the promotion of Information Society in Castille and Leon region from several positions: Director of the Technical School of Telecommunications, R&D General Manager of a Telecommunications Technological Centre, and also CEO of a cable telecommunications operator. Now, his research interests are biomedical signal, Telemedicine, Information Society, and to contribute to the promotion of the entrepreneurial character of University.

Nuno Pedro Manarte Gonçalves is a project manager and research assistant at UTAD – University of Trás-os-Montes and Alto Douro. He holds a BSc degree in Management (UTAD), with a strong marketing component where he wrote a final monograph on the subject of Database Marketing. He also completed a professional training course in website design. He is an Internet, mobile, and social media marketing enthusiast, and has a keen interest for new technologies. Previous work experience includes working as a freelance graphic designer; as a manager in a local newspaper, where he oversaw the development of a new website and a new subscriber database; and some experience in sales.

Özalp Vayvay, Ph.D., is working of Industrial Engineering Department at Marmara University. He is currently the Chairman of the Engineering Management Department at Marmara University. His current research interests include new product design, technology management, business process reengineering, enterprise resource planning systems, operations management, and supply chain management. Dr. Vayvay has been involved in R&D projects and education programs for an over the past 12 years.

Paul Strahl, for many years, has been working within the "e-Business" space, having created Fuji Xerox Australia's e-Business processes within the Document Supplies Division. As e-Business Manager, Paul introduced Web 2.0 to the company, along with an industry-first data driven online sales model. Paul has developed a worldwide "virtual" team consisting of best of breed expertise in the areas of architecture, coding, semantics, and natural language processing. Paul is a member of a multidisciplinary team at Semantic Transformations Pty Ltd.

Pedro Pina is a lawyer and a law teacher in the Oliveira do Hospital School of Technology and Management at the Polytechnic Institute of Coimbra. He holds a law degree from the University of Coimbra Law School and a post-graduation in Territorial Development, Urbanism and Environmental Law from the Territorial Development, Urbanism and Environmental Law Studies Center (CEDOUA) at the University of Coimbra Law School. He holds a master degree in Procedural Law Studies from the University of Coimbra Law School and is currently a PhD student in the Doctoral Programme "Law, Justice, and Citizenship in the Twenty First Century" from the University of Coimbra Law School and Economics School.

Ramiro Gonçalves is an Associate Professor of Computer Science at the Trás-os-Montes e Alto Douro University, Vila Real, Portugal. He received his PhD in Computer Science from Trás-os-Montes e Alto Douro University, Portugal. He has fifteen years of experience as Information Systems' technology consultant. His current research focuses on electronic commerce and management Information Systems. It is a member of several scientific committees and has participated in several panels of the Master and Doctoral degree. Has several papers published in journals and proceeding of conferences.

Ron Beckett's industry background is in R&D and manufacturing management associated with the aerospace industry. He has an ongoing interest in creative organisational change associated with inter-enterprise collaboration between firms and between sectors, managing innovation as a business process, and leveraging accessible knowledge and technology. Ron is continuing to research these topics with industry and university colleagues, and has published about 80 related articles or book chapters. He is currently the Managing Director of a management research and consultancy enterprise called the Reinvention Network that helps client firms during transitional growth periods, and is an Adjunct Professor at the University of Western Sydney, College of Business.

Rui Rijo is an Associate Professor of Computer Science at the Polytechnic Institute of Leiria. He has more than ten years of experience as contact centers' technology consultant in Tokyo (Japan), Macau (China), Hong-Kong (China), São Paulo (Brazil), Kuala Lumpur (Malaysia), Madrid (Spain), Amsterdam (Holland), and Lisbon (Portugal). His current research interests include project management, software engineer, and voice over IP communications.

Sam De Silva is a Partner at Taylor Walton LLP. Taylor Walton is one of the largest law firms in the South East region outside London and has recently been voted UK Corporate Law Firm of the Year by the readers of leading corporate finance magazine, ACQ. Silva specialises in data protection, e-commerce and technology projects including outsourcing (IT, BPO and off-shoring), system development and supply, system integration, software licensing and support, and services agreements. He advises clients in both the public and private sector and has acted for both suppliers and users of technology. He has had experience and is admitted to practice law in New Zealand, Australia, and the United Kingdom. Silva has published widely and speaks regularly on outsourcing and technology contracts and is an Associate Lecturer at the University of Surrey for the Surrey European Management School. He has also developed an online course on IT contracts for Central Law Training. Dr De Silva is also on the Law and Information Technology Committee of the English Law Society.

Serdal Bayram, PhD Candidate, received a BSc degree in Computer Engineering from Marmara University, Turkey in 2004. In 2007, he was awarded an MSc degree in Computer Engineering from Marmara University. Since 2007, he has been studying for PhD program in Engineering Management department at the same university. Since 2003, he has been working in CIO (Corporate Information Office) for Siemens in Istanbul, Turkey. Firstly, he started to be a Software Engineer in Web applications and then he continued to work as Project Manager in several internal enterprise applications. Now, his position in Siemens is Solution Consultant.

Stephan Olariu received his BSc, MSc and PhD all in Computer Science from McGill University in Montreal. Over the years Prof. Olariu has held many different roles and responsibilities as a member of numerous organizations and teams. Much of his experience has been with the design and implementation of robust protocols for wireless networks, and in particular, sensor networks and their applications. Professor Olariu is applying mathematical modeling and analytical frameworks to the resolution of problems ranging from securing communications, to predicting the behavior of complex systems, to evaluating performance of wireless networks.

Tanja Urbančič is Dean of the School of Engineering and Management at the University of Nova Gorica, Slovenia, and Head of Center for Systems and Information Technologies at the University of Nova Gorica. She is also a research fellow at the Department of Knowledge Technologies at the Jožef Stefan Institute. She received her PhD in Computer Science from the University of Ljubljana. Her current professional and research interest is mainly in knowledge management, especially in its applications to education, medicine, and public health. She is a co-author of several book chapters and journal papers in IEEE Transactions on SCM, Engineering Applications of Artificial Intelligence, Journal of Intelligent and Fuzzy Systems, Journal of Biomedical Informatics, among others.

Weiming Yang received the Bachelors of Science in Applied Mathematics in 2003 from Chengdu University of Technology, China. He received his first Master's degree of Science in Applied Mathematics at 2005 from University of Toledo, OH and second Master's degree of Science in Statistics in 2009 from Old Dominion University. He worked as a research assistant at ISTART lab at Old Dominion University as instructor from 2007 to 2008. He is currently working toward the PhD degree in Statistics with the Department of Mathematics and Statistics, Old Dominion University, Norfolk, VA, USA. His research interests are in the areas of binary longitudinal data, time series, estimating equation, and correlation estimation. He received the Graduate Teaching Assistant Fellowship for 2008-2009.

Wolfgang A. Halang, born 1951 in Essen, Germany, received a doctorate in mathematics from Ruhr-Universität Bochum in 1976, and a second one in computer science from Universität Dortmund in 1980.

He worked both in industry (Coca-Cola GmbH and Bayer AG) and academia (University of Petroleum and Minerals, Saudi Arabia, and University of Illinois at Urbana-Champaign), before he was appointed to the Chair of Applications-oriented Computing Science and head of the Department of Computing Science at the University of Groningen in the Netherlands. Since 1992 he holds the Chair of Computer Engineering in the Faculty of Electrical and Computer Engineering at Fernuniversität in Hagen, Germany, whose dean he was from 2002 to 2006. He was a visiting professor at the University of Maribor, Slovenia, 1997, and the University of Rome II in 1999. His research interests comprise all major areas of hard real-time computing with special emphasis on safety-related systems. He is the founder and was European editor-in-chief of the journal Real-Time Systems, member of the editorial boards of 4 further journals, co-director of the 1992 NATO Advanced Study Institute on Real-Time Computing, has authored 10 books and over 350 refereed book chapters, journal publications, and conference contributions, has edited 16 books, holds 12 patents, has given some 80 guest lectures in more than 20 countries, and is active and held offices in various professional organisations and technical committees as well as involved in the programme committees of almost 200 conferences.

Xenia Ziouvelou is a senior research scientist at the Research in Innovation & Entrepreneurship (RIE) Research Group and a teaching fellow at Athens Information Technology (AIT) since 2007. She holds a PhD in Industrial Economics focusing on the strategic analysis of electronic markets and an MSc in International Business both from the Department of Economics of the Lancaster University (UK). She has also been awarded with a B.Sc in Business Administration from the American College of Greece (GR).

Yi Zhao received her BEng degree in Computer Software Engineering in 1995, and her MEng degree in Image Processing and Pattern Recognition in 1998 both from Northwestern Polytechnic University, Xi'an, China, and her PhD degree in Pattern Recognition and Intelligent System from Shanghai Jiaotong University in 2001. In the same year she moved to Germany, where she is working with the Chair of Computer Engineering at Fernuniversität in Hagen. Her research interests include Semantic Web mining, security in Semantic Web services, knowledge discovery, and data mining.

Index

CPSIA information can be obtained at www.ICGtesting.com

263193BV00001B/65-122/P

9 781609 607654